ENCYCLOPEDIA OF
# TWENTIETH-CENTURY JOURNALISTS

GARLAND REFERENCE LIBRARY
OF THE HUMANITIES
(VOL. 493)

# ENCYCLOPEDIA OF TWENTIETH-CENTURY JOURNALISTS

*William H. Taft*

Garland Publishing, Inc.
New York & London
1986

**Library of Congress Cataloging-in-Publication Data**

Taft, William H. (William Howard), 1915-Oct. 24-
Encyclopedia of twentieth-century journalists.

(Garland reference library of the humanities ; vol. 493)
1. Journalists—United States—Biography—Dictionaries.
I. Title. II. Title: Encyclopedia of 20th-century journalists.
III. Series: Garland reference library of the humanities ;
v. 493.
PN4871.T34 1986 070'.92'2 [B] 84-48011
ISBN 0-8240-8961-8 (alk. paper)

Cover design by Alison Lew

Printed on acid-free, 250-year-life paper
Manufactured in the United States of America

To my wife, Myrtle

# CONTENTS

# INTRODUCTION

Americans have regularly been intrigued by the messengers with the news, whether they are seen in the movies, viewed on television, heard over the radio, or read about in newspapers and magazines.

In the nineteenth century, when the newspaper was the supreme source of information for the masses, the editors were popular personalities. The *New York Tribune* was "Greeley's newspaper," and the eccentric editor's name was well known throughout the nation. And it was as "Bennett's paper" that the *New York Herald*, the most successful publication of its time, was frequently referred to. Later we had "Pulitzer's paper" and "Hearst's paper," and people in the New York area knew exactly which paper was which.

Years later there was a change of attitude, and reporters, newspaper editors, and others associated with handling the news were relegated to the background. It was the message we wanted, not the messenger. Few reporters were given bylines for their articles. For many decades neither *Time* nor *Newsweek* let the public know who prepared the material millions of Americans read weekly. Today, however, both the writers and the researchers on these magazines are acknowledged at the ends of the articles.

When radio came along, a few announcers were prominent; some programs became exceedingly popular. Each Sunday evening, for example, millions of Americans turned their radio dial to Walter Winchell's "Jergen's Journal," on which they heard inside gossip about what their heroes and other famous people were doing or what was happening to them. With his rapid delivery, Winchell gave the impression that you were there with him, experiencing the news as it occurred.

During World War II radio became the basic source for on-the-scene coverage of the battlefront. The Edward R. Murrows were the new breed of information reporters.

With the arrival of television, the news announcers, and eventually the commentators and panelists, became well known to millions. Often, news leaders moved into other areas of the media world: a columnist, for example, might appear on a panel show.

More recently the syndication of the columnists, political cartoonists, and comic artists who provide material that so many Americans enjoy has brought them even greater public awareness. Under the syndicate operation more than a thousand newspapers carry Jack Anderson's comments each day, making him known to vast numbers of newspaper readers. "Beetle Bailey," "Blondie," "Dear Ann," and "Dear Abby" are other leading features in the nation's newspapers.

Created by Charles Schulz, the cartoon "Peanuts," with Charlie Brown and his friends, is popular with individuals from all age groups. Appearing in more than two thousand newspapers daily, the "Peanuts" characters have spawned books, toys, television shows, and stage shows and been brought before the public in many other ways.

Throughout our country's history, individuals have searched out others to honor, to pay homage to, to read and to hear about. And it has been the primary objective of the mass media to provide such information—in the press, over the air, and through pictures. We hope that at no time will we lose interest in what others are doing. It is, after all, history in the making.

With that in mind, let us take a closer look at this collection of personalities in the media world.

Every encyclopedia that provides biographical sketches will create considerable debate on why some individuals were included and why other individuals were not included.

How was this collection assembled? First, a time limit was necessary to restrict the size of the volume and so the post–World War II period has received the greatest emphasis. The majority of the persons included here are alive and working in the media world; however, a significant number of individuals who have died since World War II but who made major contributions to this field are included. A small number who died earlier are included because they played major roles in the media scene and often set the stage for others' later successes.

Next came the specific categories within the broad spectrum of the all-encompassing term "media." It was easier to eliminate some large groups first, with the hope that later volumes will focus on their contributions. Into this group fell advertising, public relations, management, and a broad group of the "behind-the-scene" operators, executives, and producers.

It is obvious that not every editor, publisher, photographer, bureau chief, columnist, commentator, cartoonist, or artist could be profiled. Inclusion was based upon significance of achievement as well as reputation.

Some book authors are included, but mainly those who started their careers in media, and their books have been listed. Often media personalities can sell books on their names alone. Much of their writing reflects on their involvement in national issues and events and often utilizes inside information to clear up obscure situations or to increase our knowledge of such incidents. Watergate is a prime example.

Many of the individuals listed here have achieved success in several areas. Quite a few of the leading broadcasters and successful magazine editors, for example, began their journalistic careers on newspapers. Seldom, however, have news program or magazine leaders turned to newspapers.

Recognition by one's peers often helped decide whether an individual was included. We have culled the names of people who have gotten major awards like the Pulitzer or other specialized ones for our listing.

Where does one obtain such a list? *Who's Who in America* is the best broad-based source of leading Americans in all fields. Its Chicago publisher also produces *Who's Who in the East, Who's Who in the South and Southwest, Who's Who in the West,* and *Who's Who in the Midwest.* There is also *Who's Who of American Women,* and those in Government, Finance and Industry, Religion, American Law, and in the World. A Northbrook, Illinois, firm publishes *Who's Who Among Black Americans.*

Entries were also obtained from journalism histories, such as Edwin and Michael Emery, *The Press in America*; Frank Luther Mott, *American Journalism*; Ernest Hynds, *American Newspapers in the Eighties*, and William H. Taft, *American Magazines for the '80's.*

Publications that focus on the media provide week-to-week data which were helpful in updating entries. These include *Editor & Publisher, Broadcasting, Television/Radio Age, Advertising Age, Folio, Publishers Weekly, Magazine Age, Madison Avenue,* and two newsletters: *Magazine Industry Newsletter* and *Gallagher's Report.*

Reviews, and city publications that focus on the media, with emphasis on their areas, include *Columbia Journalism Review, Washington Journalism Review, Washingtonian Journalism Quarterly,* and the *St. Louis Journalism Review.*

*Contemporary Authors*, published in Detroit by Gale Research Co., offers data about current writers, including journalists and television personalities. In some instances, more detailed interviews are included, along with references to other sources.

*Current Biography* offers monthly reports, collected at the end of each year.

*Time, Newsweek,* and *U.S. News & World Report* also provide media coverage, as to a lesser extent does *TV Guide.* Some major newspapers operate services and syndicates with well-known reporters commenting on media. These include Scripps-Howard, Knight-Ridder, and Gannett. There are also the New York Times Service, Los Angeles Times–Washington Post, Copley, and others.

Occasionally, corporations, newspapers, magazines, and radio and/or television stations publish their own histories.

Information was obtained about award winners through *Winners: The Blue Ribbon Encyclopedia of Awards,* published by Facts on File, Inc. This volume, by Claire Walter, provides information on many awards and lists winners in various categories. One section covers journalism.

Each December *Editor & Publisher* has an annual directory of journalism awards and fellowships. This is printed in the magazine, but may be purchased separately. It "contains basic information relative to competition that is open to reporters, photographers, editors, columnists, cartoonists, sportswriters, others in nationwide and regional prize opportunities." It provides information on submitting entries.

*Quill* magazine, in its June number, lists awards by Sigma Delta Chi and other well-known organizations. Several years ago the society adopted a longer name: Society of Professional Journalists, Sigma Delta Chi. Throughout this volume, however, I have used the shorter name, Sigma Delta Chi.

My objective with this publication is to provide the reader with a collection of sketches that reflects the media, that includes the majority of the better-known personalities, and that covers men and women who occupy key positions and who bear the responsibility for providing Americans with the necessary information to know and understand what is happening in the world.

# AWARDS

As indicated in the introduction, there are sources that list the awards available to media personalities. The following covers many of the references given in the sketches.

The *AAAS–Westinghouse Science Writing Award*, available for nearly 40 years, is awarded to science reporters. The *Aldo Beckman Award* is conferred by the White House Correspondents' Association for outstanding coverage of the White House. The *American Society of Journalists and Authors Award* is given to magazine and book writers.

In "the spirit of Heywood Broun," the Newspaper Guild gives an award in his name to a reporter with "an abiding concern for the underdog and the underprivileged." Broun, a columnist, helped establish the Guild.

The *James Wright Brown Award* is for excellence in public service reporting and honors the late publisher and chairman of *Editor & Publisher*. It is given by the Deadline Club of New York City. The *Louis Cassels Award* is given by the Religious Newswriters Association for religious reporting in newspapers. Columbia University handles the *Alfred I. du Pont Awards*, which are given in six categories. The *John Fischetti Editorial Cartoon Awards*, which honors the late Chicago cartoonist, is given to a cartoonist for outstanding work on current social and political subjects.

The *Golden Press and Mike Awards* are sponsored by the American Legion Auxiliary for features and editorials of interest to youth.

*Emmy Awards* are given by the Academy of Television Arts and Sciences in several categories.

The *Golden Quill Award* is given by the International Society of Weekly Newspaper Editors "for strong and effective commentary." The *Sidney Hillman Award* recognizes top writing about civil liberties and improved race and labor relations. For newspapers and broadcast personnel, the Scripps-Howard Foundation gives the *Roy W. Howard Public Service Award*.

The Anti-Defamation League of B'nai B'rith presents the *Hubert H. Humphrey First Amendment Freedoms Prize* to an individual or an organization for study of the First Amendment. The Inter American Press Association has *IAPA Awards* for reporting on Latin American affairs, defense of the freedom of the press, and courageous journalism.

A group of journalists who traveled with Robert F. Kennedy on his final campaign have established an award in his name "in recognition of outstanding achievement in portraying the problems of the disadvantaged."

The *A.J. Liebling Award* honors the noted media critic and is given to a career reporter with a record of excellence. The *Gerald S. Loeb Award*, handled by the University of California (Los Angeles) Graduate School of Business, recognizes reporting and commentary on business matters. The *Elijah Parish Lovejoy Award*, supervised by Colby College, is for "those who have contributed to this country's journalistic achievements."

The National Conference of Christians and Jews provides the *Mass Media Gold Medal* for promotion of better understanding among religions and races, fairness, and for professional journalism. The Scripps-Howard foundation has honored its longtime Memphis editor with the *Edward J. Meeman Award*, given for reporting on environmental subjects. Another Scripps-Howard editor and columnist has been honored with the *Lowell Mellett Award*, which is conferred for "critical evaluation of journalism."

The *Henry L. Mencken Prize* has been created "in the spirit and tradition of the *Baltimore Sun*." Each year, the University of Missouri School of Journalism awards medals to individuals, newspapers, magazines, and radio and/or television stations. The *Frank Luther Mott–Kappa Tau Alpha Award* honors the best book involving research about the media. The *Edward R. Murrow Award* is "for news coverage throughout the year, spot news, and continuing coverage." The *National Headliners Awards* have been given for over 50 years for reporting, editorials, photography, cartoons, documentaries, and other categories. The *National Magazine Awards*, established by the American Society of Magazine Editors and administered by the Columbia University School of Journalism, include several categories. They are financed by a grant from the Magazine Publishers Association.

The *National Press Club Awards* are given for excellence in the reporting of events, issues, and politics of particular benefit to hometown readers. For business publications and professional journals, there are the *James H. Neal Editorial Achievement Awards*, given by the American Business Press. They are considered "the Pulitzer Prize of the business press."

Since 1940, the *Overseas Press Club Awards* have recognized outstanding work in reporting and news photography. The *George Foster Peabody Awards* also date from 1940 and are considered the most prestigious in broadcasting. They are administered by the University of Georgia School of Journalism and Mass Communication.

The *George Polk Memorial Awards* honor a CBS correspondent who was killed in 1948 while covering the Greek civil war. The Long Island University Department of Journalism supervises the awards, which are for commentary, photography, books, magazines, and other media and honor "courage and resourcefulness in gathering information and skill in relating the story."

The *J.C. Penney–University of Missouri Awards* are for "life-style, consumer affairs and fashion reporting," with categories based on small, medium, and large circulation papers. Newspapers and magazines are included, and special awards are offered in television.

For more than 40 years, photographers have submitted their pictures to the *Pictures of the Year Competition*, supervised by the University of Missouri School of Journalism. There are various categories.

The Pulitzer Prizes are, of course, the grandfather of all media awards. They have long been administered by the Pulitzer Graduate School of Journalism at Columbia University. The categories have been expanded since they were established in 1917 with funds provided by a bequest from Joseph Pulitzer.

The Scripps-Howard Foundation has honored a former columnist with the *Ernie Pyle Award* for "newspaper writing that most nearly exemplifies the style and craft of the late Ernie Pyle." The *Reuben Award* is given by the National Cartoonists Society for editorial cartoons and comic strips and panels. The Sigma Delta Chi awards, in various categories, recognize distinguished service in journalism. In honor of the longtime United Press White House correspondent, the *Merriman Smith Award* has been established to recognize excellence in presidential news coverage.

# THE ENCYCLOPEDIA

**ABBOTT, Robert Sengstacke** (1870–1940)
A pioneer in Black journalism, Robert S. Abbott founded the weekly *Chicago Defender* in 1905. The newspaper reached a circulation of 230,000 ten years later but suffered heavy losses during the Depression. It became a daily in 1956. Its circulation today is about 20,000.

Abbott, born in Georgia, learned printing at the Hampton Institute. After his father's death, his mother married John H. H. Sengstacke, the son of a German merchant, who owned a small newspaper. Abbott worked on this paper and studied law in Chicago before he established his own publication.

Like some other publishers, Abbott resorted to sensationalism to attract readers, with headlines and articles that featured race problems and threats to Blacks. Before his death, however, Abbott had toned down his approach, shifting to better coverage of social and cultural news and the latest in fashions. A nephew, John H. Sengstacke, took over the *Defender*.

**ABEL, Elie** (1920– )
During four decades Elie Abel made the circle: after graduation from the Columbia University School of Journalism, he returned there in 1969 as dean and the Godfrey Lowell Cabot professor, a position he held for ten years.

In 1941 Abel was with the *Windsor Star* (Ontario). By 1945 he was the assistant city editor of the *Montreal Gazette* and in 1946 was in Berlin representing the North American Newspaper Alliance. In 1947 he was the United Nations correspondent for the Overseas News Agency, and two years later he began a 10-year association with the *New York Times* as a national correspondent.

Abel turned to the electronic medium in 1961 after serving as the Washington Bureau chief for the *Detroit News* for two years. He joined the National Broadcasting Co. and four years later was the network's London Bureau chief. He returned to Washington in 1967 as a diplomatic correspondent before going to Columbia University in 1969. Abel became the Harry and Norman Chandler professor of journalism at Stanford University in 1979.

In addition to his professorships, Abel won the George Foster Peabody award for outstanding radio news in 1968 and the Overseas Press Club award for interpretation of foreign news in 1969.

He wrote *The Missile Crisis; Roots of Involvement, The U.S. In Asia, 1784–*

1971 (with Marvin Kalb); and *Special Envoy to Churchill and Stalin* (with Averell Harriman). He edited *What's News: The Media in American Society.*

**ADAMS, Ansel** (1902–1984)

Starting with a Kodak Brownie box camera at the age of 14, Ansel Adams early realized the potential of the camera and turned a hobby into an art. Since that first snapshot taken in Yosemite National Park in 1916, Adams' followers, by the millions, have read his books and bought copies of his pictures. Thousands have attended his workshop and hundreds of thousands his exhibitions.

Adams became famous for his black-and-white pictures of the West. His "Moonrise, Hernandez, New Mexico" was sold originally for about $200. Recently, a print sold for $71,500. His more famous shots include "Aspens, Northern New Mexico," "Monolith, the Face of Half Dome," and other pictures taken in national parks, especially in Yosemite.

Adams' first one-man show was held in San Francisco's M.H. de Young Memorial Museum in 1932. In reflecting on the automation in photography today, Adams recalled that the early craftsmen "worked like dogs until they got what they wanted."

After he had been active in the Sierra Club for nearly 40 years, a club member observed that "It's hard to tell which has shaped the other more, Ansel Adams or the Sierra Club." Adams certainly was no favorite of the Reagan Administration, especially James Watt. He presented many of his views on the Reagan projects in an interview with *Playboy* magazine in 1983.

Explaining to *Playboy* readers his choice of subjects to photograph, Adams said: "If what I see in my mind excites me, there is a good chance it will make a good photograph. It is an intuitive sense and also an ability that comes from a lot of practice."

Adams has been credited with developing the Zone System, which was described in *Playboy* as follows: "Simplified, the Zone System enables a photographer to anticipate and control the tonal range of a print. The zones are essentially shades of gray ranging from black, which is zero, to white, which is ten. They correspond to exposure settings on the camera and can be used to identify the relative brightness of separate parts of the subject being photographed as they will appear on the print. In effect, the Zone System is a more accurate extension of the visualization concept."

Adams' large format, 20″ × 24″ Polaroid portrait of President Jimmy Carter became the first presidential photograph in the National Portrait Gallery. Adams was awarded the Presidential Medal of Freedom for work in photography and environmental interests. Other awards came from the Sierra Club and the Royal Photography Society.

Adams wrote many books, including *Yosemite Valley; These We Inherit, America's Parklands; New Ansel Adams Photography Series; Polaroid Land Professional Photography Manual; Photograph of the Southwest; The Portfolios of Ansel Adams; Ansel Adams: Yosemite and the Range of Light; The Camera;* and *The Negative.*

**ADAMS, Eddie (Edward Thomas)** (1933– )
Eddie Adams is best known for his on-the-spot photographs of a street corner execution of a Viet Cong lieutenant by the Vietnamese Chief of Police in 1968, for which he won a Pulitzer Prize.

Adams first worked on a newspaper in his hometown, New Kensington, Pennsylvania, later in Battle Creek, Michigan, and in Philadelphia from 1950 to 1962 before he joined the Associated Press. After a brief stay at *Time* magazine, Adams returned to the Associated Press until 1980. He is now a free-lance photographer, based in New York.

Adams returned to Vietnam in 1983. After his photographs became famous, he feared for the future of General Nguyen Hgoc Loan, who killed the Viet Cong officer. He discovered that the General reached America on his own and today operates a coffee and pizza shop in Virginia. Adams visited the General, who told him, "You were doing your job, and I was doing mine." These photographs are on display in the Vietnam War Museum.

Adams won the World Press Photography award in 1969. He also won awards from Sigma Delta Chi, the Overseas Press Club, Associated Press Managing Editors, and many regional groups. In addition, he has won the George Polk Memorial Award and the National Press Photographer Award. In 1975 he was named Photographer of the Year. Later came the Robert Capa Memorial Award and the American Society of Magazine Photographers Anniversary Award.

**ADAMS, Franklin Pierce** (1881–1960)
Better known as "F.P.A.," Franklin P. Adams was one of America's pioneer columnists who gained national recognition prior to World War II. Early in his life, 1903–04, Adams worked on the *Chicago Journal*. From there he went to the New York *Evening Mail*, where he wrote until 1913 a column titled "Always in Good Humor."

The next year, 1914, Adams joined the *Tribune* where "The Conning Tower" column appeared until 1921. For almost another decade, 1922 to 1931, his column was published in the *World*. When the *World* ceased publishing under that name, Adams moved to the *Herald Tribune* until switching to the *Post* in 1937. His column ended in 1941.

During World War I Adams served in military intelligence and wrote some columns for the *Stars and Stripes*, then under the editorship of Harold Ross, who later founded *The New Yorker*.

Don Marquis called Adams a master at column writing. He often spoofed timely topics. In addition to his own opinions, comments, and poetry, Adams received considerable material from his readers. Later in his career he appeared on the "Information Please" radio show.

Adams collaborated with O. Henry in a musical comedy titled *Lo*. He wrote the following books: *Tobogganing on Parnassus*; *In Other Words*; *By and Large*; *Weights and Measures*; *Something Else Again*; *Overset*; *So There!*; *So Much Velvet*; *Half a Loaf*; *Christopher Columbus*; *The Diary of Our Own*

*Samuel Pepys; The Melancholy Lute; Innocent Merriment; Nods and Becks*; and *F.P.A. Book of Pretorians*.

**ADAMS, George Matthew** (1878–1962)
George Matthew Adams today is not well known to newspaper readers, yet his work, shortly after the turn of the century, changed the content of many publications.

Adams created a syndicate under his name, buying features and distributing them. Many how-to articles were thus circulated to millions of readers. Today there are many syndicates that bring comics, columnists, and other features to the press.

Adams' birthplace was purchased by Henry Ford and restored in his Greenfield Village in Dearborn, Michigan.

**ADAMS, John Hanly** (1918– )
Following his graduation in journalism from the University of Missouri, John Hanly Adams began his career in 1940 on the *Eugene Daily News* (Oregon). After a brief career in the West, Adams joined *U. S. News & World Report* in Washington.

Adams advanced from associate executive editor to managing editor to executive editor and to director by 1979. He became editor of the Editor's Copy Syndicate in 1979 and the next year became a contributing editor to *Nation's Business*. He is an editorial consultant in Washington and a member of the White House Correspondents Association.

**ADAMS, Richey Darell** (1942– )
During the 1960s and 1970s, Richey Darell Adams won many awards in broadcasting. After working for the USIA Voice of America in Washington from 1965 to 1969, Adams became the news correspondent for radio station WTOP before going to National Public Radio in 1971 where he stayed until 1974.

Adams turned to WTOP-TV in 1974 and then, in 1976, became the editorial director for WDVM-TV in Washington.

Sigma Delta Chi honored him in 1977, the same year he was cited for outstanding television editorializing by both the Chesapeake and the Virginia Associated Press groups. Two years later, he won an award from the Academy of Television and Sciences (Emmy) for community service.

**ADDAMS, Charles Samuel** (1912– )
Readers of *The New Yorker* and viewers of early television shows are well acquainted with the cartoons and characters created by Charles Addams.

Addams, who has drawn for *The New Yorker* since 1935, has won numerous awards, such as the *Yale Record* Humor Citation and the Mystery Writers of America Special Recognition. He has published books on his "family"; his most recent book is titled *Creature Comforts*.

**ADEL, Judith** (1945– )
Judith Adel has had a successful career in the magazine field, winning many design awards for her creativity. She began her career as an editorial

assistant in 1963 for *Machinery* magazine and became its managing editor in 1967. From 1972 to 1973, she was production manager for *World* and later art director for the short-lived *Saturday Review/World* from 1973 to 1977.

Adel is the founder and creative director of the Savage Group, a design studio in New York. In 1977, she became the associate art director of *Business Week*. She has written several books.

**AGRONSKY, Martin** (1915– )
"Agronsky & Company," one of the popular Sunday television talk shows, is moderated by Martin Agronsky, who began as a reporter on the *Palestine Post*, 1936–37.

After several years as a free-lance journalist, Agronsky joined NBC in New York and in Europe, 1940–43. In 1943, he moved to the ABC Network, where he remained until 1964.

Agronsky worked for a time with the "Today Show." From 1964 to 1969, he was with the CBS Network in Paris, and since that time he has been a television commentator in Washington for the Post–Newsweek stations.

Agronsky has won many awards, including the Heywood Broun for radio reporting in 1948; the Peabody for distinguished reporting in 1952; the Alfred Dupont for television reporting in 1962, the same year he won the National Headliner Award. He won the Venice Film Festival 1963 award for "Polaris Submarine—Journal of an Undersea Voyage" and an Emmy Award for a "CBS Special."

He is co-author of *Let Us Begin: The First 100 Days of the Kennedy Administration*. He also has written magazine articles. The *Cleveland Plain Dealer* once wrote that "Agronsky would have made a classic trial lawyer."

**AJEMIAN, Robert Myron** (1925– )
After working from 1948 to 1951 as a sportswriter for the *Boston Evening American*, Robert M. Ajemian joined Time Inc. in New York, first as a *Life* reporter. He later represented *Time* and *Life* in Denver, 1954–56, worked in national affairs for *Life*, and in 1959–61, was Bureau Chief for the two periodicals in Chicago.

Ajemian moved to Paris in 1961 and spent two years there representing *Life*. He returned to New York City as political editor, later moving to assistant managing editor, and in 1972, to corporate affairs for Time Inc. From 1974 to 1977, Ajemian was a national political correspondent for *Time*. Then, in 1978, he became Washington Bureau chief.

He served in the Navy during World War II.

**ALBRIGHT, Joseph Medill Patterson** (1937– )
More than 20 years after Joseph Albright worked during the summers as a reporter for the *Denver Post* (Colorado), he won the Sigma Delta Chi prize for distinguished Washington reporting in 1979 and again in 1981. Since 1976, Albright has been the Cox Newspapers' correspondent in the national capital.

Earlier, Albright worked on the *Chicago Sun-Times* and spent a decade with *Newsday*, the last two years, 1969–71, as the publication's Washington Bureau chief. He also wrote for the *San Francisco Chronicle* and contributed to the *New York Times Magazine* in the 1970s.

In recent years, he was cited for outstanding reporting and public service by the National Press Club, Scripps-Howard, and the Headliner Club.

**ALEXANDER, Holmes** (1906– )

For three decades, conservative comments by Holmes Alexander have appeared in about 100 newspapers. From article writing, in 1932, Alexander advanced to the senior editorship of *Kiplinger's Magazine.*

Alexander's interest in politics was greater than his early interest in teaching. When he was 24, he was elected to the Maryland House of Delegates, serving until 1935. While there, he continued to write articles on political issues.

Early impressed by H. L. Mencken, Alexander turned to writing, confessing "an overfondness for words." For some time he wrote both factual and fictional articles for national periodicals. He has written novels and biographies of Martin Van Buren, Aaron Burr, and Alexander Hamilton.

After his World War II service, Alexander returned to free-lance writing and book reviews. In 1955, he told a radio audience that "conservatism is representative of all the things Americans really cherish." He retired from writing his column in 1981. Among his honors was the George Washington Honor Medal in 1973.

**ALEXANDER, Shana** (1925– )

In 1970 when Shana Alexander was editor of *McCall's*, 1964–71, she wrote: "I am quite sure that being a woman now, particularly an American woman, is more interesting, more challenging, more exciting and rewarding—and more complicated than it has ever been before."

This experience was one of many in Alexander's career. Two of her earlier jobs involved publications with specific involvement with limited audiences: *PM* newspaper, 1944–46, and *Flair* magazine, 1950.

For a decade she reported for *Life* magazine and later wrote a column, "The Feminine Eye." After a year as a Norton Simon Communications Inc. vice-president, Alexander became a television commentator, becoming nationally famous for her stimulating debates with James C. Kilpatrick on CBS's "60 Minutes" from 1975 to 1979. She also has contributed to *Newsweek.*

Alexander has won many awards, from Sigma Delta Chi, University of Southern California, to the Newswomen's Club. She was the *Los Angeles Times* "Woman of the Year" in 1969 and the winner of the Matrix award in 1973.

Her books include a *State-by-State Guide to Women's Legal Rights, Talking Woman, Anyone's Daughter,* and *Appearance of Evil: The Trial of*

*Patty Hearst.* She also wrote *Very Much a Lady—The Untold Story of Jean Harris and Dr. Herman Tarnower.*

**ALLBRITTON, Joe Lewis** (1924- )
Banking, real estate, and insurance provided the $200 to $300 million that Joe Lewis Allbritton supposedly is worth. However, he is better known outside his Houston operations for his brief ownership of the *Washington Star*, which he acquired in 1974 and sold four years later to Time Inc. for $20 million. Founded in 1952, the *Star* long occupied a key role in recording Washington's history. Allbritton brought in more top talent, including three Pulitizer Prize winners, yet the *Star* failed to turn a profit.

The *Trenton Times* (New Jersey) was bought by Allbritton for $12 million from the Washington Post Co., which had spent seven years trying to make the paper profitable. Allbritton also owns other newspapers and television and radio stations, including the *Westfield News* and *Pennysaver*, (Mass.); *Amherst Record* (Mass.); *Irwin Standard-Observer* (Pennsylvaina); *West Springfield News* (Mass.). His stations are in Charleston, S.C., Washington, D.C., Lynchburg, Va. and Kansas City, Kansas.

**ALLEN, Frederick Lewis** (1890–1954)
Probably better known for his many informative books concerning the American scene, Frederick Lewis Allen began his editing career on the *Atlantic Monthly* in 1914.

Two years later, he was the managing editor of *Century* magazine. He worked with the Council of National Defense during World War I, returning to the magazine business after several years with Harvard.

Allen became an assistant editor of *Harper's* magazine in 1923, associate editor in 1931, and editor from 1941 to 1953. He then served briefly as the director of the Ford Foundation.

Two of Allen's best known books are *Only Yesterday* and *Since Yesterday*; others include *The Lords of Creation, The Great Pierpont Morgan, Metropolis, I Remember Distinctly*, and *The Big Change.*

**ALLEN, George Howard** (1914- )
Magazine publishing has highlighted the career of George Allen who, early in his life, had been an assistant to the president of the New York-based National Theatre Supply Co.

Allen worked for radio station WOR; the Treasury Department during World War II as a radio consultant; and from 1944 to 1946, the Cooperative Analysis of Broadcasting in New York.

For many years Allen held executive positions with *McCall's* and later with Meredith Publishing Co. in Des Moines. He was publisher of *Better Homes & Gardens* and *Successful Farming* at Meredith. By 1966, he had joined Fawcett Publishers Inc. in New York, advancing to the senior vice-presidency for CBS Publications and to publisher for *Woman's Day*, a magazine he was associated with from 1966 to 1980.

Allen has won numerous awards from advertising and public relations organizations. In 1980, he was "Publisher of the Year" and the recipient of the Henry Jackson Fisher Award from the magazine industry.

**ALLEN, Larry** (1908–1975)
Excellent coverage of World War II for the Associated Press resulted in a Pultizer Prize for Larry Allen, who had started as a reporter in 1926 for the *Baltimore News*. He also worked for the *Washington Herald*, *Huntington Herald*, and *Charleston Mail*, the latter two in West Virginia.

Allen worked for the Associated Press from 1933 to 1960, with assignments in Charleston, Washington, Tel Aviv, Moscow, Singapore, Indochina, and other news centers. For defending freedom of the press while a prisoner of war, Allen was awarded the Bronze Star in 1945. Two years later, King George VI bestowed the Order of British Empire on him.

Allen organized the American Press Service, which specialized in covering Latin America, in 1960.

Among his other awards was the National Headliner Award in 1941 for his coverage of the British fleet operations.

**ALLEN, Maryon Pittman** (1925– )
Alabama newspaper readers have long appreciated the writings of Maryon Pittman Allen, who was a US senator in 1978 when she succeeded her late husband, James B. Allen.

An early career involved medical and insurance jobs, but in 1962, she became the woman's editor of the *Birmingham Sun* (Alabama). She became a columnist, winning Alabama Press Association awards in 1962 and 1963 for her "Reflections of a News Hen."

Pittman also won recognition for her work in typography, fashion reporting, and food stories. She remains associated with the J. D. Pittman Partnership Co.

**ALLEN, Steve** (1921– )
Steve Allen's full name is Stephen Valentine Patrick William Allen. But the world knows him as Steve Allen, the creator of the "Tonight Show" for the National Broadcasting Co. in 1954. He remained with the show through 1956.

Allen later was host, or moderator, of the "Steve Allen Show," "What's My Line?," "I've Got a Secret," "Laughback," and other shows. He won a Peabody Award for his more serious television show, "Meeting of the Minds."

Allen began his career as a radio announcer on Phoenix station KOY in 1942. He was later drafted for military service, but asthma ended his service after five months. Soon he was in Los Angeles working on several radio stations, where he became a disc jockey on a CBS affiliate there. In 1950, the "Steve Allen Show" opened in New York.

Since 1946, when Allen's first book, a book of verse, appeared, he has written dozens of other volumes. Several have been autobiographical.

Others concern national and international issues. One of his biographers said Allen's "creative juices never stop flowing."

Allen's books include *Fourteen For Tonight, Bop Fables, The Funnyman, Wry on the Rocks, The Girls on the Tenth Floor, The Question Man, Mark It and Strike It, Not all Your Laughter, Not all Your Tears, Letter to a Conservative, The Ground Is Our Table, Bigger Than a Breadbox, A Flash of Swallows, The Wake, Princess Snip-Snip, Curses, Schmock-Schmock!, What to Say When It Rains, Meeting of Minds, Chopped Up Chinese, Ripoff, Explaining China, Funny People, The Talk Show Murders,* and *Beloved Son: The Story of the Jesus Cults.*

**ALSOP Brothers**

The Alsop brothers, Joseph and Stewart, earned their place in journalism by excellent reporting. They frequently worked together, but also produced works of their own.

Joseph Wright Alsop (1910– ) graduated from Harvard, Stewart (1914–1974) from Yale. Both served in World War II. Joseph was sent to the Far East, where he was captured by the Japanese and later released and served with General Chennault. Stewart served in the European Theater, where he was a parachutist with the Office of Strategic Services.

*Time* magazine once described Joseph as "aggressive, facile, gregarious," and Stewart as "scholarly, quiet."

Joseph began his reporting experiences on the *New York Herald Tribune* in 1932. He later moved to Washington and from 1937 to 1940 he coauthored, with Robert T. Kinter, a syndicated column, "Capitol Parade."

In 1946, the brothers joined to write the "Matter of Fact" column for the *Herald Tribune*, which continued to 1958. In 1950 and 1952, they won the Overseas Press Club Award for the "best interpretation of foreign news."

Stewart began his career as an editor at Doubleday Doran & Co. He was said to have "excellent contacts in the White House and the intelligence community," being especially close to the Central Intelligence Agency. His last book was *Stay of Execution* in 1973. He contributed to *Life* and *Atlantic* magazines and, from 1958 to 1962, he was a contributing editor to the *Saturday Evening Post*. For the next six years, he was the *Saturday Evening Post* Washington editor. He then became a contributing editor to *Newsweek*.

**ANDERSON, Bradley Jay** (1924– )

Although the name Bradley Jay Anderson may not be immediately recognized by many Americans, the name of his artistic creation, "Marmaduke," certainly will be.

Starting as a free-lance magazine cartoonist in 1950, Anderson worked briefly for a public relations firm before starting "Marmaduke" in 1954. He also created another cartoon, "Grandpa's Boy" that year.

Marmaduke, a large, too-friendly dog, has also become the subject for many of his books. The daily cartoon is carried in hundreds of newspapers.

Anderson, who served in the Navy during World War II, has displayed his art in several major exhibitions. Some works are in permanent collections.

**ANDERSON, Curtiss Martin** (1928– )
Magazines have been the focus of Curtiss Martin Anderson's life. For his work he was recognized in 1963 as one of the Ten Outstanding Young Men in the United States.

For a decade, Anderson held various editorial positions at *Better Homes & Gardens*; he was also the editor of *Vacation Ideas* and *Home Building Ideas*, books published by the Meredith firm.

Anderson joined *Ladies' Home Journal* in Philadelphia in 1960 and became editor-in-chief in 1962. Two years later, he was writing for *McCall's*, but soon became editor of *Venture—The Traveler's World* between 1964 and 1971. Other positions were with Hallmark Cards in Kansas City and *Diversion* and *Look* magazines before he joined the Hearst Corporation in 1979 as editorial director. In recent years, he has worked for Hearst in its magazine development. He has also written, *Collection from the American Past* and co-authored *Why You Care Enough*.

**ANDERSON, Jack Northman** (1922– )
Generally credited with being the most widely read political columnist in America, Jack Anderson is either admired or damned for his work. More than 900 newspapers carry his daily column, with an estimated 40 million readers.

Anderson has long been active in the Mormon Church. This began after his family moved from California to Salt Lake City when Jack was two. At the age of 12, he edited a Boy Scout page for the *Deseret News* (Utah). In high school, he wrote for the *Tribune* on space rates.

After serving his two years of Mormon missionary work, Jack enrolled in the Merchant Marines Officers' Training School. Later he became a newspaper correspondent in China for the *Deseret News*. In 1945, he was inducted into the Army at Chunking and served for two years.

Anderson's career started slowly. He became a reporter in 1947 for Drew Pearson and his "Washington Merry-Go-Round" column. After working a decade with little public recognition, and threatening to quit, he received more bylines and, in 1965, equal credit as a partner. He became the sole owner of the column when Pearson died in 1969.

Anderson has been involved in numerous major exposes, such as the Bernard Goldfine–Sherman Adams vicuna coat gift; Truman's "Five Percenters"; the outside activities of Congressman Adam Clayton Powell, Jr., Senator Thomas J. Dodd, and others; and the Dita Beard–ITT secret memos.

Anderson once said that the mere presence of Pearson and himself in Washington kept many politicians honest, not because of any desire to be good, but because of their fear of being caught.

After previous nominations, Anderson finally won the Pulitzer Prize in

1972 for his revelation of administration policies during the India–Pakistan crisis.

"Investigative reporting has never been popular with editors and publishers," Anderson said."They usually belong to the same social world as the people we're exposing." Anderson considers himself the leading muckraker of today.

Anderson is a rarity in Washington: a Mormon who neither smokes nor drinks. He has written several books, including biographies of Joseph McCarthy and Estes Kefauver, and *The Anderson Papers*. Other Anderson books include *Washington Expose* and *Invention of New Jersey*, and he co-authored *McCarthy the Man, the Senator, the Ism; The Kefauver Story; U.S.A. Second Class Power?; Case Against Congress; American Government-Like It Is; Confessions of a Muckraker*; and *The Cambodia File*. He also appears regularly on radio and television shows, and he is in great demand as a public speaker.

But the conflict rages on. Seymour Hersh believes Anderson "has done some amazing reporting. You need somebody like him around." Ron Nissen, a regular reader, thinks "he's doing a very creditable job, a valuable job." Some enemies claim he overplays many stories. And Jody Powell, for example, said "I wouldn't trust him as far as I could throw him left-handed, and that's an understatement." But there are many millions who feel otherwise and regularly wait for Jack Anderson's latest probe of activities in Washington and around the world.

**ANDERSON, William Eugene** (1926– )

Success as an investigative reporter has brought many awards to William Eugene Anderson. His career began as a reporter on the *Indianapolis Star* (Indiana) from 1950 to 1956.

He then turned from newspapering to work as director of news for a local radio station and for two years, 1965–67, he was administrative assistant to the mayor of Indianapolis. A year as the advertising director of a local bank ended Anderson's non-newspaper work.

Anderson returned to the *Star* in 1969, and in 1975 he won the following awards for outstanding investigative reporting: the Pulitzer Prize, the George Polk Award, the National Headliner Award, the Drew Pearson Award, and a Sigma Delta Chi award.

Anderson wrote a series with *Star* reporter Harley Bierce and coordinator Richard Cady on city police corruption. It was a six-month probe. Anderson feels such reporting is needed in journalism, despite the dangers and the pressures.

**ANDREWS, James Frederick** (1936–1980)

The co-founder of the Universal Press Syndicate in 1970, James Andrews previously had been a stockbroker, managing editor of *Ave Maria* magazine in South Bend, and a reporter for the *Catholic Reporter* in Kansas City, Missouri.

Andrews helped build this syndicate into a major operation, unusual inasmuch as it is located in the Kansas City area rather than in New York. He numbered among his clients Dear Abby, Sylvia Porter, Doonesbury, Geech, Cathy, Gary Wills, William Buckley, Jr., and the Mini Page.

**ANDRIOLA, Alfred J.** (1912–1983)
The "Charlie Chan" and "Kenny Drake" cartoon strips are better known than their creator, Alfred J. Andriola. Chan began in 1938, the first to have an Asian as the primary character.

Andriola served as an assistant to Milton Caniff in drawing "Terry and the Pirates."

Andriola won the Reuben Award, Silver T-Square award from the National Cartoonists Society in 1970 and the Jester award from the Comic Council in 1966.

**ANNENBERG, Walter H.** (1908– )
When Moses Annenberg died in 1942, he left Triangle Publications to his son, Walter, and his five daughters. In 1956, Walter Annenberg founded *TV Guide*, and in 1982, his fortune was estimated by *Quill* magazine as being between $600 million and $1 billion.

Annenberg announced in 1983 that his Rancho Mirage, California estate would eventually become a museum. This estate, which includes 205 acres and a home designed by Quincy Jones, contains an art collection, including the works of Van Gogh, Cezanne, Monet, Renoir, and Gauguin, valued at $200 million.

Once the owner of the *Philadelphia Inquirer* and the *Daily News*, both Pennsylvania papers, as well as television, radio, and cable operations, Annenberg now owns *TV Guide*, *Seventeen*, and the *Daily Racing Form*. For a brief time he published *Panorama*, a magazine ahead of its time, but there were too few "upscale television viewers" to make it profitable.

Rance Crain, reporting on an interview with Annenberg in *Advertising Age* in late 1983, quoted the eastern publisher as saying he "misjudged the economics of the time involving *Good Food* [one of his earlier experiments] and perhaps I was a bit impetuous in closing that up." Annenberg added that he had misjudged the market for *Panorama*, which "was editorially good," and concluded that "we don't underestimate other people and trust that they will not underestimate us."

Occasionally, Annenberg writes a commentary for *TV Guide* to voice his opinions on current issues. A week before the 1980 presidential election he called for a Ronald Reagan victory, stating that such a victory "would promise to restore self-confidence and the self-respect that until recent years have been the foundation of the American spirit." He had known Reagan since the 1930s.

In 1969, Annenberg became the United States ambassador to the Court of St. James. He worked diligently to succeed in this position, spending considerable money to renovate the embassy. He was respected by British business leaders, but at first he was rejected by others. This negative press gradually shifted to a more friendly attitude and by the time he left, five and one-half years later, he was praised for his work. In all his encounters, he was aided by his wife, Lee, who later served as Reagan's Chief of Protocol, with the rank of ambassador.

A biographer, John Cooney, wrote that these years had changed Annenberg. His service began with "enormous trepidation," but he returned to America "relaxed and mellowed." When Queen Elizabeth II visited America in 1976 she knighted Annenberg, who is still called "Mr. Ambassador" by his associates.

Annenberg has given away millions of dollars. He has donated $250 million to the University of Pennsylvania, which includes funds for the Annenberg Center and the Annenberg School of Communications. A similar school has been established at the University of Southern California. He has promised $150 million over a 15-year period to the Corporation for Public Broadcasting. Others have benefited from his generosity, such as the Child Day Care Center at Desert Hospital in Palm Springs and the Peddie School. He has received many awards and honors for his civil leadership activities.

All his projects have not been favorably received, however. For example, he once created a "News Watch" column for *TV Guide* designed to monitor the network news for fairness. However, his choice of "monitors" was rather loaded on the conservative side.

**ARLEDGE, Roone** (1931– )

The creator of "Wide World of Sports" and the "National Football League Monday Night Football," Roone Arledge has been president of ABC News and ABC Sports since 1977. He has been involved in controversy over events coverage and has been credited with many innovations in the television industry.

To some observers, Arledge is "The P.T. Barnum of television news." Apparently he has a sense of what the public wants. A controversy arose the day Elvis Presley died. Would this lead the evening ABC News or would the Panama Canal Treaty? ABC went with Presley; CBS went with Panama. Later, when Bing Crosby died, CBS also went first with that story.

Slow motion, stop action, instant replay, split screens, hand-held cameras, and more interviews. These are some of the changes Arledge used to revitalize the television screen.

Arledge believes anchor persons should go to the scene of the news from time to time. He was involved in the Harry Reasoner–Barbara Walters co-anchorship of ABC Evening News, and he has been responsible for bringing, to his network, Carl Bernstein, David Brinkley, Britt Hume, Max Robinson, Hughes Rudd, Pierre Salinger, Lynn Sheer, Sander Vanocur, and others, while making Howard Cosell a household word. He also tried to hire Dan Rather and Tom Brokaw.

After completing his studies at Columbia University, Arledge joined the old Dumont network in the early 1950s before service in the Korean War. Later, he was the stage director and a producer with NBC from 1955 to 1960. He once told Roger Piantodosi, in an interview published in the

*Washington Journalism Review*, that he originally "wanted to work at *Time* or *Newsweek* or one of those publications, something like that. But television was just getting started, and it occurred to me that a lot of things I really enjoyed, television was able to do."

Arledge joined ABC Sports in 1960, and by 1968 he was president. His more recent success has been the growth of "Nightline" with Ted Koppel, which has cut into the Johnny Carson audience on NBC. ABC bid $225 million for the 1984 Olympics.

Arledge received a Gold Medal from the International Radio and Television Society in 1983 for 23 years of service to the profession. He has won at least ten Emmy awards as well as the TV Guide Award, the Cannes Film Festival Grand Prize, National Headliner' citation, and several George Foster Peabody recognitions.

**ARLEN, Michael J.** (1930– )

Although better known as the author of books, Michael J. Arlen began his career in 1952 as a reporter for *Life* magazine. Since 1957 he has been a contributor and television critic for *The New Yorker*. He also has served on the faculty of the Bread Loaf Writers Conference and as a juror for the Columbia University-Dupont awards in broadcast journalism.

Arlen once described the war in Vietnam as the "living room war" with its television coverage of on-the-scene killings and combat action.

In 1968 Arlen won the Screen Directors Guild award for his television criticism and in 1976 the National Book Award for contemporary affairs. His books include *Living-Room War*; *Exiles: An American Verdict*; *Passage to Ararat*; *The View from Highway 1*; *Thirty Seconds*, and *The Camera Age*.

**ARMSTRONG, Joe** (1943– )

A varied career preceded Joe Armstrong's rise to the position of editor–publisher of the *New York* magazine. Armstrong, admitted to the Texas bar in 1968, spent the next four years with a New York banking firm. He next entered the publishing arena, first as assistant to the publisher of *Family Weekly*. A shift occurred in 1973 when Armstrong began a four-year stint with Straight Arrow Publishers, serving first as advertising director of the firm's *Rolling Stone* magazine and later as president and publisher.

Armstrong's career with *New York* started in 1977. Two years later he was president–editor. In 1969, he was named "Outstanding Young Man in America" by the Junior Chamber of Commerce. Today he is with a new magazine, *Movies*.

**ARMSTRONG, Richard Alford** (1929– )

By way of Mississippi and Alabama, Richard Armstrong moved to become the executive editor of *Fortune* magazine.

Following his journalism studies at the University of Missouri, Armstrong spent four years on the *Gadsden Times* (Alabama), with time off for service in the Korean War where he was awarded the Bronze Star. Then he became a contributing editor for *Time*, followed by seven years with the

*Saturday Evening Post*, 1962–69. He was managing editor for *USA-I*, which was unsuccessful.

Armstrong has been with *Fortune* since 1969.

**ARMSTRONG, Tom** (1932?– )

A modest baby boom in America inspired Tom Armstrong to create the comic strip, "Marvin," which first appeared in late 1982.

Armstrong's "comic baby" experienced a rapid growth, gaining nearly 300 newspaper outlets within six months. The cartoonist said, "Marvin is ugly, but cuty." His wife believes Marvin "is so ugly only a mother could love him." However, millions of readers do. His wife tests many of Armstrong's ideas for the strip.

As with other cartoonists, Armstrong's strips are often autobiographical, based on members of his family. His first book, *Marvin: A Star Is Born*, appeared in 1983. Soon there will be Marvin dolls, posters, puzzles, toys, and the like.

**ARNETT, Peter** (1934– )

Outstanding coverage of the Vietnam War brought international recognition and a Pulitzer Prize for Peter Arnett, then an Associated Press reporter. In 1983, he revisited Vietnam as national correspondent for the Cable News Network.

"I happen to believe that war reporting is an essential service undertaken in the great majority by serious-minded men and women," Arnett wrote about this visit. Such reporters "are not the eyes, the ears, the arbiters of the world's problems. We are an imperfect window on our troubled times, providing at least the glimmer of truth from places where darkness rules," he added.

Arnett was a reporter in New Zealand and Australia in the 1950s and served in the New Zealand Army from 1952 to 1954.

When Arnett won a Sigma Delta Chi award in 1970 he said, "an aggressive, cantankerous and unlovely press corps has enabled the world to see the war in Vietnam for what it was."

Arnett served as an Associated Press correspondent for 20 years and won a citation from the Overseas Press Club, as well as the George Polk Memorial Award.

**ARNO, Peter** (1904–1968)

For more than half a century, readers of *The New Yorker* have found the same aristocratic old gentleman looking at them from the magazine once a year.

Peter Arno created this personality when the magazine began in 1925. *The New Yorker* reprints the same cover for each anniversary.

Arno's career as a writer and producer of musical revues has been overlooked, however. He also was a designer for Paramount Studio and he designed automobiles. A pianist, Arno also found success as a photographer.

Arno's illustrations and paintings appeared in other American and foreign publications.They were exhibited in many cities in the United States and in London and Paris.

**ASCOLI, Max** (1898–1978)
Max Ascoli established *The Reporter* magazine in 1949. It was sold to *Harper's*, which discontinued it in 1968, because Ascoli could not "accommodate his views to the changing mood over American intervention in Indochina."

Ascoli brought most of his family's fortune to America in 1931, escaping Mussolini's rule in Italy. He taught at the New School for Social Research in New York and, with a few associates, designed *The Reporter* as "a liberal fortnightly of facts and ideas dealing with national and international affairs."

Ascoli wrote several books, including *Intelligence in Politics* and *The Power of Freedom*.

**ASHMORE, Harry Scott** (1916–     )
A Southerner by birth and by professional experience, Harry Ashmore became better known across America for his editorials in the *Arkansas Gazette* in Little Rock during the 1950s integration struggles, for which he won a Pulitzer Prize.

After varied assignments on a newspaper in his hometown of Greenville, South Carolina, and later in Charlotte, North Carolina, where he became editor of the *News* in 1947, Ashmore moved to the *Arkansas Gazette* in 1947. He edited the editorial page. He took a leave of absence to assist Adlai E. Stevenson in the 1955–56 presidential campaign.

Ashmore began a new career as consultant for the Center for Study of Democratic Institutions Fund for Republic in 1959. For several years he was editor-in-chief for the *Encyclopedia Britannica*. He continues as a senior fellow at the Center.

Two of his books, *The Negro and the Schools* (1954) and *An Epitaph for Dixie* (1958), were well received. The latter was called, by a New York reveiwer, "probably the best book written about the South by a Southerner in recent years."

In addition to the Pulitzer Prize, Ashmore won the Freedom House and the Sidney Hillman awards. He was a Nieman fellow at Harvard in 1941–42.

**ATHERTON, James Kenneth Ward** (1927–     )
A frequent winner of the White House Press Photographers Association annual contest, James Atherton has, in recent years, operated a used book shop in Kensington, Maryland which continuing his photography career.

Atherton currently is a staff photographer for the *Washington Post*. He began as a Telephoto operator for Acme Newspapers in 1949 and spent the next 20 years as a Washington photographer for the United Press International. In 1973, he moved to the *Post* as a staff photographer.

Atherton won the Picture of the Year Award for general news coverage in 1964. Other awards came from the Headliner Club, the Washington-Baltimore Newspaper Guild, and Kent State University.

**ATKINSON, Brooks** (1894–1984)
Brooks Atkinson began his newspaper career on the *Springfield Daily News* (Massachusetts) in 1917.

Atkinson moved to the *Boston Transcript* in 1919 as a reporter and assistant to the drama critic. Two years were spent as associate editor of the *Harvard Alumni Bulletin* before he joined the *New York Times* for a long career.

In 1922, Atkinson edited the *Times' Book Review* section. He was a drama critic from 1925 to 1942 and again from 1946 to 1960 after serving as a war correspondent in China and Moscow. In 1947 he won a Pulitzer Prize for his stories about Russia.

Atkinson became a critic-at-large from 1960 to 1965, writing a column twice a week. His reviews were said to make or break a play or a performer. He claimed he only tried to be truthful, and refrained from close contacts with theater personalities to keep neutral. Nevertheless, he received awards from the Actor's Equity Association and the League of Off-Broadway Theatres. In addition, a theater was named for him. Atkinson wrote many books, including *Skyline Promenades*; *A Potpourri*; *Henry Thoreau: The Cosmic Yankee*; *East of the Hudson: The Cingalese Prince*; *Cleo for Short*; *Broadway Scrapbook*; *Once Around the Sun*; *Tuesdays and Fridays*; *Brief Chronicles*; *Broadway*; and *The Lively Years*. He edited *College in a Yard*; *The Pace Report*; *Walden and Other Writings*, and *Sean O'Casey Reader*. He was the co-author of *This Bright Land, A Personal View*.

He was named to the Theatre Hall of Fame and Museum in 1973.

**ATTWOOD, William Hollingsworth** (1919– )
Born in Paris, William H. Attwood spent his early years there before coming to America. At Princeton, Attwood worked on the *Daily Princetonian* and, during the summers, on newspapers.

Service in World War II was followed by a three-year stint on the *New York Herald Tribune* as a correspondent in Washington and Paris and at the United Nations. Attwood also wrote magazine articles. In 1949, he became a European correspondent for *Collier's* and moved to *Look* two years later to serve a decade in various editorial positions. This work resulted in a Headliner' Club Award in 1955 for outstanding magazine work.

Attwood wrote speeches for Adlai Stevenson in 1956 and 1960 and for John F. Kennedy after he had won the Democratic nomination. Attwood served as ambassador to Guinea and later to Kenya, in addition to a brief tour as special adviser to the United Nations.

Attwood returned to the publishing world in 1966 with Cowles Communications, which then included *Look*, *Family Circle*, *Venture*, and *Insider Newsletter*. During this time he was involved in a controversy with Jacqueline Kennedy over the serialization of the William Manchester biography of her husband.

He resigned from Cowles in 1970 to become the president–publisher of *Newsday*, a position he held until 1978. He serves on the executive committee of the International Center of Photography, U.S. National Commission for UNESCO. In addition to his Headliner' Club awards, Attwood won the George Polk Memorial Award in 1956 and the New York Newspaper Guild Page One Award in 1960. He has written several books, including *The Man Who Could Grow Hair; or Inside Andorra*; and *The Reds and the Blacks; A Personal Adventure.*

**AUCHINCLOSS Brothers**
David Auchincloss (1943– ) entered the *Newsweek* training program in 1967, and ten years later became the publisher, after being the executive vice-president for a year. He was with the International Investor, Inc., in New York in 1981–1982. In 1982, he was appointed president and publisher of the *Altantic Monthly.*

Kenneth Auchincloss (1937– ) was involved in several political jobs in the early 1960s before going to Princeton University as assistant to the trustees for the Institute for Advanced Study. He joined *Newsweek* in 1966 and became the managing editor in 1975.

**AUTH, Tony** (1942– )
Political cartoonist Tony Auth began his career as a medical illustrator at Rancho Los Amigos Hospital in Downey, California, where he worked from 1964 to 1971. Auth moved to the *Philadelphia Inquirer* (Pennsylvania) in 1971 as editorial cartoonist, and in 1976 he won the Pulitzer Prize for his work.

Associated with the Washington Post Writers Group, Auth provides a "light touch on serious subjects." In addition to his Pulitzer Prize, Auth has won awards from the Overseas Press Club and Sigma Delta Chi. He published an anthology in 1978, *Behind the Lines.*

**BACKLUND, Ralph Theodore** (1918– )
Broadcasting and magazine interests have kept Ralph T. Backlund busy. In 1946, he began as a newswriter on station WCCO in Minneapolis, Minnesota, and in 1950 began an eight-year association with CBS, beginning as a producer of public affairs programs for the radio network.

Backlund turned to magazines, becoming associate editor for *Horizon* and later its managing editor, 1958–66. He served with the Department of State, 1966–69, as a special assistant for arts in the Bureau of Educational and Cultural Affairs.

Today Backlund is the executive editor of *Smithsonian* magazine, having joined its board of editors in 1969. He moved to his present post in 1976.

Backlund, who served in both World War II and the Korean War, won the Heywood Broun Award in 1948.

**BAGDIKIAN, Ben Haig** (1920– )
His job as an ombudsman, or in-house critic, for the *Washington Post* earned Ben Bagdikian his recognition in the newspaper world. In 1941, he was a reporter for the *Springfield Morning Union* (Massachusetts). He served in World War II and became a staffer with the *Providence Journal*, 1947–62, serving as a reporter, foreign correspondent, and Washington correspondent.

During the past two decades, Bagdikian has written for the *Saturday Evening Post*, the *Washington Post*, and the *Columbia Journalism Review*. From 1967 to 1969, he was project director for a study of the future news media in America for the Rand Corporation. He has written several books and has won numerous awards, including a Guggenheim fellowship in 1961–62.

Bagdikian's comments have stirred up frequent debates. He said "newspaper corporations, like all others, hate to have their linen washed in public." He frequently upset the *Washington Post* editors, claiming he was "writing for the readers" and not for the newspaper.

In recent years, Bagdikian has continued his writing about the newspaper business while teaching at the University of California in Berkeley.

Bagdikian's books include *In the Midst of Plenty: The Poor in America; The Information Machines: Their Impact on Men and the Media; The Shame of the Prisons; The Effete Conspiracy; Caged: Eight Prisoners and Their Keepers*; and *The Media Monopoly*.

**BAILEY, Charles Waldo II** (1929– )
For more than three decades, Charles Bailey's career was with the *Minneapolis Tribune* (Minnesota). He began as a reporter in 1950 and later represented the newspaper in Washington. He remained in the capital until 1972, and was four years the bureau chief.

Bailey returned to Minneapolis as editor in 1972. A decade later he resigned in a dispute with the owner and publisher over their required 15 percent cut in staff. He had served as editor of the *Star and Tribune*, which was the result of a merger between the morning and afternoon Minneapolis newspapers.

In resigning, Bailey wrote in the *Washington Journalism Review* about his experiences. "I think there are some new threats to the independence and public utility of newspaper editors," he noted. "One is the growing tendency to encourage, in fact, to require, editors to become businessmen—to be part of a 'management team,' to concentrate on things that involve business rather than journalism."

Bailey feared that "an awful lot of newspapers are standing on the shore instead of wading out to make waves."

**BAILLIE, Hugh** (1890–1966)
Hugh Baillie and the United Press Associations were one and the same for 40 years.

Baillie began his career on the *Los Angeles Herald* in 1910; and later on he joined the *Record*. He managed United Press bureaus on the West Coast and, in 1920, became general manager. Four years later he was United Press sales manager. Baillie continued to advance, reaching the wire service organization presidency in 1935. For the next two decades he was the top executive at United Press.

Baillie interviewed many of the world's leaders, including Stalin, Mussolini, Hirohito, Adenauer, Chiang Kai-shek, and Douglas MacArthur. He directed the press coverage of World War II and the Korean War.

The Missouri School of Journalism honored Baillie with its Distinguished Service in Journalism Award in 1953, two years before he retired. Baillie also wrote *Two Battlefronts, Men at Crisis* and *High Tension*.

**BAKER, George** (1915–1975)

Millions of World War II servicemen remember George Baker, or at least his cartoon, "The Sad Sack," which was printed in *Yank*.

Baker began cartooning in Hollywood with the Walt Disney Studio, working on such memorable classics as *Pinocchio, Dumbo, Bambi*, and *Fantasia*.

"The Sad Sack" was syndicated after World War II. The characters were continued in books, on radio programs, and in motion pictures. Baker was awarded a Legion of Merit.

**BAKER, Marilyn** (1929– )

Reporting for the press and for television stations has brought many awards to Marilyn Baker. Baker started as a reporter on the *Los Angeles Examiner* in 1945. From 1949 to 1959 she was editor of *Spectator* in Los Angeles and Beverly Hills.

Her television career began in 1968 when she took over as news director for Cameron Broadcasting in Los Angeles and Palm Springs. She then moved to KQED-TV in San Francisco where she stayed until 1974.

Baker created the first investigative unit in local television news in 1974 and won awards for such reporting on station KPIX-TV. Two of her major citations included Emmy awards for feature reporting in 1975 and 1977 and the George Foster Peabody Award in 1974. She now operates Baker Enterprises in San Francisco.

**BAKER, Russell (Wayne)** (1929– )

His book, *Growing Up*, added to Russell Baker's newspaper fame and increased his nationwide audience. The *Washington Post* called this memoir "the stuff of American legend . . . an incandescent work of memory, imagination and artistry."

Baker's "universality of his vision" brought him a Pulitzer Prize in 1979 for his commentary in the *New York Times*. Earlier Baker had told Nora Ephron that he had had "an unhappy life, thank God." His book, however, made his childhood in Virginia and Maryland exciting to readers.

After graduation from Johns Hopkins University, where he edited the campus newspaper, Baker became a police reporter on the *Baltimore Sun*

(Maryland). When he returned to visit the campus staff at Johns Hopkins in 1983 he told them that, in his day, "We were the C students. The bright group went into banking."

On the *Sun*, Baker became a rewrite man and, in 1952, chief of the London bureau. James B. Reston offered him a job with the *New York Times* Washington Bureau in 1954. By 1961, Baker "had done enough reporting" so he wrote a book, *An American In Washington*, termed "an irreverent guide to survival in the capital."

Offered a chance to return to the *Sun*, Baker's boss gave him the chance to write the "Topics" column on the *Times* in New York. Baker later said he modeled his column on E.B. White's humorous editorials in *The New Yorker*.

Baker told Ronald Steel, in a GEO interview, that "the hardest thing is deciding what subject to deal with. What are people interested in today that I'm interested in?"

Other awards include the Mark Sullivan Memorial Award in 1976 and the George Polk award for commentary in 1979. Baker has written such books as *No Cause for Panic; All Things Considered; Our Next President; Poor Russell's Almanac; The Upside Down Man*, and *So This Is Depravity*.

**BALK, Alfred William** (1930– )

Alfred Balk has been a reporter, a producer, a magazine writer, and an editor. Beginning on the *Rock Island*, Illinois *Argus* in 1946, Balk moved to Chicago in 1952 to become a newswriter–producer at WBBM.

Balk later worked for the *Sun Times* (Illinois) and the J. Walter Thompson advertising agency in Chicago. He then turned to magazines, where he remains today as editor–publisher of *World Press Review*. Before this association, Balk was with the *Saturday Evening Post* and the *Saturday Review*.

Books written by Balk include *The Religious Business; The Free List: Property Without Taxes; A Free and Responsible Press* and as co-author of *Our Troubled Press*.

Balk is a consultant to the Ford and Markle foundations and vice-president of the Media Commentary Council.

**BARBOUR, William Albert** (1921– )

Before becoming president of the Chilton Company, William Barbour was editor of the *Cape May County Gazette* and the *Moorestown News Chronicle*, both in New Jersey.

Joining the Chilton firm as an assistant editor in 1952, Barbour became managing editor in 1953, editor in 1951, and publisher in 1961. He advanced through the vice-presidency level to become president and chief operating officer in 1972.

Barbour's comments on the status of the business press in America, an area in which he is a recognized authority, are often quoted. For the years ahead, this Air Force veteran of World War II visualizes more specialization and more audience segmentation. He also predicts greater use of electronic delivery systems that could complement conventional print editions.

**BARNARD, William Calvert** (1914– )
Long a member of the Associated Press news gathering organization, William Barnard, in 1981, became the general executive for the group's 24 western states.

Barnard began his reporting career on the *Corpus Christi Caller-Times* (Texas) in 1935 and in 1941 moved to the feature editor's position on the *San Antonio Express-News* (Texas). The next year Barnard joined the Associated Press as writer and state editor in the Dallas Bureau. He covered the Korean War and other Far East news until his return to Dallas in 1954 as Bureau Chief.

Before moving to San Francisco in 1971, Barnard was an Associated Press executive in the New York headquarters.

**BARNETT, David Leon** (1922– )
Newspapers and magazine assignments prepared David Barnett for his present position as senior editor of *U.S. News & World Report.*

Barnett, in 1947, was a member of the *Richmond News-Leader* (Virginia) staff. Later he served as chief of the newspaper's state house bureau and handled political news. He was also regional correspondent for *Business Week* from 1951 to 1954.

After a few years as assistant city editor, Barnett became the Washington correspondent for the North American Newspaper Alliance and for ten years, 1966–76, its Bureau Chief.

In 1976, Barnett became the associate editor of *U.S. News.* In 1985 he became an assistant managing editor. During World War II he served in the Air Force.

**BARRON, Clarence Walker** (1855–1925)
Clarence Barron, early in his career, worked on the *Daily News* and the *Transcript* in Boston. He founded the News Bureau there to obtain financial stories, which he rewrote and sold to clients. He was the Boston correspondent for the *Wall Street Journal*, and in 1902 acquired its owner, Dow Jones & Co.

Barron, at 5 feet, 6 inches and 300 pounds, was quite visible in financial circles, where he established a reputation as a top interviewer. He wrote about the leaders, some of whom later became known as the "Robber Barons."

Barron has been credited with turning the *Wall Street Journal* into a "hard-hitting, influential paper" and an industrial watchdog.

**BARTHOLOMEW, Frank H.** (1898– )
As president of the United Press Association, Frank Bartholomew presided over the merger of this group and the International News Service in 1958. Today it is the United Press International.

Bartholomew joined the United Press in Portland in 1921 and moved through the executive levels, becoming emeritus chairman of the board in 1972.

The significant events in this nation's history covered by Bartholomew included many Pacific battles as well as the climax to World War II, the surrender of the Japanese on the USS *Missouri* in 1945. He also covered the atomic bomb tests, the fall of Shanghai, the Korean War, and other events. After his UPI career, Bartholomew invested in California vineyards.

**BARTLEY, Robert Leroy** (1937– )
The editor of the *Wall Street Journal* began his reporting career on the *Grinnell Herald-Reporter* (Iowa) in 1959, after graduating from Iowa State University.

By 1962, Bartley was associated with the *Wall Street Journal* as a reporter in Chicago and later in Philadelphia, where editor Vermont Royster later claimed he and associate editor Joe Evans "gave him some books to review and were so pleased with his performance that we invited him to come to New York ." He also described Bartley as a good reporter with "brashness and brightness."

To prepare Bartley for higher editorial assignments, the newspaper sent him to Vietnam, Japan, and Washington before bringing him back to New York. When Evans died suddenly in 1971, Bartley became the associate editor and in 1979 the editor of the *Wall Street Journal*.

**BATCHELOR, Clarence D.** (1888–1977)
Among the pioneer newspaper editorial cartoonists was Clarence Batchelor, who won a Pulitzer Prize in 1937. He also won the Headliner Award and Page One award. Twenty-five years earlier, in 1912, he had won a $200 prize from the American Medical Association for the best cartoons concerning public health.

In 1911, Batchelor worked in the *Kansas City Star* and for several years was a free-lance artist. He was trained at the Chicago Art Institute.

Before joining the *New York Daily News*, were he worked from 1930 to 1969, Batchelor was a cartoonist for the New York-based Ledger Syndicate.

Batchelor once said "a political cartoonist should have in him a little of the clown, the poet, the historian, the artist, and the dreamer."

**BATIUK, Thomas Martin** (1947– )
The name Thomas Batiuk may not be as well known to most newspaper readers as his comic strip creation.

Batiuk has been drawing "Funky Winkerbean," syndicated by the Field Newspaper group, since 1972. In 1979, he added "John Darling," in which he is assisted by Tom Armstrong. Several Winkerbean books have been published. His book, *You Know You've Got Trouble When Your School Mascot Is a Scapegoat*, appeared in 1984.

**BATTEN, Frank** (1927– )
Frank Batten took over Landmark Communications in 1954 in Norfolk, Virginia. According to a *Quill* magazine report in late 1982, Batten today is worth between $100 and $200 million.

Batten's holdings include television stations, cable operations, and newspapers in Virginia and North Carolina. He began as an assistant secretary-treasurer with Norfolk Newspapers, Inc., in 1952. By 1966, he had become the chairman of the board and the firm's chief operating officer.

**BATTEN, James Knox** (1936– )
From a reporter's position on the *Charlotte Observer* (North Carolina) in 1957, James Batten has moved up in the Knight-Ridder organization to its presidency.

Batten spent five years in the Knight Newspapers' Washington Bureau, where he concentrated on Southern politics and civil rights reporting. He earned degrees from Davidson College and Princeton.

From 1970 to 1972, Batten was assistant city editor of the *Detroit Free Press* before returning to the *Charlotte Observer* as executive editor. In 1975, he joined the Knight-Ridder corporate staff and, in 1980, became a senior vice-president.

Batten has won the George Polk Memorial Award, for regional reporting, and the Sidney Hillman Foundation Award.

**BAUKHAGE, Hilmar Robert** (1889–1976)
Baukhage, well known to radio listeners in the 1940–50 era, claimed to be the first person to broadcast news directly from the White House. This broadcast, in 1941, broke the news about Pearl Harbor.

A long career with Consolidated Press, 1919–32, followed Baukhage's newspaper experience in Paris, London, and Washington. After other newspaper and magazine jobs, Baukhage became a news commentator for NBC on the Farm and Home Hour in 1934. In 1939, he was broadcasting news from Berlin. He worked for ABC from 1942 to 1951 and then with the Mutual Broadcasting System from 1951 to 1954.

Among Baukhage's many awards was the National Headliner Club honor in 1945. He was a co-author of *I Was There* and the editor of *American Military Leaders of World War I* and *World War II*.

**BAUMAN, George Duncan** (1912– )
The Department of Defense awarded its highest civilian honor, the Secretary of Defense's Medal for Distinguished Public Service, to George Duncan Bauman, publisher of the *St. Louis Globe-Democrat* (Missouri). The 1983 citation noted his newspaper's role "as a fearless and outspoken advocate of a strong nation." He was also named the Man of the Year in St. Louis in 1983. He is now retired, following the sale of the *Globe-Democrat* in 1984.

Bauman was a reporter on the *Chicago Herald Examiner* from 1931 to 1939. By 1943, he had joined the *Globe-Democrat*, serving as personnel manager, business manager, and in 1967, publisher. Throughout his career, Bauman has been active in civic affairs in St. Louis and throughout Missouri.

He has received honorary university degrees, numerous citations, and other awards. Much of his non-newspaper interests have been with such organizations as the Boys Club, United Way, and Catholic Charities.

**BAXTER, Michael John** (1944– )
The George Polk Memorial Award was given to Michael Baxter in 1973 for his reporting on the *Miami Herald* (Florida). This was followed by other citations, including the Associated Press Managing Editors Public Service Award and the Investigative Reporting Award. His alma mater, the University of Nebraska, gave Baxter its Distinguished Journalism Award in 1975.

Baxter began his newspaper career on the *Lincoln Evening Star* (Nebraska) in 1962. In 1968, he moved to the *Miami Herald* and eight years later became its city editor.

**BEAN, Gerald A.** (1943– )
A native of Illinois, Gerald Bean first worked as a summer reporting intern in 1965 on the *Rockford Register Star* (Illinois). This began a long association with the Gannett organization.

Bean became president–publisher of Gannett's *San Bernardino Sun* (California) and vice-president of the Gannett West newspaper group in 1983.

Before joining the start-up team that launched *USA TODAY* in late 1982, Bean had moved up in Rockford through editing and production positions to become president–publisher. He was general manager of *USA TODAY* before he moved to California.

**BEAR, Charles Benson** (1919– )
Since 1945, Charles Bear has been associated with Time Inc. Following graduation from Grinnell and the Fletcher School of Law and Diplomacy, and after a brief job with the Gallup Poll, Bear in 1945 became the business manager of Time–Life International.

Other Time Inc. assignments included business manager of *Fortune* magazine; associate publisher and general manager of *Architectural Forum*; vice-president of International Time Inc. and several vice-presidencies; he became the director in 1977.

Bear served in the Air Force in World War II and currently is a member of the Friends of Earth Foundation and on the International Marketing Institute and Grinnell College boards.

**BEATTY, Morgan** (1902–1975)
Morgan Beatty is better remembered as a radio correspondent and news analyst, although he began his career as a reporter on the *Ft. Smith Southwest American* (Arkansas) in 1920.

Later Beatty worked on the *Arkansas Gazette* before joining the Associated Press for service in Atlanta, New York, Cleveland, and Albany between 1927 and 1942.

During World War II, Beatty was a foreign correspondent for the National Broadcasting Co. He later served the network in Chicago, New York, and London. Among his many honors were the Dupont Award in 1945 and the Headliner Award in 1948. He wrote one book, *Our Nation's Capital.*

**BEAUDET, Eugene Charles** (1924– )
A career in business journalism has brought numerous citations for Eugene Beaudet, since 1950, the editor of *Iron Age* magazine. Beaudet has won several Jesse H. Neal and C. D. Crane awards, all for outstanding contributions to business journalism.

Beaudet, who served in the Navy during World War II, was a copywriter for McCann-Erickson Inc. from 1948 to 1950.

**BEAUFORT, John David** (1912– )
The *Christian Science Monitor* has been home for John Beaufort since 1930. He is now a contributing drama critic and feature writer for this Boston-based publication.

Beaufort covered the Pacific during World War II, returning to become chief of the *Monitor*'s New York Bureau.

For his critical reports Beaufort has won the Critics Award. A member of many associations, Beaufort wrote for several magazines and foreign newspapers as well as for the *Monitor*, and won the Critics Award for his drama criticism. He told *Who's Who in America* that "adult education is learning to live and living to learn and sharing what life had taught you."

**BECK, Joan Wagner** (1923– )
Joan Beck earned two journalism degrees from Northwestern in 1945–47. Subsequently, she spent a brief time as a radio script writer for the Voice of America and as a copywriter for Marshall Field & Co.

In 1950, Beck joined the *Chicago Tribune* as a feature writer. Since that time, she has written an award-winning syndicated column for young readers, along with her *Tribune* stories.

Beck's awards include several from Chicago organizations, as well as a citation from the Associated Press for features. National awards have come from Alpha Chi Omega and the J. C. Penney–University of Missouri competition. Her books include *How to Raise a Brighter Child* and *Effective Parenting*, and she is the co-author of *Is My Baby All Right?*

**BECKMAN, Aldo Bruce** (1934– )
As Washington Bureau Chief for the *Chicago Tribune* since 1977, Aldo Beckman has won several awards.

Beckman began his career with the United Press International as a reporter in Chicago in 1958. A year later, he joined the *Tribune* and moved to Washington as a correspondent in 1965. From 1970 to 1977, he was the newspaper's White House correspondent, and won the Merriman Smith citation. He also served as president of the White House Correspondents Association.

Other recognition includes the Edward Scott Beck Award in 1966 and 1972, and the Alumni Achievement Award from his alma mater, Western Illinois University, in 1973.

**BEEBE, Lucius Morris** (1902–1966)
Lucius Beebe may best be remembered for his interest in trains and his attempts to regain their earlier prestige for travel. His earlier career, however, included positions with the *Boston Telegram* and *Transcript* and the *New York Herald Tribune* for 30 years (1921–51).

Americans became more familiar with the history of the West when Beebe moved to Virginia City, Nevada in 1952 and published the *Territorial Enterprise*. Eight years later, he was a *San Francisco Chronicle* staffer. He wrote for many magazines, including *Gourmet*.

Beebe's first book, which appeared in 1921, was *Fallen Stars*. Many of his poems were collected into books as were his biographical sketches of poets. His love for trains and for the West led him to write many books about these topics, such as the *Legends of the Comstock Lode*. In 1965–1966, he produced the two-volume *The Trains We Rode*.

**BELL, Elliott** (1902–1983)
A prominent economist and a former editor of *Business Week*, Elliott V. Bell died in 1983 at the age of 80.

Recalling highlights of his career, *Advertising Age* noted that early in Bell's career, he was a financial reporter for the *New York Herald Tribune* and the *New York Times*.

While working for the New York papers, he was the American correspondent for the *Banker*, a London periodical. He also wrote for other magazines.

In the 1940s, he assisted presidential candidates Wendell Willkie and Thomas Dewey in their campaigns. From 1943 to 1949, Bell was New York State Superintendent of Banks. He resigned that position to become the chairman of McGraw-Hill Publishing Co. and editor–publisher of *Business Week*.

**BELL, Stephen Scott** (1935–     )
Steve Bell, a correspondent for ABC News since 1967, began his career at radio stations in Oakaloosa and Ames, Iowa; Chicago; and Omaha. In 1965, he was an anchorman at radio station WNEW in New York.

With ABC, Bell covered Vietnam and Asia as well as the White House, and since 1975, he has been the news anchorman on "Good Morning, America."

For his outstanding work, Bell has won several Emmy nominations, the Oversea Press Club Award, and the Headliners Award. He appears on television from Washington.

**BELLAMY, William Butler** (1920– )
San Antonio is the newspaper home for William Bellamy, who began his career in 1946 with the Express Publishing Co. The next year, he was sports editor for the *News* and by 1952 managing editor of the *Express*. In 1984 he retired but continued as a consultant.

Bellamy moved up to publisher of the *San Antonio Light* (Texas) and vice-president of the Hearst Corp. He won an award from the San Antonio Bar Association and was named the "Most Outstanding Young Texan." For his newspaper writing, Bellamy has won a Sigma Delta Chi award as well as Hearst National Writing and Texas Headliner citations. He continues to live in San Antonio where he is active in several civic organizations.

**BELLOWS, James Gilbert** (1922– )
Newspaper work has taken James Bellows from his home in Detroit to the managing editorship of the *Miami News* (Florida), 1958–61, and for three years, an editorship of the *New York Herald Tribune*.

From New York, Bellows moved to the *Los Angeles Times*, where he was an associate editor from 1966 to 1974. In 1974, he was brought back to Washington where he spent three years in a futile attempt to save the *Star*. He adopted a daily magazine approach for the *Star*, among his other innovations, and invented the "Ear," a gossip column that often took jabs at the rival *Washington Post*.

Bellows returned to the *Los Angeles Herald Examiner* in 1977 and now is managing editor of the television show, "Entertainment Today," after 35 years in print journalism.

Bellows said he "would tell youngsters contemplating a career in print journalism to work on developing their writing skills and idea-generating abilities. These are in equal demand by newspapers, television, movies, book publishing, magazines, and so many other fields where writing is central."

**BENN, Nathan Herman** (1950– )
Nathan Benn has won the National Press Photographers Picture of the Year competition in 1973, 1974, and 1978. After starting his photographic career on the *Miami News* in 1969, Benn worked briefly on the *Palm Beach Post-Times*, in Florida before joining the *National Geographic* magazine in Washington in 1972.

Benn, a member of the White House News Photographers Association, has contributed to several books and has written *We Americans* and *American Healing Arts*.

**BENNACK, Frank Anthony Jr.** (1933– )
"All the innovations and improvements and advances will go gurgling down the drain unless we're able to maintain a constant flow of bright, talented, dedicated people to give them meaning," said Frank Bennack, Jr., president of the Hearst Corp.

Bennack began his career in 1950 in advertising, working on the *San Antonio Light* (Texas). He became the publisher in 1967 and, in 1974, the general manager for the Hearst newspapers. In 1978, he became the president and chief operating officer for Hearst.

Bennack was active in several charitable organizations in Texas before moving to New York. In 1974–75, he was president of the Rotarians.

**BENNETT, Lerone, Jr.** (1928– )
Lerone Bennett, Jr. began his writing career as a reporter on the *Atlanta Daily World* (Georgia) in 1949, moving to the city editor's position in 1952. The next year, he was an associate editor for *Ebony* magazine in Chicago and since 1958 he has been the publication's senior editor.

Bennett has won several awards for his journalistic activities, including the Book of the Year Award from the Capital Press Club and the Patron Saints Award from the Society of Midland Authors. He has written several books, including *Before the Mayflower: A History of the Negro in America, 1619–1964*. Another book was *What Manner of Man; A Biography of Martin Luther King, Jr.*

**BENTLEY, Helen** (1923– )
Helen Bentley became interested in journalism early in life, working as a part-time reporter on the *Ely Record* (Nevada), in 1939, while she was still in high school. Later, she earned her journalism degree from the University of Missouri, working as a waitress, an assistant in photography, and a stringer for the United Press.

Bentley worked for the United Press in Indiana, the *Lewiston Tribune* (Idaho), and, in 1945, the *Baltimore Sun* (Maryland), where she specialized in labor news. She became the first woman reporter to cover maritime news. According to one of her biographers, she developed "a vocabulary as salty as the sea and as pungent as stack gas." She also produced her own television show and wrote free-lance. President Richard Nixon appointed her to head the Federal Maritime Commission in 1969.

An anecdote about her career involves the occasion when she punched the jaw of a dockworker who had "likened her nose to a ski jump."

Bentley received numerous honors, including recognition by the AFL-CIO Maritime Port Council of Greater New York; the Ironworkers and Shipbuilders Council; the United Seamen's Service; the New York Freight Forwarders and Brokers Association; the American Legion; the Navy League; and the Society of Naval Architects and Marine Engineers. She received the Freedoms Foundation George Washington Honor Medal and was named "GOP Woman of the Year" in 1972.

**BERGER, Eric** (1906– )
For many years, millions of Americans have read publications directed by Eric Berger, who joined Scholastic Magazines, Inc., in New York in 1941. He had worked earlier on the *Brooklyn Eagle* and *Times*, and later with National Science Publications in New York.

A year after joining the Scholastic firm, Berger became the editor of *World Week*, and in 1943 he entered the Army. He returned to *Senior Scholastic* as associate editor. He also edited *Literary Cavalcade*. In 1959, the firm acquired *Science World* and Berger became editor.

Berger has been an editorial consultant since 1973. He was awarded a Freedoms Foundation citation for his articles on democracy.

**BERGMAN, Jules Verne** (1929– )
An Emmy award winner and the author of several books, Jules Bergman is better known as a broadcast journalist.

Bergman, early in his career, worked with CBS News and *Time* magazine in New York. In 1953, he became a writer for ABC News. Later he was a senior writer and reporter, and in 1959, he became the network's science writer. His books are mostly on flying, including *90 Seconds to Space; Anyone Can Fly; Fire; Danger in Sports Crashes*, and *Illusions of Safety*. A more recent volume, however, was *Weekend Athletes*.

**BERNAYS, Edward L.** (1891– )
The father of modern public relations, Edward L. Bernays was born in Vienna. During his long career in America he has been awarded many honorary degrees and been recognized by New York City and several foreign nations.

Since 1919 he has been involved in public relations, working with the arts, governments, corporations, trade groups, individuals, etc. In 1923 he taught the first course in public relations at New York University. Later he taught at other institutions, including the University of Hawaii and Boston University. He has served as a consultant with several Federal agencies, including the State Department, Department of Commerce, and Health, Education and Welfare Department. In World War I he was with the U.S. Committee on Public Information.

A pioneer book, *Crystalizing Public Opinion*, appeared in 1923. Bernays changed the field from its press-agentry image to its counseling role today. He continued to write other volumes, including *Public Relations, Your Future in Public Relations*, and, in 1965, *Biography of an Idea, Memoirs of Public Relations Counsel Edward L. Bernays*. He edited *The Engineering of Consent* along with many articles for periodicals. In 1946 he established the Edward L. Bernays Foundation.

France honored him with its Officer of Public Information award. Denmark awarded him its King Christian medal, and in 1961 New York City granted him its bronze medallion of honor. He was termed a "battler for democratic causes." Many professional associations also have paid him honors.

**BERNSTEIN, Carl** (1944– )
Carl Bernstein and his colleague, Bob Woodward, became famous for their Watergate coverage that brought the resignation of President Richard Nixon. The term "Woodstein" became famous, too, in media circles.

Before joining the *Washington Post*, Bernstein rose from a copyboy, a position he obtained when he was 16, to a reporter on the *Washington Star* between 1960 and 1965. After a year on the *Elizabeth Journal* (New Jersey), Bernstein began his career on the *Post*, where he remained until 1976. Three years later, he was the Washington Bureau chief for ABC.

Bernstein and Woodward were described by historian J. Anthony Lukas as "a kind of journalistic centaur with an aristocratic Republican head and runty Jewish hindquarters." Chalmers Roberts thought Bernstein "an easy and imaginative writer."

These two men later wrote fuller accounts in their bestsellers, *All The President's Men* and *The Final Days*. These books, especially *The Final Days*, aroused considerable opposition. James J. Kilpatrick labeled the latter as "brutal, needless, tasteless, and profitable." Kilpatrick, however, had been a Nixon faithful until the end.

Many awards resulted from these accounts, including the Drew Pearson prize for investigative reporting; the George Polk Memorial Award; the Worth Bingham Prize; and the Heywood Broun Award. He was also honored by the Newspaper Guild and Sigma Delta Chi; the Sidney Hillman Foundation; and the University of Missouri School of Journalism.

**BERNSTEIN, Theodore Menline** (1904–1979)

Theodore Bernstein's goal was to improve newspaper grammar and style. He was on the *New York Times* staff from 1925 to his death in 1979, when he was the managing editor.

During those years, Bernstein was a news editor, founding editor for the newspaper's international edition in Paris in 1960, and director of the book division for several years. He was the executive editor of the *New York Times Encyclopedic Almanac* for several years, spending his later years as a consulting editor.

Among his many books to improve the use of words were *Headlines and Deadlines*, *Watch Your Language*, *More Language That Needs Watching*, *The Careful Writers*, and *Dos, Donts and Maybes of English Usage*. From 1972 to 1979 he wrote a syndicated column, "Bernstein on Words." Bernstein was a consultant for the *Random House Dictionary* and the *American Heritage Dictionary*.

**BERNSTEIN, Victor Heine** (1904– )

After having held a reporting position from 1926 to 1930 on the *Providence News* and *Woodland Democrat* (California), Victor Bernstein became a contributor to the *New York Times* Sunday edition. Between 1937 and 1949, Bernstein served as foreign correspondent for the Jewish Telegraph Agency, as well as foreign editor for *PM* newspaper and the *New York Star*.

Later (1952–63), Bernstein was managing editor of *The Nation*. He has been a free-lance writer and editor since 1964.

Bernstein wrote the *Final Judgment, the Story of Nuremberg*, with Justin Gray, and *The Inside Story of the Legion*. Many of his reports covered the prewar persecution of Jews in Europe.

**BERRY, Jim** (1931– )
While with the Navy, Jim Berry said "A year on the destroyer gave me a chance to practice my drawing and painting." He feels his artistic interest developed at this time. Later, he worked briefly as an animator for television and for training programs for a management firm.

In 1963, Berry started his "Berry's World," which is syndicated to more than 600 newspapers. He has won the National Cartoonists Society Reuben award on five occasions as well as the National Headliner Club citation for "consistently outstanding editorial cartoons." Ohio Wesleyan has cited him as a distinguished alumnus.

He has published one book, *Berry's World*, a collection of his cartoons.

**BERRYMAN, James Thomas** (1902–1971)
James Berryman followed his father as a political cartoonist on the *Washington Star*. The younger Berryman joined the *Post* in 1924, and, in 1950, won a Pulitzer Prize. His father had won such an award in 1944.

After some academic training in journalism and art, Berryman had a short reporting stint on the *Albuquerque State Tribune* (New Mexico). The next year he became a staff artist on the *Washington Star* and, later, an editorial illustrator and sports cartoonist. Starting in 1944, his editorial cartoons were syndicated.

In addition to drawing cartoons, Berryman wrote many articles. His art works were printed in several periodicals. He won awards from the Red Cross and the U.S. Treasury for his work during World War II. He was honored by other groups, including the American Legion and the Infantile Paralysis Foundation. He also received a Freedoms Foundation Award.

**BESSIE, Simon Michael** (1916– )
Simon Bessie has been active in magazine and book publishing since he held a brief reporting job on the *Newark Star Eagle* (New Jersey) in 1936. Before becoming editor of *Market Research Monthly* in 1938, Bessie was in the RKO-Radio Pictures research department.

During World War II, Bessie was a correspondent for *Look* magazine. Later he became an editor at Harper & Bros. In 1959, he was the cofounder of Atheneaum, and subsequently its president. In 1975, he returned to Harper & Row as senior vice-president and director.

Bessie has been active in the American Book Publishers' Council and the Association of American Publishers. For several years he headed the Freedom to Read Committee. During World War II, he served in Algiers, Sicily, and Italy, working in psychological warfare. His book, *Jazz Journalism* (1938), was a pioneer study of this journalistic era.

**BIERCE, Ambrose** (1842–1914?)
Best remembered by readers today for his famed *The Devil's Dictionary*, Ambrose Bierce was a contributor to magazines and newspapers. His career in writing articles began after distinguished service in the Civil War. After this conflict, Bierce went to California where he spent much of his life.

For a brief time, 1872–1876, Bierce worked in London where he contributed to magazines and wrote several books. When he returned to San Francisco he joined Hearst's *Examiner* as a columnist, 1887–1897. Then he became a Washington correspondent for Hearst's *New York American*. He also contributed articles to *Overland Monthly* and edited *Argonaut and Wasp* and the *News Letter*.

Among his books are *Cobwebs from An Empty Skull*; *The Fiend's Delight*; *Nuggets and Dust Panned Out in California*; *The Monk and the Hangman's Daughter* (with G. A. Danziger); *Black Beetles in Amber*; *Can Such Things Be?*; *In the Midst of Life*, earlier titled *Tales of Soldiers and Civilians*; *Fantastic Fables*; *Shapes of Clay*; *The Cynic's Word Book*, later retitled *The Devil's Dictionary*; *The Shadow on the Dial and Other Essays*; *Write It Right*; and, in 1912, his collected works appeared in 12 volumes.

Bierce's death remains a mystery. According to some writers, he became upset over the way he thought the American civilization was moving and he moved to Mexico in 1913. He was last heard from in Mexico in early 1914.

**BIERCE, Harley R.** (1941– )
An award winner for his outstanding reporting, Harley R. Bierce founded the Investigative Reporters and Editors, Inc. organization in 1975 and served as its executive editor for several years.

Bierce worked on the *Indianapolis Star* (Indiana) from 1968 to 1978. Since that time, he has been president of Bierce Associates, Inc., in Indianapolis.

Among Bierce's awards are the Pulitzer Prize for local special reporting in 1975; the Drew Pearson Memorial Award; the George Polk Memorial Award; the Sigma Delta Chi Distinguished Service Award, and the National Headliner Award.

**BILLS, Sheryl J.** (1945– )
Sheryl Bills, since 1982 the managing editor of the Life section of *USA TODAY*, began her newspaper experience on the *Cincinnati Enquirer*. Bills covered many areas before becoming its *Sunday Magazine* editor in 1975.

After a year of directing the *Sunday Magazine*, Bills moved to the editorship of the newspaper's "People Today" section. She continued to advance on the *Enquirer* and for two years served as the managing editor, one of the few women in America to occupy such a high position on a big-city newspaper.

Bills was one of seven planning editors in the development of Gannett's *USA TODAY*.

**BINGHAM Family**
The Bingham name has long been associated with media interests in Louisville, Kentucky, especially as owners of the *Courier-Journal* and the *Louisville Times* since Judge Robert Worth Bingham (1871–1937) acquired them in 1917. His son, Barry Bingham, took over the operations in 1937.

Two of the Bingham sons were killed in accidents, and in 1971, Barry Bingham, Jr. took over.

Barry Bingham, Jr. was a management trainee with CBS in New York in 1959, and then worked in 1960 with NBC there as a researcher. He has been in Louisville with the newspapers as editor and publisher and as president of station WHAS since 1971.

Bingham took a sabbatical in 1984–85 to study and think "about where the communications industry is going and how we (the Louisville papers) can fit into wherever it is going."

In 1984 he won "The First" Prize by the local chapter of Sigma Delta Chi that honored excellence in the craft.

**BIRNIE, William Alfred Hart** (1910– )

William Birnie, long associated with the *Woman's Home Companion*, began as a newspaper reporter on the *Berkshire Evening Eagle* in Pittsfield, Massachusetts, in 1933 and then spent four years, 1935–38, on the *New York World-Telegram*.

A writer of magazine articles in his spare time, Birnie, in 1938, became an associate editor of the *American* magazine. Several of his articles have been reprinted in *Reader's Digest*.

In 1942, Birnie moved to another Crowell-Collier magazine, the *Woman's Home Companion*, as managing editor, becoming the editor the next year and, in 1952, the publisher. Birnie is credited with improving the magazine by adding many departments of concern to post-World War II readers.

Birnie left Crowell-Collier in 1957 and for three years was foreign affairs attaché to the USIA in Germany. He joined *Reader's Digest* in 1960, remaining until 1976.

**BISHER, James Furman** (1918– )

Sports fans throughout the South are well acquainted with the newspaper stories and books by James Bisher, who began his career on the *Lumbertown Voice* (North Carolina) in 1938.

He was a writer on the *High Point Enterprise* and *Charlotte News* for several years before becoming sports editor of the *Atlanta Constitution* in 1950. Seven years later, he was with the *Atlanta Journal*, where he writes today.

Bisher has won many sports awards from such groups as the Thoroughbred Breeders Association as well as more than 15 Associated Press sportswriting citations. Bisher has written books about Arnold Palmer, Henry Aaron, and the Masters Golf Tournament. Many of his articles have appeared in the *Best Sports Stories of the Year*.

**BISHOP, Jim** (1907– )

Best known to most readers for his "Day books," Jim Bishop began his newspaper career as a copyboy on the *New York News* in 1929. The next year he became a reporter for the *New York Mirror*, where he assisted columnist Mark Hellinger for two years; he was later to write a biography of him.

Bishop's more famous books include *The Day Lincoln Was Shot, The Day Christ Died, A Day in the Life of Kennedy, The Day Kennedy Was Shot, F.D.R.'s Last Year, A Day with President Johnson*, and *The Days of Martin Luther King, Jr.* His latest book (1980) was *A Bishop's Confession.*

After his newspaper career, Bishop worked on *Collier's, Liberty*, and the *Catholic Digest*, where he started the Catholic Digest Book Club. Bishop has been awarded several honorary university degrees and has been cited for his work with Catholic organizations.

**BISSELL, Charles Overman** (1908– )
As editorial cartoonist on the *Nashville Tennessean* since 1943, Charles Bissell has won several major awards. He began his career in art as a lithographer in 1924 and in 1943 joined the *Tennessean* staff. From 1945 to 1970, he was the art director for the paper's Sunday magazine.

The Headliner Club in 1963 recognized Bissell's cartoons, as did Sigma Delta Chi, which presented him its Distinguished Service Award in 1964. He created a cartoon feature, "Bissell's Brave New World," in 1962, which ran to 1976.

**BISSELL, Phil (Charles P.)** (1926– )
An editorial and sports cartoonist since his first job on the *Christian Science Monitor* in 1949, Phil Bissell's works are on permanent display in the Basketball Hall of Fame, the Baseball Hall of Fame, the International Swimming Hall of Fame, and the Eisenhower Library.

Bissell worked for the *Boston Globe* from 1953 to 1965, and then became a free-lance commercial artist for two years. He joined the *Worcester Telegram and Evening Gazette* in 1967, and stayed for 12 years. For the next two years, he was the *Boston Herald American* sports cartoonist. He has been a free-lance cartoonist since 1977.

**BLACK, Cathleen** (1944– )
In 1968, a new magazine, *New York*, was published. In 1980, Cathleen Black became its publisher. From 1980 to 1983, Black brought stability to this city periodical that had undergone frequent editorial changes during its growing period.

Black was in charge of the magazine's 15th anniversary edition, which featured "A Day in the Life of New York" as its theme. She was named the Outstanding Women of Communications in 1982 for her contributions to the publishing industry in a program sponsored by the March of Dimes.

Before joining *New York*, Black worked as an ad sales representative with *Holiday* magazine, 1966–69, and with *Travel and Leisure*, in 1970.

In 1983, Black became president of *USA Today*, the No. 2 position in this Gannett-owned national daily newspaper, working in both Washington and New York. She was promoted to publisher in 1984. In discussing her new position Black said, "It will give me a chance to learn about radio, television, outdoor and newspapers. This is a quantum leap in management responsibility for me."

**BLACK, Creed Carter** (1925– )
A native Kentuckian, Creed Black is publisher of the *Lexington Herald and Leader* (Kentucky), a Knight-Ridder newspaper. In 1962, he was president of the National Conference of Editorial Writers and also serves as president of the American Society of Newspaper Editors.

Black was a reporter on the *Paducah Sun-Democrat* (Kentucky) at age 17. During World War II, he worked on *Stars and Stripes*. In 1949, he was a copyeditor at the *Chicago Sun-Times* and, later, the *Chicago Herald-American*.

In the 1950s, Black became an editorial writer on the *Nashville Tennessean* and executive editor of the *Savannah Morning News* and *Evening Press* (Georgia).

He spent four years with the *Wilmington Morning News and Evening Journal* before returning to Chicago as the managing editor of the *Daily News* from 1964 to 1968. He served briefly in the Nixon Administration as assistant secretary for legislation in the Department of Health, Education & Welfare.

From 1970 to 1977, Black was responsible for the editorial page of the *Philadelphia Inquirer* before moving to the Lexington position.

**BLACKWELL, Betsy Talbot** (1906–1984)
For many years, Betsy Blackwell was editor of *Mademoiselle*, raising the magazine "up from an awkward miss in pigtails to a poised young lady."

She was the fashion editor for *Mademoiselle* when the magazine began in 1935; two years later, she was editor. Before that, she worked briefly as a fashion reporter for *The Breath of the Avenue*, before joining *Charm* magazine where she worked from 1923 to 1931, as fashion editor and later beauty editor.

Among Blackwell's honors is the Neiman-Marcus Award for Distinguished Service in the Field of Fashion in 1942.

**BLAKESLEE, Alton Lauren** (1913– )
A pioneer science writer, Alton Blakeslee has, for several decades, made science more understandable for millions of newspaper readers.

Blakeslee began his reporting life in Wilmington, Delaware in 1935; in 1939 he joined the Associated Press. He worked in Baltimore and New York before becoming a science reporter and later the science editor for this wire association.

Blakeslee won numerous awards, including citations from the American Chemical Society, the University of Missouri, Sigma Delta Chi, the American Psychiatric Association and the American Heart Association. He has also won the George Westinghouse Science Writing Award, the George Polk Award, and the Lasker Medical Journalism Award.

His books include *What You Should Know about Heart Disease* and *Your Heart Has Nine Lives*.

**BLEIBERG, Robert Marvin** (1924– )
Robert Bleiberg, in 1954, became the editor of *Barron's Weekly*, the youngest man to occupy this position. In 1980, he became publisher and, a year later, editorial director and vice-president of the parent firm Dow Jones & Co., Inc.

He started his career as an associate editor of *Prudden's Digest of Investment and Banking Opinions* in New York, in 1946 before going to *Barron's*.

According to Dana L.Thomas, writing in *The Media Moguls*, "Bleiberg writes in the elegant, rotund style of a latter-day Samuel Johnson and his social and political credos have the musty odor of the 18th century. He is a no-holds-barred proponent of undiluted, straight whiskey."

**BLEIWEISS, Herbert Irving** (1931– )
Herbert Bleiweiss, who has had a successful career as a magazine art director, currently is the executive art director for *Good Housekeeping*. He has won many awards, including awards from the Art Directors Club in New York, Los Angeles, and London, as well as the Society of Illustrators.

Bleiweiss began as an art director for New York advertising agencies; he joined *McCall's* in 1962. After five years at *McCall's*, he moved to the *Ladies' Home Journal* in 1967; in 1975, he took his present position with *Good Housekeeping*.

His art directing has included work on *Needle and Craft*, *American Home Crafts*, and *Country Living* magazines. In recent years he wrote *A Patchwork Point of View*; *Redo It Yourself*; and *The Pillow Book*.

**BLIVEN Family**
Bruce Bliven (1889–1977) worked on the *San Francisco Bulletin* from 1909 to 1914. He taught briefly at the University of Southern California and then spent a year with *Printer's Ink* magazine.

Bliven's varied career continued, with editorial work on the *New York Globe* and *New Republic*. From 1927 to 1947, he was also a correspondent for the *Manchester Guardian*. From 1956 until his death, Bliven lectured at Stanford and contributed articles to several magazines.

He wrote the following books: *The Wonderful Writing Machine*; *Battle for Manhattan*; *Under the Guns*; *Book Traveller*; *Volunteers, One and All*; *The Finishing Touch*; *The Story of D-Day*; *The American Revolution*; *From Pearl Harbor to Okinawa*; and *From Casablanca to Berlin*. He was co-author of *New York: The Story of the World's Most Exciting City*.

Bruce Bliven, Jr. (1916– ) has had a successful magazine, newspaper, and book writing career. In 1936, he was a reporter on the *Manchester Guardian* (England). In 1937, he worked on the *New Republic*, and from 1939 to 1942, he was an editorial writer on the *New York Post*.

For his service in World War II, he won a Bronze Star with an oak leaf cluster. Several of his books were based on this conflict.

Since 1946, Bliven has contributed to *The New Yorker* and other periodicals.

**BLOCK Family**

The sons of William Block have become major newspaper publishers in Pittsburgh, Pennsylvania and Toledo, Ohio. *Quill* magazine, in 1982, estimated that the brothers were worth between $200 and $300 million, with their ownership of the *Toledo Blade*, the *Pittsburgh Post-Gazette*, two smaller newspapers, and television and radio stations. They inherited the larger newspapers from their father.

Paul Block, Jr. (1911– ) started his newspaper training as a reporter with the *Blade* in 1935. He had advanced to political writer, assistant editor, and co-publisher by 1942. Active in civic affairs, he served four years as chairman of the Toledo Development Commission. He also has served on the boards of the Medical College of Ohio at Toledo and the U.S. Metric Board. A chemist who maintains his interest in chemical research, he earned his Ph.D. degree from Columbia University.

William Block (1915– ) worked in the circulation and other departments of the *Blade* from 1937 to 1939 before becoming its general manager. Then he moved to Pittsburgh, where he has worked with the Communications Foundation, the Symphony Society, and the World Affairs Council.

He was in World War II and served in the military government in Korea from 1945 to 1946.

William Block, Jr., became director of operation for the *Blade* in 1984, after holding other positions with the paper. Allan Block co-ordinates electronic technology planning for the *Blade*.

The brothers are now co-publishers of the *Blade* and *Post-Gazette*.

**BLOCK, Herbert Lawrence** (1909– )

Herblock, as Herbert Block is better known to newspaper readers, has kept presidents and other government officials on their best behavior since he joined the *Washington Post* in 1946.

His outstanding editorial cartoons, which are syndicated to several hundred newspapers, have won Herblock the Pulitzer Prize in 1942, 1954, and 1979.

Herblock considers his cartoons to be "a signed expression of personal opinion . . . like a column or other signed articles—as distinguished from the editorials, which express the policy of the *Post*," according to Chalmers Roberts in his history of the *Post*.

Herblock studied at the Art Institute (Chicago) on a scholarship before becoming editorial cartoonist on the *Daily News* in 1929. Four years later, he began a decade with the Newspaper Enterprise Association, which syndicated his cartoons out of Cleveland. After Army service in World War II, he joined the *Post*.

The *Post* has given Herblock the independence he prefers, as well as the opportunity to record national events at close hand. He once said he took "a whack at each side" in political campaigns, yet often his cartoons express the opposite views of those taken by newspapers that carry his work. According to Roberts, "Herblock rained hammer blows at Nixon and his crew, drawing some of the most powerful cartoons of his career."

His 1954 Pulitzer winner was based on Stalin's death. Herblock captioned his drawing, "You Were Always a Good Friend of Mine, Joseph," in a cartoon that showed the grim reaper welcoming the Russian leader.

In addition to his Pulitzers, Herblock has won the Newspaper Guild, Heywood Broun, Sigma Delta Chi, and Sidney Hillman awards. He won the Reuben from the National Cartoonists Society and the Lauterbach Award for work on civil liberties, and the Golden Key, Capital Press Club, Bill of Rights, Headliner and Power of Printing awards. He was given a medal by the University of Missouri School of Journalism.

His cartoons have been collected in books, the first one appearing in 1952. Other Herblock books include *The Herblock Book; Herblock's Here and Now; Herblock's Special for Today: Straight Herblock; The Herblock Gallery; Herblock's State of the Union*; and *Herblock Special Report*. He also designed the postage stamp the government issued to observe the 175th anniversary of the Bill of Rights.

**BOCCARDI, Louis D.** (1937– )

In 1967 Louis D. Boccardi joined the Associated Press as executive assistant to the general news editor. In late 1984 he became president and general manager of this news-gathering organization.

Prior to joining the AP, Boccardi worked as a reporter and desk editor of the *New York World Telegraph and Sun* from 1959 to 1964. After this newspaper was merged into the *World Journal Tribune*, Boccardi became the assistant managing editor. When the publication ceased in 1967 he moved to the AP.

From 1966 to 1973 Boccardi was a visiting faculty member in the Fordham University Communication Arts division. In 1967 this university gave him its Alumni Achievement Award and the following year its Outstanding Alumnus Award.

Boccardi has served as a Pulitzer prize juror and on committees of the American Newspaper Publishers Association and the Newspaper Advertising Bureau. He also has been active in the Columbia University School of Journalism program.

**BOMBECK, Erma Louise** (1927– )

Erma Bombeck is among the most widely read columnists in America today. Her daily comments encourage housewives and parents alike. Others have become fans after reading her best-selling books, such as her first, *At Wit's End* (1967) and others, including those with such "unusual" titles as *Aunt Erma's Cope Book: How to Get from Monday to Friday in 12 Days*, that arrived in 1979. Her latest book is *Motherhood: The Second Oldest Profession*, which appeared in 1983. Additional books include *Just Wait till You Have Children of Your Own; I Lost Everything in the Post-Natal Depression; The Grass Is Always Greener over the Septic Tank*, and *If Life Is a Bowl of*

*Cherries, Then What Am I Doing in the Pits?* She continues to produce her columns and books in her Arizona home in Paradise Valley. She told David Hinckley, of the *New York Daily News*, that her typewriter "is an old friend who calls me by my first name and is trained to stop after 450 words." In recent years, she has added a secretary and a maid, but prefers to do her own cooking.

Bombeck told Hinckley that "to me, writer's block is like North Dakota. It doesn't exist—although sometimes when I need a rest I'd like to get it, for maybe three to four months."

Bombeck always knew she would be a journalist. After high school, she worked on the *Dayton Journal-Herald* (Ohio) as a copygirl in 1944 and returned there in 1949 after finishing college. After the birth of her first child, she became a full-time mother.

The writing urge prevailed, however, and in 1964, she started a humor column in the *Kettering-Oakwood Times*, earning $3 a week. As she recalled the job, Bombeck said she was "too old for a paper route, too young for Social Security, and too tired for an affair." The next year, the Dayton newspaper rehired her for two columns a week. Soon she was a syndicated columnist appearing in more than 800 newspapers. She was also a contributing editor to *Good Housekeeping* for several years.

One of her books, *The Grass Is Always Greener over the Septic Tank*, became a CBS television movie featuring Carol Burnett. This was her first bestseller.

She appears regularly on "Good Morning, America" and is also seen on talk shows. She lives with her husband, a high school principal, in Phoenix, Arizona. *Newsweek*, in 1978, estimated her annual earnings in excess of $500,000.

**BONFILS, Helen** (1889–1972)

The Bonfils name has long been associated with the *Denver Post* (Colorado). Helen Bonfils inherited the newspaper from her father, Fred G. Bonfils, and directed its operation until her death.

Bonfils established a private foundation to handle the *Post*, devoting the profits to civic projects. She was the founder of the Bonfils Theatre, the Bonfils Tumor Clinic, and the Belle Bonfils Blood Bank, all in Denver. She also assisted the Denver Center for the Performing Arts.

For years, she waged a campaign to prevent outside newspaper publishing firms from acquiring the *Post*. Eventually, the *Post* was acquired by the Times-Mirror Company, owner of the *Los Angeles Times*.

**BONSIGNORE, Joseph John** (1920– )

The *Smithsonian* magazine, established in 1969 in Washington, D.C., is one of the nation's most successful publications. Joseph Bonsignore worked with the periodical from the start and became associate publisher in 1976 and publisher in 1981.

Previously, Bonsignore had worked from 1945 to 1969 as manager of editorial production for Time Inc. in Chicago. Today he is a consultant for new periodicals.

In Chicago he was active in the Christian Family Movement and the Civil Rights Organization.

**BOONE, Gray Davis** (1938– )
Gray Boone, the wife of James Buford Boone, Jr., has been the publisher of *Antiques Monthly* magazine in Tuscaloosa, Alabama since 1967. In 1978, she took over *Horizon* magazine.

Boone was honored with a Gray Boone Day in Tuscaloosa in 1979. Her work with antiques has involved the *Gray Letter* and a syndicated weekly newspaper column. A restorer of historic homes, she has been associated with the Colonial Williamsburg Forum, the Cooper-Hewitt Museum, the Alabama Historical Commission, and several colleges.

**BOONE, James Buford, Sr.** (1909–1983)
James Boone, Sr. had a significant career in Southern journalism. Starting as a reporter on the *Macon Telegraph and News* (Georgia) in 1929, be became city editor in 1938 and managing editor in 1940.

From 1942 to 1946, Boone was a special agent for the Federal Bureau of Investigation before returning to the *Telegraph* as editor. In 1947, he became the publisher of the *Tuscaloosa News* (Alabama) and eventually its president and chairman of the board of Tuscaloosa Newspaper, Inc.

Boone received a Pulitzer Prize for editorial writing in 1957 for articles on the Autherine Lucy case at the University of Alabama. He was also given the George Washington medal for editorial writing by the Freedoms Foundation; other honors included the Lovejoy Award, the Algernon Sydney Sullivan Award from the University of Alabama, and the alumnus award from Mercer University.

**BORG, Malcolm Austin** (1938– )
Malcolm Borg, the head of the family that owns the *Bergen County Record* (New Jersey), is worth between $100 and $200 million, according to *Quill* magazine. The family also owns four television stations.

Borg was with the *Record* in Hackensack in 1959. He held several positions as he advanced from reporter to president and chief operating officer in 1971, a position he held until 1978.

Borg's interests include the Boy Scouts, the Regional Kidney Center, the New Jersey Health Care Administration Board, the Department of Health, the Boys Club, and the Community Chest.

In recognition of his many civic activities, he has been awarded citations from B'nai B'rith, the Salvation Army, Toastmasters, and other groups.

**BORLAND, Harold Glen** (1900–1978)
Similar to the training experienced by many other book writers, Hal Borland began as a newspaperman, working on the *Denver Post* in 1918. He was on the *Flager News* (Colorado) before going east to work in Brooklyn and, later, was with the United Press.

Borland has held editorial positions on other newspapers, working in

Asheville, North Carolina, Stratton, Colorado, Philadelphia, Pennsylvania, New York, New York, and Pittsburgh, Pennsylvania.

Borland is best remembered for his many books, starting with *Heaps of Gold* in 1922. He wrote plays, novels, poems, and many books about country experiences and wildlife. For years he was a contributing editor of *Audubon* magazine.

Among his honors were the Columbia University Journalism award and the John Burroughs and Edward J. Meeman Conservation Writing award.

Other books: *Rocky Mountain Tipi Tales, Valor, Wapiti Pete, What Is America?* (play), *America Is Americans, An American Year, High, Wide and Lonesome*—and on & on—probably 40 in all.

His last book was *A Countryman's Woodland* in 1982, that appeared after his death.

**BOURKE-WHITE, Margaret** (1906–1971)
One of the better-known women photographers of this century, Margaret Bourke-White became famous for her pictures in *Life* magazine.

From 1927 to 1971, she worked as an industrial photographer, taking pictures for *Fortune* magazine from 1929 to 1922 and for *Life* until 1971. She was an accredited war correspondent and photographer for *Life* in World War II and the Korean War.

Bourke-White's photographs have been shown in the Library of Congress, the Cleveland Museum of Art, the Museum of Modern Art, and other art centers. She also wrote *Eyes on Russia* and *U.S.S.R., A Portfolio of Photographs*, and with Erskine Caldwell, her second husband, *You Have Seen Their Faces* and *North of the Danube*. She also produced *Shooting the Russian War; They Called It Purple Heart Valley; Dear Fatherland Rest Quietly; Halfway to Freedom, A Study of New India*; and as co-author, *A Report on The American Jesuits*. Her last book, in 1963 was an autobiography, *Portrait of Myself*.

**BOYCE, Carroll Wilson** (1923– )
Business journalism has been the major area for Carroll Boyce's work since he became an editorial assistant to the managing editor of *Factory* magazine in 1946. He was editor of *Fleet Owner* magazine, 1959–69 and 1973–77. He is now the emeritus editor of this McGraw-Hill periodical.

Between 1969 and 1973, Boyce was director of the truck division of the Motor Vehicle Manufacturers Association in Washington. He returned to McGraw-Hill and became editor of *Trucks 26-Plus* magazine and, since 1979, president of Transportation Forecasts and Planning Inc.

In the mid-1960s, Boyce received three Public Service to Safety awards from the National Safety Council and three Jesse H. Neal Awards for business journalism. He wrote two books, *How to Plan Pensions* and *Materials Handling Casebook*.

**BOYER, Jean** (1919– )
As publisher of the Gannett-owned *Visalia Times-Delta* in California, Jean Boyer reached the high mark of her newspaper career that began in 1947

when she served as a circulation clerk and secretary to the *Times-Delta* publisher. In 1956, she became the office manager, and in early 1978, the publisher.

Boyer is active in the Christian Science Church, the California Newspaper Youth Foundation, the YMCA, and other organizations.

**BOYLE, Harold Vincent** (1911–1974)
Hal Boyle spent his career writing for the Associated Press, earning a reputation for his humor and his interest in servicemen.

He joined the AP as a copyboy in his home city of Kansas City in 1928 and was its correspondent in Columbia while he earned degrees from the University of Missouri. After service in Kansas City and St. Louis, Boyle was moved by the Associated Press to New York where he remained until he was sent to cover the Mediterranean and European battlefronts.

"Leaves from War Correspondent's Notebook" was his title for a column that was printed in the hundreds of newspapers that used the service.

Boyle won a Pulitzer Prize in 1945 for his distinguished correspondence. That same year, he was selected as one of the 10 most outstanding young men by the Junior Chamber of Commerce. His columns have been collected in book form, under the title *Help, Help, Another Day.* After his death in 1974, his colleagues established a scholarship in journalism in his honor at the University of Missouri.

**BRADFORD, Barbara Taylor** (1933– )
Born in England, Barbara Bradford was a reporter on the *Yorkshire Evening Post* (England) in 1949 and the women's editor there from 1951 to 1953. She edited *Women's Own* for a year before joining the *London Evening News* and, later, the *London American.*

In America, Bradford edited the *National Design Center Magazine* from 1965 to 1969. In 1968, she became a syndicated columnist. In addition, she is the author of numerous books on decorating. Other books include one about children's verse, and *How to Be the Perfect Wife.* Barbara Bradford wrote *Complete Encyclopedia of Homemaking Ideas*; *A Garland of Children's Verse*; *Easy Steps to Successful Decorating*; *Decorating Ideas for Casual Living*; *How to Solve Your Decorating Problem*; *Making Space Grow*; and *A Woman of Substance.*

She has won the Distinguished Editorial Award and a National Press Award from the National Society of Interior Designers.

**BRADLEE, Ben** (1921– )
Ben Bradlee and the *Washington Post* are synonymous in the newspaper world. His career there was highlighted by the Watergate episode and the subsequent motion picture about the fall of President Richard Nixon.

After World War II service in the Navy, Bradlee worked briefly for the American Civil Liberties Union in New York and later, with friends, started the *New Hampshire Sunday News* in Manchester. In 1948, he sold his interest in this paper and joined the *Washington Post* as a police and federal courts reporter. After three years, Bradlee joined the U.S. Embassy in Paris as press attaché.

Bradlee moved to *Newsweek* as European correspondent in 1953 and was transferred to Washington four years later, obtaining many scoops when his one-time neighbor, John F. Kennedy, became the President. In 1975, Bradlee recalled these experiences in his book, *Conversations With Kennedy*, which covered the years 1959 to 1963.

The Washington Post Co. bought *Newsweek* in 1961. In 1965, *Post* publisher Katharine Graham convinced Bradlee to join the newspaper's staff. He soon became the managing editor and, in 1968, he became the executive editor.

The Nixon Administration had brushed it off as a "third-rate burglary," but Bradlee's *Post* used 80 column inches to report the break-in of the Democratic National Committee's office in Watergate. The rest of the story, recorded in articles and books by Bob Woodward and Carl Bernstein, is well known.

Bradlee and the *Post* were denied access to news sources by the Nixon Administration. Chambers Roberts, in his *Post* history, quotes Bradlee as saying, "the older I get, the more finely tuned my sense of conflict of interest seems to become. I don't think executive editors in charge of news should have anything to do with editorials; I don't think editors should be officers of the company. I don't think editors should join any civic groups, clubs, institutions. I truly believe that people on the business side of newspapers shouldn't either."

**BRADY, James**

"If you want to write, you've got to read. Besides, I'm innately curious about the world around me," says James Brady, who, in 1983, became editor-at-large for *Advertising Age*, and a writer of a weekly column.

Brady was in charge of *Women's Wear Daily*, working under John Fairchild from 1964 to 1971. He then moved to *Harper's Bazaar* in 1971 and said he had been given 14 months to move the magazine around. But after a short time, he was "canned."

Brady's next move was to the Murdoch-owned tabloid *Star* and later to Murdoch's *New York* magazine before the publisher made him a columnist for his *New York Post*.

A former associate told a *Folio* writer, "Brady is to writing what Spencer Tracy was to acting." Brady believes "an editor has to be able to do a lot of things, He's got to plan, conceptualize, motivate, be able to say 'no,' establish contact with writer."

When he moved to *Advertising Age*, Brady dropped his *Post* column, but continues as a correspondent for WCBS-TV in New York. In his first *Advertising Age* column he concluded: "Journalism has been good to me. Editorships, publishing jobs, columns, television gigs, Emmy Awards, the raw material that in digested form was turned into books including *Superchic, Paris One* and *Nielsen's Children*. Journalism got me to Washington, to London, to Paris, and back to New York," where he remains today.

**BRADY, Raymond John**
Broadcast journalism, with an emphasis on business news, has placed Raymond Brady in the public eye. He began his career as a reporter on the *Long Branch Daily Record* (New Jersey) in 1950. Three years later he was a writer for AT&T.

Brady started as a business writer with *Forbes* magazine in 1954. From 1956 to 1961, he was an assistant editor. He moved to *Barron's Weekly* as an associate editor, and by 1961, he was editor of *Dun's Review*.

Brady entered television as a business commentator for WCBS in New York in 1972. He also served as a CBS radio commentator from 1975 to 1979, and since 1978, he has provided CBS-TV Morning News viewers with the latest business information. He is a member of the board of governors of the New York Financial Writers Association.

**BRAND, Stewart** (1938– )
The name Stewart Brand may not be as quickly recognized as his major product, *The Whole Earth Catalog*, which first appeared in 1968. According to David Armstrong in his book, *A Trumpet to Arms*, Brand was influenced by Buckminster Fuller and the L.L. Bean Catalog and "had little use for politics, feeling that it only pitted people against one another." Brand is a pragmatist, a problem-solver. Also according to Armstrong, the first *Whole Earth Catalog* "was positively nostalgic for the future and, in its writers' speculations and fantasies, displayed an almost tangible hunger for another, newer, better world, one its contributors had as yet only glimpsed."

The *Catalog* survived three years. Brand then founded the nonprofit Point Foundation and gave a million dollars to ecology groups and other organizations. He started the *CoEvolution Quarterly* in 1974, and issued the *Next Whole Earth Catalog* in 1980. Brand plans a *Software Catalog*, which has brought a $1.3 million bid from Doubleday. Brand now lives in a rebuilt tugboat in Sausalito, California.

**BRANDON, Brumsic, Jr.** (1927– )
The comic strip "Luther" has brought fame for its creator, Brumsic Brandon, who began his career as a free-lance cartoonist in 1945.

Brandon worked as an illustrator for several business groups and as a design animator for Bray Studios Inc. in New York between 1957 and 1970. He began "Luther" in 1969. He has published several books based on the strip: *Luther From Inner City*; *Luther Tells It As It Is*; *Right On, Luther*; *Luther Raps*; *Outta Sight, Luther*; *Luther's Got Class*.

Since 1976, Brandon has been a political cartoonist for *Black Media* in New York. He has also served on the advisory board for the Afro-American Bicentennial Corporation, 1975–76.

**BRANDT, Raymond Peter** (1896–1974)
As the Washington bureau chief for the *St. Louis Post-Dispatch* (Missouri) from 1934 to 1961, Raymond Brandt's stories were widely read and quoted.

Brandt's career began on the *Post-Dispatch* as a reporter in 1917. He went to Washington as a correspondent for the newspaper in 1923 and became bureau chief in 1934.

In recognition of his outstanding reporting, Brandt was honored with the first Raymond Clapper Memorial Award in 1945. The University of Missouri School of Journalism awarded him its medal in 1939. He served as president of the National Press Club and the Gridiron Club in Washington.

**BRANT, Irving Newton** (1885–1976)
Although Irving Brant is best remembered for his books on James Madison, he began his career as a reporter on the *Iowa City Republican* in 1909.

Later Brant moved to the *Clinton Herald* and to the *Des Moines Register and Tribune* (Iowa). By 1918, he was in charge of the editorial page of the *St. Louis Star* (Missouri); he continued to work for this paper and the merged *Star-Times* until 1941.

Brant was an editorial writer for the *Chicago Sun* when it was established in 1941 and later served the newspaper as a foreign correspondent. He then turned his attention to writing books, winning several awards from historical associations. His study of James Madison resulted in "six-volumes series, with later books for more general audiences." His last book, in 1971, was *The History of American Presidental Elections.*

**BRESLIN, Jimmy** (1930– )
Jimmy Breslin, in 1948, worked on the *Long Island Press* (New York) with sportswriting as his major objective. He worked for several other newspapers in the 1950s, including the *New York Journal-American*, where he said he was miserable.

Breslin has written many books. His first, in 1962, was *Sunny Jim: The Life of America's Most Beloved Horseman, James Fitzsimmons.* The next year he wrote about the New York Mets baseball team. Later he wrote *The Gang that Couldn't Shoot Straight*, which was made into a movie; *World without End, Amen*; and *How The Good Guys Finally Won.*

Breslin became a *New York Herald Tribune* columnist in 1963 and remained with the merged *World Journal-Tribune* until it folded in 1967. He later wrote longer stories for *New York* magazine and, briefly, for the *New York Post.*

With Norman Mailer, who was running for mayor, Breslin entered the New York City Democratic primary as a candidate for president of the New York City Council. Their platform called for New York City to become a separate state. They lost. However in 1972, Breslin was a McGovern delegate to the Democratic National Convention.

Although he never won a Pulitzer Prize, Breslin has been recognized by Sigma Delta Chi and the New York Reporters Association and has won the Meyer Berger Award for local reporting. James Brady calls Breslin one of the best writers today, adding, "too bad he isn't a member of the Establishment. The Pulitzer jury might look at him if he were."

**BRICKLIN, Mark Harris** (1939– )
After a year teaching English, Mark Bricklin, in 1962 became the city editor of the *Philadelphia Tribune* (Pennsylvania), a position he held until 1971. During that same time he was also a free-lance writer and a photographer.

Bricklin, who joined the Rodale Press in 1971, became vice-president four years later. Since 1974, he has been the executive editor of *Prevention* magazine, one of the fastest growing periodicals in America. As a result of this association with *Prevention*, Bricklin has written two books, *The Practical Encyclopedia of Natural Healing* and *Lose Weight Naturally*.

**BRINKLEY, David McClure** (1920– )
David Brinkley began as a reporter on his hometown newspaper, the *Wilmington Star-News* (North Carolina) in 1938. Three years later, he was a reporter with the United Press in the South.

Brinkley moved into radio and television in 1943, first as a news writer for NBC in Washington and then as a Washington correspondent in 1951.

For some 14 years, Brinkley and Chet Huntley led NBC News to top nightly ratings. The team continued until Huntley retired in 1970.

In her book, *The Evening Stars*, Barbara Matusow wrote: "There seemed to be two David Brinkleys. One faithful and mischievous, the other remote, sour, even forbidding."

While at NBC, Brinkley received ten Emmys and two Peabody awards. He joined ABC in 1981. He started "This Week With David Brinkley" in late 1981, a guest-panel confrontation program, assisted by George Will and ABC's White House correspondent, Sam Donaldson. The program has been called "brilliant, sensational, a break-through, a breath of fresh air" by network executives.

**BRODER, David Salzer** (1929– )
A long newspaper career has placed David Broder on the *Washington Post* as a syndicated columnist. Broder began on the *Bloomington Pantagraph* (Illinois) in 1953. Two years later, he joined the *Congressional Quarterly* staff in Washington, D.C. for a five-year stint.

Broder worked for the *Washington Star* from 1960 to 1965, when he joined the Washington bureau of the *New York Times* for a year. A reporter's position in 1966 on the *Post* began a long association with this newspaper. He became associate editor in 1975.

In 1973, Broder won a Pulitzer Prize in journalism. He has won several fellowships, including the John F. Kennedy School of Government at Harvard fellowship, 1969–70. He won Newspaper Guild awards in 1961, 1973, and 1974. A prolific magazine article writer, Broder also wrote *The Party's Over: The Failure of Politics in America* in 1972, and *Changing of the Guard: Power and Leadership in America*.

**BROEG, Bob** (1918– )
Missourians know Robert William Broeg for his big-time sports coverage in the *St. Louis Post-Dispatch* (Missouri), where he has been on the staff since 1945.

Broeg began with the Associated Press in Columbia, Missouri in 1939 and worked for the service in nearby Jefferson City and in Boston until 1942. Then he returned home to his first St. Louis, Missouri job, on the *Star-Times*. In 1958, he was president of the Baseball Writers Association.

His awards include those from the National Sportscasters and the University of Missouri. In 1978, he was elected to the Missouri Hall of Fame.

He has written several books, including two on Stan Musial. They include *Don't Bring That Up*; *Stan Musial: The Man's Own Story*; *Super Stars of Baseball*; *Ol' Mizzou, a Story of Missouri Football*; *We Saw Stars*; *The Man Stan . . . Musial, Now and Then*; *Football Greats*.

**BROKAW, Thomas John** (1940– )

Tom Brokaw has been in the news so frequently since he took the anchor position with Roger Mudd on the "NBC Nightly News" in 1982 that he "can't even voice an opinion when he's off the air."

Brokaw began early in broadcasting. During high school, he worked after class as an announcer for a Tankton, South Dakota station. From 1962 to 1965, he presented the morning news on Omaha station KMTV. The next year, he served as news editor and anchorman at Atlanta station WSB-TV before moving to KNBC-TV in Los Angeles where he remained until 1973.

The National Broadcasting Company named Brokaw its White House correspondent in 1973. He took a cut in pay to get to Washington, and he has called himself a "political junkie," anxious to be in the midst of politics. Three years later, he moved to New York as the anchorman for the "Saturday Night News" and soon became more visible as host for the "NBC Today Show."

During these growing years with NBC, Brokaw worked on many documentaries. His coverage of the White House coincided with the Watergate era.

Brokaw's salary, variously reported as between $1.2 and $2 million annually, has been commented on by both columnists and critics. In a *Current Biography* sketch, Brokaw was described as "a non-nonsense newsman with solid journalistic credentials and more than twenty years experience in television news broadcasting."

Brokaw is well known for his forthrightness. Seen by some as an "inexperienced lightweight" when he first reached Washington, Brokaw once asked President Gerald Ford about stories that suggested the new President was not "intelligent enough" to hold that position.

Unlike some broadcasters, Brokaw has refused to read commercials on the air, a practice he termed "repulsive" in a *Time* interview. In 1977, he told TV critic, Gary Deeb, that, "I've never done anything purely for the money."

Some flak was raised when Brokaw, in 1979, received a Small Business Administration federal loan guarantee to buy a Rapid City, South Dakota radio station. Later he admitted he had "made a minor mistake in judgment."

He has been given the Golden Mike Award and the Alumni Achievement Award from the University of South Dakota.

Brokaw wrote an introduction for *The Best of Photo-journalism 5: People, Places and Events of 1979*, in which he paid tribute to the world's great photographers, noting: "These rumpled bundles of concentration, energy and devotion live a kind of guerilla life-style, constantly on the move ready to shoot from any position at a moment's notice. They have an extraordinary feel for life in so many forms, and they have a vision that permits them to see what too many ordinary journalists overlook." These same comments, no doubt, apply to the photographers who prepare pictures for the television networks.

**BROKENSHIRE, Norman Ernest** (1898–1965)
"King of the announcers" identified Norman Brokenshire to audiences in the early years of radio. He began work in radio in 1924, not many years after its invention and has been credited with many "firsts" in the industry.

After service in World War I and a variety of jobs, Brokenshire answered an ad in 1924 for "a college man with knowledge of musical terminology." Although not fully qualified, he became an announcer on station WJZ and handled many miscellaneous chores as well.

Among his "firsts" was the use of his name as an announcer, since announcers had previously remained anonymous. He was the first to cover a political convention—the Democratic Convention in New York in 1924—and he developed the present-day "soap opera" concept.

Brokenshire's career had many ups and down through the years. He was the announcer for "The Chesterfield Hour," "Eddie Cantor's Follies," "Major Bowles' Amateur Hour," and other leading radio shows. Many will recall his voice on CBS's "Inner Sanctum" and NBC's "Theatre Guild of the Air" in the 1940s.

He wrote one book, *This Is Norman Brokenshire*.

**BRONSON, William Howard Jr.** (1936– )
William Bronson has spent his life in Louisiana where today he is regional vice-president of Gannett's Central Region and publisher of the *Shreveport Times* (Louisiana).

Bronson began his career on the *Times* as a production engineer in 1960. He was promoted to production manager and later labor manager, and by 1972, he was president and general manager of The Newspaper Production Co. Later he became its publisher.

Throughout his career, he has been active in local and state projects and in Southern newspaper development. He has been active in the leadership of the Boy Scouts and the YMCA. Currently, he is a board member on the Council for a Better Louisiana and the local chapter of the National Conference of Christians and Jews.

Within his own profession, Bronson has served on committees in the American Newspaper Publishers Association and the Southern Newspaper Publishers Association.

**BROUN, Heywood** (1888–1939)
One of the most highly controversial columnists of the 1920s and the 1930s Heywood Broun is best remembered for his work in organizing the American Newspaper Guild.

Broun began as a reporter on the *New York Morning Telegraph* at $20 a week in 1908. Four years later, he was with the *New York Herald Tribune*, and by 1921, he had joined the *World*.

Broun worked for Scripps-Howard Newspapers from 1928 until shortly before his death. Roy Howard fired him at a time Broun was making $49,000 a year writing his column, "It Seems To Me." Broun then joined the *Post*, but wrote only one column before his death.

Richard O'Connor's biography of Broun termed the writer "perhaps the most towering of the journalistic legends predating the Second World War." He was called rumpled, easy-going, a prophet of liberalism. Broun had graduated from Harvard and had become a member of the famed Algonquin Round Table. He had also been a baseball writer, a drama critic who lectured at Columbia University, and a book reviewer.

In his column, Broun campaigned for many causes, such as clemency for Sacco and Vanzetti. But his most lasting effort was the organization of the American Newspaper Guild. In a 1933 column he called for a "newspaper writer' union." The formal organizing convention was held the next year.

O'Connor added that although the Guild won minimum wage scales, "the Guild minimum became the publishers' maximum and the result was that newspaper people of talent and ambition were impelled sooner or later to leave journalism."

During World War I, he served as a war correspondent. Broun wrote the following books: *A.E.F.–with General Pershing and the American Forces; Seeing Things at Night; Pieces of Hate; The Boy Grew Older; Gandle Follows His Nose*, and *Anthony Comstock*. He co-authored *Roundsman of the Lord* and *Christians Only*.

**BROWN, Helen Gurley** (1922– )
"The Iron Butterfly," Helen Gurley Brown, took over an ailing *Cosmopolitan* magazine in 1965 and revamped it into one of the country's most successful periodicals. The "Cosmopolitan Girl" continues to have a unique appeal, both to readers and advertisers, as millions of readers turn to Brown's magazine to learn more about today's morality and the role of women in everyday life.

In late 1982, Brown was honored as one of the Outstanding Women in Communications because of her success with *Cosmopolitan*.

From her youth, Brown wanted to write. She said she had held 18 secretarial positions between the ages of fifteen and twenty-five, including jobs with the William Morris Agency, the *Los Angeles Daily News*, and an advertising agency where she learned to be a copywriter. She won awards for her work in advertising in 1957, 1958, and 1959.

Brown published her first book, *Sex and the Single Girl*, in 1962. It was an immediate bestseller. Two years later, she wrote *Sex and the Office*, and in 1966, *Helen Gurley Brown's Outrageous Opinions*. In 1969 she published

*Helen Gurley Brown's Single Girl's Cookbook*; in 1983, she wrote *Having It All*.

Brown became an advertising writer in 1958 as an account executive for Kenyon & Eckhardt in California. The next year she married David Brown, then a film studio executive.

Brown's books attract a large audience. She has also written a syndicated column for newspapers and magazines, she had her own television show, briefly, and she has appeared on many talk shows. These activities, and the plans she and her husband developed for a new magazine, to be called *Femme*, led to Hearst officials hiring her to revive *Cosmopolitan*. She had never before edited a magazine.

Brown directs *Cosmopolitan* to the working women, between 18 and 34, and to those who "think single."

Nora Ephron said Brown took over *Cosmopolitan*, "turned it around, breathed new life and new image into it, became the only editor in America to resurrect a dying magazine." Chris Welles wrote that "*Cosmopolitan* functions as a kind of Baedeker of happy mate-hunting grounds."

**BROWN Family**

The Brown family has been associated with *Editor & Publisher* magazine since James W. Brown, Sr. acquired it in 1912. The senior Brown (1873–1959) worked on Detroit newspapers before entering the magazine arena. James Brown Jr. (1902–1910) began on the circulation department in 1925 and became the president–publisher in 1947. He left *Editor & Publisher* briefly to work as sales manager of the Chicago Tribune-New York News Syndicate and worked two years in publisher relations for *Parade*, returning to *Editor & Publisher* in 1953.

Robert U. Brown (1912–     ) began his media career as a reporter on the *Trenton Times* in 1935. He also worked briefly on the *Auburn Citizen-Advertiser* (New York) and with the United Press in Philadelphia.

Brown became a reporter on *Editor & Publisher* in 1936 and, by 1944, was editor. In 1952, he became president of the firm and, six years, later its publisher.

In late 1983, Brown was cited for "Professionalism in Communications" at an event hosted by *Advertising/Communications Times*. The citation noted, "As president and editor of *Editor & Publisher* he has been our Boswell, our critic and our common communicator since the mid-1930s, and has reported, commented upon and encouraged every facet and development of a much needed revolution in the newspaper business."

**BROWNE, Dik** (1917–     )

Dik Browne is best known to the newspaper reading public through his work with Mort Walker since 1954 on the "Hi and Lois" comic.

In 1973, Browne created the hapless Viking "Hagar the Horrible." Special governmental offficials from Norway and Iceland were guests for the 10th anniversary party for "Hagar," which now appears in 13 languages and 58 countries. The strip was voted the best foreign comic by the British Cartoonist Club in 1983.

**BROWNE, Malcolm Wilde** (1931– )
A long-time writer for the Associated Press, Malcolm Browne won a Pulitzer Prize for his foreign correspondence in 1964, as well as numerous other citations.

Early in his life, Browne was a consulting chemist and a technical writer before joining the *Middletown Daily Record* (New York) in 1958. Two years later, he was with the Associated Press in Baltimore, and from 1961 to 1965, he covered the Vietnam War for this wire group.

Browne became the ABC Saigon correspondent for a year (1965–66), and then spent two years as a free-lance writer before joining the *New York Times* for assignments in Argentina, Southern Asia, and Europe.

In 1977, Browne became a science correspondent. Four years later, he was the senior editor of *Discover*, the Time Inc. science magazine.

In addition to his Pulitzer, Browne has won the World Press Photo Award from the Hague; the Overseas Press Club and Sigma Delta Chi awards; the Louis M. Lyons Award; and the Edward R. Murrow Memorial fellowship. The National Headliner Club and the Associated Press Managing Editors have also honored him.

**BROYLES, William** (1944– )
During the past decade, William Broyles has edited three major magazines: *The Texas Monthly*, *California*, and *Newsweek*.

Broyles, an Oxford University graduate, worked a year in the Houston Public Schools system before taking the editorship of a new magazine in Austin, the *Texas Monthly*, in 1972. Under his editorship, the monthly won three National Magazine Awards and was recognized as a leader in this specialized field.

*Texas Monthly* publisher, Michael R. Levy, hired him after a stiff writing examination, since Broyles had had no previous magazine experience. Levy acquired *New West* in 1980, renamed it *California*, and challenged Broyles to revamp it. Soon the Western Coast publication moved upward both in circulation and in advertising.

Katharine Graham, owner of *Newsweek* and the *Washington Post*, invited Broyles to dinner during a visit to San Francisco and surprised him by offering him the editorship of the New York-based *Newsweek*. He said, "It took me about a third of a second to say yes." He took over the magazine in 1982, although he was obviously an "outsider" to the New York-dominated magazine crowd.

Broyles told *Folio* magazine he was concentrating on "long-term strategy" for *Newsweek*. He told *Advertising Age* that "I have never said that I intended to do anything but build upon, stay within, the basic newsweekly *Newsweek* tradition. This is a durable, successful medium and I think we can improve the execution of it—that's true of any institution. But I never had any revolutionary ideas."

Broyles added that "it's [*Newsweek*] a very durable form that will outlast you and me, just as it outlasted Henry Luce."

"*Newsweek* is up against some real problems [in its battle with *Time* for circulation leadership] but at least Broyles has combat training," commented one writer. He was correct. Broyles was decorated with the Bronze Star for service with the Marines in 1969–71.

Broyles discussed his new role with members of the American Society of Magazine Editors and said he planned to reach out on issues significant to "committed minorities." Because of his background, he also sought fuller coverage of the West and the Southwest.

Writing in the *Washington Journalism Review* in 1983, Charlene Canape noted early changes. "*Newsweek*'s graphics are now cleaner and bolder, the cover hypes are more terse and hard-hitting. Since Broyles took over, *Newsweek* has run several attention-grabbing cover stories. These were not recaps of last week's news, but investigative pieces aimed at creating headlines in the rest of the press."

Broyles' decision to place a photograph of Princess Grace of Monaco on the cover after her death, instead of a picture of the Beirut massacre, upset some insiders. However, *Newsweek* sold more single-copy sales with this issue than with any in its 50-year history.

After 16 months as editor, Broyles quit *Newsweek*. "I did what I came to do, and now I'm going to do what I want to do," he told Bill Abrams of the *Wall Street Journal*. Broyles said he produced "better coverage of America beyond the Eastern seaboard," reflecting his Western orientation.

In addition to his National Magazine awards, Broyles has won the J.C. Penney–University of Missouri Award for magazine writing.

**BRUCKER, Herbert** ((1898–1977)
As editor of the *Hartford Courant* (Connecticut) for many years, Herbert Brucker has won many awards for his writing and has been recognized for his concern with problems in journalism.

Brucker began as a reporter in 1925 on the *Springfield Union*. He worked on several early magazines, including *World's Work* and the *Review of Reviews*, and then moved into the teaching profession as Assistant to the Dean of the Columbia University School of Journalism. He became a professor before he ended his career there in 1944.

During World War II, Brucker worked in the Office of War Information Bureau of Overseas Publications, going to the Hartford newspaper in 1944. He remained there until 1966, when he took over the directorship of a professional journalism fellowship program at Stanford University. He wrote a syndicated newspaper column from 1968 to 1977.

One of his books, *Freedom of Information*, caused considerable debate among journalists in the late forties. He also wrote *The Changing American Newspaper*; *Journalist: Eyewitness to History*; and *Communication Is Power: Unchanging Values in a Changing Journalism*. In 1959, he received the John Peter Zenger award.

**BRUNS, Franklin R., Jr.** (1912–1979)
Franklin R. Bruns, Jr. was one of the nation's best known philatelic journalist. A syndicated newspaper columnist also worked for both the Smithsonian Institution and the Post Office Department.

Bruns spent 20 years, from 1932 to 1952, as the stamp editor for the *New York Sun* and its successor, the *World-Telegram-Sun*, before becoming the assistant curator in the Division of Philately for the Smithsonian Institution in 1951. He served there until 1957 and, later, from 1972 to 1979.

While on the *Sun*'s staff, his columns received awards for being the best in the field. He also won the Philatelic Journalist of America Award. He was president of the American Philatelic Congress and worked with many other philatelic groups.

Bruns worked with the Post Office philatelic program from 1957 to 1962. He also wrote many books about stamps and the art of stamp collecting. He once wrote that "Stamps are tiny storybooks—each carrying a message for those who look for it."

In 1972, he won the Lagerloef Award and in 1974 the H. L. Lindquist Award.

**BUCHANAN, Patrick Joseph** (1938– )

Since 1978, Patrick Buchanan has been writing a syndicated newspaper column and has been a commentator on the NBC Radio Network, expressing his conservative views to millions. Prior to that he was a special feature writer for the *New York Times* from 1975 to 1978.

Buchanan was an editorial writer and, later, an assistant editorial editor of the *St. Louis Globe-Democrat* (Missouri) from 1962 to 1966. Between 1966 and 1973, Buchanan was an executive assistant to Richard M. Nixon, and in 1974, he acted as a consultant to Nixon and Ford.

Buchanan was chosen by Walter Annenberg to be an "observer" for a *TV Guide* "News Watch," column which was published briefly in 1974.

**BUCHWACH, Buck Aaron** (1921– )

Buck Buchwach was born in Oregon, but he has made his career in Hawaii. In 1946, he became a reporter on the *Honolulu Advertiser*. He moved to become city editor, managing editor, and executive editor by 1971, a position he holds today.

Buchwach was named the Communications Father of the Year in Honolulu in 1958. Other citations have come to him for his work in gaining statehood for Hawaii and for his humanitarian projects in the state. The American Political Science Association gave him its award for distinguished reporting.

In addition to his editing duties, Buchwach has been a vice-president and the director of the Hawaii Newspaper Agency since 1963 and president of BeeBee Associations since 1950.

**BUCHWALD, Art** (1925– )

Art Buchwald, called by some "the most comic American observer of the European scene since Mark Twain," ran away from home when he was 17, joined the Marines, and used his $250 bonus check after the war to buy a one-way ticket to France.

By 1949, a career was underway. Buchwald submitted a trial column to the European edition of the *New York Herald Tribune*. It was titled "Paris after Dark," and later a book appeared under this title. Later he started another column, "Mostly about People."

"Europe's Lighter Side" became the title of the combined columns when Buchwald's successful articles were introduced to American readers through the *New York Herald Tribune* in 1952. Several years later, *Time* said the column had "an institutional quality."

Buchwald's satire upsets many readers, especially those who fail to realize the writer's objectives. Since 1950, his material has been collected in books. Their titles reflect his humor: *The Brave Coward; I Chose Capitol Punishment; Have I Ever Lied to You?; I Never Danced at the White House; I am Not a Crook; Down the Seine and Up the Potomac;* and *The Buchwald Stops Here.*

*While Reagan Slept*, another collection of his columns, appeared in 1983, and according to one reviewer, Buchwald "seeks the ultimate motivation behind the Reagan administration and all who worship it."

**BUCKLEY, William F., Jr.** (1925- )

"An Aristocrat for All Seasons" is only one of the many titles given William F. Buckley, Jr. In 1952, he was an associate editor for the *American Mercury*, a position he left when the magazine took an anti-Semitic stance. In 1955, Buckley founded his own magazine, *National Review.*

Today, Buckley is an editor, the author of successful fiction and nonfiction, a political activist, a television star with his own "Firing Line" program, and as always, a critic. Arthur M. Schlesinger, Jr. once called him "the scourge of American liberalism." When the *National Review* celebrated its 25th anniversary in 1980, one of the largest gatherings of the nation's conservative leaders occurred in New York.

Buckley spent many of his early years in France and England. He attended Roman Catholic private schools and, when only six, wrote the King of England demanding that Great Britain pay its war debt to America. Buckley has continued to voice his opinions ever since.

Buckley served in the Army in World War II and later earned a degree from Yale. He taught Spanish there briefly. His reaction to this experience has been recalled in his book, *God and Man at Yale: The Superstitions of Academic Freedom.*

Buckley's *National Review*, published with his sister Priscilla, is concerned with politics and letters. He wrote in the initial issue that his magazine stood "athwart history, yelling 'Stop' at a time when no one is inclined to do so, or to have much patience with those who urge it."

Through the *National Review*, Buckley has attacked the John Birch Society for its "false analysis and conspiratorial mania." In 1965, Buckley ran for mayor of New York City, coming in third with nearly 15 percent of the vote.

Throughout his career, Buckley has written for many magazines. In 1962, he started a syndicated newspaper column, "On the Right."

His television show, "Firing Line," has been carried on 170 stations associated with the Corporation for Public Broadcasting. His guests have included Groucho Marx, Jimmy Carter, Huey Newton, and Ronald Reagan.

In recent years, Buckley has written several well-received novels. Other books by Buckley, after his Yale volume, include *McCarthy and His Enemies; The Unmaking of a Mayor; The Jeweler's Eye; The Governor Listeth; Cruising Speed; Inveighing Who Will Go; Four Reforms; United Nations Journal; Executive Eve; Saving the Queen; Airborne; Stained Glass; A Hymnal; Who's on First; The Committee and Its Critics; Odyssey of a Friend, American Conservative Thought in the Twentieth Century; Racing at Sea; The Intellectual; What Is Conservatism?; Dialogues in Americanism; Violence in the Streets; The Beatles Book; Spectrum of Catholic Attitude; Great Ideas Today Annual*; and *Essays on Hayek*. Several of these were edited or co-authored. In addition, he has been awarded a number of honorary university degrees.

Writing in *Vanity Fair* in 1983, John Leonard recalled his experience working on the *National Review* with Buckley: "He taught me to use big words. He also introduced me to Whittaker Chambers, the translator of Bambi, who explained at lunch one day that Allen Ginsberg was the only Beat with real talent. And he sent me to Cuba to see about Castro's revolution."

Leonard added: Buckley "breathes politics. Citizenship for most of us is a hobby; for him it is a calling."

**BUFFETT, Warren Edward** (1930– )

Diversified investments in newspapers, including the *Washington Post*, and textile manufacturing have made Warren Buffett worth between $200 and $300 million, according to *Quill* magazine.

Writing about the *Washington Post*, Howard Bray noted that Buffett "is a major influence on the company's affairs. For this multi-millionaire, newspapers were first a business, like candy, trading stamps, or insurance. He was by no means indifferent to the quality of his publications. He respected well-edited newspapers and first-class writing in their own right, but he also expected higher profits to be the reward of higher quality."

One of Buffett's weekly publications investigated Boy's Town and revealed that the institution had millions of dollars in endowment. Buffett's contribution to the study was to urge the reporters to obtain IRS annual reports about Boy's Town. The investigation won many awards for the writers.

Buffett owns about 15 percent of the Washington Post Co. Other associations include the *Buffalo Evening News* (New York) and Blue Chip Stamps. He lives in Omaha, where he is active in Boys' Club projects.

**BULKELEY, Christy C.** (1942– )

Christy Bulkeley, one of the few women to become a newspaper publisher, has been active in journalism since she completed her studies at the University of Missouri in 1964.

Early training on the *Rochester Times-Union* (New York) included editorial writing, political and county government reporting, and general assignments. After eight years there, she became the editor-publisher-president of the *Saratoga Springs Saratogian* (New York) in 1974. Two years later, she had the same titles on the *Danville Commercial-News* (Illinois).

In Danville, she has worked with the Area Economic Development Corporiation Board, the YWCA, the United Way, The Executive Club, and the Community College Foundation. She has been recognized for her work with the Illinois Municipal Human Relations Association Award, the presidency of WICI (Women in Communications Inc.) and its Headliner Award, as well as the Leader of the Future Award from the National Council of Women.

In 1984 she returned to Saratoga Springs, and in 1985 she went to Rochester as a vice-president for the Gannett Foundation.

Bulkeley's professional work has brought her many assignments with the American Newspaper Publishers Association, the American Society of Newspaper Editors, Sigma Delta Chi, and other organizations. She serves on journalism advisory boards at the University of Missouri, Eastern Illinois University, and Texas Christian University.

**BURGHEIM, Richard A.** (1933- )

At Harvard University, Richard Burgheim was the sports editor for the *Crimson.* After service in the U.S. Coast Guard and a brief reporting job on the *Norfolk Virginian-Pilot*, he joined Time Inc. in 1960.

Burgheim spent his first 12 years with *Time*, rising to associate editor. He specialized in stories about television and show business personalities, writing profiles on Julie Andrews, Bob Hope, Johnny Carson, and others. He also served on juries for the Emmy and Tony awards.

The potential for cable and pay television occupied Burgheim's attention in 1972–73, while Time Inc. studied the future. Burgheim also lectured on cable television at Harvard and was a consultant to the Ford Foundation.

Burgheim moved to *People* magazine, working with the founding group in the seventies. He has been credited with "developing *People*'s cover format and contributing to the development of the magazine's editorial style."

In mid-1981, Burgheim was in charge of the editorial development of a new Time Inc. product, *TV-Cable Week*, and became its managing editor. However after only five months, Time Inc. closed the magazine following a $47 million loss. Management blamed the setback on "the cool reception given the national magazine by cable-system operators."

**BURKS, Edward C.** (1921–1983)

"'Ned' Burks was an award-winning foreign correspondent who explored the odd reaches of the planet, frequently traveling by train. In a career that spanned more than four decades, Mr. Burks also covered baseball, a lifelong passion, as well as local politics and Washington news."

In these words, the *New York Times* reported the death of one of their reporters and editors. He had been with the *Times* for 24 years.

Before coming to New York, Burks had worked on the *Baltimore Sun* (Maryland) in the Fifties, covering among other stories, the revolt in Hungary in 1956. He started his newspaper work on the *Altavista Journal* (Virginia) in 1940 and later worked in Danville and Lynchburg before going to Baltimore.

Among his more exciting reporting experience was his expulsion from the Dominican Republic in 1960 for his series exposing the regime of Rafael Trujillo.

**BURNETT, Robert** (1927– )
Named "Publisher of the Year" in 1982, Robert Burnett, who is the president and chief operating officer of Meredith Corporation, said, "When I think something has to be said, I say it." Apparently his colleagues agreed with him.

Burnett told *Advertising Age* that "magazines are based on enduring values. People look at them to be educated, to be informed, to be reflective and to be entertained—at their leisure. Magazines perform that function better than any other medium."

Burnett serves on the board of Grinnell College and is associated with a bank, an insurance firm, and other organizations.

**BUSHINSKY, Jay** (1932– )
Jay (Joseph Mason) Bushinsky has been a foreign correspondent in Tel Aviv, Israel for many years. He began his newspaper career as a reporter for the *Middletown Times Herald/Record* (New York) in 1963, and was then a copyeditor on the *Miami Herald* (Florida) for two years. He joined the *Chicago Daily News* Foreign Service in 1966 as a Tel Aviv correspondent to cover the Middle East; during part of that time, he also was a correspondent for Westinghouse Broadcasting Co.

Bushinsky has been a correspondent for the *Chicago Sun-Times* since 1978. He shared a Chicago Newspaper Guild Award in 1978 for the expose of Nazi war criminals in America and another award, in 1973, for the Best Radio Spot News Reporting from Abroad to Group W for coverage of the Mideast war.

**BUSHMILLER, Ernie** (1905–1982)
Early in his career, Ernie Bushmiller was a cartoonist for the old *New York World* and the *New York Graphic*, as well as a comedy writer for Harold Lloyd, the silent movie star.

In 1931, Bushmiller began the syndicated comedy strips "Fritzi Ritz" and the better-known "Nancy." These have been translated and published in many countries, and "Nancy" remains one of the most widely read of all comics.

**BUTLER, Eugene** (1894– )
Agricultural journalism has brought many awards to Eugene Butler, who began a long career on the *Progressive Farmer* in 1917. From 1953 to 1968, he edited the magazine's Texas edition and managed the Dallas office.

Butler became president of the publication in 1953, a position he held until 1968. Since 1964, he has been chairman of the board. Among his many awards are several for outstanding contributions to Texas agriculture from the Texas Cottonseed Crushers Association, the American Seed Trade Association, the Texas Federation of Co-ops, the National Future Farmers Association, and the Texas Forestry Association.

In 1975, Butler was named the "Farm Editor of the Year" by the Texas Farmers Union. Texas A&M University gave him its Centennial Award for outstanding contributions to the state agricultural programs in 1976, and Mississippi State University awarded him its alumni citation in 1978.

**BYLINSKY, Gene Michael** (1930– )
Gene Bylinsky has won many awards for science and medical reporting. Starting as a staff reporter on the *Wall Street Journal* in Dallas in 1957, he was moved to San Francisco in 1957 and to the newspaper's home office in New York in 1961. In 1962, he was in Washington as the science writer for *National Observer.*

Bylinsky worked as a science writer for four years, 1962–66, for the Newhouse Newspapers in Washington before returning to New York to become associate editor of *Fortune.*

He won the Albert Lasker Medical Journalism Award in 1970; Sigma Delta Chi awards in 1970 and 1972; and American Medical Association commendations and medical journal awards on four occasions. The American Chemical Society in 1976 gave him its James T. Grady Award for his success in interpreting chemistry to the public. He wrote *The Innovation Millionaires.*

**CAEN, Herb** (1916– )
Few person have done more to promote San Francisco than has Herb Caen, a columnist for newspapers there since 1938. Few persons are as well known in California, except for politicians, than is Caen.

Caen said in 1984 that he was probably "the longest running columnist in America." He met Walter Winchell, then the nation's most read columnist, in New York in 1948. Winchell said Caen imitated him better than anybody else.

A native Californian, Caen first worked on the *San Francisco Chronicle* from 1938 to 1950. For the next eight years, he was a columnist for the *Examiner.* He returned to the *Chronicle* in 1958, where he continues his column today.

In addition to his widely read and quoted column, Caen has written several books. His first, in 1948, was simply called *The San Francisco Book.* Caen's other books: *Baghdad-by-the Bay; Baghdad; Don't Call It Frisco; Caen's Guide to San Francisco; Only in San Francisco;* (co-) *City on Golden Hills; The Cable Car and the Dragon; One Man's San Francisco.* He has published guide books, as well as an account of the cable car, a San Francisco fixture. He served in World War II.

**CAMPBELL, Robert Duff** (1917– )
Robert Campbell has been associated with *Newsweek* since 1949. Prior to that he was an ad salesman for Macfadden Publications in Los Angeles after a two-year stint with a textile company in Chicago.

Campbell moved up to be managing director for international editions and then to executive vice-president and, in 1972, publisher. Since 1976, he has been president and chairman of the board. He also is a director of the parent company, The Washington Post Co.

Campbell rose to the rank of brigadier-general in the Air Force in World War II and later served in Korea and Vietnam.

**CANHAM, Erwin D.** (1904–1982)
As editor of the *Christian Science Monitor* (Boston, Massachusetts) from 1945 to 1964 and editor-in-chief until he was given emeritus status in 1974, Erwin D. Canham's goal had been "to help give humankind the tools with which to work out its salvation."

A newspaper historian wrote that Canham and his newspaper "pioneered in interpretive reporting and analysis of national and world affairs."

Canham grew up in journalistic surroundings. When only eight, he helped his father, a reporter for the *Lewiston Sun* (Maine). He learned to set type and became a reporter on another Maine weekly during the manpower shortage in World War I years.

In 1925, Canham, after receiving his degree from Bates College, immediately joined the *Christian Science Monitor* as a reporter. He covered many major events, including the League of Nations' sessions. For several years, 1932–35, he headed the *Monitor*'s Washington Bureau.

During Canham's tenure on the *Monitor*, he took three years off to accept a Rhodes scholarship for study at Oxford.

He became president of the U.S. Chamber of Commerce, after serving on its board of directors and on several major committees. Government service brought Canham many assignments. He was a delegate to the United Nations Geneva Conference on freedom of information in 1948; chairman of the U.S. advisory commission on information for the U.S. Information Agency.

He had also headed the American Society of Newspaper Editors and served as a commentator and moderator on Boston radio and television programs.

Canham had won the John Peter Zenger Award and was decorated by the British Empire, France, Greece, Germany, and Austria. He was the co-author of *Awakening: The World at Mid-Century* and *The World at Mid-Century* and *The Christian Science Way of Life, with a Christian Scientist's Life*. He edited *Man's Great Future*. In addition, Canham wrote *New Frontiers for Freedom* and *Commitment to Freedom*.

**CANIFF, Milton Arthur** (1907– )
While still in his teens, Milton Caniff began his long and successful career as a cartoonist. In 1921, he worked summers on the *Dayton Journal-Herald* (Ohio). Later he worked on the *Miami Daily News* (Florida), the *Columbus Dispatch* (Ohio), and for the Associated Press Feature Service in New York.

Caniff created several widely read comics including "Terry and the Pirates" in 1934, "Male Call" during World War II and "Steve Canyon" in 1947. They have been syndicated around the world since 1934. Caniff said in 1984 that "By the time I went to Kindergarten, I was at least drawing something resembling the human figure."

In view of this wide audience, Caniff has received numerous awards, including a War Department Citation for "Male Call," which he donated to military publications during World War II, and Air Force awards and the American Legion "Good Guy Award." He won Reuben Awards in 1946 and 1971.

The Boy Scouts, Goodwill Industries, and the Freedoms Foundation have recognized his work with special citations. His home state, Ohio, selected him for special recognition, and Ohio State University has a Milton Caniff Research Library. In 1981, Caniff was named to the National Comic Strip Hall of Fame. During his 75th year, Caniff was honored by the National Cartoonists Society when it devoted *The Cartoonist* magazine to him.

**CAPA, Cornell** (1918– )

Born in Budapest, Cornell Capa came to the United States and became a naturalized citizen. In 1946, he began a long association with *Life* magazine, working as a staff photographer and a contributing photographer until 1967. Since 1954, he has been a member of Magnum Photos, Inc., a cooperative group of photographers.

Capa has been the executive director of the International Center of Photography in New York since 1974, and he was honored by the city with the Mayor's Award of Honor for Arts and Culture in 1978. He has also written several books. Capa's books include *Farewell to Eden* and *Margin of Life*. He edited *Concerned Photographer I* and *II*, *Images of War*, *Israel the Reality* and others.

**CAPA, Robert** (1918–1954)

Photographer Robert Capa won worldwide recognition for his outstanding, on-the-scene pictures of the Spanish Civil War and the Normandy Invasion.

Covering wars had become his profession, with service in China, Sicily, Italy, and other countries, but he met his death in 1954 when he stepped on a land mine while covering the exit of the French forces in Vietnam.

Ten years after his death a book, *Images of War*, appeared, which included his most outstanding photographs.

**CAPEN, Richard G., Jr.** (1934– )

Richard Capen, Jr. became chairman and publisher of the *Miami Herald* (Florida) in 1982. Three years earlier, he had joined the Knight-Ridder group as the overseer of a number of their middle-sized and smaller newspapers.

Capen was associated with Copley Newspapers in La Jolla, California, from 1961 to 1979. He first directed the group's public affairs and eventually became senior vice-president.

In his latest assignment, Capen is responsible for the city group of Knight-Ridder publications. This is one of the three leading newspaper groups in America today.

Capen is also a Naval Reserve officer.

**CARBINE, Patricia Theresa** (1931– )
Since 1972, Patricia Carbine and her magazine, *Ms.*, have reflected the changes in the status of women in America.

The University of Missouri School of Journalism honored Carbine "as a chronicler of and contributor to change for women in the past decade" and for her dedication "to humanizing and equalizing the way its readers think of themselves, relate to one another and view the future."

Carbine started on *Look* magazine as a researcher in 1953, rising to the executive editorship before 1970. For the next two years, she was editor of *McCall's*. In 1969, she occupied the highest position ever held by a woman on a general interest magazine up to that time.

She became publisher and editor-in-chief of *Ms.* when it was started in 1972. She also founded the Ms. Foundation for Women, Inc. and the Ms. Foundation for Education and Communications, Inc. She is a trustee of her alma mater, Rosemont College. She has held offices in the American Society of Magazine Editors and the Magazine Publishers Association. She was named one of the Outstanding Women in Communications in 1982.

**CARPENTER, Elizabeth Sutherland** (1920– )
Elizabeth "Liz" Carpenter, for years, was associated with journalistic activities in Washington, especially through her relationship with the Lyndon B. Johnson family.

Carpenter started as a United Press reporter in Philadelphia in 1944. From 1945 to 1961, she and her husband operated a Washington news bureau, which represented a number of newspapers.

Between 1961 and 1963, Carpenter was an executive assistant to Vice-President Johnson and, in 1963, became press secretary to Mrs. Johnson. She remains a consultant with the L.B. Johnson Library in Austin, where she lives. She was also vice-president of Hill & Knowlton, Inc., in Washington for four years.

*The Ladies' Home Journal* in 1977 named her "Woman of the Year" in the field of politics and public affairs. She was president of the Women's National Press group and won a National Headliner Award in 1962.

**CARTER, Don Earl** (1917– )
Don Carter began his newspaper career in his native state, Georgia, on the *Atlanta Journal* as a reporter in 1938. He became the farm editor, and by 1951, he was the city editor, serving until 1959.

From 1959 to 1961, Carter was the executive director of The Newspaper Fund, founded by Dow Jones & Co., which worked closely with journalism students across the country. The Fund provides financial assistance for many students and projects.

When Dow Jones started its weekly *National Observer* in 1961, Carter became the first managing editor, a position he held until he became the executive editor of the *Hackensack Record* and *Paterson Morning Call* (New Jersey) in 1967.

Carter returned to the *Macon Telegraph and News* in 1971 as executive editor and vice-president. He was the publisher and president of the *Lexington Herald and Leader* (Kentucky), 1975–77. He has been a vice-president of Knight-Ridder Newspapers, Inc., since 1976.

Carter served in the Army during World War II and was awarded a Bronze Star.

He has been recognized for his service to journalism education by Theta Sigma Phi, the University of Nebraska, and the University of Texas. He has also held leadership positions as president of the Associated Press Managing Editors Association and the American Council on Education for Journalism.

**CARTER, Hodding** (1907–1972)

Hodding Carter emerged from his home state of Louisiana as the liberal voice of the South. Through his newspaper work, his lectures, and his books and articles, he has become well known across America.

Carter began as a reporter on the *New Orleans Item-Tribune* in 1929, and the next year he joined the United Press there. After a year with the Associated Press in Jackson, Mississippi, Carter and his wife, Betty, founded the *Hammond Daily Courier* (Louisiana), which they operated until 1936. He maintained a campaign against Senator Huey Long.

In Greenville, Mississippi, the Carters began the *Delta Star* and two years later Carter bought the *Delta Democrat-Times* and became its editor-publisher. In 1939, he was a Nieman fellow at Harvard University.

During World War II, Carter served with the Army Bureau of Public Relations, 1940–41, and later was editor of *Stars and Stripes* and *Yank*, retiring as a major in 1945.

"Big Hod," as his family called him, won a Pulitzer Prize in 1946 for editorials urging racial moderation in the South. He also won a Southern Literary award, the Bowdoin Prize, and the Journalism Alumni Award from Columbia University; he was a Sigma Delta Chi fellow and won a William A. White Foundation national citation for journalistic merit.

Carter wrote many books, including *Lower Mississippi*; *The Winds of Fear*; *Flood Crest*; *John Law Wasn't So Wrong*; *Southern Legacy*; *Where Main Street Meets the River*; *Robert E. Lee and The Road of Honor*; *Marquis De Lafayette, Bright Sword for Freedom*; *The Angry Scar*; *So Great a Good*; *Doomed Road of Empire*; *First Person Rural*; *The Ballad of Catfood Grimes and Other Verse*; *So the Heffners Left McComb*; *The Commandos of World War II*; *Their Words Were Bullets*, and *Man and the River: The Mississippi*. He was the co-author of *Civilian Defense of the United States* and *Gulf Coast Country*.

Carter devoted considerable time to educational interests, becoming involved with Bowdoin College, Tulane University, and George Peabody College.

**CARTER, John Mack** (1928– )
John Mack Carter, named "Publisher of the Year" by Brandeis University in 1977, earned this title and other awards for his outstanding work as editor of three major women's magazines.

From 1961 to 1965, Carter was editor of *McCall's*; from 1965 to 1974, *Ladies' Home Journal*, and since 1975 *Good Housekeeping*. Carter at one time edited *American Home* and was an assistant editor of *Better Homes and Gardens*.

*Time* and *Newsweek* have called Carter a phenomenon in publishing history, and in a *Folio* magazine personality sketch he was designated "one of the best editors in publishing today."

Carter feels "it's critical to be in tune. You can't possibly get to the top—and stay there—unless you are." He edits every issue of *Good Housekeeping*, "both before and after it's printed." He asks for total dedication from his staff and achieves it through his own dedication.

Carter's alma mater, the University of Missouri, presented him its Honor Award for Distinguished Service in Journalism. Women in Communications, Inc., awarded him its "Headliner of the Year" title.

In 1970, Carter faced a revolt of women "liberators" on the *Ladies' Home Journal*, who demanded "an immediate stop to the publication of articles that are irrelevant, unstimulating and demeaning to the women of America." Thirty women occupied Carter's office, where he listened for 11 hours to their demands. Later he provided a supplement to the magazine for the women to publish their articles. The *Ladies' Home Journal* slogan at that time was "Never underestimate the power of a woman."

Carter has served on the National Commission for the Observance of International Women's Year. He is active in the American Cancer Society, the Christian Church Foundation, and Religion in American Life.

In addition to his *Good Housekeeping* editorship, Carter is director of magazine development for Hearst.

**CARTER, William Hodding III** (1935– )
Hodding Carter III began his career on his father's newspaper, the *Greenville Delta Democrat-Times* (Mississippi) in 1959, becoming the editor in 1965. In 1977, he was an assistant secretary of state for public affairs and became known to television viewers as the State Department spokesman in Washington. He was extremely visible during the Iranian crisis.

With his newspaper background, Carter had an "exceptionally good relationship" with the media. He left the State Department in 1980, after the family newspaper had been sold for a reported $16 million. The next year Carter became the anchorman and commentator of a Public Broadcasting Service weekly series, "Inside Story." He also is a columnist for the *Wall Street Journal*. Carter told *People* magazine in 1981 that "I learned from my father what courage was really about—it was being afraid but doing what you had to do."

After graduation from Princeton in 1957, Carter spent two years in the Marine Corps. He returned to Greenville after his father suffered failing eyesight and depression after the death of his youngest son. He became an editorial writer there.

Carter has long been active in the Democratic Party, serving as co-chairman of the Young Democrat Clubs in Mississippi for several years. He helped to organize the Loyal Democrats of Mississippi in 1968 and worked on Lyndon B. Johnson's staff in 1964. In 1976, he worked with the Carter campaign. He sought a biracial party in his state, an idea that ran counter to the traditional party leaders' goals there. His book, *The South Strikes Back*, reflects his goals.

**CASH, Wilbur Joseph** (1900–1941)
A freelance writer and newspaperman, W. J. Cash may be best remembered for his one book, *The Mind of the South*, published in 1941. Here Cash recorded his interpretations of the feelings of White Southerners, their prejudices and standards. No doubt this volume helped bring about improved racial relations in the South.

Cash's biographer, Joseph Morrison, wrote: "During this second half of the twentieth century, it (Cash's book) has been accepted by virtually everyone that studies of the South—and, by extension, of the Negro revolution—must begin where Cash left off."

Cash in 1923 was a member of the *Charlotte Observer* (North Carolina) staff. For two years he taught English and French in North Carolina before joining the *Chicago Post* in 1924. This was followed in 1925 with free-lance newspaper work. By 1926 he was with the *Charlotte News*, eventually becoming associate editor.

Cash contributed to many periodicals, including the *American Mercury*, *Nation* and others. He had received a Guggenheim fellowship to write a novel in Mexico in 1941. He later took his own life in Mexico.

**CASSELS, Louis Welborn** (1922–1974)
Louis Cassels spent his reporting career with the United Press International, joining the service as a correspondent in New York, in 1946, and later moving to Washington where he spent the rest of his life.

He became a religious news columnist in 1956 and covered major church events around the world.

Cassels believed that newspapers had an obligation to report religious controversies, whether they occurred within a congregation or involved social and political issues.

For his outstanding reporting, Cassels won the Christopher Award; the School Bell Award from the National Education Association; the Faith and Freedom Award in religious journalism; the Front Page Award for domestic reporting, and other citations.

As one might expect, many of Cassels' books were about religious concerns. He wrote *Christian Primer*; *What's the Difference?*; *Your Bible*; *The*

*Real Jesus; The Reality of God; Haircuts and Holiness; A Feast for the Time of Fasting; This Fellow Jesus; Forbid Them Not; Coontail Lagoon: Preludes to Prayer; A Bad Investment*; and *Faiths of America*.

**CASTLEBERRY, Vivian Lou** (1922– )
A leader in Southern journalism, Vivian Castleberry currently is women's editor and on the editorial board of the *Dallas Times Herald* (Texas).

Castleberry began as an editorial assistant with the Petroleum Engineering Publishing Co.; she later worked for Cousins Publishing Co. and *Texas A.&M. Bulletin*, where she was women's editor. In 1954, she joined the *Times Herald* as home editor.

For her achievements with the Dallas Council of World Affairs, Dallas International Cultural and Social Circle, and other organizations, she has won awards from the Dallas Press Club, the Headliner Club, the Southwestern Journalism Forum, the Business and Professional Women's Club, the Soroptomist Club, and the Dallas Women's Center, as well as three United Press International awards for women's news reporting.

**CATER, Douglass** (1923– )
Douglass Cater's career has included writing, editing, government service, and, since 1982, a college presidency.

From 1950 to 1963 Cater was the Washington editor for the *Reporter* magazine. He served another year as its national affairs editor before becoming a special assistant to President Lyndon Johnson. In the early fifties he had held similar positions with the Secretary of the Army and the Mutual Security Agency. During World War II he served with the OSS.

Prior to becoming president of Washington College in Maryland in 1982 Cater taught at Princeton, the University of California at San Francisco and Stanford. Since 1978 he also has been a senior fellow with the Aspen Institute.

Cater's books include *Ethics in a Business Society* (with Marquis Childs); *The Fourth Branch of Government; Power in Washington; Dana: The Irrelevant Man*, and *Television Violence and the Child*. He helped edit *The Future of Public Broadcasting, Television as a Cultural Force*, and *Television as a Social Force*.

Among his awards Cater won a Guggenheim fellowship in 1955 and an Eisenhower exchange fellow two years later. He won a George Polk Memorial award and a New York Newspaper Guild Page One award, both in 1961.

**CATLEDGE, Turner** (1901–1983)
Turner Catledge, who began his newspaper career in the South, joined the *New York Times* in 1929. In 1951, he became the managing editor, and by 1964, he was the newspaper's first executive editor, a position he held until he stepped down in 1968. After his retirement, he returned to the South; he died in New Orleans.

Catledge started writing as an assistant to the Missisippi State University agricultural editor in the early Twenties. In 1922, he was editor of the weekly *Tunica Times* (Mississippi). The plant was burned down after he published an anti-Ku Klux Klan series written by the *Times'* owner Clayton Rand.

Catledge moved to Tupelo en route to the *Memphis Press* (Tennessee) in 1924. Soon after that he joined the *Commercial Appeal*, the Scripps-Howard companion paper there.

His success in the East can be traced directly to Herbert Hoover. In 1927, as Secretary of Commerce, Hoover toured the Mississippi Valley to assess flood damage. He was impressed by Catledge's knowledge of the area and urged his friend, Adolph Ochs of the *New York Times*, to hire him. Ochs did not act at that time, but when Hoover became President he again recommended that the *Times* hire Catledge.

Before he was employed by the *Times*, Catledge worked on the *Baltimore Sun* (Maryland), where the Mississippian once said he "learned to write better, to dress better, to act better."

By 1929 Catledge was associated with the *Times*, moving up rapidly as he managed to settle many internal disputes among staff members. He called for writing with brevity, simplicity, and clarity.

Catledge became the executive editor for both the Sunday and the daily editions. He opposed government censorship and published such stories as a series on the CIA's foreign operations, the planned invasion of Cuba in 1961, and Harrison Salisbury's dispatches from Hanoi, which upset some readers.

A Turner Catledge Chair of Communications has been established at his alma mater, with a $400,000 gift from the *Times*.

**CAVE, Ray** (1929- )

In 1952, Cave was with the *Baltimore Sun* doing police and investigative reporting, becoming a foreign correspondent in North Africa before he assumed the duties of assistant city editor for the *Sun*. During his association with the *Sun*, Cave was also a special correspondent for *Time* and *Sports Illustrated*. He served in the Army during the Korean War.

Ray Cave joined Time Inc. in 1959 to write for *Sports Illustrated*. Three years later, he switched to editing and, after several promotions, became executive editor in 1974.

After 17 years with *Sports Illustrated* as managing editor, Cave moved to *Time* in 1977, the position he holds today.

**CHAMBERS, James Floyd, Jr.** (1913- )

James Chambers, Jr., began newspaper work as a copyboy and later became a reporter on the *Dallas Dispatch* (Texas) in 1934. He handled sports for several years before becoming city editor in 1940. A year as the public relations director for the Chamber of Commerce and three years with the North American Aviation Corp. preceded Chambers's appointment as the executive news editor of the *Times Herald* in 1945.

By 1960, Chambers was the firm's president. Among the major stories he reported was the Bikini atom bomb tests in 1946.

Among his professional achievements was the presidency of the Texas Daily Newspaper Association.

He was also the ghost writer for several books, including those "by" Byron Nelson and Doak Walker.

**CHANCELLOR, John William** (1927– )

"Some of the tension could be taken out of press conferences, and more information imparted, if Presidents would be willing to give up the fiction that they are omniscient," so wrote John Chancellor in his review of presidential press conferences for *TV Guide* readers.

After service in the Army from 1945 to 1947, Chancellor began on the *Chicago Sun-Times* in 1948 as a copyboy, working up to a reporter, a rewrite, and then a feature writer.

In 1950, Chancellor made his first connection with the NBC, becoming a staffer with the network's station WNBQ in Chicago. During his time there, Chancellor won a Sigma Delta Chi award in 1955 for outstanding reporting. Three years later, the Fund for the Republic gave him the Robert E. Sherwood Award for his television commentary on Southern migrants in the North.

Significant events followed. Chancellor covered the Adlai E. Stevenson 1956 campaign. The next year, he covered the Little Rock desegregation story, which won him other citations.

His foreign assignments began with a trip to the Vienna Bureau with NBC News. Later he covered London, Paris, and Moscow, coming home for the 1960 presidential campaign. He reluctantly and briefly served as a communicator for the "Today" show, following Dave Garroway who had left the program.

Another brief tour, 1966–67, was with the Voice of America. He soon returned to NBC where he remains today. For many years he was the anchorman for the "NBC Nightly News" until he stepped down to become the show's commentator. Chancellor has always considered himself a reporter.

In 1982, Chancellor was named Broadcaster of the Year by the International Radio and Television Society. That same year he told *Newsweek*, "I had money and I had fame but the last thing I wanted was to be a 65-year-old anchor man. So I decided it was time to take control of my life."

In 1983, Chancellor and Walter R. Mears wrote *The News Business*.

**CHANDLER Family**

"No single family dominates any major region of this country as the Chandlers have dominated California," wrote David Halberstam. It started with Harry Chandler, "the classic entrepreneurial wheeler-dealer." Harry Chandler (1864–1944) had moved from his native New Hampshire to California, and with his son, Norman, and his grandson, Otis, made the *Los Angeles Times* one of the nation's best newspapers.

Norman Chandler (1899–1975), in 1922, married Dorothy Buffum, who was described by Halberstam as a "restless, highly energized woman of soaring ambition, ambition for her husband, for herself, above all for her son (Otis)." Actively involved with the Los Angeles Philharmonic Association and the Music Center, at one time she was the vice-president in charge of corporate relations at the *Times*.

The *Times* remained "parochial and reactionary, a voice of the property holdings of the Chandlers and their close friends" during the Forties and Fifties. Subsequently Norman Chandler, always a conservative, became a long-time Nixon supporter. Halberstam thought Los Angeles then "was a more isolated island in America." The daily newspaper had a bad reputation, especially among eastern publishers, so much so that for a brief time the *New York Times* published a western edition in direct competition with the *Los Angeles Times*.

Otis Chandler joined the Times Mirror Co. in 1953. By 1960, he was the publisher, a position he held for the next 20 years. Today, he is chairman of the board and editor-in-chief.

When he took control of the *Times*, the newspaper underwent a major transition. Joining the *Washington Post*, the two newspapers established a news service that expanded their worldwide coverage. Although he had gone through the *Times'* training program, Dennis Holder observed that Otis "had the wisdom to know what he didn't know" and to hire experienced personnel as top staffers and executives. Additional editorial personnel were added, along with more news bureaus. The newspaper has one of the largest electronic news editing systems now in service and has made plans for plant expansion that will cost in the millions.

Norman Chandler had stepped down to devote more time to expanding the company's other interests, although he had apparently enjoyed being the *Times'* publisher. Today the Chandler family wealth has been estimated at between $600 million and $1 billion. Family holdings include the *Times*, *Newsday*, the *Denver Post*, the *Dallas Times Herald*, and the *Hartford Courant*; television stations and cable TV; book publishing firms; newsprint and forest product companies, and real estate.

The *Times* has won the Pulitzer Prize three times, the first, in 1966, for its coverage of the Watts riots; the second, in 1969, for its international reporting and public service activities; and more recently, in 1976, for editorial writing.

Otis Chandler served in the Air Force in the Fifties. He is a big-game hunter and his office is lined with stuffed animals. As James Brady wrote in *Advertising Age*, "the big, profitable, largely provincial and relatively undistinguished paper he took over in 1960 is today, by whatever reckoning, ranked in the top five, perhaps in the top three American dailies. It is more profitable than ever and it is very, very big. Daily circulation is 1,081,050; Sunday circulation is 1,340,743." Otis has been recognized with the Lovejoy Award.

Dennis Holder, writing in the *Washington Journalism Review*, notes that although the *Times* is more than a century old, today's paper "is much younger, a newcomer even in its own hometown. The *Times* as we know it was born barely 22 years ago on April 11, 1960," the date Otis Chandler took control.

Chandler won the Joseph Quinn Memorial Award by the Greater Los Angeles Press Club in 1984 for his efforts over two decades to make the *Times* one of the nation's best papers.

**CHAPMAN, Alvah Herman Jr.** (1921– )
Alvah Chapman, Jr., a third-generation newspaper executive, is chairman and chief executive officer of Knight-Ridder Newspapers, Inc., a firm that publishes 32 daily newspapers.

Chapman started on the *Columbus Ledger-Enquirer* (Georgia) in 1945, and within three years had become business manager. This followed his service in World War II as a bomber pilot, for which he won the Distinguished Flying Cross, the Air Medal, the Croix de Guerre, and the European combat ribbon, most of them with extra clusters.

In 1953, Chapman became the executive vice-president and general manager of the *St. Petersburg Times*, and four years later became a part owner as well as the president-publisher of the *Savannah Morning News* and *Evening Press*.

Chapman joined the Knight group in Miami in 1960. He was vice-president and general manager of the *Herald* in 1962, and in 1969, its president.

Named Dade County "Outstanding Citizen of the Year," Chapman has been frequently honored in Miami. He won the NCCJ's Silver Medallion in Brotherhood in 1974; the Religious Heritage of America Award in 1975 and 1978; the *Miami News*' Business Leader of the Year in 1980, and the American Jewish Committee's Institute of Human Relations Award in 1982.

Chapman has been active in other Florida projects, including Goodwill Industries, United Funds, Orange Bowl, and Miami Citizens against Crime.

**CHARNEY, Nicholas H.** (1914– )
Nicholas Charney and John Veronis founded *Psychology Today* in 1967. During the magazine's early history, Charney said he hoped to make *Psychology Today* "lively, clear, and technically accurate."

Charney said he was "irritated with pompous unnecessary vocabularies generated by some psychologists in their attempts to be objective and precise." He preferred to make psychology "a fascinating and alive subject."

For two years, 1971–73, Charney was part owner of *Saturday Review*, and for the next two years, the publisher of *Book Digest*. In 1976, he founded *Videofashion Monthly* and serves as its editor.

**CHASE, Barry O.** (1945– )
As director of news and public affairs programming for the Public Broadcasting Service (PBS), Barry O. Chase has many duties in a position he has held since 1976.

Following graduation from Harvard Law School, Chase worked with Wilmer, Cutler and Pickering from 1970 to 1976. During those years, Chase was involved with communications-related issues, including litigation, subpoena of newsmen, comparative renewal proceedings, fairness, political endorsements, personal attack, paid political advertising, CATV, and matters affecting license renewal applications.

In 1976, Chase became the associate general counsel for PBS. In addition to federal issues, Chase was concerned with programming, funding, and leasing and other assorted projects.

Two years later, Chase moved to his present position, where he is responsible for development, coordination, and the acceptance/rejection of all PBS news, public affairs, science, sports, and minority-interest programs.

**CHASE, Sylvia** (1938– )

Sylvia Chase began her career in politics, first as an aide to the California State Assembly Committee on Finance and later to Senator Thomas Rees, from 1961 to 1965.

After assisting in other California campaigns, Chase became a coordinator for the Kennedy presidential drive in 1968. By 1969, Chase had entered broadcasting, as an action reporter on Los Angeles Station KNX. Two years later, she was a correspondent and anchorperson for CBS News in New York. She moved to ABC News in 1977.

"Chase may be the cagiest interviewer of them all," wrote Mark Ribowsky in *TV Guide* early in 1983. She is a "pussy-cat on the surface who gently yet deftly brings out the natural emotions in an interview without calling attention to herself or playing the role of adversary."

Chase received the Public Service Award from the American Trial Lawyers Association in 1970; an Emmy in 1978; and the Headliner, Front Page, and Gainsrugh awards in 1979.

**CHASSLER, Seymour Murray** (1919– )

Editing magazines has kept Seymour Chassler busy since his first position as associate editor of *Coronet* from 1945 to 1948. This followed three years as a writer for *March of Time* films, 1942–45.

Chassler served as the picture editor for *Pageant* magazine from 1948 to 1950, and after five years in a similar role for *Collier's*, returned to *Pageant* as managing editor and later executive editor, a position he held until 1959.

After a brief association with *This Week* magazine, Chassler started his long career with *Redbook*, first as executive editor in 1960, eventually becoming editor-in-chief, his current position.

Chassler is vice-president of the Redbook Publishing and the McCall Publishing companies. He has served on committees concerned with women interests, the United Nations, and the National Women's Political Caucus. He is an honorary trustee for the Elizabeth Cady Stanton Foundation.

Chassler won the Graflex Award, in 1952, for his contributions to photojournalism and the Headliner Award from Women in Communications, Inc., in 1979. He has long been active in the programs of the American Society of Magazine Editors.

**CHILDS, Marquis** (1903– ) died June 30, 1990

For more than 40 years, from 1926 to 1968, Marquis Childs worked for the *St. Louis Post-Dispatch* (Missouri), the last six years as chief of the newspaper's Washington Bureau.

Childs' other work includes several years with the United Press; he was also a columnist with the United Feature Syndicate. Childs has won many awards including the first Pulitzer Prize for commentary, in 1969. Sigma Delta Chi named him the best Washington Correspondent in 1944. Sweden and Germany have also decorated him.

Childs has been president of both the Overseas Writers and the Gridiron clubs.

In 1982, Childs published *The Mighty Mississippi: Biography of a River*, a subject he has been close to, since he was born in the Mississippi River town of Clinton, Iowa. He also wrote *Sweden the Middle Way; They Hate Roosevelt; Washington Calling; This Is Democracy; This Is Your War; I Wrote from Washington; The Cabin; The Farmer Takes a Hand; The Ragged Edge; Eisenhower, Captive Hero; The Peacemakers; Taint of Innocence*; and *Witness to Power*. He co-edited *Ethics in Business Society* and *Walter Lippmann and His Times*. He has taught at several universities and, in 1983, was a visiting professor at the University of Texas, lecturing on the government and the press.

**CHRISTOPHER, Robert Collins** (1924– )

Robert Christopher has administered the Pulitzer Prize committee activities at Columbia University since 1981, a position that followed a long career in the magazine world.

Christopher, in 1949–1950, was on the staff of the *Investment Dealers Digest*. He was associated with *Time* from 1950 to 1963, rising to senior editor for the United States and World Business sections. He served a year as director of economic research for the Corning Glass Work and still serves as a director for the firm's foundation.

In 1963, Christopher returned to magazine work, becoming the foreign editor of *Newsweek* until 1969, when he became the executive editor. He was later a contributing editor, and in 1979, he became managing editor of GEO magazine.

**CHUNG, Constance Yu-hwa** (1946– )

"NBC's Early-Morning Star" was *Newsweek's* headline when Connie Chung took her new anchor job on the "NBC News at Sunrise" in 1983. This move from Los Angeles was a major change in her more than 13 years on the air.

Chung started as a television news reporter on WTTG-TV in Washington in 1969. She joined CBS there in 1971, and in 1976, she became the news anchor at CBS's station WNXT-TV in Los Angeles.

While in Los Angeles, Chung said she thought "anchor people who are real journalists often feel guilty about just anchoring. If they don't go out and do some reporting they become just readers. No journalist wants to be just that."

According to *Newsweek*, Chung took a $250,000 pay cut from her $700,000 Los Angeles salary when she moved to New York. She has been labeled a workaholic, with the desire to cover a presidential campaign. She accompanied President Richard Nixon when he visited the Soviet Union.

She started her eastern duties with NBC with a heavy schedule. She was to handle "Sunrise" report for the "Today" show, and anchor the "NBC Nightly News" on Saturday.

Chung has been honored by the AAUW; the U.S. Humane Society, for making the public aware of the cruelties of seal harvesting; the National Association of Media Women; and The Chinese-American Citizens Alliance. She was the Outstanding Young Woman of the Year in 1975 and won an Emmy Award in 1978.

**CIOFFI, Louis James** (1926– )

Radio and television news reporting by Louis Cioffi has brought him awards from the Overseas Press Club and the Headliner Club in the Seventies.

Lou Cioffi began with CBS News in 1947 as a copyboy, and moved up to writer and editor by 1952. He was a war correspondent in Korea before moving to the Paris Bureau in 1961, when he joined ABC News as chief of the European and Far East bureaus for four years. He also worked with the ABC German Bureau.

Cioffi has been the ABC United Nations chief in New York since 1977.

**CLAIBORNE, Craig** (1920– )

Craig Claiborne has become nationally famous as a journalist, a chef, and a gourmet as food editor for the *New York Times*.

Claiborne's evaluations of hundreds of eating places in New York were published as his *Guide to Dining Out in New York* in 1964, and in updated editions since. It is a bestseller.

Claiborne was born in Sunflower, Mississippi, where his mother was known as a "fantastic cook." After service in the Navy during World War II and the Korean War, he said he "only knew that he liked to cook and liked to write." He has been very successful in this combined endeavor.

From 1946 to 1949, Claiborne was with ABC in Chicago, working in public relations for the Don McNeill's Breakfast Club before moving to New York where he began his "cooking career."

Claiborne told interviewer Jack Ryan several years ago that "I decided that if I wanted to eat good food I'd have to cook it myself. The more I tried the more hooked I became and it's never worn off." He studied at the Ecolé Hoteliere in Switzerland, 1953–54, adding to his knowledge of French cuisine.

Back in America, Claiborne eventually joined *Gourmet* magazine as a receptionist before moving to the editorial staff. In 1957, he was hired by another Southerner, Turner Catledge, then vice-president of the *New York Times*. He is the author of several cookbooks, his latest being *Craig Claiborne's The New York Times Cookbook* with Pierre Franey, and he writes a weekly food column, also with Franey, for *The New York Times Magazine*.

In 1984 he and Pierre Franey collected 600 recipes "that reflect the changing tastes of today" into a new book *Cooking With Craig Claiborne and Pierre Franey*. Other books by Claiborne include *Classic French Cuisine; Cooking with Herbs and Spices; New York International Cook Book; Craig Claiborne's Kitchen Primer; New York Times Menu Cook Book; Veal Cookery; New York Times Cook Book; The Gourmet Diet Cook Book; A Feast Made for Laughter, a Memoir with Recipes*; and four volumes of *Favorites from the New York Times*. He co-authored with Virginia Lee *The Chinese Cook Book*.

**CLARK, Matt** (1930– )

Matt Clark has been the medicine editor for *Newsweek*, since 1961, and contributes articles to other periodicals.

Clark was a reporter on the *Boston Traveler* (Massachusetts) from 1953 to 1956 before becoming its science editor. Two years later, he was on the staff of *Medical News*; subsequently, he joined *Newsweek* (Long Island, New York).

Clark's writing has been honored by many groups, and his honors include the Albert Lasker Medical Journalism Award; the Howard W. Blakeslee Award, from the American Heart Association; an editorial award from the Association for Advancement of Medical Instrumentation; the J. C. Penney–University of Missouri magazine award in health; and the American Medical Association medical journalism award. Others include the Claude Bernard Science Journalism Award, from the National Society for Medical Research; the Page One Award, from the New York Newspaper Guild; and the Deadline Club and the American Cancer Society media awards.

**CLAYTON, James Edwin** (1929– )

James Clayton joined the *Washington Post* in 1956 as a reporter and moved upward to become the newspaper's associate editor in 1974.

Prior to his work on the *Post*, Clayton reported for *Southern Illinoisan* in Carbondale from 1951 to 1952. His work in Washington brought him numerous awards, including several from the Newspaper Guild as well as an award from Sigma Delta Chi for Washington Correspondence. He also won the Worth Bingham prize and the George Polk Memorial Award for editorial writing.

Clayton has lectured at Northwestern and Johns Hopkins universities and has written a book, *The Making of Justice*. He served in the Korean War.

**CLENDINEN, James Augustus** (1910– )

In 1958, James Clendinen became the editor of the *Tampa Tribune* (Florida) and, in 1974, the chairman of the editorial board. Before joining the

*Tribune* staff in 1935, Clendinen worked for the nearby *Clearwater Evening Sun* for five years.

Clendinen has regularly won editorial writing awards from the Florida Daily Newspaper Association and the Freedoms Foundation. National recognition has also come from the Headliner Club, Sigma Delta Chi, and the American Bar Association. He was the founder and the first president of the Florida Society of Editors.

**COBBS, John Lewis** (1917– )
Joining *Business Week* as the finance editor in 1942, John Cobbs, in 1966, became the editor of this weekly magazine. Before that, he served briefly as a research assistant to the National Industrial Conference Board.

Cobbs is actively involved in outside public projects, such as the Chappaqua Board of Education and the Chappaqua Public Library.

In 1958, he won the National Educational Association's School Bell Award. He has also been honored for his editing by Sigma Delta Chi and the Overseas Press Club. In 1972, he won the G.M. Loeb Achievement Award.

**CODEL, Martin** (1902–1973)
When he was only 15, Martin Codel became a reporter on the *Duluth News-Tribune* (Minnesota). Later he worked on the *Gibbing Tribune*, the *Detroit Journal*, and the *Detroit News* (Michigan).

In 1925, Codel joined the Associated Press in New York; he stayed a year and then worked two years on the *U.S. Daily* in Washington before joining the North American Newspaper Alliance.

Codel, after shifting his interest to radio in 1930, organized the Radio News Bureau. The following year, he made his major contribution to the media world when he founded *Broadcasting* magazine and served as its publisher until 1944.

Codel next established *Television Digest and Electronic Reports*, publishing this from 1945 to 1959. After that, he served as a consultant in television and radio. One of his jobs was to survey European and Latin American television for Time-Life.

**COGLEY, John** (1916–1976)
Starting as the editor of *Today* magazine, John Cogley, in 1950, became the executive editor of *Commonweal*. From 1965 to 1966, he was the *New York Times'* religious news editor.

Another phase of Cogley's career found him as editor of *The Center Magazine*, 1967–75, and as a senior fellow and an associate with the Center for Study of Democratic Institutions in Santa Barbara, California.

Cogley was "into politics" with the campaign staffs of John F. Kennedy, in 1960, and of Eugene McCarthy, in 1968. He served in the Air Force during World War II. Cogley wrote five books, *Report on Blacklisting*; *Religion in a Secular Age*; *Catholic America*; *A Canterbury Tale* and edited *Religion in America*; and *Natural Law and Modern Society*. He also contributed to encyclopedias, and won the Catholic Press Association award in 1965 for his coverage of the Vatican Council.

**COHEN, Stanley E.** (1919– )
In 1983, Stanley E. Cohen was elected to the Washington Journalism Hall of Fame by Sigma Delta Chi. The Hall of Fame honors persons "who have earned the highest esteem and affection of their colleagues in the news media in the nation's capital as a result of their exemplary professional achievements, outstanding service to other members of the profession and lifelong dedication to the highest standards of journalism."

Now the editor for *Advertising Age's Focus*, Cohen began his Washington reporting career with *Broadcasting* magazine in 1942. The following year he joined *Advertising Age* as Washington Bureau Chief.

Cohen received the Consumer Federation of America's National Consumer Media Award in 1979. He writes on business and government relations, with an emphasis on consumerism.

**COLBURN, John H.** (1912–1983)
Colburn began his 55-year journalism career in 1930 as a reporter on his hometown *Columbus Dispatch* (Ohio). Five years later, he joined the Associated Press, first in Columbus, but later, during World War II, in London, Stockholm, and Paris.

Returning to the United States in 1946, Colburn became a general executive at the Associated Press New York headquarters, where he remained until 1949. He next became the managing editor of the *Richmond Times-Dispatch* (Virginia). Between 1963 and 1972, Colburn went west to be the editor and publisher of the *Wichita Eagle and Beacon* (Kansas).

Colburn returned to Virginia in 1972 and joined Landmark Communications, Inc., becoming president in 1975.

Professional colleagues elected him to the presidency of the Associated Press Managing Editors and to directorships of the American Society of Newspaper Editors, the American Newspaper Publishers Association, the ANPA Research Institute, and the ANPA Foundation.

**COLLINGWOOD, Charles** (1917– )
Charles Collingwood was a war correspondent for the United Press in London from 1939 to 1941. After the war, Collingwood became a CBS commentator, serving as the United Nations Correspondent, 1946–48, as a White House correspondent, 1948–52, and as chief of the London News Bureau, 1957–60. He was the network's chief foreign correspondent from 1966 to 1975.

Collingwood was given two Headliner Club awards, and two Peabody awards for best foreign reporting and for his televised tour of the White House with Mrs. John Kennedy.

Other awards include the Alexander Hadden Medal for promoting world understanding and the English Speaking Union's Better Understanding Award. France and England have also honored him.

He has written one novel, *The Defector*.

**COMPTON, Ann Woodruff** (1947– )
Ann Compton was a reporter and anchorwoman for WDBJ-TV in Roa-

noke, Virginia in 1969, and from 1971 to 1973, she was a political reporter and the state capitol bureau chief in Richmond, Virginia.

ABC News hired her as a radio anchorwoman in New York. The next year she became the network's White House correspondent, the first woman correspondent to be assigned by a network to cover the White House. Av Westin wrote that "being a women there was an asset because it gave Ann greater visibility over what she described as 'the gray pin-stripe suits.' "She continues with ABC in Washington.

**CONRAD, Paul** (1924– )
One of the nation's best-known syndicated editorial cartoonists, Paul Conrad began his career on the *Denver Post* (Colorado) in 1950. He remained there until 1964, when he moved to the *Los Angeles Times*. His cartoons have been syndicated since 1973.

Conrad, who has exhibited his sculpture and his cartoons in one-man shows, won the Pulitzer Prize in 1964, in 1971, and again in 1984. He has also won a Sigma Delta Chi prize three times and has won recognition from the Overseas Press Club. He served in World War II.

Conrad believes that cartoons should call for changes in life today, and summed up cartooning this way: "You've got to wrap up the point or a drama that may have been playing for months, or even years, on a stage as wide as the world; and you've got to apply the needle in places familiar to everyone—but in such a manner that even the person needled has a laugh at himself."

**CONSIDINE, Robert Bernard** (1906–1975)
Bob Considine, one of the nation's best-known reporters in the Forties, began his newspaper career on the *Washington Post* in 1930, and later worked on the *Herald*, also in Washington.

His long association with Hearst's International News Service began in the Thirties. A syndicated sports columnist, he also wrote features and covered major news events for Hearst newspapers, including the *New York American* and *Mirror*.

Considine served the International News Service as a war correspondent in England and other areas during World War II, and later was a war correspondent in Korea. He won several best foreign correspondence awards from the Overseas Press Club and the George R. Holmes Memorial Award. He was also honored by the Catholic Writers Guild and the Catholic Institute of the Press.

Considine wrote *MacArthur the Magnificent*; *Innocents at Home*; *Panama Canal*; *Man against Fire*; *the Brink's Robbery*, and *It's All News to Me*. He co-authored *Thirty Seconds over Tokyo*; *Where's Sammy*; *General Wainwright's Story*; *The Babe Ruth Story*; *Christmas Stocking*, *Jack Dempsey Story*; and *Ask Me Anything*. Several of these books later became motion pictures.

**CONVERSE, Gordon Noble** (1926– )
Gordon Converse has won over 60 awards for his photographs. His long career as a photographer has been with the *Christian Science Monitor* (Massachusetts), where he began in 1946.

Converse's pictures have been exhibited in one-man shows in several universities and museums. Syracuse University presented Converse with a citation, as did the Freedoms Foundation. He won Photographer of the Year awards in 1959, 1964, and 1965.

*All Mankind* was published in 1983 by the *Christian Science Monitor* as part of its 75th anniversary celebration. The book was prepared by Converse and three of his newspaper colleagues, R. Norman Matheny, Barth Falkenberg, and Peter Main. It includes 154 photographs representing more than one hundred countries.

**CONY, Edward Roger** (1923– )

Edward Cony joined the *Wall Street Journal* in 1953, first working as a reporter in its San Francisco Bureau. Earlier, Cony had worked for two years as a reporter on the *Portland Oregonian.*

Cony moved to Los Angeles as the *Journal*'s news bureau manager. From 1953 to 1960, he was the newspaper's Southeastern news bureau manager in Jacksonville, Florida. He moved to New York in 1960 as the news editor, winning the Pulitzer Prize for reporting that same year.

In 1964, Cony became the assistant managing editor of the *Journal*'s Pacific Coast edition. He returned to New York as managing editor and, in 1970, became the executive editor. By 1972, he had reached the vice-presidency, a position he holds today.

According to Jerry M. Rosenberg in his book about this publication, "Cony played a leading part in starting the *Asian Wall Street Journal* in late 1976 and the *Asian Wall Street Journal Weekly* in 1979 and in negotiating acquisition of minority interests in newspapers in Singapore and Malaysia."

**COOK, Fred James** (1911– )

Starting in 1933 as a reporter, and later city editor of the *Asbury Park Press* (New Jersey) Fred Cook became the editor of the *New Jersey Courier* in Toms River in 1936. His major newspaper work, however, was with the *New York World-Telegram and Sun*, where he worked from 1944 to 1959.

Cook has published several hundred magazine articles, mostly since he became a free-lance writer in 1959. His articles have appeared in the *Nation, Reader's Digest, New York Times Sunday Magazine, American Heritage, Saturday Review, New York*, and others.

Among his 35 books are many directed to a younger audience. His major volumes include *The Unfinished Story of Alger Hiss; What Manner of Men: Forgotten Heroes of the American Revolution; The Warfare State; Barry Goldwater: Extremist of the Right; The FBI Nobody Knows: The Corrupted Land: The Social Morality of Modern America; The Secret Rulers: Criminal Syndicates and How They Control the U.S. Underworld; The Plot Against the Patient; What So Proudly We Hail; A Two-Dollar Bet Means Murder; The New Jersey Colony; The Nightmare Decade: The Life and Times of Senator Joe McCarthy; Julia's Story: The Tragedy of an Unnecessary Death; The Ku Klux Klan: America's Recurring Nightmare*, and *The Great Energy Scam: Private Billions vs. Public Good.*

Cook won New York Newspaper Guild Page One awards in 1958, 1959, and 1960, with a special award in 1980 for crusading journalism. In 1960 he was awarded the Sidney Hillman Foundation citation for the best magazine article of the year.

**COOPER, Kent** (1880–1965)
A long-time general manager of the Associated Press, Kent Cooper, campaigned throughout his life for the "right to publish" and the "right to know." After Cooper called for this concept in 1945, Harold L. Cross wrote an often-quoted book with the title *The People's Right to Know.*

Cooper worked from 1901 to 1909 as a reporter in Indianapolis, and in 1910, he began his long career with the Associated Press, first as a traveling inspector, but soon as chief of the traffic department.

By 1920, Cooper was the assistant general manager and, five years later, the general manager in charge of news service and personnel. Among his major achievements for the world's largest newsgathering organization was the establishment of the Associated Press in South America in 1918 and the start of the Wirephoto system in 1935. He also established the Associated Press in Great Britain, Germany, and other nations.

**COPLEY Family**
James Copley (1916–1973) was called a "giant voice in American journalism and a great American citizen who actively stood for the great principles of his beloved country" when he was named to the California Newspaper Hall of Fame. He started his long career with Copley Press Inc. in Illinois in 1942. He served in World War II and was presented the Maria Moors Cabot Award in 1959 and 1967.

Helen Copley (1922– ) inherited the Copley newspapers from her husband, James S. Copley. Before they were married she had been his secretary for 13 years. *Quill* magazine estimated the family fortune as being worth between $100 and $200 million.

Today, Helen Copley is the chairman of the board of Copley News Service and the Union-Tribune Publishing Co. and is the publisher of the *San Diego Union* and *Evening Tribune.*

The Copleys were active in San Diego projects and were recognized for their contributions by awards from the Freedoms Foundation, the San Diego Museum of Art, and the Scripps Clinic and Research Foundation. Helen Copley, in 1983, became the first woman to be honored by the San Diego-Imperial March of Dimes Chapter for "significant contributions to the community."

**CORNELL, George Washington II** (1920– )
Religious journalism brought fame to George Cornell, who has been writing a column for the Associated Press since 1951. Born in Oklahoma, Cornell worked briefly on the *Oklahoma City Daily Oklahoman,* 1943–44, before joining the Associated Press as a newsman in New York in 1947. He served in the Infantry during World War II.

Cornell has written several books with religious backgrounds. The first, in 1957, was *They Knew Jesus*. The latest, in 1975, was *The Untamed God*.

Cornell's first award, in 1953, came from the National Religious Public Relations Council. Later citations included the Religion Newswriters Association Supple Memorial Award, the Jim Merrell Religious Liberty Memorial Award, and the William E. Laidt Award.

**COSTA, Joseph** (1904- )
One of the best-known authorities on news photography, Joseph Costa was a staffer on the New York *Morning World* from 1920 to 1927. He moved, in 1927, to the *New York News*, which was then famous for its pictorial coverage of daily events. He remained there until 1946.

Costa, in 1946, joined the Hearst-owned King Features Syndicate as photo supervisor and chief photographer for the group's *Sunday Mirror Magazine*. He held these positions until 1963.

Throughout his career, Costa contributed articles on photography to periodicals. He was the executive editor of the *National Press Photographers Magazine* from 1946 to 1967, when he became editor emeritus.

In 1983, Costa received the Photographic Administrators, Inc., award for education in photography. He has been on the Ball State University faculty in recent years.

Costa has been associated with the Famous Photographers School and has lectured at several universities, including East Texas State, Ball State, Missouri, and Kent State, earning citations from several of them. He has written one book *Beginning Guide to Color Photography* and edited *The Complete Book on Press Photography*. He lives in Carmel, California.

**COUGHLAN, John Robert** (1914- )
Robert Coughlan joined *Fortune* magazine in 1937 and became associate editor in 1938. He moved to another Time Inc. publication and served on *Life*'s staff from 1943 to 1949 as text editor and until 1970 as writer–editor.

Coughlan served from 1971 to 1973 as an editorial associate with the Kennedy Foundation, and now writes for other periodicals. His first recognition was the Benjamin Franklin Award in 1953. Later, he was cited for excellence by the Overseas Press Club and Sigma Delta Chi. He has been honored by the National Editorial Writers Association, and has won the Newspaper Guild's Heywood Broun Award, the Putman Award, and an award of recognition from Northwestern University.

In 1967, The National Association of Independent Schools recognized his work. Coughlan has written *The Wine of Genius; The Private World of William Faulkner* and *Elizabeth and Catherine* as well as books about such subjects as Michelangelo. He collaborated with Rose Kennedy in the writing of her memoirs in 1974.

**COUSINS, Margaret** (1905- )
Magazine writing and editing kept Margaret (Sue) Cousins active for nearly four decades working for some of the nation's leading publications.

Cousins began her career in 1927 in Dallas on her father's *Southern*

*Pharmaceutical Journal*, becoming its editor in 1932. In 1938, she moved to New York to work on *Pictorial Review*, and in 1942, she began a long association with *Good Housekeeping*, remaining there until 1958 and advancing to the post of managing editor. Earlier, she had contributed poems and short stories to this magazine.

During those early years, Cousins wrote many short stories. In an interview in 1953, she said, "Sometimes I'm a frustrated writer, sometimes I'm a frustrated editor. But either way, I know one thing; a good story, give it time, will always sell itself."

After several years as the managing editor of *McCall's*, Cousins became the fiction and book editor for *Ladies' Home Journal*, 1971–73. She continued to write books, the last a juvenile volume, *Thomas Alva Edison*.

Among her honors are the Achievement Medal from Alpha Chi Omega and the Distinguished Alumnae Award from the University of Texas. She won the J. C. Penney–University of Missouri writing award in 1969.

**COUSINS, Norman** (1915– )

The *Saturday Review* and Norman Cousins were synonymous for years, although the latter appears to have survived more successfully. He once said that this association was "a love affair with the readers." The magazine ranked a close second after his family.

Cousins has been given many honorary degrees, citations, honors, and awards in recognition of his outstanding career in the publishing world and his desire for worldwide peace. In recent years, his books about his health problems have become bestsellers. *The Anatomy of an Illness as Perceived by the Patient* was at the top of the bestseller list in 1979, and his latest, *The Healing Heart*, arrived in 1983. Other Cousins' books are *The Good Inheritance: The Democratic Chance; Modern Man Is Obsolete; Talks with Nehru; Who Speaks for Man?; In God We Trust: The Religious Beliefs of the Founding Fathers; Writing for Love or Money; Doctor Schweitzer of Lambarene; In Place of Folly; Present Tense; The Improbable Triumvirate; The Celebration of Life*. He edited *A Treasury of Democracy* and co-authored with William Rose Bénet *An Anthology of the Poetry of Freedom*.

Early in his career, Cousins was the managing editor of *Current History*. In 1940, he became editor of *Saturday Review*, a magazine established in 1924 by the founders of *Time*, Briton Hadden and Henry R. Luce. Cousins' philosophy and concern about international peace was best demonstrated in his introductory column when he took over the *Saturday Review*:

"Too bad there can't be one great ice storm all over—over those battlefields in Europe especially. Because when men have to fight to keep alive against the cold, they stop thinking about fighting other men . . . we lose electricity, we can't listen to the radio . . . go to movies . . . so we have to sit around a fire and swap ideas."

Cousins continued as editor of *Saturday Review* until 1971 and, briefly, between 1973 and 1977. During his tenure, the magazine's circulation increased from 26,000 to 600,000. The publication underwent several ownership changes, resulting in a shift of emphasis, which confused both its readers and advertisers. It was nearly defunct in 1982. Meanwhile,

Cousins experimented with *The World*, which later merged with the *Saturday Review*.

A shift to a teaching career came for Cousins in 1978 when he became a senior lecturer at the University of California in Los Angeles School of Medicine, teaching a humanities course. He said he wanted students to gain "the ability to feel deeply for human beings, the compassion and ability to inspire trust in a patient that is a doctor's most potent resource."

For several years, Cousins was president of the United World Federalists, a group dedicated to global government. Later, he served as international president of the World Association of World Federalists.

These and other projects reflect his ever-present goal to achieve peace. He has worked behind the scene as an unofficial ambassador in cases involving the White House, the Vatican, and the Kremlin. He helped organize the Citizens Committee for a Nuclear Test Ban.

Cousins took his campaigns to his *Saturday Review* readers, where many joined in helping the victims of Hiroshima. *Saturday Review* readers paid the cost for rehabilitating 24 Japanese women, the "Hiroshima maidens," who had been maimed by atomic radiation.

**COWLES, Fleur Fenton** (1910– )

In magazine circles, Fleur Cowles is best remembered for her editorship of *Flair*, which survived for a year in the early 1950s. *Flair*, a "class" magazine, was somewhat ahead of its time.

Cowles said *Flair* would combine "for the first time under one set of covers the best in the arts, literature, fashion, humor, decoration, travel and entertainment." Its printing challenged the publisher, with many die cuts, different size pages and paper textures and, for that time, a new binding technique. These elements added to *Flair*'s cost and helped bring about its early demise.

Cowles was also associate editor of *Look* and *Quick* magazines. As early as age eleven, she had developed a desire to write, recording her impressions of life about her. After studying at the School of Fine and Applied Arts, she worked in Gimbel's advertising department. Later, she wrote a daily column for the *New York World-Telegram*, but by 1936, she had her own advertising agency.

She held several governmental positions during World War II, and in 1946, she married Gardner Cowles, president of Cowles Magazines, Inc. In addition to *Flair*, her work on *Quick*, a weekly 4- by 6-inch pictorial, helped make it an early success.

Cowles was decorated by the French Government in 1951. She has won awards for service to the fashion industry, the Urban League, and various medical organizations.

**COWLES Family**

The Cowles Publishing family began with Gardner Cowles, Sr., with newspaper holdings in Des Moines, Iowa. When *Quill* magazine listed wealthy media leaders in late 1982, it reported the Cowles family as being worth between $200 and $300 millions.

In addition to the *Des Moines Register* (Iowa) and the *Minneapolis Star and Tribune* (Minnesota), the company owns interests in magazine and book publishing. It was reported in the *Washington Journalism Review* in 1983 that "about 50 members of the Cowles family directly or indirectly control more than 80 per cent of the company's stock."

Gardner Cowles, Sr. bought the *Des Moines Register and Leader* in 1903 for $300,000. He acquired the *Tribune* in 1911, the *Star* in 1924, and the *Leader* in 1927. He merged them into the *Register and Tribune.*

John Cowles, Sr. (1898–1983) was the second boy in the family and Gardner "Mike" Cowles, Jr. was his brother. They urged their father to buy the *Minneapolis Star* in 1935 for $1 million. "Mike" launched *Look* in 1937, while John took over the Minneapolis newspaper. The family pruchased the *Minneapolis Journal* for $2½ million and merged it with the *Star.*

John Cowles once defended the newspaper monopoly trend as making newspapers "better able to resist the constant pressure of immediacy." He added that "nobody has a monopoly on responsibility." Like Henry Ward Beecher, John considered the newspaper to be "an educational institution," reflecting its role in providing information to millions of Americans.

In 1983, John was removed as president and chief operating officer of Cowles Media Co. and as publisher of the Minneapolis newspaper. He was replaced by his cousin, David Kruidenier, who had been directing the Des Moines Register and Tribune Co. Profits had declined and some family members were reportedly upset over Cowles' sale of the *Buffalo Courier-Express* and his firing of Minneapolis publisher Donald R. Dwight. Cowles remained on the board.

William Hutchinson Cowles (1902–1971) held several positions with the firm, but established his career at the *Spokane Chronicle.* His son, William Cowles III (1932– ), has been president of the Spokane Chronicle Co. since 1968. He is also president-publisher of several farm publications, such as the *Farmer-Stockman* in Oregon, Idaho, Utah, and Montana. He is active in Washington State affairs and civic projects.

**COX Family**

James M. Cox (1870–1957), the Democratic nominee for President in 1920, founded the family fortune, which *Quill* magazine estimated in 1982 to be worth between $1 and $2 billion.

His son, James M. Cox, Jr. (1903–1974) entered newspaper work on the *Dayton Daily News* (Ohio) in 1929. He became chairman of Dayton Newspapers, Inc., in 1958. Under his leadership, the holdings were enlarged to include the Cox Broadcasting Corp. and newspapers in Atlanta, Miami, and Palm Beach, in addition to the Ohio holdings.

The *Quill* article noted that two sisters, Barbara Cox Anthony and Ann Cox Chambers, inherited 95 percent of Cox Enterprises when their father, James Cox, died in 1957 and their brother, James, Jr., died in 1974.

The Cox operations include one of the nation's top ten newspaper group, the fifth largest cable television system, and other holdings, including an oil refinery.

**CRAIN Family**

*Advertising Age*, started in 1930, is the major magazine owned today by the Crain family. G. D. Crain, Jr. (1885–1973) always wanted to be a publisher, even during his school days in his native city, Louisville, Kentucky. He started early on the *Herald* and became city editor when he was 21.

Later, Crain did free-lance work, providing editorial material for some 200 business publications. In 1916, he started *Hospital Management*, and later *Class*, which today is called *Industrial Marketing*. But it was *Advertising Age*, started in 1930, that led to the family success in publishing. Crain's brother, Murray E. Crain, was the New York correspondent.

The elder son of the founder, Rance Crain, joined the firm in 1960, working in Washington and New York, as well as in the home office in Chicago. He was editor of *Business Insurance* when it was started in 1967. He has been president of Crain Communications, Inc. since 1973.

Rance Crain noted in the 50th anniversary edition of *Advertising Age* that "our challenge as we embark upon our second 50 years is to remain alert, aggressive and responsive to the needs of our readers."

Keith E. Crain joined the sales staff of the family's *Automotive News* in 1964, became vice-president in 1969, and publisher in 1971. Murray E. Crain, who died in 1958, was managing editor for *Advertising Age* in the Thirties.

**CRANE, Royston Campbell** (1901–1977)

"Wash Tubbs," "Captain Easy," and "Buz Sawyer" are characters from comic strips created by Royston Crane. He began his work with the art department of the *Fort Worth Record* in 1919 and then moved to a reporter's position with the *Austin American*.

By 1922, Crane was in New York with the *World*. He spent the rest of his career drawing his widely syndicated cartoons. In 1950, he won the National Cartoonists Society Reuben Award. In 1961, the Banshees presented him its Gold Medal Award as outstanding cartoonist of the year.

Among his many other awards was a Gold Medal from the U.S. Navy for public service.

**CRAWFORD, Kenneth** (1902–1983)

For nearly one-half a century, Ken Crawford worked in journalism and made a distinguished career for himself. Much of this time was spent with *Newsweek*.

Crawford started with the United Press in 1924 and worked in St. Louis, Cleveland, Lansing, and Indianapolis before becoming a Washington correspondent in 1929. He was a columnist for the *Buffalo Times* for three years; from 1932 to 1940, he was the Washington correspondent for the *New York Post*.

Three years were spent with the experimental *PM* newspaper before he joined *Newsweek* in 1943. Crawford became a war correspondent in North Africa, Italy, the Middle East, England, and France in 1943–44. From 1944 to 1970, he was the magazine's Washington correspondent and political columnist, and later was a free-lancer.

During his years in Washington, Crawford "won the confidence of presidents from Roosevelt to Nixon." During the Thirties, he wrote regularly for *The Nation* and *New Republic*, according to *Newsweek*'s account of his death in early 1983. He wrote two books, *The Pressure Boys* and *Report on North Africa*.

Crawford won a Navy commendation and a French Liberation Medal.

**CRONKITE, Walter** (1916– )
America's best-known newsman, Walter Cronkite, appeared nightly on the "CBS Evening News" for years, until he stepped down in 1981. In his final show he said, "For almost two decades, we've been meeting like this in the evening, and I'll miss that. But those who have made anything of this departure, I'm afraid have made too much." Thus ended a 19-year run.

On reading a story in *American Boy* while he was in junior high school, Cronkite decided he, too, wanted to be a foreign correspondent. He worked on school publications and studied journalism at the University of Texas, working part-time as campus correspondent for the *Houston Post*. He also did sports announcing and reporting for the Scripps-Howard Houston Bureau. Finding reporting more exciting than the classroom, he dropped out of college to become a full-time newspaperman.

Cronkite began as a reporter and worked for the United Press in Houston, Kansas City, Dallas, Austin, and El Paso; he was a war correspondent between 1942 and 1945. He was the United Press bureau manager in Moscow, from 1946 to 1948. He also was the United Press chief correspondent for the Nuremberg war crimes trial.

Cronkite subsequently joined the CBS News, and in 1952, headed the network's coverage of the presidential campaign. His evening news show began on April 16, 1962. Three years later he told John Cashman that "I am a reporter and I am giving the viewer a front page that I hope is interesting and informative. We're giving them the news, not telling them how to think." A decade later he told the *Christian Science Monitor*, "I feel no compulsion to be a pundit. . . . I am a news presenter, a news broadcaster, an anchorman, a managing editor—not a commentator or analyst."

American public opinion shifted more toward an anti-Vietnam view after Cronkite reported on his trip to Vietnam in 1968. He predicted a stalemate, noting that "we have been too often disappointed by the optimism of the American leaders, both in Vietnam and in Washington, to have faith any longer in the silver linings they find in the darkest clouds."

Cronkite was chief correspondent for many CBS programs, such as "Reports about South Africa," "Eisenhower," and "D-Day Plus 20 Years." He hosted the "Eyewitness to History," "Twentieth Century" and "Twenty-First Century" series, as well as the "You Are There" documentaries.

In discussing America's educational crisis in 1983, Cronkite wrote: "I almost flunked physics in college. But I realized how essential this subject was when I was describing the space program and flights to the moon on television. I had to work hard to educate myself on all the technical aspects before every telecast." He recalled "the Seventies was the Decade of the Environment. The Eighties could be the Decade of Education," in comments written for the American Express Gold Cardmembers Newsletter, *For Members Only.*

The cover on *Panorama,* a short-lived, high-class television magazine, once featured a cover painting showing Cronkite, Frank Reynolds, and John Chancellor on Mount Rushmore, replacing the presidents. The message was clear.

"Old Faithful," the title often applied to Cronkite, was justified by his millions of viewers. For many, his grandfatherly appearance restored their faith in television. To Barbara Matusow, "the most legendary aspect of his personality was his fanatical competiveness." In her book, *The Evening Stars,* she wrote that his "star-sized ego" was the secret weapon that made possible his on-air longevity. When he stepped down from the evening show, one of his rivals, ABC News, took a full-page ad to praise his "extraordinary contributions" to the industry.

Cronkite won numerous awards, including the Peabody in 1962; the William A. White Journalism Award, 1969; Emmys on several occasions; the George Polk Award, 1971; the Alfred I. Dupont–Columbia University Award, 1978; and the Gold Medal from the International Radio and Television Society, 1974.

He wrote *Challenge of Change* and, *South by Southeast* (with Ray Ellis), a book based on his boating experience.

**CROWTHER, Bosley** (1905–1981)

For several decades, Bosley Crowther was a critic for the *New York Times,* a newspaper he joined in 1928 as a reporter and rewrite staffer.

Crowther became critic emeritus in 1968 after having been drama editor, screen critic, and editor. In 1953, he won the Screen Director Award. He wrote three books *The Lion's Share: The Story of an Entertainment Empire; Hollywood Rajah;* and *The Great Films* and contributed articles to magazines.

**CUNNINGHAM, Emory** (1921– )

"The Norman Vincent Peale of publishing" is a title often applied to Emory Cunningham for his work on the *Progressive Farmer* and *Southern Living* magazines.

Cunningham has been the publisher of the two magazines since 1967. He joined the sales staff of *Progressive Farmer* in 1948.

For years, Cunningham has been a spokesman for the South. In an interview in the *Madison Avenue Magazine,* he voiced the concept that "Southerners display a more positive and upbeat attitude toward life than Northerners do." He directed *Southern Living* "toward what our readers can accomplish in their own towns."

*Southern Living* has become the voice of the South much as *Sunset* represents the West. *Progressive Farmer* similarly covers the South, as it has for the past century.

Cunningham was named "Man of the Year" in Birmingham in 1971 and

"Man of the Year in Service to Agriculture" there in 1975. Advertising and sales groups awarded him titles in 1976 and 1978. He has been active in the work of the Magazine Publishers Association, winning its Henry Johnson Fisher Award in 1975. He is also active in civic and educational affairs.

**CURLEY, John Joseph, Jr.** (1938– )
John Curley, a one-time editor of *USA TODAY*, a Gannett-owned national daily newspaper, is now the president of its newspaper division.

Curley started his career as a reporter for the Associated Press, working in New York, Trenton, and Newark from 1961 to 1966. For the next two years, he was a reporter and editor on newspapers in Asbury Park and Perth Amboy, New Jersey.

In late 1969, Curley joined Gannett as a suburban editor of the *Rochester Times Union*. The next year, he was editor of the *Bridgewater Courier-News* (New Jersey). He joined Gannett's Washington Bureau in 1974.

In 1975, Curley assumed the general managership of Gannett News Service and, in 1979, he became the vice-president for news. Other duties were added, and in early 1981, he became the editor of *USA TODAY* during its planning stages. In 1984 he became president and chief operating officer.

Curley served in the Army from 1960 to 1962. A trustee for both Dickerson College and the Washington Journalism Center, he belongs to several press clubs.

**CURTIS, Charlotte** (?– )
After serving as society editor for the *Columbus Citizen* (Ohio) from 1950 to 1961, Charlotte Curtis joined the *New York Times* as a reporter. She moved up to women's news editor, Family Style editor, and Opposite-Editorial (OPED) page editor, when she replaced Harrison Salisbury who retired.

Curtis has been a radio commentator in Columbus and New York. She was active with the Columbus Symphony Orchestra and with both the Columbus and New York Junior League programs.

Curtis has won many awards, including awards from the New York Newspaper Women's Club, the Ohio Newspaper Women's Association, and the American Newspaper Women's Club. In 1979, she won the Ohio Humanitarian Award from the American Civil Liberties Union. She wrote a book, *First Lady*, in 1963, and another in 1976, *The Rich and Other Atrocities*.

**CURTIS, J. Montgomery** (1905–1982)
A long association with the American Press Institute and the Knight-Ridder group marks the journalistic career of J. Montgomery Curtis.

While in high school, Curtis began work as a reporter. He started in his home state on the *Wheeling News Register* (West Virginia) in 1928. Then he worked on the *Morgantown Dominion News* (West Virginia) before moving to the *Buffalo Evening News* (New York) as a reporter, and advanced to city editor.

Curtis joined the American Press Institute in 1947 at a time when it was affiliated with the Columbia University School of Journalism. Before he left the Institute, 20 years later, he "made a career of telling United States editors what was wrong with their newspapers—and making them enjoy it."

Filling a newly created post of vice-president for development with Knight-Ridder, Curtis left the Institute in 1967. Because of his "widely respected expertise, clear English, and light touch," Curtis became the "house critic" for Knight-Ridder. He retired in 1978. A scholarship fund was established at West Virginia University in his honor.

**DABNEY, Virginius** (1901– )

A native Virginian, as his name suggests, Virginius Dabney has devoted his life to the Richmond, Virginia newspapers and to his books about his native state and its leaders.

Dabney, in 1922, became a reporter on the *Richmond News-Leader*. Then from 1928 to 1934, he was on the editorial staff of the *Times-Dispatch* before becoming chief editorial writer and, from 1936 to 1969, editor.

A list of Dabney's awards would include the Pulitzer Prize for editorial writing in 1947; two Sigma Delta Chi awards; the Thomas Jefferson Award for Public Service; and the Lee Editorial Award from the Virginia Press Association.

Dabney was president of the American Society of Newspaper Editors, 1957–58, and the Virginia Historical Society, 1969–72. His first book, in 1932, was *Liberalism in the South*. His last, in 1981, was *The Jefferson Scandals*. Dabney also wrote *Below the Potomac; Dry Messiah: The Life of Bishop Cannon; Virginia: The New Dominion; Richmond: The Story of a City; Across the Years: Memories of a Virginian*; and *Mr. Jefferson's University*.

**DALEY, Arthur John** (1904–1974)

One of the nation's best remembered sports writer is Arthur Daley. As the sports columnist for the *New York Times*, Daley won the Pulitzer Prize in 1956 "for his outstanding coverage and commentary on the world of sports."

Daley's interest in sportswriting began while he was still a student at Fordham University. After graduation, in 1926, he joined the *Times* staff. He has also contributed articles to *Collier's, the Literary Digest*, and *Reader's Digest*.

When John Kieran died in 1942, Daley took over the "Sports of the Times" column, which he wrote until his death. During those years he won the Grantland Rice award in 1961; he was named Sportswriter of the Year in 1963; and he won the Professional Football Writers' Distinguished Writing Award in 1970. He also wrote several books, including the first with Kieran, in 1948, *The Story of the Olympic Games*. Later he wrote *Times at Bat: A Half Century of Baseball*.

**DALLIS, Nicholas Peter** (1911– )

Nicholas Dallis created three comic strips. First there was "Rex Morgan, M.D." in 1948. Next came "Judge Parker" in 1952, and finally "Apartment 3-G" in 1961.

A medical doctor, Dallis specialized in psychiatry in Detroit and Toledo from 1941 to 1959. The American Medical Association awarded him its Public Health Education honor in 1954. In 1973, Dallis received the Kiwanis Decency Award. His work for the handicapped brought him a Distinguished Service Award from the President's Committee on the Employment of Handicapped in 1954.

**DALY, John Charles, Jr.** (1914– )
A career in broadcasting with CBS and ABC brought John Charles Daly, Jr. before millions of viewers.

From 1937 to 1949, Daly worked for CBS, first as a correspondent and news analyst, handling special events and the White House. From 1943 to 1944, he was in the Middle East and Italy, and from 1945 to 1949 worked in Europe and South America.

Daly moved to ABC in 1949 as a correspondent, analyst, and moderator. Later he became vice-president in charge of news, special events, and public affairs. From 1967 to 1968, when he retired, he was the director of the Voice of America. Since 1971 he has been a consultant for Citibank in New York City and since 1976 the forum moderator for the American Enterprise Institute.

**DANIEL, E. Clifton** (1912– )
Born in North Carolina, Clifton Daniel wrote news items for his hometown *Zebulan Record* while he was still in high school. He expanded this interest at the University of North Carolina.

For three years, 1934 to 1937, he worked for the *Raleigh News and Observer* (North Carolina). Then he joined the Associated Press in New York, working also in Switzerland and England. He switched to the *New York Times* as a London correspondent in 1944. He covered the Allies' advance into Germany and later reported from the Middle East and Russia. For his work in Moscow, Daniel won the Overseas Press Club Award for best reporting from abroad.

Daniel returned to America and, in 1957, became the assistant to the managing editor Turner Catledge. Later he became managing editor in charge of the news department. He often said, "Either *we* shall lead the world, or the *Communists* will."

In 1956, Daniel and Margaret Truman were married in Missouri. They share an enjoyment for music, theater, ballet and writing. In 1984 his book, *Lords, Ladies and Gentlemen* appeared. She has written several popular mystery novels, with Washington themes.

**DANIELS, Derick January** (1928– )
After a newspaper career that started in 1950, Derick Daniels joined the Knight Newspaper group before moving to the presidency of Playboy Enterprise, Inc., in 1976.

Daniels was a reporter on the *Durham Herald* (North Carolina) in 1950, but soon moved to the *St. Petersburg Times* (Florida). After four years on the *Atlanta Constitution* (Georgia), he moved to the *Miami Herald* (Florida), where he remained until 1961.

His association with Knight started in Detroit, where he was with the *Free Press* from 1961 to 1973. He became a vice-president, and from 1973 to 1976, he was president of Knight News Service.

Daniels became the chief operating officer for the Playboy organization in 1976. He has been in charge of the firm during its recovery from its early 1970s "plunge into hotels, record making and movie production." The organization was also forced to sell its British gaming business, long a source of profits.

**DANIELS Family**

The Daniels family long has been associated with the *Raleigh News and Observer* (North Carolina). The first was Josephus Daniels (1862–1948). In 1885 he became the editor of the *State Chronicle* and, in 1895, merged it with the *News and Observer*. He also served as Secretary of the Navy under President Woodrow Wilson and was once U.S. ambassador to Mexico.

His son, Jonathan Worth Daniels (1902– ) reported for the *Louisville Times* (Kentucky) before joining the family newspaper, where he worked in Washington before becoming editor. He became editor emeritus in 1970.

Daniels, who reported from the press gallery during Coolidge's days and later became a member of Franklin D. Roosevelt's "palace guard," wrote many books, starting in 1930. They included *Clash of Angels*; *A Southerner Discovers the South*; *A Southerner Discovers New England*; *Tar Heels: A Portrait of North Carolina*; *Frontier on the Potomac: The Man of Independence*; *The End of Innocence*; *Prince of Carpetbaggers*; *Stonewall Jackson*; *Mosby—The Gray Ghost of the Confederacy*; *Robert E. Lee*; *October Recollections*; *The Devil's Backbone: The Story of the Natchez Trace*; *They Will Be Heard*; and *The Time between the Wars*.

Frank Arthur Daniels (1904– ), another son, worked in the mechanical, circulation, and advertising departments, starting in 1927. By 1956, he was president. He has been publisher since 1966 and chairman of the board since 1971.

The family has been active in civic and state affairs for decades.

Josephus Daniels, Jr. (1894–1964) was with the *News and Observer* from 1918 until his death. He was business manager and advertising manager by 1921, president in 1948, and chairman of the board in 1956.

**DANZIG, Frederick Paul** (1925– )

For more than a decade, Fred Danzig was a reporter and columnist for the United Press in New York. He worked first as a copyboy for the Associated Press there and briefly for the *Herkeimer Evening Telegram* and *Port Chester Daily Item* (New York).

Danzig became the senior editor for *Advertising Age* in New York in 1962. In 1969, he became executive editor. In late 1983, he was named editor of the weekly "Op-Ed" section, and in 1984 became editor.

Danzig, who served in World War II, was awarded a Bronze Star and the Purple Heart. Among his civic activities are the United Civic Organization and the Huntley Civic Association in Eastchester. He is co-author of *How to be Heard: Making the Media Work for You*.

**DARLING, Jay** (1876–1962)
Jay N. "Ding" Darling became one of America's better-known cartoonists early in this century. His work appeared in the *Des Moines Tribune* (Iowa) for several decades and brought him Pulitzer Prizes in 1923 and 1942.

Darling was a reporter and cartoonist in Sioux City, Iowa at the turn of the century. By 1906, he was with the *Des Moines Register* (Iowa). He moved to New York to work on the *Globe* for two years, 1911–13, but returned to the *Register* where he remained until his retirement in 1949.

Darling was a honorary president of the National Wildlife Federation, and was honored with a postage stamp in 1983 on the 50th anniversary of the Migratory Bird Hunting and Conservation Stamp Act.

**DAVIDSON, Jeff** (1937– )
Jeff Davidson worked as a radio announcer during his college days in Kentucky and Texas. In 1962, he became the director of national sales and programming at WNYS-TV in Syracuse, New York.

Subsequently, Davidson worked on television stations in Wheeling, Pittsburgh, Washington, and Louisville. By 1976, he was president and general manager for Atlanta WXIA-TV, which was the "Television Station of the Year" in 1978 and 1981. He was "Broadcast Citizen of the Year" in 1982.

In 1981, Davidson became vice-president and general manager of Gannett Broadcasting Group, handling the group's seven television and thirteen radio stations, along with Gateway Productions in New York.

Davidson has been honored by Morris Brown College, the Southern Baptist Convention, the National Urban League, and the Georgia Association of Broadcasters. Louisville gave him its Distinguished Citizen Award. He holds several civic positions in Atlanta.

**DAVIDSON, Ralph Parsons** (1927– )
Ralph Davidson has been the publisher of *Time* magazine since 1972. He joined Time Inc. in 1954 as an advertising salesman for *Life*. From 1956 to 1962, he was advertising director for *Time* in London.

Returning to New York, Davidson became the managing director of Time-Life International in 1967. He has been active in the United Student Aid Funds, the National Urban League, the World Wildlife Fund, and the Keep America Beautiful program.

**DAVIES, Michael John** (1944– )
Although a native of England, Michael Davies grew up in Savannah, Georgia. After earning journalism degrees from Georgia State and Northwestern University, he worked on the *Savannah Morning News*, the *Atlanta Times*, and the *Atlanta Constitution*, all in Georgia.

A brief period was spent in Chicago with the Lloyd Hollister Newspapers before he became editor of *Scene* magazine and the managing editor of the *Louisville Times* (Kentucky), where he remained until 1976. The following two years were spent in the same capacity on the Louisville *Courier-Journal*.

Davies spent five years with the *Kansas City Star* and *Times*, serving as president of the firm and editor of the newspapers. During his years in Kansas City, the newspapers received two Pulitzer prizes, one for local coverage of the Hyatt Regency hotel disaster and the other for national reporting.

Davies became the chairman and chief operating office of the *Hartford Courant* (Connecticut) in 1983. He is also the incoming vice-president of the Associated Press Managing Editors group.

**DAVIS, Jim** (1946?– )

"Garfield," five years old in 1983, has become one of the nation's best-known comic strips. The cynical cat appears in more than 1,400 newspapers around the world and books about him are read by millions.

In recalling the first five years of Garfield's success, Davis told *Editor & Publisher* that he grew up on an Indiana farm where some 30 cats also lived. But he said Garfield was not modeled after "rural cats."

"The biggest inspirations for Garfield were big, fat, angry house cats—the kind whose owners tell you, 'don't sit there, that's the cat's chair.' "

Davis worked in an advertising agency in 1969 and later was an assistant to cartoonist Tom K. Ryan on the "Tumbleweed" comic strip. In 1977, after Davis had developed Garfield, it was rejected by two syndicates before United Features signed him. The strip began on June 19, 1978.

Garfield had a rough start, with only 50 newspapers carrying the "cat" during the first year. However, when the *Chicago Sun-Times* dropped Garfield they received 1,300 phone calls and hundreds of letters calling for his reinstatement, a clear indication the strip had a devoted following.

Fifty million viewers saw his first television special, "Here Comes Garfield," followed later by "Garfield on the Town." Davis said Garfield "is being introduced to approximately 50,000 new readers every day. I'm going to continue to play off his fat, lazy, cynical, lasagna-loving, dog-hating characteristics."

Garfield has appeared in eight books. Once seven of these books appeared simultaneously on the best-seller list. Among his titles are *Garfield at Large, Garfield Gains Weight, Garfield Sits Around the House, The Second Garfield Treasury, Garfield Takes the Cake, Garfield Weighs In,* and *Garfield Loses His Feet.*

**DEALEY Family**

Edward Musgrove Dealey (1892–1969) became a reporter on the *Dallas News* (Texas) in 1915. He moved to the presidency of the A.H. Belo Corp., the newspaper's publishing firm, in 1940 and was board chairman until his death.

Edward Dealey served as president for both the Texas Newspaper Publishers Association and the Southern Newspaper Publishers Association. He was active in the American Newspaper Publishers Association and the Associated Press.

His son, Joseph MacDonald Dealey (1919– ), began his reporting career on the *News* in 1942. By 1960, he was president of the firm and board chairman, and he became publisher in 1980.

Joe, too, has been active with national and state press groups as well as state and city civic organizations, such as the Red Cross, the Community Council, the United Fund, the Dallas Theater Center, and the University of Texas Development Fund and Chancellor's Council.

In 1983, Joe won the DeWitt Carter Reddick Award from the University of Texas for his role in community affairs. He called for employees to get out "in the hustings and rub elbows with persons involved in important and worthwhile civic endeavors."

Joe M. Dealey, Jr. (1948– ) was a fourth-generation member of the family involved with the *News*. In 1970, he had become a personnel assistant and later a management trainee. By 1976 he was on the editorial staff, covering foreign and military topics. Dealey resigned as vice-president and secretary of the Belo firm in late 1983 "to pursue other business interests and objectives."

**DEEB, Gary James** (1945– )
"The Terror of the Tube" is the title *Time* magazine gave Gary Deeb, who "views television from inside and outside." Nearly 200 newspapers carry his syndicated comments about the television industry.

In 1962, Deeb was an announcer at Buffalo station WNED-TV; he subsequently worked for four other stations in that city. In 1969, Deeb became a reporter for the *Buffalo Evening News* (New York), and the paper's TV columnist, a job he kept until 1973. Then he joined the *Chicago Tribune* as television critic and columnist. In 1980, he moved to the *Sun-Times*, leaving this $250,000 job in 1983 to host a weekly television magazine show.

In addition to his column, which he plans to continue, Deeb writes for magazines, including *Playboy*, *Variety*, and *Saturday Review*. *Editor & Publisher* reported that "one of his continuing campaigns has been to alert viewers to the butchery of movies on television to allow for a saturation of commercials."

Deeb voiced pleasure "that the networks have felt forced to 'play the trump cards'—news and information programming that the new technologies (cable, pay TV, and home video) cannot match."

**DEEMS, Richard Emmet** (1913– )
An early career in circulation started Richard Deems on his way to the presidency and chairmanship of the Hearst magazine organization.

Deems was with the Interstate News Services in 1930 and two years later, *The New Yorker* Circulation Department. Between 1933 and 1939, he worked for *Esquire* in a similar capacity, before joining *Harper's Bazaar* in 1939.

He worked in advertising for *Harper's Bazaar*, becoming vice-president in charge of advertising for the Hearst magazines, a position he held from 1952 to 1955. He advanced to executive vice-president, to president, and from 1976 to 1978, to chairman of Hearst Corporation.

Deems has been associated with several corporations. He is a trustee for the William Randolph Hearst Foundation and the Hearst Foundation, as well as for other organizations. He served in the Army in the early 1950s.

He has received several awards, including the Neallie Sullivan Award from the San Francisco Art Institute National Endowment for Arts grantee. He also has been cited for his work by the Whitney Museum of American Art and the Denver Art Museum.

**DELAPLANE, Stanton Hill** (1907– )
A California newspaper columnist, Stanton Delaplane won a Pulitzer Prize for regional reporting in 1941. He began his reporting career on the *San Francisco Chronicle* in 1936, where he continues today.

Delaplane was an organizer of the California Young Democrats and was editor of their publication in the Thirties. After his World War II service, he worked for a year as the *Chronicle*'s war correspondent.

In addition to his Pulitzer, Delaplane has been honored with the National Headliner Award and other citations. He has been president of the San Francisco Press Club and has written one book, *Pacific Pathways.*

**DELICH, Helen** ( ? – )
As the maritime editor of the *Baltimore Sun* (Maryland), Helen Delich has won recognition for her "outstanding service to the Port of Baltimore and State of Maryland."

Following her graduation from the University of Missouri, where she worked as a waitress and as a news stringer and a photographic assistant in the School of Journalism, Delich joined the United Press in Fort Wayne. A brief tour followed on the *Lewiston Tribune* (Idaho) before Delich joined the *Baltimore Sun* in 1954 for general assignment reporting.

Shortly after that, she became the first woman to cover an American Federation of Labor convention. Soon she became the first woman to become an editor, other than society editor, on the *Sun.*

She has won many awards for writing and for her television show, "The Port That Built a City and State." She was appointed to the Federal Maritime Commission by President Nixon.

For some time she wrote a column, "Around the Waterfront." It has been said that "she is known to be familiar with the kind of language longshoremen use, and can translate it into several languages," including Yugoslavian dialects.

**DENTON, Herbert Howard, Jr.** (1943– )
An Arkansas native who received his education in Massachusetts, Herbert Denton was one of the early Black reporters hired by the *Washington Post.*

After graduating cum laude from Harvard, Denton joined the *Post* in 1968. He became the Maryland editor five years later and, in 1976, the city editor.

Denton's early association with the *Post* began while he was at Harvard, where he worked on the *Crimson.* One of his colleagues on this campus newspaper was Donald Graham, whose family owns the *Post.* Denton and Graham were drafted together in 1966 and were together in basic training. Later they were together in Vietnam, where Denton was awarded a Bronze Star.

"Young reporters want to know how far they can go; it's important that there be Black stars in the firmament," according to Denton.

**DESFOR, Max** (1913– )
After spending 45 years with the Associated Press, plus five years with the *U.S. News & World Report*, Max Desfor retired for the second time in 1983.
He began with the AP in New York in 1933 as a messenger. Later he served in Baltimore, Washington, the Pacific, and India and in Rome and Tokyo.
Desfor won a Pulitzer Prize for his photo coverage of the Korean War. Other photography awards won by Desfor include the Graflex Diamond honor in 1951. He also has been cited for his work by *Editor & Publisher*, the White House Photographers Association, and the National Press Photographers Association.
Although retired as a full-time staffer with *U.S. News*, Desfor continues to work as a consultant on special projects.

**DIAMANDIS, Peter George** (1931– )
In 1983, Peter Diamandis became president of the CBS Consumer Publishing Division, with its ten magazines. Diamandis had been involved with a number of periodicals in recent years. According to the *Media Industry Newsletter*, Diamandis' new assignment was "to shake up the division, wipe out its sluggishness, and focus on profits" for the CBS Division.
Diamandis, who served in the Navy during the Korean conflict, was in the agency business between 1963 and 1970. He became the publisher of *Mademoiselle* in 1970 and three years later became president of American Essence, Inc. By 1975, he was with MLA Advertising Inc. In 1977 he became the publisher of *New York* and *New West* magazines, and the next year he held a similar position with *Self*.
In 1980 Diamandis became the publisher of GEO magazine. In that same year he was named the Marketing Man of the Year by the American Management Association.

**DICKERSON, Nancy** (1929?– )
As the first woman correspondent on the CBS News staff in the Fifties, Nancy Dickerson has been active in journalism for many years.
Dickerson was a producer for CBS News from 1956 to 1960 before becoming a news correspondent in 1960. In 1963, she joined NBC as a correspondent. She has been a news analyst for "Inside Washington," a nationally syndicated television program, since 1971.
Before she entered television, Dickerson worked briefly as a staff assistant on the Senate Foreign Relations Committee, with research and editorial duties. This experience helped her obtain the producer's position for "The Leading Question," in 1954. Later she was associate producer of "Face the Nation." She had her own CBS radio show in the 1960s, "One Woman's Washington."
Dickerson has covered presidential campaigns since 1960. She reported

President John F. Kennedy's funeral, the Civil Rights March on Washington, and the inaugurals of Kennedy, Johnson, and Nixon.

Dickerson has been honored by LaSalle College, Albert Einstein College, and Yeshiva University, as well as by Sigma Delta Chi and the New England Woman's Press Association. She once said, "I've always been charmed by political maneuvering. It amuses me—it delights me." Her latest book is *Among Those Present.*

**DIGGES, Sam Cook** (1916– )
After a brief career as an advertising salesman and a columnist for the *Washington Daily News* from 1937 to 1942, Sam Cook Digges entered television, becoming a time salesman on Washington station WMAL-TV, where he remained until he joined CBS in 1949. Within five years he was general manager for the network's station WCBS-TV in New York.

Digges continued to move up with CBS until his retirement in 1981. He was executive vice-president of CBS-owned AM stations from 1967 to 1970, when he became president of the CBS Radio Division. He served for years on the Advertising Council and the Radio Advertising Bureau. In 1977, he was named the Communicator of the Year by Sales and Marketing Executives International.

Digges' alma mater, the University of Missouri, awarded him its Journalism Medal and its Faculty-Alumni Gold Medal. He also served on the board of Stephens College. He served from 1944 to 1945 in the U.S. Merchant Marine.

**DILLIARD, Irving** (1904– )
For four decades, Irving Dilliard was associated with the *St. Louis Post-Dispatch* (Missouri), where he began as a correspondent in 1923. From 1930 to 1949 and from 1957 to 1960, Dilliard was an editorial writer. Between 1949 and 1957 he edited the editorial page.

During his newspaper career, Dilliard lectured frequently at such universities as Brandeis, Colby, Illinois, New Mexico, Oregon, DePauw, Kansas, Nevada, California, and Princeton.

For his service in World War II, Dilliard was awarded a Bronze Star. He also was cited by the British Empire and by France. He served as national president of Sigma Delta Chi and as historian for Phi Beta Kappa.

Dilliard wrote *Building the Constitution; The Development of Free Press in Germany: An Aspect of American Military Government; I'm from Missouri; Editor; Mr. Justice Brandeis, Great American; The Spirit of Liberty; Papers and Addresses of Learned Hand;* and *One Man's Stand for Freedom: Mr. Justice Black and the Bill of Rights.* He has also contributed articles to encyclopedias.

**DILLMAN, Grant** (1918– )
Forty years of service with the United Press ended in 1983 for Grant Dillman when he retired. He had witnessed changes in the wire service

operations, including its merger with the International News Service and changes in ownership.

Dillman joined the United Press in Columbus, Ohio in 1942, and three years later, he was in Washington. He told *Editor & Publisher* that he "has had a hand in just about everything from Harry Truman's beer parties to Ronald Reagan's California wine parties." Dillman also recalled helping teach President Richard Nixon "the value of giving us something new to write in overnight stories."

After being night editor for several years, Dillman served as the bureau's news editor for 10 years. He became bureau chief in 1973. Reflecting on his career, Dillman feels that "the White House press people do their damnedest to project a positive image of their man and use us in any way they can to minimize the bad news and emphasize the good news from their standpoint."

**DIX, Dorothy** (1870–1951)

Elizabeth Meriwether Gilmer was known to the American reading public for years as Dorothy Dix, the forerunner of many of today's advice columnists.

From 1896 to 1901, Gilmer was the editor of the woman's department of the *New Orleans Picayune* (Louisiana). She moved to the *New York Journal* in 1901, writing her column three times a week. She became "one of the greatest sob sisters of her time" and for 15 years covered many sensational news events.

In 1917, her column was syndicated, and by the mid-1920s, it was carried in nearly 300 newspapers.

Early in her youth, Gilmer wrote stories. She sold her first article for $3 and obtained the *Picayune* job. She selected her own writing name, and according to *Current Biography*, she chose "Dorothy because she liked it, and Dix in honor of the old family slave Dick, who had saved the Meriwether family silver."

Even when she was seventy, she continued her daily work, having returned to New Orleans. She wrote many books of advice for women, including *How to Win and Hold a Husband.*

**DODD, Edward Benton** (1902– )

The successful artist who created "Mark Trail" in 1946, Ed Dodd has won many citations for this informative and educational cartoon strip.

Before he became a cartoonist, Dodd worked in a boys' camp and a New York military academy. From 1930 to 1945, he drew a humor panel, "Back Home Again."

The success of "Mark Trail" is evident in Dodd's awards from such groups as the National Forestry Association, the Wisconsin Humane Society, the National Wildlife Federation, and the Detroit Sportsman's Congress. In 1948, Sigma Delta Chi named "Mark Trail" the best strip.

Among his books about outdoor life and conservation are *Mark Trail's Book of North American Mammals; Mark Trail Outdoor Tips; Flapfoot;*

*Clipper; Today's World of Conservation; Mark Trail's Fishing Tips; Mark Trail's Hunting Tips;* and *Mark Trail's Camping Tips.*

**DONALDSON, Sam** (1934– )
Termed "the brashest of the new breed of television reporters," with a reputation as a "wild man," Sam Donaldson has been with ABC News since 1967.

After six years as a radio–television news reporter and anchorman on WTOP in Washington, Donaldson moved to ABC News as Capitol Hill correspondent in 1967. Ten years later he became the White House correspondent.

*Playboy*, in an interview in 1983, called Donaldson "a maverick who has been credited with revitalizing Washington press coverage in an era in which some reporters have contented themselves with official briefings and press handouts."

Donaldson has covered the House, Senate, Vietnam, and Watergate. He professes to having "strong opinions." He believes that "too many policy decisions have been made by men in closed rooms. When bullets fly, people do, and TV pictures ram that message home."

Donaldson has also been described as "the junkyard dog of the White House press corps," by Roger Piantadosi in the *Washington Journalism Review.* "He is a clown, walking nonchalantly across the top of the assignment desk, or falling out of his briefing room chair. Off camera, at work, he is alternately known as a bully and a hero."

**DONOVAN, Hedley** (1914– )
Now a retired consultant to Time Inc., Hedley Donovan spent more than 30 years with this corporation. After five years as a *Washington Post* reporter, Donovan, in 1945, was a writer for *Fortune* magazine, where he specialized in political articles.

Donovan advanced to the managing editorship in 1953 and was editor-in-chief from 1964 to 1979. In 1979 he became a senior advisor to President Ronald Reagan.

Henry R. Luce, co-founder of *Time* and founder of other Time Inc. publications, selected Donovan to be his successor. Donovan came well prepared for the assignment. He had been a Rhodes Scholar and, at Oxford, had served as a campus correspondent for the United Press. He left employment at the *Washington Post* for World War II service in Naval Intelligence.

Donovan is a trustee for New York University, Mt. Holyoke College, the National Center for Humanities, the Carnegie Endowment for International Peace, and the Ford Foundation. He has won numerous awards, including the Loeb Journalism Award, and has been honored by New York University and the University of Minnesota.

Donovan's daughter, Helen, is an assistant managing editor on the *Sunday Boston Globe.* He says he's "delighted with her career." He admits he could help her get a job, "but once they've got their first interview, they're on their own."

**DOTSON, Robert Charles** (1946– )
The recipient of nearly 50 national and international awards for television news work, Robert Dotson has spent most of his life working in the South.

Dotson worked on KMBC-TV in Kansas City as a reporter and photographer and as documentary producer from 1967 to 1968. He then worked in Oklahoma City, Oklahoma, Cleveland, Ohio, and in 1977, in Dallas, Texas, as a NBC network correspondent. He is now in Atlanta, Georgia.

Dotson was a correspondent for the NBC "Today" Show in 1979. Among his many awards are an Emmy and a Robert F. Kennedy Journalism citation for his documentaries.

**DOWIE, Mark** (1939– )
Canadian-born Mark Dowie worked in banking and investments in San Francisco for many years. In 1976, he became the publisher of *Mother Jones* magazine and, in 1980, its editor.

The magazine, named for Mary "Mother" Jones, who was a pioneering socialist organizer, won a National Magazine Award in 1977 and again in 1979. The publication was established in 1976 and Dowie was an early staffer. He has voiced pride over some of *Mother Jones'* investigative stories, such as the exposure of problems with the Pinto. He once said, "Investigations should be long term. They should be deep. They should be politically motivated. They should be advocacy journalism."

Dowie is director for the Center for Investigative Reporting. He has written one book, *Transitions to Freedom*, and many articles for professional journals.

**DOWNES, Bruce** (1899–1966)
Publishing and photography were highlights in the career of Bruce Downes, who began his newspaper career as a drama critic on the *Brooklyn Times* in 1921. He was a feature writer on the *Jacksonville Journal* (Florida) in 1927, and two years later, he was with the *Brooklyn Citizen* (New York) as city editor and later managing editor until 1943.

Downes was the associate photography editor for *Collier's* between 1936 and 1943. He was eastern editor for *Popular Photography* magazine 1944–50, and its editor and publisher, 1951–66.

Downes also was the editor and publisher of *Photography Annual* and *Photography Directory and Buying Guides*, as well as many other books on this subject.

**DOWNS, Hugh Malcolm** (1921– )
One of America's better-known television personalities, Hugh Downs was the host of NBC "Today" Show. He began his long and successful career in 1939 as an announcer on radio station WLOK in Lima, Ohio for $7.50 a week.

By 1940, Downs was with WWJ in Detroit, while he attended Wayne University. He served briefly in the Infantry during World War II before receiving a medical discharge. Downs joined NBC-owned station WMAQ in Chicago in 1943 as announcer, interviewer, and disk jockey. By 1954, he was in New York to work with Arlene Francis on the NBC-TV "Home Show." He announced the "Sid Caesar" show and, in 1957, joined Jack Paar's "Tonight Show."

Downs has been described as low-keyed, calm, self-assured, and soft-spoken. He demonstrated his talents when he took over the "Tonight Show" following Paar's sudden departure in the middle of a program to protest NBC's censorship of one of his jokes.

In recent years, Downs hosted the Public Broadcasting Service's "Over Easy Show" designed for senior citizens. Currently, he is the host of the ABC "20/20 Show."

Downs has been active in medical and scientific projects, UNICEF programs, and other projects. He won the Fame Award for several years as the best announcer on the air.

**DRAKE, Donald Charles** (1935- )

Donald Drake started his newspaper career as a copyboy for the *New York Herald Tribune* in 1954. Within two years he was a reporter on the *Mt. Kisco Patent Trader* (New York).

Drake moved to the *New Haven Register* (Connecticut) and then spent seven years with *Newsday* before he joined the *Philadelphia Inquirer* (Pennsylvania) in 1965. He continues there as a medical writer.

Drake has won many major awards for his medical writing, including two Howard W. Blakeslee Awards, from the American Heart Association; the Claude Bernard Award, from the National Society for Medical Research; and the Russell L. Cecil Writing Award, from the Arthritis Foundation.

Other honors have come from the Philadelphia Press Association, the Keystone Press, and the Associated Press Managing Editors.

**DREW, Elizabeth** (1935- )

Elizabeth Drew is one of the few journalists to be recognized with awards for both print and broadcast work. Drew has written for *The New Yorker*, *Reporter*, *New Republic*, *New York Times Magazine*, and *Atlantic*, and she has written several significant books as well. Several of these originally appeared in shorter form in *The New Yorker*, where she has been a writer since 1973.

Drew is widely recognized for her research abilities. Early in her career she was an associate editor for the *Writer* before becoming associated with *Congressional Quarterly*, where she rose to senior editor. She also served as Washington editor for *Atlantic* from 1967 to 1973.

In 1971, Drew hosted a "Thirty Minutes with . . ." television program over WETA-TV in Washington. Eventually, more than 150 PBS stations carried the program.

Drew kept a diary, a daily record of the Watergate scandal, and her book, *Washington Journal: The Events of 1973–75*, was widely praised for its accuracy and thoroughness. This prompted her to repeat the process in the 1976 presidential campaign, which resulted in *American Journal: The*

*Events of 1976*. This, too, was serialized in *The New Yorker*. Later she wrote a book, *Senator*, in which she recreated the atmosphere of the Senate. She also has written *Politics and Money* and *Portrait of an Election*.

Drew appears as a guest on "Agronsky & Company," as well as on "Meet the Press" and "Face the Nation." The *Ladies' Home Journal* in 1977 named her "Woman of the Year in Communications." She has received the Wellesley Alumnae Achievement Award and the Award for Excellence from the Society of Magazine Writers. The University of Missouri gave her its Journalism Medal in 1979.

In an interview in *USA TODAY* in 1983, Drew discussed the problems of congressmen and their relationship to campaign contributors. She said, "Members of Congress are afraid to write a bill because they believe it will irritate or antagonize an interest group from whom they want contributions or whom they fear will give money to an opponent." She won the Sidney Hillman Award for her book on campaign financing.

**DRUMMOND, Roscoe** (1902–1983)
A long career with the *Christian Science Monitor* preceded Roscoe Drummond's success as a syndicated newspaper columnist. Drummond began as a reporter on the *Monitor* in 1924 and held many positions until 1940. As *Editor & Publisher* noted, Drummond "went on to become assistant city editor, assistant to the executive editor, chief editorial writer, European editorial manager, general news editor, editorial board member, and executive editor before he served as *Monitor* Washington Bureau chief from 1940 to 1953."

His newspaper column, "State of the Nation," which appeared for 25 years in 150 newspapers, helped establish Drummond's reputation. He headed the Washington Bureau of the *New York Herald Tribune* for two years.

Drummond won several awards early in his career and wrote many articles for American and British periodicals. He co-authored one book, *Duel at the Brink*. He may have been the shortest reporter in Washington, since he was just under five feet tall.

**DRYFOOS, Orvil E.** (1912–1963)
A rare individual, Orvil Dryfoos once admitted that he selected a career in journalism because of his "marriage to the daughter of the publisher of the *New York Times*," Marian Sulzberger, in 1941.

In 1961, Dryfoos succeeded Arthur Hays Sulzberger as publisher of the *Times*. His interest in newspaper work started in preparatory school, where he wrote a sports column, but later he became a broker and a member of the New York Stock Exchange.

Dryfoos' association with the *Times* began when he became assistant to the publisher in 1943. Four years later, he was the firm's president. Before this climb upward, Dryfoos served as a cub reporter, worked in the city room, and spent some time on the make-up desk.

Dryfoos maintained an active interest in many civic projects, including the Times Neediest Cases Fund; he was also a trustee for the Baron de

Hirsch Fund, he worked for New York World's Fair, and he was on the board of Fordham University and Dartmouth College.

**DUBOIS, Jules** (1910–1966)

For nearly 20 years, Jules Dubois was the Latin American correspondent for the *Chicago Tribune.* Before joining the *Tribune*'s staff, Dubois worked for several newspapers, starting in 1927 on the *New York Herald Tribune.* Between 1929 and 1947 he worked on various assignments for the *Panama Star and Herald* and the *Panama Times.*

During World War II, Dubois served six years in the Army before retiring as a colonel. He received the Medal of Merit and special recognition from Brazil, Peru, Panama, the Dominican Republic, Ecuador, and Uruguay.

Dubois also received the Tom Wallace Award from the Inter-American Press Association and the William Allen White Award for his coverage of Latin America.

**DUNCAN, David Douglas** (1916– )

One of the world's best-known photographers, David Duncan began his career in 1934 when he covered a Tucson hotel fire with a 39-cent Bakelite camera that his sister had given him.

By 1983, Duncan had written and provided the photographs for 15 books. His latest, *The World of Allah,* is based on pictures made during a decade in the Middle East for *Life* magazine.

Duncan was educated in archaeology, but made a career in photojournalism. Some of the pictures he took on an expedition to Chile and Peru appeared in the *National Geographic* in 1941 through 1943.

During World War II, he served with the Marine Corps, eventually photographing battles in the Pacific. He also covered the Japanese surrender on the *USS Missouri.* He retired as lieutenant-colonel, with a Legion of Merit and other crosses and stars and three Air Medals.

In early 1946, he joined *Life.* His coverage of the war in Korea was another milestone. His pictures first appeared in *Life* and later in his book, *This Is War!* One reviewer observed that Duncan had "caught war's essence as well as most of its facets."

Duncan became a free-lance photographer in 1955. His pictures appeared in *Collier's,* the *Saturday Evening Post,* and *Life.* One year he was assigned to photograph the Kremlin art treasures.

Duncan wrote in the *Saturday Review* in 1968, "I am no kook, hippie, hawk, or dove. I am just a veteran combat photographer and foreign correspondent who cares intensely about my country and the role we are playing—and assigning to ourselves—in the world of today."

A list of his awards include the Overseas Press Club Award, the U.S. Camera Gold Award, and the Robert Capa Gold Medal. In an interview in 1983, Duncan said, "It's been a great life. If you live long enough you get to know a hell of a lot of people."

**DUSCHA, Julius Carl** (1924– )
Currently the director of the Washington Journalism Center, Julius Duscha had a varied career in reporting before taking this position in 1968.

Duscha was a reporter on the *St. Paul Pioneer Press* (Minnesota) in 1943. He worked in publicity for the Democratic National Committee in 1948 and 1952, and later wrote for the AFL Labor League for Political Education for three years. He also worked for the *International Machinist* and was an editorial writer for the Lindsay-Schaub Newspapers in Illinois before joining the *Washington Post* as a reporter in 1958. He remained there until 1966.

Before taking the Center directorship, Duscha was involved in the Stanford Professional Journalism Fellowship program. Sigma Delta Chi honored him in 1961 as a distinguished Washington correspondent.

Duscha wrote *Taxpayers' Hayride: The Farm Problem from the New Deal to the Billie Sol Estes Case*; *Arms, Money and Politics*; and *The Campus Press*. He also has been a frequent contributor to magazines, including *New Republic, Harper's, Progressive, New York Times Magazine*, and others.

**EBERT, Roger** (1942– )
Roger Ebert was editor of the *Daily Illini* during his University of Illinois years in Chicago. Earlier he had been a staff writer for the *Champaign-Urbana News-Gazette* (Illinois). However, it was on television that Ebert and his colleague, Gene Siskel, became known to millions of viewers.

Earlier, these two men had a "Sneak Previews" show on Public Broadcasting. They have switched to "At The Movies" on commerical television, continuing their dialog about what is going on in the movie industry.

Ebert became a feature writer in 1967 and later was film critic for the *Chicago Sun-Times*. In 1975, he won a Pulitzer Prize, the first and only film critic to be so honored. Ebert wrote briefly for *US* magazine.

In addition to his Pulitzer, Ebert has won awards from the Overseas Press Club, the Chicago Headline Club, and the Chicago Newspaper Guild. In 1979 he won an Emmy. He wrote *An Illini Century* and *Beyond Narrative: The Future of the Feature Film*. He also wrote the script for *Beyond the Valley of the Dolls*.

**EDDY, Bob** (1917– )
Bob Eddy, who has been a visiting journalism professor at Nebraska and Syracuse universities, began as a copyeditor on the *St. Paul Pioneer Press* (Minnesota) in 1939. By 1962, he had worked on the *Minneapolis Star*, the *St. Paul Dispatch*, and eventually the combined *Dispatch and Pioneer Press* (Minnesota), where he was an editorial writer.

Eddy joined the *Hartford Courant* (Connecticut) as assistant to the publisher in 1962 and became editor in 1966. He also served as the publisher for six years. In 1976, Eddy received the Distinguished Alumnus Award from the University of Minnesota. He has been involved in several Hartford civic projects.

**EDSON, Guy** (1901–1966)
"Streaky," "The Gumps," and "Dondi" are all associated with the life of Guy Edson. In 1920, he was a free-lance cartoonist and, from 1925 to 1928, he worked on the *New York Graphic.* He then worked briefly for the Paul Block chain of newspapers and later became a feature cartoonist for the King Features Syndicate. For four years he was a sports cartoonist for the *New York Daily News.*

Edson created a Sunday comic, "Streaky," in 1933. From 1935 until his death he drew "The Gumps." In 1955, he was the co-creator of "Dondi," which was considered the best story strip in 1962 and 1963. Edson also wrote several books and made some motion picture cartoons, including "Dondi" and "Dondi Goes Native in Brooklyn."

**EDWARDS, Douglas** (1917– )
In 1955, Douglas Edwards received the Peabody Award for news, and in 1982, he was inducted into the National Broadcasters Hall of Fame for his work in anchoring "a daily TV news broadcast without interruption since August 1948."

Edwards began his career as a junior announcer for WHET, a radio station in Troy, Alabama, in 1932. Three years later he was on the news staff of Atlanta station WSB before moving to Detroit station WXYZ. His first association with CBS, in 1942, was on the "World Today" and "Report to the Nation" broadcasts in New York. For a year, 1945–46, he was a CBS foreign correspondent in Europe and the Middle East.

**EISENSTAEDT, Alfred** (1898– )
"The eyes of Alfred Eisenstaedt see things very fast," reported *Life* magazine in the Fifties. "Eisenstaedt lives for photography," the magazine added, noting his durable zeal, his enthusiasm, and his professionalism, although, as Jacob Deschin once wrote, "after 25 years of professionalism, Eisenstaedt is still an amateur at heart, excited about his medium, full of delight in persons and things and as enthusiastic as a beginner."

Eisenstaedt was one of the original *Life* photographers. Starting in 1936, he covered nearly 2,000 assignments for *Life.* His career began in 1927 when he made a poetic study of shadows in photographing a Czech tennis player. He worked for the Associated Press photo agency in Europe, developing what was then a new style that stressed natural lighting.

He recalled the early years of *Life*, where, he said, it was so wonderful to work: "Before, the editors would always tell you what they wanted. But at *Life* you were on your own." He was known for his many outstanding photographic essays and pictures. Many of these continue to appear in books, periodicals, and museums.

To some he is best remembered for his pictures of such individuals as Marilyn Monroe, Ernest Hemingway, Sophia Loren, Jackie Kennedy, and Henry Kissinger. Some may also recall his post-World War II celebration scenes taken in New York City.

Of his nature photographs, Eisenstaedt says, "It's my avocation, too.

Ninety percent of it I do for myself." Although he changed to color when *Life* did, he claims, "When I dream, I dream in black-and-white."

More than 90 *Life* covers were shot by Eisenstaedt. He has been named Photographer of the Year, and in 1978, he received the Lifetime Achievement in Photography Award from the American Society of Magazine Photographers. He has written several books, the latest being *Eisenstaedt's Guide to Photography*. Eisenstaedt's other books include *Witness to Our Time; The Eye of Eisenstaedt; Martha's Vineyard; Witness to Nature; Wimbledon: A Celebration; People*; and *Celebrity Photos*.

**ELFIN, Mel** (1929– )

After a year in the Air Force (1952–53), Mel Elfin became a reporter on the *Long Island Daily Press* in 1954; subsequently he became the assistant city editor. He joined *Newsweek* in 1958 and from 1964 to 1965 was its general editor, becoming chief of its Washington Bureau in 1965.

Elfin won the George Polk Memorial Award for his reporting in 1957. He has also been honored by the New York Newspaper Guild, with its Page One Award, and by the Education Writers Association. He has written many articles, and was the co-author with others of *Bricks and Mortarboards*.

**ELIOT, George Fielding** (1894–1971)

Although George Fielding Eliot began his career as a magazine fiction writer in 1926, he later earned his place in journalism as a military specialist.

As early as 1939, Eliot was writing about military and naval affairs for the *New York Herald Tribune*, and during World War II, he was the military analyst for CBS. He worked for MBS from 1950 to 1953.

Eliot was a columnist on the *New York Post* for several years and, in 1950, began a 17-year career as a syndicated columnist on military topics.

His books included *The Ramparts We Watch; Bombs Bursting in Air; Hour of Triumph; The Strength We Need; Hate, Hope and High Explosive; If Russia Strikes; Victory without War; Sylvanus Thayer of West Point; Reserve Forces and the Kennedy Strategy*; and *Franklin Buchanan*. He co-authored *If War Comes* and wrote one novel, *Caleb Pettengill, USN*.

In 1962, the University of Missouri awarded Eliot its Journalism Medal for his contributions to the profession.

**ELISOFON, Eliot** (1911–1973)

During his first three decades as a photographer, Eliot Elisofon estimated he traveled 2 million miles around the world. In 1942, he joined *Life* magazine.

As a young student his interest was in painting, which eventually led him to photography. He borrowed his sister's camera until he could buy a $14 one for himself, and in 1935, he gave up a job with the New York Workmen's Compensation Bureau to become a professional photographer.

Later Elisofon recalled that he learned "to point a camera at things that I thought needed attention." He covered World War II in Europe and North Africa for *Life*. Later he joined the Pacific Fleet on assignment.

An experimental photographer, Elisofon once told *The New Yorker* that "I've never believed that color in pictures ought to be a facsimile of the real thing. Good artists take what they like from reality and discard the rest."

Eventually Elisofon was the color consultant for a number of motion pictures, starting with *Moulin Rouge*, in 1953. He has continued to paint, and his work has been shown in many countries.

As cameraman for expeditions to the Dutch New Guinea and other areas, he was sent by ABC-TV to Africa in the mid-1960s. His first book, *Food Is a Four-Letter Word*, appeared in 1948 and others included *Color Photography*; *The Sculpture of Africa*; *The Nile*; *Africa's Animals*; *Java Diary*; *A Week in Agata's World: Poland*; and *Hollywood Style*. He contributed articles to the *Smithsonian* magazine and the *National Geographic*.

**ELLERBEE, Linda** (1944– )
Starting as a disk jockey on Chicago station WVON in 1964, Linda Ellerbee became program director for KSJO in San Francisco in 1967 and moved to Alaska in 1969 for a three-year reporting assignment with station WJNO and the Associated Press.

After a year with Houston station WHOU-TV, 1972–73, Ellerbee moved to New York with WCBS-TV. She switched to NBC News in 1978 and has been a co-anchorperson on the Weekend NBC News.

**ELLIOTT, Osborn** (1924– )
Osborn Elliott has been a magazine editor, a deputy mayor of New York City, and an educator.

Raised in "an old, socially prominent New York 'WASP' family," Elliott early in life became acquainted with such personalities as Walter Lippmann, John Gunther, and Robert Moses. After World War II service in the Navy, he joined the *New York Journal of Commerce* staff in 1946.

His work on the *Journal of Commerce* involved reporting, editing, and column writing. "Journalism changed his whole life," wrote Merle Miller. "It has become the ruling passion of his life."

Early in 1949, Elliott joined *Time* as a business writer, and in 1955, he joined *Newsweek* as a senior business editor. Four years later, he was voted one of the ten outstanding young men in America by the U.S. Junior Chamber of Commerce. That same year he published his first book, *Men at the Top*.

Elliott became *Newsweek*'s executive editor in 1961. There he gave writers bylines, a practice then rejected by *Time*. More polling projects of Americans and their opinions were handled as Elliott moved *Newsweek* into "advocacy journalism." By the end of the decade, he was president, chief executive officer, and board chairman.

Taking a terrific cut in pay, Elliott left *Newsweek* in 1976 to become Mayor Abraham Beame's deputy to help rebuild the city's financial base.

He held the job for a year. He has been dean of the Columbia University School of Journalism since 1979.

Honors include being a trustee for the New York Public Library, the Asia Society, the American Museum of Natural History, and the Carnegie Endowment for International Peace. Ohio University awarded him its Van Anda Award in 1969. In 1980, Elliott wrote *The World of Oz*, his autobiography.

**ENGELHARDT, Thomas Alexander** (1930– )

After Daniel R. Fitzpatrick had drawn editorial cartoons for 45 years for the *St. Louis Post-Dispatch* (Missouri), he retired in 1950. He was replaced by Bill Mauldin. In 1962, Tom Engelhardt became the permanent replacement for these two Pulitzer Prize-winning cartoonists.

Engelhardt was a free-lance cartoonist and artist from 1957 to 1960 and then worked briefly for the Newspaper Enterprise Association in Cleveland. From there he returned to St. Louis, the city of his birth.

When Engelhardt joined the *Post-Dispatch*, it was thought he would "bring a greater local flavor to the newspaper's editorial page cartoons after the international-minded Mauldin left to join the *Chicago Sun-Times*," which he did.

"I would like to be able to hit forcefully what I consider to be wrongdoing, hypocrisy, and injustice," he once said. "A cartoon should make an editorial point first and foremost. Then I would like to see this done with an imaginative viewpoint or analogy. Next it should be done with good design and good drawing, and if possible it also should be humorous."

**EPSTEIN, Eleni Sakes** (1925– )

A career as a fashion editor has brought recognition to Eleni Epstein who began her career in journalism as a copygirl. She became a member of the women's staff on the *Washington Star* in 1945, becoming its fashion editor in 1946, a position she held until 1981.

During her editorship, Epstein won many awards, including the J.C. Penney–University of Missouri Fashion Writing Award in 1961. Other honors have come from the New York Fashion Reporters and the American Legion Post in Washington, the latter as Woman of the Year. She also has been honored by the Greek and Italian governments.

**ETHRIDGE, Mark Foster** (1896–1981)

Mark Ethridge began as a reporter on the *Meridian Star* (Mississippi) in 1913, his home town. He later worked on the *Columbus Enquirer* and *Macon Telegraph* in Georgia.

In the early Twenties, Ethridge joined the *New York Sun* and the Consolidated Press. Still later, he was the assistant general manager of the *Washington Post*. For two years, 1934–36, he was president and publisher of the *Richmond Times-Dispatch* (Virginia) and from 1936 to 1942 was with the *Louisville Courier-Journal* and *Times* (Kentucky).

Ethridge later worked as editor of *Newsday*. Other activities involved the Ford Foundation and the U.N. Commission to Study Greek Border Disputes. He served in World War I.

**EVANS Family**

The name Evans has long been associated with the *Nashville Tennessean.*

Silliman Evans (1894–1955) began his career as a reporter in 1913, working with the United Press, the International News Service, the *Dallas Morning News*, and the *Ft. Worth Star-Telegram* (Texas). Later he was involved in business activities and the airline industry. He was a director on the *Tennessean.*

Silliman Evans, Jr. (1925–1961) spent his life with the Nashville newspaper. He started in 1947, after three years of service in the Air Force. He was its publisher until his death.

The *Tennessean* was sold to the Gannett group for $50 million in 1979.

**EVANS, Medford Stanton** (1934– )

A career that included newspapers, magazines, and radio work has brought many awards to Medford Evans, who was an assistant editor of *Freeman* in 1955. He was on the editorial staff of *National Review* from 1955 to 1968. During much of that time, Evans was also on the staff of *Human Events* and has contribued to that magazine since 1968.

Evans wrote editorials and later served as the editor of the *Indianapolis News* (Indiana), 1959–60. Since 1971, he has been with the CBS "Radio Spectrum" series.

He has won four Freedoms Foundation awards for editorial writing, and The National Headliner Club cited him for his outstanding editorial pages.

Evans has written *Revolt on the Campus; The Fringe on Top; The Liberal Establishment; The Politics of Surrenders; The Lawbreakers; The Future of Conservatism*; and *Assassination of Joe McCarthy.*

**EVANS, Rowland, Jr.** (1921– )

After serving on the staff of the *New York Herald Tribune* from 1955 to 1963, Rowland Evans, Jr. became a syndicated columnist, working with Robert Novak in Washington.

Evans and Novak's book, *Lyndon B. Johnson: The Exercise of Power*, was well received in 1967 and was considered by many to be the best biography of the president. Evans also has written *Nixon in the White House: The Frustration of Power* and *The Reagan Revolution.*

In addition to his columns and books, Evans has contributed to the *Saturday Evening Post, Harper's, The Reporter*, and *New Republic.* He also appears as a panelist and commentator on television shows.

**FABER, John Henry** (1918– )

A long-time photographer and executive, John Faber was a technical sales representative for Eastman Kodak Co. for 33 years before his retirement in 1983. He was also the historian for the National Press Photographers Association for many years.

Faber has been a special advisor to the curator of photography at the Smithsonian Institution on news photography history since 1960. One of his books is *Great Moments in News Photography*.

Faber's career with Eastman began in 1950. Earlier he had been the chief photographer for the Alabama Ordnance Works and the Bechtel-McCone-Parsons Corp., in Birmingham. From 1946 to 1950, he was director of photography for the *Birmingham News* (Alabama) and its WAFM-TV station.

At his Mountain Lakes, New Jersey home, Faber's library walls are covered with citations and awards. In 1961, for example, he received the President's Medal from the National Press Photographers Association. He also has won the Joseph A. Sprague Memorial highest honor award and the Joseph Costa Award. The New York Photographers Association and Eastman have also honored his works.

Faber's first book, *Industrial Photography*, appeared in 1948, and he has written articles for newspapers and periodicals. His other books include *Humor in News Photography*; *Travel Photography*; and *Great News Photos and the Stories behind Them*.

**FAIRCHILD, John Burr** (1927– )

John Fairchild is best known as the publisher of *Women's Wear Daily* (*WWD*), a publication once termed "the American fashion industry's gossipy and irreverent trade journal."

Fairchild took over the *WWD* publishing task in 1960. Prior to that he had served in the Army from 1947 to 1948 and worked in the research department of the J.L. Hudson Company in Detroit.

Fairchild Publications was founded by John's grandfather, Edmund Fairchild. John joined the firm in 1951 as a reporter in New York and for six years headed the *WWD* Paris Bureau. By 1960, he was in New York as the publisher. Six years later, he succeeded his father, Louis W. Fairchild, as president, and in 1970, became the board chairman when his uncle, Edgar Fairchild, retired.

During his tour in Paris, Fairchild "earned fame—or notoriety—by panning top designers' collections, printing sketches before release dates, and reporting often unverified gossip on Parisian high society," according to a 1971 sketch in *Current Biography*. Despite this, he has been honored by the French government.

Fairchild has continued to make changes in *WWD*, adding reviews, market news, gossip columns, and the like. Some designers have been praised, others have been ridiculed.

Fairchild's firm publishes other magazines, including *W*, for women and M, for men. In 1966, Fairchild Publications merged with Capital Cities Broadcasting Co., and Fairchild became an executive vice-president with that group. He has written *The Fashionable Savages* and *The Moonflower Couple*.

**FANNING, Katherine Woodruff** (1927– )

Katherine Fanning's latest assignment, starting in mid-1983, was to turn the highly respected, but money-losing *Christian Science Monitor* around.

Fanning went to Alaska after she divorced Marshall Field IV of the *Chicago Sun-Times* in 1963 and became the librarian on the *Anchorage Daily News*, thus starting her journalism career. In 1966, she married Lawrence Fanning and they bought the Anchorage newspaper. Lawrence Fanning had worked on the *San Francisco Chronicle* and the *Chicago Sun-Times* before he moved to Alaska.

The *Anchorage Daily News* was losing money when her husband died in 1971. She succeeded in pushing the daily ahead, however, and won a Pulitzer Prize in 1976 for exposing the illicit activities of the Teamsters Union in Alaska. She sold the *Anchorage Daily News* to the McClatchy group in 1983, before moving to Boston to join the *Monitor*.

The *Monitor*'s circulation had declined, and in 1982, it lost $10 million. In seeking younger readers, Fanning made changes quickly in content and layout and in the organization of departments, and dropped regional editions for a single national edition.

In Alaska, Fanning was active in many projects, including Urban Beautification and Educational Broadcasting commissions, Repertory Theater, and the Community Chest. She is chairperson for the American Society of Newspaper Editors' ethics committee. As *Time* noted, her *Monitor* job gives her "the most prestigious top-editor post in American newspapering now held by a woman."

**FEIFFER, Jules** (1929– )

Cartoons by Jules Feiffer have been syndicated to newspapers across America since 1959. They are well known and quickly recognized for their satire and their unique approach to the social and political issues of the day. Some individuals in the 1960s viewed him as "the most talented social commentator in cartooning in our generation."

Feiffer studied at the Art Student's League and Pratt Institute in New York. From 1946 to 1951, he assisted cartoonist Will Eisner in drawing "The Spirit" strip. For several years Feiffer drew his own Sunday feature, "Clifford."

During his two years in the Signal Corps, Feiffer worked as a cartoon animator. He held many jobs until 1956, when his work appeared in the weekly, *The Village Voice*. He donated the satirical strip, "Sick, Sick, Sick," to the *Voice*.

In addition to his syndication today, Feiffer's cartoons appear regularly in American and English publications. His books include *Sick, Sick, Sick; Passionella and Other Stories; The Explainers*; and *Boy, Girl, Boy, Girl*. He also wrote *Feiffer's Album; The Unexpurgated Memoirs of Bernard Mergendeiler; Feiffer on Civil Rights; Pictures at a Prosecution; Feiffer on Nixon: The Cartoon Presidency*; and *Ackroyd*. He wrote several plays, including *Crawling Arnold; Little Murders; God Bless; The White House Murder Case; Knock-Knock*; and *Grownups*. He also wrote several revues, including *The Explainer* and *Hold Me!* He was also involved in the *Little Murders* and *Popeye* screenplays, and *Tantrum*, a cartoon novel. He wrote a novel, *Harry, The Rat with Women*. In 1958, he earned what he termed his first "regular money," $500 a month from *Playboy*. Feiffer once called Hugh Hefner the best cartoon editor he ever had.

Awards have been frequent, starting with the Academy Award for animated cartoon in 1961. This recognized his work with "Munro," a four-year-old boy accidentally drafted into the Army. Other awards include the George Polk Memorial Award and the Outer Circle Drama Critics citation.

Feiffer once said, "The most important thing to me is being an amateur, retaining the level of the professional. By amateur I mean doing what I like to do."

**FEININGER, Andreas** (1906– )
Long before French-born Andreas Feininger joined *Life* magazine as a photographer, he studied architecture. He became a journeyman cabinet-maker and worked in Germany before his start as a photographer who eventually specialized in architecture and industrial work.

By 1940, Feininger had turned to full-time photography, with the Black Star Photo Agency in New York, and from 1943 to 1962, he was a *Life* staff photographer.

Feininger has had one-man exhibitions of his pictures at the Smithsonian Institution and the International Center of Photography, and many of his articles have appeared in photography magazines. He is a charter member of the American Society of Magazine Photographers. In addition to writing 34 books, he has conducted research on telephotography. Among Feininger's books are *The Anatomy of Nature*; *The Roots of Art*; *The Face of New York*; *The Creative Photographer*; *The Complete Photographer*; *Total Photography*; *Advanced Photography*; *Total Picture Control*; *Trees*; *Shells*; *Photographic Seeing*; *The Mountains of the Mind: A Fantastic Journey*, and others.

Feininger once said that "the world is full of things that the eye doesn't see; the camera sees more and oftentimes better."

**FELKER, Clay S.** (1925– )
Few individuals have been involved with so many major magazines in so many capacities as Clay Felker has. He was born into a journalistic-oriented family: His father, Clay T. Felker, was managing editor of *The Sporting News*, and his mother, Cora F. Felker, was a women's section editor.

While earning his degree at Duke, Felker edited the campus newspaper. A colleague, Peter Maas, recalled that even then Felker was "hard-driving, energetic—the paper was all he talked about." After Duke, he joined Time Inc. and reported for *Life*. He also helped develop *Sports Illustrated*.

From 1957 to 1962 Felker was the feature editor of *Esquire*, but his desire to have his own magazine prompted his move to Viking Press as a consulting editor and later to the editorship of *Infinity*, the American Society of Magazine Photographers' publication. He joined the *New York Herald Tribune* as a consultant in 1963 and the following year became editor of the newspaper's new supplemental magazine, *New York*.

When several New York newspapers merged into the *World Journal-Tribune* in 1966, Felker became the associate editor in charge of future planning. He was also editor of the newspaper's supplement, *Book Week*, while continuing to direct *New York*.

When that paper folded in 1967, Felker, Jimmy Breslin, and others acquired the name *New York*. They produced the first copy of the magazine, in 1968, with Milton Glaser and other colleagues from their *Herald Tribune* days. Felker moved *New York* ahead, and by 1971, the magazine had become profitable. For a time the staff was also in charge of *New West* magazine.

However, internal disputes involving Felker and staffers resulted in the departure of several major writers. Felker left in 1977.

From 1974 to 1977, Felker was also editor and publisher of the *Village Voice*. He became a partial owner, but when he overspent he was out after his partners sold their interests to Rupert Murdoch. Felker reportedly received a hefty out-of-court settlement.

Felker then returned to *Esquire*, when he promised to make it "the best magazine for men in the world," but not "a skin magazine." However, after two years of experimentation, and a $7 million deficit, *Esquire* was sold to two young Tennessee publishers, Christopher Whittle and Phillip Moffitt.

Felker often had disputes with staffers, which prompted Murdoch to say: "Clay never realized there are simple ways to deal with a board of directors. He could have had them to lunch twice a year with Teddy Kennedy or somebody. Instead, he made enemies of them one by one. He was afraid of them."

For a time, in the early 1980s, Felker was editor of the experimental *New York Daily News Tonight* edition. He said then that "newspapers have a more promising future than magazines. . . . Because newspapers come out so frequently, they establish a very strong emotional bond with their readers." In spite of this, there have been rumors that Felker was once again planning another New York-based publication.

**FEY, Harold** (1898– )

Trained for the ministry, Harold Fey spent much of his life working on religious publications. Fey, a minister in Nebraska in the 1940s, later taught in Manila before becoming editor of *World Call* in Indianapolis, Indiana in 1932. Three years later, he was editor of *Fellowship* magazine in New York.

Fey's career really started after he became a field editor for *Christian Century* in Chicago in 1940. By 1956, he was the editor and, after 1964, a contributing editor. He was also president of the Christian Century Foundation.

During these years Fey wrote book reviews, lectured at universities, worked with other groups, and won many awards, including the Distinguished Service Award from the National Congress of American Indians. The Christian Church gave Fey its Leadership in Christian Journalism Award. He wrote *The Lord's Supper: Seven Meanings*; *Cooperation in Compassion*; *Life—New Style*; *With Solemn Reverence*; and *Kirby Page, Social Evangelist*. He co-authored *Indians and Other Americans* with D'Arcy McNickle.

**FIELD Family**

Five members of the Field family have carried the first name of Marshall. The first Marshall Field (1835–1906) established the store under his name in Chicago in the 1880s. His investments in banks, railroads, and real estate started the family fortune. He also provided funds for the Field Museum of Natural History and left the family between $100 and $175 million.

Marshall Field II (1868–1905) died at the age of 37, possibly from a shooting accident.

Marshall Field III (1893–1956) became the first Field to be directly involved in journalism. In his early years, the press considered him to be a playboy. He moved to New York City where he spent considerable time playing polo, racing hounds, and driving speedboats. During that time he also invested some $5 million in *PM*, an experimental newspaper that refused to carry advertisements. When he was 50 he received the last of his grandfather's inheritance, possibly $160 million. On Dec. 4, 1941, he started the *Chicago Sun*. At that time he said, "I am going to end the un-American morning monopoly now enjoyed by the *Chicago Tribune*." Some name-calling between the *Sun* and the *Tribune* followed, and for years the *Tribune* prevented the *Sun* from obtaining an Associated Press wire service. Years later, the Supreme Court ruled for the *Sun*, resulting in changes in the Associated Press rules for membership.

In 1948, Field bought the *Daily Times* for its printing plant. The next year, he merged it into the *Sun-Times* in an effort to cut heavy losses. He also expanded his operations into other areas, buying the Pocket Books and Simon and Schuster book firms and creating Field Enterprises, Inc., with its *World Book Encyclopedia* and *Parade*, the latter a picture weekly that sold for 5¢ on newsstands. He turned the newspapers over to his son in 1950.

Marshall Field IV (1916–1965) was more concerned with a profitable operation. Soon he had the *Sun-Times* in the black. He sold the book business and later sold *Parade* to John Hay Whitney for $10 million. The money was part of the $24 million used in 1959 to buy the *Daily News* from John S. Knight. He also created the Field Newspaper Syndicate.

After five years of training, Marshall Field V (1941– ) became the youngest publisher of a major United States newspaper at age 29. Before he stepped down in 1980, turning the publishing over to James Hoge, Field closed the *Daily News* after reported losses of $11 million annually. In 1983, the *Sun-Times* was sold to Rupert Murdoch.

**FISCHER, John** (1910–1978)

John Fischer started writing for *Harper's* magazine in 1944 and served as its editor from 1953, when he succeeded Frederick Lewis Allen, until 1967, when he was replaced by Willie Morris. He remained a contributing editor until 1978.

A journalism student in Oklahoma, Fischer worked summers on newspapers in Amarillo, Texas, and Carlsbad, New Mexico, with a year on the *Daily Oklahoman* in Oklahoma City before he went to Oxford as a Rhodes Scholar. He later worked as a United Press and Associated Press correspondent in Europe and in Washington.

From time to time he held federal appointments, including positions with the Department of Agriculture and a United Nations Relief and Rehabilitation Administration mission in the Ukraine. His articles about his visit to Russia later appeared in book form. At that time (1947), Fischer suggested we "speak firmly and carry a big stick in our relations with Russia."

In addition to his articles for *Harper's*, Fischer wrote for other magazines, including *Reader's Digest* and *Life*. His last and sixth book was *From the High Plains*, published in 1978; earlier books included *Why They Behave Like Russians; Master Plan, U.S.A.; The Stupidity Problem; Six in the Easy Chair*; and *Vital Signs, U.S.A.* He was also an aide to Adlai E. Stevenson in the 1952 campaign.

**FISCHETTI, John** (1916–1980)

For many years John Fischetti was the editorial cartoonist for the *Chicago Daily News*, with his work syndicated across America. After some work with Walt Disney on animated films, Fischetti joined the *Chicago Sun*. He also drew cartoons for *Esquire, Saturday Evening Post, Collier's*, and *Coronet*.

In 1950, Fischetti drew for the Newspaper Enterprise Association, moving to the *New York Herald Tribune* in 1962. Later, in Chicago, his cartoons were syndicated by the Publishers' Newspaper Syndicate.

Fischetti once said, "I blow off a lot of steam. Something happens and I think how awful it is or how good. The average person kicks the kid or throws the tricycle out of the driveway. I sit down and draw." Many of his cartoons were based on social satire, which he termed "serious comments in comic clothes."

Fischetti won a Pulitzer Prize in 1969 and on four occasions was named the Best Editorial Cartoonist by the National Cartoonists Society. He won awards from the American Civil Liberties Union and the New York Newspaper Guild, as well as two citations from Sigma Delta Chi. The John Fischetti Editorial Cartoon Competition has been established in his honor with $2,500 prizes for cartoons on current social and political subjects.

**FISHBEIN, Morris** (1889–1976)

Medical journalism placed Morris Fishbein in the limelight for many years. He was associated with several publications of the American Medical Association, especially the *Journal of the American Medical Association* (JAMA).

After completing his medical degree, Fishbein served on the *JAMA* staff from 1913 to 1949, eventually becoming its editor. He was also editor of *Hygeia* for many years and worked on *Post-graduate Medicine, Excerpta Medica, Medical World News*, and *Family Health* magazines.

Fishbein edited the medical section for the *Britannica Book of the Year* for more than three decades. He received honors from Italy, Cuba, Spain, the Netherlands, and Greece and was cited by President Harry Truman with the Certificate of Merit.

Fishbein wrote many books. Among his later ones are *Joseph Bolivar DeLee: Crusading Obstetrician; Handy Home Medical Adviser; Heart Care;*

*Modern Home Medical Adviser*; and his autobiography, *Morris Fishbein, M.D.* He edited *Modern Family Health Guide.*

**FITZPATRICK, Daniel Robert** (1891–1969)
With the exception of two years spent on the *Chicago Evening News*, 1911–13, Daniel Fitzpatrick spent his career on the *St. Louis Post-Dispatch* (Missouri), drawing editorial cartoons until his retirement in 1958.

During those years Fitzpatrick received the Pulitzer Prize for editorial cartoons in 1926 and in 1954. In 1924, he received the John Frederick Lewis prize for caricature. And in 1958, the University of Missouri honored him with its Journalism Medal.

**FLANAGAN, Alvin C.** (1915– )
A long career in broadcasting on the West Coast led to Alvin Flanagan's appointment as president of the Gannett Broadcasting Group. He directs seven television and thirteen radio stations, plus Gateway Productions.

Flanagan's early years included a two-year tour as a crew member of a Norwegian tanker, construction work on Boulder Dam, and a radio assignment with the U.S. Office of Education. After more radio training at the University of Florida, Flanagan worked briefly in Pittsburgh and New York before three years of World War II service in the Marine Corps.

When television was in its infancy in the late Forties, Flanagan became an independent packager of shows in Los Angeles, and soon was program manager for Don Lee Television. In 1948, he was station manager for KFMB-TV in San Diego. Two years later, he was program manager for ABC's television western division.

Other changes followed before Flanagan became president of Crosby-Brown Productions. Later he was president of Mullins Broadcasting Co., which merged in 1972 with Combined Communications Corp. of Phoenix, Arizona. In 1979, Combined was merged into Gannett and Flanagan acquired his present title.

Flanagan serves in an advisory capacity for the University of Colorado and The Wharton School. He has been active in many community projects. He once said broadcasting success comes from "pride and guts to produce the news and information programs that give you 'localism'—a reputation for being a real part of your own community."

**FLANAGAN, Dennis** (1919– )
Dennis Flanagan joined the staff of *Life* magazine in 1941. He remained there until 1947, when he became the managing editor of *Scientific American*. Three years later, he was editor and part owner of this publication, which is one of the oldest in the nation.

From 1977 to 1979, Flanagan was president of the American Society of Magazine Editors.

**FLEESON, Doris** ( ? –1970)
One of the pioneer women political reporters, Doris Fleeson first worked on the *Pittsburg Sun* (Kansas) in 1923. She later became the society editor

of the *Evanston News-Index* (Illinois) and city editor of the *Great Neck News* (Long Island, New York) before going to the *New York Daily News* in 1927.

Fleeson's political reporting began when she was assigned to the Albany Bureau. In 1933, she helped establish the American Newspaper Guild, which then sought a $35-a-week minimum pay for reporters.

Fleeson and her reporter-husband, John O'Donnell, moved to the *News'* Washington Bureau in 1933. She accompanied Franklin D. Roosevelt on his campaign tours. She left the *Daily News* in 1943 to become a war correspondent for the *Woman's Home Companion* in Europe.

After World War II, Fleeson wrote a column for the *Washington Star*, *Boston Globe* (Massachusetts), *Kansas City Star* (Missouri), *St. Louis Post-Dispatch* (Missouri) and *Chicago Daily News*. The column was eventually syndicated.

She won the New York Newspaper Women's Club award twice for outstanding reporting; Theta Sigma Phi gave her its Headliner Award, and in 1953, the University of Missouri awarded her its Journalism Medal. For "exceptionally meritorious work" she won the Raymond Clapper Award in 1954. The University of Kansas gave her its distinguished alumna citation.

Fleeson has said, "I think reporters need to use their legs always, and see the people and talk with the people."

**FLEISCHMANN Family**

Raoul Fleischmann (1885–1969) made *The New Yorker* possible by helping Harold Ross, its editor, keep the publication afloat in its early years. Fleischmann had been with the family bakery and related businesses from 1906 to 1925. He formed the F-R Publishing Co. in 1924 to handle *The New Yorker*.

Peter F. Fleischmann (1922– ) has been with *The New Yorker* since 1955, moving to the presidency in 1968 and the chairman of the board in 1969.

**FLEMING, Robert H.** (1912–1984)

Robert H. Fleming spent 35 years in the media world, working on newspapers, radio, and television stations before he turned to the federal government, where he once was deputy press secretary to President Lyndon Johnson.

Fleming began as a sports reporter for the *Madison Capital Times* (Wisconsin) while he was in college in 1931. From 1945 to 1953 he was a political reporter for the *Milwaukee Journal*. From 1953 to 1957 he was midwest bureau chief for *Newsweek* magazine. He turned to ABC as a correspondent in 1957; in 1961 he was the network's Washington Bureau chief. In 1966 he worked with President Johnson and two years later he was with the USIA. From 1969 to 1981 he worked for the House Select Committee on Crime.

The University of Wisconsin awarded him its Distinguished Service Award in 1959.

He served in the Army during World War II. He also was a Nieman Fellow at Harvard University.

**FLYNT, Larry Claxton** (1942– )
Keeping himself before the public has proved both successful and tragic for Larry Flynt, founder of *Hustler*, "a magazine that nobody quotes."

Prior to entering the publishing world Flynt worked in a Dayton General Motors factory.

During the presidency of Jimmy Carter, Flynt became a friend of Ruth Carter Stapleton and professed to being a "born-again Christian." He published articles in *Hustler* that pointed out the abuses parents were inflicting on their children. Later on, Flynt rejected his religious conversion.

Flynt founded the *Ohio* magazine and, since 1974, has published both *Hustler* and *Chic*. Between 1958 and 1964 he served in both the Army and Navy. He bought the *Los Angeles Free Press*, but then let it die.

In 1978 he was shot after testifying at an obscenity trial in the South. He has since been confined to a wheelchair.

**FORBES Family**
Bertie Forbes (1880–1954) reached New York from his native Scotland, by way of Africa, in 1904 with some newspaper experience. He worked for the *New York Journal of Commerce* and, later, the *Commercial and Financial Chronicle* before joining the *New York American* in 1911.

His own publication, *Forbes*, was established in 1917 as a "Magazine of Business." However, he continued to write a syndicated daily newspaper commentary that appeared in 50 publications until 1941. In his initial editorial in *Forbes*, he wrote: "Business was originated to produce happiness, not to pile up millions." During his career he also wrote eight books: *Finance, Business and the Business of Life; Men Who Are Making America; Forbes Epigrams; Men Who Are Making the West; Automotive Giants of America; How to Get the Most Out of Business; Little Bits About Big Men*; *499 Scottish Stories*. In 1948 he edited *America's Fifty Foremost Business Leaders*.

In recalling the early years, *Forbes'* 50th anniversary edition carried a profile of B.C., as he was called. He interviewed many of the business leaders of his era, including John D. Rockefeller and Frank Woolworth, which was unique for the times. He was critical of any businessman who would "grind employees and then donate a million dollars to perpetuate his name." The magazine experienced difficulties in the Thirties when two competitors, *Business Week* and *Fortune*, arrived.

Malcolm Forbes (1919– ) briefly published the *Fairfield Times* in Lancaster, Ohio, in the early Forties. After World War II service, when he was awarded the Bronze Star, Forbes joined the magazine in New York. He was its publisher and editor from 1954 to 1957. He has been publisher and editor-in-chief since 1957, and president since 1964.

Malcolm Forbes may be better known to the general public for his non-magazine activities. He took up ballooning in 1972 when he was 52. He has set several records in flights across America. Earlier, when he was 48, he took up motorcycling. Today he owns a New Jersey firm that is one of the largest cycle centers in the East.

Forbes is the sole owner of the magazine. He told a *Playboy* interviewer in 1979 that "our annual stockholder's meeting tends to be brief," and added that "money may be an immense facilitator, but it still comes down to your capacity to enjoy, to eat, to love, to read, to see, to feel. All those things are no greater for a rich man than for a poor man." He loves to discuss capitalism and refers to his magazine as "Capitalist Tool." He often is called the "happy millionaire." He published *The Sayings of Chairman Malcolm: The Capitalist's Handbook*, in 1978. Other books include *The Forbes Scrapbook of Thoughts on the Business of Life* and *Fact and Comment*.

To offset what he calls "spending money on trivia," Forbes, in 1982, gave $4 million to Princeton to honor his father. The family fortune has been estimated at $100 to $200 million, which includes the magazine, real estate, art, castles, and "collectibles."

**FOUHY, Edward Michael** (1934– )
After service in the Marine Corps in 1956–59, Edward Fouhy became a news writer with station WBZ-TV in Boston. By 1963 he was the news director.

Fouhy joined CBS News in 1966 and in 1978 he was the network's bureau chief in Washington. CBS moved him to New York City in 1981 as vice-president and director of news operations.

Between these tours with CBS, Fouhy was the producer of the NBC Nightly News, 1974–76. He became the network's bureau director for news in Washington the following year.

Fouhy won an Emmy award and the Drew Pearson Memorial Award in 1973.

**FRANK, Reuven** (1920– )
Between 1947 and 1950, Reuven Frank was a reporter and night city editor for the *Newark Evening News* (New Jersey). He joined the NBC news staff in 1950. In 1967, he was executive vice-president, and from 1968 to 1972 president, becoming the network's senior executive producer in 1972, a position he currently holds. During those years he was associated with many NBC shows, including the "Camel News Caravan," and "Huntley-Brinkley," as well as presidential conventions, campaigns, and inaugurations, and documentaries. His "The Tunnel," about East Berlin, was widely acclaimed.

Sigma Delta Chi cited his television news writing in 1955. He also has been given the Robert E. Sherwood Award, George Polk Award, and the Columbia University Journalism Alumni Award for distinguished service. He has six Emmy awards for best news programs and one Emmy for best documentary. In 1971, the University of Missouri awarded him its Journalism Medal, designating him the Broadcasting Man of the Year.

Frank was to step down in May 1984 as president of NBC News. After turning his attention to producing news programs, he was expected to retire after the 1984 presidential elections.

**FRANKEL, Max** (1930– )
Max Frankel has been associated with the *New York Times* since 1952, and,

from 1968 to 1973, he was the chief of the newspaper's Washington Bureau; he later spent three years as the Sunday editor.

Frankel has been editor of the *Times*' editorial page since 1977. He won a Pulitzer Prize in 1973 for international reporting.

**FREDERICK, Pauline** ( ? – )

In the mid-Thirties, Pauline Frederick was a reporter for *United States News*, covering the Department of State in Washington. She next worked for the North American Newspaper Alliance. With six years of writing experience, she moved to radio where she became the first woman to win the DuPont News Commentator Award.

Frederick worked for H.R. Baukhage in preparing scripts. He advised her to "stay away from radio. It doesn't like women." She did not, of course. She worked with NBC and continued with some newspaper work in Washington until 1945, when she became a war correspondent for North American Newspaper Alliance, covering the Nuremberg trial and other major events. The next year she joined ABC News and remained until 1953, when she rejoined NBC. She became well known for her interviews and for her program, "Pauline Frederick Reporting."

Frederick moderated the second Ford–Carter debate in 1976. In recent years, she has been an analyst for National Public Radio. Her many awards include the Theta Sigma Phi National Headliner title as Outstanding Woman in Radio. Several universities have recognized her work, including the University of Southern California, Pennsylvania, and Ohio. The University of Missouri awarded her its Journalism Medal.

**FRIEDHEIM, Jerry Warden** (1934– )

After newspaper work as a reporter and editor in Joplin and Columbia, Missouri, from 1956 to 1962, Jerry Friedheim taught at the University of Missouri for a year.

Friedheim's next "career" was political. He was an aide to Missouri Congressman Durward Hall for a year, and from 1963 to 1969, he was an assistant to Texas Senator John Tower. For the next three years, he was in the Department of Defense as assistant secretary for public affairs. Another year was spent with public and government affairs for AMTRAK.

Friedheim's current "career" started in 1975 when he became the vice-president and general manager for the American Newspaper Publishers Association and the ANPA Foundation. In this capacity, he maintains contacts with journalism schools, educators, and American newspapers. He also directs the association magazine, *Presstime*. Friedheim served in the Army from 1956 to 1958.

**FRIEDRICH, Otto** (1929– )

In 1983, *Time* magazine, the oldest of the nation's news weeklies, celebrated its 60th year. Assigned the task of reviewing more than 3,000 previous issues for this anniversary edition was Otto Friedrich, senior editor since 1971.

Friedrich began his career in newspaper work as a member of the *Stars & Stripes* staff. From 1953 to 1954, he worked for the United Press in Paris and London before joining the *New York Daily News* telegraph desk.

Friedrich's magazine career started in 1957, when he joined the foreign department of *Newsweek*. Five years later, he was the foreign editor for the *Saturday Evening Post*, where he remained untill 1971, moving to the managing editorship. He later wrote a definitive book on the *Post*'s struggle to survive, *The Decline and Fall*.

In 1970, he won the George Polk Memorial Award.

Friedrich wrote many books, some with his wife; some were for juvenile readers. These include *The Poor in Spirit*; *The Loner*; *Decline and Fall*; *The Rose Garden*; *Going Crazy*; *Clover*; *The Easter Bunny That Overslept*; *Clean Clarence*; *Sir Alva and the Wicked Wizard*; *The Marshmallow Ghosts*; *The Wishing Well in the Woods*; *Noah Shark's Ark*; *The Christmas Star*; *The April Umbrella*; and *The League of Unusual Animals*.

**FRIENDLY, Alfred** (1912–1983)

Alfred Friendly began his career in 1936 with the *Washington Daily News* and shifted to the *Washington Post* in 1939. He was managing editor of the *Post* from 1955 to 1965 and then he became a roving foreign correspondent, operating from London from 1967 to 1971, when he retired. He was succeeded by Ben Bradlee.

Howard Bray, in his *Post* history, writes that Friendly and Katharine Graham, the owner of the *Washington Post*, were almost like brother and sister. "He regarded her father, Eugene Meyer, as 'my spiritual godfather.'" Friendly had changed his name from "Rosenbaum," saying "It was hard enough to get in someone's door if you were a reporter. It was even harder if you had a Jewish name."

As the result of his front-line dispatches during the Arab-Israeli War for the *Post*, Friendly won the Pulitzer Prize in 1967.

Shortly before he took his life, apparently because he was suffering from cancer, Friendly created the International Free Press Development Fellowships program. It is financed through the Alfred Friendly Foundation, with the money he made with his *Post* stock. The Institute of International Education in Washington administers the program.

**FRIENDLY, Fred** (1915– )

A career that began in radio in 1937 won fame for Fred W. Friendly, who collaborated with Edward R. Murrow in several award-winning television documentaries and shows.

In 1938, Friendly was a radio announcer in Providence, where he utilized his interest in history to develop a series of biographies of famous personalities. In World War II, he won the Legion of Merit and other citations, participating in B-29 and P-61 flight missions.

Following the war, Friendly joined NBC for a quiz show, "Who Said That?" Friendly suggested to Murrow that they record the voices of the world's leaders. Their "Hear It Now" series won a Peabody citation in 1951.

The realistic "See It Now" show began in 1951 under Murrow–Friendly leadership. This show won the George Peabody Award and a Robert E. Sherwood television award of $20,000. It was on this program that many viewers believe Senator Joe McCarthy suffered his first setback.

Av Westin once wrote that "Friendly was a demanding boss, a stickler for good lighting who insisted that directors who worked for him spend time getting the polished effect that proper lighting can bring to a subject's face."

Friendly became the Edward R. Murrow Professor of Broadcasting at Columbia University. He has written several books, including the widely acclaimed *Minnesota Rag*. He also wrote *Due to Circumstances beyond Our Control* and *The Good Guys, the Bad Guys and the First Amendment*. For a number of years (1964–81), Friendly was advisor on communications at the Ford Foundation.

He was elected vice-president of the American Judicature Society, a national organization for improvement of the courts, in late 1983. This appointment permits Friendly to continue his study of the judicial system. He earlier originated and directed Media Law Seminars.

**FUERBRINGER, Otto** (1910– )

After serving as a reporter on his hometown *St. Louis Post-Dispatch* (Missouri) from 1932 to 1942, Otto Fuerbringer moved to New York as a writer for *Time* magazine.

Fuerbringer advanced to senior editor and, in 1960, to managing editor. From 1968 to 1975, he was vice-president of Time Inc. He was editor of the group's Magazine Development unit from 1972 to 1975, and since then became a consultant. Briefly (1977–79), he edited *Horizon* magazine.

Fuerbringer once said, "Television has had little effect on news magazines. There is some evidence that television helps the news magazine by whetting the appetite for more detailed and comprehensive coverage, especially of big events." Circulation and ad revenues of news magazines in recent years tend to support his views.

In W. A. Swanberg's *Luce and His Empire*, Fuerbringer was described as "the tall, crusty son of a Missouri Lutheran seminary official was a driver and a martinet. Both his toughness and Toryism were suggested by two of his many nicknames: the Iron Chancellor and Otto Fingerbanger."

Swanberg added that Fuerbringer considered the Vietnam War to be holy, agreeing with Luce and often changing *Time*'s correspondents' copy "to conform to the Luce–Fuerbringer–Pentagon win-the-war line."

**FULLER, (Edwin) Keith** (1923– )

Keith Fuller retired in 1984 after long service as the president and general manager of the Associated Press (AP), the world's largest newsgathering organization.

Fuller, in 1940, began as a cub reporter on the *Beaumont Enterprise* (Texas) at $13.50 a week. Fuller later joined the *Dallas Morning News* (Texas ) in 1947 as a reporter and, two years later, was with the AP. For several years he worked in Mississippi, Texas, New Mexico, Arkansas, and Colorado, holding positions from correspondent to bureau chief.

In 1960, Fuller joined the New York AP office as a general executive. From 1964 to 1972, he was assistant general manager before advancing to vice-president and deputy general manager and finally to his current position.

One of Fuller's early tasks was as supervisory editor of the AP book, *The Torch Is Passed*, which covered the death of President John F. Kennedy. During World War II, he served in the Air Force in Germany and was a prisoner of war.

**FUOSS, Robert** (1912–1980)
During most of his journalistic career, Robert Fuoss was associated with either the *Saturday Evening Post* or the *Reader's Digest*.

From 1942 to 1945, Fuoss was managing editor of the *Saturday Evening Post*. He was executive editor, 1956–61, and editor-in-chief, 1961–62. For a year, 1964–65, he was a senior editor with the *Reader's Digest*.

For two years (1962–64), Fuoss was vice-president in charge of public relations for the Federated Department Stores, Inc. In 1961, he received the Overseas Press Club distinguished service award.

**FURNAS, Joseph Chamberlain** (1905– )
"—And Sudden Death" became one of the most widely-read articles ever to appear in *Reader's Digest*. Written by J. C. Furnas, it was to be "a short, hard-hitting article which would dramatize the necessity of safe driving." *Reader's Digest* publisher DeWitt Wallace in 1935 wanted to "shock the country into realization of the thousands of highway tragedies, many of them due to reckless or careless driving."

Proofs of Furnas's article were sent to five thousand newspapers, offering them the right to reprint after it appeared in *Reader's Digest*. Within three months the magazine's reprints appeared, with thousands of copies distributed through companies, clubs, and other groups.

Furnas's career, however, is reflected in his many books, including *The Prophet's Chamber*; *Many People Prize It*; *So You're Going to Stop Smoking*; *Anatomy of Paradise*; *Voyage to Windwood: The Life of Robert Louis Stevenson*; *How America Lives* (with the editorial staff of the *Ladies' Home Journal*); *Goodbye to Uncle Tom*; *The Road to Harpers Ferry*; *The Devil's Rainbow*; *The Life and Times of the Late Demon Rum*; *Lightfoot Island*; *The Americans*; *Great Times*; *Stormy Weather* and *Fanny Kemble*.

Furnas won the Anisfield-Wolff award for non-fiction, and the George Freedley award.

**GAINES, William Maxwell** (1922– )
*MAD* magazine, begun in 1952, is unique in American publishing. Alfred E. Neuman, *MAD*'s patron saint, is better known than his creator and publisher, William Gaines. Gaines' father, Max Gaines, started Educa-

tional Comics and also developed the concept of putting newspaper comic strips together into books.

Young Gaines started *MAD* as a comic book with Alfred E. Neuman the symbol, using his slogan, "What, me worry?" Neuman has been described as a "lop-headed, jug-eared, gap-tooth idiot boy."

Gaines' magazine circulation reached 2.3 million in the mid-1970s. However, in recent years it has been closer to 1 million. It has published many parodies, including ones on the *Wall Street Journal*, the *National Enquirer*, and *The Runner's Book*.

Gaines once said that "when Nixon came along we had something to work with," but Reagan "is so personally likable that he's hard to hate." Gaines was once described as "a 265-pound eccentric who hates neckties, loves King Kong and has shoulder-length hair and a full beard, created an undercurrent of mistrust and skepticism among teenagers in the '60s and '70s."

*MAD* is now owned by Warner Communications.

**GALLAGHER, James Wes** (1911– )

Wes Gallagher and the Associated Press formed a successful team for nearly four decades. After working as a reporter in 1935 on the *Baton Rouge State Times* (Louisiana), Gallagher joined the *Rochester Democrat and Chronicle* staff later that year.

In 1937, Gallagher began his career with the Associated Press in Buffalo. Two years later he went to Albany en route to New York City. By 1940 he was a foreign correspondent for the wire service, working in Africa and Europe. Historian Michael Emery called Gallagher "AP's leading World War II war correspondent and postwar foreign bureau chief."

Gallagher became the AP acting chief in 1945 and six years later its general executive. In 1954 he was assistant manager and from 1972 to 1976 he was president. In 1976 he became a director for the Gannett Company. Since his retirement to California he has been active with the Santa Barbara Boys' Club, serving as president for several years.

Among his honors are the William Allen White, the George Polk, Carr Van Anda, and John Peter Zenger awards. The University of Missouri School of Journalism awarded him its medal in 1976. In 1945 he was selected by the U.S. Chamber of Commerce as one of the Outstanding Young Men in the nation.

He has written one book, *Back Door to Berlin*.

**GALLO, William Victor** (1922– )

From 1969 to 1973, William Gallo was named the best sports cartoonist by the National Cartoonist Society.

Gallo joined the *New York Daily News* in 1941 and became the newspaper's sports cartoonist in 1960. His cartoons are represented in the Baseball Hall of Fame in Cooperstown. He has been president of the New York Boxing Writers and the National Cartoonists Society. The New York Newspaper Guild has given Gallo nine Page One awards.

**GALLUP Family**
The Gallup Survey probably is the best-known such study to reach the American public. George Gallup (1901–1984) established his American Institute of Public Opinion in 1935. He developed the concept while teaching journalism at Drake, Northwestern, and Columbia universities.

Gallup turned his Iowa doctoral dissertation into a career. He offered "A New Technique for Objective Methods for Measuring Reader Interest in Newspapers." His methods were originally tested on newspapers in Des Moines, Cleveland, and St. Louis.

From 1932 to 1947, Gallup worked in research for the Young and Rubicam advertising agency. After he started his surveys, his results were syndicated to newspapers across America. In recent years, they have been collected in books.

Gallup was the founder of the Quill and Scroll Society for high school journalists. He has been named to the Hall of Fame in Distribution and the Market Research Hall of Fame. Many other groups have recognized his work, including Sigma Delta Chi, Sigma Xi, the National Press Club, the National Municipal League, and the American Marketing Association.

George H. Gallup III (1930– ) became president of the Gallup Poll in 1963. He has been active in professional and other associations.

**GANNETT, Frank Ernest** (1876–1957)
Today the Gannett Group is one of the leading media corporations in America. However, few individuals are aware of its origin.

Frank Gannett, who spent his life in New York State, was editor and manager of the *Ithaca Daily News* at the turn of the century. He expanded his operations and eventually owned newspapers in Elmira, Rochester, Albany, Utica, Newburgh, Ogdenburg, Saratoga Springs, Olean, and Niagara Falls in New York. He also owned newspapers outside of New York, in Pittsburgh, Pennsylvania, Plainfield, New Jersey, and Hartford, Connecticut.

Gannett was also a promoter of the Teletypesetter, long since replaced by the computerized cold-type operation in the back shops.

Gannett has been given awards by the Catholic War Veterans, the Veterans of Foreign Wars, and others, along with several professional groups. The president of the New York State Publishers' Association from 1921 to 1927, he once headed the New York Associated Dailies.

Gannett established the Frank E. Gannett Newspaper Foundation, Inc., which continues to operate. He also wrote three books, *Britain Sees It Through 1944*, *The Fuse Sputters in Europe*, and *Winging Around the World.*

**GARNER, William Simpson** (1935– )
William Garner served in the Army, with three years as cartoonist and illustrator for the *Pacific Stars & Stripes* in Tokyo. After working for a Texas advertising agency, he spent 13 years with the *Star* in Washington. He returned to Washington in 1983, joining the *Washington Times*, after six years as editorial cartoonist for the *Memphis Commercial Appeal* (Tennes-

see). While in Memphis, he won a National Headliner Award for "consistently outstanding editorial cartoons." His cartoons are syndicated nationally.

A painter, Garner has had his work shown in several galleries.

**GARRETT, Wilber E. "Bill"** (1930- )

Bill Garrett got his start in photography when, as a child, he mowed the lawn of a retired school principal, who gave him an old Eastman folding camera. He then "started shooting pictures of my relatives and friends and events in the neighborhood."

Beginning as a photographer for Hallmark Greeting Card Co. in his native Kansas City, Bill Garrett continued his career as a photographer in the Navy during the Korean War.

When Gilbert Hovey Grosvenor was honored with a Journalism Medal by the University of Missouri for the *National Geographic* he met Garrett, then completing his journalism degree work there, and offered him a position in Washington. Garrett joined the *National Geographic* in 1954 as picture editor. Today he is editor of the magazine, and twenty-five years later, he has received a similar medal from his alma mater.

Garrett's other awards include the Magazine Photographer of the Year in 1968; the Joseph A. Sprague Memorial Award in 1967; and the Newhouse Citation, from Syracuse University, in 1963; the Overseas Press Club and the White House Press Association have also honored him. Garrett lectures at seminars and at workshops, and obviously, is no deskbound editor.

"It's never dull working with Bill. He's always pushing for new approaches in photography, realistic approaches. And he's terribly committed to journalism," according to a *National Geographic* colleague, Thomas R. Smith.

**GAYLORD Family**

Edward K. Gaylord (1873–1973) operated the *Oklahoma City Daily Oklahoman* from 1903 until his death at the age of 101.

His son, Edward Gaylord (1919- ) now directs the operation of the Gaylord Broadcasting Co., Mistletoe Express Service, Oklahoma Publishing Co., Gayno Inc., Gaylord Production Co., a coal firm, and a ranch.

Edward L. Gaylord, chairman of Oklahoma Publishing Co., Oklahoma City, was chosen by the American Academy of Achievement as one of the 1984 "giants of accomplishment" to receive the Golden Plate Award, according to *Editor & Publisher* magazine.

Gaylord serves on many boards and, for a decade, was a leader in the work of the Oklahoma State Fair. He is also on the board of the National Cowboy Hall of Fame and Western Heritage Center. He has been named to the Oklahoma Hall of Fame.

The Gaylord media and real estate holdings have been estimated to be worth from $200 to $300 million. Included are newspapers, television and radio stations, and other operations.

**GELB, Leslie Howard** (1937– )
Before becoming a *New York Times* correspondent in Washington in 1973, Leslie Gelb held a number of jobs. From 1962 to 1965, he was a teacher, and he then spent 1966–67 working with Senator Jacob K. Javits.

Gelb, in 1967–68, was with the Defense Department before moving to the Brookings Institute where he remained until he became a newspaperman. In 1977–79, he represented the *Times* in the State Department.

Gelb moved to the Carnegie Endowment for International Peace program before going back to the *Times* in 1981 as its national security correspondent.

Gelb won the Woodrow Wilson Award in 1980. He wrote *The Irony of Vietnam: The System Worked.*

**GERMOND, Jack W.** (1928– )
For more than 30 years, Jack Germond has been a reporter, with his major emphasis on national politics in Washington. And since 1977, he and Jules Witcover have covered the national scene in their syndicated newspaper column.

Germond worked for Gannett Newspapers for twenty years, four as the chief of the Washington Bureau. In 1974, he joined the *Washington Star* and in 1981 became a columnist with the *Baltimore Evening Sun* (Maryland). He appears frequently on televised panel shows. He and Witcover wrote *Blue Smoke & Mirrors.* In addition, he has written articles that have appeared in the *New York Times Magazine* and other publications.

**GEYELIN, Philip Laussat** (1923–1979)
Joining the Washington Bureau of the Associated Press in 1946, Philip L. Geyelin built his career on the *Wall Street Journal* and the *Washington Post* and as a syndicated columnist.

He received a Pulitzer Prize for editorial writing in 1970. *Time* once called him the best editorial writer of his day. He was a staffer and diplomatic correspondent for the *Wall Street Journal* (New York) from 1947 to 1967. He then joined the *Washington Post*'s editorial staff. He and Ben Bradlee had been friends for years, and Bradlee had tried to hire him earlier.

According to *Post* historian Chalmers Roberts, "Geyelin's prescription for reasoned editorials sometimes left readers uncertain. The prime examples were editorials before presidential elections." Geyelin explained: "We did not exactly endorse and we did not exactly not endorse. We added things up on both sides of the ledger and then declined to offer a bottom line."

Geyelin served in the Marine Corps from 1943 to 1946.

**GEYER, Georgia Anne** (1935– )
For more than 20 years, Georgia Geyer earned her credentials as a foreign correspondent, after beginning as a reporter on the *Southtown Economist* in Chicago in 1958.

The next year she moved to the *Chicago Daily News* and in 1964 became the newspaper's Latin American correspondent; from 1967 to 1975, she was its roving foreign correspondent and columnist. From 1975 to 1980, her column was syndicated through the Los Angeles Times Syndicate. Since 1980, she has been with the Universal Press Syndicate.

In her 1983 autobiography, *Buying the Night Flight*, Geyer recalled her early years and her interviews with the world's leaders. She wrote, "With only a few exceptions they tend to be egomanics; they issue tiresome pronouncements."

Geyer has won awards from the American Newspaper Guild, the Press Editors Association, the Overseas Press Club, and the National Council of Jewish Women. She also won Theta Sigma Phi's National Headliner Award. Northwestern University gave her its alumni award and Columbia University its Maria Moors Cabot honor.

She has written other books: *The New Latins*, *The New 100 Years War*, and *The Young Russians*. She has written for the *Atlantic*, *The Nation*, *The Progressive*, *New Republic*, and others.

In reflecting on her 25 years in journalism, Geyer wrote two columns on her career. She asked: "What do Americans want in the world? That's the question that I still cannot answer."

**GIALANELLA, Philip T.** (1930– )
A career of more than two decades in publishing has made Philip Gialanella the publisher of the *Honolulu Star-Bulletin*. He is also president of the Hawaii Newspaper Agency and the Gannett Pacific Newspaper Group.

Gialanella's career began with Gannett in 1957 as promotion director of the *Binghamton Evening Press* (New York) and WINR-TV. He later was vice-president and general manager of the *Dover Daily Advance* (Delaware) and the *Hartford Times* (Connecticut).

In 1970, Gialanella was president-publisher of the *Newburgh News* (New York). The next year, he was in Hawaii, beginning his climb upward.

In Hawaii, Gialanella works closely with the United Way, the Symphony Society, and the Boys Choir. He is a member of the Board of the Pacific and Asian Affairs Council.

**GIFFORD, Frank Newton** (1930– )
A long football career (1952–63) with the New York Giants made Frank Gifford well known in the sports world. After leaving football, Gifford became a sports announcer on radio and television. From 1967 to 1969 he was with CBS Radio in New York. For several years, he was a pre-game host for CBS and, in 1971, he joined the ABC Network, where he continues today.

In addition to the honors he received for his career in football, Gifford has received the Gil Hodges Memorial sports award, an Emmy award for outstanding sports personality, and other citations. He has written *Frank Gifford's NFL-AFL Football Guide*; *Frank Gifford's Football Guide Book*; and, with Charles Mangel, *Gifford on Coverage*.

**GILL, Brendan** (1914– )
In 1936, Brendan Gill became a contributor to *The New Yorker*. In 1960, he became the magazine's film critic and, in 1968, the magazine's drama critic.

In New York, Gill is associated with the Institute for Art and Urban Resources, the Landmarks Conservancy, the Commission on Cultural Affairs, the Whitney Museum of American Art, Pratt Institute, and other groups.

Gill has written a number of books since his first, *Death in April*, appeared in 1950. During the 50th anniversary of *The New Yorker*, Gill, in 1975, wrote *Here at The New Yorker*, which related highlights of his association with this publication. Nora Ephron, writing in her *Scribble Scribble*, termed it "one of the most offensive books I have read in a long time." In 1980, Gill published *The Dream Come True* and *Wooings*. Gill also has written *The Trouble of One House*; *The Day the Money Stopped*; *Cole*; *Tallulah*; *Happy Times*; and *Ways of Loving*.

**GILLESPIE, Marcia Ann** (1944?– )
During the first decade (1970–80) of *Essence*'s life, Marcia Ann Gillespie was the magazine's editor, beginning as the managing editor, and becoming the editor a year later, at age 26. In 1982, she was named one of the Outstanding Women in Communications.

Gillespie considers *Essence* a "magazine for today's Black women." According to a *Folio* article, Gillespie "has transformed it from an undefined fledging publication into the fastest growing women's magazine in the country."

She said, "I had wanted to combat the negative imagery which for centuries had been foisted on Blacks. . . . I didn't want little Black girls growing up as I had thinking only white women were beautiful." Gillespie told University of Missouri journalism students that *Essence* was "the first of the new breed of Black magazines in the '70s," although it had roots in the late 1960s Black power movement. The magazine was designed to "shock" readers.

*Essence* won a National Magazine Award in 1975 for fiction.

**GILMER, Elizabeth Meriwether** (1870–1951)
See DIX, Dorothy.

**GINGRICH, Arnold** (1903–1976)
When Arnold Gingrich died, it was reported that "he developed from scratch what it took others generations to acquire—a totally aristocratic outlook and mode of living."

Gingrich was editor of *Esquire* from 1933 to 1945 and returned later to be publisher, senior vice-president, and editor-in-chief of that magazine, as well as *Gentleman's Quarterly*, until his death.

For decades, Gingrich's name was synonymous with *Esquire*. As one of its founding fathers, he worked with David Smart and William Weintraub. From the beginning Gingrich attracted leading writers to the publication, especially his fishing buddy, Ernest Hemingway. Gingrich was also responsible for acquiring E. Simms Campbell's cartoons after meeting the Black youth in his home in Harlem. Campbell's cartoons appeared in every issue from that time until his death. He also created the magazine's symbol, Colonel Blimp, or "Esky."

Gingrich paid Hemingway $200 for first-edition short stories. By using Hemingway, he was able to lure other noted writers to *Esquire*. A controversial editor, his last controversy involved a lengthy article by Harrison Salisbury, which was sponsored by the Xerox Corporation. Some competitors attacked the practice of a corporation paying for a magazine article, but Gingrich said, "I feel proud of our author, and for that matter proud of our sponsor, and by no means ashamed of ourselves."

Gingrich wrote articles and many books. These include *A Thousand Mornings of Music; Nothing but People: The Early Days at Esquire; The Joys of Trout; The Fishing in Print; Cast Down the Laurel; The Well-Tempered Angler; Toys of a Lifetime*; and *Business and the Arts*.

**GINN, John Charles** (1937- )

John Ginn, now a publisher and newspaper executive, began as a reporter on the *Charlotte Observer* (North Carolina) in 1959. He moved to the *Kingsport Times-News* (Tennessee) in 1963 as editor, but returned the next year to Charlotte as editor of the *News*, a position he held until 1969.

Ginn was director of corporate development for the *Des Moines Register and Tribune* (Iowa), 1972–73, but returned to the South to edit and publish the *Jackson Sun* (Tennessee) for a year before taking his current position as president and publisher of the *Anderson Independent and Daily Mail* (South Carolina).

Ginn has predicted that newspapers in 1990 will put "more emphasis on meeting the information need of our readers. Readers want more news about subjects like health and nutrition, medical science, human interest occurrence, home maintenance, repairs, religion, hobbies, free-time activities, home furnishing and decoration, personal finance, recipes and hunting and fishing."

Ginn, a member of the Pulitzer Prize jury, has lectured frequently before professional groups. He has received awards for the best editorials from the Tennessee Press Association in 1964, 1973, and 1974.

In Anderson, Ginn has been active in civic affairs, working with the Chamber of Commerce, Anderson College, and the YMCA. He also serves as a vice-president for Harte-Hanks Communications, Inc. and president of the Century Group of Harte-Hanks. He served in the Air Force from 1959 to 1961.

**GLASER, Milton** (1929- )

One of the better-known graphic artists in the magazine field, Milton Glaser is associated with Clay Felker for their new and redesigned publications.

*Newsweek* called him "one of the true geniuses in the image-making trade." For many years, between 1954 and 1974, he was president of the Push Pin Studios in New York City, which produced a variety of objects.

Glaser, in 1973, redesigned *Paris Match* magazine as an overnight assignment. He has also taught at the School of Visual Arts and Cooper Union.

Glaser, once a Fulbright scholar in Italy, has worked in designing since the early Fifties. He was a co-founder of *New York* magazine and served in several executive capacities there from 1968 to 1977. In addition, he was vice-president and design director of the *Village Voice* for several years.

In 1977, he started Milton Glaser, Inc. Since 1972, he has been associated with the International Design Conference in Aspen, Colorado.

Cooper Union, where Glaser studied from 1948 to 1951, awarded him its St. Gauden's Medal in 1972, the same year he won the American Institute of Graphic Arts Gold Medal. He has been named to the Art Directors Club Hall of Fame.

Glaser designed the observation deck of the World Trade Center Twin Towers in New York City. He has also designed record album covers, book jackets, posters, and other projects.

He wrote *Milton Glaser: Graphic Designer* and *The Milton Glaser Poster Book* and co-authored *If Apples Had Teeth* and *The Underground Gourmet.*

**GOLDBERG, Reuben Lucius** (1883–1970)

"Rube" Goldberg's cartoons became well known to newspaper readers in the period between 1921 and 1964. Later, he became a sculptor, with a one-man show at the Smithsonian Institution in 1970.

Goldberg was first a sports cartoonist for the *San Francisco Chronicle* and then the *Bulletin* between 1904 and 1907. He moved to the *New York Evening Mail*, where he remained until 1921. At that time, his cartoons were syndicated across the nation. He halted these in 1964 to spend the rest of his life sculpting.

Many of his early cartoons featured "inventions" and contraptions that added his name to our vocabulary. As comics' historian Jerry Robinson wrote, "A 'Rube Goldberg' contraption has become part of the American vocabulary. Goldberg was a social satirist." He won a Pulitzer Prize in 1948 and the Reuben award in 1968; this award was named for him by the National Cartoonist Society, a group he helped establish.

Goldberg created such characters as Boob McNutt and Mike and Ike. He also created a series, "Foolish Questions," featuring such questions as "Have an accident?" The answer: "No, thanks, just had one."

Goldberg wrote *Soup to Nuts; Rube Goldberg's Guide to Europe; How to Remove Cotton from a Bottle of Aspirin; I Made My Bed*; and *Rube Goldberg vs. The Machine Age.*

**GOLDEN, Harry** (1902–1981)

As the founder and editor of the *Carolina Israelite* newspaper and author of such bestsellers as *Only in America* and *For 2 Cents Plain*, Harry Golden was inducted posthumously into the North Carolina Journalism Hall of Fame in 1983.

Golden was with the *New York Post* and *Mirror* before he started the *Carolina Israelite* in 1942 in Charlotte. It had become famous around the nation before Golden halted publication in 1968.

Golden's satiric proposals to end segregation in the South were partially responsible for this recognition. For example, his "Golden Vertical Negro Plan," in 1956, eliminated all seats in schools, forcing everyone to stand. He believed "Southerners seemed to object only to sitting, not standing, beside Negroes."

Three groups named him Man of the Year, including Carver College, Johnson C. Smith College, and Temple Emanu-EL, in New York. His last book, published in 1974, was *Long Live Columbus*. Other books included *Enjoy, Enjoy*; *Carl Sandburg*; *You're Entitle*; *Forgotten Pioneer*; *Mr. Kennedy and the Negroes*; *So What Else is New*; *A Little Girl Is Dead*; *Eat, Eat My Child*; *The Lynching of Leo Frank*; *The Right Time*; *So Long as You're Healthy*; *The Israelis*; *The Greatest Jewish City in the World*; *Golden Book of Jewish Humor*; and *The Southern Landsman*.

**GOLDENSON, Leonard H.** (1905– )
After practicing law for several years in the early Thirties, Leonard Goldenson worked for Paramount Pictures in New York until 1952. He held several positions, including that of chairman and president of United Paramount Theatres, Inc. He became involved with television in 1939, through one of Paramount's operations in Chicago.

Goldenson's major contribution to the media came in 1953, when he put together what is known today as the ABC Network. It was first named American Broadcasting-Paramount Theatres, Inc. When opponents claimed there was no need for a third network, Goldenson disagreed and started a series of innovations, such as being the first network to sell individual minutes to advertisers rather than requiring them to sponsor an entire show.

Early in the network's history, Goldenson obtained Walt Disney shows and eventually ABC picked up millions of viewers for its Mickey Mouse Club shows.

Thirty years later, in 1983, Goldenson was quoted in the *Washington Post* as saying, "It's fighting against all odds that made ABC what it is today," and Frederick Pierce, now ABC president, added: "We were the last ones into the ball game and had no choice other than to establish one area at a time by being different and innovative."

Goldenson founded the United Cerebral Palsy Association in 1946. He works for other groups, too, such as the Children's Cancer Research Foundation in Boston, Will Rogers Memorial Hospital, the Jacob Geriatric Center, and the World Rehabilitation Fund.

**GOODMAN, Ellen Holtz** (1941– )
A winner of the Pulitzer Prize for commentary in 1980, Ellen Goodman has been a syndicated columnist for the Washington Post Writers Group since 1976.

From time to time, Goodman appears on television shows as a commentator. She began her career as a researcher and reporter for *Newsweek* (New York) from 1963 to 1965. For the next two years, she was a feature writer for the *Detroit Free Press* (Michigan). Goodman moved to the *Boston*

*Globe* (Massachusetts) in 1967 as a feature writer and columnist. She still writes from there, with her syndicated column appearing across the nation in nearly 400 papers.

In mid-1984 she said, "Things keep changing and things keep happening. I never really run out of ideas. I guess as long as I'm interested, I'll be interesting."

In addition to her Pulitzer, Goodman was named New England Newspaper Woman of the Year in 1968. She has also been honored as Columnist of the Year by the New England Women's Press Association. She has written one book, *Close to Home.*

**GORKIN, Jess C.** (1913– )
For almost 30 years (1949–78), Jess Gorkin was editor of *Parade*, a Sunday newspaper supplement, retiring from that position in 1978. According to journalism historian Ernest C. Hynds, "Gorkin contends that *Parade* has changed the Sunday magazine field from an entertainment device and filler to a vehicle for serious and meaningful news."

Since 1979, Gorkin has been editor of *50 Plus.* He wrote that "the derogatory stereotype of 'old geezers' and 'old biddies' is beginning to be replaced by a truer image of the enormous diversity among today's older Americans."

During his early career Gorkin was associate editor of *Look*, 1937–41. He was also with the Office of War Information, 1942–46, before he joined *Parade* as managing editor in 1947. Gorkin won the Christopher Award in 1956 and citations from the Overseas Press Club and the American Legion.

**GOROG, William** (1925?– )
President of the Magazine Publishers Association (MPA) since late 1982, William Gorog has been termed a "business-oriented chief executive who lives, travels, thinks, and consorts with other top businessmen." According to an interview in *Folio* magazine, Gorog came to his new position without any magazine experience, thus with an "unprejudiced approach to the MPA and its challenge."

Gorog served in the Korean War, after training as an engineer at West Point. Before accepting the MPA presidency, Gorog was the chief operating officer of the Bulova Watch Co. He was a co-founder of Data Corporation, which, in 1969, merged with the Mead Corporation. He also worked with President Gerald Ford on the Economic Policy Board.

Gorog looks upon his MPA presidency as involving a three-sided project: education, technology, and government. When he took the new position he said he was joining "the right industry at the right time."

**GOULD, Chester** (1900– )
"Dick Tracy" is one of America's oldest and best-known comic strips, and combines crime and adventure. Chester Gould, its creator, started young, winning a $5 prize in a cartoon contest when he was 12 years old. This sparked an ambition to be a cartoonist.

After college, Gould went to Chicago in 1921 and worked on many newspapers, including the *Journal*, *Herald Examiner*, *American*, and *Daily News*, meanwhile always trying to sell his comic ideas.

In 1931, Gould created "Plainsclothes Tracy." Joseph M. Patterson, co-publisher of the *Chicago Tribune* and the *New York Daily News*, changed the title to "Dick Tracy," a slang term for detective. Early on, the strip often upset editors and readers with its violence.

Some of Gould's more famous subjects have earned their place in history, however; they include Flyface, Pruneface, Flattop, Mumbles, the Mole, and especially B.O. Plenty and his family.

Gould told a *Wall Street Journal* reporter in 1974 that "the only reason a comic strip gets in the paper is that it helps to sell newspapers. I've tried to make people want to see tomorrow's paper. They may not like Gould but I want them to say, 'How's that crazy bastard gonna end it?' "

In 1974 Gould hired Rich Fletcher as his drawing assistant, although he seldom vacations, claiming he is always fighting deadlines. There are still some problems with such a comic, since a television show can tell a story in 30 minutes, whereas "Dick Tracy" takes 13 weeks to complete a story.

Gould has won recognition from the Police Athletic League and the Associated Police Communications Officers. He won a Reuben Award in 1959, and his work has been displayed in the Smithsonian Institution.

**GRAHAM, Donald Edward** (1945– )
Donald Graham joined the *Washington Post* in 1971. He served as assistant managing editor for sports, assistant general manager, executive vice-president and general manager and, since 1979, publisher.

**GRAHAM, Fred Patterson** (1931– )
Combining a career as a lawyer and a broadcaster, Fred Graham now is heard by millions on the CBS News from Washington, where he has been stationed since 1972.

Graham studied law at Vanderbilt and Oxford and practiced in Nashville, Tennessee before he became the chief counsel on the Subcommittee on Constitutional Amendments for the U.S. Senate in 1963. For the next two years, he worked for the assistant secretary of labor, and in 1965, he entered journalism as the Supreme Court correspondent for the *New York Times*, remaining with the newspaper until he joined CBS.

Graham received the George Foster Peabody Award in 1975. He has received three Emmy awards for his broadcasting activities. A trustee for the Reporters Committee for Freedom of the Press, he has written three books, *The Self-Inflicted Wound*, *Press Freedom Under Pressure* and *Alias Program*. He served in the Marine Corps from 1953 to 1956.

**GRAHAM, Katharine Meyer** (1917– )
Katharine Meyer Graham has been described as one of the most powerful women in America, primarily because of her ownership of the *Washington Post* and *Newsweek*. Born in New York City, Katharine Meyer attended

Vassar and, in 1938, graduated from the University of Chicago. During her college years she worked briefly as a newspaper reporter. In 1940, she married Phil Graham.

Her father, Eugene Meyer, acquired the *Post* in 1933 for $825,000 at auction. Control of the newspaper passed to Phil Graham in 1948. However, Graham, a manic-depressive, committed suicide in 1963, placing his widow in control. She once said her "credentials were pathetically thin" when this occurred.

Anecdotes usually picture Katharine Graham as a shy, modest person, well known in Washington, but little known outside the city. Early she avoided personal confrontations when possible. Later Chalmers Roberts wrote, "she finally mastered speechmaking" and "became as adept as her father and husband in dealing with those in the business world who thought her newspaper too liberal."

With her policy of backing her editors, Katharine Graham gave her newspaper the chance to expose Watergate. Caroline Bird credits her with a "brilliant performance" in this episode, feeling she handled Watergate better than her husband might have. Phil was thought to have been "too politically involved."

Katharine Graham gained national recognition along with the *Post.* James Reston said the *Post* is now "an immensely better paper than it was when she took over." Her media colleagues elected her the first woman director and later the first woman president of the American Newspaper Publishers Association. She has demonstrated, in practice, her father's belief that "a newspaper should serve the conscience of its community" while extending the *Post*'s influence well beyond Washington.

The *Post* organization acquired *Newsweek* in 1961. She contributed $20,000 to help found *Ms.* magazine. Although the *Post*'s operations now are handled by her son, Katharine Graham is still an influence. She and her newspaper have won numerous awards and citations, acknowledging their leadership in the newspaper world.

**GRAHAM, Philip** (1915–1963)

Early in his life, Philip Graham was a law secretary to Justice Stanley Reed and, later, Justice Felix Frankfurter. Later he became the publisher and president of the *Washington Post.* During World War II he served in the Air Force, rising from private to major and winning a Legion of Merit.

According to historian Dana Thomas, "Graham resented the fact that he had achieved his position as publisher by marriage, and he tried feverishly to prove himself on his own." Alfred Friendly, the *Post*'s managing editor, once said Graham "could out-sleuth the paper's star reporters, out-think its sagest pundits, out-wit its most genial spoofers, and out-write its fanciest—or most fancied stylists." He was said to have had "a natural affinity with writers and editors." He was a close personal friend of John F. Kennedy.

Graham joined the *Post* after World War II as associate publisher and took over as publisher and president in 1961. A manic-depressive, he took his own life in 1963.

**GRAUE, Fremont David** (1926– )
"Alley Oop" was created by V.T. Hamlin and taken over by Fremont Graue, an assistant to Hamlin for 23 years, in 1973. "Alley Oop" celebrated its 50th anniversary in 1983.

Oop, the story of a caveman and his girlfriend, Oola, appears in more than 700 newspapers. As Graue recalls, Hamlin "was a history buff and tremendously interested in paleontology and prehistoric things. He did a great deal of research before doing a strip. I maintain the tradition of keeping things that appear in the strip as accurate as I can."

The strip's gimmick is a time machine, whereby Graue "can push the characters around through various places in time," thus permitting him to keep Oop up-to-date. Graue's career has been with Oop, except for a brief period in the *Pittsburgh Post-Gazette* art department.

**GRAUER, Ben** (1908–1977)
For many years, New Year's Eve, Times Square, and Ben Grauer were a team. Millions of Americans waited for Grauer to announce the New Year on his television show. Long before this assignment, however, Grauer had established himself in the media.

For a decade (1915–25) Grauer was in motion pictures and the theater. In 1930, he joined NBC, where he remained until 1973. During that time he covered many special events, such as the Olympics, political conventions and inaugurations, conferences, and wars. For example, he covered the NBC Symphony under Toscanini from 1940 to 1954.

Grauer was an announcer, commentator, host, narrator, and a co-producer for NBC. He won the George Sandham Prize from the College of the City of New York in 1930 and a Peabody Award for convention-election coverage in 1972. A Ben Grauer scholarship has been established at the Columbia University School of Journalism.

Grauer wrote *March on Pharoah* and *Bernal Diaz Reborn.*

**GRAVES, Earl Gilbert** (1935– )
Before starting *Black Enterprise* magazine in 1970, Earl Graves was an administrative assistant to Senator Robert F. Kennedy from 1965 to 1968. From 1968 to 1970, he operated his own management consulting firm.

In establishing *Black Enterprise*, Graves called it the "*Fortune* of the Black World." He added, "Black-owned media can be proud of what they have achieved. But it has to be a bitter pride."

Today Graves operates a number of other companies involved in marketing, research, and broadcasting. He is also a member of many organizations, including the Greater New York Council of Boy Scouts, the Corporate Fund Performing Arts at Kennedy Center, the American Museum of Natural History, and the Planetarium Authority. He is also a trustee of Tuskegee Institute.

*Ebony* magazine once listed Graves as one of the 100 influential Blacks in America. The National Association of Black Manufacturers gave him its Key Award. President Richard Nixon named him one of the Ten Most Outstanding Minority Businessmen in the country in 1973, and *Time* called him one of 200 future leaders of the country. He has won other citations for his work.

In the late Seventies, Graves voiced a fear that "the mood of this country toward equal opportunity for Black Americans and Black-owned businesses is getting worse, not better."

**GRAVES, Ralph** (1924– )

After graduation from Harvard in 1948, Ralph Graves joined *Life* magazine as a researcher, but soon became a reporter for *Time-Life* in San Francisco. During the Fifties, Graves wrote for *Life* in New York and Chicago, and in 1959 became senior editor.

By 1961, Graves was the assistant managing editor of *Life*; by 1967, he was the senior staff editor for all Time Inc. magazines. From 1969 to the termination of *Life* in 1972, he was its managing editor. Later *Life* was resumed as a monthly. A new assignment followed, that of corporate editor of Time Inc.'s Film and Cable Television projects.

Graves continued to move up the corporate ladder, becoming associate publisher of *Time*, the corporate editor for all the firm's publications and film-cable activities, and finally, editorial director of Time Inc. and a member of the board.

Graves is also a board member of the Universal Press Syndicate and three Time Inc. subsidiaries: Book-of-the-Month Club, Inc., Home Box Office, and Time-Life Books Inc. He is chairman of the board of directors of the New York City Citizens Crime Commission.

He has published two novels, *Thanks for the Ride* and *The Lost Eagles.* He served in the Air Force during World War II.

**GREEN, Abel** (1900–1973)

*Variety*, a tabloid covering the entertainment world, was founded by Sime Silverman. However, Abel Green joined the publication in 1929 and helped organize news coverage of Europe, Africa, and South America.

Green, who wrote a film story about Silverman, also wrote many books and magazine articles on the theater. They included *Tin Pan Alley* and *Outward Bound and Gagged.* He wrote *Show Biz* with Joe Laurie, Jr., and edited *Variety Music Cavalcade* and *The Spice of Variety.*

**GREENBERG, Paul** (1937– )

Paul Greenberg has spent most of his journalistic career with the *Pine Bluff Commercial* (Arkansas). For a brief period (1966–67), he worked as an editorial writer for the *Chicago Daily News.*

Greenberg lectured on American history at Hunter College in 1962, and since 1978, he has lectured at the University of Arkansas. His first tour in Pine Bluff began in 1962 and his current tour in 1967. His column has been syndicated since 1970.

In 1967, Greenberg won the Pulitzer Prize for editorial writing. When he returned to his alma mater to receive the University of Missouri Journalism Medal, he said, "The press must be tough enough to ring the alarm, to point the finger, to become a bloody nuisance." But he thought it was all worth the effort "if you can nab a Richard Nixon climbing out of the window with something far more valuable than the family silver."

Other awards include the Grenville Clark Editorial Award for the best editorial concerning world peace through law in 1964, and in 1981, he won the American Society of Newspaper Editors' Distinguished Writing Award for Commentary.

Greenberg believes that "when a newspaper finds everyone agreeing with it, it's because the paper never says anything to disagree with."

**GREENE, Robert William** (1929– )

A two-time Pulitzer Prize winner, Robert Greene is considered by some to be the father of team investigative reporting. Greene began his reporting career on the *Jersey Journal* in 1949 and became a senior investigator for the New York City Anti-Crime Committee in 1950. After five years he returned to reporting, working on *Newsday* in Garden City, New York.

Greene refined his concept for team investigative reporting on *Newsday* and in 1967, he became the leader of *Newsday*'s team. By 1970, he was a senior editor.

Greene and the team approach won nationwide recognition in the six-month investigation of the murder of Dan Bolles, an *Arizona Republic* reporter. During this investigation, 36 reporters from print and broadcast media participated, to produce a 23-part series about crime in Arizona.

In 1976, the Investigative Reporters and Editors Group was organized, with Greene as president. In addition to his Pulitzers (1970 and 1973), Greene has won the George Polk Award, the John Peter Zenger Award, and the James Wright Brown Award. Greene's latest book, *American Beat*, a collection of his articles, arrived in 1984. The Book-of-the-Month Club Bulletin referred to Greene as "part Sam Spade, part Mark Twain and part All-American boy." He also wrote *Naked Came the Stranger* and *The Heroin Trail*. Tom Wolfe called him "a virtuoso of the things that bring journalism alive: literary talent, hard reporting, a taste for mixing it up with the people of all sorts, and a willingness to let out a barbaric yawp now and again."

Greene feels that the reporter's job "is getting facts. But beyond that I think one most important thing is to attempt to purvey the truth, not just what somebody says to be the truth. The truth isn't always easy to get, and always we must balance the truth and our need to get it against the methods we must use."

**GREENFIELD, Jeff** (1943– )

Jeff Greenfield is a television commentator and magazine writer. He created a hassle with a *TV Guide* article in late 1983 when he "blamed" the "Howdy Doody" show for instigating the cultural upheavals of the Sixties.

"With the passing of time, we shall never know whether the enormous instability wrought by *Howdy Doody* was an act of fate, the accidental impact of images on an impressionable generation, or a fiendishly clever plot wrought by fiendishly clever manipulators in alien lands," Greenfield wrote. He claims readers missed his satire.

In 1983, Greenfield joined ABC as a political and media analyst. He has worked for CBS on the Charles Kuralt's "CBS News Sunday Morning" since 1979.

Earlier, Greenfield was a speech writer for New York Mayor John V. Lindsay, and writes a weekly political column syndicated to newspapers.

According to the *Kansas City Star* television-radio critic, Gerald B. Jordan, "Greenfield is the best counterpunch the commercial networks have when critics decry the scarcity of self-criticism on television."

His books include *No Peace, No Place*; *Raintree*; *The Real Campaign: The Media and the Battle for the White House*; *Television: The First Fifty Years*; *Tiny Giant: Nate Archibald*; *Playing to Win: An Insider's Guide to Politics*; and *The World's Greatest Team: A Portrait of the Boston Celtics*. In his book on television, Greenfield wrote: "Television is the pervasive American pastime; cutting through geographic, ethnic, class, and cultural diversity, it is the single binding threat of this country, the one experience that touches young and old, rich and poor, learned and illiterate."

**GREENFIELD, Meg** (1930– )

Meg Greenfield has been editor of the *Washington Post*'s editorial page since 1979. Before joining the *Post* in 1968, Greenfield worked for the *Reporter* magazine from 1957 to 1968, working the last three years as its Washington editor.

In 1982, Greenfield upset a number of Washington residents when she wrote an internal *Post* memo indicating that she would have nothing more to do with public relations people. Her plan was endorsed by her boss, Ben Bradlee.

Writing in the *Washington Journalism Review*, Roger Piantadosi noted: "Greenfield has few peers in contemporary journalism: as editor of the *Washington Post*'s editorial page she shapes the skeptically liberal editorial policy of that powerful and influential newspaper.

"She is the arbiter of argument in a town that was founded on it. Her own pungent writing unquestionably affects the national debate more than any other editorial voice in the country."

Greenfield won the Pulitzer Prize in 1978 for editorial writing. Her publisher, Katharine Graham, once called her thinking "independent and uninfluenced by trends or molds. Her judgment is very dispassionate."

She has also been a columnist for *Newsweek* since 1974.

**GREGORY, Bettina** (1946– )

Bettina Gregory is included among the top investigative reporters in network television today. She began her reporting career on radio and television stations in Ithaca, New York in 1972, and moved the next year to be anchorwoman for Freeport (New York) station WGBB. She later joined WCBS in New York.

Gregory worked a year as a free-lance reporter and editor for the Associated Press in New York and then spent a year with the *New York Times* before joining ABC in 1974. She moved to Washington in 1977, became the White House correspondent in 1979, and a senior general assignment correspondent in 1980.

In a *TV Guide* story in 1983, Mark Ribowsky wrote: "ABC industry people still talk about her marvelous expose of the GSA a few years ago. More recently she took a gritty look at New York's heroin traffic and broke the story of a nuclear-power plant's deficiencies." Gregory won the Clarion Award given by the Women in Communications, Inc.

**GRIMES, William H.** (1892–1972)
Under the editorship of William Grimes, there were many changes on the *Wall Street Journal*. Grimes joined the staff in 1923, as a Washington correspondent. By 1934, he was the managing editor and, in 1941, the editor.

Between 1913 and 1920, Grimes worked on Ohio newspapers. He then joined the United Press in Washington for a year before moving to the news service's New York office.

Grimes won a Pulitzer Prize for editorial writing in 1946, the first won by the *Journal*. For years, the Pulitzer committee had refused to consider the publication a "newspaper."

A *Wall Street Journal* colleague, Vermont Royster, once described Grimes as a man "who sometimes had to keep enthusiasm from running riot and who in the meantime was slowly turning the *Wall Street Journal*'s editorial page into a voice of national influence." Grimes was also instrumental in hiring many staffers who helped to make the publication the nation's circulation leader for daily newspapers. He retired as editor in 1948.

**GROSS, Ben S.** (1891–1979)
Ben Gross began his newspaper career as a reporter, but became better known to the radio and television public as a commentator and a critic in the 1930–40 era.

In 1911, Gross worked for the *Birmingham News* (Alabama) as a reporter. After being admitted to the bar in 1915, he was an attorney for several years, but returned to newspaper work with a reporting job on the *Bronx Home News* (New York) in 1919.

Other jobs followed on the *World Traveler* magazine, *New York Morning Telegraph*, and *New York American*. He worked for the Associated Press before joining the *New York Daily News* where he was the radio–television editor and critic from 1925 to 1971.

From time to time, Gross was a commentator for NBC and other stations. He served in World War I and wrote several books and many magazine articles. Gross wrote *I Looked and Listened* and co-authored *What this Town Needs* with Charles Zerner and *Men, Mikes and Money* with M.H. Aylesworth.

**GROSSMAN, Lawrence K.** (1931– )
As president and chief operating officer for the Public Broadcasting System since 1976, Lawrence Grossman helped develop the first nationwide satellite system. He also helped establish "The MacNeil–Lehrer News Hour" and the widely praised "Vietnam: A Television History."

Grossman started in 1953 with *Look* magazine in editorial and promotion work. He joined the advertising division of the CBS Network in 1956, and switched to NBC as vice-president for advertising in 1962. He operated his own advertising and production firm from 1966 to 1976.

He was associate editor for *Somehow It Works, A Candid Portrait of the 1964 Presidential Election.*

**GROSVENOR Family**
Since 1899, there has been a Grosvenor associated with the *National Geographic* magazine and the society that produces this publication and its books, atlases, globes, maps, and other products.

Gilbert Grosvenor (1875–1966) took over the *National Geographic* in 1899 when its circulation was under a thousand. He became known as the "Geographer to Millions." In an obituary, he was described as "this kindly, mild-mannered but purposeful man, of frail but sprightly frame, who combined business acumen, intellectual curiosity, and a regard for tradition into a warm personality that radiated charm."

He was the magazine's editor until 1954, president from 1920 to 1954, and chairman of the board from 1954 until his death.

Melville Bell Grosvenor (1901–1982) was *National Geographic* editor from 1957 to 1967. Then he became editor-in-chief and board chairman. After serving in the Navy from 1923 to 1924, Melville joined the *National Geographic* as an apprentice and worked in various departments. He took the first color pictures used in the magazine from a blimp over New York City in 1930. He also produced the society's first "Atlas of the World" and its first globe. He wrote many articles for the publication and edited many of the Society's books. He promoted additional exploration and research projects and held many affiliations with other organizations and civic groups.

Gilbert Melville Grosvenor (1931– ) joined the *National Geographic* staff in 1954 as a picture editor. He was in the Army shortly after that, 1954–56, but returned to become involved in writing, photography, and editing. He developed the concept for *World*, a publication for children the Society started in 1975.

Gilbert is the third-generation Grosvenor to edit the magazine and the fifth-generation president of the Society. In 1961, he won the National Press Photographers Association Award for his coverage of Eisenhower's tour of Asia, Africa, and Europe. He also won the University of Southern California Distinguished Achievement Award in Periodical Journalism in 1977. He was editor from 1970 to 1980, when he became the Society's president. He, too, has been active in many projects, foundations, schools, and hospitals.

**GRUNWALD, Henry Anatole** (1922– )
In 1979, Henry Grunwald became editor-in-chief for all Time Inc. publications, which was the peak of a career that began in 1944 when Grunwald worked part-time as a night copyboy for *Time* magazine.

Grunwald moved up rapidly. By 1951 he was a senior editor, the youngest person to hold that title at *Time*. He edited most of *Time*'s departments on different occasions and was the first editor of the Essay section. He also wrote many cover stories and, in 1968, became managing editor.

Under Grunwald's leadership, *Time* added new sections, including Environment, Behavior, The Sexes, and Energy. Bylines were provided for the writers and more color photographs were used. He has also written for *Life, Fortune* and *Horizon* magazines. He has written *Salinger, A Critical and Personal Portrait*; *Churchill, The Life Triumphant* and *The Age of Elegance.*

In addition to his Time Inc. work, Grunwald is a director of the World Press Freedom Committee and the Metropolitan Opera Guild.

**GUCCIONE, Bob** (1930– )
Bob Guccione prepared for the priesthood during his youth in Brooklyn, but left the seminary after several months.

Before Guccione made his fortune as the founder of *Penthouse* and *Omni* magazines, he tried many jobs, from writing greeting cards and direct mail advertising copy to drawing cartoons for British newspapers. In England he sold collections of pinup pictures by mail.

According to Dana Thomas, Guccione in 1969 offered an American edition of *Penthouse*, which he had started in England, to "outdo Hefner in the lavish display of sexuality." Hefner responded with *Oui*, which was closer to *Penthouse* than was *Playboy*, at that time. *Penthouse* set a record sales of nearly 6 million copies in 1984 with its pictures of Miss America.

Guccione also founded *Viva*, which had a short existence. He produced and directed a film, *Caligula*, in 1979. In 1983, *Forbes* magazine listed him as being worth at least $225 million.

**GUGGENHEIM, Harry F.** (1890– )
Harry Guggenheim, an industrial and foundation executive, became involved in publishing when he and his wife, Alicia Patterson Guggenheim, started *Newsday* in 1939.

This Long Island newspaper won its first Pulitzer Prize in 1954 for meritorious public service. Its typography has also brought the newspaper special recognition.

After Alicia Guggenheim died in 1963, her husband assumed the duties of publisher. In 1970, he sold *Newsday* to the Times Mirror Company of Los Angeles.

**GUINDON, Richard** (1935– )
In the 1960s, after returning from service in the Army, Richard Guindon began to draw professionally. He first created "Hugger Mugger," which was syndicated to more than 100 college newspapers. In 1972, he joined the

*Minneapolis Tribune* as a cartoonist and, in 1982, moved to the *Detroit Free Press.*

He began the "Guindon" panel in 1977. Currently more than 70 newspapers are carrying "Guindon," which seeks to "poke fun at a variety of people, things and ideas"; many are "absolutely absurd situations," according to some readers. He has poked fun in his panel by having a person sentenced to death in "People's Court," a woman arrested for making more than one trip to a salad bar, and another arrested for taking a loaded shopping cart through the "10 items or less line."

Guindon has his "self-consciousness in public" with his ideas. "I was raised to believe there were things you just didn't do. You don't raise a fuss. And I embarrass easily." He gave his characters serious names, such as Roger Fenster and Eunice Benson.

**GUISEWITE, Cathy Lee** (1950– )
Early in her career, Cathy Guisewite held jobs in advertising, but in 1976, she created a comic strip and named it "Cathy"; it became an immediate success.

Guisewite notes that "Cathy is always trying to be organized and it seems that no matter how organized you try to be, the more cluttered and unorganized things become." Her characters combine many individuals she has known.

"She's funny enough to make you laugh, but subtle enough to make you think, too," said Marlene Connor, a Literary Guild editor. The Guild has produced a hardcover volume that combines several Cathy books. Connor felt that Cathy "has replaced Mary Tyler Moore as the spokeswoman for the upwardly-mobile, single, career-minded woman of the eighties."

"Cathy" has been considered a catalyst for other comic strips about women as well as responsible for changes in the treatment of women by older, male cartoonists.

Guisewite was included in a San Mateo, California museum cartoon exhibit in 1982 as one of the "10 influential 20th Century cartoon artists." The museum leaders thought Guisewite "depicts realistically yet humorously the trials of trying to survive as a 'Woman of the '80s.'" She works out of Santa Barbara.

**GUITTAR, Lee John** (1931– )
*Denver Post* publisher Lee Guittar was named the Colorado Publisher of the Year in 1982, after only one year on his new job.

Guittar began his career with General Electric in 1955 and spent ten years with this company in community and government relations programs. Before joining the *Miami Herald* as personnel and circulation director in 1967, Guittar handled employee and public relations for the Tidewater Oil Co. in New York.

In 1972, Guittar moved to the *Detroit Free Press* (Michigan) where he spent two years as vice-president and business manager and three years as president. He moved to the *Dallas Times Herald* (Texas) in 1977 as publisher. Shortly after the Times Mirror Co. purchased the *Denver Post* (Colorado), Guittar was made publisher.

**GUTHMAN, Edwin O.** (1919– )
Edwin Guthman began his newspaper career in his hometown, Seattle, following World War II Army service. A reporter for the now defunct *Star* from 1946 to 1947, he moved to the *Times* (Washington), where he worked until 1961. He won a Pulitzer Prize in 1949 for articles that cleared a University of Washington professor of charges that he was a communist. This was the first Pulitzer won by anyone in the State of Washington.

Guthman was a press assistant for Senator Robert Kennedy in 1965 before returning to the position of national news editor for the *Los Angeles Times*, a position he held until 1977, when he became editor of the *Philadelphia Inquirer* (Pennsylvania). A Nieman Fellow at Harvard, 1950–51, Guthman has written one book, *We Band of Brothers*.

**HADDEN, Briton** (1898–1929)
Briton Hadden and Henry Luce were Yale sophomores together before they were sent to Camp Jackson in South Carolina for officers' training in World War I days. They had little time to serve before the Armistice was declared.

After the war, Hadden joined the *New York World* staff in 1920. In 1921, both Hadden and Luce were working on the *Baltimore News* (Maryland). The next year, they were in New York planning what would eventually become *Time* magazine.

Hadden and Luce raised sufficient capital to start *Time*, dividing their duties, with one the editor and the other business manager. After five years, they reversed their roles. Both men had worked on student publications at Yale and had long been interested in starting a new magazine.

In 1924, the two started another magazine, the *Saturday Review of Literature*. That same year the firm reported a profit of $674.15, with *Time* reporting a circulation of 70,000. The next year the company moved to Cleveland. Hadden, however, was not happy there and returned to New York City.

Hadden died at age 31. According to Time Inc. historian Robert T. Elson, Hadden "had endowed the magazine with its style. He was an innovator."

**HALBERSTAM, David** (1934– )
Early in his life David Halberstam worked on Southern newspapers, the *West Point Daily Times Leader* (Mississippi) and the *Nashville Tennessean*. He also wrote for *Reporter* magazine.

Halberstam also began writing books at this time, his first novel, *The Noblest Roman*, being published in 1961.

By 1960, Halberstam was with the *New York Times'* Washington Bureau, and in 1961, he was assigned to the Congo (now Zaire). His work there brought him a New York Newspaper Guild Page One Award. The next year, Halberstam was in Vietnam where the accuracy of his reports on the deteriorating situation upset many government leaders. President John Kennedy sought to have him removed from Vietnam, but *Times* publisher Arthur Sulzberger defended him.

Halberstam won a George Polk Memorial Award in 1963 and shared the 1964 Pulitzer for reporting. He also shared the first Louis M. Lyons Award. He wrote about Vietnam in a book, *The Making of a Quagmire*. The *Nation* reported that this book "had an electrifying effect on a new generation of dissenters. It opened the eyes of a wider public to the sordid activities concealed by official fustian."

Continuing with the *Times*, he was sent to Poland and was later ordered to leave because of his comments about the Communist leaders. He went to Paris before returning to New York. A contributing editor to *Harper's* in 1967, he worked with editor Willie Morris. Halberstam continues to write books, including the award-winning *The Powers That Be*, a massive study of media leaders. He also wrote *One Very Hot Day*; *The Unfinished Odyssey of Robert Kennedy*; *Ho* (Ho Chi Minh); and *The Best and the Brightest*.

In 1983, Halberstam was one of three media leaders elected to receive the Fellow of the Society Award of Sigma Delta Chi.

**HALE, William Harlan** (1910–1974)

A varied career for William Hale involved magazines and the federal government. In 1932–33, he was associate editor of *Vanity Fair* and later, a *Washington Post* columnist briefly before joining *Fortune* for a year.

During World War II, Hale worked for the Office of War Information in New York, directing radio broadcasts to Germany. After the war, Hale became editor of the *New Republic*, and from 1948 to 1958, he was with the *Reporter*. Another tour of editing found Hale with *Horizon* magazine and Horizon Books. At one time he was the press attaché and chief information officer for the United States in Vienna.

Hale wrote the following books: *Challenge to Defeat*; *Hannibal Hooker*; *The March of Freedom*; *Horace Greeley Voice of the People*; *Innocence Abroad*; *The Horizon Book of Ancient Greece*; *The Horizon Book of Eating and Drinking through the Ages*; and *Ghosts of Berlin*.

**HALL Family**

Long associated with the *Montgomery Advertiser* (Alabama), Grover Cleveland Hall (1888–1941) started in the traditional way, working as a printer's devil on the *Dothan Daily Siftings*, a paper owned by his uncle, in 1905.

Within two years, Hall had moved to the *Enterprise Ledger* as editor, but returned to the *Siftings* as editor in 1908. The next year he was managing editor of the *Selma Times*, and moved again to the *Pensacola Journal* (Florida) as editorial writer.

Hall first became associated with the *Montgomery Advertiser* in 1910 as associate editor. By 1926, he was editor, a position he held until his death. He won a Pulitzer Prize in 1928 for editorials against "gangism, flogging, and racial and religious intolerance." Writing about the Hall family in 1950, Charles Scarrett at the University of Missouri noted that "Hall was responsible for the Twentieth Century evolution of that tradition and the shaping of it to fit into a markedly changed Alabama, a New South, and fast-moving America in his long fight with the Ku Klux Klan."

Grover Cleveland Hall, Jr. (1915–1971) said his father was "both the creation and the creator" of the *Advertiser*. He followed his father as associate editor of the newspaper in 1947. He was its editor from 1948 to 1956, and editor-in-chief until his death. He was active in professional organizations.

**HALLER, Ellis M.** (1915–1981)
From 1956 until his death, Ellis Haller was associated with *U.S. News & World Report*, editing business and financial articles. Eventually he served as assistant managing editor.

Prior to his magazine work in Washington, Haller worked for the *Watertown Daily Times* (New York) and the *Wall Street Journal*, first in New York City and later in its Chicago and Washington bureaus.

Haller lectured on typography at Syracuse University and the American Press Institute. He was honored by the National Management Association in 1955, and worked closely with other professional organizations.

**HALSMAN, Philippe** (1906–1979)
Portrait photographer Philippe Halsman will be remembered for his pictures of such world leaders as Winston Churchill, Mrs. Eleanor Roosevelt, the Kennedys, Albert Einstein, and several other presidents.

Halsman's pictures have been included in many exhibits and are in permanent collections in several countries. His portraits of Adlai Stevenson, John Steinbeck, and Albert Einstein have appeared on United States postage stamps.

In 1958, Halsman was named one of the 10 greatest photographers in the world. He was given the Newhouse Award and the Golden Plate Award.

Halsman's books include *The Frenchman*; *Piccoli*; *Dali's Mustache*; *Philippe Halsman's Jumpbook*; *Halsman on the Creation of Photographic Ideas*; *Sight and Insight*; and *Catalogue of Halsman Exhibitions*.

He had also directed several films, and lectured on photography.

**HANNA, Gordon** (1920– )
After 41 years working for the Scripps-Howard Newspapers, Gordon Hanna retired in 1983. His alma mater, a year earlier, had named him to the Texas Tech University Mass Communications Hall of Fame.

Hanna began on the *Port Arthur News* (Texas) in 1939 and moved to the *Houston Press* in 1942. From 1944 to 1945 he was in the Air Force, returning to the *Press* where he became the city editor in 1949.

After five years as city editor in Houston, Hanna moved to the *Memphis Commercial Appeal* (Tennessee) as managing editor and remained there until 1959. During the next nine years he edited the *Evansville Press* (Indiana) before returning to Memphis as editor.

Hanna became the general editorial manager for the Scripps-Howard Newspapers in 1976, the position he held until he retired.

**HANSON, Joseph J.** (1930– )
*Folio*, the magazine for magazine management, was established in 1972 by Joe Hanson, who feels "magazines are filling the 'need to know revolution' that has been sweeping the nation."

Hanson's career has been in management. He began in Cleveland as sales manager for a publishing firm, 1954–55. In 1958, he was vice-president of Management Publishing Corp. in Connecticut. After seven years he was president of Market Publications, Inc., in New Canaan (Connecticut), a position he held for 11 years.

For several years Hanson was chairman of the board of the Marketplace firm before starting *Folio.*

Hanson won a Jesse H. Neal Award for distinguished journalism in 1975, the Florida Magazine Association Award in 1978, and the Lee C. Williams Award in 1979. He has lectured widely in America and abroad, and has addressed the World Congress of the International Federation of the Periodical Press.

**HARING, Howard Jack** (1924– )
A varied career on newspapers and magazines prepared Howard Haring for his current position as senior editor of *Guideposts*, a religiously oriented publication that has some 3.5 million subscribers, co-founded by Norman Vincent Peale and his wife.

Haring, in 1949, was a reporter on the *Providence Journal-Bulletin* (Rhode Island). The next year he was editor of the *Boyertown Times* (Pennsylvania) before going to the *Allentown Morning Call* (Pennsylvania). Between 1954 and 1958, he was a sports columnist and television magazine editor of the *Washington Star.*

After four years with the *Saturday Evening Post* and another six years with the *Ladies' Home Journal*, he was executive editor of *Boys' Life* and editor of *Exploring* before he joined *Guideposts.* He has edited books for the Curtis Publishing Co., Scribner's, and Reader's Digest Books.

He served in World War II in the Army.

**HARRIS, Louis** (1921– )
Lou Harris' interest in journalism and politics began during his high school days. He worked on newspapers then and while attending the University of North Carolina. After graduation, he worked from 1946 to 1956 with Elmo Roper and Associates. Since 1956 Lou Harris has directed his firm, Louis Harris and Associates, in marketing and public opinion research. His Harris Poll is well known in America.

When Harris joined the Roper firm, he helped to write newspaper columns and radio scripts. Soon he turned to political research. In 1958, he was hired by Senator John F. Kennedy and was instrumental in convincing Kennedy to enter the West Virginia presidential primary.

Harris was associated with CBS News from 1962 to 1968, and in 1964, developed the Voter Profile Analysis in cooperation with IBM and CBS. Since 1971 he has been with ABC News. For five years his columns appeared in the *Washington Post* and in *Newsweek*, and since 1969, they have been syndicated. Harris has also been associated with the Life Poll in 1969–71.

Harris co-authored *The Negro Revolution in America*, and wrote *Is There a Republican Majority?*; *Black and White*; and *Black-Jewish Relations in New York City: The Anguish of Change*. He has also written numerous articles.

During World War II he served in the Navy.

**HARRIS, T. George** (1924– )
George Harris began as a newspaper reporter, but later switched to magazine editing. In 1942, he was a reporter on the *Clarksville Leaf-Chronicle* (Tennessee); from 1949 to 1955, he was a *Time* correspondent, and from 1955 to 1958, its Midwest Bureau chief. He moved to New York as a contributing editor in 1958 with *Time*, and from 1960 to 1962 was its Northwest Bureau chief.

Harris was senior editor of *Look* for the next six years and then served seven years as editor-in-chief of *Psychology Today*, making it a "hot book" in the industry. Meanwhile, he has served as consultant for several publications.

In 1981, Harris became editor of the newly established *American Health*. In this magazine, Harris said, "We're providing people with news to use about the one resource they've got, the beautiful, intelligent bundle of tissue we all walk around in."

His alma mater, the University of Kentucky, named him to its Hall of Fame, and in 1955, he was named Chicago's Outstanding Young Man of the Year.

**HART, John Lewis** (1931– )
John Hart's cartoons first appeared in the *Saturday Evening Post* in 1954 and his comic strip, "B.C.," was syndicated in 1958. Since 1964, his other strip, "The Wizard of Id," has appeared in hundreds of newspapers.

The National Cartoonists Society recognized him as the creator of the best humor strip in 1967. He has also been honored by groups in Italy and France. His strips have been collected into more than 20 books.

During the Korean War he served in the Air Force.

**HARTE Family**
Several members of the Harte family have been associated with newspapers, especially in Texas.

Houston Harte (1893–1972) began his journalism career on the *Los Angeles Examiner* in 1912, before coming to Missouri where he worked on the *Knobnoster Gem*, 1914, and the *Boonville Republic*, 1915–20. In 1920, he became publisher of the *San Angelo Evening Standard* (Texas), where he remained until 1962. He served the Associated Press in many capacities. In 1931, the University of Missouri presented him its Journalism Medal.

He served in World War I.

Houston Harriman Harte (1927– ) was a partner in the *Snyder Daily News* (Texas) in 1950 and its editor from 1952 to 1954. He spent two years with the *Des Moines Register and Tribune* (Iowa), and then became president of the San Angelo Standard, Inc. In 1966, he was president and, in 1971, chairman of the board of Harte-Hanks Communications, Inc.

He has been active in programs of the Boy Scouts, Air Force Academy, East Texas State University, and Stillman College.

He served in the Navy, 1945–46.

Edward Holmead Harte (1922– ) worked for the *Kansas City Star* (Missouri), 1948–50. In 1950, he was a partner on the *Snyder Daily News* (Texas) and, in 1962, he became the publisher of the *Corpus Christi Caller Times* (Texas).

**HARTMAN, David** (1935– )

Once called "perhaps the most successful chatsman since Dave Garroway," David Hartman pushed ABC's "Good Morning, America" television show ahead of the NBC "Today Show" in 1979.

Hartman began his stage career in the late Fifties after three years in the Air Force, where he appeared in several musical comedies. In later years, Hartman appeared in "My Fair Lady" and "Hello Dolly!" before he turned to motion pictures and television.

In 1975, Hartman became the host of "Good Morning, America." This show combines news and entertainment and regularly interviews celebrities. Hartman calls it "the best job in the world." His listeners know his fondness for sports, since many well-known sports leaders appear with Hartman.

**HARVEY, Paul** (1918– )

According to Sanford Ungar, Paul Harvey is "one of the best-known and perhaps most influential personalities in the history of American radio."

Now a news analyst, author, and columnist, Harvey began in the early Forties with stations in Tulsa, Oklahoma, Salina, Kansas, St. Louis, Missouri, and Michigan, Indiana. His first broadcast was at the age of 14 in Tulsa.

Since 1944 Harvey has been an analyst and commentator with ABC network, and since 1954, a syndicated columnist. From his radio start in Chicago, Harvey has had a greater following in grass roots areas than in big cities. Even his newspaper column appears more frequently in smaller newspapers. Some persons feel he is anti-New York.

When Franklin D. Roosevelt died, Harvey received 25,000 requests for transcripts of his broadcast of the event. By 1970, his morning radio broadcasts were rated tops in the nation.

Ungar reports that Harvey was a close friend of J. Edgar Hoover and Senator Joseph McCarthy. He has been "most often identified with the political right" and has called for military growth and agreed with Vice-President Spiro Agnew in his Nixon-supported criticisms of the media, especially of broadcasting. His one son, Paul, Jr., however, was a conscientious objector.

Harvey has won many awards, especially from the DAV, the VFW, the American Legion, and the Freedoms Foundation. He was named the Top Commentator of the Year in 1962 by *Radio-TV Daily*. In 1975, he won the

John Peter Zenger Freedom Award and, in 1979, he was named to the National Association of Broadcasters Hall of Fame. He had earlier been named to the Oklahoma Hall of Fame. Although he never completed college, Harvey has been awarded many honorary degrees, especially from smaller institutions.

Harvey's books include *Remember These Things*; *Autumn of Liberty*; *The Rest of the Story*; *You Said It, Paul Harvey*; and *Our Lives, Our Fortunes, Our Sacred Honor*.

There's not much grim news from Harvey, according to *Orlando Sentinel* (Florida) writer Howard Means. "'Paul Harvey News' is a promotion for old values vs. new ones. It is a kind of theater of scantily clad ideas where those values do battle."

**HARWOOD, Richard Lee** (1925– )

After working for the *Nashville Tennessean* and the *Louisville Courier-Journal* and *Times* (Kentucky) between 1947 and 1969, Richard Harwood became a national correspondent for the *Washington Post*.

In 1968, Harwood was the national editor and later assistant managing editor before spending two years (1974–76) as vice-president of the Trenton Times Newspapers in New Jersey. However, in 1976 he returned to the *Post*, where he is deputy managing editor.

Harwood was a Nieman Fellow at Harvard, 1955–56, and a Carnegie Fellow at Columbia University, 1965–66. In 1957, he was given a citation by the National Education Writers Association. Other awards include the George Polk Memorial Award and the Sigma Delta Chi distinguished service medal.

He served in the Marine Corps from 1942 to 1946.

**HASEN, Irwin** (1918– )

In 1955, Irwin Hasen and the late Gus Edson created the comic strip "Dondi." As Hasen recalls, the men did not become too involved in political, sexual, or religious topics during the first decade of "Dondi." Some controversy arose in 1983 when Hasen worked a retarded boy in the strip. When the *Pittsburgh Press* withheld "Dondi" for a time, the artist was baffled. Hasen said he had "no intention of maligning mentally handicapped people. To make a point, you have to have anti-heroes." Hasen feels it is necessary to address some of the problems of the day, "given the society we live in."

**HATLO, Jimmy** (1898–1963)

In 1914, Jimmy Hatlo was a sports and editorial cartoonist for the *Los Angeles Times*. After four years there, he took a similar job with the *San Francisco Call-Bulletin*, and Hearst newspapers, where he remained until 1939.

Hatlo's lasting fame started in 1939 when he began two comic features, "They'll Do It Every Time" and "Little Iodine." Eventually five books of these cartoons were published and, in 1946, Mary Pickford and Buddy Rogers produced a "Little Iodine" motion picture.

**HAYNIE, Hugh** (1927- )

Hugh Haynie has been an editorial cartoonist with the *Richmond Times-Dispatch* (Virginia) (1950–53), *Greensboro Daily News* (North Carolina) (1953–55, 1956–58), and the *Atlanta Journal* (Georgia) (1955–56) before he joined the *Louisville Courier Journal* (Kentucky) in 1958.

Haynie's cartoons are now nationally processed by the Los Angeles Times Syndicate. For his outstanding work, he was named one of the Ten Outstanding Young Men in the United States by the Junior Chamber of Commerce in 1965. He also has won the Headliner Award, the Freedoms Foundation Award, and the Sigma Delta Chi Distinguished Service Award.

His alma mater, the College of William and Mary, gave him its alumni medal for service and loyalty in 1972.

He served in the U.S. Coast Guard, 1944–46 and 1951–52.

**HEALY, George William Jr.** (1905–1980)

In 1926, George Healy, Jr. joined the *New Orleans Times-Picayune* (Louisiana) where he spent the rest of his life. Earlier he had worked briefly for the Associated Press and several newspapers while attending the University of Mississippi. He also worked for the *Knoxville Sentinel* (Tennessee).

Healy moved up to become city editor, managing editor, and in 1952, to begin a 20-year assignment as editor of the *Times-Picayune*. Meanwhile, he held several executive positions with the Times-Picayune Publishing Co.

During World War II, Healy worked as a consultant on domestic problems for the Office of War Information. Later, he was decorated by the Dominican Republic, Belgium, and Italy. He was active in local affairs and professional organizations.

**HEARST Family**

The Hearst family, according to a 1982 *Quill* magazine report, is worth between $1 and 2 billion, based on the group's eight newspapers, twenty magazines, ten television and radio stations, and two book publishing firms, as well as their real estate holdings.

Of William Randolph Hearst (1863–1951), "it is entirely safe to say that no more controversial figure ever existed in the journalism business," according to Hearst biographers Kenneth Stewart and John Tebbel.

Hearst's father, George, acquired the *San Francisco Examiner* in 1880. Young Hearst took over as editor in 1887, after several years at Harvard. In 1895 he moved east, with the purchase of the *New York Journal*. The famous circulation battle with Pulitzer's *World* during the Spanish-American War followed. Later came the Yellow Journalism era, so closely allied to these two men.

According to journalism historians Edwin and Michael Emery, it is difficult to assess Hearst's role because of the "complex nature of his personality, the variegated social and political impact of his many ventures, and the length and extent of his career." One needs also to look at his political activities, which were apparently designed to place Hearst in the White House. He ran for mayor of New York and for governor of the state. He lost. He did win a place in Congress, running from a "safe" district where the count could be assured. His newspapers were used to promote these campaigns, as well as the campaigns of others he supported.

In the firm's official obituary, this sentence appeared: "It was a strange portrait, obscured by myth and legend, confused by controversy and distortion." In his day he operated the "world's biggest publishing empire in terms of newspapers and their combined circulation."

Other members of the Hearst family have continued operations, cutting back on the non-profitable newspapers and expanding in other areas.

George Randolph Hearst, Sr. (1904–1972) was publisher of the *San Francisco Examiner*, 1924–27, and vice-president of the *Los Angeles Examiner*, 1929–53. He also served as an executive in the Hearst Corp. He was also on the board of directors of the Palm Springs Boys Club.

William Randolph Hearst, Jr. (1908– ) took over the operation of the group upon the death of his father. In 1928, he had joined the organization as a police station cub reporter in New York, working for the *American*, and by 1937 he was the publisher. From 1943 to 1945 he served as a war correspondent. In 1955, he was editor-in-chief of all Hearst newspapers.

As a youngster, Hearst worked on the *New York Mirror* during summer vacations. Like his father, he too failed to complete his university courses. Young Hearst became closely involved in covering the European phase of World War II.

When the senior Hearst died in 1951, Hearst, Jr. became president of Hearst Consolidated Publications. He made many changes, not only in the top personnel, but also in the contents of the newspapers, stressing local coverage and effective reporting.

In 1955, Hearst, Frank Conniff, and J. Kingsbury Smith visited Russia on a "journalistic trip." They interviewed many Russian leaders, including Nikita Khrushchev. The series of articles won for Hearst the first Pulitzer Prize ever awarded this group. The writers also won an Overseas Press Club Award.

Hearst is now chairman of the executive committee and director of the Hearst Corporation. On his 75th birthday he said, "My main most consistent piece of work is the Sunday column. The idea is to keep the Hearst name in the readers' minds. . . . I was encouraged by my mother and close newspaper friends to write the column after Pop died." During his reporting days, Hearst, Jr. interviewed many of the world's great leaders, including DeGaulle, Mrs. Gandhi, the Emperor of Japan, and many prime ministers and heads of state.

John Randolph Hearst (1909–1958) worked on the *Atlanta Georgian* in 1927 and was later with *Cosmopolitan*, *Photoplay*, and Harper's Bazaar–Cosmopolitan Book Club. In 1932, he became publisher of the *New York Mirror* and, in 1936, publisher of the *Evening Journal*. He was assistant general manager for Hearst Newspapers in 1941.

Randolph Apperson Hearst (1915– ) also worked in the early Thirties on the *Atlanta Georgian*. He soon moved to the *San Francisco Call-*

*Bulletin*, becoming publisher in 1950. In 1972, he was president of the *San Francisco Examiner*. He has held several executive positions with the corporation and, since 1972, has been president of the Hearst Foundation.

From 1942 to 1945 he served in the Air Force.

George Randolph Hearst, Jr. (1927– ) joined the *Los Angeles Examiner* staff in 1948 and worked two years in San Francisco on the *Examiner* before returning to the *Herald-Express* in Los Angeles in 1956. By 1962, he was the publisher and, since 1977, he has been a vice-president for Hearst Corporation.

He was in the Navy, 1945–46, and the Army, 1950–54.

**HEBERT, F. Edward** (1901–1979)

A long career in New Orleans brought many recognition awards for F. Edward Hebert. He began as a sports reporter on the *Times-Picayune* (Louisiana) in 1919 and, by 1925, had become the assistant sports editor for the *New Orleans State* (Louisiana).

Hebert remained with the *State*. He was city editor when the newspaper waged its attack on the Huey Long political machine that for years dominated Louisiana.

Later Hebert entered Congress, where he was chairman of the Armed Services Investigation Subcommittee. He received several awards from the City of New Orleans, the Army, Navy, and Air Force, as well as veterans' associations. He wrote *I Went, I Saw, I Heard*; *Last of the Titans* and *The Life and Times of F. Edward Hebert*.

**HECHINGER, Fred Michael** (1920– )

For many years, Fred Hechinger was education editor for the *New York Times*. A decade, 1959–69, in this position was followed by a decade on the editorial board of the *Times*. Since 1978, he has been a columnist and president of the New York Times Company Foundation.

Hechinger has worked as a correspondent for the *London Times*, education columnist for the *Washington Post*, and in various positions with the *Bridgeport Herald* (Connecticut). He served briefly, in the late Forties, as a foreign correspondent for the Overseas News Agency and from 1946 to 1950 as a special writer for *This Week* magazine.

Hechinger was born in Germany and became a naturalized citizen in 1943. Among his many honors is the British Empire Medal. He also won the George Polk Memorial Award, 1950–51, and the Fairbanks Award and the Townsend Harris Medal, along with two editorial writing citations from the Society of Silurians.

His books include *An Adventure in Education*; *New Approaches*; *Worrying about College*; *The Big Red Schoolhouse*; *The New York Times Guide to N.Y.C. Private Schools*; *Pre-School Education Today*; and *Growing Up In America*. He co-authored *Tenn-age Tyranny*, and has contributed many articles to magazines, such as *Harper's*, *McCall's*, and the now-defunct *Reporter*.

**HECHT, Ben** (1894–1964)
In 1910 the co-author of *The Front Page*, Ben Hecht, began his journalistic career on the *Chicago Journal*. Later he joined the *Chicago Daily News*, remaining with the daily from 1914 to 1923. In 1918–1919 he directed the *News'* Berlin operations. He was described as "a Bohemian member of the literary group that flourished in Chicago just after the First World War." Briefly, 1923–1925, he published the *Chicago Literary Times*.

Among his many books and plays, *The Front Page*, written in collaboration with Charles MacArthur, is best remembered. It reflected life on the Chicago newspapers during the Twenties. The two men later wrote *Ladies and Gentlemen* and *Twentieth Century*. They also worked on motion pictures, *Crime Without Passion* and *The Scoundrel*.

Hecht's books include *The Master Poisoner* and other plays (with Maxwell Bodenheim); *The Wonder Hat* (with Kenneth Goodman; *Erik Dorn*; *Gargoyles*; *Fantazius Mallare*; *1001 Afternoons in Chicago*; *The Egotist* (drama); *Tales of Chicago Streets*; *Humpty Dumpty*; *The Florentine Dagger*; *The Kingdom of Evil*; *Count Bruga*; *Broken Necks* (short stories); *A Jew in Love*; *The Champion from Far Away*; *Lily of the Valley* (play); *Jumbo* (play); *We Will Never Die* (pageant); *1001 Afternoons in New York*; *The Collected Stories of Ben Hecht*; *To Quito and Back*; *Actors Blood*; *A Book of the Century*, his autobiography; *Charlie*; *A Treasury of Ben Hecht*; *Gaily, Gaily*; *Letters from Bohemia*, and *Great Magoo* (a play, with Gene Fowler.)

Among other motion pictures he was associated with were *Wuthering Heights*, *Angels over Broadway*, *Notorious*, *Spellbound*, *Viva Villa*, *Scarface*, *Gunga Din*, *Spectre of the Rose*, *Actors and Sin*, *Ride the Pink Horse*, *Nothing Sacred*, *Jumbo*, and *Underworld*.

**HECHT, George Joseph** (1895–1980)
Millions of Americans have read *Parents* magazine, founded by the Hecht family in 1926. The publication remained in the family until 1978 when it was sold to *Grunner & Jahr.

Hecht founded *Better Times* magazine in 1919 and served as its editor until 1931. Other magazines under Hecht's leadership were *Expecting*, *Baby Care*, *Children's Digest*, *Young Miss*, and *Humpty Dumpty's*.

Hecht worked closely with various child welfare projects, and at one time, he was chairman of the National Committee for the Observance of Mother's Day.

**HEFNER, Christie** (1952– )
*Playboy* magazine was established when Christie Hefner was only one year old, but in recent years, she has been preparing to take control of her father's Playboy Enterprises.

Christie has said, "People have come to expect a little more than the fact that I might actually be able to string four or five sentences together without screwing up the grammar." She admits that she's "not just another employee."

Christie, a feminist, believes "women are capable of working on a project that is aimed for men. God knows, men have worked on products aimed at women for generations."

Within eight years of her graduation summa cum laude from Brandeis University, Christie was named president of the organization. Before then she had worked briefly on the *Boston Phoenix*. With the Playboy firm, one of her early tasks was to develop and publish a series of *Playboy Guides*. She has been credited with having "a talent for leadership" in her new role.

Christie has been subjected to many in-depth interviews for other periodicals and has been in great demand for talks. *Next* magazine once called her one of the 100 most powerful people for the 1980s.

**HEFNER, Hugh M.** (1926– )

"The first magazine publisher to fully appreciate the profits to be made from stroking the human libido" is Dana Thomas' description of Hugh M. Hefner, who started *Playboy* magazine in 1953.

During his high school and University of Illinois years, Hefner was involved with student publications and with cartooning. In Chicago, after graduation, Hefner worked in several jobs, writing copy for a department store and promotion copy for *Esquire* magazine. When *Esquire* wanted to transfer him to its New York office, Hefner resigned rather than accept $5 less a week than he demanded.

Remaining in Chicago, Hefner became circulation manager for *Children's Activities* magazine. Meanwhile, he mortgaged his furniture and borrowed money from friends to publish the first issue of *Playboy*, which appeared in December, 1953 and featured Marilyn Monroe's famed picture. Hefner is said to have had only $600 of his own money in the initial project. By the 1960s he was regularly writing "The Playboy Philosophy" column in which he voiced many of his opinions and views.

Hefner continued to expand his activities. He added movie and television productions and acquired hotels and expanded his Playboy Clubs across America. He had a successful club operation in England, until he was forced by the British government to sell out because of gambling irregularities. In the 1970s, he moved from his Chicago mansion to a 5½-acre estate in Los Angeles, from which he directs operations today.

Hefner, in 1965, was named an outstanding citizen of Chicago, and the Southern California chapter of the American Civil Liberties Union named him Man of the Year in 1971. He won the humanitarian award in 1972 from the National Association for the Advancement of Colored People. For his work related to individual freedom, he was given a First Amendment Freedom Award by the B'nai B'rith Anti-Defamation League.

When *Playboy* reached its 25th birthday, Los Angeles Mayor Tom Bradley and Chicago Mayor Michael Bilandic both proclaimed "Hugh M. Hefner Days."

Hefner has claimed "there's been a reluctance in some quarters to give *Playboy* its due." He admits he is "more creatively oriented than business oriented." In the late 1970s, he told *Folio* magazine that "today the public is closer to where *Playboy* is than at any time since we started publishing."

Hefner continues his concern for *Playboy*, while Christie Hefner and others seek to establish a firmer control over the business, faced with circulation decline and other problems.

**HEISKELL, Andrew** (1915- )
Born in Italy, Andrew Heiskell was educated in European schools. He spent a year at the Harvard School of Business before he decided against a business career.

Heiskell worked a year as a *New York Herald Tribune* reporter before becoming the associate editor of *Life* in 1937. He became the magazine's science and medicine editor and, in 1946, the publisher. He had worked briefly in the *Life* Paris office, and when he returned to New York, he helped move *Life* into more in-depth coverage of scientific and cultural subjects.

Heiskell became vice-president of Time Inc. in 1949 and chairman of the board from 1960 and 1969. In 1969, he added the title of chief operating officer. Upon his retirement from these duties in 1980, after four decades with Time Inc., John Meyers wrote in *Time*: "In many ways he has been a towering figure in the publishing business. No one could claim to know it better, to have contributed more to it, or, at 6 ft. 5½ in., to have dominated it so literally."

Two years after his retirement, Heiskell said, in accepting the Henry Johnson Fisher Award as Publisher of the Year from the Magazine Publishers Association, "In this business, it's not only important to enjoy yourself for your own sake, but equally for your product's sake." Under his leadership, Time Inc. launched *Discover, Money*, and *People* and revived *Life*.

Heiskell is chairman of the New York Public Library and the Bryant Park Restoration Corp. and is on the executive committee of the Brookings Institute.

**HEISKELL, John N.** (1872–1972)
For 70 years, John N. Heiskell edited the *Arkansas Gazette* in Little Rock. For a few days, between January 6 and January 19, 1913, he was a U.S. Senator, appointed by the governor.

During his long career with the *Gazette*, Heiskell was awarded a citation by the American Library Association in 1957 for his service to the Little Rock Public Library. Both Syracuse and Columbia universities awarded him medals in 1958, and four years later, the University of Missouri awarded him its Journalism Medal. He also won the Lovejoy and the John Peter Zenger awards and recognition from Sigma Delta Chi.

**"HELOISE" (Heloise Bowles)** (?–1977)
After a brief career as a columnist on the *Honolulu Advertiser*, 1959–62, Heloise Bowles began her "Hints From Heloise" in 1962. This column was syndicated until her death in 1977, when her daughter took it over.

Many of Heloise's "hints'" were collected into books, with six published during her lifetime. She was also given many awards, including the

Key to the City by Fort Worth, Texas, New Orleans, Louisiana, and Waco, Texas. She worked with the blind and was honored for her non-journalistic activities.

**HEMINGWAY, Ernest** (1899–1961)
Ernest Hemingway is probably best remembered for his books and short stories, yet his early career, when he learned the art of writing, was with newspapers and magazines. During his high school days in Oak Park, Illinois, he wrote for the newspaper and literary magazine.

Years after he worked for seven months on the *Kansas City Star*, Hemingway said "Those were the best rules I ever learned for the business of writing. I've never forgotten them." He was referring to the stylesheet written by the *Star*'s founder, William Rockhill Nelson.

Later Hemingway worked on the *Toronto Daily Star* (Canada), the *Chicago Tribune*, and the *Co-operative Commonwealth*, in Chicago. He was with the North American Newspaper Alliance and at one time represented the picture newspaper, *PM*, in the Far East during World War II. Among the magazines that printed his material were *Esquire, Ken, Collier's, Look* and *Life*.

Hemingway reported World War I and II and the Spanish Civil War. He preferred to invent his material rather than to describe events, and no doubt used money from non-fiction writing to support his fiction.

Among his many books are *Across the River and Into the Trees*; *A Farewell to Arms*; *A Moveable Feast*; *Death in the Afternoon*; *The Fifth Column and the First Forty Nine Stories*; *For Whom the Bell Tolls*; *Green Hills of Africa*; *In Our Time*; *Men at War* (anthology); *Men Without Women*; *The Old Man and the Sea*; *The Sun Also Rises*; *Three Stories and Ten Poems*; *Spanish Earth*; *To Have and Have Not*; *Torrents of Spring*, and *Winner Take Nothing*.

In 1953 Hemingway won a Pulitzer Prize and was named a Honorary Game Warden in Kenya. The next year he won the Nobel Prize in Literature.

**HENDIN, David Bruce** (1945– )
David Hendin joined the Newspaper Enterprise Association as a science editor in 1969, at which time he also wrote a syndicated column, "Man and His World." For five years he wrote the NEA "Medical Consumer" column. Of his ten books, one, *Death As a Fact of Life*, has been a bestseller.

Hendin became the executive editor and vice-president of United Media Enterprises in 1971 and, in 1983, senior vice-president for the United Features Syndicate/Newspaper Enterprise Association.

Hendin's responsibilities include the company's Sunday comic printing business, reader service and patterns, and a new literary agency.

Hendin is a member of the University of Missouri School of Journalism off-campus faculty and has also lectured at the Columbia University School of Journalism. He received the American Association of Blood

Banks Award and the Claude Bernard Science Journalism Award in 1972, and medical journalism awards from the American Medical Association and the American Heart Association Blakeslee Award in 1973. Four years later, he won the Book of the Year Award from the American Medical Writers Association.

He is a member of several organizations and has a special interest in coin collecting.

Among Hendin's books are *Everything You Need to Know about Abortion*; *The Doctor's Save-Your-Heart Diet*; *Death As a Fact of Life*; *Save Your Child's Life*; *The Life Givers*; *A Guide to Ancient Jewish Coins*; *The World Almanac Whole Health Guide*; *The Genetic Connection*; and *Collecting Coins*.

Assuming his new titles in 1983, Hendin said that his organization receives from 7,000 to 10,000 submissions a year, with only six to ten chosen.

**HENRY, Bill** (1890–1970)
From 1911 to 1970, Bill Henry was associated with the *Los Angeles Times* and was the *Times'* war correspondent in France and the South Pacific during World War II. He also reported for the CBS Network in 1941. Later, he worked as a news analyst for the NBC Network.

Henry was an administrative aide on President Richard Nixon's round-the-world goodwill trip in 1956. He had a similar role on Nixon's African tour in 1957. Henry won honors from the Headliner Club and the Freedoms Foundation, both for his newspaper columns and his radio reporting. At one time he was president of the President Radio Correspondents Association in 1947.

In 1948, he wrote the *History of the Olympic Games*.

**HENRY, William Alfred III** (1950– )
From 1971 to 1980, William Henry III worked for the *Boston Globe*, serving in several capacities, as education writer, art critic, political reporter, editorial writer, columnist, and critic-at-large. He also worked briefly for the *New York Daily News*, as book reviewer and critic-at-large. In 1981, Henry became an associate editor of *Time*.

During his newspaper career, Henry received the Story of The Year Award from the New England Associated Press and Best Feature of the Year Award from the New England United Press International; he was also co-recipient of an editorial prize from United Press International.

He has written several books and has been a university lecturer; throughout his life, he has been active in civic projects.

**HENTOFF, Nathan Irving** (1925– )
Jazz was the highlight of Nat Hentoff's early career as reflected in his publications and activities. Since 1960 he has been a staff writer for *The New Yorker*. He co-founded *The Jazz Review* in 1958 and had been an associate editor on *Down Beat*. Since 1957 he also has been a columnist and staffer on *The Village Voice*. He also writes a weekly column on civil liberties for the *Washington Post*.

In 1950 Hentoff was a Fulbright fellow at the Sorbonne in Paris. Between 1944 and 1953 he was a writer, producer, and announcer for radio station WMEX. other activities include a role as music adviser for CBS-TV "The Sound of Jazz" and "The Sound of Miles Davis."

Currently Hentoff works with the Reporters Committee for Freedom of the Press and the Freedom-to-Write Committee of PEN.

Hentoff's books include *Hear Me Talkin' to Ya* (edited with Nat Shapiro); *The Jazz Makers*; *Jazz* (with Albert McCarthy); *The Collected Essays of A. J. Muste*; *The Jazz Life*; *Peace Agitator: The Story of A. J. Muste*; *The New Equality*; *Jazz Country*; *Call the Keeper*; *Our Children Are Dying*; *Onwards*; *A Doctor Among the Addicts*; *I'm Really Dragged but Nothing Gets Me Down*; *Journey Into Jazz*; *A Political Life: The Education of John V. Lindsay*; *In The Country of Ourselves*; *State Secrets: Police Surveillance in America*; *This School Is Driving Me Crazy*; *Jazz Is*; *Does Anyone Give a Damn? Nat Hentoff on Education*; *The First Freedom: The Tumultuous History of Free Speech in America*; *Does This School Have Capital Punishment?*; *Blues for Charles Darwin* and *The Day They Came to Arrest the Book*, and *The Man from Internal Affairs*. He also has contributed to other books.

**HERSEY, John** (1914- )

Although John Hersey may better be recognized for his many books, he was associated with *Time* and *Life* magazines for many years. For one summer, 1937, he was the private secretary for Sinclair Lewis.

In 1937 Hersey joined *Time* as a staff writer, remaining there until 1944 when he became *Life*'s senior editor. From 1942 to 1946 he was a war and foreign correspondent for *Time*, *Life*, and *The New Yorker*. Since 1950 Hersey has been associated with Yale, first as a fellow at Berkeley College there and later at Pierson College. He has lectured at the Salzburg Seminar in American Studies, Massachusetts Institute of Technology, and the American Academy in Rome.

The Pulitzer Award went to Hersey in 1945, followed by the Sidney Hillman Foundation award in 1951 and the Howland Medal from Yale in 1952. For five years, 1975–1980, he was president of the Authors League of America, and, since 1981, he has been chancellor of the American Academy and Institute of Arts and Letters.

William Swanberg wrote that Hersey was "a man whose compassion could cross national boundaries." Born in China, he came to America when he was 10. At one time he was considered a possible successor to Henry Luce at Time Inc. Hersey's *Hiroshima* originally appeared in *The New Yorker*, which devoted the entire issue to this story that created a sensation and quickly appeared in book form.

Among his books are *Men on Bataan*; *Into the Valley*; *A Bell for Adano*; *Hiroshima*; *The Wall*; *The Marmot Drive*; *A Single Pebble*; *The War Lover*; *The Child Buyer*; *Here to Stay*; *White Lotus*; *Too Far to Walk*; *Under the Eye of the Storm*; *The Algiers Motel Incident*; *Letter to the Alumni*; *The Conspiracy*; *The Writer's Craft*; *My Petition for More Space*; *The President*; *The Walnut Door*, and *Aspects of the Presidency*.

**HERSH, Seymour** (1937– )
*The Price of Power* is a 700-page study of Henry Kissinger in the White House, and Seymour Hersh, the author of this 1983 study, has been called by some "the best investigative reporter alive."

After earning a degree in history from the University of Chicago, Hersh's first journalistic experience was with the City News Bureau in that city as a police reporter, 1959–60. For a brief time, he and a colleague operated a newspaper in Evergreen Park, Chicago. The paper failed.

Hersh worked for the United Press International in Pierre, South Dakota and later for the Associated Press in Chicago. The AP sent him to Washington in 1965 where he covered the Pentagon, making contacts that assisted him in uncovering the My Lai story and William Calley's role in it. His story was privately syndicated.

Hersh worked for the *New York Times* in Washington, 1972–75, and in New York with the newspaper until 1978. For his My Lai story Hersh won the international reporting Pulitzer Prize in 1970, along with the Worth Bingham and Sigma Delta Chi awards. Other recognition included the George Polk Memorial Award; the Scripps-Howard Public Service and the Polk awards for stories of the B-52 bombing of Cambodia; and the Sidney Hillman and Polk awards for his exposure of domestic CIA spying. He has often been at odds with the CIA over his reports. He also won the John Peter Zenger Freedom of the Press Award and the Drew Pearson Award.

Hersh's books include *Chemical and Biological Warfare: America's Hidden Arsenal*; *My Lai 4: A Report on the Massacre and Its Aftermath*; and *Cover-Up: The Army's Secret Investigation of the Massacre of My Lai 4*.

In relating his problem in writing *The Price of Power*, Hersh told Peter Gorner of the *Chicago Tribune*, "I'm broke and this (book) is a gamble. I left the *Times*, a good job with great security, and that international air travel card." He added that "Travel ate up my $250,000 advance first. I finally had to borrow $61,000 from my banker."

Hersh is now a national correspondent for the *Atlantic Monthly*.

**HERSHEY, Lenore** (?– )
Lenore Hershey has been associated with *McCall's* and the *Ladies' Home Journal* for three decades. From 1952 to 1968, she was editor of *McCall's*; in 1968, she became the managing editor and later executive editor of the *Ladies' Home Journal*; and in 1973, she became editor-in-chief of the *Journal*, a position she held until 1981.

When Hershey became editor she promised "to produce the kind of magazine that will amplify, enlarge and illuminate the life of its readers."

In a 1980, *Boston Globe* story by Marian Christy, Hershey was called "one of the most influential women in America." Christy added that "she rules the *Journal* with an iron hand and although the word 'ladies' is paramount in her professional life, she herself wavers between feminism and classical femininity."

Hershey said, "I don't think of myself as a working woman. I am a woman who works." She added, "I am impatient with ineptitude and lack of dedication, but compared to male bosses, I am less secret. My door is always open."

Hershey has held many civic positions, working with the President's Commission for Observance of the International Women's Year, the National Center for Voluntary Action, the Child Study Association, and others. Her alma mater named her to the Hunter College Hall of Fame. The *World Almanac* calls her one of the 25 most influential women in America.

She writes short stories and articles.

**HEWITT, Don** (1922– )

As executive producer of CBS "60 Minutes," Don Hewitt reaches millions of the television viewers each Sunday evening with his all-star cast.

Av Westin credits Hewitt with finding "a way to make four grown men speak with his voice and to share his interests in the world." Hewitt accepts or rejects each story proposal for this network show.

In 1960, Hewitt produced the first Kennedy–Nixon television debate, and has been associated with "A Conversation with Kennedy" and a similar show with President Johnson. From 1961 to 1964, he produced the CBS Evening News with Walter Cronkite. He also traveled with Eisenhower and Kennedy on their European tours.

Hewitt took over "60 Minutes" in 1967. He wrote, in a defense of this top-rated show in a *Newsweek* 1983 report, "We are nobody's darling." He cited many persons and groups that refuse to have any contact with the show, including the World Jewish Congress, the Palestine Liberation Organization, the National Council of Churches, and the National Rifle Association.

In replying to newspaper critics, Hewitt noted: "We didn't invent gossip columns, advice to the lovelorn, horoscopes, banner headlines, 'Maggie and Jiggs,' 'Barney Google,' crossword puzzles, the quote of the day and Wingo, a bingo-style numbers game. Newspapers did."

**HIBBS, Ben** (1901–1975)

Ben Hibbs became a leader in the magazine world during his long association with the Curtis Publishing Co., the largest such company in America at that time. He began work, however, as a newspaperman, serving the *Fort Morgan Times* (Colorado), the *Goodland News-Republic* (Kansas), and the *Arkansas City Traveler* (Kansas) from 1923 to 1928, with two years out for a college teaching assignment.

Hibbs moved to Philadelphia as associate editor of the *Country Gentleman*; in 1940, he became editor. Two years later, he moved to the Curtis-owned *Saturday Evening Post* as editor, remaining until 1963. Leaving Curtis, Hibbs spent nine years with *Reader's Digest* as a senior editor.

The Universities of Pennsylvania and Kansas honored Hibbs as did the National Education Association. He also won a George Washington Medal from the Freedoms Foundation.

**HICKEY, Maurice** (1935?– )
In 1983, Maurice Hickey became president of the Gannett-West Newspaper Group while still publisher of the *Reno Gazette-Journal* (Nevada).

Hickey is now in charge of 22 Gannett newspapers in 14 western and midwestern states, having spent nearly 20 years with Gannett, many in top management positions. He began his career in 1958 in his hometown as a reporter for the *Biddlefield Journal-Tribune* (Maine).

After that, Hickey worked on Norfolk and Philadelphia newspapers before going to the *Elmira Star-Gazette* (New York) a Gannett publication, in 1964. Other positions followed, including work with *Cocoa TODAY*, the Rochester (New York) newspapers, the *Lansing State Journal* (Michigan), and newspapers in Rockford, Illinois. In 1980, he became president of GANSAT, the Gannett Satellite Information Network.

In assuming his more recent assignment, Hickey said, "I do believe in a balanced newspaper" where good news stands alongside bad. He added that a newspaper should be a "good citizen."

**HIGGINS, Marguerite** (1920–1966)
As a war correspondent for the *New York Herald Tribune*, Marguerite Higgins became well known to American readers for her coverage of the wars in Korea and Vietnam. She joined the newspaper in 1942 and became a war correspondent two years later, the chief of the Berlin Bureau in 1947, and the chief of the Tokyo Bureau in 1950. Between the two wars, Higgins served as a diplomatic correspondent in Washington.

Higgins told General Douglas MacArthur, who objected to her presence in Korea, that "I am not working in Korea as a woman. I am there as a war correspondent." He eventually let her return to Korea and subsequently gave her an exclusive interview.

Higgins witnessed the death of the first American soldier in Korea and was there when Seoul fell in 1950. She shared the hardships of covering this war with male reporters and soldiers.

She moved to Vietnam, where she was a "hawk" in this conflict. She expressed her feeling that the atomic bomb should be used, if necessary, to halt the advance of Communism. She contacted an Asiatic infection there in 1965, and died a slow death the next year.

Higgins won a Pulitzer Prize in 1951.

Her books include *War in Korea—Report of a Woman Combat Correspondent; News Is a Singular Thing; Red Plush and Black Bread*; and *Our Vietnam Nightmare*. She co-authored *Overtime in Heaven: Adventures in the Foreign Service.*

**HIGHTOWER, John M.** (1909– )
John Hightower, who spent a career with the Associated Press, has won many awards, including a Pulitzer Prize. After a brief time as editor of *Drug Topics* magazine, 1929–30, he became a reporter with the *Knoxville News-Sentinel* (Tennessee).

In 1933, Hightower joined the AP in Nashville, Tennessee, and he worked in the Washington Bureau from 1936 to 1971. During those years, he covered many significant events, such as United Nations conferences around the world and the Kennedy-Khrushchev meeting. He also covered the Navy and State departments.

Hightower won the Raymond Clapper and Sigma Delta Chi awards, the first newsman to win these major awards in the same year, 1951. His style has been called "explanatory–interpretive."

**HILL, Pamela** (1938– )
As a television producer, Pamela Hill has won awards for her work with NBC and ABC. From 1961 to 1964, she worked for the Nelson Rockefeller presidential campaign and then joined NBC News as a researcher and, eventually, worked as a producer to 1973. With ABC News in New York since 1973, she has produced several series, winning an Emmy in 1974.

Hill has also won a George Foster Peabody Award and the du Pont Award from Columbia University, along with the Clarion, Christopher, National Press Club, Gabriel and Headliner awards. The New York State Broadcasting group honored her in 1975.

**HILLS, Lee** (1906– )
After more than a half-century in newspaper work, Lee Hills became publisher emeritus of the *Detroit Free Press* (Michigan) and editorial chairman emeritus of the *Miami Herald* (Florida) in 1981. He had been editorial chairman of Knight-Ridder Newspapers Inc.

When Hills received the William A. White Foundation Award in 1983, he called for better reporting of the "process of change, the causes and trends behind the individual events, putting them in both historical and social perspective."

Hills won a 1956 Pulitzer Prize for his coverage of the UAW-Ford-General Motors negotiations for a guaranteed annual wage. He started his career in Utah in 1924 on the *Price News-Advertiser*. He also worked on the *Oklahoma City Times*, the *Oklahoma News*, the *Cleveland Press* (Ohio), the *Indianapolis Times* (Indiana), and the *Memphis Press-Scimitar* (Tennessee).

In 1942, Hills became managing editor of the *Miami Herald* and, from 1970 to 1972, he was publisher. When he was with the *Detroit Free Press*, he was editor, publisher, president, and, from 1979 to 1981, editorial chairman. He has held several executive positions with Knight-Ridder group.

In professional circles, Hills has been president of the American Society of Newspaper Editors, the Associated Press Managing Editors Association, the Florida Associated Press Association, and Sigma Delta Chi.

**HIRSCH, George A.** (1934– )
"The name of the publishing game is the economics of circulation," said George A. Hirsch, who established *New Times* in 1973. When the magazine stopped publication 1978, Hirsch said, "To meet the skyrocketing costs of putting out a magazine, all publishers have been forced to raise subscription prices."

Earlier, 1962–67, Hirsch worked for Time-Life International. For the next four years, he was with *New York* magazine, serving as president, treasurer, and director, before starting *New Times*.

Hirsch, since 1978, has been the publisher of *The Runner* magazine. As a magna cum laude graduate of Princeton, Hirsch is now a member of the University Alumni Council and on the publication board of its *Alumni Weekly*.

From 1957 to 1960, he served in the Navy.

**HOBBY, Oveta Culp** (1905– )
To some individuals, Oveta Hobby is best known for her newspaper career in Texas. To others, she is better known for her work as the first director of the Women's Army Corps (WACS) and, later, as Secretary of the Department of Health, Education and Welfare.

Following her 1931 marriage to William Hobby, publisher of the *Houston Post* and one-time Texas governor, she became the research editor on the newspaper. By 1938, she was executive vice-president. In 1941, she took a $1-a-year position with the War Department Bureau of Public Relations. The next year she organized the Women's Auxiliary Corps, eventually becoming a colonel and retiring in 1945. In 1952, she became the *Post*'s co-editor and publisher.

*Texas Business* magazine, in 1983, named Mrs. Hobby as the only woman on its list of "The 20 most powerful Texans." The magazine noted that "the 77-year-old mother of Lt. Gov. Bill Hobby is less active than she once was in corporate and civic affairs. But she still calls the shots in her family's publishing and broadcasting empire which includes the *Houston Post* and several radio and television stations."

The family fortune was estimated at between $100 and $200 million by *Quill* in 1982. In 1983, the *Post* was acquired by The Toronto Sun Publishing Corp. for a reported $100 million.

Hobby's civic and political activities have kept her busy. She was an early campaigner for Dwight Eisenhower and has promoted the Houston Symphony, the University of Texas and Rice University, the Sam Rayburn Foundation, the Eleanor Roosevelt Memorial Foundation, and other groups.

She has won the University of Missouri Journalism Medal and the Texas Press Association service award. Her son, William P. Hobby, has been involved in Texas politics and, from 1965 to 1983, was president of the Houston Post Co. and the firm's radio–television operations.

**HOGE, James** (1935– )
James Hoge has been described as a man "who takes chances, a man who will try almost anything. Some think him a bit of a dilettante. Some say he is easily bored. But all agree that he possesses a cool, reckless courage."

Thus Dennis Holder pictured the *Chicago Sun-Times* publisher in a *Washington Journalism Review* sketch. Holder added that Hoge "is one of the bright younger stars in journalism."

While working for his master's degree at the University of Chicago,

Hoge worked part-time on the *Sun-Times*, handling a variety of routine assignments. When he could not obtain a full-time position with this newspaper, Hoge spent a year in Washington on an American Political Science Association fellowship.

The *Sun-Times* eventually named him (1963–65) a Washington correspondent and brought him back to Chicago in 1965 as city editor. Later, he became executive vice-president and editor-in-chief. Journalism historian Ernest Hynds noted that "Hoge slowly updated the look and feel of the paper by adding younger writers, more sections, reviews and investigative pieces and by seeking Pulitzer awards."

Hoge was also in charge of the Field-owned *Daily News* in Chicago, but was unable to prevent its demise, although columnist Mike Royko said he gave it "one hell of a try." He once said newspapers "ought to make sure they protect their basic franchise, which is the presentation of newsworthy information and analysis."

Hoge has been active in civic projects and professional groups. After Rupert Murdoch bought the *Sun-Times*, Hoge moved to New York in 1984 as publisher of the *News*.

**HOHENBERG, John** (1906– )
John Hohenberg has spent a lifetime in journalistic projects, including newspaper work, teaching, and from 1954 to 1976, administrating the Pulitzer prizes.

Hohenberg, 1923–24, was a *Seattle Star* (Washington) reporter before he joined the *New York World*. He moved to the *New York Evening Post* as a foreign correspondent and later to the *Journal-American* and later rejoined the *New York Post*.

In 1949, Hohenberg, began a journalism teaching career at Columbia University, becoming emeritus in 1974. The Pulitzer prizes are administrated there. In 1976, the committee awarded him a special Pulitzer Prize for services to American journalism.

Since retiring from Columbia, Hohenberg has been a visiting professor at several universities.

His books include *The Pulitzer Prize Story*, updated in *The Pulitzer Prize Story II*; *The Professional Journalist*; *Foreign Correspondence—The Great Reporters and Their Times*; *The New Front Page*; *Between Two Worlds: Policy, Press and Public Opinion in Asian-American Relations*; *The News Media*; *Free Press/Free People: The Best Cause*; *New Era in the Pacific*; *An Adventure in Public Diplomacy*; *The Pulitzer Prizes: A History of the Awards*; and *A Crisis for the American Press*.

**HOPPER, Hedda** (1890–1966)
For years, Hedda Hopper and Louella Parsons waged a bitter battle for scoops as they covered the movie industry in Hollywood. Both wrote syndicated columns, featuring gossip about well-known stars.

Known for her famous hats, Hopper once wrote a book titled *From under My Hat*; she also wrote another book, *The Whole Truth and Nothing*

*But*. In addition to her column, which was syndicated by the Chicago-Tribune-New York Daily News Service, Hopper wrote many magazine articles.

**HOROWITZ, David Charles** (1937-    )
Combining a newspaper and broadcasting career, David Horowitz, in 1966, became associated with NBC News in Los Angeles as a correspondent, education editor, consumer authority, and ombudsman. In 1982, he had his own Horowitz/Consumer Buyline show.

Horowitz started as a reporter on the *Peoria Journal Star*, 1957–60. For a year, he worked for Lerner Newspapers and the Chicago City News Bureau before joining KRNT radio and television stations in Des Moines, Iowa. He was briefly with the ABC Radio Network in New York before spending a year, 1963–64, at NBC News as a Far East correspondent. After another assignment as public affairs director of WMCA in New York, Horowitz moved to Los Angeles.

Horowitz received Emmy awards in 1974, 1976, and 1977 for his success in consumer reporting. He has also been cited by the Los Angeles City and County for public service.

In 1979 he wrote *Fight Back* and *Don't Get Ripped Off*.

**HOSOKAWA, William K.** (1915-    )
After two years with the *Singapore Herald* and the *Far Eastern Review* in Shanghai, William Hosokawa returned to the United States for a career on western newspapers. Between 1942 and 1946, he was with the *Heart Mountain Sentinel* (Wyoming) and the *Des Moines Register* (Iowa). He joined the *Denver Post* (Colorado) in 1946 and continues there today.

Hosokawa wrote a history of the *Post*, *Thunder in the Rockies*, and later *35 Years in the Frying Pan*, in which he recalled his activities as a war correspondent, editor of the daily's *Empire* magazine, and other assignments. He became editorial page editor in 1977.

Hosokawa has been a lecturer in journalism at the University of Colorado and the University of Northern Colorado. The Japanese-American Citizens League in 1952 gave him its distinguished achievement award. He has also been honored by the Cowboy Hall of Fame and Sigma Delta Chi.

**HOTTELET, Richard C.** (1917-    )
After a four-year association with the United Press, from 1938 to 1942, Richard C. Hottelet worked two years for the Office of War Information in London.

In 1944, he began a long association with CBS, working first as a war correspondent in London, Moscow, Berlin, and Bonn. He returned to CBS News in New York City in 1956 and, since 1960, he has covered the United Nations.

Hottelet was honored by Brooklyn College in 1957.

**HOWARD, Jack Rohe** (1910– )
For most of his career, Jack Howard has been associated with the Scripps-Howard organization. This came after he had worked for the *Japan Advertiser* and *Shanghai Evening Post and Mercury* (China) 1932–33.

Howard joined the *Indianapolis Times* (Indiana) in 1933, and by 1935, he was with the *Washington Daily News*. Howard next turned to radio, with Knoxville station WNOX (Tennesee) and Continental Radio Co., in Washington, DC and New York which eventually became Scripps-Howard Broadcasting Co.

In 1939, Howard was assistant executive editor for the Scripps-Howard Newspapers. With the exception of his World War II service, 1942–45, Howard has been the president of Scripps-Howard Broadcasting Co.

Since 1976, he has been chairman of the board and a member of the executive committee with control over the group's newspapers, broadcasting facilities, syndicates, and the United Press International, until it was sold.

In professional circles, Howard has been president of the American Press Association and a director of the American Newspaper Publishers Association.

**HOWARD, Roy Wilson** (1883–1964)
The "Howard" of Scripps-Howard began his long and successful newspaper career with the *Indianapolis News* (Indiana) in 1902 as a reporter. He then worked for the *Indianapolis Star* before moving to the *St. Louis Post-Dispatch* (Missouri) as assistant telegraph editor.

After a brief tour as news editor of the *Cincinnati Post* (Ohio), Howard became the correspondent of the Scripps-McRae League in 1906 and the next year, when only 25, he became the New York manager of the United Press. By 1936, he was UP president, a position he held until 1952. He was also associated with the Newspaper Enterprise Association and was national president of Sigma Delta Chi.

During his career with Scripps-Howard, he was involved in the acquisition of the *New York Telegram* in 1927; the *New York World* in 1931, and the *New York Sun* in 1950. He was head of the *World-Telegram and Sun* until his death. He was chairman of the board of Scripps-Howard Newspaper from 1921 to 1953 and chairman of the executive committee from 1953 until his death.

The University of Missouri awarded him its Journalism Medal. Howard helped establish additional UP bureaus in Europe and in South America. He was involved with the wire service's premature announcement of the end of World War I, but UP survived this false armistice report. Howard provided staffers with bylines, a practice not then followed by the Associated Press.

**HOWE, Edgar Watson** (1853–1937)
"The Sage of Potato Hill," as Ed Howe was best known around the nation, spent most of his lifetime in Atchison, Kansas, where he was

editor and publisher of the *Daily Globe* from 1977 to 1911 and held the same titles with *E. W. Howe's Monthly* from 1911 until his death.

Calder Pickett, Howe's biographer, noted that Howe was without peer, one of the nation's top country reporters, a writer who placed brevity high on his list of writing talents. Howe became disturbed by what was occurring in America, especially in the twenties and thirties, because of "the ascendancy of the radicals and the decline of the conservatives." He was upset by Paul Whiteman and jazz, by Franklin D. Roosevelt, and by other changes in the nation. His pithy comments were widely reprinted in newspapers across America.

Before going to Kansas, Howe published the *Golden Globe* in Golden, Colorado. He learned typesetting in Missouri in his teen years and felt prepared for the Colorado task even though he was only 19 at that time.

Two of his many books became well-known, *The Story of a Country Town* and *Plain People*. His other books included *The Confession of John Whitlock*; *Daily Notes of a Trip Around the World*; *Travel Letters from New Zealand*; *Country Town Sayings*; *The Hundred Stories of a Country Town*; *Ventures in Common Sense*; *The Anthology of Another Town*; *An Autobiography*; *When a Woman Enjoys Herself*; *The Indignations of E. W. Howe*; *About Nothing by Nobody*; *In Defense of Men*; *An Ante-Mortem Statement*; *A Man Story*; *A Moonlight Boy*; *The Mystery of the Locks*; *The Blessings of Business*; *Success Easier Than Failure*; *Notes for My Biographer*; *Preaching from the Audience*; *Her Fifth Marriage and Other Stories*; and *Sinner Sermons*.

**HOWE, Quincy** (1900–1977)

Quincy Howe earned his reputation in radio and magazine activities, beginning with the *Atlantic Monthly* in 1922 and becoming editor of *Living Age* by 1929. From 1935 to 1942, he worked for Simon & Schuster publishers.

Howe started his radio career as a news analyst for CBS (1942–50). After teaching briefly at the University of Illinois, Howe joined ABC as a news analyst, working for the network from 1954 to 1963. He worked for other New York stations as well.

For a time (1961–65), Howe edited *Atlas* magazine and *World Press*. Later he became a contributing editor to the *Atlas World Press Review*.

In 1955, Howe won the George Peabody Award for his radio-television news analysis. Four years later, he won an Overseas Press Club award and, later, the Columbia-Catherwood Award for international news coverage.

Howe's books include *World Diary*; *England Expects Every American To Do His Duty*; *Blood Is Cheaper Than Water*; *The New and How to Understand It*; *Ashes of Victory: World War II and Its Aftermath*; and two volumes of *World History of Our Own Times*.

**HOWEY, Walter C.** (1882–1954)

Other than several years (1902–04), spent on the *Fort Dodge Messenger* (Iowa) and the *Des Moines Daily Capital* (Iowa), Walter C. Howey spent most of his career working on Hearst publications.

In 1904, Howey joined the *Chicago American* and two years later became city editor of the *Inter Ocean* in Chicago. From 1907 to 1912, Howey was with the *Tribune*, earning $8000 a year. He moved to the *Herald-Examiner* when Hearst offered him $35,000. He left Chicago for the *Boston American* in 1922.

Howey was one of the founders of the Hearst-owned *New York Mirror* in 1924, when Hearst finally decided that the tabloid was here to stay, five years after the establishment of the *Daily News*. Howey later became editor of the *Boston Record-American* and, in 1942, editor of the *Chicago Herald-American*. He was also supervising editor of Hearst's *American Weekly* Sunday supplement.

In addition to his newspaper career, Howey invented several electrical engraving systems.

According to journalism historian, John Tebbel, Howey "was the inspiration for Hildy Johnson's city-room nemesis in *The Front Page*." William Swanberg termed Howey "a brilliant screwball." The aging Hearst once asked Howey to "check carefully on all news stories about scientific advancements in the prolongation of life, and send him reports." Howey was one of the three executors of the Hearst will.

**HOYT, Palmer** (1897–1979)

Palmer Hoyt worked on the *Portland Oregonian* during summers in the early Twenties while attending the University of Oregon. He served in World War I in France and returned to work on the *Pendleton East Oregonian*. He also wrote pulp fiction, with stories based on sports, horror, detective, and Western themes.

Hoyt rejoined the *Oregonian* and, in 1929, was its movie reviewer. He moved to night city editor and, by 1934, managing editor. In 1943, Hoyt was head of the Domestic division of the Office of War Information in Washington, seeking to get news quicker to the public.

When Hoyt joined the *Denver Post* he told the staff, "Print the news as fairly as you can; comment on the news adequately, and never let the two functions mix." This had not been the newspaper's policy under the flamboyant Tammen-Bonfils leadership.

As Bill Hosokawa wrote in *Thunder in the Rockies*, "Hoyt had never tried to please everyone. He was his own man." He wanted respectability, credibility, and vitality for the *Post*.

Hoyt retired in 1970. He wrote a book, *A Gentleman of Broadway*, about Damon Runyon.

**HUBENTHAL, Karl Samuel** (1917– )

A cartoonist since 1935, Karl Hubenthal has worked since 1952 as a syndicated editorial cartoonist for Hearst newspapers.

Before joining Hearst, Hubenthal worked for the *Los Angeles Herald-Express* in 1935. After doing sports cartoons and free-lance magazine illustrations, he returned to Los Angeles as sports cartoonist for the *Examiner*, a Hearst newspaper, from 1949 to 1956.

Hubenthal was named the Best Sports Cartoonist at the New York

World's Fair in 1940. For many years, he has received awards from the Freedoms Foundation. In 1959, he won the Headliner Award. On three occasions, in 1962, 1968, and 1970, he was the National Cartoonists Society's Best Editorial Cartoonist.

He served with the Marine Corps, 1944–46.

**HUGHES, Emmet John** (1920– )
During his career, Emmet Hughes has been a foreign correspondent and editor for *Time*, *Life*, and *Fortune*. He published his first book, *The Church and the Liberal Society*, shortly after he graduated from Princeton. The book was an expanded version of his senior honor's thesis.

During World War II, Hughes was press attaché in Spain. He was in the Army with the Office of Strategic Services and with the Office of War Information.

In 1946, Hughes joined Time-Life Bureau in Rome, and two years later, became the Berlin Bureau chief before returning to New York as *Life*'s articles editor. He worked in Dwight Eisenhower's campaigns, 1952 and 1956, as a speechwriter. He also helped to write the President's first inaugural address. Hughes wrote *The Ordeal of Power* about these experiences.

In 1960, he left the Luce organization to work for the Rockefeller family as a senior adviser on public relations. In 1962, he became a columnist for *Newsweek*.

**HUGHES, John** (1930– )
Early in his career, John Hughes worked for newspapers in South Africa and London, and was also associated with the Reuters' news agency.

Hughes spent 25 years, from 1954 to 1979, with the *Christian Science Monitor*, the last nine years as editor and manager, and for a few years, he was the newspaper's correspondent in Africa and the Far East.

During his years with the *Monitor*, Hughes expanded coverage and hired younger reporters to cover more youth-oriented topics, according to Ernest Hynds. More "problem-solving journalism" was encouraged. Between 1977 and 1981 he was publisher of Hughes Newspapers Inc. in Orleans, Massachusetts.

Hughes won a Pulitzer Prize for International Reporting in 1967. He was also honored by the Overseas Press Club and Sigma Delta Chi. Since 1981 he has been with the United States Information Agency.

**HUGHES, Lawrence M.** (1900–1982)
As the creator of the first daily newspaper advertising news column, Lawrence Hughes was for years associated with *Advertising Age* and *Sales Management* magazines.

In the early 1940s, Hughes was executive editor of *Advertising Age*, where he expanded the magazine's coverage of the industry. He was instrumental in establishing what is known today as the Agency Income Annual Edition.

Later, Hughes spent 30 years with *Sales Management.* Following his retirement, he was a columnist for *Air Transport World* and contributed articles to other publications.

**HULME, Etta** ( – )
Etta Hulme began drawing in the animation department of the Walt Disney Studios in 1945. She was there for only a short time, but she later said, "I think animation is the best experience a cartoonist can have. You get a feeling for movement and facial expression," according to an *Editor & Publisher* interview with David Astor in late 1983.

She was a free-lancer on the weekly *Texas Observer* in the mid-Fifties and, in 1972, was hired full time by the *Fort Worth Star-Telegram* (Texas) to provide six cartoons weekly. She won a Reuben award for editorial cartoons in 1982. Her cartoons are syndicated nationally.

Hulme's philosophy is "moderate-to-liberal; probably more toward moderate than liberal." She added, "I don't think you can really convert anybody. But you might point out a facet of an issue people are unaware of. That's a worthy aim."

**HUME, BRIT** (1943– )
Brit Hume was associated for several years with Jack Anderson, in the columnist's many activities, and working on the ITT and Dita Beard exposure. Hume was also involved in getting facts on cartoonist Al Capp and assaults on coeds.

Hume was a reporter on the *Hartford Times* (Connecticut) 1965–66, before joining the *Baltimore Sun* (Maryland) in 1967. He free lanced for a brief period and then joined Anderson in 1970. During his free-lance days he was a fellow at the Washington Journalism Center.

After the Anderson years, Hume joined ABC News, where he has served as a correspondent since 1976. In 1974, he wrote *Inside Story.*

**HUNT, George P.** (1918– )
George Hunt has spent his journalistic career with Time Inc. beginning in 1941 as an office boy; later he became a writer for *Fortune.* From 1948 to 1969, he was a member of *Life*'s staff, serving as correspondent, writer, bureau chief, and managing editor. From 1971 to 1973, Hunt was editor of Time-Life Film.

In accepting a National Magazine Award for *Life*, he discussed surveys and reports and added: "I should hope that nowhere are the results and demands of such studies affecting the judgments and decisions of editors . . . editors do care about the desires of their readers. But they care about them in the sense of feeling a responsibility toward them, a responsibility to give them what they, the editors, believe to be new, timely, thoughtful, provocative, beautiful, educational, historical."

**HUNTLEY, Chester Robert** (1911–1974)
The Huntley-Brinkley NBC News report led the television ratings for years until Chet Huntley retired in 1970. As Edwin and Michael Emery

wrote in their book, *The Press in America*: "Many Americans grew up with Huntley reading the news from New York and Brinkley adding his part from Washington, each time signing off with the somewhat silly and often imitated 'Good Night, David. Good Night, Chet.' "

Huntley worked 20 years on the West Coast and left Los Angeles for New York in 1956. During his earlier years, as well as during his last years, Huntley lived and worked in Montana.

While a student at the University of Washington in 1933, Huntley obtained a job on Seattle radio station KPCB. He was with Spokane station KHQ for a year 1936–37, and later worked in Portland and Los Angeles. For 12 years, starting in 1939, he was with CBS on the network's Los Angeles station as a newscaster and an analyst. In 1951, he was with the ABC Los Angeles station and, in 1955, he was with NBC in New York, where he handled many controversial subjects. He assisted in war bond campaigns during World War II.

Huntley and Brinkley worked the 1956 presidential conventions as a team, and Av Westin later wrote that some persons at NBC "backed Huntley, preferring the scholarly style, his good looks and the hint of Edward R. Murrow's authority in his voice. Others pushed for Brinkley, who was known for his wit, his superb writing ability and his dry, offbeat delivery on the air."

Huntley remained with NBC until 1970, and then became involved with the Big Sky Montana Inc. development company.

He won George Foster Peabody awards in 1942 and 1954, and awards from Ohio State University and New York University, as well as the University of Missouri Journalism Medal. Huntley was also active in outside projects, such as the Boy Scouts and the United Nations.

**INGERSOLL, Ralph M.** (1900–1984)

Ralph Ingersoll began as a reporter for *The New Yorker* in 1925 and, for five years, was its managing editor. In 1930, he moved to *Fortune* as associate editor, later becoming managing editor.

Ingersoll continued to advance at Time Inc., becoming vice-president and general manager for the corporations's magazines—*Time, Life, Fortune* and *Architectural Forum*—and the radio and cinema productions of "The March of Time."

For two years, 1937–39, Ingersoll was publisher of *Time*. From 1948 to 1959, he was president of the R.J. Co., Inc., which was involved in newspaper investments. He also has been involved with other management concerns and a number of newspapers.

Shortly before World War II, he helped to organize and finance the experimental PM newspaper. He has written nine books, the first in 1924, which are *In and Under Mexico*; *Report on England*; *America Is Worth Fighting For*; *Action on All Fronts*; *The Battle Is the Payoff*; *Top Secret*; *The Great Ones*; *Wine of Violence*; and *Point of Departure*.

Serving in the Army during World War II, Ingersoll won the Legion of Merit.

**INTERLANDI, Frank** ( - )

Nine years with the *Des Moines Register* and Tribune syndicate prepared Frank Interlandi for his move, in 1962, to the Los Angeles Times Syndicate. That same year he was voted the best cartoonist by Sigma Delta Chi.

Interlandi's cartoons have been described as "like casual charcoal sketches, with heavy lines and little definition of facial features." He also has been called "an artist of rare intensity." Today he works in Laguna Beach, California, surrounded by Thomas Nast originals.

**ISAACS, Norman Ellis** (1908- )

"The relationship between readers and newspapers is markedly different from what held in the '30s, '40s, and 50s," said Norman Isaacs in 1982, after he retired as director of the National News Council. Isaacs had called for such an organization in 1969 when he was president of the American Society of Newspaper Editors. He told that group he wanted "to establish some type of grievance committee."

Isaacs spent four decades in newspaper activities. He worked on the *Indianapolis Star*, *Times*, and *News* (Indiana) between 1925 and 1945, before he became the managing editor of the *St. Louis Star-Times* (Missouri). In 1951, Isaacs moved to Lousiville, Kentucky, where he spent the rest of his newspaper career on the *Times* (1951–61), and then as vice-president and executive editor of the *Courier-Journal* and *Times* from 1962 until his retirement in 1971.

Isaacs became chairman of the National News Council in 1977 after a brief tour as president and publisher of the Wilmington News Journal (Delaware) Co. Isaacs also became involved in the academic world as associate dean and editor-in-resident at Columbia University School of Journalism from 1971 to 1980.

Among his honors are the Dartmouth College Amos Tuck Award, the William Allen White Journalism Award, and the Southern Methodist University Medal. He has been active in many civic and professional affairs.

**JACKSON, Keith MacKenzie** (1928- )

Most sports fans are acquainted with Keith Jackson, a sports commentator, writer, and producer for ABC-TV in New York since 1964. Jackson worked for Seattle radio-television station KOMO for a decade (1954–64) before moving to ABC Radio as news correspondent for five years (1964–69). He has also been sports director for radio station KABC.

Washington State University gave Jackson its distinguished alumnus award. He has also won the Sylvania and Headliner honors. The Southern California News Directors Association gave Jackson its Golden Mike Award in 1972, and for several years, Jackson was the National Sportscaster of the Year.

**JAROFF, Leon** (1927- )

When Time Inc. established *Discover*, a science monthly, Leon Jaroff became the managing editor. Jaroff, who began as an editorial trainee for

*Life* in 1951, later was a *Life* correspondent in Detroit and Chicago. He switched to *Time* in 1958 as a Chicago correspondent. He later worked in Los Angeles before becoming Detroit Bureau chief in 1960.

By 1964, Jaroff was again in New York working for *Time*'s business section, and in 1966, he turned to science writing, preparing cover stories on the U.S. space and moon landing programs. In 1970, he became senior editor in charge of *Time*'s back-of-the-book section that includes Sports, Science, Behavior, The Sexes, Medicine and Environment units.

Jaroff's stories have won awards from the American Association for the Advancement of Science, the American Medical Association, and the American Institute of Physics. Before joining Time Inc., he worked briefly on *Material & Methods*, a technical magazine.

**JARRETT, Vernon D.** (1921– )
Vernon Jarrett has successfully combined newspaper and television careers. His newspaper career started in 1946 on the *Chicago Defender* as a reporter.

Jarrett, in 1970, started a column on the editorial page of the *Chicago Tribune*, and in 1983, moved to the *Chicago Sun-Times*. His opinion editorial page column deals with urban affairs, race relations, and politics.

For many years, Jarrett has been the producer and host of a Sunday morning talk show, "Black on Black," on Chicago station WLS-TV. He has been a member of the Pulitzer panel of jurors and twice has been nominated for reporting awards. He has won many awards for reporting.

**JASPIN, Elliot Gary** (1946– )
Investigative reporting has brought Elliot Jaspin recognition for his work on the *Philadelphia Daily News* (Pennsylvania) and other newspapers.

Jaspin, in 1971, worked on the *Augusta Kennebec Journal* (Maine). He next worked as an investigative reporter on the *Pottsville Republican* and the *Leighton Times News*, both in Pennsylvania. Since 1979, he has been with the *Philadelphia Daily News*.

Jaspin has won three Keystone Press awards for his reporting. He also won the Edward J. Meeman and the Silver Gavel awards, and in 1979, he won a Pulitzer Prize for local reporting. The University of Missouri awarded him its Journalism Medal in 1978, and the Associated Press Managing Editors, on two occasions, has recognized his work.

**JENNINGS, Peter** (1938– )
After several years broadcasting from London on "ABC World News Tonight," Peter Jennings, in 1983, became the lone anchor on the show.

ABC tried a similar experiment in 1965 when it placed Jennings against CBS Walter Cronkite and NBC Chet Huntley and David Brinkley. But as Jennings said in 1983, "I was as clearly unqualified for the job then as I am clearly qualified for it now."

Jennings began broadcasting when he was 10 on a Canadian radio show. His Canadian accent "gave his delivery a pleasant distinction," Av Westin wrote. While stationed in London, Jennings covered the Middle East crises, interviewing many of the involved leaders.

In a *TV Guide* story by Doug Hill, Jennings was compared to the James Bond character in the movies. "With his urbane good looks, the lingering traces of his Canadian accent and his impeccably tailored suits, he bears more than a passing resemblance to the actor who plays Bond, Roger Moore."

For a time Jennings was with the Canadian Broadcasting Co. in Montreal and later with CJOH-TV in Ottawa, but by 1964, he was with ABC News.

**JINKS, Larry** (1929- )
As vice-president of Knight-Ridder Newspapers in charge of the Metro Group, Larry Jinks is responsible for the group's 10 largest newspaper publishing operations. He is also responsible for the group's Washington Bureau and News Wire.

Jinks worked on newspapers in Muskogee, Oklahoma and in Greensboro and Charlotte, North Carolina. By 1960, he was the assistant city editor of the *Miami Herald* (Florida) moving to the executive editor's role in 1972. From 1977 to 1981, he was editor of the *San Jose Mercury News* (California).

Jinks received a distinguished service award in journalism from his alma mater, Columbia University, in 1982. He has been president of the Associated Press Managing Editors and the Florida Society of Newspaper Editors. He is a board member of the American Society of Newspaper Editors.

He served in the Army from 1951 to 1953.

**JOHNSON, Gerald White** (1890–1980)
For more than 26 years, Gerald Johnson contributed articles to the *New Republic,* while he also wrote editorials, taught journalism, and authored many books and won national recognition for his journalistic skills.

Johnson established the *Thomasville Davidsonian* (North Carolina) in 1910 and later worked on newspapers in Lexington and Greensboro before joining the School of Journalism faculty at Chapel Hill (University of North Carolina) in 1924.

Johnson's big-city career began as an editorial writer for the *Baltimore Evening Sun* (Maryland), 1926–39, and with *The Sun* for the next four years. Later, he was a news commentator for WAAM-TV.

Among his awards were the du Pont Commentators Award, 1953; the Sidney Hillman Foundation Award; the George Foster Peabody Award; the Gold Medal from the State of North Carolina, and the Andrew White Medal from Loyola College.

He wrote many books, including the following written between 1950 and his death: *Incredible Tale: This American People; Pattern for Liberty—Lunatic Fringe; Peril and Promise; The Lines Are Drawn; America: A History for Peter* (three volumes); *The Man Who Feels Left Behind; Hod-Carrier;*

*Communism: An American's View; Franklin D. Roosevelt; The Imperial Republic;* and *America Watching.*

He served with the Army in World War I.

**JOHNSON, Haynes B.** (1931– )

After two years, 1956–57, as a reporter for the *Wilmington* (Del.) *News-Journal* Haynes Johnson moved to Washington where he continues his career.

Johnson worked on the *Star* from 1957 to 1969 when he moved to the *Post.* First a national correspondent, Johnson later became the assistant managing editor and, since 1977, has been a columnist.

Among Johnson's numerous awards is the Pulitzer Prize for national reporting in 1966. He also has been cited by the Washington Newspaper Guild. For national reporting he won the Headliner and Sigma Delta Chi awards. Johnson has written or co-authored nine books, the most recent being *In The Absence of Power.* Other books include *Dusk at the Mountain; The Bay of Pigs; The Working White House,* and the following edited or co-authored volumes: *Fulbright: The Dissenter; Army in Anguish; The Unions; Lyndon;* and *The Fall of a President.*

From time to time, Johnson appears as a commentator on the NBC "Today Show" and PBS "Washington Week in Review."

Johnson once wrote that newspapers have "two functions, both vital: to report what is the news of the day, fully and fairly, and also to go beyond these events and draw a larger portrait."

He served in the Army from 1952 to 1955.

**JOHNSON, John H.** (1918– )

"The Man Who Turned *Ebony* Into Gold" is the title *Reader's Digest* gave a story on John Johnson in 1975. Other sources have called him "the most prosperous and influential publisher in American Negro history."

Johnson's career began in 1942 when he established *Negro Digest* in Chicago. This later became *Black World.* Since that time, Johnson has continued to move ahead, establishing other publications, winning many awards, and receiving many honorary degrees.

Johnson has often related his Horatio Alger story, telling how he borrowed $500 on his mother's furniture to help establish *Ebony* in 1945. In 1972, Johnson received the Henry Johnson Fisher Award naming him the Publisher of the Year. The award is given by the Magazine Publishers Association. Johnson said at the time, "Businessmen speak of cautious optimism. Perhaps we should think in terms of responsible daring. We have to anticipate what the reader will want tomorrow by walking a step ahead of him. In fact, we have to anticipate the reader's desires by leading him, step by step, to what he really wants."

Early in the history of *Negro Digest,* Johnson ran a series of articles by whites titled "If I Were a Negro." Among the authors were Eleanor Roosevelt, Marshall Field III, and Edward G. Robinson.

"Failure is a word I don't accept" is Johnson's philosophy. In an interview in the *Harvard Business Review*, Johnson admitted he had "a certain amount of fear" when he started a new magazine. With *Ebony* the problem for years was to obtain sufficient advertisements from so-called "white firms" that for years rejected his calls.

*Ebony* was Johnson's greatest success. On its 20th anniversary, *Ebony* carried a promotional message noting that its "editorial deals with present day and historical events centered around the lives of Negro Americans."

After *Ebony*'s success, Johnson started other publications. In 1950, it was *Tan*, later renamed *Black Stars*. In 1951, *Jet* was started "to give a brief weekly summary of all that is happening in the Black community." It has been highly successful.

*Ebony Jr.* arrived in 1972 for children six to twelve years old.

The Johnson family fortune has been estimated at $100 to 200 million by *Quill* magazine. It includes magazines, a radio station, an insurance company, a cosmetic business, and real estate. He is probably the wealthiest Black in America. In 1983 the company became the nation's largest black-owned firm in America.

Currently Johnson is preparing his daughter, Linda, to run the firm. She is now vice-president. In a 1983 interview, Johnson told the Associated Press about his early days in Arkansas before he moved to Chicago. "I read Dale Carnegie. . . . I read books on public speaking. I practiced in the mirror." Today he is in great demand as a speaker.

His publishing empire occupies a 11-story building on Michigan Avenue in Chicago. More than 250 paintings and pieces of sculpture by Black artists are scattered about the building. One room contains all the awards he and his publications have won. Each floor has a different color scheme.

Johnson is chairman and chief operating officer of the Supreme Insurance Co., where he once worked as an errand boy. He is also chairman of WJPC, the first and only Black-owned radio station in Chicago, and board member for several corporations, including Bell & Howell, Greyhound, Zenith, and Twentieth-Century-Fox Film.

In 1951, Johnson was selected one of the "Ten Outstanding Young Men of the Year," by the U.S. Junior Chamber of Commerce. He has won many other honors, including the John Russwurm Award, the Spingarn Medal from the AACP, and the Horatio Alger Award. The University of Missouri gave him its Journalism Medal in 1973. Many other institutions have honored him, including the University of Chicago, Columbia University, and Babson College. Sixteen schools have given him honorary degrees.

**JOHNSON, Wyatt Thomas, Jr.** (1941– )
Tom Johnson began his association with newspapers as a reporter and management trainee on the *Macon Telegraph and News* (Georgia), in 1965. Between 1965 and 1970, Johnson was a White House fellow, working with President Lyndon Johnson's press secretary, Bill Moyers, before he became a special assistant to the President and eventually an executive assistant.

Johnson returned to the media world as executive vice-president of the

Texas Broadcasting Corp. in Austin, 1970–73. He moved to the *Dallas Times-Herald* (Texas) as executive editor, vice-president and publisher from 1975 to 1977. At that time, he became the publisher and chief operating officer of the *Los Angeles Times*, where he remains today. In 1984 he returned to Dallas as chairman and chief executive officer of the *Times-Herald*.

Writing in the *National Forum* about American journalism, Johnson admitted that some of the public no longer believes in the press, although he said criticism will never stop. "I would be worried if it did. The give-and-take between the press and other public and private institutions in this country is inevitable, and desirable."

Johnson suspects "that critics of the press freedom will continue to have considerable public support until that same public perceives the media to be as open and as forthcoming as the media expect others to be."

**JONES, Jenkin Lloyd** (1911– )

Jenkin Jones has spent his career in Tulsa, Oklahoma, where he started as a reporter on the *Tribune* in 1933. He became the managing editor in 1938, the editor in 1941, and the publisher in 1963.

Jones was president of the American Society of Newspaper Editors in 1957 and of the U.S. Chamber of Commerce in 1969. He has been named to the Oklahoma Hall of Fame and has been honored by the William Allen White Journalism Award. He has also been cited by the American Legion and Freedoms Foundation and honored by the Universities of Wisconsin and Oklahoma and by Oklahoma State.

He served in the Navy during World War II.

**JONES, Family**

The *Tulsa Democrat* (Oklahoma) was acquired by Richard Jones, Sr. (1873–1963) in 1919. He changed the name to *Tribune*. Eventually Richard Lloyd Jones, Jr. (1909–1982) became the president and chairman of the board. He is a brother of Jenkin Jones, the publisher.

The senior Jones worked for the *Stamford Telegram* (Connecticut), the *Washington Times*, *Cosmopolitan*, and *Collier's*. He owned the *Madison State Journal* (Wisconsin) before he acquired the Tulsa newspaper.

Richard Jones, Jr. was inducted into the Oklahoma Aviation and Space Hall of Fame in 1981.

He was active in professional groups, holding offices in the Associated Press, and Bureau of Advertising of the American Newspaper Publishers Association. He was also president of the Southern Newspaper Publishers Association.

He served in the Navy during World War II and later was with the Tulsa Airport Authority for 30 years.

**JONES, William Hugh** (1939– )

After a tour with the Marine Corps, 1958–61, William Jones joined the *Chicago Tribune* staff. In 1965, he became the managing editor, where he remains today.

Jones won a Pulitzer Prize in 1971 for local reporting. This was for an investigation of ambulance service in Chicago. He has also won more than two dozen other awards, including a 1968 honor from the Headliner Club for a "Save Our Lake" series on pollution and ecology he wrote with Casey Bukro.

Northwestern University gave Jones its Alumni Association Award of Merit in 1972, and the University of Wisconsin-Milwaukee similarly honored him in 1975.

**JUDGE, Joseph** (1928– )

An amateur archeologist, artist, and bird watcher, Joseph Judge has been associate editor of *National Geographic* magazine since 1978, after several earlier assignments. He has written many articles for this monthly.

Judge was a *Life* reporter after graduation from Catholic University, where his work on the school yearbook had impressed the magazine staffers in New York. For a year he was a producer-director for Washington station WTOP-TV. From 1954 to 1963, he was a confidential assistant to the Secretary of Labor and later was awarded the department's Meritorious Service and Distinguished Service awards.

Judge now is in charge of the *National Geographic* writers, editors, and researchers and its News Service. He is also chairman of the Planning Council, where story ideas are reviewed.

Judge's interest in history was reflected in his first *National Geographic* story, on Jefferson's home, Monticello, in Virginia. "He has a lot of curiosity, a lot of drive," said a colleague. He is also interested in community affairs.

His alma mater, Catholic University, awarded him its Alumni Association Distinguished Achievement Award in 1975.

He served in the Army in the early fifties.

**KAEL, Pauline** (1919– )

Pauline Kael worked briefly, 1966–67, as the movie critic for the *New Republic* magazine before joining *The New Yorker* in 1968, where she continues to write reviews, working six months of each year.

Kael's first movie review appeared in a San Francisco magazine in 1953. It was her opinion of Charlie Chaplin's "Limelight," which she called "Slimelight." Before her magazine career, she wrote a bestseller in 1965, *I Lost It at the Movies*, a collection of her reviews.

Her successful book made it possible for her to free lance for magazines. She worked for *McCall's* briefly, but was fired for panning "The Sound of Music." She has written six books: *I Lost It at the Movies*; *Kiss Kiss Bang Bang*; *Going Steady*; *Deeper into Movies*; *Reeling*; and *When the Lights Go Down*.

Kael won the George Polk memorial Award for criticism in 1970; the Guggenheim fellowship for European study in 1964; the National Book Award for *Deeper Into Movies* in 1974; and the Front Page Award from the Newswomen's Club in New York in 1974.

**KAISER, Robert Greeley** (1943- )
A winner of several major awards, Robert Kaiser has been with the *Washington Post* since 1967. From 1967 to 1970, Kaiser reported from Saigon before transferring to Moscow where he remained until 1974.

Kaiser returned to Washington as the *Post*'s national correspondent in 1975.

While overseas, he won a Front Page Award from the Baltimore-Washington Newspaper Guild for his reporting. Two years later he won another award from the Overseas Press Club.

Kaiser co-authored *Great American Dreams* and *Russia From the Inside.* He also wrote *Cold Winter, Cold War* and *Russia: The People and the Power.*

**KALB, Marvin** (1930- )
For many years associated with the CBS Network, Marvin Kalb switched to NBC in 1980. With CBS News in Moscow, 1960–63, Kalb was highly successful, partially because of his fluency in the Russian language.

Kalb was the CBS diplomatic correspondent in Washington from 1963 to 1980. He was a panel member of "Meet the Press."

Kalb has won several Overseas Press Club awards for his radio and television analysis.

His books include *Eastern Exposure; Dragon in the Kremlin* and *The Volga: A Political Journey Through Russia.* He was the co-author of *Roots of Involvement: The U.S. in Asia 1784–1971* and *Kissinger.*

He served in the Army, 1953–55.

**KALTENBORN, H. V.** (1878–1965)
H. V. Kaltenborn, a pioneer radio and television reporter, became widely known when President Harry Truman imitated his voice during the Missourian's campaign for the White House.

Kaltenborn began his newspaper career as city editor of the *Merrill Advocate* (Wisconsin) in 1899 and was with the *Brooklyn Eagle* (New York) from 1902 to 1930. In 1922, he was a radio broadcaster when radio was only two years old. In 1929, he was a CBS news analyst, and in 1940, he switched to NBC.

During his lengthy career, Kaltenborn covered political conventions, international conferences, and World War II. He served in the Spanish-American War, 1898–99, and in the 1930s he covered the civil war in Spain.

Kaltenborn has been honored by the National Federation of Press Women, Radio Institute of Ohio State University, and the National Civic Federation. He contributed to many magazines. His books include *We Look at the World; Kaltenborn Edits the News; I Broadcast the Crisis; Kaltenborn Edits the War News; Europe Now; Fifty Fabulous Years;* and *It Seems Like Yesterday.*

**KAUFFMANN, Samuel Hay** (1898–1971)
In 1952, The *Washington Star* celebrated its centennial, and for most of those one hundred years, the *Star* had been owned by the Noyes and the Kauffmann families.

Samuel H. Kauffmann was an assistant advertising manager on the *Star* in 1926. He moved up through the ranks to become president by 1963. From that year until his death he was chairman of the board. His son, John, replaced him. The Sixties were not good for the *Star*, and in 1971, it was sold to Texan Joe L. Allbritton.

**KEANE, Bill** (1922– )
"Family Circus" has a daily newspaper readership of more than 50 million. In 1983, its creator, Bill Keane, was named the "Cartoonist of the Year," winning his Reuben Award over Jim Davis ("Garfield") and Garry Trudeau ("Doonesbury").

Keane began as a syndicated cartoonist in 1954 with "Channel Chuckles." In 1960, he started "Family Circus." In accepting his Reuben Award Keane said, "I don't try to make my cartoons especially funny. I would rather have the readers react with a warm smile, a tug at the heart or a lump in the throat as they recall doing the same things in their own families."

Keane, who works in his home, says his family provides much of the "fodder" for his strip. "I try to show the love that exists between different family members in the home, which is the happiest place in the world."

In 1945, he was a cartoonist for *Stars & Stripes*, having served in the Army from 1942 to 1945. For two years, he was president of the National Cartoonists Society. His "Family Circus" characters have also appeared in television holiday specials. To mark the panel's 25th anniversary in 1985, Keane's book, *The Family Circus Album* was released.

**KEATING, William J.** (1927– )
A career in his home state of Ohio has brought William J. Keating to the position of president and publisher of the *Cincinnati Enquirer*. Keating also is president of Gannett Central Newspaper Group, which includes seventeen dailies in six states.

Keating was trained in law and, in 1974, was honored with the University of Cincinnati William Howard Taft Medal for Notable Achievement. The next year, his alma mater awarded him a honorary doctorate degree. He was associated with the State of Ohio as an assistant attorney general and later was a municipal and, eventually, a county judge. From 1971 to 1974, he served in Congress.

In 1974, Keating joined the *Enquirer* as president and chief operating officer, becoming president and publisher in 1979. He has been active in the Associated Press, serving on its board; the American Society of Newspaper Editors, the American Newspaper Publishers Association, the Newspaper Advertising Bureau, and the Ohio Newspaper Association. In addition, he has been involved in civic projects in Cincinnati, including the University of Cincinnati, the Cincinnati Symphony Orchestra, and several hospitals. He served in the Navy during World War II.

**KEETON, Kathy** (1939– )
For her achievement as editor of two magazines, Kathy Keeton was named one of the Outstanding Women in Communications in late 1982.

Keeton first edited *Viva*, which was published by the Penthouse organization. It had only a brief career, and lost $14 million, which Keeton blamed on "the prejudices of the bloody distributors [who] thought it was a dirty magazine for women."

With Bob Guccione the publisher, as he was with *Viva*, Keeton is editor of the more successful *Omni*, which was started in 1978. She said *Omni* is "intended to stimulate and evoke curiosity." Guccione calls it "an original if not controversial mixture of science fact, fiction, fantasy and the paranormal."

Keeton is now president of *Omni* and vice-chairman of Penthouse International.

**KELLY, Stephen E.** (1919–1978)
"A modest, witty, blue-eyed man with rusty hair" describes Stephen Kelly, who became president of the Magazine Publishers Association in 1969, a position he held until his death.

In his memory, the MPA annually awards a $25,000 prize to honor creative excellence in advertising campaigns in magazines.

After Navy service in World War II, Kelly joined Time Inc. in merchandising. By 1954, he was the New York manager for *Sports Illustrated*, eventually becoming its advertising sales director. He was later the publisher of *McCall's* and still later publisher of *Holiday* and the *Saturday Evening Post*.

Kelly considered the early 1970s the time of "the second great revolution in advertising—the return to print." In an *Advertising Age* review of Kelly's career, industry leaders spoke of his enthusiastic support for magazines that "rubbed off" on others. "He was a vigorous leader in all areas, particularly on the Washington Scene."

**KELLY, Walter Crawford** (1913–1973)
During the 1950s, Walt Kelly's "Pogo" was read by more than 50 million newspaper readers in America and abroad. He became so popular that, in 1952, there was a "I Go Pogo" campaign to place him in the White House.

Kelly used satire and a good sense of timing to depict current affairs, speaking through a group of unusual characters living in a Southern swamp. He had started his career while in high school, reporting for the *Bridgeport Post* (Connecticut). From 1935 to 1941, he was an animator at Walt Disney Studios. Six years later, he helped create children's comic books, in which Pogo first appeared. He told *Life* magazine, in 1952, that Pogo was "the reasonable, patient, soft-hearted, naive, friendly, little person we all think we are."

For a brief time (1948–49) Kelly was the political cartoonist for the short-lived *New York Star*.

Pogo was continued by the syndicate for two years after Kelly's death.

**KEMPTON, James Murray** (1918– )
As editor, columnist, and commentator, James M. Kempton has reached many audiences in America. He began in publicity work for the American

Labor Party in 1941, but soon joined the *New York Post* as a labor reporter. Between 1949 and 1965, he was the daily's labor columnist. On the *Post*, he noted, he "could say whatever I damned well pleased."

For a brief time (1963–64) Kempton was editor of the *New Republic* and, for two years, a columnist on the *World-Telegram* before returning to the *Post* in 1965. Two years were spent with the *New York Review of Books* before Kempton joined CBS Network as a commentator in 1970.

Kempton won the Sydney Hillman Foundation Award for reporting in 1950 and the George Polk Memorial Award in 1966. He was also recognized by the Newspaper Guild and the American Academy and Institute of Arts and Letters. He has written *Part of Our Time* and *American Comes of Middle Age.*

*Current Biography* notes that Kempton is "a master phrase-maker with a sharp ear and a sharp ear and a sharper pen." His journalism has been notable "for its compactness, its terse, arresting lead paragraphs, and its epigrammatic, allusive, and at times haunting style."

**KENNEDY, Edward** (1906– )

Edward Kennedy left the Carnegie Institute of Technology in Pittsburgh, where he was studying architecture, to become a reporter on the *Syracuse Journal* (New York) but soon moved to the *Newark Star-Eagle* (New Jersey), where he covered the famed Hall-Mills double murder trial in the middle Twenties. He was one of the youngest reporters among the 200 covering the case.

Kennedy then joined the Paul Block Newspapers and for two years he wrote on political affairs from Washington. He had his first exposure to foreign correspondent work when he worked briefly on the *Paris Herald* in France.

Kennedy returned as city editor of the *Newark Ledger* before joining the Associated Press in Pittsburgh in 1932. Later he was transferred to Washington and in 1935 to Paris. He covered the Spanish Civil War in 1937 and remained in Europe and Africa covering wars and political issues until he was returned to the United States following V-E Day.

As the Associated Press chief of the western front in World War II, Kennedy witnessed the German surrender at Rheims. He was part of a "pool" arrangement.

He released the story a day ahead of the release date, the official V-E Day, for which action violent opinions were voiced by his colleagues, who termed his action "the most disgraceful, deliberate, and unethical double cross in the history of journalism."

Kennedy, however, called it needless political censorship to withhold the agreement so long, especially since the German radio had already released the story. Ten years later he continued to defend his action.

Upon his return to America he was placed on "leave" by the wire service. Eventually he became the managing editor of the *Santa Barbara News-Press* (California). Each time he was asked about the incident he replied, "I'd do it again."

He was killed in an automobile accident.

**KENNERLY, David Hume** (1947– )
David Kennerly became widely known for his pictures taken as the White House official photographer during President Gerald Ford's years in office. Born in Oregon, Kennerly had worked as a photographer on the *Oregon Journal* and the *Oregonian* before joining the United Press International in 1967, working in Saigon in 1971–72. Kennerly was a *Time* photographer in Southeast Asia in 1973 and worked in Washington, 1973–74. According to an *Editor & Publisher* story in 1983, Kennerly "considers Lafayette Park his front yard." He plans to be married there.

He has written one book, *Shooter*.

For feature photography in Vietnam he won a Pulitzer Prize in 1972. Later he won an award from the World Press Photo group for his pictures from Cambodia.

**KENNY, Nicholas N.** (1895–1975)
Nick Kenny is known for his journalistic as well as his musical career. He began journalism as a sportswriter and a columnist on the *Bayonne Times* (New Jersey), in 1920. By 1924, he was with the *New York Journal* and, in 1927, the *Daily News*. From 1930 to 1963, he was a radio columnist for the Hearst *Daily Mirror* in New York.

After his *Mirror* work, Kenny moved to Sarasota, Florida, where he contributed a column to the *Herald Tribune*.

To some Americans he is better remembered for his songs, including "There's A Gold Mine in the Sky" and "Love Letters in the Sand." He also wrote two books, *Collected Poems of Nick Kenny* and *Poems to Inspire*.

Kenny served in World War I, and during World War II he was decorated by the Army and Navy for his canteen work in entertaining servicemen.

**KENT, Frank Richardson** (1877–1958)
Frank R. Kent has been described by Edwin and Michael Emery as one of the writers who was a "master of the practical political scene of the 1920's," but who was "not responsive to the social and economic shifts that brought the widespread increase in governmental activity in the New Deal Era."

Kent's career was associated with the *Baltimore Sun* (Maryland), where he started in 1898. He held various positions. For a decade he was a political reporter, and, in 1911, he was the managing editor. In 1922, he became the newspaper's London correspondent.

Kent reached a nationwide audience when his column was syndicated to more than 100 newspapers. He served on the Columbia University School of Journalism Advisory Board.

His books include *The Story of Maryland Politics; The Great Game of Politics; History of the Democratic Party; Political Behavior; Without Gloves;* and *The Story of Alexander Brown & Sons*.

**KERR, Walter F.** (1913– )
As drama critic for the *New York Herald Tribune* from 1951 to 1966, and for the *New York Times* since 1966, Walter Kerr has influenced theatergoers

for years. As early as 13 he had displayed an interest in being a critic, reviewing films for his Evanston, Illinois, high school newspaper.

Kerr continued his interest in drama at Northwestern University, where he worked on periodicals while writing two musicals. For several years, 1938–49, he taught drama at Catholic University, Washington. He wrote several plays that eventually reached Broadway.

He took a "temporary" job in 1951 with the *Herald Tribune*. He stayed there until he moved to the *Times*. Kerr won a Pulitzer Prize for criticism in 1978 and has won other awards for his theatrical work. For two years he was president of the New York Critics' Circle.

His books include *How to Write a Play; Criticism and Censorship; Pieces at Eight; The Decline of Pleasure; The Theatre in Spite of Itself; Tragedy and Comedy; Thirty Plays Hath November; God on the Gymnasium Floor; The Silent Clowns;* and *Journey to the Center of the Theater*. He also wrote two plays, *Sing Out, Sweet Land* and *Touch and Go*, and many articles.

**KESSLER, Ronald B.** (1943– )

In 1964, Ronald Kessler was a reporter on the *Worcester Telegram* (Massachusetts). From 1964 to 1968, he was on the staff of the *Boston Herald-Traveler*, and for the next two years, he was a bureau reporter for the *Wall Street Journal* in New York.

Investigative reporting has been Ronald Kessler's specialty since he joined the *Washington Post*, in 1970. He was named the Washingtonian of the Year by *Washington Magazine*, two years later. Among his investigations were the U.S. Postal Service and Nixon's real estate transactions in California.

Kessler has been described as cautious and thorough with a "quiet, sympathetic manner." He once said "It takes a real gut desire to get at the truth. It goes beyond a professional interest in getting good stories."

In 1973, Kessler received the George Polk Memorial Award for community service, and in 1979, for national reporting. In 1967, he won a United Press International news-writing award and the Sevellon Brown Associated Press Award. Other honors have come from the American Political Science Association and the Washington-Baltimore Newspaper Guild.

**KETCHAM, Henry King** (1920– )

"Dennis the Menace" has appeared in newspapers around the world since 1951. His creator, Henry "Hank" Ketcham, worked in Hollywood with the Walter Lantz productions and Walt Disney Productions between 1938 and 1942. He then did free-lance work until "Dennis" was born. He received the Billy de Beck Award from the National Cartoonist Society as the outstanding cartoonist in 1952, and a collection of his cartoons has been placed in the Boston University Library.

Ketcham sold his first cartoon in 1952 to the *Saturday Evening Post*. The title for his current cartoon came from a remark by his wife about their 4½-year-old son, "Hank, our son Dennis is a menace." No doubt his neighbor, Mr. Wilson, would agree.

During his World War II Navy days, Ketcham was a chief photographer specialist.

**KEY, Ted** (1912– )

"Hazel," a cartoon that appeared from 1943 to 1969 in the *Saturday Evening Post*, was syndicated in 1969. Ted Key, Hazel's creator, began his career on the now-defunct humor magazine *Judge*, in 1937. After that, he was a writer and cartoonist, with his work appearing in the *Saturday Evening Post, Look, The New Yorker, This Week*, and other periodicals. Later his "Diz and Liz" were featured in *Jack and Jill* magazine. From time to time, Key also wrote radio scripts.

Nearly 20 books have appeared featuring Hazel, plus a motion picture and a television special.

Key was in the Army Signal Corps, 1944–46.

**KILGALLEN, Dorothy** (1913–1965)

Following the career of her famous father, James L. Kilgallen, Dorothy Kilgallen began as a cub reporter on the *New York Evening Journal* in 1931. Winning a byline after only two weeks on the job inspired her to make journalism her career.

In 1936, Kilgallen participated in a round-the-world flight by commercial routes. The trip, which took 24 days, was later reported more fully in her book, *Girl around the World*.

By 1938, she had become a Broadway columnist for the Hearst *Journal-American*, and she also wrote for magazines.

Kilgallen started her radio career in 1941, with a weekly CBS "Voice of Broadway" show. In 1947, she was with ABC in her "Star Time" program. She and her husband, Dick Kollman, for a time had a "Breakfast with Dorothy and Dick" show. She also appeared on television with "Leave It to the Girls" and the better-known "What's My Line?"

She died in an accident in 1965.

**KILGALLEN, James L.** (1888–1982)

Damon Runyon once described James L. Kilgallen as "an editor's dream of a reporter." Kilgallen retired from an exciting newspaper career in 1966; he continued, however, to occasionally file stories for the Hearst Feature Service.

When he was 16, Kilgallen entered journalism on the *Drover's Journal* in Chicago. He worked on the *Chicago Tribune* and eventually was employed by all three major wire services, the Associated Press, the United Press, and the International News Service. He spent his last 38 years with the Hearst-owned INS.

Kilgallen owned the *Laramie Daily Boomerang* (Wyoming) before World War I. An *Editor & Publisher* story noted that Kilgallen "used to sit his baby daughter Dorothy at a typewriter at a front window and let sidewalk passers-by watch her pound the keys with her little fists." He outlived her by many years, "but he proudly watched her grow into a reporter, columnist, and radio and television personality with national exposure and international renown."

Among the major stories he covered was the Lindbergh baby kidnapping; he also covered World War II in Europe.

**KILGORE, Bernard** (1908–1967)
While a student at DePauw University, Bernard Kilgore studied economics and edited the campus newspaper. After graduation, he began his *Wall Street Journal* career at $45 a week, in 1929. Soon he joined the rewrite desk.

Kilgore was the *Journal*'s news editor on the Pacific Coast, 1930–32, before returning to New York City as financial columnist, 1933–35. The next four years he was chief of the daily's Washington Bureau, where he started the weekly "Washington Wire."

Kilgore was vice-president and general manager by 1942. The next year he was vice-president of the parent firm, Dow Jones & Co., Inc., and in 1945, its president.

As Jerry M. Rosenberg wrote in his book, *Inside the Wall Street Journal*, "For Kilgore reader interest and profitability went hand in hand. He sought a broad spectrum of business news, one that included political and sociological trends . . . one of Kilgore's most urgent priorities was top-quality writing. Style and comprehensibility became his obsessions." He did not tolerate sloppiness.

Under Kilgore's leadership, the *Journal*'s circulation moved from 30,000 to more than a million. Rosenberg believes such growth came from Kilgore's "creative energy." He was a trustee on the *Daily Princetonian* and on the board of DePauw University.

Kilgore wrote one book, *Do You Belong in Journalism?*

**KILPATRICK, James Jackson, Jr.** (1920– )
After a long career on the *Richmond News Leader* (Virginia) James Kilpatrick began a nationally syndicated column in 1964 devoted to political commentary. He also serves as a contributing editor to *National Review* and has been a regular on the "Agronsky & Co" television show. For many years, he provided the conservative comments on the CBS "60 Minutes" show opposite Shana Alexander.

Kilpatrick began as a reporter on the *Richmond News Leader* in 1941, after graduating from the University of Missouri. By 1949 he was the chief editorial writer and two years later its editor. During his high school days in Oklahoma City, he edited the student newspaper and worked summers during his university years on the *Oklahoma City Times*.

While in Richmond, he created the Beadle Bumble Fund, "to deflate an occasional overblown bureaucrat, to unstuff a few stuffed shirts and to promote the repeal of foolish and needless laws. There is entirely too much law and order in the world."

Long a friend of President Richard Nixon, Kilpatrick, in late 1973, wrote: "The time has come, much as a long-time admirer regrets to say it, to proceed with the impeachment and trial of Richard Nixon."

His alma mater, the University of Missouri, gave him its Journalism Medal in 1953. He has also been cited by Sigma Delta Chi and other groups for his commentaries. He won the William Allen White Medal in 1979 for distinguished service to journalism. In 1978, he returned to his native state, Oklahoma, where he was named to the Hall of Fame.

His books include *The Sovereign States; The Smut Peddlers; The Southern*

*Case for School Segregation*; and *The Foxes' Union*. He was editor or co-author of *A Political Bestiary*; *We the States*; and *The Lasting South*.

**KING, Frank O.** (1883–1969)
For more than 60 years, the comic strip "Gasoline Alley" has appeared in newspapers around the world, and before he died in 1969 at the age of 86, creator Frank O. King had developed three generations of the Wallet family.

Readers were excited when Skeezix was placed on Wallet's doorstep on Valentine's Day, 1921. King's approach since that time has differed from most other cartoonists—he permitted his characters to age.

King's career began on the *Minneapolis Times* (Minnesota) when he was 18. While studying art in Chicago, he also worked on the *Examiner*, and later the *Tribune*, where he experimented with comics. Before "Gasoline Alley" arrived, King had created "Bobby Make-Believe" and "The Rectangle."

In 1957, the National Cartoonists Society named "Gasoline Alley" the best strip of the year. In 1958, King was voted Cartoonist of the Year. He won other awards and wrote books about his basic characters. These were *Skeezix and Uncle Walt*; *Skeezix and Pal*; *Skeezix at the Circus*; and *Skeezix Out West*.

**KING, Larry** (1934?– )
"The Larry King Show" has expanded to include more than 275 Mutual Broadcasting System radio stations and more than 110 television outlets. In mid-1983, King was termed "the reigning monarch of late-night radio" by Gail Shister of Knight-Ridder Newspapers.

King has been in radio since 1957 in Miami, where he was first a handyman around the station. Soon he was on the air, hosting his own shows and conducting his famous interviews. King's radio show starts at midnight and continues until 5:30 each morning. The audience has been estimated at three and one-half million. This radio show began in 1978 with only 28 stations.

King claims his interview technique has not changed. "He does no preparation for guests, preferring the wide-eyed spontaneity that often emerges in first meetings," according to Shister.

Telephone calls to King's radio show are not screened, but those to his television show are. "TV is a more frightened medium," according to King. He compares his technique to that of the newspaper editor who screens the letters to the paper to decide which to print.

**KING, Thomas H.** (1934– )
For many years, Thomas King was group vice-president of McGraw-Hill Publications, after joining McGraw-Hill as a sales representative in 1956. He worked in Boston, Chicago, and Detroit. In 1975, he acquired his highest title at McGraw-Hill. In 1982, he became president of the American Business Press, a trade association.

King said he took the ABP position because "I didn't feel I was where the action was, and that bothered me. There were also limits to my power."

**KING, Warren Thomas** (1916–1978)
For 22 years (1955–77) Warren King served as editorial cartoonist for the *New York Daily News*. Prior to that, King freelanced, illustrating books, magazines, movies, and advertisements in New York. During those same years (1940–61), he was the editorial cartoonist for the National Association of Manufacturers.

Many of King's works are permanently displayed in the Pentagon and the Air Force Academy. They have also been exhibited in several countries. Freedoms Foundation awarded King medals of honor in 1953, 1959, and 1965 and its George Washington Honor Medal in 1963. The Foundation also gave him a certificate of merit in 1960. He has also been recognized with awards from the Newspaper Guild, on two occasions, and the Silurians, on three occasions. The Headliner Club and Overseas Press Club have also honored him.

**KINGSBURY-SMITH, Joseph** (1908– )
A long-time Hearst staffer, Joseph Kingsbury-Smith began with the International News Service as a copyboy and cub reporter in 1924. He then worked for the United Press, but later returned to the INS. After working in London, he returned to the United States to cover the Senate and the State, War, and Navy departments. He was again in Europe as general manager for INS and News Photos operations, 1944–55.

Moving up the executive ladder, Kingsbury-Smith was vice-president and director of Hearst in 1955, and publisher of the *New York Journal-American* from 1959 to 1966, when he became the chief foreign writer for Hearst newspapers and King Features Syndicate.

Since 1976, he has been the national editor for all Hearst newspapers. He won the Pulitzer Prize for international reporting in 1956 and has received awards from the Headliner Club, on three occasions, and from Sigma Delta Chi. He won the George R. Holmes Memorial Award, on several occasions, and the George Polk Award, in 1950.

**KINSLEY, Michael** (1951– )
Michael Kinsley was a National Magazine Award winner for General Excellence, in recognition of his 1½-years of work in "saving" *Harper's* magazine from sure death. To help in this rescue, Kinsley took a cut in his own pay, dropping from $80,000 to $55,000 annually.

"I have never had one word of thanks from this [*Harper's*] board" he was quoted as telling *Newsweek* in mid-1983. So Kinsley returned to the *New Republic* were he was once senior editor. In his new position, he writes the publication's best-known column, "TRB," which had been written by Richard Strout.

**KINTNER, Robert E.** (1909–1980)
Two years after obtaining his Swarthmore College degree in 1931, Robert Kintner was a financial news reporter on the *New York Herald Tribune*. For a time (1937–41), Kintner and Joseph Alsop, Jr. wrote a column, "The Capital Parade," which was carried in nearly 100 newspapers. They also wrote two books, *Men Around the President* and *American White Paper: The Story of American Diplomacy and the Second World War.*

Kintner served in the Army during World War II. In 1944, he joined the ABC Network as a vice-president and, by 1950, was president of the organization. He was vice-president of NBC in 1958, president in 1958, and after 1966, chairman. For a short time (1966–67), Kintner was a special assistant to President Lyndon B. Johnson.

Kintner won the Keystone Award from the National Association of Radio and Television Broadcasters.

**KIPLINGER, Austin H.** (1918– )
In 1939, Austin Kiplinger was a reporter for the family's *Washington Letter*. Between 1940 and 1945, he worked a year on the *San Francisco Chronicle* and then served in World War II as a Navy pilot.

After the war, Kiplinger worked with several non-family operations, including the *Chicago Journal of Commerce* and the ABC and NBC networks in Chicago as a commentator. By 1956, he was back in Washington, where he became president of the Kiplinger Washington Editors in 1959, editor of the *Washington Letter* in 1961, publisher of *Changing Times* from 1957 to 1979, and editor-in-chief since 1979 of *Changing Times*.

The son of Willard Kiplinger, Austin has been active in Washington projects concerning youth, health, and welfare activities, as well as the National Symphony Orchestra. Since 1967, he has worked with the Washington Journalism Center.

Austin's son, Knight A. Kiplinger, became vice-president of Kiplinger Washington Editors in 1983. He earlier had been associated with the Ottaway News Service.

**KIPLINGER, Willard Monroe** (1891–1967)
Willard Kiplinger, who made his "Letters" known the world over, began as a reporter on the *Ohio State Journal* in Columbus in 1912. Two years later, he joined the Associated Press there, and between 1916 and 1919, he was with the AP in Washington as a special reporter on economical topics.

In 1923, Kiplinger borrowed $300 and established the *Kiplinger Washington Letter*, at first a two-page mimeographed report. It included prophetic opinion, along with factual information. By 1946, it had a circulation of 125,000.

Later the firm added the *Kiplinger Tax Letter*, the *Foreign Trade Letter*, the *Agricultural Letter*, and the *Florida Letter*. The *Kiplinger Magazine* was started in 1947 and later renamed *Changing Times*.

Kiplinger was honored in 1937 with an honorary degree from Ohio State University. He wrote four books and articles for magazines. His books included *Inflation Ahead*; *Washington Is Like That*; *Boom and Inflation Ahead*; and *Your Guide to a Higher Income*. He also established the Washington Journalism Center.

**KIRKPATRICK, Clayton** (1915– )
After a brief time as a reporter for the Chicago City News Bureau in 1938, Clayton Kirkpatrick joined the *Tribune* staff. He moved up to become city editor, managing editor, editor, and since 1979, president of the Chicago Tribune Co.

Kirkpatrick "instituted a wide range of changes to improve the content, appearance and overall image of the paper," according to historian Ernest Hynds. The "turning point" in the *Tribune*'s history came under Kirkpatrick. According to Edwin and Michael Emery, Kirkpatrick expanded the staff, bringing in many younger writers. Between 1971 and 1976, the newspaper won three Pulitzer Prizes.

In Lloyd Wendt's monumental history of the *Tribune* he refers to Kirkpatrick as being "almost evangelical in his journalistic purity," who "demanded and got pristine editorial content." Kirkpatrick "made it clear that he did not intend to follow traditionalism in the manner of his predecessors." He added sections and called for more in-depth reporting.

In 1974, Kirkpatrick supervised the transformation of the morning *Tribune* into a 24-hour-a-day operation. He called the move "one of the biggest challenges to any American newspaper in this century."

Kirkpatrick won the William Allen White Journalism Award in 1977, and later, the Lovejoy Award and the National Press Club Fourth Estate honor.

**KNIGHT, John S.** (1895–1981)
For more than three decades, John S. Knight expressed his opinions in his column, "The Editor's Notebook," that appeared in his group's publications.

Knight began his newspaper career in the Twenties on the *Akron Beacon-Journal* (Ohio). Later, the organization acquired the *Miami Herald* (Florida), the *Detroit Free Press* (Michigan), the *Charlotte Observer* and *News* (North Carolina) and the *Philadelphia Inquirer* and *News* (Pennsylvania).

Knight won the Pulitzer Prize for editorial writing in 1968. He was twice president of the American Society of Newspaper Editors, and he helped establish the Inter American Press Association before he retired in 1976.

In 1944, Knight acquired the *Chicago Daily News*, but later sold it to Marshall Field IV. He merged his newspapers with the Ridder publications in 1974, to create the Knight-Ridder operations.

James L. Knight (1909– * ), a brother of John S. Knight, was listed by *Quill* magazine as being worth between $100 and $200 million. He is the largest shareholder in the Knight-Ridder group.

* died Feb. 5, 1991

**KOBLER, John** (1910– )
John Kobler worked for the *New York Evening Journal*, the International News Service, King Features Syndicate, and the *New York Daily Mirror* between 1931 and 1939. He served as the editor of the experimental *PM* newspaper, 1940–42.

During World War II, Kobler was a civilian intelligence officer in Africa and Europe. He was later attached to the American embassy in Paris.

Kobler turned to magazine work after the war, becoming a contributor to *The New Yorker, Life,* the *Saturday Evening Post, Collier's,* and other magazines. In 1957, he became a contributing editor to *SEP*, and, by 1965, was editor-at-large. His books include *Trial of Ruth Snyder and Judd Gray; Some Like It Gory; Afternoon in the Attic; The Reluctant Surgeon, A Biography of John Hunter; Luce: His Time, Life and Fortune; Capone; Ardent Spirits; The Rise and Fall of Prohibition;* and *Damned in Paradise: The Life of John Barrymore.*

**KOHLMEIER, Louis Martin, Jr.** (1926– )
Since 1952, Louis Kohlmeier has been associated with the *Wall Street Journal* with the exception of a brief time, 1958–59, when he worked on the *St. Louis Globe-Democrat* (Missouri).

Kohlmeier first worked in St. Louis and then in Chicago for the *Journal.* In 1960, he joined the newspaper's Washington Bureau. He won a Pulitzer Award for national reporting in 1964 for his story that revealed the conflict of interest that involved Lady Bird Johnson and her Texas broadcasting holdings. The report noted that, as President, Lyndon Johnson received more favorable treatment from the Federal Communications Commission.

Kohlmeier also won a National Headliner Club reporting award in 1959 and, five years later, he was honored by Sigma Delta Chi. He wrote a book about Federal regulations, *The Regulators Watchdog Agencies and the Public Interest.*

**KONDRACKE, Morton** (1940?– )
Morton Kondracke, currently a nationally syndicated columnist with United Features, started on the *Chicago Sun-Times* in 1963, moved to the newspaper's Washington Bureau in 1968, becoming White House correspondent in 1974.

Kondracke has contributed to *The Economist* and *Public Opinion* magazine and has been a commentator on National Public Radio's "All Things Considered" and "Communique." He also has been on NBC-TV "Meet the Press" and CBS-TV "Face the Nation." In 1983, he was a panelist on WRC-TV's "The McLaughlin Group." He has his own radio show on WRC-AM.

**KOPPEL, Ted** (1953– )
For more than 20 years, Ted Koppel has been with ABC News, more recently as anchor of "ABC News Nightline," which started in 1980.

Before joining ABC in 1963, Koppel worked for WMCA radio in New York.

In 1965, Koppel switched to ABC Radio and covered such major events as the civil rights movement in Selma, Alabama. By 1967, he was in Vietnam, and the next year he was the Miami Bureau chief. The following three years ABC placed him in Hong Kong, before returning him as chief diplomatic correspondent in 1971.

Koppel said that coverage of the State Department "taught me to listen very carefully because diplomats are very good at misleading you."

Koppel has received many awards, including the University of Missouri Journalism Medal in 1983. In accepting this award, he told the students to ask themselves what is important and not to lose sight of that. He added that television can offer perspective by reducing years into instants. Television has the potential, he added, to be a real teaching medium.

For his "Nightline" analyses of Reagan's victory, Koppel won an Emmy in 1981. He also won the Alfred I. du Pont Award from Columbia University and the Christopher Award for his Iran hostage reporting. The Overseas Press Club has also honored him.

**KOSNER, Edward A.** (1937– )
For five years (1958–63), Edward Kosner worked for the *New York Post*, first in rewrite and later as assistant city editor. The next year, he became the associate editor of *Newsweek*, where he remained until 1979. Kosner moved from general editor to national affairs editor to managing editor and, finally, to editor of the weekly.

In 1980, Kosner left *Newsweek* to become editor of the weekly *New York*, where he promised to build "a new community of writers."

He has won various journalism awards and currently is a member of the executive committee of the American Society of Magazine Editors.

**KOTULAK, Ronald** (1935– )
Science writing has brought many awards to Ronald Kotulak, a member of the *Chicago Tribune* staff since 1959. After serving the newspaper in several capacities, he became science editor in 1965.

In one year, 1968, Kotulak won three major awards from the American Medical Association, the American Chemical Society, and the National Society for Medical Research. In 1976, the American Health Foundation gave Kotulak its Lifeline Award, the same year he won the Edward Scott Beck Award from the *Tribune*. His alma mater, the University of Michigan, gave him its Outstanding Achievement Award, in 1968, in recognition of his scientific writing.

**KOTZ, Nathan Kallison** (1932– )
During an extensive career with the *Des Moines Register* (Iowa), starting in 1958, Nick Kotz has won many national awards, including the Pulitzer Prize.

Kotz served the *Register* and other Cowles Publications as Washington correspondent between 1964 and 1970, when he joined the *Washington Post* for a three-year tour. Since 1973, he has been a free-lance writer and has served on several boards, including the Fund for Investigative Reporting. Kotz has also taught part-time at the American University since 1978.

For his national reporting, Kotz won the Pulitzer Prize and the Sigma Delta Chi and the Robert F. Kennedy Journalism awards in 1968. Previously (1966), he won the Raymond Clapper Memorial Award and a Sigma Delta Chi distinguished service medal.

Kotz wrote *Let Them Eat Promises: The Politics of Hunger in America*; and *A Passion for Equality: George Wiley and the Movement*. He co-authored *The Unions*.

He was in the Marine Corps from 1956 to 1958.

**KRAFT, Joseph** (1924– )

Since 1963, Joseph Kraft has been a syndicated columnist reporting the Washington scene. From 1951 to 1952, he was an editorial writer for the *Washington Post* and, for the next four years, he was a staff writer for the *New York Times*.

Kraft returned to Washington in 1962 as the Washington correspondent for *Harper's* magazine. The next year his column started its syndication. He frequently appears on television talk shows and continues to contribute articles to periodicals. He has written four books: *The Struggle for Algeria, The Grand Design, Profiles in Power* and *The Chinese Difference*. Kraft was a speech writer for John F. Kennedy.

As a liberal columnist Kraft follows the Walter Lippmann tradition. In 1984, he started to work directly for the *Los Angeles Times*. He also won the Legion d'Honneur from the French Government in 1984. He continues to write from Washington.

**KRASLOW, David** (1926– )

Sportswriting on the *Miami News* (Florida), 1947–48, started David Kraslow on his journalistic career. He moved to the *Miami Herald* in 1948, where he remained until 1963 as a sportswriter, reporter, and Washington correspondent.

For the next nine years, Kraslow worked for the *Los Angeles Times* as its Washington correspondent, news editor, and, later, Washington Bureau chief. For two years, he was editor of the *Washington Star-News* before joining the Cox newspapers as bureau chief in 1974. The Cox newspapers are in Dayton, Ohio, Atlanta, Georgia, Miami and Palm Beach, Florida, and Springfield, Ohio.

According to James H. Dygert's study of *The Investigative Journalist*, "Kraslow was the first to write a story about the CIA-backed preparations for the disastrous Bay of Pigs invasion of Cuba but his paper didn't publish it."

In 1977, Kraslow became the publisher of the *Miami News*. He won the George Polk, the Raymond Clapper, and the Dumont awards in 1969.

He is active in civic affairs, including the United Way, Center for the Fine Arts, and the University of Miami.

**KREMENTZ, Jill** (1940– )
A well-known photographer, Jill Krementz was involved in eight books: *Sweet Pea—A Black Girl Growing Up in the Rural South, A Very Young Dancer, A Very Young Rider, A Very Young Gymnast, A Very Young Circus Flyer* and *A Very Young Skater*. She also provided the photographs for *The Face of South Vietnam* and *Words and Their Masters*.

Krementz was with *Harper's Bazaar*, 1959–60, and with *Glamour* the next year. She spent a year, 1961, in New Delhi with the Indian Industries Fair, working in public relations. She was also a reporter for the short-lived *Show* magazine.

In 1964, Krementz moved to the *New York Herald Tribune* as staff photographer. She went around the world, working in Vietnam. She then became associate editor of *Status-Diplomat* magazine, a contributing editor to *New York* magazine (1967–68), and finally joined Time-Life Inc. (1969–70). Since 1974, she has been a contributing photographer for *People* magazine.

Krementz's photography has been exhibited in art centers, shows, and galleries.

**KROCK, Arthur** (1887–1974)
For many years, Arthur Krock was associated with newspapers in Louisville, Kentucky, New York, and Washington.

He began as a reporter in 1907 on the *Louisville Times*. Three years later, he was the correspondent for both the *Times* and the *Courier-Journal*. He returned to Louisville as editorial manager for the two dailies, and from 1919–23, he was editor-in-chief of the *Times*.

Krock was in New York with the *World* from 1923 to 1927 as assistant to the president. Then he joined the *New York Times* and, from 1923 to 1953, was its Washington correspondent. He was a commentator on the capital city until 1967.

Krock won the Pulitzer Prize in 1935, 1938, and 1951. From 1940 to 1953, he was a member of the Pulitzer Prize Board. He also won awards from France and Norway. In 1970, Krock won the Presidential Medal of Freedom and the next year was cited by Freedoms Foundation.

He wrote *Memoirs: Sixty Years on The Firing Line, The Editorials of Henry Watterson, The Nation,* and *The Consent of the Governed and Other Deceits*.

**KRUIDENIER, David** (1921– )
Kruidenier worked for the Minneapolis, Minnesota newspapers from 1948 to 1952 before going to Des Moines, Iowa. By 1971, he was president and publisher, and in 1978, chairman of the board and publisher in Des Moines. Since 1973, he has also been vice-chairman of the board of the Minneapolis Cowles-directed publications.

Now for the first time in its history, the Cowles Media Co. has a non-Cowles at its helm. David Kruidenier became president in 1983, replacing John Cowles, Jr. who was pressured to resign. In 1984 he became chairman.

Kruidenier faced several problems when he took over his new assignment. He had been chairman of the Des Moines Register and Tribune Co., in Iowa, and the Iowa newspapers own 13 percent of the Minneapolis-based Cowles firm. Also, both the Des Moines operation and the flagship *Minneapolis Star & Tribune* had suffered declining profits in the 1982–83 period. He was involved in selling the paper to Gannett for $200 million.

Active in Des Moines and Midwest civic affairs, Kruidenier works with the Civic Center, Drake University, the Menninger Foundation, the American Federation of the Arts, and the Midwest Research Institute.

He served in the Air Force in World War II.

**KUEKES, Edward D.** (1901– )
A career cartoonist, Edward Kuekes spent his lifetime in the Cleveland area. From 1922 to 1949, he was a cartoonist with the *Plain Dealer*, becoming the chief editorial cartoonist from 1949 until he became emeritus in 1966. Since that time he has worked as a cartoonist for Metro Newspapers Inc., in Cleveland.

Kuekes created such features as the "Cartoonist Looks at the News." His has won frequent awards, starting with recognition by the Newspaper Guild in 1947. Others have come from the National Safety Council, and the Disabled American Veterans. He won many citations from Freedoms Foundation between 1949 and 1969, and the Pulitzer Prize for Cartooning in 1953. He was a student at Baldwin-Wallace College, which later gave him its Alumni Merit Award. Some 450 of his original cartoons are at the college, and 5,000 cartoons are in a collection at Syracuse University.

Wayne State University recognized Kuekes' work with its Political Cartoon Award in 1960. Other honors have come from the Treasury Department, the Cleveland Dental Society, and Eisenhower's People to People Program.

**KUPCINET, Irv** (1912– )
Midwest newspaper readers and television viewers are well acquainted with the work of Irv Kupcinet, who started his career as a sportswriter on the *Chicago Daily Times* in 1935.

In 1943, Kupcinet joined the *Sun-Times* as a columnist. He has been host to "Kup's Show" for some time, and in 1960, he won an Emmy award as the best moderator of a television show.

**KURALT, Charles B.** (1934– )
"On the Road" has brought CBS' Charles Kuralt before millions of viewers and has taken him more than one-half a million miles across America. The show began in 1967.

Kuralt has been with CBS since 1957. Earlier he worked as a reporter and columnist on the *Charlotte News* (North Carolina), where he won the Ernie Pyle Memorial Award for feature writing. He also has won Emmy awards in 1969 and 1978, and the George Foster Peabody Award in 1969 and 1976.

Kuralt has handled many CBS specials and for a time was the co-host of "CBS News Sunday Morning." He also hosted the earlier "Eyewitness to History" program.

*Newsweek* once referred to Kuralt as "our beloved visiting uncle." The magazine added, in mid-1983, that "only Charles Kuralt can make us choke up over the significance of the commonplace."

Kuralt told the *Christian Science Monitor* in a 1979 interview that he "loved to read [while growing up in North Carolina] and what there was in the house to read was *National Geographic* and the complete works of Dickens and O. Henry."

In high school, Kuralt won an American Legion "Voice of Democracy" contest, which included a trip to Washington to meet President Harry Truman, but Kuralt was more impressed by his hero, Edward R. Murrow, who read the student's oration over CBS Radio.

He wrote *To the Top of the World* and *Dateline America.*

**KURTIS, William (Bill) H.** (1940– )

*On Assignment*, a 1983 book, relates the highlights of the career of Bill Kurtis, anchor for the "CBS Morning News." In this book he tells "some of the stories he reported on during his nine years as WBBM, the CBS outlet in Chicago. Those stories are not exactly the bread-and-butter of everyday TV reporting, involving as they do controversial subjects and often uncomfortable insights into events that have been superficially treated elsewhere, if at all," according to an interview with Kurtis in *Publishers Weekly.*

After service in the Marine Corps, Kurtis joined WBBM-TV as a news reporter and later became the anchorman. He was also with CBS News in Los Angeles between 1970 and 1973. In 1970, he won an Emmy for reporting the Chicago conspiracy trial. He also reported the fall of Saigon and the Belfast investigations. He was cited for his excellence as a performer on camera, and also won an award from the Overseas Press Club.

The *Publishers Weekly*'s interview described Kurtis' writing as "smooth and professional and sometimes, as in the introduction about his boyhood in Kansas, something more than that." He told the magazine he plans a novel, based, at least in part, on his Kansas years. He concluded that he loves "the idea of books and writing. They give you that invaluable luxury: to say what you want, and all the time in the world to say it." This is obviously in contrast to presenting the morning news on television.

**KWITNY, Jonathan** (1941– )

"Fight for what you believe in, even if most other people disagree" is the philosophy that *Wall Street Journal* writer Jonathan Kwitny practices in his reporting and books. "You may be right and you may win," he added.

Following his graduation in journalism from the University of Missouri and his graduate degree work in history at New York University, Kwitny joined the *Perth Amboy Evening News* (later the *News Tribune*) in 1963. From 1964 to 1966 he was with the Peace Corps, teaching English and literature in a high school in Benin City, Nigeria.

Between "vagabond" tours in 1966–67 and 1970–71, Kwitny again worked briefly on the *New Tribune* as well as the *New York Post*. His vagabond tours took him backpacking around Africa and Asia.

In 1971 he joined the *Wall Street Journal*. In addition to his in-depth reports for this newspaper, Kwitny had written the following books:

The *Fountain Pen Conspiracy; The Mullendore Murder Case; Shakedown; Vicious Circles: The Mafia in the Marketplace*; and *Endless Enemies: The Making of an Unfriendly World*.

He was awarded the University of Missouri Journalism Medal in 1982.

**LAKE, John Bryon** (1920– )

In 1984, John Lake retired as publisher and executive vice-president of the Times Publishing Co. in St. Petersburg, Florida. He had been with this award-winning publication since 1960.

Lake was an advertising salesman for the *Lancaster Eagle-Gazette* (Ohio) from 1947 to 1956, and he continued in advertising on the *Elizabeth Daily Journal* (New Jersey) until he moved to Florida. In St. Petersburg, Lake served as president of the Semit Corporation and as a member of the Florida Council of 100.

He is a trustee of the Poynter Fund and on the board of the University of South Florida Foundation.

He served in the Air Force in Korea, 1952–53.

**LAMBERT, William G.** (1920– )

While a reporter on the *Portland Oregonian*, William Lambert won the 1957 Pulitzer Prize for local reporting. He worked on the *Oregon City Enterprise-Courier* from 1945 to 1950, when he joined the *Oregonian*.

Lambert shifted to television in 1961 as news director of Portland station KPTV, and a year later, joined *Time* magazine. He worked eight years on *Life* as associate editor and writer, and from 1971 to 1973, was a staffer for Time-Life News Service. Lambert returned to newspaper work in 1974 as a writer for the *Philadelphia Inquirer* (Pennsylvania).

Lambert also won the Heywood Broun Award in 1957 and, ten years later, the Sigma Delta Chi Award. Other honors include the Worth Bingham prize for distinguished reporting, the George Polk Award for magazine reporting, and Headliner Club and Page One awards.

**LAMBRO, Donald** (1940– )

Beginning as a reporter on the *Boston Traveler* in 1963, Donald Lambro today is a nationally syndicated columnist with United Features Syndicate.

After several years as a free-lancer, Lambro joined the United Press International as statehouse reporter in Hartford, Connecticut, before moving to the Washington Bureau in 1970. After a decade on this job, he started his syndicated column.

Since 1982 he has appeared on the Associated Press Radio network, "Donald Lambro Watching Washington." He was also involved in a one-hour special on Public Television, "Star Spangled Spenders."

Lambro wrote *The Federal Rathole; The Conscience of a Young Conservative;* and *Fat City: How Washington Wastes Your Taxes.*

**LANDERS, Ann** (1918– )
Since 1955, Mrs. Esther P. Lederer has been providing helpful advice and information for millions of Americans under the name "Ann Landers." She is an identical twin to Mrs. Morton Phillips, who writes under the name "Abigail Van Buren."

The name "Ann Landers" had been used by the *Chicago Sun-Times* for the column. When the writer, Ruth Crowley, died, Lederer won the position in a competition among persons working on the newspaper and their relatives. She said she "happened to be at the right place at the right time."

"Ann Landers" appears in a thousand newspapers with answers to letters received each month from readers. Although "Dear Ann" Lederer never completed college, she has been awarded honorary degrees from five institutions, and many associations have honored her. She has held many national offices in such groups as the Anti-Defamation League, the National Foundation of Infantile Paralysis, the TV Christmas Seal Campaign, Dialogue for the Blind, the American Cancer Society, the Harvard Medical Society, the Menninger Foundation, and the League of Women Voters.

She has written *The Ann Landers Encyclopedia*, as well as *Since You Asked Me, Teen-agers and Sex, Truth is Stranger. . .*, and *Ann Landers Speaks Out.*

**LANE, Family**
Laurence Lane (1890–1967) was a hardware salesman in Des Moines, Iowa and St. Louis, Missouri before he joined the Meredith Publishing Co. in Des Moines, moving from salesman to advertising director between 1913 and 1928. Lane's career turned to *Sunset* magazine in 1928 when the publication was near bankruptcy.

Lane had become acquainted with the West during his travels for Meredith's *Better Homes & Gardens.* After he took over *Sunset* it prospered, and today is a leader in its field. It became one of the first magazine firms to publish its own books. The senior Lane was president and chairman of the company.

He served in World War I.

Laurence W. Lane, Jr. (1919– ) has been with the firm since 1930. In 1974, he became the chairman of the board. He is active in many corporations and has been associated with the National Parks, Stanford University, the Department of State, the Colonial Williamsburg Foundation, and other groups.

He served in the Navy during World War II.

**LANGE, Dorothea** (1895–1965)
Dorothea Lange became famous for one special picture, her "Migrant Mother," taken during the Dust Storm era in the mid-Thirties. The

subject (Florence Thompson) later became bitter over the fame Lange achieved, especially since the photograph has been widely reprinted and has become symbolic of an era in American history.

Lange began her career in Palisades, California. She later had her first one-person show in San Francisco and, in 1941, won a Guggenheim Fellowship. It was during her work with the Federal Government that she made her Depression photographs.

She wrote, with her husband, Paul Schuster Taylor, *American Exodus: A Record of Human Erosion.*

**LANKER, Brian Timothy** (1947– )
Few newspaper photographers have won as many major awards as has Brian Lanker, since 1974 the chief photographer for the *Eugene Reporter-Guard* (Oregon). Before that, Lanker worked from 1966 to 1969 on the *Phoenix Gazette* (Arizona) and, for the next five years, with the *Topeka Capital Journal* (Kansas).

In 1973, Lanker won a Pulitzer Prize for feature photography. The National Press Photographers Association has twice named him the National Newspaper Photographer of the Year. For six straight years, between 1968 and 1973, he was the Regional Photographer of the Year. His more recent prize was the Joseph Sprague Memorial Award, in 1979.

**LARDNER, Ring W.** (1885–1933)
The Ring Lardner influence continues among sportswriters today. Lardner was a reporter on the *South Bend Times* (Indiana) in 1905, and later worked with the *Chicago Inter-Ocean, Examiner,* and *Tribune,* before he became editor of *Sporting News* in 1910.

Lardner continued to travel about the country, writing about sports, working for the *Boston American, Chicago American, Chicago Examiner,* and the *Chicago Tribune,* several for the second time.

From 1919 on, Lardner's sport comments were syndicated. He wrote 14 books and a play, *June Moon,* in association with George S. Kaufman.

Among Lardner's books are *Bib Ballads; You Know Me, Al; Gullible's Travels; Own Your Own Home; Treat 'Em Rough; The Real Dope; My Four Weeks in France; The Young Immigrants; Symptoms of Being 35; The Big Town; How to Write Short Stories; What of It?; The Love Nest; The Story of a Wonder Man;* and *Round Up.*

**LARSEN, Roy Edward** (1899–1979)
Roy Larsen joined *Time* magazine in 1922, during the formative years when Britton Hadden and Henry Luce were "creating" this newsweekly. Larsen was the circulation manager until 1927. He eventually replaced Luce as president of Time Inc. in 1939, a position he held until 1960. He was vice-chairman of the board from 1961 until he retired in 1979.

Larsen worked on the *Harvard Advocate,* turning the literary magazine into a profit-making periodical. On Time Inc., he was also involved with the March of Time, and was publisher of *Life* in its early days.

Larsen was involved in many civic and governmental activities. He assisted the United Hospital fund (New York); the Fund for the Advancement of Education; the Ford Foundation, the New York Public Library, Harvard, the Nature Conservancy, and several White House conferences concerning education.

**LARSON, Gary**
The success of Gary Larson's comic panel, "The Far Side," became evident in early 1985 when three of his books appeared on the *New York Times* best-seller list. These books, taken from his panels, included *The Far Side Gallery, In Search of The Far Side*, and *Beyond The Far Side*.
Larson's panel appears in more than 200 newspapers.

**LAURENCE, William L.** (1888–1977)
One of the early science writers on American newspapers, William Laurence won Pulitzer prizes in 1937 and 1946. The second award came for his eye-witness account of the atom bombing of Nagasaki. In 1945, he was the only journalist present when the first atomic bomb was tested in New Mexico, and he witnessed other tests in Nevada and in the Pacific.
Laurence was working for the *New York World*, 1926–39, before he became the science reporter on the *New York Times*. From 1956 to 1964, when he retired, he was the *Times*' science editor.
Laurence was the science consultant for the New York World's Fair, 1964–65.
Laurence was awarded the George Westinghouse Distinguished Science Award in 1946; the University of Missouri Journalism Medal in 1947; and the George Polk, Page One, and Lasker awards in 1950. The American Chemical Society and the Medical Writers also cited his outstanding reporting.
He fought in World War I with the Army.

**LAURIE, James Andrew** (1947– )
James Laurie was a free-lance writer and reporter for Metromedia Radio-TV in Washington in 1969. From 1970 to 1971, he was in Vietnam, and from 1971 to 1975, he worked for NBC News reporting that war. The network moved him to Tokyo in 1975, and in 1978 he was with ABC News in Hong Kong.
Laurie opened the first American radio and television bureau in Peking in 1981 as chief of ABC News operations. In 1982, he became the network's chief Asia correspondent in Tokyo.
Laurie won the George Foster Peabody Award in 1976 for his report on the fall of Saigon and the Du Pont Award for his ABC documentary on Cambodia in 1981.

**LAVINE, John** (1941– )
John Lavine, in 1983, became president of the Inland Daily Press Association. He followed his father in the newspaper business, operating a number of small Wisconsin dailies. Two years before his father died, he purchased the *Chappewa Falls Herald-Telegram* for his son, who remarked

many years later, "all of a sudden I went from being an improvished graduate student with no debts to a publisher with lots of debts."

In an *Editor & Publisher* interview, Celeste Huenergard described Lavine's years following his start as a publisher. "He added two other papers to the stable of small Wisconsin dailies he began to publish almost 20 years ago; served as the country's youngest regent for the University of Wisconsin system; put in a stint with a movie company; wrote editorials three times a week for King Syndicate; traveled the world on political and editorial assignments; attended the signing of the Panama Canal Treaty at the request of Vice-President Mondale; and earned the respect of his colleagues as a tireless supporter of civil and human rights, environmental issues, education, and free press."

Lavine has been editor-in-residence at several universities and has been cited by the Associated Press Managing Editors for his work. He once clocked a Wisconsin governor speeding and wrote a personal, signed column about it in his newspaper.

His Wisconsin newspapers today include the *Baraboo News-Republic*; the *Shawano Evening Leader*; the *Portage Daily Register*, and the *Chappewa Falls Herald-Telegram.*

**LAWRENCE, David** (1888–1973)

David Lawrence, in 1910, worked for the Associated Press in Washington and later was the local correspondent for the *New York Evening Post.* In 1919, he created the Consolidated Press, which was a pioneer service in syndicated dispatches by wire rather than by mail, and his column was published in more than 300 newspapers. While conducting this service, Lawrence started the *United States Daily* in 1926 as a national newspaper, a forerunner to *USA Today.*

Lawrence created the *U.S. News & World Report* and developed it into the only newsweekly to originate in Washington.

Seven years later, he renamed his publication *United States News* and made it a weekly. In 1946, he launched *World Report*, and in early 1948, he merged the publications into today's *U.S. News & World Report.*

Lawrence thought "there was no magazine with an adequate explanation and correlation of what the day-to-day actions of government really mean to the economic life of the individual and his enterprises," so he set out to remedy this shortage. The magazine became employee-owned in 1962.

President Richard Nixon named him among the "greats of the profession": when he presented Lawrence with the Medal of Freedom. The University of Missouri awarded him its Journalism Medal. He wrote *The True Story of Woodrow Wilson*; *The Other Side of Government*; *Beyond the New Deal*; *Stumbling Into Socialism*; *Nine Honest Men*; *Who Were the Eleven Million?*; and *Diary of a Washington Correspondent.*

**LAWRENCE, David, Jr.** (1942– )

David Lawrence, Jr. has spent his career with newspapers, starting as a reporter in 1963 on the *St. Petersburg Times* (Florida). In 1967, he was the

News/Style editor for the *Washington Post*, but he returned South to the *Palm Beach Post* in 1969 as managing editor. He worked from 1971 to 1975 on the *Philadelphia Daily News* (Pennsylvania) and from 1975 to 1978 as executive editor and editor of the *Charlotte Observer* (North Carolina). Lawrence became executive editor of the *Detroit Free Press* (Michigan) in 1978.

**LEARD, John Earnshaw** (1916– )
A pioneer in the modern technological revolution in the newspaper business, John E. Leard first worked on the *Lewiston Sun-Journal* (Maine) in 1937. After traveling in South America under a Pulitzer scholarship from Columbia University, Leard joined the *Richmond News Leader* (Virginia) as an editorial assistant.

Leard moved up to being a reporter in 1941, and to city editor in 1963. Between these assignments, Leard worked on the *Atlantic Monthly* in Boston and the *New Haven Register* (Connecticut). In 1963, he became the managing editor of the *Richmond Times-Dispatch*, and in 1969, the executive director of both Richmond newspapers.

Leard has been president of the Associated Press Managing Editors. He is a trustee for Bates College and has been active in other civic and professional groups.

He served in the Army in World War II.

**LEE, Michael Edward** (1942– )
Michael Lee started as a reporter on Austin, Texas station KHFI in 1965 and, later, worked for station WFAA there. He moved to San Francisco station KPIX-TV in 1968, where he remained until 1975.

Lee joined CBS News in 1975, later serving in Beirut before going to London in 1977 where he worked until he joined ABC News as a correspondent in 1980.

Among his awards were several from the Overseas Press Club. He also won recognition for his coverage of the Lebanese Civil War and the Iran Revolution.

**LEHRER, James Charles** (1934– )
James Lehrer began his career in print journalism, working as a reporter on the *Dallas Morning News* (Texas), 1959–61. He moved to the *Dallas Times Herald* in 1961, becoming city editor before he joined Dallas station KERA-TV in 1970. After two years as a producer and correspondent, Lehrer joined the Public Broadcasting Service in Washington, where he is best known today for The MacNeil/Lehrer News Hour, which has become one of the leading evening programs, appearing on some 300 Public Television stations.

While he was in Dallas, Lehrer also taught creative writing at Southern Methodist University, and has written two books, *Viva Max* and *We Were Dreamers*. Among his awards are the Columbia-Dupont, George Polk, George Peabody, and Emmy citations. He also has won the University of Missouri Journalism Medal.

**LEHRMAN, Nat** (1929- )
Nat Lehrman has been associated with the Playboy operations since 1963, and today he is president of the publishing division of Playboy Enterprises, Inc.

Early in his career Lehrman served in the Army in Japan (1953–55) and was a travel writer and editor for the American Automobile Association. From 1957 to 1963, he worked for the West Park Publications, a New York magazine publisher. In 1963, Lehrman became associate editor of *Playboy* and, in 1967, senior editor. By 1972, he was editor of new publications for the firm, moving up to his present position after service on both *Playboy* and *Oui*.

Lehrman wrote *Masters and Johnson Explained.* He has taught creative writing at Columbia College in Chicago.

He served in the Army, 1953–55.

**LELAND, Timothy** (1937- )
A career on the *Boston Globe* has brought many awards to Timothy Leland, who joined the newspaper as science editor in 1965. Before joining the *Globe*, Leland worked on the *Boston Herald*, 1963–64.

He moved to the State House as bureau chief in 1966 and became an investigative reporter in 1970. He won a Pulitzer Prize in investigative reporting in 1972. Since 1981, he has been the daily's managing editor.

He has also won awards from Sigma Delta Chi and Associated Press Managing Editors and has been cited with an Sevellon Brown award and by other groups.

**LEONARD, William Augustus II** (1916- )
An executive with CBS News for many years, Bill Leonard warned in 1983 that "there's a tendency, just a tendency, for the competitive forces within the TV industry to overwhelm what used to be the primary—to inform, to get at the truth—not to amuse or arouse or tickle. . . . I don't say that is happening, but that is the tendency."

Leonard started as a reporter in 1937 on the *Bridgeport Post-Telegram* (Connecticut). After a brief tour in advertising research, he joined CBS in New York City in 1945, where he has remained. He has been an executive producer, vice-president of programing, vice-president of the Washington operations, and since 1979, president.

He has received the Albert Lasker Award for medical journalism and the Ed Stout Award for his Latin America reporting. It was Leonard who selected Dan Rather to replace Walter Cronkite on the CBS Evening News and it was Leonard who helped to select the initial casting for the network's "60 Minutes" program.

Leonard served in the Navy during World War II.

**LERNER, Louis A.** (1935–1984)
Louis A. Lerner's career included positions on his father's Lerner Newspapers, Inc., in Chicago and an ambassadorship to Norway.

Lerner began his newspaper work on the *North Town News* (Chicago) in

1954 and became a correspondent in Scandinavia for Accredited Home Newspapers of America in 1956–1958. He returned as an executive for the Lerner newspapers in 1959, holding that position until 1977. By 1980 he had purchased the chain of suburban newspapers from his mother and his father's estate.

President Jimmy Carter named him ambassador to Norway in 1977. He served until 1980. He was honored by Norway and Portugal.

Lerner was active in civic affairs in the Chicago area, associated with the Lyric Opera Guild, Public Library, Catholic Interracial Council, Better Business Bureau, and other organizations.

**LEVINE, Ellen R.** (1943– )

The editor-in-chief of *Woman's Day* in 1982, Ellen Levine had previously worked with *Cosmopolitan* magazine, with Helen Gurley Brown in the food and decorating section. She had also created and edited *Cosmopolitan Living.*

She has appeared on ABC's "Good Morning" program.

Levine told Ira Ellenthal, in a *Folio* magazine interview, "I believe strongly that, in order to edit effectively, we can't lose sight of what pleases the reader. No matter how brilliantly a piece is written or photographed, it's worthless if readers don't like it."

**LEVINE, Irving Raskin** (n.d.– )

Like so many television newscasters, Irving R. Levine began as a newspaper reporter. He worked on the *Providence Journal* (Rhode Island) while attending Brown University. He served in the Army Signal Corps in World War II, and in 1947, he became the foreign news editor for International News Service in Vienna.

Levine joined the NBC News staff in 1950 and continues with this network. He covered the Korean War and was the network's chief correspondent in Moscow from 1955 to 1959. He was the first American the Russian government accredited to work there. In addition to his NBC duties, he reported for *The Times of London* and *Variety* magazine while in Russia.

Levine later served in Rome and London before going to Washington in 1971. He has filed reports from around the world.

Levine has won many citations from the Overseas Press Club and the Headliner Club. He has also won an Emmy, and for his economics reporting, the Martin R. Gainsbrugh Award. The U.S. Junior Chamber of Commerce selected him as one of the ten Outstanding Young Men in America.

He has written many articles. His books include *Main Street, USSR*; *Travel Guide to Russia*; *Main Street, Italy*; and *The New Worker in Soviet Russia.*

**LEVY, Michael Richard** (1946– )

In 1973, the initial issue of *Texas Monthly* appeared in Austin. Michael R. Levy was the president and publisher and William Broyles, later editor of *Newsweek*, was the editor.

Levy has been described as "forged in the Texas entrepreneur and good-ole-boy mold. While he can be both brash and bullish, he also can be delightful," according to Christy Marshall's account in *Advertising Age*. Friends have described Levy as "a super person, a dedicated and loyal friend" and a "most work-oriented person."

Levy began work as a lawyer after he graduated from the University of Texas in 1972. That same year, he established Mediatex Communications Corp. and, in 1973, published his first magazine. Earlier he had worked for the *Philadelphia* city magazine for nine months. While there, he decided to start his own publication, believing it would be better to have a state- rather than a city-oriented publication. As a youngster, Levy had sold magazine subscriptions door-to-door in Dallas.

In 1980, Levy bought *New West* for $3 million and renamed it *California*.

The *Texas Monthly* won a National Magazine Award in 1974, the first such periodical to win this prestigious citation outside of those on the East or West coasts.

**LEWIS, Anthony** (1927– )

A *New York Times* columnist, Anthony Lewis won the Lovejoy Award in 1983 to go with the two Pulitzer Prizes for national reporting he won in 1955 and 1963.

In his acceptance speech for the Lovejoy Award, Lewis said, in part: "The more serious threat to freedom, the one that should concern us urgently as journalists and citizens, is the secrecy campaign being carried on by President Reagan and his Administration.

"I am convinced that they are more than isolated steps. They reflect a methodical, consistent and relentless effort to close off the sources of public knowledge on basic questions of national policy; to upset the Madisonian premise that American citizens must be able to examine public characters and measures."

Lewis' Lovejoy recognition cited him "for his distinctive writing and for his unusual courage in stating his views on a variety of issues." He first worked on the *Times* from 1948 to 1952 before he spent a year with the Democratic National Committee.

From 1952 to 1955, Lewis was a *Washington Daily News* reporter before joining the *New York Times'* Washington Bureau where he remained until 1964. He was chief of the newspaper's London Bureau from 1965 to 1972. He has been writing his column since 1969.

Other honors include the Heywood Broun Award and the Nieman Fellowship, 1956–57. He has written two books, *Gideon's Trumpet* and *Portrait of a Decade: The Second American Revolution*, and many articles for professional journals.

**LEWIS, Claude Aubrey** (1936– )

Claude Lewis was a *Newsweek* reporter from 1953 to 1963 before he spent a year with the *New York Herald Tribune*. He then joined ABC-TV in Philadelphia, Pennsylvania as a reporter-writer and served another year in that city with the Westinghouse Broadcasting Co.

By 1967, Lewis had become a columnist for the *Philadelphia Bulletin* and, in 1975, its associate editor.

He started the *National Leader* in 1982 and a year later said he believed "a lot more is riding on the success of the year-old Black weekly than showing a profit." The tabloid is published in Philadelphia for a nationwide audience.

Lewis won a meritorious service award from Lincoln University in Missouri in 1975 to go with his other honors.

**LEWIS, Edward** (1940– )

Edward Lewis' background was in banking, having worked for First National City Bank in New York from 1966 to 1969. Prior to that he worked briefly as an analyst in the Albuquerque, New Mexico city manager's office.

While with the bank, Lewis attended a conference on Black capitalism and heard a proposal for a Black woman's magazine. He and three partners established *Essence* in 1969, raising about $2 million from several New York banks and corporations. Playboy Enterprises also provided some capital. He called *Essence* a magazine designed "to make Black women feel good about themselves."

After some early problems, Lewis selected Marcia Ann Gillespie to be *Essence*'s editor. She moved the periodical ahead, making it a success.

Lewis is on the boards of several national organizations. The National Association of Media Women gave him its Decision Makers Award in 1975. Earlier, he had been named Businessman of the Year by Blackfrica Promotions, Inc.

**LEWIS, Fulton, Jr.** (1903–1966)

In the early Twenties, Fulton Lewis, Jr. began as a reporter on the *Washington Herald*, where he eventually became the city editor. From 1928 to 1937, Lewis was with the Washington Bureau of Universal Service and the International News Service.

Lewis went on the air over the Mutual Broadcasting System in 1937 with his nightly news comments, and for years he was heard nightly over the radio and his newspaper column, syndicated through King Features, was read weekly.

Lewis is remembered for his active work in getting the U.S. House and Senate to open their chambers to radio newsmen, as they had been opened for the press. He was among the ten Outstanding Young Men in America in 1939 and 1940, and was in great demand for lectures. He wrote many magazine articles, and was the founder of the Radio Correspondents Association. He also won the Alfred I. du Pont and Sigma Delta Chi awards for his radio work.

He covered World War II for Mutual.

**LEWIS, Sinclair** (1884–1951)

Before Sinclair Lewis became famous for his novels, he had a brief career as a writer for newspapers and magazines as well as for the Associated Press.

Lewis was a reporter on the *New Haven Journal and Courier* (Connecticut). He also worked for a time on the *San Francisco Bulletin* and edited *Translantic Tales, Yolta Review* and *Adventure* shortly after the turn of the century.

Lewis's books included *Our Mr. Wrenn; The Trail of the Hawk; The Job; The Innocents; Free Air; Main Street; Babbitt; Arrowsmith; Mantrap; Elmer Gantry; The Man Who Knew Coolidge; Dodsworth; Ann Vickers; Work of Art; It Can't Happen Here; Prodigal Parents; Bethel Merriday; Gideon Planish; Cass Timberlane; Kingsblood Royal; World So Wide*; and *Jayhawker* (with Lloyd Lewis). He was also involved with several stage productions and a number of short stories were published in magazines.

In 1930 Lewis was awarded the Nobel Prize in Literature.

**LIBERMAN, Alexander** (1912– )
For more than 40 years, Alexander Liberman has been associated with the Conde Nast organization. As Maureen McFadden wrote in *Magazine Age*, "Liberman has worked outside of the public eye to bring about changes in editorial, graphics, and positioning of many of Conde Nast's most successful publications."

Liberman began his magazine career as art director for *Vu Paris*, 1931–36, and was director of *Vogue* in 1936. Since 1943, he has been the art director and, briefly, the editorial director for Conde Nast Publications. He was involved with the founding of *Self* in 1979, the company's acquisition of *Gentlemen's Quarterly*, and the re-starting of *Vanity Fair*.

Liberman is also a photographer, painter, and sculptor. His works have been exhibited at the Museum of Modern Art and some are in the museum's permanent collection. He also has written two books, *The Artist in His Studio* and *Greece, Gods and Art*.

When he reached 70, Liberman said he had no plans for retiring. He still loves magazines. "They have fluidity and a contact with an awareness of life that actually parallels the flow of life."

**LICHTY, George M.** (1905– )
George M. Lichty had worked two years as a sports cartoonist for the *Chicago Daily Times* before he started his cartoon, "Grin and Bear It," which has been around since 1932.

"Grin and Bear It" is currently syndicated by the Field Newspaper Syndicate in Chicago.

**LIEBLING, Abbott Joseph** (1904–1963)
A. J. Liebling has been described by J. Anthony Lukas as "*The New Yorker*'s press critic, gourmand, boxing writer, war correspondent, labor reporter, medievalist, Francophile, chronicler of Broadway, and resident epicure."

Before joining *The New Yorker*, Liebling worked from 1931 to 1935 on the *New York World-Telegram* under Roy Howard. He also worked, prior to that (1926–39), on the *Providence Evening Bulletin* and *Journal* (Rhode Island). He once worked for Hearst, where he was told "the public is interested in just three things: blood, money and the female organ of sexual intercourse."

After joining *The New Yorker*, he was the publication's correspondent during World War II in France, England, and North Africa. Between 1945 and his death, Liebling wrote the "Wayward Press" article for the magazine. This was probably the first column that criticized the American press.

Lukas quoted Liebling about his three kinds of writers of news: "1. The reporter, who writes what he sees; 2. The interpretive reporter, who writes what he sees and what he construes to be its meaning; 3. The expert, who writes what he construes to be the meaning of what he hasn't seen." Liebling had little love for publishers or "experts."

A recent biography by Raymond Sokolov, *Wayward Reporter*, tells of Liebling's massive production. He had nearly 500 manuscripts published, and some 20 books including, *Back Where I Came From*; *The Telephone Booth Indian*; *The Road Back to Paris*; *Mink and Red Herring*; *The Republic of Silence*; *Chicago: Second City*; *The Honest Rainmaker*; *The Sweet Science*; *Normandy Revisited*; *The End of Louisiana*; *The Press*; and *Between Meals*. He co-authored *They All Sang*.

Sokolov feels that Liebling "was the first important writer to work in the area between fiction and objective reporting, where Truman Capote and Norman Mailer followed him."

**LIPPMANN, Walter** (1889–1974)

"While philosophy may be his love, journalism has been his mistress, and the amazing thing is that he has managed to be faithful to both." So James Reston, *New York Times*' columnist, once described Walter Lippmann.

Lippmann is remembered for his volume of writing, through his newspaper work and his books. In 1914, he was associate editor of the *New Republic*, which he had helped found. For a decade, 1921–31, he was editor of the *New York World* until it ceased operation under that title. Lippmann then joined the *New York Herald Tribune*, where Ernest Hynds said the newspaper "turned him loose in the early 1930's to explain, interpret and voice his opinions about the affairs of Washington and the world." Hynds called Lippmann the "first of the true political columnists."

Among Lippmann's best-remembered books are two that appeared early, *Liberty and the News*, 1920, and *Public Opinion*, 1922. His other books include *A Preface to Politics*; *Drift and Mastery*; *The Stakes of Diplomacy*; *The Political Scene*; *Liberty and the News*; *Public Opinion*; *Phantom Public*; *Men of Destiny*; *American Inquisitors*; *A Preface of Morals*; *Interpretations*; *The Method of Freedom*; *The New Imperative*; *The Good Society*; *Some Notes on War and Peace*; *U.S. Foreign Policy: Shield of the Republic*; *U.S. War Aims*; *The Cold War*; *Isolation and Alliances*; *The Public Philosophy*; *The Communist World and Ours*; *The Coming Test with Russia*; *The Western Unity and the Common Market*; and *The Essential Lippmann*. He co-authored *The United States in World Affairs*.

For his syndicated column, "Today and Tomorrow," Lippmann won two Pulitzer prizes. The 1958 award cited "the wisdom, perception and high sense of responsibility with which he has commented for many years on national and international affairs." The second, in 1962, was for "wise and responsible international reporting." Lippmann also won the George Foster Peabody Award in 1962; the Medal of Freedom in 1964; and the National Institute of Arts and Letters Gold Medal in 1965. He was decorated by the United States, Belgium, Norway, and the Netherlands. He was also awarded a number of honorary degrees.

Lippmann once wrote that "the theory of a free press is that the truth will emerge from free reporting and free discussion, not that it will be presented perfectly and instantly in any one account."

**LISAGOR, Peter Irvin** (1915–1976)
For his outstanding coverage of Washington for the *Chicago Daily News*, from 1950 until his death in 1976, Peter Lisagor won many national awards. These included two Newspaper Guild Page One honors, a Peabody Award in broadcasting in 1974, Headliner Award 1974, and the Edward Weintel Prize for diplomatic reporting in 1976. The University of Missouri awarded him a posthumous Journalism Medal in 1977.

Lisagor spent most of his newspaper career with the *Daily News*, having joined the newspaper in 1939 as a sports reporter. Later he was the United Nations' correspondent and diplomatic writer, before taking over the Washington Bureau in 1959.

Lisagor's only non-*Daily News* work included a brief tour with United Press International and, later, as news editor for the *Paris Post* in 1945.

While serving in the Army during World War II, Lisagor was managing editor of *Stars & Stripes* in London and, later, in Paris.

**LLOYD, Kate Rand** (n.d.– )
Kate Lloyd worked for *Vogue* from 1945 to 1954 and returned in 1963 as senior editor. While on *Vogue*, Lloyd rose from a staff writer to managing editor. For a few years she was feature editor and later managing editor of *Glamour* (1954–63). She remained with the monthly magazine until she became editor-in-chief of *Working Woman*.

In her new role with *Working Woman*, Lloyd seeks to make women feel more productive, confident, and healthy. "She [working woman] must be satisfied that the thousands of decisions she makes, minute-by-minute or year-by-year, are generally sound ones."

In 1982, Lloyd was named one of the Outstanding Women in Communications. In 1945, she received the first prize from *Vogue Prix de Paris*. The YWCA Woman of Achievement Award was presented to her in 1978. She had edited several *Vogue* and *Glamour* books.

She was on the advisory board of the First Women's Bank in New York City and has helped other groups in a similar capacity.

**LOCHER, Richard Earl** (1929– )
Richard Locher requires from 60 to 70 hours each week to draw "Dick Tracy," "Clout Street," and a syndicated editorial cartoon, for which he won the Pulitzer Prize in 1983. It is carried in 65 newspapers.

Locher in the mid-Fifties was an artist working on the "Buck Rogers" comic strip; and he worked on "Dick Tracy" from 1957 to 1961, returning, in early 1983, to "Dick Tracy" when Rich Fletcher died. This strip is carried in 450 newspapers. Lochner's own comic, "Clout Street," deals with local city politics, but became nationally distributed in 1983. He had also worked with the Martin Aerospace Co. in Denver and was art director for Hansen Company in Chicago and New York. In 1968, he founded Novamark Corp. Since 1972 he has been working for the *Chicago Tribune.*

Locher also enjoys painting and sculpture. He has been an Air Force test pilot and helped with the design of the B-58 bomber. He also is an inventor and has won other awards for his art.

**LOCHNER, Louis Paul** (1887–1975)
Louis Lochner was the first foreign correspondent to follow the German Army into Poland when Hitler launched his attack in 1939.

From 1909 to 1919, he was involved with various alumni and college publications positions, beginning as a reporter in 1919. Lochner had a long career with the Associated Press, covering World War II and during some of those years (1942–44), he was also an analyst and commentator for NBC. He won a Pulitzer Prize in 1939 for his foreign correspondence.

He wrote seven books, his last being *Herbert Hoover and Germany*; and he also won Overseas Press Awards in 1950 and 1955.

He was active in the Lutheran Church after World War II.

**LOEB, Marshall Robert** (1929-     )
The managing editor of *Money* magazine, Marshall Loeb has won every major award for economic and financial journalism.

After completing his journalism studies at the University of Missouri, Loeb studied at Goettingen University in West Germany. Early in the Forties, Loeb worked as a sports reporter on the weekly *Garfield News* and *Austinite* in Chicago. From 1951 to 1954, he was a United Press correspondent in Frankfurt and, in 1955, he became a reporter for the *St. Louis Globe-Democrat* (Missouri).

Loeb began his long association with Time Inc. in 1956 as a contributing editor for *Time* magazine. By 1965, he was the senior editor. He later worked with the organization's task force to consider a daily newspaper, returning to the magazine to edit *Time*'s Business section and, still later, the Nation section. In 1978, he was editor of the Economy and Business and Energy sections. The next year, Loeb became *Time*'s first economics editor, and since 1980, he has been managing editor of *Money*; in 1984, he became editor of the magazine development program.

Among Loeb's honors are the Gerald M. Loeb Award from UCLA, 1974 and the John Hancock Award and the University of Missouri INGAA awards, 1966. He has been honored by the Champion Media Award for Economic Understanding; the Dallas Press Club; Sigma Delta Chi; and other groups.

In addition to his writing, Loeb provides a daily commentary for CBS Radio network on financial topics. His book, *Money Guide*, appeared in 1984.

**LOEB, William** (1905–1981)
"I don't care what people think of me, so long as they think" was William Loeb's philosophy while he published the influential *Manchester Union Leader* (New Hampshire). The *Wall Street Journal* reported in late 1983 that "presidential candidates are discovering a big change in politics here [Manchester]. They don't have William Loeb to kick them around anymore."

Loeb took over the *Union Leader*, a newspaper that provided an outlet for his views, in 1946. Even during his college days Loeb had been in the public eye, resigning when his fraternity refused to admit a Jewish applicant, and he invited labor leader William Green to address students at Williams College when such a proposal was considered inappropriate.

Loeb's journalistic training included reporting on Springfield, Massachusetts newspapers and serving as a stringer for the *New York World*. He then worked as a reporter with Hearst National News Service and, from time to time, explored sales and public relations positions.

Loeb bought the *St. Albans Daily Messenger* (Vermont) in 1941 and, later, the *Burlington Daily News* (Massachusetts). The *Union Leader* came next. In 1948, he acquired the *New Hampshire Sunday News*, which became the Sunday edition of the *Union Leader*.

Loeb's editorials reflected his conservatism. According to some sources, Loeb viewed himself "as a sort of last-bastion defender of the traditional American way of life." He was instrumental in the defeat of Senator Edmund Muskie in his 1972 campaign for the presidency; he preferred Robert Taft over Dwight Eisenhower, and Barry Goldwater over Nelson Rockefeller. His attacks on the Kennedys prompted Robert F. Kennedy to reply: "If there's anyone more reckless with the truth, I don't know him." Loeb had called President John F. Kennedy "the number one liar in the United States."

In the publishing industry, Loeb pioneered in employee profit-sharing. His widow, Nackey Scripps Loeb, continues the tradition, although not with the same "passion" for causes or candidates. She has campaigned against homosexuality and against a national holiday for Martin Luther King, Jr.

**LOORY, Stuart Hugh** (1932– )
Stuart Loory has combined newspaper and television work to win many awards. He began on the *Newark News* (New Jersey), in 1955, and by 1959, he was working for the *New York Herald Tribune*. He was the newspaper's science writer for two years before moving to Washington as its correspondent. He worked in Moscow from 1964 to 1965.

While working on the *Herald Tribune*, Loory was also with Metromedia Radio stations. He wrote science stories for the *New York Times*, briefly, and from 1967 to 1971, he was White House correspondent for the *Los Angeles Times*.

Loory was executive editor for WNBC-TV News in 1973 and, for the next two years, he taught public affairs reporting at Ohio State University. Next, he joined the *Chicago Sun-Times*, where he remained until 1980 when he joined the Cable News Network.

Among his awards are the Raymond Clapper Award; the George Polk Award; and the DuMont Award; and several awards from his alma mater, Columbia University. He was also honored by the Overseas Press Club.

**LOWER, Elmer** (1913– )

One of the few individuals to have held executive positions with all three major broadcasting networks, Elmer Lower began his career in newspaper work in the Thirties.

After graduating from the University of Missouri, Lower was associated with newspapers in Kentucky and Michigan and with the United Press in Missouri and Ohio before moving to Washington. From 1939 to 1942, he was with the Associated Press in Chicago and New York, and for part of World War II he was with the Office of War Information. Following the war, Lower was six years a foreign correspondent for *Life* magazine.

Lower spent several years in Germany in the office of the U.S. High Commissioner before he started his broadcasting career with CBS News in 1953. Next, he joined NBC News in 1959 as chief of the Washington Bureau.

By 1963, Lower was president of ABC News, a post he held until his retirement in 1977. During that period he brought many noted newscasters to ABC, including Frank Reynolds, Ted Koppel, Sam Donaldson, Peter Jennings, Ann Compton, and Barbara Walters.

Following his work with the networks, Lower became a visiting journalism professor at several universities. During one year, 1982–83, he was dean of his alma mater's School of Journalism in Missouri. The school had awarded him its Journalism Medal in 1959.

For his 50-year career in journalism, Lower was one of three media leaders elected to receive the Fellow of the Society Award from Sigma Delta Chi, in 1983.

**LUCAS, Jim G.** (1914–1970)

Jim Lucas covered three wars in his time, World War II, Korean War, and the Vietnam War. He won a Pulitzer Prize and two Ernie Pyle awards, as well as the George Polk Memorial Award and the National Headliner Award. The American Legion and other groups also recognized his reporting talents.

Lucas started as a reporter on the *Muskogee Phoenix* (Oklahoma) and *Times-Democrat*. He was also a news broadcaster on a Muskogee radio station and then joined the *Tulsa Tribune* (Oklahoma) in 1938. He was a Marine correspondent in the Pacific from 1942 to 1945, and then joined the Scripps-Howard Newspaper Alliance, where he worked until his death.

Lucas wrote two books, *Combat Correspondents* and *Dateline—Vietnam* and co-authored *Battle for Tarawa.*

**LUCE, Clare Boothe** (n.d.- )
Clare Boothe Luce has been called the "patron saint of female success" by her biographer, Wilfred Sheed. She worked with magazines, wrote books and plays, and served in Congress from 1943 to 1947. She was ambassador to Italy from 1953 to 1957.

Before her marriage to Time Inc. president Henry R. Luce, in 1935, Clare Luce was associate editor of *Vogue* magazine in 1930 and associate editor and later managing editor of *Vanity Fair* from 1931 to 1934. She was a newspaper columnist in 1934 and, since 1935, has considered herself a playwright. She was also a member of the board of editors of *Encyclopedia Britannica* and a consultant in American Letters for the Library of Congress.

During an "Evening with Clare Boothe Luce" in Washington in 1983, she voiced fears for the nation's future. She believes people are as they were before World War II, insofar as they fail to want to know more about the future.

Sheed also termed her a pioneer, "cutting her way through a man's world that most women were scared even to enter, and making clearings for others in the future." He credits Clare Luce with developing the concept for *Life* magazine, which is usually credited to her husband.

She wrote the following books, plays, and movies: *Stuffed Shirts*; *Europe in the Spring*; *Abide with Me*; *The Women*; *Kiss the Boys Goodbye*; *Margin for Error*; *Child of the Morning*; *Slam the Door Softly*; and *Come to the Stable.*

In 1982 she was named one of the Outstanding Women in Communications. She has been awarded several honorary degrees, and has also won the Fourth Estate Award, the Sylvanus Thayer Award, and others. She now lives in Honolulu.

**LUCE, Henry Robinson** (1898–1967)
When Henry R. Luce died, the competition, *Newsweek*, reported "There has been no one like him in the history of modern journalism." *Newsweek* also put his picture on its cover. With Briton Hadden, Luce started *Time* in 1923, creating the foundation for Time Inc., today's largest publishing enterprise.

Luce objected to the title "press lord," since he associated this with such men as William Randolph Hearst. He was, according to *Newsweek*, an eminent Victorian, Anglo-American, a person surrounded by legends and stories. He was given 18 honorary degrees.

Born of missionaries in China, Luce was educated in England and attended Oxford, and later Yale, where he met Hadden. Luce worked on the *Yale Daily News* as editor in 1916. The two men trained for World War I service together, and after the conflict, Luce worked on the *Chicago Daily News* briefly. Both men were with the *Baltimore News* (Maryland) in the early Twenties, when they conceived the concept for *Time.*

*Time* was the pioneer in the newsweekly field, as well as a pioneer in "group journalism," which depends on many writers and one editor. It was also a pioneer in its emphasis on personalities. *Time*, too, coined many words that are now part of our language.

Luce's widely quoted philosophy reflected his attitude toward *Time*: "I am a Protestant, a Republican and a free-enterpriser, which means I am biased in favor of God, Eisenhower and the stockholders of Time Inc. and if anyone who objects doesn't know this by now, why the hell are they still spending 35 cents for the magazine." And as one of his biographers, William Swanson, noted, "It was his magazine. He could print what he wanted."

Emmet John Hughes, who worked for Time Inc. for 12 years, wrote of Luce: "He was a truly American intellectual. He was more authentically so than many self-proclaimed intellectuals whose disdain for him, most of his life, was matched by his scorn for them." Hughes added: "He was a fiercely American zealot."

Luce believed "publishing is a business, but journalism never was and is not essentially a business. Nor is it a profession. Journalism is an art—the art of collecting various kinds of information (news) which a few people possess and of transmitting it to a larger number of people who we supposed to desire to share it."

"Luce and his magazines have more effect on the American character than the whole educational system put together," wrote Dr. Robert Hutchins.

In 1965, Luce won the Henry Johnson Fisher award as Publisher of the Year. He was honored by many countries, including China, France, Denmark, Germany, Greece, and the Netherlands. He was a trustee for several groups and was active in many civic projects.

**LUCE, Henry III** (1925– )

Henry Luce III began as a reporter for the *Cleveland Press* in 1949 and, two years later, joined the Time Inc., first as a Washington correspondent. He worked for *Time* from 1953 to 1955 and later directed the new building department.

By 1960, Luce III was the assistant to the publisher, but soon took over circulation for *Fortune*, *Architectural Forum*, and *House & Home*. He became the corporation's vice-president in 1964 and a director in 1967.

Luce III returned to the magazines in 1966, to spend two years with the London Bureau. Returning to New York, he was publisher of *Fortune* for a year and publisher of *Time* from 1969 to 1972. Since that time he has been director of corporate planning.

**MAILER, Norman** (1923– )

When Norman Mailer joined the Army during World War II, he said he was "determined to write the great war novel." In 1948, *The Naked and the Dead* appeared and for weeks this war novel headed the best-seller list.

Norman Mailer's successful literary career has been achieved through his best-selling books. His 22nd volume, *Ancient Evenings*, appeared in 1983, and he has written many other books including *Barbery Shore; The Deer Park; Advertisements for Myself; Deaths for the Ladies and Other Disasters; The Presidential Papers; An American Dream; Cannibals and Christians; Why Are We in Viet Nam?; Miami and the Siege of Chicago; Of a Fire on the Moon; The Prisoner of Sex; Existential Errands; St. George and the Godfather; Marilyn; The Faith of Graffiti; The Fight; Some Honorable Men; Genius and Lust; A Transit to Narcissus; The Executioner's Song; Of a Small and Modest Malignancy; Wicked and Bristling with Dots; Of Women and Their Elegance;* and *Tough Guys Don't Dance.*

He has won two Pulitzer Prizes, in 1968 and 1980, and two National Book Awards.

Mailer's newspaper career involved his role as a co-founder of the *Village Voice* in New York in 1955. Most of his life, however, has been with books. On the side, he ran for mayor of New York in 1969, the same year his *The Armies of the Night* won a Pulitzer Prize. This book concerned the march on the Pentagon.

**MANKIEWICZ, Frank Fabian** (1924– )

Before Frank Mankiewicz became a syndicated columnist and a television news commentator, he worked on newspapers in Washington and in Los Angeles. For five years (1955–61), he practiced law in Beverly Hills after he had served in the Army during World War II.

Mankiewicz moved into politics as director of the Peace Corps in Peru, 1962–64, and director in Latin America, 1964–66. For the next two years, he was Senator Robert F. Kennedy's press secretary.

Mankiewicz was a syndicated columnist and news commentator from 1968 to 1971 before taking a year off to help Senator George McGovern run for president. He returned to writing, joining the *Washington Post*, in 1976. The next year he became president of National Public Radio. He resigned in 1983, following budget cuts in NPR's operations, and is now involved in public relations.

He has written four books and many magazine articles. Mankiewicz's books: *Perfectly Clear: Nixon from Whittier to Watergate; U.S. v. Richard M. Nixon: The Final Crisis; With Fidel: A Portrait of Castro and Cuba; Remote Control, Television and the Manipulation of American Life.*

**MANNES, Marya** (1904– )

For many years, starting in 1952, Marya Mannes was with the *Reporter* magazine. This followed an earlier career with other periodicals.

Mannes, in the early Twenties, was a reviewer for *Creative Art* magazine and then wrote articles for *Theatre Arts.* From 1933 to 1936 she was the feature editor for *Vogue.* During World War II she worked with the Office of War Information and the Office of Strategic Services in the government.

Following the war, Mannes was a reporter for *The New Yorker* in Spain, Portugal, and Jerusalem. She returned to the states in 1946 and for a brief time was feature editor for *Glamour* magazine. She has published several collections of essays.

**MARBUT, Robert Gordon** (1935– )
For more than a decade, Robert Marbut has been the president and chief operating officer for the Harte-Hanks Newspapers in San Antonio, Texas. In discussing the future of newspapers, Marbut, in 1983, said, "I don't think we can ever be innovative enough; it's an unreachable frontier. The important thing for newspapers is to stay with the mainstream in the 80s."

In 1957, Marbut was an engineer with Esso Standard Oil Co. in Baton Rouge; in 1963, he was a management trainee with the Copley Newspapers in Los Angeles. He held several engineering and planning jobs in La Jolla, California, in the mid-Sixties.

Marbut began his association with Harte-Hanks as vice-president in San Antonio in 1970, moving to the top position in 1971. He has been active in professional groups, including the Associated Press and the American Newspaper Publishers Association and its Foundation and Research Institute. He was also president of the Southern Newspaper Publishers Association.

He has taught at several colleges and helped the Up with People musical group that travels nationwide. He has also written articles for magazines and professional publications.

He was in the Air Force from 1958 to 1961.

**MARCIL, William Christ** (1936– )
"The newspaper business has confidence in the free enterprise system and in the competitive marketplace, because we have a competitive service that the American reader and advertiser want and need," according to William Marcil, who was president of the American Newspaper Publishers Association from 1983 to 1984.

Marcil's career has focused mostly on newspapers and broadcasting stations in Minnesota and the Dakotas. He began with a Minneapolis finance firm, 1959–61, but switched to journalism with an advertising position on the *Fargo Forum* (North Dakota) in 1961. He became president of the Forum Publishing Company in 1969.

The company also operates radio and television stations in Sioux Falls and Aberdeen, South Dakota; Fargo, Devil's Lake, and Grand Forks, North Dakota; and Grand Island, Nebraska.

In 1983, Marcil took over the ANPA presidency. He observed then that "newspapers are indeed a part of our daily lives. They are a staying power for freedom and a mighty force in helping make our democracy work. We should cherish the freedoms our Forefathers gave us—and we should guard them tenaciously."

In civic affairs, Marcil works with the Boy Scouts and the North Dakota State University.

He was in the Army from 1958 to 1959.

**MARIMOW, William Kalmon** (1947– )
Born in Philadelphia, William Marimow has spent his life there, working initially with the Chilton Company before joining the *Bulletin* in 1970. Two years later he moved to the *Inquirer* as a staff writer.

In 1977, Marimow won awards from the Philadelphia Press Association, the Associated Press Managing Editors of Pennsylvania, and Sigma Delta Chi. The next year he won the Pulitzer Prize for distinguished public service. The American Bar Association gave him its Silver Gavel Award in 1978.

Other recognitions for Marimow's reporting include the Roy W. Howard Public Service Award, the Robert F. Kennedy Journalism Award, several Sigma Delta Chi awards, and several awards from Pennsylvania press groups.

**MARKEL, Lester** (1894–1977)
Although Lester Markel spent most of his career on the *New York Times*, he started as a reporter on the *New York Herald Tribune* in 1914. He moved up quickly to become assistant managing editor in 1919.

The *Times*' owner, Adolph Ochs, in 1923 offered Markel a chance to reorganize the Sunday supplements. Taking over a staff of three editors, one secretary, and one office boy, Markel quickly moved the operation to nearly one hundred staffers. The *Times Magazine* was expanded, the News of the Week in Review unit was added, and the Book Review section was enlarged. Other new units have been created from time to time.

Markel remained the Sunday editor until 1965, when he became associate editor for the *Times*. He retired in 1969 and, until his death, he was associated with Fairleigh-Dickinson University. He moderated a television program "News in Perspective" and was helpful in establishing the International Press Institute in 1951. His books include *Background and Foreground* and *What You Don't Know Can Hurt You*.

**MARQUARDT, Frederic S.** (1905– )
In the early Twenties, Frederic Marquardt became a reporter on the *Utica Daily Press* (New York). He was in the Philippines from 1928 to 1935, and from 1936 to 1937, he was with the *Canton Repository* (Ohio), but returned to Manila to work for the International News Service from 1939 to 1941. Later he reported on the Far East for the *Chicago Sun* and *Sun-Times*.

During World War II, Marquardt worked with the Office of War Information in the Pacific. After the war, he joined the *Phoenix Gazette* (1950–54), and then moved to the *Arizona Republic*, where he became senior editor in 1979.

In Arizona, Marquardt has been involved with the Governor's Committee on Aging, the Heard Museum of Anthropology, the Arizona Academy, Lincoln Foundation, and other groups. He has been a visiting editor-in-residence at Texas Tech University and Northern Arizona University.

The Army presented him the Medal of Freedom for meritorious civilian service in 1945. He was also given the Philippine Legion of Honor.

He has been active in several professional groups.

**MARTIN, Judith** ( - )

The "Miss Manners" column has a wide circulation through its syndication to newspapers across America. Miss Manners, or Judith Martin, seeks to provide answers to questions from her readers.

Educated at Wellesley College and with a father who works for the United Nations, Martin has had a varied background, especially the so-called "elite" scene.

She joined the *Washington Post* in 1959.

Among her books are *The Name on the White House Floor* and *Miss Manners' Guide to Excruciatingly Correct Behavior.*

**MARTY, Martin E.** (1928- )

One of the nation's best known religious editors, Martin E. Marty is a Lutheran clergyman and a noted church historian. After his ordination, Marty was pastor of churches in Illinois and in Washington, D.C.

Since 1963, he has been a professor of modern Christianity history at the University of Chicago Divinity School, as well as co-editor of *Church History.* Since 1956, he has been an associate editor of *Christian Century.*

Marty has written nearly 20 books and numerous articles for religious periodicals. His books include *A Short History of Christianity*; *The New Shape of American Religion*; *The Improper Opinion*; *The Infidel*; *Baptism*; *The Hidden Discipline*; *Second Chance for American Protestants*; *Church Unity and Church Mission*; *Varieties of Unbelief*; *The Search for a Usable Future*; *The Modern Schism*; *Righteous Empire*; *Protestantism*; *You Are Promise*; *The Fire We Can Light*; *The Pro and Con Book of Religious America*; *A Nation of Behavers*; and *Religion, Awaking and Revolution.*

He is in great demand as a lecturer and a television panelist, appearing before both Protestant and Catholic groups. *Life* magazine, in 1962, named him one of the "One Hundred Most Important Young Men and Women in America."

**MARTZ, Lawrence C.** ( - )

Lawrence Martz worked for the *Pontiac Press* (Michigan) for two years and for the *Detroit News* (Michigan) and the *Wall Street Journal* before he joined *Newsweek.*

While a student at Dartmouth College, Martz was managing editor of the campus daily and editor of the humor magazine. In 1962, he became associate editor of *Newsweek.* He was involved in launching a new section, The Cities, in 1969 and has been responsible for the Business and Finance section, as well as the National Affairs section.

With two colleagues, Martz handled *Newsweek*'s special issue, "The Negro in America: What Must Be Done," which won a National Magazine

Award in 1968. He also won a 1969 University of Missouri–J.C. Penney Award for a cover story, "The Beauty Business."

**MATTHEWS, Herbert L.** (1900–1977)
Herbert Matthews worked for the *New York Times* for 45 years, having joined the staff in 1922. Much of this time was spent in foreign service and as a war correspondent. In 1929, he was in Peking; in 1936, he was in Addis Ababa, traveling with the Italian Army. He reported the Spanish Civil War in the late Thirties and then covered World War II.

After postwar service in London, Matthews returned to New York and worked on the editorial staff from 1949 to 1967. On several occasions he interviewed Castro in Cuba. Gay Talese, writing in *The Kingdom and the Power*, feels that Matthews influenced Castro's career.

Talese described Matthews as "an individualist inspired by a touch of idealism and self-absorption." He added that "he was not a reporter's reporter, he was a *writer's* reporter." Talese believed "there was something in the chemistry of Herbert Matthews that could activate readers, provoking them to extravagant praise or scorn."

In addition to citations from Italy, Bolivia, France, Brazil, and Colombia, Matthews received the Maria Moors Cabot Award in 1956; the George Polk Memorial Award in 1957; and the New York Newspaper Guild Page One Award in 1957. He wrote 11 books *Eyewitness in Abyssiania*; *Two Wars and More to Come*; *The Fruits of Fascism*; *The Education of a Correspondent*; *The Yoke and the Arrows*; *The Cuban Story*; *Cuba*; *Fidel Castro*; *A World in Revolution*; *Half of Spain Died*; *Revolution in Cuba*. He wrote, with Edith Matthews, his wife, *Assignment to Austerity*.

**MATTHEWS, Thomas Stanley** (1901– )
T.S. Matthews' career was mostly associated with *Time* magazine, although he started on the *New Republic* as a proofreader and make-up man in 1925. Two years later, he was associate editor, writing reviews, editorials, and other articles.

*Time* was in its sixth year when Henry Luce, its co-founder, offered Matthews a position as book critic in 1929. He spent eight years in this position before becoming an assistant managing editor in charge of the "Back-of-the-Book departments." He moved up to the editor's post when Luce stepped down in 1949.

According to W.A. Swanberg, in his *Luce and His Empire*, Luce later sought to oust Matthews from the publication. However, Luce had difficulty firing anyone who had been with the operation for as long as Matthews had. According to Swanberg, Matthews was sent to London to study the possibility for a *Time-in-Britain* edition. Matthews had expected to be there some time and had joined several clubs and paid his apartment rent well in advance when Luce decided to let him go. According to various sources, Matthews sent the following telegram to Luce: "Why did you keep me standing on tiptoe so long if you weren't going to kiss me?" With that, Matthews left the magazine and later embarrassed Luce in his memoirs.

**MAULDIN, William Henry** (1921– )
During World War II, millions of American servicemen read Bill Mauldin's cartoons that featured Willie and Joe and the Infantry. Today, millions of American newspaper readers see his daily editorial cartoon that appears in 250 newspapers.

Mauldin studied cartooning at the Chicago Academy of Fine Arts. He says he keeps a Sears Roebuck catalog handy to help draw body positions. Mauldin, called a legend early in his career, joined the Army in 1940 and eventually became the *Stars & Stripes* cartoonist in Europe. He traveled about the war front in his own jeep. At 23, he won a Pulitzer Prize, and he returned home in 1945, more famous than most generals. Many of his Army cartoons appeared in his first book, *Up Front.*

When Eisenhower died, Mauldin's cartoon featured a cemetery with the caption, "It's Ike himself—pass the word." Although Kennedy was not a Mauldin favorite, the assassination prompted another famous Mauldin cartoon. He drew a sketch of Lincoln in his memorial, his hands covering his bowed face, with tears falling. It carried no caption. He did not like Nixon and once told *Rolling Stone* magazine that "he's a clown with evil eyes and Rudolph Hess eyebrows."

Mauldin could not tolerate those he termed "professional veterans" and, in 1971, suggested drafting the American Legion to finish the war in Vietnam.

Mauldin was cartoonist for the *St. Louis Post-Dispatch* for a time, but he moved to the *Chicago Sun-Times* in 1962, where his drawings are now syndicated. Mauldin won a second Pulitzer Prize in 1959. In 1962, he was voted Cartoonist of the Year by the National Cartoonists Society. Sigma Delta Chi has honored him three times, and in 1983, he received the Governor's Award, the highest artistic honor his home state, New Mexico, grants. Mauldin has written 12 books and illustrated many magazine articles. Mauldin's books: *Star Spangled Banter*; *Sicily Sketch Book*; *Mud, Mules and Mountains*; *This Damn Tree Leaks*; *Up Front*; *Back Home*; *A Sort of a Saga*; *Bill Mauldin's Army*; *Bill Mauldin in Korea*; *What's Got Your Back Up?*; *I've Decided I Want My Seat Back*; and *The Brass Ring.*

**MAURY, Reuben** (1899–1981)
After three years practicing law in his home city of Butte, Montana, Reuben Maury joined the *New York Daily News* as a reporter in 1923 and continued with that newspaper for years.

Maury became the movie critic in 1926 and, later that year, the chief editorial writer, a position he held until he became an editorial consultant in 1973. In 1940, he received the Pulitzer Prize for editorial writing, in 1954, he was awarded the Christopher editorial honor.

Since that time, Maury has received the George Sokolsky Award from the American League against Communism in 1965; and the Freedoms Foundation certificate in 1973. He wrote four books and contributed to many periodicals. His books were *The Wars of the Godly: The Story of Religious Conflict in America*; *Americans to Remember*; *What Made the U.S. Great*; and, with Karl Pfeiffer, *Effective Editorial Writing.*

**MAYES, Herbert Raymond** (1900– )
Herb Mayes was selected Editor of the Year in 1960 by the Magazine Editors Council. That same year, he received a Distinguished Achievement Award in the field of periodicals from the University of Southern California.

Mayes began his magazine career in 1920 as editor of *The Inland Merchant* magazine. Four years later, he was editor of the business paper division of the Western Newspaper Union.

For eight years, 1926–34, Mayes edited *The American Druggist* before moving to a similar position on *Pictorial Review.* He moved up to become managing editor of *Good Housekeeping* in 1937 and was editor there from 1938 to 1958.

Mayes joined *McCall's* as editor in 1959. He became president of the corporation in 1961, and since 1966, has been a consultant to Norton Simon, Inc. He has written three books. *Alger, A Biography Without a Hero*; *Editor's Choice* and *An Editor's Treasury.*

**MAYNARD, Robert C.** (1937– )
One of the nation's most successful Black journalists, Robert Maynard acquired the *Oakland Tribune* in 1983 for $22.5 million, having been editor and publisher of the California daily when it was owned by Gannett.

Maynard was a reporter for the *Afro-American News* in Baltimore, Maryland in 1956. He worked on the *York Gazette and Daily* (Pennsylvania), 1961–67, before he became a *Washington Post* reporter in 1967. He was associate editor, ombudsman, and editorial writer there before he moved to Oakland in 1979.

*Newsweek* quoted Maynard as being convinced he could move the *Tribune* to a break-even point within a year, but the newspaper lost $3 million in 1982. The *Tribune,* founded about 110 years ago, was owned for more than half a century by the Knowland family. Maynard is the first Black to own a metropolitan general circulation daily.

He has been active in professional associations and was a Nieman Fellow at Harvard.

**McBRIDE, Mary Margaret** (1899–1976)
From a one-room schoolhouse in rural Missouri to New York City, Mary Margaret McBride pursued a successful career in newspaper and radio work. Early in her career, she voiced confidence in her ability to write, and was one of the early women graduates from the University of Missouri journalism program.

McBride worked on the *Mexico Ledger* (Missouri) before becoming a reporter in 1919 on the *Cleveland Press* (Ohio). Soon she moved to the *New York Evening Mail,* where she worked from 1920 to 1924. During this time, she also wrote articles for *Good Housekeeping, Cosmopolitan, Pictorial Review,* and other periodicals. She and Paul Whiteman collaborated on a *Saturday Evening Post* four-part serial titled "Jazz."

Books, mostly about travel, occupied her time between 1929 and 1932. To earn more money, she turned to radio station WOR and, under the name "Martha Deane," provided household hints. She was also woman's page editor for the Newspaper Enterprise Association.

McBride also had a CBS program under her own name. After five years on the air, she was earning $100,000 annually during the Depression. More than 125,000 persons requested tickets to attend her 10th anniversary program in Madison Square Garden. By 1948, her radio audience had reached 6 million, for her NBC program.

McBride moved to ABC in 1950. Known as the "First Lady of Radio," she received more than 250,000 fan letters annually. She also had a syndicated newspaper column with the Associated Press for several years.

She received many honors, including the Journalism medal from her alma mater, the University of Missouri. Her home state governor proclaimed a Margaret McBride Day in Missouri; the *Radio Guide* in 1940 cited her distinguished service to radio; and the All-American Rose in 1943 was named for her.

Including some co-authored volumes, McBride wrote 15 books. She wrote *The Story of Dwight Morrow*; *How Dear to My Heart*; *America for Me*; *Tune In for Elizabeth*; *Harvest of American Cooking*; *A Long Way from Missouri*; *Out of the Air*; *The Growing Up of Mary Elizabeth*; and co-authored others.

**McCLENDON, Sarah Newcomb** (1910– )

Television viewers of presidential press conferences are acquainted with the questions asked by Sarah McClendon. She began her career in her hometown of Tyler, Texas on the *Courier-Times* and *Morning Telegraph* 1931–39. After a few years with the *Beumount Enterprise* (Texas), she became the Washington correspondent for the *Philadelphia Daily News*.

In 1946, she established the Sarah McClendon News Service in Washington and, in 1969, expanded it to provide service to radio and television stations across the nation. She served in the WACs during World War II.

McClendon has appeared on many talk shows and her book, *My Eight Presidents*, won a writer's award.

Her alma mater, the University of Missouri, and the Texas Press Women have honored her. She has also been recognized by the Headliner Club and Women in Communications for her reporting. She won the 1983 Woman of Conscience Award from the National Council of Women of the United States for her constant fight for "the people's right to know."

**McCORMICK–PATTERSON Families**

*Quill* magazine, in 1982, estimated that the McCormick–Patterson group of descendants of Joseph Medill, who made the *Chicago Tribune* one of the nation's leading newspapers, are worth between $200 and $300 million.

They include Maryland McCormick (the widow of Robert R. McCormick); Ruth McCormick Tankersley, James Patterson, Joseph Albright, and Kathrine McCormick Barnes. For a fuller account of the McCormick–Patterson families, one should consult Lloyd Wendt's comprehensive history, *Chicago Tribune, The Rise of a Great American Newspaper*.

One should also note Robert Rutherford McCormick (1880–1955), who earned the title Colonel in World War I and carried it the rest of his life. He is best remembered as the outspoken editor of the *Tribune* and for his strong Republicanism.

Early in his career, McCormick practiced law and served as a member of the Chicago City Council, the Chicago Charter Convention, and the Chicago Planning Commission; he was also president of the Sanitary District. The rest of his career was involved with the *Tribune*. Wendt, in his history, notes: "In the end the Colonel determined all policy, through sometimes major nonpolitical events were launched without his prior approval."

McCormick wrote the following books: *With the Russian Army, the Army of 1918*; *Ulysses S. Grant, the Great Soldier of America*; *Freedom of the Press*; *How We Acquired Our National Territory*; *The American Revolution and Its Effect on World Civilization*; and *The War without Grant*. His many articles were mainly political, historical, and military.

**McCORMICK, Anne O'Hare** (n.d.–1954)
Anne McCormick was one of the first women to join the *New York Times* staff. She became a staffer in 1937, but had contributed articles since 1921 on a free-lance basis.

McCormick was a foreign affairs columnist and won a Pulitzer Prize for foreign correspondence in 1937. Gay Talese noted that she was known for the "clarity of her reporting, the depth of her perception." In 1946 and 1948, she was a delegate to the UNESCO conferences.

She wrote one book, *The Hammer and Scythe*.

Among her awards are two from the Theodore Roosevelt Memorial Association and others from the University of Notre Dame, Altrusa, the Women's National Press Club, and the National Institute of Social Sciences.

**McCROHON, Maxwell** (1928– )
Maxwell McCrohon, born in Australia, worked on the *Sydney Morning Herald* from 1950 to 1952. He then served two years as the newspaper's New York correspondent before returning for five more years as a reporter and feature writer for the *Sun-Herald* in Sydney.

McCrohon joined the *Chicago American* in 1968 and later became managing editor of the Sunday edition. In 1969, he became managing editor of *Chicago Today*, when the *American* changed its name. He moved to the *Chicago Tribune* in 1972, becoming editor in 1979, his position today. McCrohon has been active in professional organizations.

**McCUTCHEON, John T., Jr.** (1917– )
A 42-year career on the *Chicago Tribune* ended for John T. McCutcheon, Jr. when he retired in late 1982.

McCutcheon worked from 1939 to 1940 as a reporter for the City News Bureau in Chicago, a training ground for many successful newsmen. In 1940, he joined the *Tribune*, where he remained until retirement.

McCutcheon edited the newspaper's famed column, "A Line O'Type or Two" from 1951 to 1957, when he became an editorial writer. By 1971, he was editor of the editorial page.

According to an account in *Editor & Publisher* in 1983, McCutcheon "was in charge of the editorial page during the period when the daily moved from a position of consistently supporting a conservative Republican spirit of view to a more independent stance." He has been active in civic and professional associations.

McCutcheon helped write the *Tribune* editorial that called for the impeachment of President Richard Nixon. The *Tribune* published some 44 pages of the testimony in this historical case.

He served in the Navy during World War II.

**MACDONALD, Donald A.** (1919– )

Donald MacDonald worked for several insurance companies and served in the Army during World War II before he joined the *Wall Street Journal* in 1953 as a advertising sales representative for the New England and Canadian territory. Later, he was the executive advertising manager and director of sales promotion and production.

MacDonald was involved with the Dow Jones purchase of *Book Digest* in 1978, but the firm was unable to turn this periodical into a profitable operation, and it was closed in 1982. The firm has been more successful with the international air edition of the *Wall Street Journal* for Europe.

Jerry M. Rosenberg refers to MacDonald as "Dow Jones' self-styled advertising 'guru.'"

MacDonald received the Silver Medal from the New York Advertising Club in 1965.

**MACDONALD, Dwight** (1906–1982)

A magazine writer, Dwight MacDonald was associated with *Fortune*, 1929–36 and *Partisan Review*, 1937–43. He also wrote for *Esquire*, *New York Review*, and *Encounter*. From 1944 to 1949, he was the editor and publisher of *Politics*.

His 20-year career with *The New Yorker*, 1951–71, brought him greater recognition for his writing. According to an obituary in that weekly when MacDonald died in 1982, "Dwight was, successively, a Stalinist, a Trotskyist, an anarchist, a pacifist, a conservative." He wrote about "big themes—culture, society, poverty in America—but his style of writing was witty, down-to-earth: conversational or epistolary." MacDonald was a visiting professor at many universities, and in 1966 he was a Guggenheim fellow.

He wrote the following books: *Henry Wallace: The Man and the Myth*; *The Root is Man*; *The Ford Foundation*; *Against the American Grain: Essays on the Effects of Mass Culture*; *Dwight Macdonald on Movies*; *Politics Past*; and *Discriminations: Essays & Afterthoughts*. He edited *Parodies, an Anthology from Chaucer to Beerbohm—and after*; *Selected Poems of Edgar Allan Poe*; *My Past & Thoughts; An Annotated Abridgement of the Memoirs of Alexander Herzen*.

**MACDONALD, Kenneth** (1905- )

Until his retirement in 1976, Kenneth MacDonald had spent more than half a century with the *Des Moines Register and Tribune* (Iowa). As Ernest Hynds wrote, MacDonald "headed the news operation for almost 40 years and also served as publisher and chief executive officer during the 1960s. During his tenure, a dozen of the newspaper's staff members earned Pulitzer Prizes."

MacDonald began his newspaper work in 1926 as a reporter. He held many editorial positions, becoming editor in 1953, editorial chairman in 1976, and chief executive officer from 1960 to 1970. He was a director of the Associated Press and served on the Pulitzer advisory board. In 1955 he was president of the American Society of Newspaper Editors.

He served in the Navy during World War II.

**McGEE, Frank** (1921–1974)

When President John F. Kennedy was assassinated in 1963, Frank McGee spent 12 straight hours on the NBC News desk. During his career he worked primarily for this network.

McGee, born in Louisiana, served in the Army during World War II. He held many jobs after that, but while studying at the University of Oklahoma, 1947–48, he became an announcer for a Shawnee radio station.

By 1950, McGee was a newscaster on Oklahoma City WKY radio and television stations. Five years later, he was with WSFA-TV in Montgomery, Alabama as news director. NBC officials were impressed by McGee's coverage of the Ku Klux Klan and brought him to the network's Washington news desk in 1957. McGee worked on "World Wide 60," "Monitor" and many specials and documentaries.

Among his many awards were the Robert E. Sherwood in 1959; *TV Guide* in 1960; the Headliner citations for both radio and television broadcasting in 1958; the George Foster Peabody in 1966; and the Emmy, 1967–68, for special events coverage.

**McGILL, Ralph** (1898–1969)

For years, the names of Ralph McGill and the *Atlanta Constitution* were synonymous. He was the daily's sports editor, and later editor and publisher, during a career that ended only with his death. He had worked on the *Nashville Banner* from 1922 to 1928.

McGill won the Pulitzer Prize for editorial writing in 1958 and in 1964 was given the Presidential Medal of Freedom. The University of Georgia School of Journalism has an annual Ralph McGill Lecture in his honor.

McGill also wrote books and won the *Atlantic* non-fiction $5,000 prize for *The South and the Southerner*.

He served with the Marines in World War I.

**McGRAW, Curtis** (1895- )

Curtis McGraw, in 1950, became the third successive McGraw to be president of McGraw-Hill Publishing Co., Inc., after James H. McGraw, Jr. took over in 1935 when the founder, James H. McGraw, Sr., resigned.

In 1982, *Quill* magazine estimated the McGraw family to be worth between $200 and $300 million. This included the six grandchildren of James McGraw, Sr. Today, the principal members of the family include Harold McGraw and his cousins, Donald McGraw and John McGraw. The family is said to own about 20 percent of the firm.

James H. McGraw, Sr., in 1899, bought the *Street Railway Journal*, and John A. Hill was editor of *The Locomotive*. These publications formed the basis for the McGraw-Hill Book Co., founded in 1909.

Harold Whittlesey McGraw, Jr. (1918– ) has been with the company since 1947, working in advertising, sales, and with a number of publications. In 1974, he became president and, two years later, chairman of the board. After serving as the chief operating officer he retired at age 65.

**McGRORY, Mary** (1918– )

Mary McGrory has been a syndicated columnist for many years, with 225 newspapers carrying her material. She began her writing on the *Boston Herald-Traveler* in 1942 and remained there until 1947.

At that time she moved to the *Washington Star*, where she was a book reviewer from 1947 to 1954. She became a feature writer on national affairs and covered such major events as the Army-McCarthy hearings.

She won the Pulitzer Prize for commentary in 1975. She has also won the George Polk Memorial Award and, in 1983, the Matrix Award from the New York Chapter of Women in Communications, Inc.

**McGURN, William Barrett** (1914– )

Barrett McGurn joined the *New York Herald Tribune* in 1935 as a copyboy but soon became a reporter. He was in Paris from 1952 to 1955, before he spent 13 years in Italy. He covered the Popes and the Vatican, but eventually returned to New York to work on the *Herald Tribune* until 1966.

While a student at Fordham, McGurn worked on the newspaper and yearbook while serving as a stringer for New York newspapers. In World War II, he worked on *Yank* magazine. He won the Overseas Press Club award in 1957 for his foreign reporting and, in 1963, was president of this organization.

In recent years McGurn has made his career with the federal government. He has been a press attaché in Rome and in Vietnam and liaison officer for the State Department to the White House and Pentagon and with the United States Information Agency. He has been director of public information for the Supreme Court since 1973.

Other journalistic awards have come from Sigma Delta Chi, the New York Newspaper Guild, and the Silurians, as well as from several religious organizations. He was cited by Fordham University and by the Italian Government, and was given the Christopher Award in 1959 for his book, *Decade in Europe*.

Among his books are *Decade in Europe*; *A Reporter Looks at the Vatican*; *I Can Tell It Now*; and *The Best from Yank*.

**McKAY, Jim** (1921– )
After a year reporting for the *Baltimore Evening Sun* (Maryland), 1946–47, Jim McKay turned to broadcasting, where he continues today. In 1947, he was a news and sports commentator for Baltimore station WMAR-TV. In 1950, he was with the CBS Network in sports, a position he held until 1961.

McKay is better known for his commentary during the Winter and Summer Olympics for 1960, 1964, 1968, 1972, 1976, 1980 and 1984. Since 1961, he has been the host for Wide World of Sports. For these and other reporting assignments, McKay received eight Emmy awards between 1960 and 1980.

McKay has won the George Polk Memorial Award in 1973 and the Engelhard Award from the Thoroughbred breeders of Kentucky in 1978. Germany and Austria have also honored him for his reporting.

He wrote *My Wide World.*

He served in the Navy in World War II.

**McKELWAY, Benjamin Mosby** (1895–1976)
Benjamin McKelway's career has involved Washington newspapers and the Associated Press. Born into a journalistic family, his father edited a church publication and other relatives were involved with several other periodicals.

McKelway began as a reporter on the *Washington Times* in 1916 and, after Army service in World War I, became an editorial writer and news editor with the *New Britain Herald* (Connecticut). A year later, in 1920, he returned to Washington with the *Herald.*

By 1921, McKelway's long career with the *Star* began. He served as a reporter, city editor, news editor, managing editor, and by 1946, editor, a position he held until 1963 when he became the editorial chairman. He was president of the American Society of Newspaper Editors in 1949 and president of the Associated Press from 1957 to 1963. He served on the Library of Congress Trust Fund Board for three years and on the American Press Institute Board. He also served other civic and professional associations.

McKelway won a Sigma Delta Chi fellowship award in 1951.

**McKINNON Family**
Clinton D. McKinnon (1906– ) established a number of publications in California and had owned radio-television stations in that state and in New Mexico. The senior McKinnon served in Congress and won many awards in California.

In 1960, Clinton McKinnon (1934– ) joined the Sentinel Newspapers in San Diego, California. Two years later, he was the owner of radio station KSON and later, KSON-FM. During the Sixties, McKinnon added the *La Jolla Light Journal* and the House of Hits music publishing firm. Later he acquired television stations in Corpus Christi and Beaumont, Texas.

The younger McKinnon has been active in San Diego and national activities, from political affairs to such religious projects as the Billy

Graham Crusade. He was Advertising Man of the Year in 1971 and Radio Station Manager of the Year in 1973 in San Diego. He has also won the Freedoms Foundation George Washington Medal.

**McMANUS, George** (1884–1954)
At one time, the comic strip "Bringing Up Father" was appearing in 750 newspapers in America, as well as in publications in 46 countries in 27 languages, reflecting the great success of its creator, George McManus, who had made Maggie and Jiggs among the best-known characters on the American scene.

McManus first had a strip called "Alma and Oliver" in the *St. Louis Republic* (Missouri) in 1899, when he was only 15. He won $3,000 on a horse race and, at the age of 21, went to New York, eventually getting a job on the *World*. There he did "The Newlyweds," "Their Only Child," "Panhandle Pete," "Rosie's Beau," "Snookums," and "Let George Do It."

McManus joined the Hearst organization in 1912, when he started writing "Bringing Up Father." Jiggs was much like McManus in appearance, although McManus once said, "I am not Jiggs, Maggie is not my wife, I have no daughter." The column has been continued by other artists.

McManus appeared on many radio and television shows and won several awards for his humor.

**McMEEL, John Paul** (1936– )
John McMeel was sales director for the Hall Syndicate from 1960 to 1967 and later held a similar position with the consolidated Publishers-Hall Syndicate until 1970. In 1970, he co-founded the Universal Press Syndicate. Its success proved that such services can operate in the Midwest, a long way from the majority of such groups in New York.

In addition to the presidency of Universal, McMeel, since 1973, has been the board chairman of Andrews & McMeel, Inc. He has been active in community affairs in the Kansas City area.

He served with the Army, 1958–59.

**McMULLAN, John** (1921– )
After more than 30 years "of crusading against crime and exposing the permissive foibles of Miami's hustlers, hoodlums and hood-winking officeholders," John McMullan retired as executive editor of the *Miami Herald* (Florida) in 1983. *Time* considered the event worth a full page in its magazine.

In discussing McMullan's retirement, the *Florida Trend* magazine called the job "one of the most visible and powerful in Florida journalism." The *Herald* is a Knight-Ridder Newspaper, serving as the group's flagship.

McMullan joined the Knight newspaper group in 1957, working in the Washington Bureau, on the *Philadelphia Inquirer*, and in Miami. He expanded the *Herald*'s domestic and foreign bureaus and was instrumental in the newspaper winning three Pulitzer Prizes during the past four years. The *Herald* also publishes a Spanish-language edition.

**MCNEESE, Gretchen** (1931– )
As senior editor of *Playboy* magazine, Gretchen McNeese assigns, edits, and supervises copy for several sections of this monthly publication.

McNeese joined the Playboy organization in 1967. She was the managing editor of the Playboy Club magazine, *VIP*, before moving to *Playboy* as associate editor. Before her magazine career, McNeese worked nine years as a reporter for the *Portland Oregonian* and two years on the *San Juan Star* as editor of its Sunday magazine.

She wrote the book *New Credit Rights for Women* for the Consumer Credit Project.

She has been active in the Equal Rights Amendment movement and the Civic Arts Council, the Civic Symphony Chorus, and the Civic Theater in the Chicago Area. She was married to Alvin H. Edgren in 1984.

**MCWILLIAMS, Carey** (1905–1980)
After working as a lawyer in California, Carey McWilliams became a contributing editor for the *Nation* magazine in 1945. In 1951, he was the associate editor; in 1952, the editorial director; and from 1955 to 1975, editor.

He will be best remembered for his many books, including *Ambrose Bierce: a Biography*; *Factories in the Field*; *Ill Fares the Land*; *Brothers Under the Skin*; *Prejudice*; *Southern California Country: An Island on the Land*; *A Mask for Privilege*; *Anti-Semitism in America*; *North from Mexico*; *The Spanish-Speaking People of the United States*; *California: The Great Exception*; *Witchhunt: The Revival of Heresy*; *The California Revolution*, and *The Education of Carey McWilliams*.

**MACNEIL, Robert** (1931– )
The MacNeil/Lehrer Report became a one-hour nightly program on Public Broadcasting in 1983. Robert MacNeil has been associated with the show since 1975.

Born in Canada, MacNeil started as a radio actor for the Canadian Broadcasting Corp. in 1950. His first television appearance was in a CBC children's show in 1954. Leaving acting, MacNeil turned to broadcasting, with a five-year association with Reuters News Service as a rewrite man and also as a stringer for CBC in London.

NBC hired MacNeil to be its news correspondent in London in 1960 and returned him to Washington in 1963 and to New York City in 1965. Prior to his association with Public Broadcasting, MacNeil was with the BBC in London. He has been the moderator for several television discussion programs.

As early as 1969, MacNeil complained that television was "a market place." In the Seventies, he and Sander Vanocur had their "A Public Affair/Election '72" and "America '73" programs. MacNeil early complained that the Nixon Administration sought to censor public broadcasting.

Before the MacNeil/Lehrer Report, MacNeil had his own show with WNET-TV in New York City in 1975. The program aired many controversial subjects. It gained its present title in 1976. After its 1,000th broadcast, in 1979, MacNeil told *New York* magazine that this program proved "that in-depth journalism has its place on television."

Among his awards are the Emmy in 1974 and the George Foster Peabody and DuPont awards in 1977.

**MacNELLY, Jeffrey Kenneth** (1947– )

A cartoon "should stick its tongue out at people, make people think and laugh," claims Jeffrey MacNelly, who has been successful with his editorial cartoons and his comic strip, "Shoe."

MacNelly was a cartoonist and staff artist for the *Chapel Hill Weekly* (North Carolina), in 1969–70, and then joined the *Richmond News Leader* (Virginia), where he stayed until he joined the *Chicago Tribune* in the early Eighties. His editorial cartoons have been syndicated to 400 newspapers.

In 1977, MacNelly started his "Shoe" comic strip, a "bird-populated" story. It is carried by 800 newspapers.

MacNelly told *Editor & Publisher* in 1983, "With political cartoons you get up in the morning and something stares at you in the newspaper. The comic strip really is my own plot and characters. I start from scratch every morning. It's like writing a play or a little series of plays all the time."

MacNelly won the Pulitzer Prize for editorial cartoons in 1972.

**MEANS, Marianne Hansen** (1934– )

Marianne Means has been a syndicated political columnist since 1965. Ten years earlier, she was a copy editor on the *Lincoln Journal* (Nebraska) and, in 1957, became the woman's editor on the *North Virginia Sun* in Arlington, Virginia.

Means moved to the Hearst Headline Service in 1959, and from 1961 to 1965 she was the group's White House correspondent. She was also a commentator on the CBS Radio Spectrum show. Among her awards are the Front Page Award from the New York Newspaper Women and the Texas Headliner Award. In 1963, she wrote *The Woman in the White House.*

**MEARS, Walter R.** (1935– )

A lifelong career with the Associated Press moved Walter Mears into the position of vice-president and executive editor for this worldwide news organization in 1984.

While attending college in Boston in 1955, Mears joined the Associated Press and worked there and later in Montpelier, Vermont, before moving to Washington in 1961, where he remained for more than 20 years.

In Washington, Mears held varied positions and at times covered the House, the Senate, and the White House, and all the presidential campaigns since 1964. He was awarded the Pulitzer Prize for his coverage of the 1976 campaign.

Mears has been called "dean of the wire-service political reporters," according to C. David Rambo, in *presstime*. Mears "never wanted to do anything else," as he continues "to make 'readable' the important but complex issues involving government and society."

With John Chancellor, Mears wrote *The News Business* in 1983. His only non-AP job was in 1974 when he served the *Detroit News* in Washington, but the next year he rejoined the AP, claiming he "couldn't take the pace. It was too slow."

**MEEMAN, Edward John** (1889–1966)
Edward Meeman began a lifelong association with Scripps-Howard as a reporter on the *Evansville Press* (Indiana) in 1907. He was the founder and editor of the *Knoxville News-Sentinel* (Tennessee) in 1926, and in 1931, he became editor of the *Memphis Press-Scimitar* (Tennessee), where he worked for 31 years before his retirement.

Scripps-Howard has named a major annual award in Meeman's honor and in recognition of his lifelong interest in ecology. He has been credited with putting the National Park in the Great Smokey Mountains and he helped start the Tennessee Valley Authority. While in Memphis, he was at least partially responsible for damping the powers of Boss Ed Crump.

Meeman claimed that "citizens working alone can do much; a newspaper working alone can do much; citizens and their newspapers working together can do anything." He was a delegate to the Atlantic Congress in 1959.

His book *The Editorial We*, was posthumously published.

**MENCKEN, H.L.** (1880–1956)
H.L. Mencken may be better remembered for his many books, yet he spent much of his lifetime working on newspapers and magazines. In 1899, Mencken was with the *Baltimore Herald* (Maryland), where he was city editor, 1903–05, before going to the *Evening Herald* and, in 1906, to the *Baltimore Sun.*

He remained with the *Sun* until 1941, but returned in 1948 to continue this association. Meanwhile, he served as a critic for *Smart Set* from 1908 to 1923 and co-editor from 1914 to 1923. He was editor of the *American Mercury*, 1924–33. For a brief time, 1921–22, he was a contributing editor to *Nation.* Books by Mencken include *Ventures Into Verse*; *George Bernard Shaw—His Plays*; *The Philosophy of Friedrich Nietzsche*; *The Artist*; *A Book of Burlesques*; *A Little Book in C Major*; *A Book of Prefaces*; *In Defense of Women*; *Damn—A Book of Calumny*; *The American Language* (with four revisions and two supplements); *Prejudices* with First, Second, Third, Fourth, Fifth and Sixth Series; *Notes on Democracy*; *Treatise on the Gods*; *Making a President*; *Treatise on Right and Wrong*; *Happy Days*; *Newspaper Days*; *Heathen Days*; *Christmas Story*; *A Mencken Chrestomathy*; *Minority Report*; *Part Author: Men vs. the Man*; *Europe After 8:15*; *The American Credo*; *Heliogabalus*; and *The Sunpapers of Baltimore.*

He edited *The Players' Ibsen*; *The Free Lance Books*; *The Charlatanry of the Learned*; and *A New Dictionary of Quotations.* He also translated *The Antichrist*, by F. W. Nietzsche.

**MERIWETHER, Heath** (1944– )
Following a four-year tour as sportswriter for his hometown *Columbia Tribune* (Missouri), Heath Meriwether started a long career with the *Miami Herald* in 1970.

Prior to joining the Florida daily newspaper, Meriwether spent three years, 1967–70, in the Navy aboard an aircraft carrier and a destroyer. In Miami, his advancement to the executive editorship in 1983 represents a trend to appointment of younger staffers to key positions.

In preparing Meriwether for his new assignment, the *Herald* shifted him from education writer to the Broward city editorship, to Palm Beach editor, to city desk assignments editor, to Broward editor, to executive city editor, to managing editor, by 1980, and later, to his current position.

**MERZ, Charles** (1893– )

Charles Merz joined the *New York Times* in 1931, after a career on magazines and with the *New York World*. Merz was editor of the *Yale Record* and, in 1915, joined *Harper's Weekly*, eventually becoming managing editor. From time to time he was the Washington correspondent for the *New Republic* and a contributor to *Harper's* monthly and *Collier's*.

Merz worked on the *New York World* for a decade (1921–31) as associate editor and overseas correspondent. He joined the *Times* the day before the *World* was merged with the *Telegram* in 1938. *Time* reported that "Merz' new, sober post will probably not dim his quick wit." His duty was to edit the editorial page.

Merz was described as being a "systematic man without ever seeming to be." He always believed that "the editor studies the news more carefully than any possible reader of his paper."

In World War I, he was in military intelligence.

**MESSICK Dale** (1906– )

In 1940, a new comic strip, "Brenda Starr, Reporter," appeared, created by Dale Messick. Although her name actually was "Dalia," she changed it to "Dale" when she encountered prejudice against female artists.

Messick's interest in drawing began when she was 10. After completing high school, she studied at the Art Institute of Chicago and subsequently held various jobs, including one designing greeting cards. Her initial contact with the *New York Daily News* publisher, Joseph M. Patterson, was not encouraging. Patterson had become a promoter of comics. She left some samples of her work with him and a syndicate official eventually hired her, although Patterson did not originally carry the strip in his newspaper.

"Brenda Starr, Reporter" started as a Sunday-only strip in 1940 and was so successful it became a daily strip in 1945. Messick had no professional journalism experience and once said, "Authenticity is something I always try to avoid." Nor has she been bothered by some inconsistency in her stories.

**MEYER, Eugene** (1875–1959)

In 1933, Eugene Meyer purchased the *Washington Post* for $825,000. According to Dana Thomas, he "spent $20 million more to lift this shabby newspaper out of the garbage dump and give it a thorough delousing before he handed it over to his daughter, Katharine Meyer Graham."

Meyer was the *Post*'s publisher until 1940, when he took the title of editor and publisher until 1947. He was chairman of the board in 1947. In 1954, Meyer and Phil Graham bought the *Washington Times-Herald.*

According to Frank Waldrop, although "Meyer ran an honest newspaper and a literate newspaper, he did not run a popular newspaper." Howard Bray wrote that Meyer's wife, Agnes Ernst, was the first woman in the *New York Morning Sun*'s newsroom. "She remained a vigorous and progressive-minded reporter and commentator through most of her life." She died in 1970, age 83.

"Meyer used his newspaper to influence people and the course of events in the direction of his ideal," according to Howard Bray, *Post* historian, Meyer spent much of his lifetime working for the federal government, serving in many capacities. He worked during the World War I era on several commissions, the War Industries Board, and for the Secretary of War, and held other important roles through the Forties.

**MICKELSON, Sig** (1913– )

Sig Mickelson has served as an executive with the CBS Network, Time-Life Broadcast, and the Encyclopedia Britannica Educational Corp. He has also been a visiting journalism professor.

Michelson joined CBS in New York in 1943, and from 1954 to 1961 he was president of CBS News. He also directed the CBS Foundation. From 1961 to 1970, he was vice-president and director of Time-Life Broadcast, Inc. in New York. For two years he was with Encyclopedia Britannica group in Chicago.

As a visiting professor, Michelson taught journalism at Northwestern University (Illinois) from 1972 to 1975 and at San Diego State University (California) from 1978 to 1979. He has been a member of the advisory council for the Aspen Program on Communications and Society since 1970; he helped to establish the group in Colorado. He has also been executive director for the Center of Communications at San Diego since 1979, and he served as an adviser to the National News Council.

Michelson founded the Radio and Television News Directors Association and the International Broadcast Institution.

**MIDDLETON, Drew** (1913– )

A long career in reporting started for Drew Middleton in 1936, when he was sports editor on the *Poughkeepsie Eagle News* (New York). He soon moved to the *Evening Star* there, and in 1939, joined the Associated Press in New York, writing sports.

Middleton covered World War II for the AP, starting with the British forces in 1939. By 1942, he was on the London staff of the *New York Times.* He continued his war coverage and covered the Nuremberg trials that followed the war. He worked for the *Times* in Russia, Germany, London, and Paris before turning to the United Nations in 1965. In 1947, he was denied re-entry into Russia. He has remained a military correspondent since 1970.

Middleton has been recognized by the Headliner Club and the U.S. Navy and won the U.S. Medal of Freedom for his reporting.

His books include *Our Share of Night; The Struggle for Germany; The Defense of Western Europe; These Are the British; The Sky Suspended; The Supreme Choice; The Atlantic Community; Retreat from Victory; Where Has Last July Gone?; Can America Win the Next War; Submarine*; and *The Duel of the Giants: China and Russia in Asia.*

**MIDGLEY, Leslie** (1915– )
Leslie Midgley has won several major broadcasting awards for his special programs on the CBS Network. Midgley began in the newspaper field as a reporter in 1935 on the *Salt Lake City Deseret News* (Utah), where he became city editor in 1937. He also worked on the *Denver Post* (Colorado), the *Louisville Courier-Journal* (Kentucky), the *Chicago Times*, and the *New York World Telegram.* He worked in New York for several years for the *New York Herald Tribune* before becoming editor of the Paris, France edition.

For a brief time, Midgley worked in magazines, with *Collier's* and *Look.* He joined CBS News as a staff producer in 1954, moved to become executive producer in 1967, and became vice-president for special programs at NBC News in 1980.

For such programs as "Face of Red China," "Senate and the Watergate Affairs," and "American Assassins," Midgley won the Peabody and Emmy awards.

**MILLER, Gene Edwards** (1928– )
For a series of stories that resulted in freedom for two persons wrongly jailed on murder charges, Gene Miller won the Pulitzer Prize in 1967. At that time he was working for the *Miami Herald* (Florida).

Miller worked on the *Fort Wayne Journal-Gazette* (Texas) in 1950 before he served in the Army, 1951–53. He joined the *Wall Street Journal* in Washington in 1953. The next year, he moved to the *Richmond News Leader* (Virginia), where he worked until he joined the *Miami Herald* in 1957. In 1967, he was a Nieman Fellow at Harvard.

He has written two books, *83 Hours Till Dawn* and *Invitation to a Lynching.*

**MILLER, Paul** (1906– )
Paul Miller, who spent most of his career with the Associated Press and the Gannett organization, served as president for both groups. He headed Gannett in 1957 and stayed on the job until he stepped down as chairman of the board in 1978. In 1983, Miller donated his personal papers to his alma mater, Oklahoma State University, where he established a scholarship and provided funds for a journalism and broadcasting building.

Miller began his reporting career on newspapers in Oklahoma between 1923 and 1930. After two years with Oklahoma State's information and service bureau, he joined the Associated Press in 1932, when he remained in various capacities through the Seventies.

Miller first worked for the AP in New York, Kansas City, and Salt Lake City. He became chief of the Harrisburg and Philadelphia Bureau in 1937 and transferred to New York in 1941. He served five years as general manager before joining Gannett. Miller later became a director and eventually president of AP, the first employee to be elected to the Board of Directors.

With Gannett in 1947, Miller worked on the group's executive staff as assistant to Frank E. Gannett, the founder, in Rochester. In 1957, he became president and chief operating officer, positions he held until 1970 when he became chairman.

Miller has traveled extensively throughout the world, writing articles and columns for Gannett. Among his honors are the William Allen White Award in 1963; the National Council of Christians and Jews Brotherhood Award in 1965; the Hall of Fame Award from the Oklahoma Heritage Association in 1973; the Ohio University Journalism Award in 1979; and his earlier, 1967, similar award from the University of Missouri. He has also been honored by his alma mater.

He belongs to many professional associations and has been involved in civic and educational projects.

**MINTZ, Morton Abner** (1922- )
Morton Mintz' reporting has brought him several major awards. He began as a writer on the *St. Louis Star-Times* (Missouri) in 1946, and became assistant city editor of the *St. Louis Globe-Democrat* (Missouri) in 1951.

Mintz joined the *Washington Post* in 1958, where he has won the Heywood Broun, Raymond Clapper, and George Polk awards, all in 1962. He won the A. J. Liebling Award in 1974, and two years later, the Worth Bingham Memorial honor.

On the *Post*, Mintz' stories have focused on the health hazards of automobile exhaust fumes and hazards in the field of drugs, including the safety of the "Pill." His disclosure of the thalidomide horrors resulted in a Senate drug probe.

**MITCHELL, Joseph (Quincy)** (1908- )
Early in his newspaper career, Joe Mitchell, a native of Fairmont, North Carolina, worked as a reporter on the *New York World*, 1929–30; the *Herald-Tribune*, 1930–31; and the *World Telegram*, 1931–38. Then he joined *The New Yorker*, where he has continued.

In the *Chapel Hill Newspaper*, Jay Jenkins has written about several prominent North Carolinians who have earned their place in American literature. He noted "Joseph Mitchell—in some ways the least known . . . and in some ways the most remarkable." He believes Mitchell was, and still is, a reporter. Noel Perrin, writing in the *Sewanee Review* in the spring of 1983, tells of Mitchell's work and how he "described the life and even the very soul of New York as perhaps no one else ever has."

"As a marvelous craftsman with words," Mitchell has taken several of *The New Yorker* pieces and turned them into books. He has written *My Ears Are Bent*; *McSorley's Wonderful Saloon*; *Old Mr. Flood*; *The Bottom of the Harbor*; and *Joe Gould's Secret.* He co-authored with Edmund Wilson *Apologies to the Iroquois, with a Study of the Mohawks in High Steel.*

**MOFFITT, Philip W.** (1944?– )
When Phillip Moffitt and Christopher Whittle took over *Esquire* magazine in 1979, the New York publishing world knew little about them. These men had founded the 13–30 Corp. in Knoxville, Tennessee, in the mid-Sixties, adopting the name from the audience their publications reach—persons from 13 to 30.

Among their publications are *Nutshell*, distributed each fall at colleges and universities; *Graduate*, for college seniors; *18 Almanac*, for high school seniors; and special editions underwritten by a single sponsor, such as *America: The Datsun Student Travel Guide.*

After acquiring *Esquire*, Moffitt and Whittle announced plans to spend $25 million on an expansion program to advance the magazine, as well as Esquire Video and Esquire Press activities; the men are often referred to as the "Muppets." Meanwhile, their profits from 13–30 Corp. continue to underwrite *Esquire*, which celebrated its 50th anniversary in 1983, a year highlighted by several special issues.

**MOLLENHOFF, Clark Raymond** (1921– )
Clark Mollenhoff won a Pulitzer Prize for national reporting in 1958 for his probe of labor union racketeering. He began as a reporter on the *Des Moines Register* and *Tribune* in 1941 while attending law school. He has combined his legal background with his reporting and teaching.

By 1950, Mollenhoff was with the Washington Bureau of Cowles Publications, after Navy service in World War II. He kept his position until 1969, when he became a special counsel to the President for one year.

Mollenhoff returned to reporting, and from 1970 to 1977, was bureau chief of the *Des Moines Register* in Washington. Then he turned to teaching journalism and law at Washington and Lee University.

In addition to his Pulitzer, Mollenhoff has won three Sigma Delta Chi awards, the Raymond Clapper and Heywood Broun awards, an Elijah Parish Lovejoy fellowship, as well as the Headliner, John Peter Zenger, and William Allen White awards.

Many of Mollenhoff's books have been based on his investigative reporting projects. They include *Washington Cover-Up; Tentacles of Power; Despoilers of Democracy; The Pentagon; George Rommey Morman in Politics; Strike Force; Game Plan for Disaster; The Man Who Pardoned Nixon; Investigative Reporting: From Courthouse to White House;* and *The Presidency That Failed.*

**MONTALBANO, William Daniel** (1940– )
Starting as a reporter on the *Newark Star-Ledger* in 1960, William Montalbano joined the *Quincy Patriot Ledger* (Massachusetts) in 1962. He spent the year 1964–65 in Argentina on the *Buenos Aires Herald* before returning to New York with the United Press International, 1965–67.

As Latin American correspondent, 1967–78, for the *Miami Herald*, Montalbano reported from that area until he returned to Miami, Florida as projects editor. In 1980, he became the Knight-Ridder Newspapers'

Bureau chief in the People's Republic of China. The next year he returned to Miami as chief of correspondents.

The Overseas Press Club has honored Montalbano on three occasions. Other citations include the Tom Wallace Award from the Inter-American Press Association in 1971; the Maria Moors Cabol prize from Columbia University in 1974; and the Ernie Pyle Award in 1975.

**MOORE, Acel** (1940- )
Awards have been frequent for Acel Moore, who started as a copyboy on the *Philadelphia Inquirer* (Pennsylvania) in 1962. He became a reporter in 1968, and continues with the daily, with time out for Army service from 1959 to 1961.

Moore was co-producer of a Public Broadcasting weekly news program, "Black Perspective on the News," between 1971 and 1978.

He won a Pulitzer Prize in 1977 and the following awards that same year: the Robert F. Kennedy Journalism Prize, the Heywood Broun Award, the Pennsylvania Prison Society Award, and the Philadelphia Bar Association Award. He was a Nieman fellow at Harvard, 1979–80.

**MOORES, Richard Arnold** (1909- )
For more than 20 years, Richard Moores has been drawing "Gasoline Alley," carrying the story of the Wallet clan, a comic strip started by Frank King in 1919. Moores had assisted King from 1956 to 1963.

Earlier in his career, between 1931 and 1936, Moores worked with Chester Gould on "Dick Tracy" and from 1936 to 1942, he drew the "Jim Hardy" strip. For a time he was with Telecomics, Inc., in Hollywood and was co-producer of the NBC Comics first cartoon shows on national television in the early Fifties.

In 1974, he was named Outstanding Cartoonist of the Year, and in 1983 he won the Reuben award from the National Cartoonists Society.

Three books have appeared, based on his comic strips. They are *Gasoline Alley*, *The Smoke from Gasoline Alley* and *Jim Hardy*. He also has illustrated many Walt Disney books.

**MORGAN, Edward P.** (1910- )
Edward P. Morgan is better remembered for his broadcasting activities, although he began, in 1932, as an unpaid sports reporter on the *Seattle Star* (Washington). From 1934 to 1953, he was with the United Press, serving from Honolulu to Mexico City to San Francisco. He was with the *Chicago Daily News* foreign service during World War II.

Morgan continued in the print medium, with *Collier's* (1946–48) as an associate editor and later as a free-lance writer in Europe until he joined CBS Network in 1951. Within four years he became director of news for radio and television.

Morgan reached his widest audience as an ABC Network news commentator in Washington in 1955–67 and again in 1969–75. For years, he was sponsored by the AFL-CIO, but Morgan said, "The program is sponsored by the unions, but I am paid by the network." While covering the White House he always asked sharp and hard questions, believing reporters should do this to get at the heart of the news.

In 1950, he assisted Edward R. Murrow in "This I Believe" for CBS. He also was a columnist for the Newsday Syndicate from 1966 to 1971.

He received a Peabody Award for radio news in 1956; the Sidney Hillman Foundation Award for radio news analysis in 1959; the University of Missouri Journalism Medal in 1965; the Alfred I. du Pont Award in 1960; and the George Polk Memorial Award in 1965. He was recognized by the Overseas Press Club in 1966, and by others.

He authored, or co-authored the following books: *Candidates*; *The Press in Washington*; *The Presidency and the Press Conference*; *Editor: This I Believe*, contributing articles for both volumes 1 and 2; and *Clearing the Air.*

**MORGAN, Neil** (1924- )
San Diego, California has provided a base for Neil Morgan's newspaper career. He worked as a columnist on the *Daily Journal* from 1946 to 1950, when he switched to the *Evening Tribune*. Since 1977, he has been associate editor of the daily and, since 1958, his column has been syndicated by the Copley News Service.

Morgan has won the Ernie Pyle Memorial and Bill Corum Memorial awards. His alma mater, Wake Forest College, has recognized his writing career with an award. In addition to being active in San Diego civic affairs, Morgan has written 12 books, mostly about the city. They include *My San Diego*; *It Began with a Roar*; *Know Your Doctor*; *Crosstown*; *Westward Tilt*; *Neil Morgan's San Diego*; *The Pacific State*; *The California Syndrome*; and *The Unconventional City*. He was the co-author of *Marines in the Margarita* and *Yesterday's San Diego*. His articles have appeared in several nationally circulated magazines.

**MORIN, Relman** (1907–1973)
For his coverage of the Korean War and the Little Rock school integration crisis, Relman Morin won the Pulitzer Prizes in 1951 and in 1958.

Early in his career, between 1923 and the start of World War II, Morin was associated with the *Los Angeles Times* and *Record*, the *Shanghai Evening Post*, and newspapers in Peking and other areas. He joined the Associated Press in 1934 and reported from many areas of the Pacific.

Morin was imprisoned in Saigon by the Japanese, but was repatriated in 1942 and returned on the *Gripsholm*, the exchange ship. After World War II, he was chief of the AP Paris Bureau before returning to Washington and New York.

Morin won the George Polk Memorial Award on two occasions and was also recognized by the Overseas Press Club and other groups.

He wrote *Circuit of Conquest*, which was termed "one of the best books on the decline and fall of Western power in the Far East." He has written *East Wind Rising*; *Churchill: Portrait of Greatness*; *Assassination: The Death of President Kennedy*; and *Dwight D. Eisenhower: A Gauge of Greatness* and contributed articles to several anthologies.

**MORRIS, John Martin** (1906– )
As an editorial cartoonist, John Morris has worked for the Associated Press since 1935. Before that he was a staff artist for the *Los Angeles Record* and, later, the *New York Journal-American.*

Morris frequently covered political conventions and United Nations meetings to provide AP cartoons for member newspapers.

The Headliner Club cited his cartoons in 1959 and the Freedoms Foundation named him for recognition almost each year between 1951 and 1970. In 1959, he was named the New Castle Citizen of the Year, and in 1972, he was named one of the top four cartoonists in the nation.

He has been active in his New York community, serving on several civic boards in Chappaqua.

**MORRIS, William S. III** (1934– )
A Georgia newspaper publisher, William Morris III acquired the *Jacksonville Times-Union and Journal* in 1983 for a reported $200 million.

From 1956 to 1960, Morris was president and publisher of Southeastern Newspapers and Augusta Newspapers. For three years, he was vice-president and director of Savannah Newspapers, Inc., and from 1963 to 1965, he returned to Southeastern. Since the mid-Sixties, Morris has been president of Southeast Newspaper Corp. and three other firms, in addition to being publisher of the *Augusta Chronicle* and *Herald.*

The Morris Communications Corp. has newspapers in Augusta, Athens, and Savannah, Georgia, Lubbock and Amarillo, Texas, and Juneau, Alaska. Morris has also been active with major publishing associations.

**MORRIS, Willie** (1934– )
While a student at the University of Texas in the early Fifties, Willie Morris recalled in his autobiography that "a riotous night of fraternity hazing that shook him from lethargy" prompted him to turn to reading with "a great undigested fury."

Morris edited the *Daily Texan* during his senior year and used this university newspaper to expose activities of the oil and gas industries. Such stories upset the administration. Morris later studied at Oxford, and in 1960, joined the *Texas Observer.* He served for three years on what was termed "the best political forum in the state."

By 1963, Morris was in New York with *Harper's* magazine. Within two years he had become executive editor and, in 1967, editor. He brought in many top writers, such as David Halberstam, Larry King, Bill Moyers, William Styron, and John Corry.

Under Morris' editorship, *Harper's* reached its peak circulation, and in the late 1960s, it absorbed *The Reporter* magazine. Morris also became vice-president, but he paid writers so well that the publication ran a deficit. His tour with *Harper's* ended when he resigned in 1971; his resignation was attributed in part to his publication of Norman Mailer's "The Prisoner of Sex" with its heavy use of four-letter words, and in part to dissension among management personnel.

In 1984, Morris was still in Oxford, Mississippi, where he told Julia Cass of the Knight-Ridder Newspapers, "Everything comes together for me here, and a writer has to be selfish. You have to be in a place where you can work. My relationship with Mississippi is sexual . . . we all love Mississippi but sometimes she doesn't love us back. She is a difficult and ardent mistress."

From 1980 to 1981, Morris was writer-in-residence at the University of Mississippi. He has been described as "a young Turner Catledge," the *New York Times* editor who also came from Mississippi. Among Morris' books are *The South Today; 100 Years after Appomattox; North toward Home; Yazoo: Integration in a Deep Southern Town; Good Old Boy; The Last of the Southern Girls; James Jones: A Friendship*; and *The Ghosts of Ole Miss and Other Essays*. Morris told *Newsweek* in 1983 that "the challenge facing the South is to retain the finer elements of the past—honor, sacrifice, courage, dignity, pride—and at the same time adapt to changes that are taking place."

**MOSKIN, John Robert** (1923– )
Starting on the *Boston Post* in 1941, John Moskin moved after his World War II service in the Army to the *Newark News*, and in 1948, to the *New York Star*. In 1949, he was editor of the *Westport Town Crier* (Connecticut).

Between 1950 and 1971, Moskin worked for three magazines that have ceased publication: *Look*, *Woman's Home Companion*, and *Collier's*. Before he took his current position as senior editor for *Atlas World Press Review* in 1976, he worked for several years on the *Saturday Review*.

Moskin has won awards throughout his editorial career; these include the Benjamin Franklin Gold Medal in 1955; the Page One Award from the New York Newspaper Guild; the Sidney Hillman Foundation awards in 1965; the Headliner Club Award in 1967; and the Overseas Press Club in 1969.

He has authored or co-authored four books: *The Decline of the American Male*; *Morality in America*; *Turncoat*; and *The U.S. Marine Corps Story*. He has also written many magazine articles.

**MOWRER, Edgar Ansel** (1892–1977)
Edgar Mowrer has been called "the dean of American foreign correspondents" largely because of his long career with the *Chicago Daily News*.

Mowrer began writing on the University of Michigan magazine. He spent some time in Paris, where his brother, Paul Scott Mowrer, was with the *Daily News*. When World War I started, the younger Mowrer began his newspaper career.

During this war, Mowrer interviewed Mussolini, served in Rome, and by 1923, was in Berlin. Eventually he had problems with the Nazis, since he was president of the Foreign Press Association in Germany and called for more freedom for writers. In 1934, Edgar replaced Paul Mowrer in Paris. From there he covered the Spanish Civil War and was a witness to the political scene that led to World War II.

After a year in Washington with the *Daily News*, Mowrer worked for two years with the Office of War Information.

Throughout his reporting days, he wrote many books, including *Immortal Italy; The American World; The Future of Politics; Germany Puts the Clock Back; The Dragon Awakes; Global War; The Nightmare of American Foreign Policy; Challenge and Decision; A Good Time to Be Alive; An End to Make Believe; Triumph and Turmoil—A Personal History of Our Time*; and *Umano and the Price of Lasting Peace.* He also wrote many magazine articles.

Between 1957 and 1960, he edited the North American material for *Western World*, published in England and France. He also wrote a syndicated newspaper column and was a consultant to Radio Free Europe.

**MOWRER, Paul Scott** (1887–1971)
Like his brother, Edgar, Paul Mowrer spent much of his time with the *Chicago Daily News.* He joined the newspaper as a reporter in 1905 and was in Paris in 1910, remaining to cover World War I and its aftermath. He returned to Chicago in 1934 and served as editor from 1935 to 1944.

Mowrer later was European editor for the *New York Post.* His earlier work for the *Daily News* won him a Pulitzer Prize in 1928 for best foreign correspondent. Sigma Delta Chi honored him in 1932, under the same category.

Mowrer wrote many books and several plays. He was a poet, as some of the titles indicate: He wrote the following collection of poems: *Hours of France, The Good Comrade, On Going to Live in New Hampshire, And Let the Glory Go, Twenty-one and Sixty-five, The Mothering Land, High Mountain Pond, School for Diplomats, The Teeming Earth and the Island Ireland.* He also wrote *Balkanized Europe—A Study of Political Analysis and Reconstruction* and *Our Foreign Affairs*. He also wrote *Six Plays* and *Fife*, a verse play.

**MUDD, Roger** (1928– )
For broadcasting positions he did not receive, Roger Mudd has created more media debates than did the appointment of those who "won" these anchor slots on the networks.

But Roger Mudd has won many titles. One-time NBC News President William J. Small called him "the premier broadcast journalist in Washington." While Barbara Matusow, in her book *The Evening Stars*, noted Mudd is "intellectual, well-read, even erudite," but he lost his CBS anchor race because of his inflexibility and his unwillingness to leave his home city, Washington, and his family.

Mudd served in the Army in World War II and after studying at Washington and Lee and the University of North Carolina, he worked on the *Richmond News Leader* (Virginia) in 1953, but was subsequently fired. Next he joined station WRNL in Richmond. In 1960, he was a reporter for WTOP radio and television stations in Washington.

Howard K. Smith, then with CBS News, hired Mudd to cover Congress in 1961. He earned special recognition for his marathon 67-day coverage of the Civil Rights Acts debates in 1964.

Mudd and Robert Trout anchored the 1964 Democratic convention for CBS. Mudd covered Robert F. Kennedy's 1968 primaries and, when the senator was assassinated, Mudd led the widow through the crowd.

"Bobby and I got to say goodbye to each other," Ethel Kennedy said later in praise of Mudd.

Mudd was associated with the documentary, "The Selling of the Pentagon." He won Emmys for his coverage of the shooting of George Wallace and the resignation of Spiro T. Agnew. He covered other major events and, in a 1980 interview with Senator Edward Kennedy, Mudd's questions prompted many observers to conclude that the senator's bid for the presidency had come to an end. This program brought Mudd the George Foster Peabody Award.

When the time came to replace Walter Cronkite, Dan Rather was named over Mudd, who replied: "I have regarded myself as a news reporter, not as a newsmaker or a celebrity." Shortly after that, Mudd signed with NBC as chief Washington correspondent. He said he had been disappointed in the way CBS had handled the situation after he had served the network for 19 years.

After 16 months, Mudd was dropped as NBC's co-anchor on the "Nightly News," with Tom Brokaw left to handle the chores. Mudd was to remain the senior political correspondent and host for documentaries. Again Mudd was "stunned." He said, "I've believed in being serious about my work and not putting any shellac on stuff."

"Mudd is seen as patriarchal, professorial and professional," according to John Weisman, writing in *TV Guide*.

**MURDOCH, Rupert** (1931– )

Although Rupert Murdoch is an Australian publisher, he has become a major personality on the American newspaper scene through his acquisition of the *New York Post*, *New York* magazine, the *Village Voice*, the *San Antonio Express and News*, the *Boston Herald-American*, and, in 1983, the *Chicago Sun-Times*, and he established the weekly tabloid *Star*, all since he came to America in 1974.

Murdoch, as a youth, worked briefly on the *London Daily Express* while attending Oxford, but when his father died, he returned to Australia. After taxes were paid on the estate, Murdoch owned only the *Adelaide News* and the *Sunday Mail* and a radio station. He used his London experience to move the newspapers ahead, and he soon owned the *Sydney Mirror*. He later established *The Australia*, a national newspaper. Eventually he acquired the *London News of the World* and the London tabloid, the *Sun*.

Murdoch appears difficult to interview. As Ira Ellenthal noted in *Folio* in 1981, "he is polite and outwardly composed—except for an occasional flare-up . . . he projects a cool, dispassionate image." Murdoch claims "publishers simply aren't providing the written word for the broad masses in America."

**MURPHY, Reg** (1934– )

A Southerner, Reg Murphy began his newspaper career on the *Macon Telegraph and News* (Georgia) between 1953 and 1960 before he became a political editor of the *Atlanta Constitution* in 1961. Murphy later became a

*Constitution* editor, in charge of the editorial page. Stanley E. Cohen wrote in *Advertising Age* that Murphy "had a reputation at the *Constitution* as a superior political reporter; as an editor, one former co-worker recalls, he was 'a very strong leader in terms of directing the editorial page and policy.'" He also has been called a "fine political writer."

In 1974, Murphy was kidnapped and the event was widely publicized. He was subsequently released after other editors had paid the ransom. The next year Murphy moved to the *San Francisco Examiner* as publisher and editor, with control over both editorial and business operations. He helped redesign the newspaper. When he took the position Murphy said, "San Francisco is ready for a newspaper that takes readers seriously."

Murphy took over as publisher of the *Baltimore Sun* in 1981. Cohen reported that Murphy faced a challenge to "retain the *Sun*'s dominant position as a fine newspaper with distinguished original reporting from its own bureaus at home and abroad, while at the same time competing effectively in the suburban bedroom communities with the *Washington Post*, *New York Times*, *Wall Street Journal* and *USA Today*." He has increased the use of color in the *Sun*.

**MURRAY, James Patrick** (1919- )

One of the nation's better known sports columnists, James Murray has been with the *Los Angeles Times* since 1961. Before that he worked on the *New Haven Register* (Connecticut), the *Los Angeles Examiner*, and, from 1948 to 1961, with Time Inc.

Murray won the Sportswriter of the Year Award in 1964 and from 1966 to 1977, the National Association of Sportscasters and Sportswriters. He won Headliner Awards in 1965 and 1976. His books are *The Best of Jim Murray* and *The Sporting World of Jim Murray*.

**MURROW, Edward R.** (1908–1965)

When Edward R. Murrow died, Eric Sevareid said, "He was a shooting star. We shall live in his afterglow—a very long time—we shall not see his like again."

Murrow became famous through such radio programs as "Hear It Now" and such television events as "See It Now." He became famous during World War II with his on-the-scene radio coverage of the blitz bombing of London.

Following his university days, Murrow was president of the National Student Federation from 1929 to 1932. He traveled widely around the nation and in Europe, visiting schools and discussing student issues. He next joined the Institute of International Education, but resigned in 1935.

Murrow started his lifelong association with CBS Network in 1935 and two years later joined the European Bureau in London. He described the German march into Poland. Soon his "This Is London" greeting was heard by millions of Americans. After the war, Murrow became a CBS vice-president in charge of news, education, and discussion programs.

With Fred W. Friendly, Murrow produced a series of record albums of "I Can Hear It Now," with original speeches and descriptions of the events and "See It Now" went into millions of American homes via television in 1951. Probably the best remembered, and no doubt the most effective program, was the one that focused on Senator Joseph McCarthy in 1954. This program eventually brought an end to the senator's career.

In 1953, Murrow started "Person to Person" and interviewed more than 500 persons before the show ended in 1959. Between 1961 and 1964, he headed the USIA.

Murrow received the President's Medal of Freedom in 1964. Among his many other awards were the Overseas Press Club, the du Pont, the George Foster Peabody, the Headliner, the Emmy, One World, the George Polk Memorial, and the L. S. Weiss Memorial. Popular on the lecture circuit, Murrow was awarded many honorary degrees.

He wrote many magazine articles and one book, *This Is London*, a collection of his 1939–40 radio broadcasts.

**NAISBITT, John** (1932– )

*Megatrends* became a best-seller in 1982 and John Naisbitt became a media notable because of this book. For some time, he has published the quarterly *Trend Report*, which costs $15,000 yearly. He also has a corporate newsletter.

Naisbitt's book represents the work of his company and its analysis of the more than 200 newspapers his staffers read daily. It has been estimated that the firm reviews a total of 6,000 periodicals each month, from all parts of America.

From a one-time sugar beet farmer in Utah, Naisbitt worked for IBM, Eastman Kodak, and later, as a special assistant, for President Lyndon Johnson. Today he is the director of the CRS Group of Houston and public director of the American Institute of Architects.

Naisbitt has been termed the "prophet of the 'information age' " and a "social forecaster." His book is a primer for the Eighties, a look into America's future. He offers among his many recommendations the idea that all persons "will need to speak English, Spanish and Computer" in the future.

Naisbitt does not believe that the United States has reached George Orwell's 1984 scenario. "What's happening in the country is that we Americans, bottom-up, are running our own lives," adding, "we are moving from an industrialized to an informational economy."

**NAST, Conde** (1874–1942)

Before becoming a publisher of his own periodicals, Conde Nast was advertising manager, 1900–05, and later business manager, 1905–07, for the Collier's publications. He was also briefly associated with *The Housekeeper*.

Nast set the foundation for his publishing house with the purchase of *Vogue* in 1909, *House & Garden* in 1915, and *Vanity Fair* in 1913. Caroline Seebohm wrote a biography of Nast, called *The Man Who Was Vogue*. A reviewer, Diana Hobby, noted in the *Washington Journalism Review* that this book was "a social history of American women; on another it is an account of brilliant advertising and technological feats in publishing, and one third of it is a collection of biographical sketches of the drivers of the golden coach, principally Conde Nast, Edna Woolman Chase and Frank Crowninshield." In other words, Nast's publications have had a major influence on American women.

**NATT, Ted M.** (1941?– )

In 1980, the *Longview Daily News* (Washington) won a Pulitzer Prize for its coverage of the Mount St. Helen's eruption. The editor of the *News* was Ted M. Natt, who became president of the Associated Press Managing Editors in 1983.

Natt became editor of the *Daily News* in 1974. He is a nephew of the previous publisher, John McClelland, Jr. From 1966 to 1967, he was a professional journalism fellowship scholar at Stanford University.

In his APME position, Natt called for improvement in the "content, writing and management of the daily newspapers." He has urged more double checking of news stories. He fears that too many writers "assume too much" when they prepare their stories.

**NAVASKY, Victor Saul** (1932– )

Since 1978, Victor Navasky has been editor of the *Nation* magazine. Before that he was a special assistant to Michigan Governor G. Mennen Williams, 1959–60. Between 1961 and 1965, he was editor and publisher of *Monocle* magazine, and for two years, he edited the *New York Times Magazine*.

A member of several organizations, Navasky has lectured at four universities and was a Guggenheim fellow, 1974–75. His book, *Kennedy Justice*, was a 1971 National Book Award nominee.

He served in the Army from 1954 to 1956.

**NELSON, John Howard (Jack)** (1929– )

John Nelson began as a reporter on the *Biloxi Daily Herald* (Mississippi) in 1947 and in 1952 joined the *Atlanta Constitution* (Georgia), where he remained until 1965.

Nelson became the Southern bureau chief for the *Los Angeles Times* in 1965, working in Atlanta before moving to its Washington Bureau in 1970. He became bureau chief in 1975, where he remains today. In 1960, he won a Pulitzer Prize for local reporting. The same year he was named one of 10 Outstanding Young Men by the U.S. Junior Chamber of Commerce.

The Drew Pearson Award was given to Nelson in 1974 for investigative reporting. He is a member of the executive committee of the Reporters Committee for Freedom of the Press and has co-authored three books: *The Censors and The Schools*; *The Orangeburg Massacre*; and *The FBI and the Berrigans*.

In 1984 Nelson told the *Wall Street Journal* that on occasions the press had covered alleged improprieties in the Reagan Administration but admitted readers objected. "People are so damn tired of seeing presidents written up negatively."

**NESSEN, Ronald H.** (1934– )
Ron Nessen became well known as press secretary for President Gerald Ford in 1974, replacing Jerald F. ter Horst, who resigned when Ford pardoned Nixon. Earlier, from 1952 to 1955, he worked for radio stations in West Virginia and Virginia.

Nessen, in 1956, worked on the *Montgomery County Sentinel* in Rockville, Maryland. A few months later, he joined the International News Service in Washington. By 1962, he had turned to television as NBC News political correspondent. He covered the presidential campaigns and so angered officials with his investigative reporting that he was subpoenaed by Vice-President Spiro T. Agnew in 1973. He refused to reveal confidential sources.

He covered the Vietnam War and later appeared on the NBC "Today Show." One of his reports, "The Plains in Reeds," won the George Polk Award. He also worked in other areas, including Mexico City and London, and once said he was "sort of their fireman at NBC. I always seemed to get the wars and the earthquakes."

When Ford named him press secretary, he cited Nessen's "skill and objectivity" and "superb reputation." Reporters were mixed about his work in the White House.

He was a free-lance writer and lecturer in the late Seventies, and in 1980, became senior vice-president for Marston and Rothenberg Public Affairs, Inc. in Washington and as associate with Robert Marston & Associates in New York City. In mid-1984 Nessen became vice-president for news for Mutual Broadcasting System.

He wrote a novel, *The Hour.*

**NEUHARTH, Allen H.** (1924– )
In 1983, Allen H. Neuharth renewed his contract with Gannett Co., Inc. His updated pay was to be $900,000 plus bonus for a contract that continues until 1989. Neuharth will then be 65 and will become a columnist, or a consultant to the corporation.

The Gannett Co., in 1983, operated 87 daily newspapers, including its nationally distributed *USA Today*, thirty-three non-daily newspapers, outdoor advertising agencies, and seven television and thirteen radio stations.

Neuharth's newspaper career began at the age of 11 when he carried the *Minneapolis Tribune* (Minnesota). Two years later, he worked in the *Alpena Journal* composing room. He edited his high school newspaper before serving in the Army during World War II.

While at the University of South Dakota, he edited the campus newspaper and held summer intern jobs on newspapers in Mitchell and Rapid City. He joined the Associated Press in Sioux Falls as a reporter after graduation.

After an unsuccessful experiment with a weekly tabloid sports publication in South Dakota, Neuharth in 1954, joined the Knight-owned *Miami Herald* (Florida) as a reporter. He became assistant managing editor in Miami, and in 1960 was assistant executive editor of the Knight-owned *Detroit Free Press* (Michigan). Three years later, he began his career with

Gannett as general manager of the group's headquarter newspapers in Rochester.

Neuharth moved up to the presidency of Gannett Florida and helped establish *TODAY* at Cape Canaveral. He moved to the presidency of the organization in 1970, eventually adding the titles of chairman and chief executive. He has also been president of the American Newspaper Publishers Association and vice-president of the International Federation of Newspaper Publishers in Paris.

Among his honors are the Horatio Alger Award and Sigma Delta Chi and Associated Press Managing Editors' First Amendment citations. His management success has resulted in recognition from the *Financial World Magazine*, *Gallagher Report*, and *Wall Street Transcript*. He has received several honorary degrees.

Neuharth said in 1983 that "newspapers are going to benefit from the growing appetite for news and information." He predicted a bright future and an era of unprecedented growth for newspapers.

**NEWHOUSE Family**

Samuel I. Newhouse (1895?–1979) created an organization that was estimated to be worth between $150 and 200 million in 1961 and between $1 and 2 billion in 1982. In 1983, the Internal Revenue Service placed an even higher estimate of the family holdings, when it sued the estate for $914 million in taxes and penalties. The IRS action released financial figures to the public, something this family-owned operation had never done.

In 1983, the Newhouse Empire included 31 daily newspapers, magazines, radio and television stations, and printing and publishing operations. Among the magazines are *Bride's*; *Gentlemen Quarterly*; *Glamour*; *Gourmet*; *House & Garden*; *Mademoiselle*; *Vogue*; and *Vanity Fair*. Random House and Knopf are two of the Newhouse-held publishing firms.

Newhouse, the son of poor Jewish immigrants from Europe, worked for $2 a week for an attorney after he completed elementary school. The attorney acquired the *Bayonne Times* (New Jersey), and told Newhouse, then 16, to "take care of the paper." Newhouse studied at night and eventually earned a law degree. Meanwhile, the *Times* prospered.

Newhouse began to acquire newspapers in the tri-state area, including the *Staten Island Advance*, the *Long Island Press*, the *Newark Star-Ledger*, and the *Long Island Star-Journal*. Then came the Syracuse dailies—the *Herald-Journal*, the *Sunday Herald-American*, and the *Post-Standard*.

The *Portland Oregonian* was acquired in 1950, for $5,500,000. He paid $6,250,000 for the St. Louis *Globe-Democrat* (Missouri) in 1955, a daily his sons sold in 1983 after several years of losses. Additional purchases have followed in Birmingham, Huntsville, and Mobile, Alabama; New Orleans, Louisiana; Springfield, Massachusetts; and Ann Arbor, Bay City, Flint, Grand Rapids, Jackson, Kalamazoo, Muskegon, and Saginaw, Michigan, a transaction that cost him more than $300 million and included the Sunday magazine supplement, *Parade*; Pascagoula, Mississippi; Jersey City and Newark, New Jersey; Staten Island, New York; Cleveland, Ohio; and Harrisburg, Georgia.

Newhouse gave millions of dollars to Syracuse University for the

Newhouse Communications Center. He was a trustee of the University, which gave him an honorary degree.

Sam Newhouse apparently was proud of the fact that he never occupied a fancy office or maintained elaborate files. To him his briefcase was adequate. He made the major corporate decisions, permitting editorial staffers to decide what went into his publications. According to *Time* magazine, the corporation is so huge that it might pay the IRS fine out of profits.

**NEWMAN, Edwin Harold** (1919– )
In 1941, Edwin Newman began his journalistic career as a dictation boy with the International News Service in Washington. He worked for the United Press just prior to his World War II service in the Navy as a communications officer.

Between 1945 and 1947, Newman worked for the New York liberal *PM* daily and the Washington news bureau operated by Esther Tufty that served out-of-town clients. His initial experience with broadcasting came in 1947, when he worked for Eric Sevareid at the CBS News Bureau. Newman spent more than three years on a free-lance basis in London, during which time he wrote magazine articles and handled special broadcasts for the BBC and NBC. He also wrote articles for the U.S.-sponsored European Recovery Program.

Newman's career with NBC started in 1952 in London. Four years later, he was the network's London chief and later worked in Rome and Paris. By 1961, he was back in America on a permanent basis. He hosted several programs and specials. Between 1965 and 1971, he was drama critic for WNBC-TV. He told *Newsday* then that "if you have any ego or ham, being a drama reviewer is a satisfying occupation." He retired in 1984 but continues as an after-dinner speaker-lecturer.

Newman won a Peabody Award in 1966 for "wit and depth of understanding," for his work on the NBC radio series "Emphasis." That year, he was president of the Association of Radio-Television News Analysts. He continues to write for magazines.

His awards include the Overseas Press Award in 1961; the University of Wisconsin School of Journalism Award in 1967; the University of Missouri Journalism Medal in 1975, and six Emmy awards. His books on "our language" have been best-sellers, and have included *Will America Be the Death of English?*; *Strictly Speaking*; *A Civil Tongue*; and *Sunday Punch*.

In 1983, Newman said the news business faces problems that only the public could change by demanding better news coverage. "The problems are not a question of bias or conspiracy among those covering news. The problem is how to get competence in the news business."

**NEWTON, Virgil Miller, Jr.** (1904–1977)
Although born in Atlanta, Georgia, Virgil Newton, Jr. made a career in the newspaper business in Florida, especially in Tampa. He started as a sports editor on the *Gainesville Sun* in 1925 and moved to the *Tampa Daily Times* in 1926 in a similar capacity.

Newton became sports editor of the *Tampa Tribune* in 1930, moved to assistant managing editor in 1935 and to managing editor in 1943, a position he held until 1969. During his reporting days, Newton won several awards, including the Free Enterprise Award from the National Association of Management in 1954 and the Freedoms Award from the Virginia Press Association in 1957.

The National Press Photographers Association named him editor of the year in 1958, and his alma mater, the University of Florida, named him the Outstanding Alumnus in 1977. Newton was active in other civic and professional organizations.

**NICHOLS, William T.** (1905– )
After working at Harvard, for a power company, and for the Tennessee Valley Authority, William I. Nichols became editor of *Sunset* magazine in San Francisco in 1937. While attending Oxford University in 1926–27, he worked with the Associated Press staff in London.

Two years later, in 1939, Nichols took over a major assignment, joining *This Week* magazine in New York City as managing editor. He moved up to editor, then publisher, and in 1969–70, senior consultant.

*This Week*, one of the pioneer Sunday newspaper supplements, had been losing money, but Nichols turned it around. Among his improvements were the "Words to Live By" column and the "Wake Up and Read" campaign.

Nichols traveled extensively in Europe for the U.S. Department of State from 1946 to 1951. In 1945, he toured Europe as one of 18 editors selected by General Dwight Eisenhower to report on Nazi atrocities.

While *This Week* editor, he said, "Our main objective is to be entertaining, to provoke interest, but underneath it all is the compulsion to be entertaining on the positive side." After his work on this magazine, Nichols worked with book associations, libraries, and other groups.

He wrote *On Growing Up* and *Fishing for Fun*, both about Herbert Hoover, and he edited *Words to Live By*.

**NORTON, Howard Melvin** (1911– )
Before joining the *Baltimore Evening Sun* (Maryland) in 1940, Howard Norton worked in the Far East and on the *Los Angeles Times*, the *San Francisco Chronicle*, the *Kansas City Star*, and the *Philadelphia Inquirer* in the years between 1933 and 1940.

On the *Sun*, Norton was the Behind-the-News editor, the foreign editor, and war correspondent. He spent five years as Washington correspondent before serving in London and Moscow. Another five years were spent with the Washington Bureau before he joined the national staff of the *U.S. News & World Report*.

While with the *Sun*, Norton won a Pulitzer Prize in 1974 for a series on unemployment compensation. His alma mater, the University of Florida, gave him its Centennial Award in 1953 and, in 1979, named him a Distinguished Alumnus.

From 1976 to 1977, Norton was the *National Courier*'s Washington

Bureau chief. The next year, he became director of publications for the National Association of Community Action Directors in Washington.

He has written five books: *Only in Russia*; *The Miracle of Jimmy Carter*; *Rosalynn—A Portrait*; *When the Angels Laughed*; and *Good News about Trouble*.

**NOSSITER, Bernard Daniel** (1926– )

Bernard Nossiter began his newspaper work as a reporter on the *New York World-Telegram and Sun* from 1952 to 1955. Then he joined the *Washington Post* as a national economics reporter.

Between 1964 and 1979, Nossiter worked in Paris, Asia, and London for the *Post*. Among his honors are the Sigma Delta Chi citation as distinguished Washington correspondent in 1961; the Overseas Press Club Award in 1966; the George Polk Award in 1969; and a Nieman Fellow in 1962–63.

He has written *The Mythmakers: An Essay on Power and Wealth*; *Soft State: A Newspaperman's Chronicle of India*; and *Britain—a Future That Works*. *The Mythmakers* won a Hillman Foundation Book award.

In 1979, Nossiter became the U.S. Bureau chief for the *New York Times*.

**NOVAK, Robert S.** (1931– )

For 20 years, Robert S. Novak has been writing political columns, much of this time with Rowland Evans, Jr. The writers also have collaborated in writing two books: *Lyndon B. Johnson: The Exercise of Power*, in 1966, and *Nixon in the White House: The Frustration of Power*, in 1971.

Novak was a reporter on the *Joliet Herald-News* (Illinois) in 1948. He moved to the *Champaign-Urbana Courier* in 1951–52, while attending the University of Illinois, and in 1954, he started a four-year tour with the Associated Press. The *Wall Street Journal* was Novak's next employer, and after five years there he moved to the *New York Herald Tribune* as a syndicated columnist. Today the Novak-Evans Column is syndicated by the Field Newspaper Firm. The team works out of their Washington office.

**OAKES, John Bertram** (1913– )

John Oakes became a reporter on the *Trenton State Gazette and Times* (New Jersey) in 1936. He spent the next four years as a political reporter on the *Washington Post*.

Oakes' long career with the *New York Times* began in 1946, when he was editor of the Review of the Week section in the Sunday edition. He later was a member of the editorial board, while contributing to the Book Review section and the Sunday magazine. From 1961 to 1978, Oakes handled the editorial page, for a year as the senior editor while serving as visiting professor in 1977–78 at the Syracuse University School of Communications.

His many decorations, awards, and citations include the George Polk Memorial Award in 1965; the Jefferson Award from the Unitarians in 1968;

and the John Muir Award from the Sierra Club in 1974 and other environmental recognitions. He wrote *The Edge of Freedom.*

**O'BRIAN, Jack** (1921– )
For three decades, Jack O'Brian has been a newspaper columnist in New York. O'Brian began with the *Buffalo Times* in 1939 and moved to the *New York World-Telegram* the next year, returning to the *Buffalo Courier-Express* to work from 1940 to 1943.

By 1943, O'Brian was working for the Associated Press in New York as a drama, movie, and music critic and a columnist. He switched to the Hearst *New York Journal-American* where he wrote his own column from 1949 to 1967; since 1967, he has been writing "Voice of Broadway" for the Hearst-owned King Features Syndicate.

O'Brian's work has brought him the Christopher Award in 1955; three Deems Taylor Awards in 1974, 76, 79, from ASCAP; the Morality in Media Award in 1971; the George M. Cohan Award from the Catholic Actors Guild in 1977; and others. On three occasions, he was nominated for a Pulitzer Prize.

He wrote *The Great Godfrey* and articles for magazines.

**OLIPHANT, Patrick** (1935– )
"I'm supposed to be angry with someone," says Pat Oliphant, a Pulitzer Prize-winning editorial cartoonist. Today he is one of the best cartoonists in America, with his work appearing in more than 500 newspapers.

Born in Australia, Oliphant began as a copyboy and press artist on the *Adelaide Advertiser*, 1953–55, and then became the newspaper's editorial cartoonist. In 1964, Oliphant succeeded Paul Conrad on the *Denver Post* (Colorado). He said, "It took a lot of courage for the *Post* to hire me. They knew nothing about me. Nobody in America was using my style." Earlier, Oliphant had made a world-wide tour to study techniques used by other editorial artists.

Oliphant won a Pulitzer Prize in 1967. He has also been cited by the International Federation of Free Journalists in London, and the California Newspaper Publishers Association. He has written three books: *The Oliphant Book, Four More Years*; and *An Informal Gathering.*

Oliphant's trademark is "Punk the Penguin," who appears in a corner of the panel. His cartoons are "famous for their toughness, his illustrations are perhaps best known for their comic detail," according to *Kansas City Times* reporter Bryon Hori in an 1984 interview with Oliphant. He is currently handled by Universal Syndicate.

In 1984 Oliphant added another cartoon, "Sunday Punk," to go with his five weekly drawings. It differs from the traditional political cartoon with its many panels.

**O'NEILL, Michael James** (1922– )
Publishers were urged "to have an open mind and a willingness to look at the information revolution in a fresh, innovative way" by Michael O'Neill, editor of the *New York Daily News* and former president of the American Society of Newspaper Editors.

O'Neill began his career in public relations, worked briefly for a Detroit radio station, and then joined the United Press in 1947. He worked for the wire service in Washington before he became the capital correspondent for the *New York Daily News* in 1956. He moved to New York as assistant managing editor in 1966, became managing editor in 1968, executive editor in 1974, and editor in 1975. He also is a vice-president and director for the newspaper.

The National Headliner Award honored O'Neill in 1956 for national affairs reporting. In addition to being ASNE president, O'Neill headed the Overseas Writers in 1965.

Ernest Hynds credits O'Neill with giving the *Daily News* "the first major overhaul since it was started in 1919." He added local editions, more specialists, more criticism and investigative projects.

He wrote *China Today* and co-authored *The Kennedy Circle.*

He served in the Army from 1943 to 1945.

**ORR, Carey** (1890–1967)
For more than 40 years, 1917–63, Carey Orr was the editorial cartoonist for the *Chicago Tribune.* Before that, he worked briefly for the *Chicago Examiner* in 1912 and the *Nashville Tennessean* and *American* from 1912 to 1917.

Orr won a Pulitzer Prize for his cartoons in 1961, the first the *Chicago Tribune* had won since 1936. He originated the "Brain Trust" cartoon characters, which reflected the *Tribune*'s Republican philosophy in those years. He also helped pioneer the daily color cartoons and, from time to time, provided cartoons for other sections of the *Tribune*, including sports. His anti-New Deal cartoons referred to the NRA as "No Relief Anywhere."

Orr won a Government Gold Medal in 1918 and several Freedoms Foundation Awards. He also taught many future cartoonists at the Chicago Academy of Fine Arts.

**OSGOOD, Charles** (1933– )
Don Kowet, writing in *TV Guide* in late 1983, described Charles Osgood as this "whimsical CBS correspondent" who loves to dress up the news with doggerel.

Charles Osgood Wood III, his full name, planned a music career as a classical pianist and organist, and during World War II, he was in the Army band. "Black Is Beautiful" is one of the more than 25 of his tunes that have been published.

Before and following World War II, Osgood worked with Washington station WGMS in a musical capacity. From 1963 to 1964 he had a brief tour as general manager of Hartford (Connecticut) station WHCT-TV. Then he joined ABC radio for "Flair Reports." Along with Ted Koppel, the two concocted a show that would compete with NBC's "Today Show," but were unable to get it going.

Osgood joined CBS-owned radio station WCBS in New York in 1967 and in 1972 joined the television unit as a correspondent while continuing his radio work. He has written two books, both collections of the "rampant doggerel" that he recites on his program. The title of the first,

*Nothing Could Be Finer Than a Crisis That Is Minor in the Morning*, indicates his sense of humor. His other book is *There's Nothing That I Wouldn't Do If You Would Be My POSSLQ*. The letters represent a Census Bureau acronym for "Persons of the Opposite Sex Sharing Living Quarters." He once told *People* magazine that he liked "to keep my humorous pieces on a high level."

**OTT, William** (1928– )

As senior vice-president of operations for Knight-Ridder Newspapers, Inc., William A. Ott is responsible for the group's newspaper business affairs.

Before joining the Knight-Ridder group, Ott edited the *Macon Telegraph* (Georgia), where he was active in many civic projects.

Ott was in Akron between 1971 and 1977 as president and publisher of the *Beacon-Journal*. He was also president of the Ohio Newspaper Association. For five years he was in charge of Knight-Ridder's 10 largest newspapers, while living in Akron (Ohio). In his current job, he operates out of Miami, Florida.

He was an Army CID agent in Korea before the war started there.

**OTTAWAY Family**

James Ottaway (1911– ) started in the newspaper business in 1933 as the national advertising manager of the *Port Huron Times Herald* (Michigan). He was associated with several newspapers until he became the publisher of the *Endicott Bulletin* (New York) in 1936. He founded Ottaway Newspapers-Radio, Inc. in 1946 and became chairman of the board. Since 1970, he had been chairman of the board of Ottaway Newspapers, Inc.

Ottaway acquired newspapers in New York, Pennsylvania, Massachusetts, Michigan, Minnesota, Kentucky, and New Hampshire. The newspaper group was acquired by Dow Jones & Co. in 1970 in a stock transaction, and Ottaway became a Dow Jones director. In 1984 he was named to the new position of "founding director" of Ottaway. During his career he has been active in civic affairs, including the Girl Scouts, Boys Club, parks, colleges, and universities. He was president of the New York State Publishers Association in 1954 and elected to the Hall of Fame in 1976 by the New York Associated Dailies.

"I've always figured that if we put out a good quality editorial product, the business end will take care of itself," he once said.

James Haller Ottaway, Jr. (1938– ) started his training on the *Danbury News-Times* (Connecticut) in 1960. He later worked on the *Middletown Times Herald-Record* (New York), and in 1963, he became editor of the *Pocono Record* (New York). From 1966 to 1970 he was publisher of the *New Bedford Standard-Times* (Massachusetts). He became president of Ottaway Newspapers, Inc. in 1970, its chief operating officer in 1976, and chairman of the board in 1979. He has been a vice-president of Dow Jones since 1980.

**OTTO, Jean Hammond** (1925– )

Jean Otto was the women's editor of the *Appleton Post-Crescent* (Wisconsin) for eight years (1960–68) before she began her long association with the *Milwaukee Journal.* By 1977, she had moved from being an editorial writer to editor of the Op-Ed page.

Otto gained wider recognition when she became the first woman to be president of the Society of Professional Journalism, Sigma Delta Chi, 1979–80.

Among her awards was the Milwaukee YWCA Outstanding Woman in Journalism title in 1977. The National Broadcast Editorial Association gave Otto its James Madison Award in 1981, and Ball State University and the National Press Photographers Association have also honored her. She has served on the American Council of Education in Journalism accrediting evaluation teams. In 1983, Otto became the editorial page editor for the Denver *Rocky Mountain News* (Colorado).

For years she has been active in the First Amendment movement, and was a founding member of the First Amendment Congress in 1979. Otto received the Inland Daily Press Association 1984 Ralph D. Casey Minnesota Award for Distinguished Service to Journalism for her contributions to journalism education and the profession.

**OTWELL, Ralph Maurice** (1926– )

Ralph Otwell has been with the *Chicago Sun-Times* since he joined the newspaper as assistant city editor in 1953, becoming managing editor in 1968 and editor in 1976.

Before his *Sun-Times* connection, Otwell worked for the Southern Newspapers Inc. in Hot Springs from 1943 to 1944, and again in 1947. He served in the Army on two occasions, 1944–47 and 1951–53.

Otwell has served with the newspaper division of Field Enterprises, Inc. and has been with the National News Council since it was founded in 1972. He has also lectured at Northwestern University School of Journalism.

The Chicago Newspaper Guild gave Otwell its Page One Award in 1964, the same year Northern Illinois University named him the "Illinois Journalist of the Year."

He works closely with professional and civic groups.

**OURSLER Family**

Fulton Oursler (1893–1952) gained national fame with one of his books, *The Greatest Story Ever Told*, a bestseller in 1949. He also spent much of his career working with Bernarr Macfadden on many of his publications.

From 1910 to 1912, Oursler worked as a reporter on the *Baltimore American* (Maryland) and was music critic for a time before he became managing editor of the *New York Music Trader* in 1920. He was editor of *Metropolitan* magazine in 1923, and from 1931 to 1942 edited *Liberty* when it was owned by Macfadden. He became a senior editor of *Reader's Digest* in 1944.

Fulton Oursler, Jr. (1932– ) joined *Reader's Digest* in 1956, and from 1968 to 1970 was the magazine's book editor. He became a senior staff editor in 1970, assistant managing editor in 1973, and managing editor in 1974. In 1984 he was the executive editor. He has written one book, *Behold This Dreamer.*

**PACE, Eric Dwight** (1936– )
After a short time, 1957–58, on the *San Angelo Standard Times* and *Evening Standard* Eric Pace became a staffer with *Life* magazine in New York in 1959. Later he worked in Bonn and Paris for *Life*, before switching to *Time* in 1963. He served in Hong Kong from 1963 to 1965.

Since 1965, Pace has been with the *New York Times*, first in New York and then in Saigon, Cairo, Paris, Beirut, and Teheran before returning to the home office in 1977.

Pace has won the George Polk Memorial Award and the New York City Newspaper Guild Page One Award, both in 1968. He has written three novels: *Saberlegs*; *Any War Will Do*; and *Nightingale*; and has contributed to many major magazines.

He served in the Army in 1957.

**PACKARD, Vance Oakley** (1914– )
Better known for his books than for his magazine career, Vance Packard began as a reporter on his campus newspaper at Pennsylvania State University in 1936. He became a *Boston Record* columnist and, from 1938 to 1942, was with the Associated Press Feature Service.

Packard turned to magazines to better prepare himself for writing books. He was with the *American* from 1942 to 1956, and briefly with *Collier's*. He also lectured at Columbia University and New York University.

Among Packard's better-known books are *The Hidden Persuaders*; *The Status Seekers*; *The Waste Makers*; *Pyramid Climbers*; *The Naked Society*; *The Sexual Wilderness*; *A Nation of Strangers*; and *The People Shapers*.

**PACKER, Fred L.** (1886–1956)
Fred Packer worked for some 20 years with the *New York Daily Mirror*, where he obtained the job as a protégé of Arthur Brisbane, Hearst's right-hand aide for many years.

Packer started on the *Los Angeles Examiner* in 1906 and switched to the *San Francisco Call-Post* from 1907 to 1918. After studying at the Chicago Art Institute, Packer joined the *New York Journal* and *American* in 1932 and the next year moved to the *Daily Mirror*.

Between 1918 and 1931 he was a commercial artist in New York, with a number of clients among the industrial leaders. He won a Pulitzer Prize for his cartoons in the *Daily Mirror* in 1952. Packer was cited by the Treasury Department and the War Production Board for his contributions to World War II. He won the Page One Award three times from the New York Newspaper Guild. He also won a Freedoms Foundation Award and a citation from the American Cancer Society. His cartoons have been placed in the Library of Congress.

**PADDLEFORD, Clementine** (1900– )
"The best known food editor in the U.S." was the title *Time* magazine applied to Clementine Paddleford in the early Fifties, a title earned through her work on magazines and newspapers.

Paddleford, in 1922, sold some articles to the *New York Sun*, and the next year wrote advertising copy for Montgomery Ward and Co. In 1924, she wrote for *Farm and Fireside* before turning to free lancing for several years.

Paddleford joined the *New York Herald Tribune* in 1936 as the food markets editor; and joined *This Week* Sunday newspaper magazine in 1940. Between 1941 and 1953, she also wrote a column for *Gourmet* magazine. Among her awards were two from the New York Newspaper Women's Club. She wrote *A Flower for My Mother* and *How America Eats.*

**PAIK, Kwanik Kenneth** (1940– )

Ken Paik has been associated with photography since his youth in Korea. After his journalism training at the University of Missouri, he joined the *Coffeyville Journal* (Kansas) in 1968. He moved to the *Kansas City Kansan* the next year and shortly after that to the *Kansas City Star*, where he remained until 1978.

In Kansas City, Paik became the photo editor before he went south to *Jacksonville Journal* and *Florida Times-Union* as director of news illustration. In Florida, Paik was an adjunct professor at the University of North Florida and a visiting professor at the Universities of South Carolina and Florida.

In 1983, Paik became the director of photography for the *Baltimore Sun* (Maryland). He serves as a judge for several national photography contests. He has been recognized with the Overseas Press Club Humanity Award, and in 1975, he was named the best photographer reporting from abroad.

He served in the Korean Marine Corps.

**PALEY, William S.** (1901– )

William S. Paley, long called "Mr. CBS," was president of this broadcasting network from 1928 to 1946 and chairman until his recent retirement.

Paley had had no previous journalistic experience when, at the age of 27, he bought the Independent Broadcasting radio chain and renamed it the Columbia Broadcasting System. Earlier he had taken over his father's Congress Cigar Co. in Philadelphia. When he noticed an increase in sales following radio advertising, he became impressed by the potential of this young medium.

When he stepped down as chairman at the age of 81, Paley promised he would "stay close to CBS." He added that "the only institution I wanted to guard against was the government." The corporation's annual revenues exceed $4 billion as a communications conglomerate.

Fred Friendly, former CBS News president, once said, " I think broadcast news was invented at CBS." "Paley ranks with the immortals in electronic communications," noted *Advertising Age* in 1983. He was a "boss who usually supported his reporters . . . over the years the Paley network has won the most prime time battles." He "stole" many stars from the other networks. Paley considered Edward R. Murrow the "most outstanding man" he had ever known.

*Esquire*'s list of "50 Who Made the Difference" noted Paley's career in 1983, citing his major shows and the personalities he brought to the nation, including "I Love Lucy," the "Ed Sullivan Show," "Playhouse 90," "M*A*S*H," Walter Cronkite, "Beverly Hillbillies," and "60 Minutes." *Esquire* writer David McClintick called Paley a "restless, energetic man, easily bored" and noted that "as long as Bill Paley has breath in his body, he will *be* CBS."

Paley, who has been involved in many civic activities, established the Paley Foundation. In addition to recognition from France and Italy, Paley won the George Foster Peabody Award in 1958 and 1961, along with other citations from professional and civic organizations.

**PANITT, Merrill** (1917– )

From the founding of *TV Guide*, in 1953, by Walter H. Annenberg, the president of Triangle, Merrill Panitt has been a guiding force in its operation. In 1956 he was the editor and in 1973 the editorial director of Triangle Magazines, which also publishes *Seventeen*.

Panitt dropped out of the Missouri School of Journalism in the Thirties to work for the United Press in nearby Jefferson City. After several years in a public relations capacity with the Missouri Public Expenditure Survey, he joined the Army. He later completed his requirements for the journalism degree.

In 1946, Panitt worked for Triangle's *Philadelphia Inquirer* as a writer and television columnist.

David M. Rubin wrote in *More* magazine in 1976 that "while Annenberg gets most of the money, his top lieutenant, Merrill Panitt, deserves most of the credit for making *TV Guide* a success." He credited Panitt with having "successfully piloted a mass magazine through a period when all mass magazines were supposed to be dying"; *TV Guide* now leads the weeklies with a circulation of nearly 18 million.

Panitt has co-authored a book, *Soldiers' Album*, and has written for national magazines. From time to time, his comments appear in *TV Guide*. In 1982, for example, Panitt warned the networks of the expansion of cable facilities. He said that "besides protecting their flanks by investing in cable, they should be trying to find ways to make broadcast television more competitive with cable." In recent years, *TV Guide* has been more critical of networks and has expanded its coverage of cable listings and added an "Insider" section about "What's Happening, Who's Hot in Television Today." This latter appears to be in competition with *People* magazine.

The Freedoms Foundation awarded Panitt its George Washington Honor Medal and the University of Southern California and the Women's National Press Club have given him awards for journalism.

**PARKER, Brant Julian** (1920– )

"The Wizard of Id" has been a nationally syndicated comic strip since 1964, when Brant Parker created it. In 1975, he created "Crock."

Like so many other artists, Parker worked for the Walt Disney Productions in 1945–47 before turning to his own comic strips, and for a decade (1954–64) he was the advertising art director for the IBM Corporation in Washington.

Parker won the National Cartoonist Society's best humor strip award in 1971 and 1977. He has won other awards and has published 13 books based on the "Wizard of Id" material.

He served in the Navy during World War II.

**PARKER, Daniel** (1893–1967)
Daniel Parker spent a lifetime writing about sports after his start as a reporter, 1912–13, on the *Waterbury Republican* (Connecticut) and the *Waterbury American*, as sportswriter for 11 years.

Parker joined the *New York Daily Mirror* in 1924 as a sportswriter, and two years later he became its sports editor and columnist.

Among Parker's many awards was the Headliner for sportswriting in 1949; the Page One Award from the New York Newspaper Guild in 1951, 1956, and 1961; the George Polk Memorial Award in 1954; and the Sportscasters and Sportswriters Award in 1960.

One of his major civic involvements was the presidency of the Damon Runyon Memorial Fund for Cancer, a national project created by Walter Winchell.

**PARKER, Dorothy** (1893–1967)
Although Dorothy Parker is better known for her public comments about issues of the times and for her articles in *The New Yorker*, she earlier worked for magazines.

From 1916 to 1917, Parker worked for *Vogue*; from 1917 to 1920, she was with *Vanity Fair*. She wrote many books, with several based on her poems. These include *Enough Rope; Sunset Gun; Laments for the Living; Death and Taxes; After Such Pleasures; Collected Poems—Not So Deep as a Well;* and *Here Lies*. She co-authored two plays, *Close Harmony* and *Ladies of the Corridor*.

**PARKINSON, Roger Palm** (1941– )
Roger Parkinson has been an executive with magazines and newspapers since he first worked with *Newsweek* between 1969 and 1975, where he began as an executive trainee and rose to become executive vice-president and director of special projects.

Parkinson was with the *Washington Post* from 1975 to 1980 as assistant to the general manager and, later, as assistant to the president and vice-president for administration. From 1980 to 1982, he was president and publisher of the *Buffalo Courier-Express* (New York) before he was selected by Cowles Media Company to be president and publisher of the Minneapolis Star and Tribune Co.

While in Washington Parkinson was also director of Graphic Communications Computer Associates from 1975 to 1980.

He served in the Army, 1966–69.

**PARKS, Gordon** (1912– )
For more than 20 years, photographs by Gordon Parks appeared in *Life* magazine. Parks' career started with a camera he bought for $12.50 in a pawnshop. He was soon photographing attractive Negro women and placing their pictures in Black newspapers.

From 1944 to 1948, Parks was on a documentary-making team with Standard Oil Co. in New Jersey; from 1948 to 1972, he was with *Life*.

Parks held many jobs during his youth. He was with the Civilian Conservation Corps and worked as a railroad porter; while working as a bar car waiter, he found a magazine that featured photographs by the Farm Security Administration staffers during the Depression years. Later he worked for this agency. Meanwhile, he learned to take pictures that revealed poverty in Chicago in a mood similar to the FSA pictures.

By 1954, Parks was a consultant for Hollywood productions, and during the Sixties he made documentaries on Black ghetto life for National Educational Television. He produced "The Weapons of Gordon Parks" on CBS Network and gained fame with "The Learning Tree." He also worked for the Office of War Information in the Forties.

He was an editorial director for *Essence* magazine, 1970–73.

In addition to the Rosenwald Fellowship in 1941, Parks has been honored by Syracuse University, the National Council of Christians and Jews, the Philadelphia Museum of Art, Ohio University, the University of Miami, and other groups. For lifetime achievement in photography, he was given the Photographic Administrators, Inc., Award in 1983.

Park's books, several of which are autobiographical, include *The Learning Tree; A Choice of Weapons; A Poet and His Camera; Whispers of Intimate Things; Born Black; In Love; Moments without Proper Names; Flavio; To Smile in Autumn*; and *Shannon*.

**PATTERSON, Alicia** (1906–1963)
The great-granddaughter of Joseph Medill, who made the *Chicago Tribune* into one of the nation's great newspapers, Alice Patterson became the founder, editor, and publisher of the Long Island tabloid *Newsday*.

Patterson was surrounded by newspaper leaders throughout her life. She was the daughter of Joseph Medill Patterson, who established the *New York Daily News* in 1919, after some years in association with his partner, Colonel Robert R. McCormick, on the *Tribune*.

Alicia Patterson began her training as a cub reporter on the *Daily News* in 1927. She later joined *Liberty* magazine, then owned by the *Tribune* firm. She wrote a number of magazine stories, many about her own experiences.

Patterson longed to publish her own newspaper, although her father had warned her about starting a tabloid. "Country folks are too accustomed to standard-sized newspapers," he said, a rather unusual statement from the nation's leading tabloid publisher. Following her marriage to Harry F. Guggenheim, they acquired the *Nassau County Journal* and renamed it *Newsday*. The first issue appeared September 9, 1940.

*Newsday* won a Pulitzer Prize in 1954 for its meritorious public service in handling local issues. In 1952, and 1955, the daily was judged the nation's best-looking tabloid. In subsequent years, it has continued to be recognized both locally and nationally.

**PATTERSON, Donald H.** (1916– )
In 1978, when Donald Patterson became the president of the Baltimore Sun newspapers he said, "The main emphasis has always been on trying to produce the best news coverage possible."

Patterson joined the *Sun*'s publishing firm, A. S. Abell Co., in 1946. He was a vice-president by 1964 and publisher by 1977.

He has been involved with local projects, serving on the board of Junior Achievement projects, the United Way, and the National Alliance of Business in Baltimore. He served with the Navy in World War II.

**PATTERSON, Eugene C.** (1923– )
As the chief operating officer of the *St. Petersburg Times* (Florida), Eugene C. Patterson once said, "Newspapers get C minus for innovation. The enemy is us. We spooked ourselves into thinking some unlikely electronic information system is threatening us, when we ought to be concentrating on doing our print jobs better."

Patterson worked as a reporter on the *Temple Daily Telegram* (Texas) and *Macon Telegraph* (Georgia), 1947–48, before he joined the United Press. He worked in South Carolina and New York and London between 1948 and 1956 for the wire service, before he became the executive editor of the *Atlanta Journal* and *Constitution* (Georgia).

Before joining the *St. Petersburg Times*, Patterson was the managing editor of the *Washington Post* from 1968 to 1971, and a professor of political science at Duke University.

Since joining the *Times*, Patterson has also been editor and president of the *Congressional Quarterly*, which the firm publishes in Washington.

Patterson was vice-president of the U.S. Civil Rights Commission in the mid-Sixties and has been a member of the Pulitzer Prize Board since 1973. He was president of the American Society of Newspaper Editors, 1977–78 and has been involved with other professional groups. He said in 1983 that "the new ideas for the future must come right out of the hats of the editors and publishers of the country. We're the ones who have to get demanding and start leaning toward innovation."

**PATTERSON, Graham C.** (1881–1969)
Graham Patterson worked in advertising following his graduation from Cornell, and then worked for a Chicago electrical firm before becoming a representative for magazines.

Patterson was publisher and president of the *Christian Herald* from 1918 to 1935, when he moved to Philadelphia as chairman of the board of *Farm Journal*, where he remained until 1966.

Patterson was also associated with *Pathfinder-Town Journal* in Washington, as publisher, until 1969.

A director of Freedoms Foundation, Patterson was, one time, president of the Rural Research Institute.

**PATTERSON, Joseph Medill** (1879–1946)
The founder of the *New York Daily News* in 1919 began his newspaper career on the *Chicago Tribune*, a newspaper made famous by his grandfather, Joseph Medill.

With another Medill grandson, Robert R. McCormick, Patterson was with the *Tribune* first in 1901. From 1914 to 1925 he was the co-editor and co-publisher of the newspaper. However, after establishing the successful New York tabloid, Patterson devoted his interest to that publication.

Before moving to New York, Patterson served in the Illinois House of Representatives in 1903–1905; then he became the Chicago commissioner of public works. In 1900, and in 1914–1915 he was a war correspondent in China, Germany, Belgium and France.

While he and McCormick were serving in World War I in France they mapped plans for the new tabloid, influenced by the success of such newspapers in England. After a few difficult months, *The News* turned the corner and eventually became the No. 1 circulation leader in America. It was popular with subway readers and with persons who preferred more pictures.

Early in his life Patterson developed socialistic leanings, reflected in two books, *A Little Brother of the Rich* and *Rebellion.* He also wrote *Dope and By-Products* and co-authored *The Fourth Estate.*

**PAULEY, Jane** (1950– )
Jane Pauley has appeared on the NBC "Today Show" since 1976. Before that, she was a reporter on Indianapolis station WISH-TV and later held several positions with WMAQ-TV in Chicago.

Following her graduation from Indiana University, Pauley helped with the presidential campaign of John V. Lindsay and later with the Indiana Democratic Central Committee. When she joined WMAQ-TV, she became the first female co-anchor in Chicago. She subsequently replaced Barbara Walters, who had moved to ABC News, at NBC.

Pauley's first "Today Show" included an interview with Walter F. Mondale, which she conducted with co-host Tom Brokaw. For some time she has been compared to Barbara Walters.

Pauley has continued to improve her interviewing techniques, although in a taping with Margaret Trudeau, she so angered the then-estranged wife of the Canadian Prime Minister that she walked off the set. In addition to "Today," Pauley has worked on NBC "News Update" and, on the weekend edition of NBC "Nightly News."

She received the Torch of Truth Award from the Indianapolis Advertising Club and the Headliner Award from the Austin, Texas Club; DePauw University has given her an honorary degree.

She is married to cartoonist Garry Trudeau of "Doonesbury" fame.

**PAYNE, Kenneth** (1890–1962)
Kenneth Payne was associated with two historically great periodicals, *The North American Review* and *Reader's Digest*. He began his writing career as a staff writer and, later, as a foreign correspondent for the Newspaper Enterprise Association, from 1913 to 1918. During the next two years, he

was associated with *People's Home Journal*, and this association was followed by brief tours with *Popular Science Monthly, McClure's*, and again, the *People's Home Journal.*

Payne was editorial director for the *North American Review* from 1928 to 1930, when he became the managing editor of *Reader's Digest.* In 1940, he became executive editor, a post he held until 1961. He was senior editor his last year, and also served as a consultant.

He was honored by the University of Wisconsin for service to journalism.

**PEALE, Norman Vincent** (1898– )

Known best for his ministry, for which he won many awards, citations, and honorary degrees, Norman Vincent Peale deserves a place in the journalistic world for his creation, with his wife, of *Guideposts*, in 1945.

With well over 3 million subscribers, *Guideposts* has been one of the most successful publications, with its slogan, "A practical guide to successful living."

Recalling the magazine's early days, Peale wrote in *Guideposts*' 35th anniversary edition of how he raised $1,200 from many friends, including Frank Gannett, J. Howard Pew, and Branch Rickey. The publication began over a grocery store in Pawling, New York. The first contributor was Eddie Rickenbacker, who wrote "I Believe in Prayer." It wasn't too easy during the early years, and once the printer was owed $30,000. Lowell Thomas told about *Guideposts*' plight in a radio broadcast and soon such problems were overcome.

Peale wrote that "magazines are a lot like people. A few difficulties or hardships are good for them, make them self-reliant and tough. We always believed the country needed and wanted the kind of material we were offering in *Guideposts*." *Guideposts*' popularity attests to Peale's ability to judge his audience.

Peale has written many books, with the *Power of Positive Thinking* voicing his basic philosophy, along with *Stay Alive All Your Life* and *Amazing Results of Positive Thinking.*

**PEARSON, Drew** (1897–1969)

Drew Pearson and Robert S. Allen were co-writers of a syndicated newspaper column, "The Washington Merry-Go-Round," in the early Thirties.

Prior to his entry into newspaper work, Pearson was director of the American Friends Service Committee, serving in Serbia, Montenegro, and Albania in the post-World War I years. He continued to work with this organization throughout his life. Pearson lectured on the Chautauqua circuit and had visited many countries, when he began to report such events as the Washington Arms Conference for a newspaper syndicate.

He wrote reports on the Geneva Naval Conference for the Consolidated Press. This press service was founded by David Lawrence, who also had owned the *United States Daily* when Pearson worked there from 1926 to 1933. Pearson also worked on the *Baltimore Sun* (Maryland) during many of these years. He continued to report on conferences, covering the creation of the United Nations in 1945, the Paris Peace Conference in 1946, and many others.

Pearson wrote his column from 1931 until his death in 1969. In later years, he was assisted by Jack Anderson, who took over the column in 1969.

Pearson had served in World War I, and in the post-World War II era, he gained nationwide fame through the organization of a Friendship Train to send supplies to Europe.

He was honored by Sigma Delta Chi in 1942 as the best of the Washington journalists, and by France and Italy, as well. He was the founder of the Intercollegiate Newspaper Association and one of his last talks was before such a group meeting in Missouri.

In addition to the two books he co-authored, *Washington Merry-Go-Round* and *Case against Congress*, Pearson wrote *More Washington Merry-Go-Round; The American Diplomatic Game; The Nine Old Men; USA—2nd Class Power?; Will Khrushchev Bury Us?*; and *The Senator*. He also wrote many magazine articles.

**PEGLER, Westbrook** (1894–1969)

For many years, Westbrook Pegler was widely read in the nation's newspapers, where his column was syndicated from 1944 to 1962. But as Edwin and Michael Emery wrote in *The Press and America*, "unhappily his work degenerated into monotonous and vicious attacks on three small groups—labor unions, New Dealers, and members of the FDR family—and Pegler switched from Scripps-Howard to Hearst sponsorship in the mid-1940s, becoming known as 'the stuck whistle of journalism.'"

Pegler won a Pulitzer Prize in 1941 for his crusading work. He had started writing about sports and eventually went to Europe during World War I for the United Press. He was in the Navy the last year of this conflict. From 1925 to 1933, he was the eastern sports editor for the *Chicago Tribune*. He then worked for several Chicago and New York newspapers before starting his column.

In addition to the Pulitzer Prize, Pegler was cited twice by the Headliner Club, and by the American Legion and the Nassau County Bar Association. He wrote *Tain't Right; Dissenting Opinions of Mister Westbrook Pegler*; and *George Spelvin, American*.

**PENN, Stanley** (1928– )

Stanley Penn joined the *Wall Street Journal* in 1952 and became an investigative reporter in the New York Bureau in 1957. He has continued with the *Journal*.

In 1967, Penn and a colleague, Monroe W. Karmin, shared a Pulitzer Prize for national affairs reporting on "the connection between American crime and gambling in the Bahamas." The team provided details in their dealings with owners of the gambling casinos.

**PERLMAN, David** (1918– )

For most of his career, David Perlman has been associated with the *San Francisco Chronicle*, where he was a reporter from 1940 to 1941. He returned in 1952 and became the science editor, a position Perlman held until he became city editor in 1977 and associate editor in 1979.

Perlman first worked on the *Bismarck Capital* (North Dakota) in 1940. He later worked on the *New York Herald Tribune* in Paris and in New York before joining the *New York Post.* He also covered Europe for two years for *Collier's.*

Perlman's interest in science has brought him many awards: The Atomic Industrial Forum Award in 1975; the Westinghouse Science Writing Award in 1976; and the Ralph Coates Roe Medal from ASME in 1978. He was president of both the Council for Advancement of Science Writing and the National Association of Science Writers.

*Newsweek* quoted Perlman as saying, "Television has stimulated the public's interest in science. People get their first exposure there. Those who want to know more turn to newspapers, then magazines." Perlman has contributed to major magazines, professional periodicals, and encyclopedias.

**PETACQUE, Art** (1924– )

A career, beginning in 1942, with the *Chicago Sun* and, later, the *Sun-Times* has resulted in many awards for Art Petacque, an investigative reporter and columnist.

Petacque won the Pulitzer Prize for general reporting in 1974 and has won seven Page One awards from the Chicago Newspaper Guild. He spent many years hunting for the killer of Senator Charles Percy's daughter and helped solve the murder. The Associated Press gave him six awards for investigative reporting. Among other honors are the State of Israel Prime Minister's Medal in 1976 and awards from several other Chicago organizations.

James H. Dygert, in *The Investigative Journalist*, notes that Petacque "exposed police shakedown, a Ku Klux Klan cell in the police department, fraudulent pyramid sales of 'distributorship' by a California cosmetics firm called Holiday Magic, and a stock swindle by President Nixon's 1968 campaign manager in Illinois, William H. Rentschler, who was subsequently convicted of fraud."

**PETERS, Charles Given Jr.** (1926– )

Before becoming editor of the *Washington Monthly* magazine in 1968, Charles Peters worked for a Charleston, West Virginia law firm between 1957 and 1962. For the next six years, he was with the Peace Corps, and from 1944 to 1946 he served in the Army.

Peters has also been involved in politics. He served in the West Virginia state legislature and assisted in the John F. Kennedy presidential campaign in that state in 1960. Twenty years later, he was named the "West Virginian of the Year." In 1978, he received an award from Columbia University.

Peters wrote *How Washington Really Works* and *The Culture of Bureaucracy.* He co-authored *Blowing the Whistle—Dissent in the Public Interest* and *The System.*

**PETERS, Michael Bartley** (1943- )
A nationally syndicated editorial cartoonist, Michael Peters' work originates at the *Dayton Daily News*, where he joined the staff in 1969. Peters was a cartoonist with the *Chicago Daily News* prior to that time.

Sigma Delta Chi recognized his work with an award in 1975.

He has written *The Nixon Chronicles* and *Clones You Idiot, I Said Clones.* Since 1975 he has been a lecturer at the Dayton Living Arts Center.

In 1984 he began a comic, "Mother Goose & Grimm."

The 1981 Pulitzer Prize winner also won a Reuben Award for editorial cartooning in 1984.

**PETERSEN, Robert** (1926- )
Robert E. Petersen owns the publishing company and a production group of the Petersen operations. Among the magazines the firm publishes are *Hot Rod*; *Motor Trend*; *Car Craft*; *Photography*; *Motorcyclist*; *Skin Diver*; *Teen*; *Hunting*; *Guns and Ammunition*; *Pacific Skipper*; *Sea*; *Rudder*; *Lakeland Boating*; *4 Wheel*; and *Off Road.* As the firm notes, each magazine is aimed at a "homogenous automotive audience of its own."

The Petersen operations, reported by *Quill* magazine to be worth between $100 and 200 million, also produce television series; commercial, trade, and automobile shows; and other programs.

Petersen has been active in California civic affairs, especially the Boys Club and the Los Angeles Library.

**PETRANEK, Stephen Lynn** (1944- )
Stephen Petranck, who has won several awards and promotions on newspapers, started work on the *Rochester Democrat and Chronicle* (New York) in 1972 as a financial writer and assistant Sunday editor.

Petranek was managing editor and, later editor, of the *Upstate* magazine from 1974 to 1977 and worked a year as editor of the *Tropic* magazine for the *Miami Herald.* He joined the *Washington Post* in 1978 as deputy editor, and became acting editor in 1981.

The University of Missouri, his alma mater, gave him a business journalism award in 1973. For his financial writing, he won the John Hancock Award in 1972 and the Frank Tripp Newswriting Award in 1973.

**PETTIT, Tom** (1953- )
After a brief tour with television stations as a reporter in Ames and Cedar Rapids, Iowa, and Minneapolis, Minnesota, Tom Pettit joined the NBC Network in 1959, working for the network on the West Coast between 1962 and 1975; he moved to Washington in 1975.

He won the Peabody Award in 1970 and Emmy awards for his reporting in 1969, 1970, and 1974. In addition, Pettit won the du Pont Columbia University Award in 1970 and 1975; the Robert F. Kennedy Journalism Award in 1970 and 1976; and a medical journalism award from the American Medical Association in 1971.

**PHILLIPS, Kevin** (1940– )
Since 1970, Kevin Phillips has written a syndicated newspaper column, and starting in 1971, he has been editor and publisher of the *American Political Report*.

Prior to his writing career, Phillips was an attorney and, from 1969–1970, a special assistant attorney general in Washington. He assisted the Nixon for President Committee in 1968. He was also an administrative assistant to Congressman Paul Fine in the Sixties.

Phillips has written three books: *The Emerging Republican Majority*; *Electoral Reform and Voter Participation*; and *Mediacracy*. He served on the *TV Guide* News Watch in 1974.

**PHILLIPS, Warren H.** (1926– )
Warren Phillips joined the *Wall Street Journal* in 1947 as a copyreader. In 1972, he became president of Dow Jones & Co., Inc., the *Journal* publisher. Between those dates, Phillips was the *Journal*'s correspondent in Germany in 1949 and chief of the London Bureau in 1950.

Phillips returned to New York in 1951, became news editor in 1953, managing editor in 1957, and executive editor in 1965. Since 1975, he has been the chief operating officer, and since 1978, chairman of the board.

During his Army service he was a copyreader on the *Stars & Stripes* European edition.

The Institute of Human Relations of the American Jewish Committee honored Phillips as "a man of vision whose fierce integrity inspires us all" in 1982. He is a member of the Pulitzer Prize Board and, in 1958, was one of the 10 Outstanding Young Men named by the U.S. Junior Chamber of Commerce. He co-authored a book, *China: Behind the Mask*.

In discussing the rise of *USA Today*, Phillips wrote in 1983 that "perhaps all of us in newspaper work ought to take some degree of comfort, even pride, in the fact that new newspapers can be started, that new kinds of newspapers can evolve, and that [the] American public still seems more receptive to use of the printed word on good old newsprint."

**PIEL, Gerald** (1916– )
Gerald Piel has long been associated with *Scientific American*, this nation's oldest science publication (established 1845). Piel started at *Life* Magazine as an office boy, becoming *Life*'s science editor in 1938. Six years later, he was an assistant to the president of Henry J. Kaiser Co. Piel acquired his knowledge of science through an extensive reading program of books and magazines. From this, Piel said, he learned there was no general publication for the lay person with an interest in science. Piel also said his work for the Kaiser firm "was a year and a half postgraduate course in business."

With this experience on *Life* and with Kaiser, Piel and two associates, Dennis Flanagan and Donald H. Miller, Jr., raised $450,000, and in 1948, acquired *Scientific American*. Eventually they turned the magazine around, pushing its American and foreign editions past the 1 million circulation mark.

Piel early had censorship problems with the federal government. The Atomic Energy Commission made him destroy copies and printing plates of an article in 1950. He told a House subcommittee in Washington in 1956 that it was a fallacy to suppress results of scientific research. The enemy "will ultimately discover these things on their own."

Piel has received nearly 20 honorary degrees; and he won the George Polk Award in 1961; the Kalinga Prize in 1962; and the Bradford Washburn Award in 1966. He was named Publisher of the Year by the Magazine Publishers Association in 1980. The University of Missouri awarded him its Journalism Medal in 1981.

Piel has written *Science in the Cause of Man* and *The Acceleration of History*.

**PIERCE, Frederick S.** (1934?– )

In 1983, Frederick S. Pierce became the third person to be president and chief operating officer of the American Broadcasting Co. He had joined the network in 1956 as supervisor of audience measure for television, and by 1961, he was director of research. He then became involved in sales development; by 1968 he was vice-president for planning. Continuing to acquire new duties and titles, he became president of ABC's television unit in 1974.

According to the *Kansas City Star* television-radio critic, Gerald B. Jordan, "Pierce is a pragmatic manager, schooled by ABC chairman Leonard Goldenson and vice-president Elton Rule." Pierce told a Kansas City audience in 1983 that "technology has done more than just change the rules of the game. It has changed the players and the stakes as well."

Pierce served with the Army Combat Engineers in the Korean War.

**PIERPOINT, Robert** (1925– )

Robert Pierpoint has reported the end of the Korean War on two occasions. His first report, in 1953, was for the CBS Radio from Panmunjon. And when CBS broadcast the final episode of M*A*S*H in 1983, Pierpoint recreated his report, this time for an estimated audience of 125 million.

In 1948, Pierpoint was a reporter with the Swedish Broadcasting Corp. and, in 1949, a CBS stringer. From 1951 to 1954, he covered the Korean conflict for CBS News. He remained in Tokyo until he came to Washington in 1957 as White House correspondent, and was president of the White House Correspondents Association. Since 1980, he has been the network's diplomatic correspondent.

Pierpoint's work earned him the Drew Pearson Foundation Award in 1973 for his investigative reporting. He has also won two Emmy awards and an award from the Overseas Press Club for radio interpretation of foreign affairs.

He served in the Navy during World War II.

**PINCUS, Walter Haskell** (1923– )

Walter Pincus has worked for newspapers, a magazine, and two networks and has been a consultant for several Senate Foreign Relations Committees.

Starting his journalism career as a special writer for the *Washington Star* in 1963, Pincus became an editor and reporter on the *Post* in 1966. After two years with the Senate committee, Pincus became the associate editor of the *New Republic* in 1972. He was executive editor from 1974 to 1975.

Pincus returned to Washington in 1975 as a special writer for the *Post*. In 1971, he was a consultant for NBC News, but moved to CBS News in a similar capacity in 1979.

His awards include the Page One in 1960; the George Orwell in 1977; and the George Polk in 1978.

He served in the Army from 1955 to 1957.

**PLIMPTON, George Ames** (1927– )
George Plimpton is well known for his books and his accounts of sporting events. In the early Fifties, he was editor-in-chief of the *Paris Review* and, from 1959 to 1961, an associate editor for *Horizon*. Since 1972, he has been an associate editor with *Harper's*; and since 1968, a contributing editor to *Sports Illustrated*. He has been a trustee for station WNET since 1973 and has been associated with several book firms.

Plimpton's books include *Rabbit's Umbrella*; *Out of My League*; *Paper Lion*; *The Bogey Man*; *Mad Ducks and Bears*; *One for the Record*; *Shadow-Box*; *One More July*; *American Journey*; *The Times of Robert Kennedy*; *Pierre's Book*; *The Fancy* and *Fireworks*. He was co-author of *Sports!*

**PODHORETZ, Norman** (1930– )
As a literary critic and editor, Norman Podhoretz has been associated with *Commentary*, a Jewish monthly journal of opinion, since 1956, becoming its editor in 1960.

Many of Podhoretz' early activities have been recalled in a collection of his essays in *Doings and Undoings: The Fifties and after in American Writing*. In 1966, he produced his "confessional autobiography," titled *Making It*. A decade later *Breaking Ranks* and *Present Danger* appeared. Podhoretz also edited *The Commentary Reader: Two Decades of Articles and Stories*.

In *Making It*, Podhoretz wrote: "What I wanted was to see my name in print, to be praised, and above all to attract attention."

Before joining *Commentary* he wrote book reviews for the publication. After Army service, he joined the magazine on a full-time basis and helped redesign it and bring back much of its earlier prestige.

Podhoretz was a Fulbright Fellow from 1950 to 1951.

**POE, Clarence** (1881–1964)
Clarence Poe joined the staff of the *Progressive Farmer* before the turn of the century. He was its editor in 1899 and in 1903, at the age of 22, became its owner. He remained president of the publication until 1953.

For his work in publicizing agricultural developments in the South Poe was honored by many state and national associations.

He wrote several books, among them the *Life of Charles B. Aycock*; *True War Tales From the South*; and *My First 80 Years*.

**POGREBIN, Letty Cottin** (1939- )
Letty Pogrebin has worked for Bernard Geis Associates, for book publishers in New York, and wrote a column for the *Ladies' Home Journal* before she joined *Ms.* magazine.

On the *Ladies' Home Journal*, Pogrebin wrote "The Working Woman"; she has been editor of *Ms.* since 1971. Her books are related to her magazine work: *How To Make It in a Man's World* and *Getting Yours: How to Make the System Work for the Working Woman.*

Pogrebin has lectured widely on women's issues and related topics. She was one of the founders of the National Women's Political Caucus and has been active in NOW, the ACLU, and other groups.

**POINSETT, Alexander C.** (1926- )
Alexander Poinsett has been associated with the Johnson Publishing Co. in Chicago since 1954, starting as associate editor of *Jet* magazine. In 1961, he became associate editor of *Ebony*, another Johnson publication.

By 1967, he had acquired his present position as senior staff editor for *Ebony*. He has received a J. C. Penney–University of Missouri Journalism Award for magazine writing, as well as other awards.

Poinsett has written *Common Folk in an Uncommon Cause* and *Black Power: Gary Style*. He has also contributed to *Ebony Pictorial History*; *The Ebony Success Library*; and *Black Americans and the Political System.*

He served in the Navy from 1944 to 1949.

**POLITZ, Alfred** (1908–1982)
"Research is useless unless it is creative. Creative research is the formulation of the hypothesis—the guess, the hunch—that you start with." That was Alfred Politz's philosophy that moved him to the head of his own firm by 1943.

Politz arrived in America from Berlin in 1937. According to his obituary in *Editor & Publisher*, Politz spoke out against (1) researchers who presented their findings in terms too complicated for advertisers to understand; (2) researchers who did not draw accurate forecasts from their results; and (3) copywriters who wrote ads to please advertisers instead of consumers.

Just before starting his own firm in 1943, Politz was fired by Compton Advertising. Later, his magazine research became acceptable to publishers. When he was 75, Politz obtained a license to fly hot air balloons.

**POLK, James Ray** (1937- )
A leader in the Investigative Reporters and Editors, Inc. group, James Polk served as president from 1978 to 1980. He began as a reporter for the Associated Press in Indianapolis in 1962 and later worked for the wire service in Milwaukee, Madison, and Washington. From 1971 to 1975 he worked for the *Washington Star*; since 1975, he has been with NBC News in Washington.

When Polk joined NBC News, he found it necessary to compress his stories. He told James Dygert, writing in *The Investigative Journalist*, that "investigative reporters are opportunists who will pick their topics according to what will attract attention. But there aren't many stories of Watergate dimensions around."

Polk was described in a 1983 *TV Guide* article by Mark Ribowsky as a "old blood-and-guts, old-fashioned, a slug-it-out guy." He noted that Polk was able to take some "dull ledger sheet or budget" and was able to "cut right through the crap."

He won the 1974 Pulitzer Prize for national reporting on illegal contributions to the Nixon 1972 re-election campaign and gifts to senators. His other awards include the Raymond Clapper Memorial and the Sigma Delta Chi awards.

**POPE, Generoso Paul, Jr.** (1927– )

More Americans buy the weekly *National Enquirer* than any other newspaper. Started in 1926 by the Hearst organization, this periodical was acquired by Generoso Paul Pope, Jr. in 1952. Since that time, he changed the weekly completely, shifting its emphasis and moving its operations from New York to Florida.

Before taking over the *Enquirer*, Pope was associated with his father's business in New York, and from 1947 to 1951, he edited *El Progresso Italo-Americano*. He has served on a number of commissions established by New York mayors and he continues to work with hospitals, children's groups, and other organizations, as well as directing the Generoso Pope, Jr. Foundation.

Pope's basic philosophy with the *National Enquirer* is to "give the people what they want to read. The *Enquirer* doesn't try to make news." He was one of the early publishers to realize the potential of supermarkets as outlets for newspapers. In spite of criticism of its policies, the weekly has raised millions of dollars for families and individuals in dire need and has prompted the mailing of thousands of cards to the ill, especially children with terminal illnesses. As one writer noted, the *Enquirer* has "been laughed at; ridiculed; sued and berated," yet its circulation stays near the 6 million figure.

Its top-selling issue was the one following the death of Elvis Presley. Someone, as yet unidentified, obtained a picture of the superstar in his coffin. This appeared on the front page and 99.4 percent of the press run was sold, nearly 7 million copies. The only copies not sold were those destroyed by persons grabbing them from dealers and at newsstands.

The *National Enquirer* began without ads and only in recent years have these messages occupied much space. The magazine has printed stories on the Kennedys, movie stars, and others. Usually criticized by the parties involved, the publication frequently is proved correct later, such as stories the breakup of Elizabeth Taylor's seventh marriage. The weekly said the marriage was "crumbling," but in a statement by her husband, Senator John Warner, it was denied. Later, of course, the couple divorced. The same series of events occurred in the Johnny Carson case.

An in-depth study of the *National Enquirer* in 1978 by the *Washington Post* noted that "Pope inspires an invigorating mixture of admiration and terror among his subordinates," who are among the highest paid journalists in the nation. Pope calls his weekly a newspaper; however, the California courts handling the Carol Burnett case termed *National Enquirer* a magazine, based on its contents. The entire operation was subjected to a Mike Wallace probe in a CBS "60 Minutes" report.

**POPE, John Edwin III** (1928- )
One of the nation's better-known sportswriters, James Pope, Jr. has been a sports editor with the *Miami Herald* (Florida) since 1967.

Beginning as sports editor of the *Athens Banner-Herald* (Georgia) in 1944, Pope, four years later, joined the United Press International as Southern sports editor, operating out of Atlanta. From 1954 to 1956, he was executive sports editor for the *Atlanta Journal*; in 1956, he started his assignment with the *Miami Herald.*

Pope has won awards for his newspaper work and his books. He won the Top Sports Column Award from the National Headliner Club in 1962 and 1979. He also has won several awards from the Thoroughbred Racing Association, including the Bill Corum Memorial recognition. He is also a member of the International Churchmen's Sports Hall of Fame.

Pope has written *Football's Greatest Coaches*; *Baseball's Great Managers*; *Encyclopedia of American Greyhound Racing*; and *Ted Williams: The Golden Year.* He co-authored *On the Line.*

**PORTER, Sylvia** (1913- )
Between 1935 and 1977, Sylvia Porter used the *New York Post* as her base newspaper; since 1978 she has been with the *Daily News.* She is internationally known for her syndicated column, published in nearly 500 newspapers, for her many magazine articles, and for her books on financial topics.

In 1976, she was named Woman of the Decade by the *Ladies' Home Journal*, and she was listed among the nation's top 25 influential women by the *World Almanac* from 1977 to 1981. She is listed in the *Woman's Almanac* among the media leaders. An article there notes that "until 1942 she wrote under the by-line 'S. F. Foster,' and most readers assumed she was a man." She turned down President Lyndon Johnson's request that she head the Export-Import Bank in 1965. Having sought, unsuccessfully, to be the first woman financial writer hired by the Associated Press, she worked for an investment counselor and wrote a column about the bond market before she joined the *Post.*

Porter has won the Headliner Club medal for financial and business reporting, as well as the William Allen White and Bob Considine awards. One writer summed her success in these words: She can make information understandable to the layman.

Among her books are *How to Make Money in Government Bonds*; *If War Comes to the American Home*; *How to Get More for Your Money*; her annual *Sylvia Porter's Income Tax Guide*; *Sylvia Porter's Money Book—How to Earn It, Spend It, Save It, Invest It, Borrow It, and Use It to Better Your Life*; and *Sylvia Porter's New Money Book for the 80s.* She has co-authored, with Jacob Lasser, *How to Live within Your Income*; *Managing Your Money*; and *Money and You.*

**POWERS, Ronald Dean** (1941– )
After a six-year reporting tour with the *St. Louis Post-Dispatch*, Ron Powers joined the *Chicago Sun-Times* in 1969 as a reporter. The next year, he became the newspaper's television critic. During his seven years as a critic, Powers was widely recognized for his comments, winning the Pulitzer Prize for criticism in 1973.

Powers has written *The Newscasters* and *Face Value*. He appears on television as a critic and writes magazine articles.

**POYNTER, Nelson** (1903–1978)
The *St. Petersburg Times* (Florida), one of the most respected newspapers in America, has been in the Poynter family since 1912.

Nelson Poynter began as a reporter in Washington in 1923 on the Scripps-Howard newspapers, and later was news editor of the *Japan Times* in Tokyo. He also worked on the *Washington Daily News* and Ohio Scripps-Howard before joining the *St. Petersburg Times* (Florida) in 1938. During his last ten years, he was also chairman of the board of the Times Publishing Co.

Poynter also owned the *Congressional Quarterly* publication and *Editorial Research Reports* in Washington, contributing to both. Ernest Hynds notes Poynter's "standard of ownership," in which he refused to create a newspaper group or to sell his newspaper to such an operation. He preferred home ownership. The Times Publishing Co. was willed to Modern Media Institute, an educational project established in 1975.

**PRATTIS, Percival Leroy** (1895–1980)
A pioneer editor of Black-oriented newspapers, Percival Prattis spent much of his career as editor of the *Pittsburgh Courier* (Pennsylvania). Prattis began as editor of the *Michigan State News* in 1919 and, in 1921, was city editor of the *Chicago Defender*.

From 1923 to 1935, Prattis was news editor of the Associated Negro Press before he spent a year with the *Amsterdam News*. He was city editor of the *Pittsburgh Courier* in 1936 and became editor in 1956. He stepped down in 1962.

Prattis is remembered as the first Black to gain admission to the Congressional Periodical Press Galleries in 1947. He served on several White House Conferences and was given the outstanding alumnus award by Hampton Institute. In addition to his column in the *Courier*, Prattis covered many national and international events. His one book was *Employment Opportunities Unlimited*. He was a collaborator on *Perspectives of the Black Press* with Henry La Brie III.

**PULITZER Family**
The descendants of Joseph Pulitzer (1847–1911) are now associated with the *St. Louis Post-Dispatch* (Missouri) and the *Arizona Daily Star*, as well as radio and television stations. *Quill* magazine estimated the family's wealth at $300 to 600 million in late 1982.

Joseph Pulitzer II (1885–1955) was sent by his father to St. Louis to learn the business in 1907. His father wrote the *Post-Dispatch* editorial page editor, George S. Johns, "This is my son, Joseph. Will you try to knock some newspaper sense into his head?" Johns succeeded. Although his brothers failed to keep the *New York World* in the family, Joseph kept the Pulitzer name alive in Missouri.

Joseph Pulitzer II served in the Navy in World War I, and in World War II, wrote articles for the *Post-Dispatch*. The newspaper won its first Pulitzer Prize, established by the senior Pulitzer through funds granted to Columbia University, in 1936 for an exposure of vote registration fraud in St. Louis. Many other awards followed, based on investigative reporting of frauds and corruption. Several individuals have won the Pulitzer while with the *Post-Dispatch*. Pulitzer supported Thomas Dewey for President in 1948, but only one of his editorial writers agreed with him, an indication of the freedom granted the staffers.

Joseph Pulitzer III (1913– ) worked briefly in 1935 as a *San Francisco News* reporter before joining the *Post-Dispatch*. Since his father's death in 1955, he has been the editor and publisher. He served in the Navy in World War II.

Michael Edgar Pulitzer (1930– ) trained as a lawyer and after work with some legal firms, he became a reporter in 1956 on the *Louisville Courier-Journal* (Kentucky). Four years later, he was with the *Post-Dispatch* and eventually became associate editor, his present position.

The University of Missouri awarded its Journalism Medal to the *Post-Dispatch* in 1932 and 1975. In 1942, the medal was awarded to Joseph Pulitzer II.

**PULLIAM Family**

Eugene C. Pulliam (1889–1975) began his career on the *Kansas City Star* in 1910 and two years later was with the *Atchison Champion* (Kansas). By 1915, he had reached Indiana, where he remained the rest of his life. He first worked with the *Franklin Star*, later the *Muncie Star and Press* and the *Indianapolis Star and News*. He eventually acquired the *Arizona Republic* and the *Phoenix Gazette*.

Pulliam won the John Peter Zenger Award in 1966 and the William Allen White Award in 1971. The Arizona Press Club gave him its Distinguished Service Award in 1973. He served with a number of civic and professional groups and received a dozen honorary degrees.

Eugene Smith Pulliam (1914– ), his son, worked with the United Press in several cities and with radio station WIRE in Indianapolis, before becoming city editor of the *Star* and, later, managing editor of the *News*. Today he serves as publisher of the two newspapers.

He was in the Navy during World War II. He, too, has been active in professional groups and once served as president of the ANPA Foundation and director of the American Press Institute.

Nina Mason Pulliam (1906– ), the widow of Eugene C. Pulliam, has been president of the Phoenix Newspapers, Inc. and publisher of the Phoenix newspapers since 1975. She lives in Phoenix. She has been active with civic groups and, in 1954, was given the Theta Sigma Phi National Headliner Award. She wrote a book, *I Traveled a Lonely Land*.

*Quill* magazine, in 1982, estimated the family wealth at between $200 and 300 million.

**PUSEY, Merlo John** (1902– )
Once described as a "splendid workhorse," Merlo John Pusey spent nearly four decades with the *Washington Post*, after working briefly for the *Washington Daily News* in 1928. Before that, he had held a variety of jobs in the West and, in 1922, worked with the *Salt Lake City Deseret News*.

On the *Post* Pusey wrote many of the newspaper's "court packing" editorials during the Franklin D. Roosevelt campaign to "pack the court." Pusey, a "classic conservative Republican," wrote a "Wartime Washington" column during World War II to explain the issues of the day.

Pusey won a Mott-Kappa Tau Alpha Book Award for his biography, *Eugene Meyer of the Post*. He also wrote *The Supreme Court Crisis*; *Big Government*; *Can We Control It?*; and *Charles Evans Hughes*.

**PYLE, Ernest Taylor** (1900–1945)
Ernie Pyle wrote many interesting columns before World War II, yet he gained lasting fame for his accounts of the infantrymen in this conflict. As Irving Dilliard wrote in the *Dictionary of American Biography*, "Pyle's informal, chatty columns were popular with newspaper readers, many of whom were beginning to make automobile tours." Dilliard was referring to Pyle's accounts of his travels across America by car, an innovation in the Thirties.

Pyle worked briefly for the *La Porte Herald Argus* (Indiana) in 1923 before making his initial contact with the Scripps-Howard organization through a job on the copydesk of the *Washington Daily News*. By 1926, he was with the *New York Evening World*, and the next year returned to the Washington newspaper. He was managing editor of the *Daily News* in 1932.

By 1935, Pyle's column was syndicated. It related his features about America and all he came in contact with on his tours. By 1940, he was in Europe, going through the North Africa campaigns and other World War II battles. He learned to love the infantryman, who he felt was being overshadowed by the glamor of the Air Force pilots. When he reported the death of an infantry captain, the story was so moving that the tabloid *Daily News* set it in large type and used the entire front page to give it top play. This may have been the only time a newspaper devoted such space to a columnist with a single story.

Pyle wrote several books, including *Ernie Pyle in England*; *Here Is Your War*; *Brave Men*; *Last Chapter*; and *Home Country*. A motion picture, "The Story of G. I. Joe," was based on his career.

Among his posthumous awards was the Medal of Merit, given jointly by the War, Navy, and State departments. Pyle was buried in the National Memorial Cemetery of the Pacific in the Punchbowl Crater near Honolulu. In 1984 the Fort Jackson (Columbia, South Carolina) Media Center was named in his honor.

On his death, President Truman said: "The nation is quickly saddened again by the death of Ernie Pyle. No man in this war has so well told the story of the American fighting man as American fighting men wanted it told. He deserves the gratitude of all his countrymen." Pyle was killed by a Japanese sniper on Ie Shima during the Okinawa campaign.

**QUIGG, Horace Dasher** (1911– )
While a journalism student at the University of Missouri, Horace Quigg worked on the nearby *Boonville Daily News* and *Cooper County Record* where he covered his first murder trial in 1930. In 1936, he joined the United Press. He spent the rest of his journalistic life with this wire agency.

While with the UP, later the UPI, Quigg worked in New York City, in the Pacific during World War II, and with Byrd's South Polar Expedition from 1946 to 1947. He later covered the Korean War and, since 1967, has been the service's senior editor in New York City.

Quigg co-authored *Four Days* and *Gemini-America's Historic Walk in Space.* In 1983, he received the Journalism Medal from his alma mater, the University of Missouri, for a "lifetime of an aggressive reporter and sensitive writer, covering world headline stories" such as the trial of Alger Hiss, Frank Costello, Dr. Samuel Sheppard, Jack Ruby, John Mitchell, Jean Harris, and Claus von Bulow.

**QUINN, Jane Bryant** (1939– )
Jane Quinn is known to newspaper and magazine readers and to television viewers for her informative comments on today's financial world. She began her work as an associate editor with *Insiders Newslettter* in 1962 and was its co-editor by 1966.

Quinn worked briefly as a senior editor for Cowles Book Co., and in 1969 became editor-in-chief of the *Business Week Letter.* Since 1974, she has been with the Washington Post Writers Group, which syndicates her financial column to 125 newspapers. In addition, she has been a contributing editor to *Woman's Day* since 1974 and to *Newsweek* since 1978; she has also been with CBS TV News since 1980. She wrote *Everybody's Money Book* in 1978, and updated it two years later.

Quinn told Fred Barnes in a *Washington Journalism Review* interview that "economics reporting requires so much specialized knowledge. I have a frightful lack of understanding of political reporting because I don't do it."

**QUINN, John C.** (1925– )
Starting as a copyboy on the *Providence Journal-Bulletin* in 1943, John C. Quinn advanced to his current position as executive vice-president and chief news executive of the Gannett Co., Inc. While on the *Journal-Bulletin*, Quinn became the day managing editor, having spent more than 23 years in Providence.

Quinn joined Gannett in 1966 as director of news for the *Rochester Democrat and Chronicle* and the *Times-Union* (New York). Later he became executive editor.

Quinn, who was president of the Associated Press Managing Editors from 1972 to 1973, has served as a Pulitzer Prize juror. He is a director of the International Press Institute and vice-chairman of the New York Fair Trial Free Press Conference. He has been named to the Rhode Island Hall of Fame.

He told *Editor & Publisher* in 1983 that "we have been hearing about the lurking threats all around us—television, cable, specialized magazines and everything else. But we may not have realized that the information explosion, by increasing the national appetite for news, has only confirmed our leadership in those areas where we perform best."

**QUINN, Sally** (1941– )
Sally Quinn's career has been associated mostly with the *Washington Post*, with a brief tour on CBS "Morning News," 1973–74, as co-anchor. But as Chalmers Roberts reports in his history of the *Post*, Quinn's work on the network "was a mismatch and Quinn returned to the *Post* to become the star of Style [section] writing about everyone from a rapist to Rosalynn and Jimmy Carter."

When Quinn recalled her first job with the *Post* at the age of 30, she said, "As an Army brat, I had spent my life going to official functions, abroad and in Washington. I was already cynical." She told interviewer June Bingham in 1983 that "everyone is using everyone; the politician uses the journalist to get publicity; the journalist uses the politicians to make news."

She wrote *We're Going to Make You a Star.*

**RAGAN, Samuel Talmadge** (1915– )
Born in North Carolina, Samuel Ragan has spent his life with publications in that state. After working briefly in Texas, in 1948 he had a column, "Southern Accent," in the *Raleigh News and Observer*, which he continued until 1969. He was also executive editor for the newspaper for a time.

In 1969, Ragan became editor and publisher of the *Southern Pines Pilot*, where he remains today. Ragan is past president of the Associated Press Managing Editors and the North Carolina News Council.

He published *The Tree in the Far Pasture*, a collection of his poems, and in 1963 he received the North Carolina Tercentenary Poetry Award. He has been honored by the DAR and other groups. He has also directed a Writer's Workshop since 1963 and has been associated with several colleges and art groups. He is a past president of the North Carolina Literary and Historical Association.

Other books include *To the Water's Edge*; *The Democratic Party: Its Aims and Purposes*; *The New Day*; and *Free Press and Fair Trial*; he co-authored *Back to Beginnings.*

**RASKIN, Abraham Henry** (1911– )
While working on a graduate degree at City College of the City University of New York, Abraham Raskin became the *New York Times* college correspondent.

Later, Raskin joined the *Times* full-time and soon became a top reporter. As *Current Biography* noted, "A feisty, hard-digging journalist in the Ben Hecht tradition, he was invariably at the center of the action in an era noted for its stormy labor relations."

During World War II, he served in the Army in the labor branch of the industrial services division, and in 1946, he returned to the *Times* as national labor correspondent. Many of his articles attracted national recognition, such as a series on Blacks in the North, and the chronically unemployed. Raskin's probing into labor activities often placed him in conflict with such men as Jimmy Hoffa.

Raskin became a member of the *Times* editorial board in 1961. He was an assistant editor of the editorial page in 1964, and since 1978, he has been associate director of the National News Council.

When the *Times* was involved in a 114-day printers' strike in 1963, Raskin wrote a 15,000 word article about the event. For this project he received a George Polk Memorial Award, a Page One Award from the New York Newspaper Guild, a Silurian Society Award, and a Heywood Broun Memorial Award.

Raskin wrote articles, including profiles of labor leaders, for several national periodicals. He was co-author of *David Dubinsky: A Life with Labor.*

Since his retirement in 1976, he has been an adjunct professor at Columbia University's Graduate School of Business.

**RASPBERRY, William James** (1935- )

When William Raspberry began his newspaper career in 1956, he worked as a reporter-editor on the *Indianapolis Recorder* (Indiana) until 1960. In 1962, following two years of Army service, Raspberry joined the *Washington Post.*

In 1974, *Time* magazine called Raspberry "the most respected Black voice on any white U.S. Newspaper." As Chalmers Roberts reported, Raspberry "got his start when [Al] Friendly and [Ben] Gilbert took him on as a teletype operator in 1962. Soon he was writing local civil rights stories and he was one of several to alternate in writing an area Potomac Watch column beginning early in 1965." He has continued with this column and has written articles for many magazines.

From 1971 to 1973, he lectured on journalism at Howard University, and he also has been a commentator on WTTG and a panelist on WRC-TV programs.

**RATHER, Dan** (1931- )

Born in Texas, Dan Rather early in his journalistic career taught at his alma mater, Sam Houston State College, worked for the United Press International and the *Houston Chronicle*, and in the mid-Fifties, joined CBS radio affiliate KTRH in Houston.

Rather's excellent on-the-scene coverage of Hurricane Carla, which hit Texas in 1961, brought him to the attention of CBS executives. Soon he was the network's Southwestern Bureau chief in Dallas. He was in that city when President John F. Kennedy was assassinated. Rather became the CBS White House correspondent and was then shifted to the London Bureau; he later covered the Vietnam War. By 1966, he was back in his

White House role. He also became co-anchorman on the CBS "60 Minutes" program.

Rather made news himself when he was selected to replace Walter Cronkite on the CBS-TV Evening News, for a salary in the millions. After two years on the job, "Rather is doing pretty damn well," wrote David Shaw in *TV Guide* in 1983. "In fact, I think the CBS Evening News is better under Rather than under Cronkite." Shaw considers Rather as genuinely kind, nice, and polite and, at times, he "even tries too hard to be kind on the air."

Gary Deeb, a TV columnist, also commented on Rather's second year, writing, "Rather is absolutely unbeatable in the audience ratings . . . is an extremely relaxed anchorman . . . very influential in the creation of that newscast each night."

Rather also had become known earlier to millions of television viewers for his "supercilious" exchange of questions and answers with President Richard Nixon in news conferences. He showed his investigative talents, covering the Watergate episode.

Rather won the Emmy award five times, along with the University of Southern California Distinguished Achievement for Broadcasting. In 1983, he won the Bob Considine Award from St. Bonaventure University, an award Walter Cronkite won earlier.

Rather is co-author of *The Palace Guard* and *The Camera Never Blinks*.

**REASONER, Harry** (1923- )

Harry Reasoner, known to millions of television viewers of the CBS "60 Minutes" show, began his career on the now-defunct *Minneapolis Times* (Minnesota). After World War II Army service, Reasoner returned to Minneapolis in 1946.

That same year Reasoner wrote his only novel, *Tell Me about Women*. He spent two years in public relations before joining CBS radio affiliate WCCO in Minneapolis. He also worked for the United States Information Agency in Manila for three years.

After more experience on Minneapolis station KEYD-TV, Reasoner joined CBS-TV in New York and quickly won praise as a newscaster and commentator. But controversy developed later when the ABC Network, where Reasoner worked from 1970 to 1978, paired him with Barbara Walters on the evening news program.

Although Barbara Matusow noted in *The Evening Stars* that Reasoner was "the kind of newscaster the average viewer could imagine chatting with at a bar," she thought he was to blame for the failure of the Reasoner–Walters team. Al Westin relates the incident of a viewer who berated Reasoner for much of what he had said on the air. Reasoner wrote her a letter: "Dear Madam. Why do you watch? Sincerely yours."

Reasoner received the University of Missouri Journalism Medal in 1970 and has won a Peabody award and several Emmys.

**REED, Rex** (1938- )

Rex Reed worked on the campus newspaper and literary magazine while a student at Louisiana State University. In 1960, he tried to get a job on the

*New York Times* as a copyboy, but was turned down. He then free lanced for five years and one of his interviews, with Buster Keaton, was bought by the *Times* for $125.

Reed eventually became a film critic for *Cosmopolitan*, *Status*, *Women's Wear Daily*, *Holiday*, and other periodicals. He had a weekly column for years in the *New York Daily News*, which has been syndicated since 1971. He once took a role in the film "Myra Breckenridge" and later called the picture one of the 10 worst films of 1970. He also appeared in "Superman."

Reed has written *Do You Sleep in the Nude?*; *Conversations in the Raw*; *Big Screen, Little Screen*; *People Are Crazy Here*; *Valentines and Vitriol*; and *Travolta to Keaton.*

**REEDY, George Edward** (1917– )
George Reedy worked as a reporter on the *Philadelphia Inquirer* (Pennsylvania) and for the United Press International before and after World War II; he was in the Air Force during the war. He was President Lyndon Johnson's press secretary in the mid-Sixties.

After Johnson retired, Reedy became president of Struthers Research and Development Corp. in Washington from 1966 to 1968. He later was a consultant and a lecturer before becoming dean and later professor of the Marquette University College of Journalism. At one time, he wrote a syndicated series of newspaper articles.

Reedy's books include *Who Will Do Our Fighting for Us?*; *The Twilight of the Presidency*; and *The Presidency in Flux.*

**REID Family**
In this century, Helen Rogers Reid, Whitelaw Reid, and Ogden Reid were involved in the operation of the *New York Herald Tribune.* This publication dated back to James Gordon Bennett, who founded the *Herald* in 1835, and to Horace Greeley, who founded the *Tribune* in 1841. The Reids merged the newspapers in 1924.

The first Whitelaw Reid (1837–1912) had established himself as a top Civil War reporter in Cincinnati before joining Greeley's *Tribune.* He gained control of the daily in 1873. His son, Ogden, and Helen Rogers Reid, bought the *Herald* in 1924 and merged the two.

When Ogden Mills Reid (1882–1947) died, Helen Rogers Reid (1882– ) became president of the newspaper. She had been active in women suffrage movement. Following college, she became the social secretary to Mrs. Whitelaw Reid and, in 1911, married Ogden Mills Reid.

During World War I, she sold ads for the *Tribune* and soon became the ad director. In 1922, she was vice-president and, in 1947, president. She has been awarded 10 honorary degrees and a gold medal in 1946 for service to New York City.

Ogden joined the *Tribune* in 1908 and held many positions preparing him for the presidency in 1912 and the editorship in 1913. He was responsible for bringing many famous writers to the newspapers, including Walter Lippmann, Joseph Alsop, and Alva Johnston. The newspaper won eight Pulitzer Prizes under his leadership.

Whitelaw Reid (1913-     ), the son of Ogden and Helen Reid, joined the newspaper in 1938 and became a foreign correspondent before service in the Navy during World War II. By 1947, he was editor of the newspaper. During his preparatory years, Reid studied at Yale as well as taking special training at the Mergenthaler Linotype Co. and what is known today as the Rochester Institute of Technology.

Ogden Rogers Reid (1925-     ) was a part-time *Herald Tribune* photographer by 1940. He was a paratrooper in World War II. In 1950, he became a reporter and columnist and, in 1953, was president of the newspaper's operations in Paris, where he helped revamp the publication. Ogden said in 1955 that "a free press will remain free only so long as its practitioners are free from fear, from yielding to pressure groups, from cowardice—free, at all times, to print whatever is believed to be right for our people and our country."

The Reids sold the *Herald Tribune* in 1958 to John Hay Whitney. It eventually was merged with other New York newspapers and then disappeared from the scene.

**RENNER, Thomas C.** (1928-     )

After service in the Air Force from 1948 to 1953, Tom Renner joined *Newsday* as a reporter. Eventually he established himself as one of the nation's leading investigative newsmen.

Renner has spent much of his time probing the activities of the Mafia in America. According to some accounts, he was the first full-time organized crime investigative reporter–specialist in the nation. Renner's stories have identified U.S. corporations doing business in supermarkets controlled by organized crime. His probes also have revealed Mafia infiltration within the Postal Service and Mafia control of credit card rackets. On *Newsday*, Renner worked with Robert Greene, and they were both involved with the Don Bolles–*Arizona Republic* investigation.

Renner has co-authored three books: *My Life in the Mafia*; *Vincent Teresa's Mafia*, and *Wall Street Swindler*. He is president of the Investigative Reporters and Editors group, and was a Nieman Fellow, 1982–83.

In assuming the IRE presidency in 1983, Renner said, "Too often we mistrust the intentions of our press, and we become paranoid about the intentions of those we report on. We become wrapped up in a quest for the Holy Grail of Journalism—the Pulitzers, Peabody, Emmy and other awards, and we forget what we are really here to do—report and inform and write, and have some fun doing it." He complained of television's portrayal of journalists as ruthless, reckless, and thoughtless and mindless animals.

**RENSE, Paige** (1934?-     )

Few women have achieved the position in the magazine world now occupied by Paige Rense. In 1983 she was editor of *Architectural Digest*, *Bon Appetit*, and *GEO*.

Rense's picture appeared in an advertisement for Rolex watches, and the copy noted that *Architectural Digest* won the National Magazine Award for visual excellence. "She added warmth and style to the recipes in *Bon Appetit* and made it the best-selling epicurean publication in the country."

Rense says, "I have only one rule for good editing: I put myself in the reader's place." Her magazines have a high audience appeal. *GEO*, a heavy financial loser in recent years, provided her greatest challenge. However, *GEO* went out of existence in 1985.

She joined *Architectural Digest* in 1970 as associate editor, and soon became editor. Joanna Powell interviewed her for an article in the *Washington Journalism Review* in mid-1983 and told how "*Architectural Digest* became the first magazine to lend its readers the vicarious thrills of visiting the houses of stars like Ted Kennedy, Liza Minnelli and Barbra Streisand." In 1975, the Knapp concern, which owns *Architectural Digest*, acquired *Bon Appetit*. Added in 1981 was *GEO*. Cleon "Bud" Knapp said Rense "became a great editor by her ability to bring a whole variety of elements together that created this package." Powell reports her style as "caring," "accessible," and "direct but not imperious."

**RESTON, James Barrett** (1909– )

Two great names in journalism were honored at the University of Notre Dame in 1983 when *New York Times* columnist James Reston gave the first Red Smith Lecture in Journalism. Smith, who died in 1982, had been a Pulitzer Prize winning sports columnist for the *Times* for years.

Reston, recipient of nearly 20 honorary degrees, was editor of the General Motors' Delco division house organ after he graduated from high school. His work at the University of Illinois completed, he became a sportswriter on the *Springfield Daily News* (Ohio). A year later he was with the Ohio State University public relations staff and the Cincinnati Reds baseball team. For three years, 1934–37, Reston worked for the Associated Press in New York and London, where the *New York Times* hired him in 1939. *Times*' publisher Arthur Hays Sulzberger brought Reston back to New York and shortly after that he was in Washington, where he has remained.

Reston has scored many exclusives in Washington. He once told *Newsweek* that "I think I know where the brains are in this town. I pick 'em. When I pick enough of them, I can write an analytical piece about whatever the problem is." He became chief of the Washington Bureau in 1941; associate editor in 1964; executive editor in 1968; vice-president in 1969; and columnist in 1974. Since 1968, he and his wife have operated the *Vineyard Gazette*.

"Scotty" Reston believes in freedom for the reporter. He remains an influential leader in the press. In 1971, before Nixon made his trip, Reston visited the People's Republic of China. Ben Bagdikian calls Reston "essentially a presenter of established policy" and J. Anthony Lukas called him a "journalistic statesman." Tom Wicker, who replaced him as chief of the *Times*' Washington Bureau, called him the "greatest reporter of our time." Lukas feels Reston trusted sources too much, noting "since Reston is a sentimental, romantic, pious man, perhaps it is not surprising that he should regard the System, as he grew up with it, with something approaching reverence."

Reston won the Pulitzer Prize for national reporting in 1945 and again in 1957. He has also won the George Polk, John Peter Zenger, Horatio Alger, and Lovejoy awards. The University of Missouri awarded him its Journalism Medal in 1961.

He has written *The Artillery of the Press: Its Influence on American Foreign Policy*; and *Sketches in the Sand.*

**REYNOLDS, Donald W.** (1906– )

As the sole owner of Donrey Media, Donald W. Reynolds operates a low-profile group, valued at $100 to 200 million by *Quill* in 1982. His group includes more than 45 daily newspapers, mostly in small communities; radio and television stations; and billboard and cable operations.

Reynolds worked on the *Kansas City Journal Post* after graduation from the University of Missouri in 1927. He was later with the *Indianapolis Times* and the *Austin American-Statesman* and was involved in the buying and selling of newspapers in Texas, Alabama, Massachusetts, and New Jersey early in his life.

Reynolds began his group with the purchase of the *Okmulgee Times* (Oklahoma) and the *Fort Smith Southwest American and Times Record* (Arkansas) in 1940. He was listed among the "media barons" by the *Atlantic* monthly as he expanded his operations across the nation. Many of his newspapers are in Oklahoma, where as a teenager he sold the *Oklahoma News* on street corners.

Reynolds once said that "I have been fortunate in that I early selected a plan for my life and doubly fortunate in having been relatively successful in following that plan."

During World War II, he worked with *Yank* magazine in Australia and London, winning the Legion of Merit, the Bronze Star, the Purple Heart, and five combat stars. In 1978, he was named the Nevada Broadcaster of the Year; in 1981 he was awarded the University of Missouri Journalism Medal. Donrey headquarters are in Fort Smith, with its western offices in Las Vegas, where Donrey operates the *Review Journal* and radio and television stations and supervises outdoor advertising.

The University of Nevada-Reno School of Journalism has been named in his honor.

Reynolds wrote a booklet, *From Rhinos to Prime Ministers*, relating his world-wide tours, his interviews with famous personalities, and other events in his career.

**REYNOLDS, Frank** (1923–1983)

"A Rock of Integrity" was *Newsweek*'s tribute to Frank Reynolds, who died in 1983 after 36 years in the broadcasting business. "An old-fashioned newsman in the flashiest medium, Reynolds had high stature within the press corps," *Newsweek* added.

Reynolds was with the Hammond, Indiana station WJOB from 1947 to 1950 before going to Chicago, where he worked for WBKB-TV and WBBM-CBS until 1963, when he joined ABC there. Two years later he was in Washington, and from 1978 until his death, he was the chief anchorman for ABC's "World News Tonight."

Al Westin wrote that "what made ABC's coverage [of a threatened coal miners' strike in West Virginia in 1978–79] was Reynolds' role as the on-the-scene anchor. Viewers saw him standing in the coal fields with pickets all around." Westin later noted that "Reynolds makes no excuses for his emotionalism [shown in his coverage of the attempted assassination of President Ronald Reagan]. He believes he was reacting as any human being might when confronted by a deluge of conflicting information pouring in from every direction." Reynolds replied that "if people are going to attack me for being human, then let them go ahead and do it. I don't give a damn."

Reynolds won a Peabody Award in 1969. He was proud of his son, Dean Reynolds, who followed in his father's footsteps and, in 1983, was the White House reporter for Cable News Network.

**REYNOLDS, Quentin** (1902–1965)
Quentin Reynolds began as a sportswriter, but established his lasting fame as a war correspondent and a writer of books. Early in his career, Reynolds was writing sports stories for the *New York World*, and later, the *World Telegram*.

By 1932, Reynolds had joined the International News Service, and the next year he was in Berlin. For a time, 1933–45, he also wrote for *Collier's* magazine and contributed articles to other magazines. He also appeared on radio and television shows.

His career, however, has been preserved through his many books, including *The Wounded Don't Cry*; *London Diary*; *Convoy*; *Only Stars Are Neutral*; *Dress Rehearsal*; *The Curtain Rises*; *Officially Dead*; *70,000 to One*; *Leave it to the People: Courtroom*; *The Wright Brothers*; *Custer's Last Stand*; *I, Willie Sutton*; *The Battle of Britain*; *The Amazing Mr. Doolittle*; *The F.B.I. Story*; *The Life of St. Patrick*; *Headquarters*; *The Fiction Factory*; *They Fought for the Sky*; *Minister of Death*; *The Eichmann Story*; *Known But to God*; and *By Quentin Reynolds*.

**RHOADS, Geraldine Emeline** (1914– )
Geraldine Rhoads was named one of the Outstanding Women in Communications in 1982 for her work with *Woman's Day* magazine.

Following college, Rhoads worked two years at her alma mater, Bryn Mawr, in the publicity department. Her magazine career started in 1939, when she became the managing editor of *The Woman* in New York City. She later worked three years as editor of *Life Story*, and from 1945 to 1952, she was editor of *Today's Woman*.

Rhoads moved to *Today's Family* and later to *Reader's Digest* as associate editor, with two years as a lecturer at Columbia University between these professional assignments. She was a producer for NBC Network briefly, but returned to the magazine world as associate editor of *Ladies' Home Journal* in 1956. She moved to the managing editorship before working for *McCall's* as executive editor from 1963 to 1966.

Rhoads' present association with *Woman's Day* began in 1966. She advanced to vice-president in 1972, and since 1977, has been vice-president of CBS Consumer Publications, which owns the magazine.

She has won the YWCA and Elizabeth Cutter Morrow awards. She remains active in civic and professional associations and, in 1975, won the Matrix Award from the New York Women in Communications, Inc., chapter.

**RHODES, Kent** (1912– )

After 45 years of professional work in the magazine world, most of them with *Reader's Digest*, Kent Rhodes became president of the Magazine Publishers Association in 1979. The MPA was founded in 1919 and Rhodes was its sixth leader.

Rhodes joined Time Inc. in 1933 and worked on developmental plans for *Life*. In 1936, he was with *Fortune* as production manager; in 1944, he joined *Reader's Digest* in a similar capacity. By 1975, he was president of *Reader's Digest*, becoming chairman the next year.

As *Madison Avenue Magazine* noted in 1979, "Rhodes gained renown for his eclectic magazine expertise, ranging from setting up overseas editions to pioneering such developments as high-speed, four-color printing; square-backed binding; and computerized subscription lists."

While in college, he was editor and publisher of the *Dartmouth Pictorial*, a position held previously by Nelson Rockefeller.

In recent years he has been associated with youth groups, especially the Outward Bound project.

**RICHARDSON, Midge Turk** (1930– )

For her work as editor of *Seventeen* magazine, Midge Richardson was honored in 1982 as one of the Outstanding Women in Communications. She spent 18 years (1948–66) as a member of the Sisters of the Immaculate Heart of Mary, teaching in Catholic schools and once serving as principal. For another year (1966–67) she was assistant to the dean of the School of Arts at New York University.

Richardson's magazine career began in 1967 when she joined *Glamour* as college editor in New York City. In 1974, she became editor-in-chief of *Co-Ed* magazine and editorial director for *Forecast* and *Co-Ed*.

Richardson joined *Seventeen* as executive editor in 1975, and she has been editor since 1979. She has been a guest on many television talk shows and has written *The Buried Life* and *Gordon Parks, A Biography for Children*.

Active in civic affairs, she worked with the Girl Scouts, International House, the YWCA, and other New York groups.

**RIDDER Family**

Long associated with the Ridder newspaper family, Bernard J. Ridder, Sr. (1913–1982) worked on the family newspapers in St. Paul and Duluth, Minnesota, Aberdeen, South Dakota, and Grand Forks, North Dakota, as early as 1934.

For nine years (1946–55) Ridder was editor and publisher of the *New York Journal of Commerce.* The Ridder group acquired the *Pasadena Star-News* (California) in 1956 and he took over as its publisher. In 1975, he became chairman of the board of Ridder Publications, Inc. When the Ridder and Knight groups merged in 1975, he became a member of the board.

Herman H. Ridder (1908–1969), in 1937, was publisher of the *St. Paul Daily News*; from 1945 to 1969, he was publisher of the *St. Paul Dispatch* and *Pioneer Press* (Minnesota). Ridder's outside interest as a breeder and owner of champion race horses led him to become president of the California Thoroughbred Breeders Association.

He served in the Marine Corps.

Bernard Herman Ridder Jr. (1916– ) has been in St. Paul as president of Ridder Publications, Inc., since 1969, becoming chairman of the board of Knight-Ridder Newspapers in 1979. He began his career on the *Duluth News-Tribune* and *St. Paul Dispatch* and *Pioneer Press.* He served in the Navy in World War II and has been honored by the University of Minnesota.

Joseph Bernard Ridder (1920– ), a brother of Bernard, Jr., also worked on the St. Paul newspapers before going to San Jose where he became publisher of the *Mercury-News* in 1952 and president in 1977. He, too, served in the Navy in World War II, and today is involved in many civic projects in California.

Paul Anthony Ridder (1940– ) is the son of Bernard Ridder, Jr. In 1962, he was with the *Aberdeen American News* and then joined the *Pasadena Star News* in 1964. Since 1964, he has been with the *San Jose Mercury News.* He became its publisher in 1977 and president two years later. In 1970 he was named the San Jose Outstanding Young Man of the Year. He, too, is involved with many civic projects.

**RISSER, James Vaulx, Jr.** (1938– )

After early training and practice in the law, James Risser became a reporter on the *Des Moines Register and Tribune* (Iowa) in 1964. In 1969, he became the newspaper's Washington correspondent, and in 1976, its bureau chief. From 1973 through 1974, he was a professional journalism fellow at Stanford University.

Risser won the Pulitzer Prize in national reporting in 1976 and in 1979. He also won the Raymond Clapper Memorial Award in 1976 and 1978 and the Worth Bingham Foundation prize for investigative reporting in 1976. Earlier, he had also won the American Political Science Association award for public affairs reporting and the Thomas L. Stokes Award for environmental reporting. Risser and a colleague, George Anthan, investigated grain scandals and commodity market irregularities in trading and among grain inspectors. Many indictments resulted in subsequent changes in the law.

He is active in civic affairs.

**RIVERA, Geraldo** (1943- )
Geraldo Rivera, who trained for the law, is a practitioner of advocacy journalism, as reflected in many of his ABC "20/20" documentaries. From 1970 to 1975, Rivera was with WABC-TV Eye Witness News, one of the most popular local broadcasts in New York City. Later he worked with "Goodnight America" and "Good Morning America," and in 1978, became a correspondent for ABC News.

On "20/20," Al Westin notes that "Rivera, say many sources, will occasionally take a sentimental rather than well-informed route." Others say that Rivera tends to "fall in love with someone, which affects his objectivity. He sees himself as the little man's agent—but at times he stretches the truth for a point of view." His first book, an outgrowth of a television special about a school for the mentally retarded, was *Willowbrook: A Report on How It Is and Why It Doesn't Have to Be That Way.* Later he wrote *A Special Kind of Courage* about children who have overcome obstacles. He also has written two children's books: *Miguel Robles, So Far* and *Puerto Rico: Island of Contrasts.*

Rivera wrote in *TV Guide* in 1984 that "Whether or not we admit in public that we are crusading, many investigative journalists apparently want to be part of the process of positive social change. We want to make a difference."

Rivera has won the Alfred I. du Pont–Columbia University citation, two Kennedy Journalism awards, and seven Emmy awards. On three occasions, the New York State Associated Press has named him Broadcaster of the Year.

He spent two years in the Merchant Marine.

**ROBB, Inez** (1901–1979)
After completing her journalism training at the University of Missouri, Inez Robb joined the *Tulsa Daily World* in 1924. In 1927, Robb was with the Sunday edition of the *New York Daily News* and, in 1928, took over the society editor's position, writing under the name "Nancy Randolph." She continued this for a decade.

In 1938, Robb joined the International News Service and wrote the "Assignment America" column. She continued this until 1969, although she switched to Scripps-Howard and United Features Syndicate in 1953. She was one of the few women reporters in World War II.

Robb won the Holmes Award in 1948 and the New York Newspaper Women's Club citation for best column in 1957. Her alma mater, the University of Missouri, gave her its Journalism Medal in 1948. She wrote *Don't Just Stand There!* She covered the coronation of George VI, and the weddings of Edward VIII and Wallis Simpson and of Queen Elizabeth and Prince Philip.

**ROBERTS, Chalmers M.** (1910- )
Chalmers Roberts spent 23 years with the *Washington Post* and later wrote *The Washington Post: Its First 100 Years.* He joined the newspaper as a staff

writer in 1949, although from 1933 to 1934 he had been a cub reporter on the daily, his first exposure to journalism.

Roberts was with the Associated Press in Pittsburgh in 1934, the *Toledo News-Bee* (Ohio) in 1936, the *Tokyo Japan Times* in 1938, and the *Washington Daily News* in 1939. At the start of World War II, he was the Sunday editor of the *Washington Times-Herald* before he joined the Office of War Information for service in London and Washington. In the service he knew Philip Graham, of the *Post* family.

After a brief tour with *Life* magazine, Roberts was with the *Washington Star* two years before he started his long tenure with the *Post*. He held many positions with the *Post*, from reporter to columnist, and since his retirement in 1971, he has contributed to the editorial page.

In his *Post* history, Roberts concluded, "Today a *Post* editor, reporter, or editorial writer can move a President or the Congress, influence the courts, cleanse a regulatory agency, affect elections, protect the public interest in myriad ways."

Roberts has been recognized by the Washington Newspaper Guild and Sigma Delta Chi for his national reporting and has won the Raymond Clapper Memorial Award and the Edward Weintal prize for diplomatic reporting.

He has written four other books: *Washington Past and Present*; *Can We Meet the Russians Half Way?*; *The Nuclear Year: The Arms Race and Arms Control*; and *First Rough Draft: A Journalist's Journal of Our Times.*

**ROBERTS, Eugene L., Jr.** ( - )

Gene Roberts worked with the *New York Times* and the *Detroit Free Press* (Michigan) before he took over the leadership of the *Philadelphia Inquirer* (Pennsylvania) as executive editor in 1973.

"I've seen plenty of editors and reporters get whipped doing what they think the boss wants. If you just give a nudge here and a little coax there, you're going to get a whole lot more creativity than if you try to write it all out," he told Paul Taylor, who wrote a profile of Roberts for the *Washington Journalism Review*. Taylor calls it a "freewheeling, serendipitous, exasperating style of management communication."

Under Roberts' leadership, the *Inquirer* has won six Pulitzer Prizes, the staff has been expanded, and the coverage increased.

**ROBINSON, Maurice Richard** (1895–1982)

Few Americans have completed high school without coming in contact with *Scholastic* magazine or some of its many related periodicals.

Maurice Robinson got his idea for such a publication interviewing the Pittsburgh superintendent of schools in 1920. While working in public relations for the Chamber of Commerce, he noted a chart in the office predicting a huge increase in student enrollment. While with the Chamber of Commerce, he edited *Pittsburgh First*. He started this operation in 1920 under the title, *Western Pennsylvania Scholastic*, which later became *Scholastic*, and still later, *Senior Scholastic*. Other publications have been added, such as *Scholastic Coach*, *Scholastic Teacher*, *Junior Scholastic*, and *World Week*, more than 30 different titles in all. The interest in journalism began when he worked on the Dartmouth College newspaper.

In 1943, Robinson moved the firm to New York.

He wrote in 1950 that "Scholastic magazines are published to promote the education for enlightened citizenship of students in the schools of the United States." In 1979, Jack K. Lippert wrote a book, *Scholastic: A Publishing Adventure*, which highlights the growth of this unique operation.

As Robinson expanded his *Scholastic* magazines he added filmstrips, instructional films, and other teaching aids.

**ROBERTS, Roy C.** (1887–1967)

After four years with the *Lawrence World* (Kansas), 1905–09, Roy Roberts joined the nearby *Kansas City Star*, where he spent the rest of his journalism career, 56 years, before he stepped down in 1965 as the chairman of the board of the Star Company.

All his time was not spent in Kansas City, however. He covered the Missouri legislature in Jefferson City for many years, and from 1915 to 1928 he worked in the newspaper's Washington Bureau. He then returned to Kansas City as managing editor and, in 1947, became president and general manager.

In 1957, the University of Missouri awarded Roberts its Journalism Medal.

**ROBINSON, Max** (1939– )

Max Robinson became the first Black anchor for a television network on the ABC Evening News in 1978. He reported from Chicago, while Frank Reynolds was in Washington and Peter Jennings in London.

Robinson had been a correspondent and cameraman for station WTOP-TV in Washington in 1965. Four years later he was an anchorman. Before going to ABC in New York in 1978, he was with WRC-TV in Washington. He also lectured at the Federal City College there from 1968 to 1972 and was a journalist-in-residence at the College of William and Mary in 1981. His success in Washington prompted ABC to hire him.

Indianapolis, Houston, Cincinnati, Atlanta, Gary, Richmond, and Atlanta have all made him an honorary citizen. When he was in Washington and later Chicago, he received many awards. The Capital Press Club in 1967 named him Journalist of the Year, and in 1967 and 1981, he won Emmy awards and recognition from Ohio State University, the National Association of Black Journalists, and the National Association of Media Women. He has been named an Honorary Citizen by Indianapolis, Houston, Cincinnati, Atlanta, and Gary (Indiana).

**ROBINSON, Raymond K.** (1920– )

Editing magazines and writing books has kept Raymond Robinson busy since he was the managing editor of *Magazine Management* in 1950. In 1956, he was editor of *Real* magazine, and in 1957, managing editor of *Pageant*; in 1959, senior editor of *Coronet*.

Robinson moved to *Good Housekeeping* as managing editor in 1961 before he joined his current employer, *Seventeen*, where he was first managing editor in 1969 and then executive editor in 1979. He continues in this position.

Robinson's interest in sports is reflected in the books he has written, including the *Mario Lanza Story*; *Ted Williams*; *Stan Musial: Baseball's Durable Man*; *Speed Kings of the Basepaths*; *Great World Series Thrillers*; *Greatest Yankees of Them All*; and *Baseball's Most Colorful Managers*.

**RODALE, Jerome Irving** (1898–1971)
J.I. Rodale founded the Rodale firm, which today has several widely circulated magazines including *Prevention*, *Organic Farming*, and *New Shelter*.

Rodale was an accountant in New York and Washington between 1916 and 1923. He has written dozens of books, mostly about food, health, gardening, and similar topics. His first, which appeared in 1938, was *Strengthening Your Memory*. He has also written *Cross-Word Puzzle Word-Finder* and *The Phrase Finder*. He also compiled several encyclopedias, including *Common Diseases* and *Healthful Living*.

His son, Robert David Rodale (1930–    ) is now the chief operating officer for Rodale Press, Inc., and editor of *Organic Gardening and Farming* since 1954 and *Prevention* since 1964. He has written *Sane Living in a Mad World* and *The Best Health Ideas I Know*. He has also edited *The Challenge of Earthworm Research* and *The Basic Book of Organic Gardening*.

**RODGERS, Joann Ellison** (1941–    )
While attending Boston University, Joann Rodgers was city editor of the *Boston University News*. She was also a reporter and reviewer for the *Quincy Patriot Ledger* before becoming a *New York Herald Tribune* stringer.

Rodgers joined the *Baltimore News American* in 1964 and soon became a science writer. She has been national science writer for the Hearst Headline Service since 1966, receiving the Lasker Medical Journalism Award, the American Medical Association Medical Journalism Award, the Blakeslee Award from the American Heart Association on two occasions, and recognition from the Arthritis Foundation and the Cystic Fibrosis Foundation for her reporting.

**ROGIN, Gilbert L.** (1929–    )
Gilbert Rogin has been associated with *Sports Illustrated* since 1955, when he first worked on the clip desk. He later became a reporter, staff writer, senior editor, and in 1979, managing editor.

Rogin has published a number of short stories, many of them in *The New Yorker*. He also has written three books: *The Fencing Master and Other Stories*; *What Happens Next?*; and *Preparation for the Ascent*. Rogin won an award in 1972 from the National Institute of Arts and Letters "in recognition of creative work in literature."

**ROLLIN, Betty** (1936– )
Since 1971, Betty Rollin has been in television, first with NBC News in New York City and, more recently, as a correspondent on ABC's "Nightline."

Rollin had been a professional stage and television actress from 1958 to 1964, before she joined *Vogue* magazine as associate features editor, where she worked under Allene Talmey, who Rollin described as having "a special ability to make those who thought they were tough cower." Talmey fired Rollin in 1964. The next year she became a senior editor for *Look*, working with Pat Carbine, who later became *Ms.* publisher. She stayed at *Look* until 1971.

She free-lanced magazine articles, with many rejections.

Rollin had already written *I Thee Wed* and *Mothers Are Funnier Than Children.* After *Vogue*, she wrote *The Non-Drinkers Drink Book.* In her latest book, *Am I Getting Paid for This?*, Rollin relates some of her experiences. This volume has been called "a book for women of all ages." Rollin recalls some of the problems women have faced in the media world, especially during the Sixties. She wrote profiles for *Look*, including one about Johnny Carson. She also wrote about her experience with breast cancer in *First, You Cry.*

Rollin continued her interviews while with NBC, including a talk session with Betty Ford. She has hosted documentaries and at one time anchored a series of daytime programs, "Women Like Us."

In her more recent volume, she noted that television journalism is "having to look nice and think at the same time." She added that "most people like to talk about themselves and a reporter is one of the few people who seems to want to listen."

**ROONEY, Andrew Aitken** (1919– )
"CBS News' resident curmudgeon" is one description of Andy Rooney, whose comments have become best-selling books in the Eighties. Since 1959, Rooney has been a writer-producer with CBS-TV News; since 1978 he has been a commentator-essayist on the network's "60 Minutes." And since 1979, his comments have been syndicated to more than 300 newspapers in a three-times-a-week column.

"Writing is hard work and we aren't doing much hard work," he told Missouri journalism students in 1983. In noting his fame from a few minutes weekly on "60 Minutes," Rooney said, "I have a lower opinion of well-known people than I used to have before I was one of them."

In 1943, Rooney was writing on *Stars & Stripes* while serving in World War II. He was the co-author, with Bud Hotton, of two books on this experience: *Air Gunner* and *The Story of the Stars and Stripes.* Later he spent a year in Hollywood, expecting to turn the second book into a movie, but nothing developed.

From 1949 to 1955, Rooney wrote for the Arthur Godfrey radio and television shows and for Victor Borge, Sam Levinson, Herb Shriner, Garry Moore, and others. Eventually another book appeared, *The Fortunes of War: Four Great Battles of World War II.*

With Harry Reasoner, Rooney was a CBS writer-producer of television specials. After Reasoner moved to ABC, Rooney wrote "Essay on War," which attacked the Vietnam conflict, but CBS refused to give it full coverage and Rooney switched briefly to Public Broadcasting Service. He narrated the show and won his third Writer's Guild of America Award. He later did 15 additional PBS shows on "The Great American Dream Machine" series. Rooney worked for ABC before going back to CBS for a variety of shows. He won a Peabody award for "Mr. Rooney Goes to Washington."

One of his Emmy-winning pieces for "60 Minutes" was "Who Owns What in America." Rooney visited the factory of "Mrs. Smith's Pies" in Pennsylvania, only to learn that there was no "Mrs. Smith."

After winning more Emmy awards, Rooney's best television essays were published in *A Few Minutes with Andy Rooney*, a best-seller. Rooney noted that "seeing our names in print lends to the dream all of us have of immortality." *More Andy Rooney* followed, placing more than a million hard-cover copies of the two volumes in circulation. *Pieces of My Mind* appeared in 1984.

Rooney's fame is such that the Associated Press reported "for the first time in his life, he is hailed by strangers on the street. People want his face on their podium or at their cocktail party and his name on their charity boards and magazine covers."

**ROSENTHAL, Abraham M.** (1922– )
A.M. Rosenthal, in 1983, was the executive editor of The *New York Times*, a newspaper he joined in 1944. Later he worked as the United Nations correspondent, eventually going to India, Poland, Switzerland, and Tokyo before returning to the New York office.

In 1960, Rosenthal won the Pulitzer Prize for international reporting. His stories from Poland resulted in his expulsion from that country. "The Polish government cannot tolerate such probing reporting," he was told.

In addition to his Pulitzer Prize for foreign reporting, Rosenthal has won the Overseas Press Club and George Polk Memorial awards and the Page One Award of the New York Newspaper Guild.

Rosenthal has written many magazine articles and features for the *New York Times Magazine*. He co-authored *One More Victim*.

**ROSS, Harold** (1892–1951)
For years, *The New Yorker* and Harold Ross were one and the same. Ross began his journalistic career as a reporter on the *Salt Lake City Tribune* (Utah) in 1906. In 1911, he was with the *Sacramento Union* (California); in 1912, the *Panama Star* and the *Herald* as he continued to move about.

Ross began to make contacts and establish himself while he was the editor of *Stars & Stripes* during World War I (1917–19). Following the war, he was editor of the American Legion weekly publication from 1921 to 1923, and of *Judge* humor magazine in 1924.

In 1925 Ross's contribution to the world of literature, *The New Yorker*, was established. He remained its editor until his death.

**ROSS, John Michael** (1919– )

Tennis and golf have been the major interests for John Ross, who became a *Brooklyn Eagle* (New York) sportswriter in 1937. After World War II Army service, 1942–46, he worked briefly for the experimental *PM* newspaper before becoming editor of the *American Lawn Tennis* magazine in 1947.

On two occasions, Ross worked for the Macfadden Publications, and from 1952 to 1960, he was a contributing editor to *American Weekly*. In 1961, Ross was editor-in-chief of *Golf* magazine; at that time he was also associated with *Golf Business* and *Golfdom*.

Ross also published the *Golf Business Almanac* and *Golf TV Guide*; since 1972, he has been with *Golf*. Also since 1974, he has been on the board of the World Golf Hall of Fame, and since 1977, executive director of the International Golf Association. He has also served in official capacities with golf and tennis associations.

Ross received the Christopher Award for the best magazine story in 1957. He co-authored *Nothing but the Truth*.

**ROSTEN, Leo C.** (1908– )

Leo Rosten's career has centered around government service, the writing of books, and teaching. In 1937 his book The *Washington Correspondents* provided a pioneer study of a typical member of this elite press corps. According to James Deakin's *Straight Stuff*, Rosten's study revealed that these Washington newsmen were well ahead of reporters across the nation, with their college background and training.

While other reporters in America tended then to be "poorly educated and poorly paid," Rosten's study noted that in Washington 52 percent of the writers had college degrees and 28 per cent of them had attended college.

Rosten's career in education included his doctorate degree studies in Europe, and professorships at several American universities, including Chicago, New York, Stanford, UCLA, Yale, Columbia, and others. His government career involved federal agencies during World War II, including the Office of War Information 1942–1944.

With grants from the Carnegie Corporation and the Rockefeller Foundation, Rosten studies the motion picture industry. His books include *The Dark Corner*; *The Return of Hyman Kaplan*; *Captain Newman, M.D.*; *The Story Behind the Painting*; *The Many Worlds of Leo Rosten*; *A Most Private Intrigue*; *The Joys of Yiddish*; *A Trumpet for Reason*; *Rome Wasn't Burned in a Day*; *People I Have Loved, Known or Admired*; *Leo Rosten's Treasury of Jewish Quotations*; *Dear "Herm"*; *The 3:10 to Anywhere*; *O Kaplan! My Kaplan*; *The Power of Positive Nonsense*; *Passions and Prejudice*; and *Hooray for Yiddish: A Book about English*.

Rosten also edited *Religions in America* in 1955, 1967, and 1975; *The Look Book*; *Infinite Riches: Gems from a Lifetime of Reading*; *Silky*; and *King Silky*. He also wrote screenplays, including *The Dark Corner*, *Sleep, My Love* and *The Velvet Touch*.

Among his awards are the George Polk Memorial and Freedom Foundations. He also was given the Alumni Achievement award by the University of Chicago.

**ROTHSTEIN, Arthur** (1915– )
During the Depression years 1935–40, Arthur Rothstein took pictures for the Farm Security Administration, a collection that has become one of the most famous in photography history.

In 1940, Rothstein was a *Look* magazine photographer, and in 1946, director of photography for *Look.*

Since 1972 Rothstein has held a similar position with *Parade* magazine. He taught photography at Columbia University Graduate School of Journalism for a decade.

Rothstein won a first in the International Photography Exposition at Syracuse University, as well as many other awards for his pictures. Among his books are *Photojournalism*; *Creative Color Photography*; *Look at Us*; *The Depression Years*; *Words and Pictures*; and *American West.*

He served in the Army in World War II, 1943–46.

**ROUECHE, Berton** (1911– )
Berton Roueche has been a staff writer for *The New Yorker* since 1944. Before 1944, he worked in his native Missouri on the *Kansas City Star*, the *St. Louis Post-Dispatch*, and the *Globe-Democrat.*

Roueche has been associated with several health groups, including the Health Research Commission in New York and the National Foundation for Infectious Disease. He won the Lasker Journalism Award for his medical reporting in 1950 and 1960; the National Council of Infant and Child Care Award; the American Medical Writers Association Award; the American Medical Association Journalism Award; and the J. C. Penney–University of Missouri journalism writing award.

His books include the following: *Black Weather*; *Eleven Blue Men*; *The Incurable Wound*; *The Last Enemy*; *The Delectable Mountains*; *The Neutral Spirit*; *A Man Named Hoffman*; *A Field Guide to Disease*; *Annals of Epidemiology*; *What's Left*; *Reports on a Diminishing America*; *The Orange Man*; *Feral*; *Fago*; and *The River World.* He edited *Curiosities of Medicine.*

**ROUNTREE, Martha** (1916– )
Martha Rountree is best known to television viewers as a panelist on talk shows, especially "Meet the Press," which she and Lawrence E. Spivak inaugurated on radio in 1945. This program won a Peabody Award in 1947. After it moved to television it continued to win other awards and citations.

Before entering television, Rountree worked briefly as a reporter on the *Tampa Tribune* (Florida). She met Spivak when he was publisher and editor of the *American Mercury*, and for several years, she was a roving editor for this monthly magazine. Eventually, Rountree was with "Press

Conference" on NBC-TV and later with ABC-TV. She was also, at one time or another, associated with such shows as "Keep Posted," "The Big Issue," "Washington Exclusive," and "Press Conference."

The National Fraternity for Women in Journalism named her the outstanding woman in television in 1951. Mrs. William Randolph Hearst, Jr. once observed in a *McCall's* story in 1951, "don't let her glamorous appearance fool you. Martha's a diesel engine under a lace handkerchief." Rountree once described herself as "a blunt-speaking, down-to-earth television news reporter, and I'm proud of it."

**ROVERE, Richard H.** (1915–1979)

In 1944, Richard Rovere began a 35-year association with *The New Yorker*. He had been associate editor of the *New Masses* from 1938 to 1939, but left when he was no longer able to defend its Communist line. He was assistant editor of *The Nation* from 1940 to 1943. He then edited *Common Sense* and helped rewrite articles on political science topics.

Upon joining *The New Yorker*, he had time to write articles for other publications. He was the United States correspondent for the *London Spectator* and also contributed to *Harper's* and wrote book reviews. Rovere was on the editorial boards of *American Scholar* and the *Washington Journalism Board*.

He wrote *Howe & Hummel: Their True and Scandalous History*; *Affairs of State: The Eisenhower Years*; *Senator Joe McCarthy*; *The American Establishment*; *The Goldwater Caper*; *Waist Deep in the Big Muddy*; and *Arrivals and Departures*. He was co-author of *The General and the President*.

**ROWAN, Carl T.** (1925– )

One of the busiest journalist in the media world today is Carl Rowan, who has written a syndicated, thrice-weekly column since 1965. He has interviewed the greats, including Eleanor Roosevelt, John F. Kennedy, Dr. Martin Luther King, Jr., and Lyndon Johnson.

Rowan, who has been awarded nearly 40 honorary degrees, began his journalism career as a public opinion surveyor for the *Baltimore Afro-American* (Maryland) and then as a copywriter on the *Minneapolis Tribune* (Minnesota) in 1948. He became a staff writer two years later, and wrote the "How Far from Slavery" series that won him many awards, including the Sidney Hillman citation for "best newspaper reporting" in 1951. This material formed the basis for his first book, *South of Freedom*, in 1952.

Rowan has won many other awards, including several from Sigma Delta Chi. The Junior Chamber of Commerce named him one of the 10 Outstanding Young Men in America in 1954. The National Conference of Christians and Jews presented him its National Brotherhood Award. He won the George Foster Peabody Award for his television special on the Race War in Rhodesia. Howard University gave him its Liberty Bell Award and he won the University of Missouri Journalism Medal in 1981.

Rowan, the only person to win the Sigma Delta Chi Medallion three years in a row, was named one of three Fellows by the society in 1983. He was also awarded another honorary degree, this from Wayne State University.

His other books include *The Pitiful and the Proud*; *Go South to Sorrow*; *Wait till Next Year*; and *Just between Us Blacks*. He continues to appear regularly on television panel shows, especially "Agronsky & Company," which is shown on 60 stations. He does a five-days-a-week radio commentary, "The Rowan Report," which has won Emmy awards, and he is a roving editor for *Reader's Digest*.

Popular on the lecture circuit, Rowan says he visits the poor sections of the cities in which he speaks. "Let me tell you, it's an eye-opener. The unemployed people recognize me, and they come up and talk."

**ROWEN, Hobart** (1918– )

"A seasoned business and economics writer and editor" is Chalmers Roberts' description of Hobart Rowen, a member of the *Washington Post* staff since 1966.

Before joining the *Post*, Rowen was a reporter with the *New York Journal of Commerce* in 1938 and was the newspaper's Washington correspondent from 1941 to 1942. For several years, he was with the information division of the War Production Board.

Rowen moved to *Newsweek* in 1944 as a Washington correspondent until 1965. During much of that time he was also the Business Trends editor. In 1966, he moved to the *Post* as its financial editor, and since 1975, he has been a columnist and an economics editor.

Rowen has won major business awards and other citations, including two Loeb honors, the John Hancock Award, and A. T. Kearney and Sigma Delta Chi recognitions. He has been the president of the Society of American Business Writers.

The author of one book, *The Free Enterprisers—Kennedy, Johnson and the Business Establishment*, Rowen also contributes articles to magazines and newspapers.

**ROYKO, Mike** (1932– )

Chicago columnist Mike Royko has been described as "the teller of the city's tales, the composer of a daily chronicle of the winners and losers in Chicago. It has been said that you either love Mike Royko or you hate him, but you can't ignore him."

Royko's writings have brought him many awards, including the Pulitzer Prize for commentary in 1972. In 1979, the University of Missouri gave him its Journalism Medal, the same year he was selected as the Man of the Year by the City of Hope Medical Center.

Before becoming a columnist on the *Chicago Sun-Times* in 1978, Royko worked as a reporter on the Chicago North Side newspapers, with the City News Bureau, and from 1959 to 1978, on the *Chicago Daily News*.

Born in Chicago, Royko says he prefers the mix of an ethnic rather than a cosmopolitan city, asking "Who wants to live in New York?" His dislikes include "the weather, cab drivers who can't speak English, and hyperactive television reporters." Royko has written several books, including *Up against It*; *I May Be Wrong but I Doubt it*; *Boss—Richard J. Daley of Chicago*; and *Slats Grobnik and Some Other Friends*.

In early 1984, Royko switched to the *Chicago Tribune* in protest to the *Sun-Times* sale to Rupert Murdoch.

**ROYSTER, Vermont C.** (1914- )

Although born in North Carolina, Vermont Connecticut Royster was named for two New England states. His great-grandfather was the first in his family to name his children after states.

Royster was on the University of North Carolina *Daily Tar Heel* staff and, after graduation, headed for New York, obtaining a job as copyboy on the *Wall Street Journal* in 1936. Shortly after that he joined the *Journal*'s Washington Bureau and, by 1948, was associate editor. During World War II he served in the Navy, returning to the *Journal*'s Washington office before going to New York. He became editor in 1958, and since 1971, he has been a columnist and contributing editor.

Since 1971, Royster has also been a professor of journalism and public affairs at his alma mater, the University of North Carolina. When he took this position he said, "There was a loss of income, but now I have the best of all possible worlds—Chapel Hill, teaching, and writing." His father had taught Greek and Latin there.

In 1983, Royster wrote *My Own, My Country's Time: A Journalist's Journey*.

Dana Thomas wrote that Royster was "one of the most colorful and provocative of the *Wall Street Journal*'s editors." Royster once said he believed "the primary reason for government is to provide police power to keep me from knocking you over the head." He also wrote that "the minute an editor withholds an opinion for fear that someone may think it 'irresponsible' or that he may be 'out of step with the times,' he ceases to perform his function."

Royster co-authored *Main Street and Beyond*. He also has written *Journey through the Soviet Union* and *A Pride of Prejudices*. He appears on radio and television programs.

Royster won a Pulitzer Prize in 1984 for distinguished commentary.

**RUKEYSER, Louis** (1933- )

"Wall $treet Week" is a television program that attracts more than 10 million viewers who want to hear what Louis Rukeyser and his guests feel about the economy and the future.

Rukeyser's father was a Hearst newspaper syndicated columnist for more than three decades, and his brothers have been involved in the communication world, so it was only natural that Louis Ruykeyser should follow in the media.

In his teens, Rukeyser contributed articles to the *New Rochelle Standard Star*. Later he was a *New York Times* and a *Herald Tribune* correspondent. During summer vacations, he worked on the *Mount Vernon Daily Argus*, and in the Fifties, while in the Army, he worked on *Stars & Stripes*.

Rukeyser joined the "big time" when he became a reporter for the *Baltimore Sun* (Maryland) in 1956 after war service. He moved about, working in London and then becoming the *Sun*'s Asian correspondent. During this time, he won two Overseas Press Club awards.

In 1965, Rukeyser became involved with broadcast journalism as the ABC News Paris correspondent. He also served ABC two years in London before returning to New York City as the network's economics editor. He told the *New York Times* in 1980, "I invented the job of economic commentary on television." Eventually he hosted a number of ABC documentaries and special reports.

"Rukeyser's World" began as a syndicated radio program on 450 stations in 1971. The Freedoms Foundation gave him its Washington Honor Medal for this show.

"Wall $treet Week" began on the Eastern Educational Network in 1970 and was later associated with the Public Broadcasting Service. In 1973, Rukeyser left ABC to do the "Week" full-time. It is broadcast from the Maryland Center for Public Broadcasting. He once explained his success to *Dial* magazine as being based on his ability to speak English, to knowing what he is talking about, and to having "a bit of flair."

*The New Yorker*, in late 1983, noted that "Wall $treet Week" was "perhaps the most popular of the weekly public affairs series appearing on National Public Television." Rukeyser told the magazine his philosophy is that "money isn't everything but it certainly is interesting, and the fact that most people take it so seriously gives rise to comedy that everyone, rich or poor, can enjoy." He calls it a family show.

**RUKEYSER, William S.** (1939- )

William Rukeyser began his career as a copyreader on the *Wall Street Journal* in 1961, and by 1963, he was working for the publication in Europe, where he also wrote for British publications, including the *London Observer*. In 1967, he joined *Fortune* magazine where he continues today.

In 1967, Rukeyser was the associate editor of *Fortune* and, five years later, the managing editor. He was also the first managing editor for *Money* magazine, when this monthly was established in 1972, a position now held by Marshall Loeb. Rukeyser wrote many articles about the business world for *Fortune*. In 1971, he became a member of the Fortune Board of Editors.

For two years, 1978–80, he was a weekly guest on the ABC-TV "Good Morning America" show, discussing personal financial topics, and for five days a week, he presented similar topics on the CBS Radio News Service.

**RULE, Elton H.** (1917- )

Elton Rule joined the ABC Network in New York City in 1952. He has remained there. He was general manager of KABC-TV from 1953 to 1960, and then moved to the presidency of the television network in 1968.

Since 1972, Rule has been the president and chief operating officer of American Broadcasting Companies, Inc. The International Radio and Television Society awarded him its gold medal in 1975 and the University of Southern California School of Business Administration, in 1978, gave Rule its outstanding achievement award.

Rule serves the Will Rogers Hospital and Research Center as a member of its advisory committee.

**RUSSELL, Fred** (1906– )

For more than half a century, Fred Russell has been writing a sports column for the *Nashville Banner* (Tennessee). He estimated that involves about 18,000 columns, and admits "I've never done a column that I didn't think couldn't have been done better."

Russell studied for the bar, but in 1929 joined the *Banner* as a reporter; by 1930, he was sports editor. Since 1967, he has been associated with the National Football Foundation and Hall of Fame. Also since 1946, he has been involved with the Heisman Trophy Committee.

In discussing his work for an article for the Associated Press Managing Editors *News* in 1983, Russell wrote: "My first principle is to try to make a column that's interesting to me. I don't know of anything more poisonous than self-boredom and I try to express my own emotion and thoughts."

His books include *50 Years of Vanderbilt Football*; *I'll Go Quietly*; *I'll Try Anything Twice*; *Funny Thing about Sport*; *Bury Me in an Old Press Box*; and *Big Bowl Football.* He has contributed articles to magazines.

Among his awards are the distinguished journalism honor from the U.S. Olympics Committee in 1976; the Grantland Rice Award for sports writing in 1955; and the National Headliner Award in 1936. He was named to the Tennessee Sports Hall of Fame in 1974.

**RYALL, George F. T.** ( ? – )

The "dean of American racing writers," George Ryall has been with *The New Yorker* since 1926. His column appears under the name "Audax Minor."

In a *Baltimore Sun* interview in 1978 by Carl Schoettler, Ryall was quoted as saying, "I'm over 80," but less than 100. "He was writing racing before there were starting gates, photo finishes, before parimutuel betting," wrote Schoettler. His first big race was the 1909 Epsom Derby.

Born in London, Ryall came to New York in 1912 and worked on The *World* under Herbert Bayard Swope, until the newspaper stopped publication in the Thirties. He adopted the "Audax Minor" signature to cover his two jobs.

**RYAN, Pat** ( ? – )

Pat Ryan was named one of the Outstanding Women in Communication in New York in 1982, and that same year, she was appointed the managing editor for *People* magazine after spending more than two decades with Time Inc.

Ryan joined *Sports Illustrated* in 1960 as a secretary and eventually became a researcher, staff writer, and senior editor. In 1978, she was a senior editor on *People* and moved up to other positions before her recent promotion.

Before entering the media world, Ryan worked as a secretary at the Belmont, Saratoga, and Aqueduct race tracks. Her father was a horse trainer.

**SAFER, Morley** (1931– )
Born in Canada, Morley Safer was a correspondent and producer with the Canadian Broadcasting Corp. from 1955 to 1960, and for the next four years, the network's London correspondent. For a brief time, Safer was a producer with the British Broadcasting Company.

Before television work, Safer was with two Ontario newspapers, the *Woodstock Sentinel Review* and the *London Free Press.* Later in England, he was on the *Oxford Mail and Times.*

CBS hired Safer in 1964 while he was in London. The next year he went to Vietnam, where he shocked American viewers with his on-the-scene descriptions of the brutalities of the conflict. President Lyndon Johnson was so provoked that he ordered a secret investigation of Safer's background.

Safer won several awards for this coverage, including the Polk, Overseas Press Club, Sigma Delta Chi, and Peabody, as well as the Paul White award from the News Directors Association. He also won two Emmys.

David Halberstam praised his Vietnam work, noting, "overnight one correspondent with one cameraman could become as important as ten or fifteen or twenty senators."

In 1967, Safer became chief of the CBS London Bureau. In late 1970, he became a member of the "60 Minutes" team where he has continued his investigative reporting. His watercolors have been exhibited in several galleries.

In 1984 Safer told the Associated Press, "I think it's just terribly important to keep that 'boy reporter' attitude, to maintain that kind of enthusiasm that keeps you looking for something new all the time."

**SAFIRE, William** (1929– )
A columnist for the *New York Times*, William Safire was at one time a speech writer for President Richard Nixon. According to Ernest Hynds, "Safire [in 1973] was expected to provide a conservative viewpoint in contrast to those of the *Times*' regular domestic-staff commentators, Reston, Wicker, and Anthony Lewis."

Early in his career (1949–51), Safire worked on the *New York Herald Tribune* as a researcher and writer for columnist Tex McCrary. He then turned to radio and television and went to Europe and the Middle East for WNBC and WWBT-TV. He was in the Army from 1952 to 1954. For five years Safire produced the NBC "Tex and Jinx" radio and television show, featuring Tex McCrary and his wife, Jinx Falkenburg.

Safire was in Moscow at the American National Exhibition when he took a now-famous picture for an Associated Press photographer that showed Nixon and Russian Premier Nikita Khrushchev debating in a kitchen showroom.

In 1961, Safire opened his own public relations service, but later sold out and joined the White House staff in 1968.

Safire worked with many Republican campaigns, from Eisenhower, in 1952, to Nixon, handling public relations, preparing speeches, creating slogans, and supervising other workers. By 1969, he was a special assistant to Nixon, and later helped Vice-President Spiro Agnew. Some liberals termed Safire a "hired gun." He has been with the *Times* since 1973.

Among his books are *The Relations Explosion*; *Plunging Into Politics*; *Safire's Political Dictionary*; *Before the Fall*; and *Full Disclosure*. He wrote the text to *Eye on Nixon*, a photographic history of the family.

**ST. JOHNS, Adela Rogers** (1894– )
Adela Rogers St. Johns has been around celebrities for most of her life. Her father was a well-known criminal lawyer who once defended Clarence Darrow on a charge of jury tampering.

In 1913, she began her life-time association with William Randolph Hearst, and his organization, as a cub reporter on the *Los Angeles Herald*. That same year she worked briefly on the *San Francisco Examiner*. She moved to feature writing, handling many topics suggested by Hearst. She also wrote "inside stories" and profiles for *Photoplay* magazine, as well as articles for *Good Housekeeping*, *Harper's Bazaar*, *Cosmopolitan*, *Saturday Evening Post*, *Liberty*, *Reader's Digest*, *American Weekly*, and other magazines. She wrote screenplays, but newspaper work was her primary concern. During her years with Hearst, she was, at one time or another, on the *Chicago American*, the *New York American*, and the International News Service.

Among her major stories was the Hauptmann trial, for which Hearst labeled her "the world's greatest girl reporter." And in the mid-Thirties she went to Washington to cover political stories, including a probe of Huey Long's activities. She was known as one of the "sob sisters" of the era. For a brief time in the Fifties, she taught at the University of California at Los Angeles. She calls herself the first woman sportswriter.

Among her books are *A Free Soul*; *Single Standard*; *Field of Honor*; *How to Write a Short Story and Sell It*; *Final Verdict*; *Tell No Man*; and her autobiography, *The Honeycomb*. Earlier she had written *Affirmative Prayer in Action*; *First Step up toward Heaven*; *Hubert Eaton and Forest Lawn*; and *Some Are Born Great*.

Approaching 90, St. Johns continued to write books. According to a *Los Angeles Times* account, one book was on "the 'missing years' of Jesus Christ, an ambitious project she began researching two decades ago and another that is to be the third and final installment of her autobiography."

She said "Humanity, as a whole, I think, does better and thinks better than they really think they do. I've only known one person who was really evil."

**SALANT, Richard S.** (1914– )
The former president of CBS News and one-time vice-chairman of NBC, Richard Salant became president of the National News Council in 1983. At that time he said, "The press must help people feel that it is accountable to someone—not to government, but to the public it serves."

Earlier in his career, Salant was an attorney, and from 1938 to 1943 he was with the federal government. For nearly a decade he was a partner in a law firm before his appointment as vice-president of CBS Inc. in 1952. By 1961, he was president of CBS News and later vice-president of CBS Inc. From 1979 to 1983, he was vice-chairman of NBC Inc. He served in the Navy during World War II.

Al Westin wrote of Salant's handling of the death of Elvis Presley and the subsequent debate with Roone Arledge, ABC News president. ABC made it the lead story on the evening program; CBS stayed with a four-minute Panama Canal Treaty story.

Salant had written in the CBS News Standards Book, "We in broadcast journalism cannot, should not and will not base our judgments on what we think the viewers and listeners are 'most interested' in, or hinge our news judgment and our news treatment on our guesses (or somebody else's surveys) as to what news the people want to hear or see, and in what form."

Arledge argued that people were interested in Presley. They had expected the Panama Canal decision. Salant replied, "Our job is not to respond to public taste. Elvis Presley was dead—so he was dead."

When Bing Crosby died, CBS made it the lead story.

**SALINGER, Pierre Emil George** (1925– )

Pierre Salinger became nationally famous during his tour as press secretary for Senator and later President John F. Kennedy, from 1959 to 1963, and briefly for Lyndon Johnson.

Since that time, Salinger has become known as "the surprise of the field of investigative reporters. Few industry people expected anything serious from him when ABC hired the former White House press secretary as a Paris correspondent in 1977," according to Mark Ribowsky in a 1982 *TV Guide* article.

Salinger began his newspaper work on the *San Francisco Chronicle* in 1946 and stayed until 1955, becoming night city editor. He also wrote for *Collier's*. After his government service, Salinger was associated with several corporations. In 1973, he became a correspondent for *L'Express* in Paris and in 1977, he joined ABC for Europe and became bureau chief two years later.

One of Salinger's greatest news stories was the inside report on the Iranian hostage crisis. Ribowsky noted that "some may think his material isn't 'smooth' but who cares since he is so effective."

Salinger served in the Navy during World War II and was given the Navy and Marine Corps medal, as well as the French Legion of Honor Medal.

Among his books are *With Kennedy*; *On Instructions of My Government*; *A Tribute to John F. Kennedy*; *A Tribute to Robert F. Kennedy*; *Je Suis un Americain*; *Le France et le Nouveau Monde*; and *America Held Hostage—The Secret Negotiations*.

**SALISBURY, Harrison Evan** (1908– )

After being expelled from the University of Minnesota for smoking in the library vestibule in 1929, Harrison Salisbury joined the United Press'

St. Paul Bureau and soon went to Chicago. He had worked for the *Minneapolis Journal* from 1928 to 1929, and on his high school and university newspapers, earlier.

The UP eventually sent him to Washington, New York, London, and in 1944, to Moscow, where he spent the next decade. He joined the *New York Times* as Moscow correspondent in 1949 and returned to New York in 1954. By 1972, he was associate editor and in 1973, he retired as editor of the Op-Ed page. He had been the first staffer to direct this section.

Salisbury was described as a "journalistic one-man band" by Turner Catledge, who added, "He has a passion to excel." He won the 1955 Pulitzer Prize for international reporting for his coverage of the Soviet Union. This series resulted in a five-year expulsion from Russia. Salisbury also covered London during the blitz, Moscow during the Cold War, but when he went to Hanoi during the Vietnam War, he upset many readers.

After his retirement, Salisbury hosted a PBS series, "Behind the Lines," and other programs. In addition to his Pulitzer, he has won the George Polk Memorial Award twice for foreign reporting. He has been honored by Sigma Delta Chi and the Overseas Press Club and the Sidney Hillman Foundation. The University of Minnesota, in 1955, presented him its distinguished achievement medal.

Salisbury has been a prolific book writer, with 23 to his credit, including *Russia on the Way*; *American in Russia*; *The Shook Up Generation*; *To Moscow and Beyond*; *Moscow Journal*; *The Northern Palmyra Affair*; *A New Russia*; *Russia*; *Orbit of China*; *Behind the Lines—Hanoi*; *The Soviet Union—the Fifty Years*; *The 900 Days: The Siege of Leningrad*; *War between Russia and China*; *The Many Americans Shall Be One*; *The Eloquence of Protest*; *To Peking and Beyond*; *The Gates of Hell*; *Travels around America*; *Black Night, White Snow*; *The Unknown War*; *Russia in Revolution 1900–1930*; *Without Fear or Favor: The New York Times and Its Times*; and *A Journey for our Times*, which sums up his career to 1983.

Writing in *For Members Only*, a newsletter from the American Express Gold Card, Salisbury noted in 1984 that "While I still believe journalism has its faults, media and other sources of information in America are certainly among the best in the world."

**SANDERS, Marlene** (1931– )

The first woman to anchor a network evening program, Marlene Sanders has worked for both ABC and NBC. She began as a writer and producer on WNEW-TV in New York City in 1955. By 1961, she was with the Westinghouse Broadcasting Co. on its "PM East-PM West" show.

Sanders credits Mike Wallace for her first television work, when she was working as his assistant in summer theater. In 1964, she became a news correspondent for ABC, and in 1971, a documentary producer. She became vice-president and director of television documentaries for ABC news from 1976 to 1978, after which she joined CBS Reports as a correspondent and producer.

Long active in gaining equality for women in journalism, Sanders produced several 1970 ABC shows on this subject, including "Women's

Liberation" and "We Have Met the Enemy and He Is Us." She also has produced "The Right to Die," "Children in Peril," and "How Much for the Handicapped?" among her many shows. Al Westin calls her "a very well-organized and professional journalist who has all the skills it takes." Since 1981, she has been the anchor on the CBS "Saturday Edition Newsbreak."

Sanders has won more than twenty-five awards, including three Emmys. The New York State Broadcasters Association, the National Press Club, and others have honored her. She is a past president of Women in Communications Inc.

In the mid-seventies, she taught radio and television news techniques at Columbia University.

**SANDESON, William Seymour** (1913- )

During the five-year period 1932–37, William Sandeson was a free-lance cartoonist for national magazines before he joined the *New Orleans Item-Tribune* (Louisiana) as an editorial cartoonist. He moved to the *St. Louis Star-Times* (Missouri), where he remained from 1941 to 1951.

Since 1951, Sandeson has been the editorial cartoonist for the *Fort Wayne News-Sentinel* (Indiana). He has received many awards, including the Freedoms Foundation honor medal for three years, and its George Washington Honor Medal on six occasions.

**SARNOFF, David** (1891–1971)

Truly a pioneer in the broadcast field, David Sarnoff was a messenger boy and later an office boy for early cable and wireless firms in 1906. He also served as the wireless operator on a number of ships during this era. He was long associated with the Marconi Company, which eventually was acquired by Radio Corporation of America in 1919. By 1930, Sarnoff was president of RCA, becoming chairman of the board from 1947 to 1969, and later its honorary chairman.

During his years in broadcasting, Sarnoff was decorated by several foreign nations and by his own government. In 1951, he received the Horatio Alger Award. Many professional organizations recognized his pioneering work, with citations and other honors. Born in Russia, Sarnoff later received many honorary degrees from American universities.

He wrote *Looking Ahead* in 1968.

**SARNOFF, Robert W.** (1918- )

Robert Sarnoff became president of the National Broadcasting Co. in 1955, a group he had joined in 1948 as an account executive. He was in the Navy during World War II and later helped to develop color for television.

For a brief time after the war, Sarnoff was an assistant to the publisher of the *Des Moines Register* and *Tribune* (Iowa) and worked for *Look* magazine before going to NBC. He was associated with some of the pioneer shows on the network, including the "Kate Smith Hour" and "Your Show of Shows." He served as the first president of the Radio and Television Executive Society from 1952 to 1953.

Erik Barnouw, in his three-volume history of broadcasting in America, described Sarnoff as a "relaxed executive. He was never pretentious. Appearing before government committees, he learned to handle himself, even though his knowledge of the industry and its history was limited."

**SAUTER, Van Gordon** (1935– )
Van Gordon Sauter became president of CBS News in 1982, having started in media as a reporter on the *New Bedford Standard-Times* (Massachusetts) in 1959. Four years later, he was a writer for the *Detroit Free Press* (Michigan), and from 1967 to 1968, he was with the *Chicago Daily News.*

Sauter's radio and television career began in 1968 when he became the news and program director of WBBM-TV CBS Radio in Chicago. In 1971, he was executive producer for radio, and by 1974, he was in Paris. Returning to New York in 1976, he became vice-president for program practices for CBS-TV. He later was in Los Angeles before assuming his current position.

Returning to his alma mater to speak in 1983, Sauter told the University of Missouri journalism students that "changes will come in news, not technology; a full hour of network evening news may be in the works sometime just beyond 1985."

Sauter's "eccentric" career has been described by Cheryl Lavin in a Knight-Ridder Newspapers feature in 1983: "He was CBS' Paris bureau chief although he doesn't speak French. He was network censor, although every fourth word he uses is an expletive. He was in charge of sports, although his body bears witness 'to a lifetime of sloth and self-indulgence.' "

Sauter's reports from the Vietnam War for the *Detroit Free Press* emphasized the soldiers rather than the battles. While with Chicago station WBBM-TV, Sauter kept a parrot in his office, which added to his growing legend.

Sauter told James Brady, writing in *Advertising Age* in 1983, that "we are paying in this business a considerable price with people without print experience. They have never had a tyrannical city editor. They haven't had the varied experiences of hard news and features and sidebars and obits. The problem isn't the writing, it's the reporting."

He co-authored *Nightmare in Detroit*, and later wrote *Fabled Land, Timeless, River Life along the Mississippi.*

**SAVITCH, Jessica** (1947–1983)
*Time* magazine reported a "Tragic Sign-Off for a Golden Girl" in its obituary of Jessica Savitch, who was killed in a freak automobile accident in 1983 at the age of 36.

Savitch had predicted her rapid network goals to the anchor position. In a story she wrote, Savitch noted the difficulty women had in balancing their television and their personal lives. "I went into the industry knowing that it would be more time-consuming and stress-provoking than the average career."

She was a rock deejay in 1962 on Atlantic City station WOND-radio while in high school. Even at that age, she was determined to be a broadcast star. She later worked for Rochester radio station WBBF, and subsequently became an associate producer for Trans-Media Inc. In 1969, she was a researcher for WCBS-News Radio in New York City. Prior to that she had made commercials and worked as a model.

The next year, she moved to Houston station WHOU-TV, returning to the East as weekend anchor on Philadelphia Station WKW-TV.

In 1974, she won the Clarion award for documentary and later the Broadcast Media Conference Award from Women in Communications Inc. She overcame her college professor's warning that "there's no place for broads in broadcasting."

By 1976, she was co-anchor of "Eyewitness News" in Philadelphia, and in 1977, she became a correspondent for NBC News in New York City.

Savitch wrote *Anchorwoman* in 1982. She continued to seek an anchor position and some reports placed her as a substitute for Jane Pauley during the latter's maternity leave from the "Today Show."

A *TV Guide* 1982 survey placed Savitch as the fourth most trusted network anchor. Her 1983 assignments had been more with the network's "News Digests."

"She has left behind a high stand of professionalism for countless young women who dream of replacing Dan Rather, Tom Brokaw or Peter Jennings," Maurice Christopher wrote in *Advertising Age*. Savitch claimed discrimination against women did not come from the viewers. "She worried about the impact on other women if she failed."

**SAWYER, Diane** (1945- )

As co-anchor of "CBS Morning News," Diane Sawyer is known to millions of television viewers. *Newsweek* devoted nearly three pages in 1983 to discussing Sawyer, who "wakes America with a blend of charm and intelligence that has perked up a tired program."

*Newsweek* described Sawyer as "brilliant, magnetic, industrious, inquisitive, disciplined, witty, gracious, charming, and loyal." She was America's Junior Miss in 1963, and later, she was a weather girl in Louisville's CBS affiliate, WLKY-TV from 1967 to 1970. She then worked in Ron Ziegler's press office and eventually spent three years, 1975–78, assisting the former president, Richard Nixon, in writing his memoirs. She returned to CBS later in 1978 as a reporter in Washington, although some voiced fear of her credibility because of the Nixon association. She covered the State Department and, in 1981, became co-anchor with Charles Kuralt on the morning segment.

Sawyer told *Newsweek*, "This job is so seductive. It really is the decathlon of news. When you've finished each morning, you feel like you deserve to be hosed down and given a gold medal." She told Marian Christy, writing for the Los Angeles Times Syndicate, that she was a journalist. "I ask questions that people don't like to answer. That tests your mettle. Asking such questions takes a conscious effort, but I do what I know I have to do."

Sawyer joined "60 Minutes" in August 1984.

**SCALI, John Alfred** (1918– )
John Scali began his career as a print journalist, working as a reporter on the *Boston Herald* in 1942 before going to the ABC Network in 1961. He joined the Boston office of the United Press in 1942, and two years later switched to the Associated Press, for which he covered World War II. He became a diplomatic correspondent with the Washington Bureau, where he served until 1961.

As diplomatic correspondent, Scali joined ABC News in 1961, to serve the next decade as a reporter. For several years, he was a special consultant for foreign affairs to the President and from 1973 to 1975, he was the United States ambassador to the United Nations in New York City.

After government service, Scali returned to ABC News as a senior correspondent in Washington. The University of Southern California gave him its Journalism Award in 1964, and the next year Boston University named him its Man of the Year. The Overseas Press Club and the National Academy of Arts and Sciences have also honored him. The American Federation of Television and Radio Artists created a John Scali Award in 1964.

**SCHERMAN, Harry** (1887–1969)
Harry Scherman founded the Book-of-the-Month Club in 1926, became its president in 1931, and its chairman of the board in 1950, a position he held until his death.

Scherman began in the media world in 1912, with a job in advertising. He was associated with several agencies before and after his World War I service. At one time, Scherman was publishing the Little Leather Library, a collection of classics that sold for a dime each.

He wrote several books, including *The Promises Men Live By: A New Approach to Economics*; *The Real Danger in Our Gold*; and *The Last Best Hope of Earth.* As these titles indicate, he was concerned with economics. He also wrote articles on this topic for magazines.

**SCHIEFFER, Bob** ( ? – )
"I have often felt that we spend too much time responding to what the government says it is going to do and too little time reporting what they are doing," Bob Schieffer told the *Washington Journalism Review* in 1983.

The CBS national correspondent began as a reporter on the *Ft. Worth Star-Telegram* (Texas) before turning to television at WBAP-TV in the Dallas–Ft. Worth area. Since 1964, he has been with CBS News in various capacities, such as Sunday evening anchorman. He has worked on many specials, along with reporting on the national political conventions.

Schieffer has won awards from Sigma Delta Chi, the Associated Broadcasters, and the Associated Press Managing Editors.

**SCHIFF, Dorothy** (1903– )
The socialite publisher Dorothy Schiff operated the *New York Post* from 1939 to 1976, when she sold the daily tabloid to Rupert Murdoch for $30 million.

"Kept organs are just no good," Schiff once remarked, when she explained her desire to make the *Post* pay for itself rather than depend on her inheritance. Before her newspaper career, Schiff took an active role in social welfare activities.

Schiff had an interest in radio stations in Brooklyn, Los Angeles, and San Francisco before taking over the *Post*, a newspaper founded in 1801 by Alexander Hamilton. Her husband, George Backer, was the publisher and president in 1936, but she took over these roles in 1942 when he resigned because of ill health. She acquired the *Bronx Home News* in 1945.

While operating the *Post*, Schiff made it the "column-happy American daily," publishing probably the greatest number of columnists among the nation's newspapers. In 1951 she wrote a column of her own, titled "Publisher's Notebook," and later "Dear Reader."

**SCHMICK, William F. III** (1941– )
As special projects editor for the Gannett News Service, William Schmick has the responsibility of supervising news coverage on the group's 86 daily newspapers.

Prior to joining the Gannett News Service, Schmick was city editor of the *Baltimore Sun* (Maryland), and the newspaper's foreign correspondent in Rome and in Africa. He has also been an "editor in residence" at James Madison University and has participated in American Press Institute seminars.

Among his awards for reporting are the Pulitzer Prize, the John Hancock Award for financial reporting, and the top investigative reporting award from the Investigative Reporters and Editors group.

**SCHMIDT, J. Scott** ( – )
When he was 14 years old, J. Scott Schmidt began his newspaper career with the *Pekin Times* (Illinois). Later, he was a reporter for the *Peoria Journal Star*.

Schmidt moved to Chicago and the *American*, renamed *Today*, in 1958 as a copy editor. By the time *Today* merged with the *Tribune*, Schmidt had become editor.

In 1975, Schmidt became the president of the Van Nuys Publishing Co. and six years later took over other Chicago Tribune Co. holdings in California, including the Palo Alto *Peninsula Times Tribune* and the *Escondido Times-Advocate*. In late 1983, he became president and the chief operating officer of Tribune Newspapers West, Inc.

The California Newspaper Association nominated Schmidt as Publisher of the Year in 1982. While in the Chicago area, he taught journalism at Northwestern University for 10 years.

**SCHOENBRUN, David** (1915– )
Early in his career, David Schoenbrun was a teacher, an editor of a trade publication, and a free-lance writer; and before his service in the Army during World War II, he was the French editor of "Voice of America." He was with CBS in Europe in 1945, where he remained until his return to

Washington in 1960. In 1963, he became associated with ABC News and Metromedia, remaining until 1980, when he joined the Independent Network News in New York City.

Schoenbrun has won three distinguished reporting awards from the Overseas Press Club and an Emmy for his television work. He has also been honored by the French government. His books include *As France Goes*; *Three Lives of Charles de Gaulle*; *Vietnam*; *The New Israelis*; *Triumph in Paris*; and *Soldiers of the Night*. He has also written magazine articles.

**SCHORR, Daniel Louis** (1916– )

Daniel Schorr spent 23 years with CBS News before his controversial exit precipitated by an incident in which Schorr gave the *Village Voice* a copy of the suppressed report of the House Committee on Intelligence.

While a high school student, Schorr was a stringer for the *Bronx Home News* and the *Jewish Daily Bulletin*. After college, he joined the *New York Journal-American* and, in 1941, the Netherlands News Agency, ANETA. He served in the Army during World War II and after more work with ANETA, he free lanced for a time. Edward R. Murrow, impressed by his writing, hired Schorr for CBS News in 1953.

Schorr reopened the Moscow Bureau for CBS in 1955. He covered Europe until 1966, when he became the network's Washington Bureau chief. He stayed there for 10 years.

Schorr's investigative reporting earned him a place on President Nixon's "enemies list." He reported shortcomings of Nixon's programs. Schorr also irritated some CBS officials when they failed to continue the Nixon attacks. He later covered the intelligence operations of the federal government, including committee hearings in Washington.

When Schorr turned over a suppressed report of the U.S. House Committee of Intelligence in 1976 to the *Village Voice* (New York City) CBS suspended him. He resigned seven months later. The report told of illegal CIA and FBI operations.

After leaving CBS, Schorr was a columnist for the Des Moines Register-Tribune Syndicate (Iowa) and a commentator on National Public Radio and Independent Television. He has been the senior Washington correspondent for the Cable News Network since 1980.

In 1984 Schorr wrote in *TV Guide* that "reporters shouldn't always tell the story" when "being responsible is more important than tomorrow's hot scoop."

Schorr has won three Emmy awards for his coverage of the Watergate scandals, along with other awards from the Overseas Press Club, the American Civil Liberties Union, and other associations. The Netherlands, Germany, and the Soviet Union have honored him. He has written *Don't Get Sick in America!* and *Clearing the Air*.

**SCHULZ, Charles M.** (1922– )

"I grew up with only one real career desire in life—and that was someday to draw my own comic strip." Obviously, Charles M. Schulz has achieved his goal and his "Peanuts" comic strip has become internationally famous.

Schulz, in his youth, was a faithful reader of comics and later took a correspondence course in art. After World War II, he sold his first cartoon to the *Saturday Evening Post* and, in 1949, he sold "Peanuts" to the United Feature Syndicate. Today, some 2,000 newspapers around the world carry his comic strip. When Schulz had heart surgery in 1981 he received thousands of cards. President Ronald Reagan called and later sent a plant.

A Charley Brown Christmas program appeared on CBS and brought Schulz an Emmy Award for children's programs in 1966. A more recent award, in 1983, was a special Christopher recognition for Charlie Brown and Snoopy. For nearly 20 years, Schulz's characters have been on television specials, and in 1983, CBS began a Charlie Brown and Snoopy Show. Also in 1983, a "Camp Snoopy" was established at Knott's Berry Farm in California.

The "Snoopy Fan Club" quickly gained 10,000 members, with its newsletter, the *Beagle Bugle*. There has also been a Broadway musical, which went on the road across America, and there are hundreds of Peanut products, especially stuffed toys. Reader interest has prompted Schulz to write the following books: *Peanuts*; *More Peanuts*; *Good Grief, More Peanuts*; *Good Ol' Charlie Brown*; *You're out of Your Mind Charlie Brown*; *But We Love You Charlie Brown*; *Peanuts Revisited*; *Go Fly a Kite Charlie Brown*; *Peanuts Every Sunday*; *You Can Do It, Charlie Brown*; *Happiness Is a Warm Puppy*; *Love Is Walking Hand in Hand*; *A Charlie Brown Christmas*; *You Need Help Charlie Brown*; *Charlie Brown's All Stars*; *You've Had It Charlie Brown*; *The Snoopy Festival*; *Snoopy and the Red Baron*; *Snoopy and His Sopwich Camel*; *The Snoopy Come Home Movie Book*; and *The Charlie Brown Dictionary*.

For those interested in drawing, Schulz advised one "must possess that rarest of all commodities, which is plain common sense." He explains that Charlie Brown "is a caricature. We all know what it's like to lose, but Charlie Brown keeps losing outrageously. It's not that he's a loser; he's really a decent little sort. But nothing seems to work out right." Schulz is a deeply religious person and often teaches Sunday School classes. "Good grief" and "rats" are among his most violent exclamations. He neither smokes nor drinks.

**SCRIPPS Family**

The grandchildren and great-grandchildren of Edward W. Scripps (1854–1920) control today's Scripps-Howard operations in newspapers and broadcast stations. *Quill* magazine, in 1982, estimated the family's worth at $300 to 600 million. This also includes the Scripps League Newspapers, headed by Edward Wyllis Scripps (1909–      ), who became chairman of the board in 1931.

E.W., the founder of what is known as Scripps-Howard today, first worked with his brother, James, who owned the *Detroit News* (Michigan). In 1878, E.W. established *The Penny Press*, which later became the *Cleveland Press* (Ohio) and served as the foundation for the group. Along with another brother, George, the Scripps were responsible for many newspapers across America. Their sister, Ellen, who died in 1932 at the age of 95, was a guiding influence, especially on E.W.

James Scripps ( – ), the eldest son of E.W., built the Scripps League in the West. Another grandson, John P. Scripps, built a chain of small California newspapers.

Charles Edwards Scripps (1920– ) was a *Cleveland Press* reporter in 1941 and has since been involved in executive positions with the group. He has been chairman of the board of the E.W. Scripps Co. since 1953.

**SEIB, Charles Bach** (1919– )
One of the few ombudsmen on American newspapers, Charles Seib served in this role on the *Washington Post* from 1974 to 1979 and ensured his freedom of views by a long-term contract, according to *Post* historian Chalmers Roberts. He was also associate editor.

Seib was a reporter in 1942 on the *Allentown Chronicle* (Pennsylvania) and with the Associated Press from 1944 to 1945. He worked with the *Philadelphia Record* for a year before going to the International News Service in 1946. Six years later, Seib was with the Gannett News Service in Washington.

His association with the *Washington Star* started in 1954, and during the last six years of his 20-year tour on the *Star*, he was its managing editor.

Seib wrote *The Woods* in 1971.

**SEIGENTHALER, John L.** (1927– )
John Seigenthaler has spent his newspaper lifetime on the *Nashville Tennessean*, where he started as a staff member in 1949. By 1962, he was editor and, since 1973, he has been publisher. He became president of the operations in 1979.

During those years, Seigenthaler occupied nearly every news and editorial position on the newspaper. Under his leadership, the *Tennessean* won many national awards, including a Pulitzer Prize and Sigma Delta Chi and National Headliner awards. Its series on the Ku Klux Klan was a runner-up for the Pulitzer Prize.

Seigenthaler has won the Sidney Hillman Prize for courage in publishing and the National Headliner Award for investigative reporting, among others. For a brief time, he was an administrative assistant to Attorney General Robert Kennedy. On the 1961 Freedom Rides he represented the Kennedy Administration, and was attacked and injured by a mob of whites.

The *Tennessean* is now owned by the Gannett Company, which started *USA Today* in 1982. Seigenthaler was given the additional assignment as editorial director for this nationally circulated newspaper and commutes weekly from Nashville to the Northern Virginia headquarters of *USA Today*. He has co-authored *Search for Justice* and *An Honorable Profession*. His son, Michael, is a reporter and an anchor on Nashville station WSMV-TV.

**SELDES, Gilbert** (1893–1970)
Gilbert Seldes left his mark on journalism through his comments in newspapers, magazines, and especially in his many books. Before World War I, which he covered as a reporter, he was a music critic on the

*Philadelphia Evening Ledger* (Pennsylvania). He later worked in Washington. For a time he was an associate editor of *Collier's*, and for several years managing editor and drama critic for *Dial* magazine. He also wrote for the *New York Evening Graphic* and for a number of years was a columnist with the *New York Journal*.

Seldes joined CBS early in its television developmental years (1937–45). For a few years, he also taught at the Annenberg School of Communications at the University of Pennsylvania.

Seldes' books include *Seven Lively Arts*; *The Stammering Century*; *The Movies and the Talkies*; *The Wings of the Eagle*; *The Years of the Locust*; *Mainline*; *Movies for the Millions*; *Your Money and Your Life*; *Proclaim Liberty*; *The Great Audience*; *Writing for Television*; *The Public Arts*; and many murder mysteries written under the pseudonym "Foster John."

**SELTZER, Louis Benson** (1897–1980)
Louis Seltzer and the *Cleveland Press* (Ohio) were media leaders for many years. At its peak, one of the nation's leading newspapers, the *Press* had been the first newspaper in what is today the Scripps-Howard Group.

Seltzer began as an office boy and later became a reporter on the *Cleveland Leader* in 1911. He then wrote ad copy for a year before obtaining a job with the *Cleveland News*; in 1916, he began his long association with the *Press*. He moved from reporter to editor and to editor-in-chief in 1928.

Seltzer's autobiography, *The Years Were Good*, recalls his long career in his native city of Cleveland. In this book, he wrote, "I wanted more than anything else in the world to be a reporter." *Life* magazine named him "Mr. Cleveland" in 1950. In addition to his writing for the *Press*, Seltzer wrote many magazine articles. He was active in several professional groups.

**SENGSTACKE, John Herman** (1912– )
John Sengstacke has been with the Robert S. Abbott Publishing Co., the firm that prints the *Chicago Defender* and the *Tri-State Defender*, since 1934. He is also involved with other publishing projects, along with life insurance and savings and loan businesses.

Sengstacke has been called "the father of the modern Negro press." When he took over the firm from his uncle, Robert S. Abbott, Sengstacke changed the *Defender* to a daily, and acquired other newspapers across the country.

He became the first Black to be named to the American Society of Newspaper Editors' board of directors, in 1970. He has been honored by the National Urban League and his alma mater, Hampton Institute. He also received a media award from the American Jewish Committee.

**SEVAREID, Arnold Eric** (1912– )
Eric Sevareid considered that his primary function in the media world was to raise questions. And he did, until his retirement in 1977. After his high school graduation he said he had "learned nothing except how to put the school paper to press." He began his newspaper work as a copyboy on the

*Minneapolis Journal* (Minnesota) in 1931, and later, at the University of Minnesota, he was active in all the liberal causes on the campus.

By 1938, Sevareid was with the Paris edition of the *New York Herald Tribune*, working also as night editor for the United Press. Edward R. Murrow, then in London, hired Sevareid in 1939 and he continued with the network until his retirement. Since 1977, he has been a CBS consultant and appears from time to time to comment on topics of the day.

In 1940, Sevareid was in Washington and later covered stories in Mexico and Brazil; by 1943, he was in China before becoming a war reporter in the European Theater. After World War II, Sevareid covered the United Nations before returning to New York and, later, Washington. He became part of the CBS Evening News in 1964 with Walter Cronkite. He continued to consider himself a writer rather than a performer.

Sevareid wrote *Canoeing with the Cree*; *This Is Eric Sevareid*; *Not So Wild a Dream*; *One Ear*; and *Small Sounds in the Night*. He edited *Candidates*, in 1960.

He has won a Page One Award from the New York Newspaper Guild for an article in *Look*, "The Final Troubled Hours of Adlai Stevenson," and the George Foster Peabody award on three occasions for his interpretation of the news. Other honors have included the du Pont, Overseas Press Club, Headliner, George Polk Memorial, and Sidney Hillman Foundation awards. The University of Minnesota gave him its Outstanding Achievement Award. In 1983 he received the National Press Club's Fourth Estate Award for lifetime contribution to American journalism.

**SHAWN, William** (1907– )

In 1983, William Shawn observed his 50th year with *The New Yorker*. He has been the editor of this weekly magazine, following Harold Ross who founded the publication, since 1952. As one writer noted, Ross had a vision for *The New Yorker*; Shawn has translated that vision into reality.

Shawn discussed the situation with *Women's Wear Daily* in 1968 in one of his rare interviews. He noted that editorial content had changed, such as the fiction; "but from the beginning it [*The New Yorker*] has had certain characteristics—as close an approximation of objectivity as we could humanly manage, straightforwardness, thoroughness, fairness, clarity, truthfulness, and accuracy."

"Our comic drawings now contain much more social and political content than they used to," Shawn added. Like Ross, Shawn wants a great magazine. He told a Dutch magazine, *Hollands Diep*, interviewer in 1976 that he and Ross agreed that they "never thought about how many people were interested in what we published. . . . We published what pleased us and we disregarded what it was fashionable to be interested in."

Shawn began his career on the *Las Vegas Optic* in 1928. He was there for less than a year before he became the photo editor for *International Illustrated News* in Chicago. Then he was hired in 1933 by Ross for *The New Yorker*.

*Newsweek*, in 1983, raised the question of Shawn's successor. "Shawn is the resident genius of the place, and it is difficult to imagine *The New*

*Yorker* without him," the magazine noted. Some speculate that Shawn does not want to retire, even at over 75. The magazine has been his life since 1933. And the publication has been profitable since 1928.

**SHEEHAN, Neil** (1936– )
Neil Sheehan joined the *New York Times* staff in 1964 and made news himself when he became involved with the newspaper's publication of the Pentagon Papers.

After serving in the Army, Sheehan worked for the United Press International in 1962, covering the Vietnam War; two years later, he switched to the *Times.*

David Halberstam, who also covered the Vietnam War, wrote that "Sheehan had been one of the early reporters whose pessimistic view of the war had angered American officials." In 1971, Sheehan's review of 33 books concerning this conflict occupied an entire *Times Book Review* issue. Sheehan just missed winning a Pulitzer Prize for his work in Vietnam.

Sheehan has been given many awards, including the Louis M. Lyons Award for conscience and integrity in journalism; the Poor Richard and Overseas Press Club honors; and the Drew Pearson citation for investigative reporting. In 1972, Sheehan won awards from Columbia University, the Sidney Hillman Foundation, the Overseas Press Club, and Sigma Delta Chi. He was a Guggenheim fellow, 1973–74, and an Adlai Stevenson fellow, 1973–75. He has also been honored by the Lehrman Institute and the Rockefeller Foundation.

Sheehan wrote the *Arnheiter Affair* and contributed to *The Pentagon Papers.*

**SHEPLEY, James Robinson** (1917– )
From 1969 to 1980, James Shepley was president of Time Inc. In 1937, he was a correspondent for the *Pittsburgh Press* and soon became a United Press International staffer in Pennsylvania and Washington. He joined *Time* magazine in 1942.

Shepley covered World War II in the Pacific area for *Time* and *Life* magazines. Later, he was a foreign policy correspondent for *Time.* He was an assistant publisher of *Life* from 1960 to 1963; publisher of *Fortune* from 1964 to 1967; and publisher of *Time* from 1967 to 1969, all positions that prepared him for the top corporation position.

Shepley co-authored *The Hydrogen Bomb.*

**SHERMAN, William S.** (1946– )
Before William Sherman was an investigative reporter for the *New York Daily News*, he worked on the *Boston Globe* and the *Village Voice* (New York). His investigative skills were well demonstrated in the Maryland shooting of George Wallace. Rather than stay around the scene, Sherman went directly to Milwaukee and learned the background of the young attacker. He once said, "If you push, you get results. But you have to do it

quietly. I don't believe in browbeating people. I'm just pleasantly persistent."

Another example occurred when, posing as a Medicaid patient, Sherman investigated a Queens, New York medical center. In his story he revealed considerable fraud, and secured several indictments.

Sherman's reporting has brought him many awards, including the George Polk Memorial and the Page One Award in 1973; other Page One citations for crusading journalism in 1974 and 1976; and recognition from the Silurians, Sigma Delta Chi, and the Women's Press Club. He won the Pulitzer Prize in 1974.

**SHERROD, Blackie** ( – )

An "almost legendary sports columnist," Blackie Sherrod switched from his position with the *Dallas Times Herald* to the *Dallas Morning News* in late 1983.

*Time* magazine noted that Sherrod worked in "a town where sports coverage can account for circulation gains or losses in the tens of thousands." The Dallas newspapers have been engaged in such a struggle for years.

Sherrod reportedly will receive $750,000 for his new five-year contract with the *Morning News*, according to *Time.*

**SHERROD, Robert Lee** (1909– )

When the *Saturday Evening Post* was fighting for its survival, Robert Sherrod was appointed its editor in 1962, after serving for a decade on its staff. In 1952, he was the Far East correspondent, in 1955, the managing editor, and in 1962, the editor. At that time, the *Post* outsold both *Life* and *Look* on the newsstands.

Sherrod began as a reporter in 1929 on the *Atlanta Constitution* and worked for the *Palm Beach Daily News* (Florida), the *Hampton Chronicle* (New York), and the *New York Herald Tribune* before he turned to magazine work.

He joined *Time* and *Life* magazines as a Washington correspondent in 1935 and served in World War II in the Pacific. In 1966 he returned as a contract writer for *Life.*

Both the Headliner and Overseas Press clubs have honored him. He has also received the Benjamin Franklin Award. His books include *Tarawa: The Story of a Battle*; *On to Westward: War in the Central Pacific*; and the text for *Life's Picture History of World War II.* He co-authored *Apollo Expeditions to the Moon.*

**SHIRER, William Lawrence** (1904– )

William Shirer is best remembered for such books as *Berlin Diary* and *The Rise and Fall of the Third Reich.* However, he began in newspaper work and later spent many years with CBS.

In 1925, Shirer was a European correspondent for the *Chicago Tribune* on its Paris edition, and he also worked for the *New York Herald*'s Paris edition. From 1934 to 1937, he worked for the Hearst-owned Universal News Service.

Edward R. Murrow hired Shirer to work for CBS, where he remained until he became a commentator on the Mutual Broadcasting System network in 1947. Shirer and Murrow disagreed as to how much personal opinion Shirer could use in his comments, so Shirer went to Mutual. Before that, Shirer reported such major events as the Nuremberg trials and the founding of the United Nations.

Shirer shared a Headliner Club award in 1938 for the reporting of the Austrian Anschluss. He later won a Peabody award for interpretation of the news and a Sidney Hillman Foundation award for his book, *The Rise and Fall of the Third Reich*. Other books include *End of a Berlin Diary*; *The Traitor*; *Midcentury Journey: The Western World through Years of Conflict*; *Stranger Come Home*; *The Challenge of Scandinavia*; *The Consul's Wife*; *The Rise and Fall of Adolf Hitler*; *The Sinking of the Bismarck*; *The Collapse of the Third Republic*; *20th Century Journal*; and *Gandhi—a Memoir*. He also contributed to magazines and was popular on the lecture circuit.

**SHOEMAKER, Vaughn** (1902– )
From 1930 to 1971, Vaughn Shoemaker's editorial cartoons appeared in newspapers across America; he retired in 1971. For a time (1927–42), Shoemaker taught at the Chicago Academy of Fine Arts, where many top cartoonists have studied. Frederick Opper created the "John Public" character; Shoemaker added the middle initial, "John Q. Public."

Shoemaker joined the *Chicago Daily News* staff in 1922 and from 1925 to 1952 was its chief cartoonist. He next spent five years with the *New York Herald Tribune* before returning to Chicago with the *American*, which later became *Today*; he was with this paper from 1961 to 1971.

Shoemaker won a Pulitzer Prize in 1938 and again in 1947. He has also won the National Headliner Award; several National Safety Council honors; Freedoms Foundation Gold medals from 1949 through 1969; and many other awards. His books have "dated titles," such as 1938 *A.D.*; 1939 *A.D.*; 1940 *A.D.*; '41 *and* '42 *A.D.*; '43 *and* '44 *A.D.*; '45 *and* '46 *A.D.*, except *The Best of Shoemaker Cartoons*. His works are in permanent collections in libraries across America and some have been displayed in galleries and on television shows.

**SIDEY, Hugh** (1927– )
During his career as *Time* magazine's Washington staffer, Hugh Sidey has covered seven presidents. Sidey, born in Iowa, listened to sportscaster "Dutch" Reagan, who eventually became one of the seven, when he reported Big Ten football games.

Sidey worked on the *Adair County Free Press* and the *Nonpariel* in Iowa before working from 1951 to 1955 with the *Omaha World-Herald*. He joined *Life* in 1955, and in 1958 switched to *Time*. For nearly a decade, he was chief of the magazine's Washington Bureau and, since 1978, a contributing editor.

Sidey traveled with Johnson to the Vietnam War front; he reported

Nixon's China trip; and he accompanied Ford and Carter on their travels around the world. In addition to being a panelist on the weekly television talk show, "Agronsky & Company," Sidey has written the following books: *John F. Kennedy, President*; *A Very Personal Presidency, Lyndon Johnson in the White House*; *These United States*; and *Portrait of a President*. Earlier, Sidey co-authored *1,000 Ideas for Better News Pictures*.

**SILK, George** (1916– )
A New Zealander, George Silk has won many awards in America for outstanding photography. Early in World War II, Silk was an official photographer with the Australia Infantry Forces in the Middle East and later in New Guinea.

Silk joined *Life* in 1943, remaining with the magazine for three decades. He covered the latter part of World War II for *Life* and, since 1973, has been a free-lance photographer.

Silk was named Photographer of the Year in 1960. He has won other such awards since. The American Society of Magazine Photographers gave him its memorial award in 1962. His pictures have appeared in encyclopedias and in fine arts exhibits.

**SILVERMAN, Fred** (1937– )
The only man to direct programming on all three major networks—ABC, CBS, and NBC—Fred Silverman, in 1983, became his own independent producer of television shows. However, he may have gained more public recognition through comments made by Johnny Carson while Silverman was his boss on NBC.

Silverman was with WGN-TV in Chicago before becoming an executive with WPIX-TV in New York. Later, he joined CBS-TV as director of daytime programs, and from 1970 to 1975, he was vice-president for programs. From 1975 to 1978 he was president of ABC Entertainment; from 1978 to 1981, he was president of NBC at a reported million dollars a year salary. As an independent film producer, he has promoted, among other shows, "Thicke of the Night," a talk show he set against "Johnny Carson."

Writing in *Advertising Age*, Diane Mermigas noted that Silverman had changed. Still the "persistent warrior" who had mellowed some, Silverman said "those executive jobs are just too time-consuming."

Silverman has been described as "aggressive, unorthodox and fiercely competitive" and, by another reporter, as having "the build of a football guard and the manner of a comedian." He moved ABC from third to top place, and through his career he has found success in such shows as "All in the Family" and its spinoffs "Maude" and "The Jeffersons"; "M*A*S*H"; "Soap"; "Charlie's Angels"; "Kojak"; "Happy Days"; "Three's Company"; and others. Silverman also lists several "he'd just as soon forget," including "Pink Lady"; "Supertrain"; and "Me and the Chimp."

Garb Deeb, in early 1984, called Silverman "the most famous executive in TV history," adding, "his name became a genuine household word and his face graced the covers of national magazines, including *Newsweek*."

**SIMONS, Howard** (1929– )
Science writing has occupied much of Howard Simons' time since he worked for Science Service in Washington from 1954 to 1959. After two years of free-lance work, Simons then became the American correspondent for the London-based *New Scientist.*

In 1961, Simons joined the *Washington Post.* A decade later he was the managing editor. Before that he served in the Army during the Korean War and later was a visiting professor at Syracuse University and an intellectual interchange scholar in Japan.

Simons has won several awards for his reporting, including the AAAS/ Westinghouse Electric Corp. Science Writing Award on two occasions, as well as the Raymond Clapper Journalism Award. He has written *Simons' List Book* and *Business and Media.* He co-authored *The Media and the Law.*

**SINGLETON, Donald Edward** (1936– )
Since 1964, Donald Singleton has been a feature writer for the *New York Daily News.* Before that, he worked on the *Dover Advance* (New Jersey), starting in 1959, the *Morristown Daily Record* in 1961, and the *Newark Evening News* in 1963.

The New York Council of Civic Affairs gave Singleton its Public Service Award in 1967. The Women's Press Club cited his work in 1970 and 1979, and the Newspaper Guild gave him its Heywood Broun Medal. He has also been honored by the Public Relations Society of America, the American Bar Association, and the New York Newspaper Reporters Association.

**SISKEL, Gene** (1946– )
Gene Siskel joined the *Chicago Tribune* staff in 1969, and since 1974, he also has served as movie critic for WBBM-TV. With Roger Ebert of the *Chicago Sun-Times,* Siskel produced the "Sneak Previews" show first for the Public Broadcasting Service and, more recently, for commercial television.

Siskel has spent his life in Chicago. He told *Advertising Age* in 1983 that "this is the most livable big city I've been around."

He was a CORO Foundation fellow in 1968.

**SMITH, Harrison** (1888–1971)
The *Saturday Review,* in reporting Harrison Smith's death, noted he "was enormously open-hearted, open-minded, and an excellent judge of good, new writing."

Smith was involved in publishing in 1911, as editor and book reviewer of *Century* magazine. For another two years he was a salesman for the Century Company before starting his own firm. He worked for several businesses before 1917, when he represented the *New York Times* in Russia.

His career with *Saturday Review* began in 1938, when he became the publisher. He was instrumental in adding Norman Cousins, Mason Brown, Bennett Cerf, Henry Canby, William Rose Benet, and others to the staff, making the magazine one of the nation's leading literary publications.

He edited one book, *From Main Street to Stockholm*, which included letters from his close friend, Sinclair Lewis. A sailing buff, he was considered "the office optimist" by his colleagues.

**SMITH, Hazel** (1914?– )
As editor of a small-town Mississippi newspaper, Hazel Brannon Smith was the first woman to win the Pulitzer Prize for editorial writing, an honor she received in 1964 for her comments on civil rights.

She began after high school as a writer of personal items on the weekly *Etowah Observer* (Alabama). She continued her journalism interest at the University of Alabama, where she worked on the campus newspaper. Borrowing money to buy the *Durant News*, she made the newspaper profitable by focusing on local coverage. She purchased the *Lexington Advertiser* in 1943, and in 1955–56, the *Flora Banner County Outlook* and *Jackson Northside Reporter*, all in Mississippi. She later became involved in a libel suit with a local sheriff who had shot a young Black man. But when she started to focus more on the civil rights movement, she lost many advertisers and eventually suffered financial setbacks.

Smith then went on a nationwide speaking tour to earn funds to continue. She once told the American Newspaper Women's Club in Washington, "You don't have to have a sheet to belong to the Klan. It's as much a state of mind as anything else." Her editorial offices were once fire-bombed.

In 1964, she was the "Mississippi Woman of the Year" by the vote of media leaders in the state. She was also the "Woman of Conscience," an award from the National Council of Women of the United States, and a documentary film, "An Independent Voice," was made of her career. She is past-president of the Mississippi Press Association and has won many other awards, including the Lovejoy and Theta Sigma Phi and the Golden Quill of the International Conference of Weekly Newspaper Editors.

Smith assisted with the editing of the *Baptist Observer*, a monthly newspaper for the largest Negro Baptist association in her home state.

**SMITH, Hedrick Laurence** (1933– )
After a 1959–62 tour with the United Press International in Minneapolis, Nashville, and Atlanta, Hedrick Smith joined the *New York Times*. The next year he was in Vietnam, before the *Times* sent him to the Middle East and Cairo from 1964 to 1966.

Smith served two tours in Washington as the *Times'* diplomatic news correspondent, 1962–64 and 1966–71, before going to Moscow as bureau chief, 1971–74. He returned as deputy national editor in 1976 and soon moved to the Washington Bureau where he was chief until 1979. Since 1980, he has been the newspaper's chief Washington correspondent.

Smith won the Pulitzer Prize in 1974 for his international reporting from Moscow and Eastern Europe. From 1969 to 1970, he was a Nieman scholar at Harvard.

He wrote *The Russians*, which won an Overseas Press Club award in 1976. He also wrote *Reagan The Man, The President* and co-authored *The Pentagon Papers*, which won a 1972 Pulitzer Prize.

**SMITH, Howard K.** (1914– )

Howard K. Smith, described as "one of television's most honored correspondents," has won all the major awards in the broadcasting medium. He has also been termed "the most outspoken and uncompromising of the network television news commentators."

Smith, recipient of more than a dozen honorary degrees, began as a reviewer of foreign dispatches for the *New Orleans Item-Tribune* (Louisiana) in the mid-Thirties. He studied in Europe and visited there frequently. In 1939, he was a United Press correspondent in London, and in 1941, he was with CBS in Berlin, working for *Time* and *Life* magazines as well. He had been a Rhodes Scholar at Oxford before the war.

After World War II, Smith covered the Nuremberg trial; he remained in Europe until he joined the Washington Bureau in 1957. CBS made him general manager in 1961. He resigned from CBS after a disagreement with the network's policy for commentators. From 1962 to 1979, Smith was news analyst for the ABC Network and, at times, he worked with Harry Reasoner on the "Evening News."

Although Smith was the first broadcast journalist to have an exclusive interview with President Richard Nixon, he was also the first to call for the President's resignation or impeachment. He moderated the first Kennedy–Nixon debate in 1960, and the Carter–Reagan debate in 1980.

Among Smith's many awards are the Overseas Press Club's honor on three occasions; the du Pont twice; and the Sigma Delta Chi, the Sylvania, the Peabody, the Emmy. He also won a special award from the George Polk Memorial for his documentary, "The Population Explosion." In 1971, the University of Missouri gave him its Journalism Medal, and later he received the Lowell Thomas citation.

Among his books are *Last Train from Berlin*; *The State of Europe*; and *Washington, D.C.: The Story of Our Nation's Capital.* He has moderated or narrated many radio and television productions. He once told an interviewer, "I've been close to a lot of drama in my life."

**SMITH, Merriman** (1913–1970)

For distinguished reporting of national affairs, the assassination of John F. Kennedy, Merriman Smith won the 1964 Pulitzer Prize. Smith was a correspondent for the United Press International from 1941 until his death.

While in college, in 1934, Smith worked for the *Atlanta Journal Sunday Magazine* (Georgia). In 1935, he was with the *Athens Daily Times* (Georgia). He soon joined the United Press and eventually moved to its Washington Bureau.

Smith covered many major events in the nation's history and traveled widely. He accompanied Franklin D. Roosevelt on 70,000 miles of his wartime travels. He was with Eisenhower in Korea, and he was with Truman when he fired MacArthur at Wake Island. He also traveled with Kennedy when the President met with Charles de Gaulle in France.

Smith was called the "abrasive dean of White House correspondents"; he covered six presidents, and ended many presidential press conferences with "Thank You, Mr. President," a right he had as the senior correspondent.

Among his books are *Thank You, Mr. President*; *A President Is Many Men*; *Meet Mr. Eisenhower*; *A President's Odyssey*; and *The Good New Days: A Not Entirely Relevant Study of Native Habits and Customs in Modern Washington*. He also wrote for magazines and appeared on television talk shows. In 1963, the University of Missouri gave him its Journalism Medal. He was president of the White House Correspondents Association and for years was one of the nation's best-known correspondents.

**SMITH, Red (Walter Wellesley)** (1905–1982)
For more than half a century, Red Smith wrote about sports. After reporting for the *Milwaukee Sentinel* (Wisconsin), 1927–28 and being a copyeditor and sportswriter on the *St. Louis Star* (Missouri) 1928–36, he spent a longer time, 1936–45, with the *Philadelphia Record* (Pennsylvania).

Sports editor Stanley Woodward, of the *New York Herald Tribune*, was so impressed with Smith's writing on the *Record* that he hired him. He described Smith as having "the best attributes of the 'gee whiz' and 'aw nuts' schools" of writing.

Smith stayed with the *Herald Tribune* until 1966, when he left to work on the soon-to-die *World-Journal-Tribune* for a year. In 1971, he joined the *New York Times* where he remained until his death. He died four days after writing his final column. His syndicated column had been used by more than 500 newspapers.

Once asked to offer advice to would-be sportswriters, Smith said: "Loving sports would be the very least recommendation . . . he should really feel he wants to be a newspaperman. Then I would suggest he get as much formal education as possible, not necessarily in journalism, but reading foreign languages, philosophy, history, economics, sociology. Then go out and hound a city editor for a job, and work on the local side of the paper under the discipline of a city desk. Learn what the newspaper business is all about. After that, it's easy to get a transfer into sports."

Smith won the Pulitzer Prize in 1976 for his "Sports of the Times" column. The University of Missouri honored him with its Journalism Medal the same year. He wrote *Out of the Red* and *Views of Sports*, as well as many magazine articles.

According to Martin F. Nolan, writing in the *Washington Journalism Review*, Smith "was not facile, but he was generous." Smith said of writing, "It's simple. You just sit there at the typewriter until the drops of blood ooze from your forehead." A Red Smith Lecture Series in Journalism has been established at the University of Notre Dame, his alma mater. James Reston, of the *Times*, gave the first lecture in 1983. A Notre Dame professor, Robert Schmuhl, said "The work of Red Smith—his mastery of the language along with his intelligence and sensitivity—should be a model for anyone entering journalism."

**SNYDER, Tom** (1936– )
Tom Snyder has received many labels during his broadcasting career, which began with a part-time job on Milwaukee radio station WRIT and

later with Philadelphia's KYW-TV in 1965. Also in 1965, he moved to KNBC-TV in Los Angeles where he took the station to No. 1 position in news coverage.

NBC hired Snyder in the early seventies and he hosted the "Tomorrow Show" until it was canceled in 1981. During that time he was also with NBC "Update," and he anchored the network's "Sunday Night News" and many specials. While with WNBC-TV in New York, his producer said Snyder could "edit his copy as he read it, almost use it as notes." He won an Emmy Award in 1974 for his work on the "Tomorrow Show."

In 1983, Snyder joined WABC-TV in New York, after a nine-month absence from the air. Today he is back in local television, as he had been in Los Angeles. He has developed a reputation for being "brash" and "unpredictable," and a promotional poster for the ABC show listed Snyder as being "charming, exciting, caustic, informed, controversial, involved, emotional, New York."

Snyder once told *Newsweek* that "I'm a commodity. I understand that."

**SOGLOW, Otto** (1900–1973)

Otto Soglow is remembered by long-time magazine readers for "The Little King," a cartoon character he created in the late Twenties. He began his cartooning career in 1925 and his works appeared in many publications, including *Life*, *Judge*, *Collier's*, and *Harper's Bazaar* and especially *The New Yorker*.

Soglow's "Little King" appeared in the *New York World* from 1925 to 1926, before it was syndicated by King Features from 1933 to 1975. He won a Reuben award for outstanding cartoonist of the year from the National Cartoonists Society in 1967.

Among his books are *Pretty Pictures*; *Everything's Rosy*; *The Little King*; and *Wasn't the Depression Terrible?*

**SOTH, Lauren Kephart** (1910– )

From 1947 to 1974, Lauren Soth worked for the *Des Moines Register* and *Tribune* (Iowa), first as an editorial writer and later as editor of the daily's editorial pages. He gained international fame through his successful efforts to bring Nikita Khrushchev to America, especially to Iowa.

Soth received the Pulitzer Prize in editorial writing in 1956, primarily for his suggestion that American and Soviet agricultural delegations exchange visits. In 1955, he visited the Soviet Union and earlier toured Europe.

Before joining the *Register* and *Tribune*, Soth taught at Iowa State University. In his youth, he had been a printer's devil on the *Holstein Advance* and later held federal appointments with the Department of Agriculture and Office of Price Administration before World War II Army service.

In addition to the Pulitzer Prize, Soth won the Headliner Club Award and was honored by the alumni association of Iowa State, as well as many agricultural organizations. He has written *Farm Trouble*; *An Embarrassment of Plenty*; and *Agriculture in an Industrial Society*.

**SPEZZANO, Vincent Edward** (1926– )
For more than 20 years, Vincent Spezzano has been associated with the Gannett Company, Inc. He is president of the group's national daily *USA Today* and corporate senior vice-president for communications.

Spezzano's boss, Allen H. Neuharth, said the executive will "be highly mobile as he coordinates all communications and public relations activities of Gannett's newspaper, broadcasting, outdoor and other operations. No Gannett executive has a better overview of all the company's activities in these areas than does he."

Earlier, he worked as a reporter on the *Geneseo Livingston Republican* (New York) 1950–51, and the *Lynchburg News* (Virginia), 1951–54, where he won a Virginia Press Association reporting award. He spent a year with the *St. Louis Globe-Democrat* (Missouri) before he joined the Gannett *Rochester Times Union* (New York) in 1955. He held other positions with the firm before becoming president and publisher of Cape Publications, Inc., Cocoa, Florida, in 1975.

Other awards for Spezzano include the Citizen of the Year title in Rochester in 1960 and a public service reporting award from the American Political Science Association in 1963. He is past president of the International Newspaper Promotion Association.

He served in the Navy during World War II.

**SPINA, Anthony J.** (1920?– )
Anthony Spina has been a member of the *Detroit Free Press* staff as a photographer since 1946. During that time, he has won many awards and his photographs have been shown in one-man shows.

Spina won the Pulitzer Prize for 1968 as a member of the *Free Press* team for its coverage of the Detroit race riots. Spina has won nearly 500 other awards from national and international organizations, including the Gold Medallion from Pope John XXIII.

Among his books are *The Making of the Pope—Pope John XXIII*; *The Pope and the Council*; *This Was the President—John F. Kennedy*; *The Press Photographer*; and *From a Distant Country—Pope John Paul* 1979. His column on photography is syndicated through the Knight-Ridder Newspapers.

**SPINK Family**
From 1912 until his death, J.G. Taylor Spink (1888–1962) was associated with *The Sporting News* and its many related publications in St. Louis, Missouri. During World War II, Spink prepared a special serviceman's edition for the troops, for which he received a citation from President Harry Truman. He published a number of guide books and wrote one other book, *Judge Landis and 25 Years of Baseball.*

Charles C. J. Spink (1916– ) joined *The Sporting News* in 1939 and took over as publisher in 1962. Since 1978, he has been chairman of the board and the publication's editor.

Young Spink has been active in many St. Louis civic affairs, such as the St. Louis Symphony, the Botanical Gardens, the Municipal Opera, and the Media Club.

**SPIVAK, Lawrence Edmund** (1906– )
"Meet the Press" started on Mutual Broadcasting System radio in 1945 and, two years later, appeared on NBC Television. Lawrence Spivak was the promoter of this long-time Sunday interview program.

Before his entry into broadcasting, Spivak was associated with several magazines. First he was business manager of *Antiques*, in 1921, and at the same time a reporter on the *Boston American*. Nine years later, he was the assistant to the publisher of *Hunting and Fishing* and *National Sportsman* magazines. He joined the *American Mercury*, founded by H. L. Mencken and George Jean Nathan, as business manager in 1934. Later he served as publisher and finally as editor until 1950.

After the *Mercury* lost considerable money, Spivak sold it and, eventually, his interest in Mercury Publications, Inc. This firm was a pioneer in paperback books, publishing Ellery Queen's Mercury Library and other mysteries and detective, fantasy, and science fiction paperbacks.

"Meet the Press" started with Spivak as the permanent panelist and Martha Rountree as the moderator. In 1948, it was with NBC Television, which took over its ownership in 1955.

"Meet the Press" attracted many celebrities to its unrehearsed format, and Spivak became known for his probing questions. Guests, although never paid, welcomed the chance to appear. Spivak once explained this, saying, "Most men in public life feel they can answer all questions put to them in a press conference without difficulty—and generally, they are right."

Among his awards was one from the Boston Press Club in 1953 for being an outstanding, conscientious journalist. He won an Emmy and two Peabody awards, along with the University of Missouri Journalism Medal in 1973 for "Meet the Press." The American Jewish Committee and the Associated Press Broadcasters have also honored Spivak. In 1984 he was named to the Hall of Fame by the Washington chapter by Sigma Delta Chi for distinguished service.

**STAHL, Lesley R.** (1941– )
Lesley Stahl has been "nicknamed Brenda Starr by her CBS colleagues for her aggressiveness," according to Barbara Matusow's book *The Evening Stars*.

When Barbara Walters took over as co-anchor on the ABC Evening News in 1976, there were only a few women who were prominent on the air with networks. Stahl was one of these, along with Judy Woodruff, Ann Compton, and Cassie Mackin. By that time Stahl was with CBS News in Washington, on both radio and television.

In the mid-sixties, Stahl was an assistant to Mayor John Lindsay's speechwriter in New York City. Her next job was with NBC News before she became a producer and reporter on WHDH-TV in Boston from 1970 to 1972. Then she moved to CBS News in Washington, where she continues.

Matusow refers to Stahl's problem, faced by many in the industry, when it was announced that Dan Rather would replace Walter Cronkite. "It was hard to feel terrific about Dan at first because Roger [Mudd] was leaving," she said.

In a talk at Pennsylvania State University in mid-1983, Stahl warned students to "beware of easy and early success. In fact, hope that you aren't discovered for the first 10 years of your career . . . the word 'meteoric' also implies a burning out."

## STAHLMAN Family

E.B. Stahlman, Jr. (1898–1974) and James Geldes Stahlman (1893–1974) were long associated with the *Nashville Banner*. E.B. was executive vice-president and co-publisher of the *Banner* for many years. He also was president of the Southern Newspaper Publishers Association from 1946 to 1947.

James Stahlman was president and publisher of the *Banner* from 1930 to 1971. He served in the Army in World War I and with the Navy in World War II. He was president of the Inter-American Press Association, the Southern Press Association, and the American Press Association. He won two Freedoms Foundation Washington medals and the American Legion Fourth Estate Award.

He was active in civic affairs, including the Boy Scouts, Vanderbilt University, and other organizations.

## STANTON, Frank (1908– )

Dr. Frank Stanton was a psychologist and researcher before he entered broadcasting. He taught psychology at Ohio State University and the title of his doctoral dissertation was "A Critique of Present Methods and a New Plan for Studying Radio Listening Behavior." The CBS Network hired him for the summer of 1934, and he never returned to teach at Ohio State. While with CBS, he was also associated with Columbia and Princeton universities.

After four years with CBS, Stanton became the network's head of the research department. He also became vice-president and general manager, in 1945, and the next year, its president. During World War II, he was a consultant in the Office of War Information and with other federal agencies.

As an administrator, Stanton sought to diversify CBS. He created three divisions in 1951: Radio, television, and laboratories; for a time, the network owned the New York Yankees baseball team. He also helped to develop the CBS Vote Profile Analysis, a sampling technique. He called for Congress, the Supreme Court, and other federal agencies to open themselves to television and radio coverage.

As *The New Yorker* editorialized, Stanton was "one of the few men to achieve success despite the handicap of a Ph.D."

Stanton co-authored *Radio Research 1941*; *Radio Research 1942–43*; and

*Communications Research* 1948–49. He won his first Peabody Award for efforts that brought about the Kennedy–Nixon debates, and his second for bettering international understanding. He also won the New York City Gold Medal and the *Printer's Ink* Gold Medal. The Radio Television News Directors Association gave him its distinguished service award.

**STAUFFER Family**

In 1906, Oscar Stauffer (1886–1980) was a reporter on the *Emporia Gazette* in Kansas, and in 1910, he was with the *Kansas City Star.* He returned to Kansas in 1915 to work on the *Peabody Gazette*, the first newspaper he owned and edited. This started a chain of newspapers that, before his death, were located in Topeka, Arkansas City, Pittsburg, and Newton, Kansas; Marshall, Hannibal, Nevada and Independence, Missouri; Grand Island, Beatrice, and York, Nebraska; Brookings, South Dakota; Glenwood Springs, Colorado; Hillsdale, Michigan; and Shawnee, Oklahoma. The group also owns radio and television stations in five states. In 1977, the University of Missouri awarded him its Journalism Medal.

His son, Stanley Howard Stauffer, (1920– ), who had worked on the *Topeka State Journal*, *Santa Maria Times* (California), and the *Denver Post* (Colorado), and for the Associated Press, became executive vice-president of Stauffer Publications, Inc., in 1955. In 1969, he became president of Stauffer Communications. He has been active in many professional organizations; he once served as president of the Kansas Press Association.

He served in the Air Force during World War II.

**STEELE, James Bruce, Jr.** (1943– )

Associations with the *Kansas City Star* from 1962 to 1967 and then with the Laborers' International Union in Washington for three years in information helped prepare James Steele, Jr. for his later work.

In 1970, he joined the *Philadelphia Inquirer* and worked on urban affairs and investigative reporting assignments.

With colleague Donald L. Bartlett, Steele examined 20,000 tax liens filed by the Internal Revenue Service. They won the Pulitzer Prize for this in 1974 by showing how the IRS had failed to collect billions of dollars due the government. James H. Dygert referred to these two men as "perhaps the most systematic and thorough investigative reporters in the United States today."

"These men" have also probed the oil companies and American foreign aid programs. They won the Heywood Broun award for public interest reporting.

Steele once said, "There is an incredible amount of information in the public record. The bad news is that it's not all in one place." He and Bartlett have turned to computers to assist in their research.

He co-authored a biography on Howard Hughes, titled *Empire.* In addition to the Pulitzer Prize and Broun award, he has won two George Polk Memorial awards; the Sigma Delta Chi, American Bar Association, and Sidney Hillman awards; and for his business reporting, the John

Hancock Award and the University of Missouri Business Journalism citation.

**STEICHEN, Edward** (1879–1973)
When he was one year old, Edward Steichen was brought to America from Luxembourg. Later he was "among the first to recognize the possibilities of the new photography," and from 1923 to 1938, he served as the chief photographer for the Condé Nast Publications. During World War II, he was a Navy combat photographer.

Steichen was interested in painting and the cross-breeding of flowers. He was director of the Department of Photography for the Museum of Modern Art in New York City, 1947–62; from 1962 until his death, he was director emeritus. He prepared several murals in New York.

In addition to many honorary degrees, he was cited by *Camera* and *Photography* magazines. The Photography Society of America, the Royal Photography Society of England, and the American Society of Magazine Photographers are among other groups that have honored Steichen. He received the nation's highest civilian award, the Presidential Medal of Freedom. He also was honored by France and Luxembourg.

In 1963 he wrote *A Life in Photography* and edited *Sandburg Photographers View Carl Sandburg.*

**STEIG, William** (1907– )
For more than half a century, William Steig has been a humorist cartoonist and an illustrator, with many of his works appearing in *The New Yorker*. His books have won many awards in the children field, including the Christopher, Newbery, and Caldecott.

According to a 1979 interview with *Publishers Weekly*, "Steig's work has moved from more realistic, captioned cartoons to image-oriented, sometimes abstract lyrical drawings." Steig has said, "When you're young, you like being funny. When you're old, it seems a little pointless."

Steig feels he became a cartoonist in 1930 by accident, prompted by the need to help his family survive the Depression. Since that time he has published many books, mostly for children, and his cartoons and wood sculptures have been displayed in collections and exhibitions.

Among his books are *About People*; *The Lonely Ones*; *All Embarrassed*; *Small Fry*; *Persistent Faces*; *Till Death Do Us Part*; *The Agony in the Kindergarten*; *The Rejected Lovers*; *Dreams of Glory*; *Roland, the Minstrel Pig*; *The Bad Island*; *An Eye for Elephants*; *Amos and Boris*; *Male/Female*; *Dominic*; *The Real Thief*; *Farmer Palmer's Wagon Ride*; *Abel's Island*; *The Amazing Bone*; *Caleb and Kate*; *Tiffky Doofky*; *Drawings*; and *Corky Rises.*

**STEINEM, Gloria** (1934– )
Gloria Steinem, a leader in the feminist movement, has been a co-founder of two major magazines on today's scene, *New York*, in 1968, and *Ms.*, in 1971.

Before her magazine work with these two, Steinem was with *Help!*, a humor publication, *Esquire*, and *Show*. In 1968, she wrote an exposé of life as a Playboy Bunny for *Esquire*, having obtained a job as a Bunny in the

New York Playboy Club.

After completing her studies at Smith College, Steinem eventually became director of the Independent Research Service in Cambridge, Massachusetts. By 1960, she was in New York, writing for *Esquire*; her Bunny exposé gained her her first byline and led to other assignments from other leading periodicals.

In an interview for *New York* magazine with Mrs. Patricia Nixon, the President's wife dropped her reserve and told Steinem, "I've never had it easy. I'm not like all you . . . all those people who had it so easy." Her article on the women's liberation movement in 1968 won for Steinem a J. C. Penney–University of Missouri Journalism Award.

In 1983 she wrote a book, *Outrageous Acts and Everyday Rebellions*, a collection of her essays. She describes it as for all men and women "who dream of a justice that has yet to come and live on the edge of history." In a review of this book, Garrison Keillor noted that Steinem's "face is among the most famous American faces; her name is one that millions of people would think of first if you said 'feminism.'" She has worked for such personalities as Robert Kennedy, Shirley Chisholm, and Cesar Chavez in campaigns. In 1972, she was named *McCall's* Woman of the Year and was given the Ohio Governor's Award for Journalism. She has also been honored by the American Civil Liberties Union, and in 1982, was one of the Outstanding Women in Communications in New York. She has been involved in many civil rights and peace campaigns, along with her fight for women equality.

On her 50th birthday in 1984, some 750 persons gathered in New York for a benefit that helped the Ms. Foundation. *Newsweek* reported that she "functions more as a dashing role model, the adventurous aunt who inspires others to follow her off the high diving board."

Her other books are *The Beach Book* and *The Thousand Indias.*

**STERN, Carl Leonard** (1937– )

Although he trained for the law, Carl Stern has been associated with NBC News in Washington since 1967. He uses his training with NBC, serving as the network's law correspondent.

Stern has won Gold Gavel awards in 1969 and 1974, as well as the Peabody and Emmy awards in 1974.

**STEVENS, Edmund William** (1910– )

Before joining the *Christian Science Monitor* in 1939, Edmund Stevens held positions in Russia as a translator. He also worked for the *Manchester Guardian* in London in the Thirties.

With the *Christian Science Monitor*, Stevens covered the Finnish War, the invasion of Norway, the Italo-Greek war, and the Ethiopian war. He covered World War II and was the *Monitor*'s Moscow correspondent, 1946–49, before moving to the Rome Bureau.

Stevens worked for several periodicals from 1955 to the late Seventies, including *Look, Time, Life*, the *Saturday Evening Post*, and the *London Sunday Times*; he was also a syndicated columnist for *Newsday*, and an NBC News radio reporter in 1971.

Stevens won a Pulitzer Prize for international reporting in 1950. He won three Overseas Press Club awards as well as the George Polk Memorial Award.

Stevens has written *Russia Is No Riddle*; *This Is Russia Uncensored*; and *North Africa Powder Keg*. In comments with his listing in *Who's Who in America*, Stevens warns that "the clouds on the horizon are mushroom-shaped." He also wrote a series of 44 articles, "This Is Russia—Uncensored."

**STEWART, Marcus C., Sr.** (1905–1983)
One of the nation's leading Black newspaper publishers, Marcus Stewart was the first of his race to be admitted into the Indiana Journalism Hall of Fame.

Stewart was editor and publisher of the *Indianapolis Recorder* (Indiana), which was founded by his father, George P. Stewart, in 1895. His mother took over after the death of her husband, and in 1957 Marcus Stewart became the editor and publisher.

The first Dr. Martin Luther King Drum Major Award went to Stewart for his contributions to the field of human rights. In 1982, he was given the Indiana Christian Leadership Conference and Black Expo awards.

**STOLLEY, Richard B.** (1928– )
For more than 30 years, Richard Stolley has been associated with Time Inc. His current position as managing editor of *Life* followed eight years with *People*, which he served as the founding managing editor in 1974.

Stolley, early in his career, worked as a sports editor on his home-town *Pekin Daily Times* (Illinois) from 1944 to 1946, and then as a *Chicago Sun-Times* reporter in 1953, the same year he joined *Life*. With *Life* he served in bureaus in Europe, the Middle East, and Africa and in Atlanta and Los Angeles. He covered numerous assignments in the Pacific as well. He served in the Navy during World War II.

Northwestern University presented him its Alumni Merit Award in 1977.

**STONE, Isidor Feinstein** (1907– )
I.F. Stone began a long journalistic career as a reporter on the *Haddonfield Progress* (New Jersey) and later the *Press* there; between 1923 and 1933 he was with the *Camden Courier-Post* (New Jersey), the *Philadelphia Record* (Pennsylvania) and the *Inquirer*. In 1933, he joined the *New York Post*, where he remained until 1939. The next two years he was associate editor of *The Nation*, before moving to Washington as its correspondent.

For another decade Stone worked on *PM*, the *New York Star*, the *New York Post*, and the *Daily Compass*. Other than the *Post*, these newspapers had short lives. In 1953, he began his own *I.F. Stone's Bi-Weekly*, which he continued until 1971, serving as editor and publisher. Upon his retirement from this project he wrote, "The compulsion to cover the universe in four pages has become too heavy a burden."

Stone once told *Newsday* that he "thought for a time of teaching philosophy, but the smell of a newspaper shop was more enticing than the spinsterish atmosphere of a college faculty." He eventually became a Socialist and did publicity for Norman Thomas.

In his writings, Stone frequently made news of his own. After stopping the newsletter, he turned to the study of Ancient Greece. In 1983, he lectured at Harvard and Georgetown universities, and since 1975, he has been a distinguished scholar in residence at American University. *Newsweek* referred to "Izzy Stone" as the "godfather of New Left journalism." The *New York Times* once said Stone had "almost an owlish resemblance to Benjamin Franklin."

Stone won the George Polk Memorial Award in 1970 and, the next year, the Columbia University Journalism Award. His books include *The Court Disposes*; *Business as Usual: The First Years of Defense*; *Underground to Palestine*; *This Is Israel*; *The Hidden History of the Korean War*; *The Truman Era*; *The Haunted Fifties*; *In a Time of Torment*; *The Killings at Kent State*; *Polemics and Prophecies*; and *The Best of I.F. Stone's Weekly*.

**STONE, Marvin** (1924– )

After being with *U.S. News & World Report* for 16 years, Marvin Stone became the magazine's editor in 1976. Since that time he has made changes, but slowly so as not to upset readers.

In the early seventies, Stone turned *U.S. News* "to more photographs and drawings on the cover instead of headlines, and broadened its coverage to include education, arts, family and culture. It also added a letters to the editor column," according to an account in the *Washington Journalism Review* in early 1983.

In 1941, Stone was a reporter on the *Huntington Herald-Dispatch* (West Virginia), a newspaper he returned to after World War II service in the Navy. By 1949, he was a European correspondent for the International News Service, and from 1952 to 1958, he was its Far Eastern director.

By 1960, Stone had joined *U.S. News* as an associate editor. In 1966 he became general editor, in 1971 associate executive editor, and in 1973 executive editor.

Among his awards are the Columbia University Journalism 50th Anniversary Honor Award and the Marshall University Distinguished Alumnus Award. For four years, the Freedoms Foundation has recognized his work through awards.

He wrote one book, *Man in Space*.

**STORKE, Thomas M.** (1876–1971)

"I believe that the first obligation of a newspaper editor is to his community," said Thomas M. Storke, after 50 years as a California editor and publisher.

In 1898, Storke became a reporter on the *Santa Barbara Daily News*. Later he joined the *Morning Press* and eventually owned the *Independent* in 1901. He sold it eight years later to a utility interest that closed it to curb Storke's criticisms.

Storke acquired the *Daily News* in 1913 and spent the rest of his career with the merged *Daily News and Independent.* He later acquired the *Morning Press*, his last competitor, and the newspaper became the *News-Press.*

Storke was the Santa Barbara postmaster from 1914 to 1921 and served briefly in the Senate (1938–39). During the late Fifties, Storke exposed the activities of the John Birch Society in stories and editorials. For this, he won the Pulitzer Prize for editorial writing in 1962, along with the Lauterbach and Lovejoy awards. In 1966, he was given the University of Missouri Journalism Medal.

He wrote in *I Write for Freedom* "I have a keen sense of history. I have always, from the very beginning, had an awareness of who and what I was. . . . I have nothing but pity for the man who doesn't know where he should stand in any fight concerning the welfare of his nation."

**STOSSEL, John** (1947–    )
With a "lightning-rod personality and commitment," John Stossel has been with the ABC News network since 1981.

Mark Ribowsky, writing in *TV Guide* in 1983, noted how Stossel had moved from "consumer exposes to tough general investigative stories." Ribowsky added, "He is an earnest, efficient worker—very involved in the editing and writing of his 20/20 pieces. He projects a sensitive, soulful-eyed image."

Stossel began his television career at a Portland station in 1969 and moved to WCBS-TV in New York in 1973. While with CBS, he won a George Polk Memorial Award and Emmy awards for four straight years. He moved to ABC in 1981.

**STOWE, Leland** (1899–    )
Leland Stowe has had a varied journalistic career, starting on the *Worcester Telegram* in 1921 as a reporter and then moving to the *New York Herald* in 1922 and to the newspaper's Paris edition in 1926. He also worked for a time with Pathé News. He covered many major events for the *Herald Tribune* in the Thirties.

By 1939, Stowe was with the *Chicago Daily News* as a war correspondent in Europe. He was the first American correspondent to reach the Nazi–Soviet front lines in the Forties. He later became a commentator for ABC and the Mutual Broadcasting System, and by 1949 he was foreign editor of *The Reporter* magazine. Next he took a tour with Radio Free Europe in Munich and began his longest assignment, as a roving editor for *Reader's Digest*, where he worked from 1955 to 1976. During some of this time, he also was a journalism professor at the University of Michigan.

Stowe won a Pulitzer Prize in 1930 for his coverage of the Paris Reparations Commission. He won the University of Missouri Journalism Medal and the Sigma Delta Chi Award in the early Forties.

Among his books are *Nazi Means War*; *No Other Road to Freedom*; *They Shall Not Sleep*; *While Time Remains*; *Target You*; *Conquest by Terror*; *The Story of Satellite Europe*; and *Crusoe of Lonesome Lake.*

**STROUD, Joe Hinton** (1936– )
Joe Stroud began his newspaper career in his home state of Arkansas, working on the *Pine Bluff Commercial* from 1959 to 1960 and on the *Arkansas Gazette* from 1960 to 1964. He became editorial page editor of the *Winston-Salem Journal-Sentinel* (North Carolina) from 1964 to 1968 before joining the *Detroit Free Press* (Michigan).

On the *Free Press*, Stroud was associate editor by 1968 and editor by 1973. Since 1978, he has also been the senior vice-president.

He has been active in civic and religious areas, including the United Methodist Church Publication Board and the *Michigan Christian Advocate*. He also worked with the Detroit Symphony and other groups.

Stroud received the School Bell Award in both North Carolina and Michigan. He also won the William Allen White and Overseas Press Club awards, and he has been active in professional organizations.

**STROUT, Richard** (1898– )
At the age of 80, Richard Strout said, "If you live long enough, people confuse ability with longevity." For forty years Strout's comments have appeared in the *Christian Science Monitor* and in the *New Republic* column, "TRB From Washington."

He served in the Army during World War I and began work on a British newspaper, the *Sheffield Independent*, in 1919. Two years later he was with the *Boston Post* and that same year, 1921, he started his career with the *Christian Science Monitor*. He moved to Washington in 1925 as the *Monitor*'s representative. The *New Republic* column, where he has voiced his liberal political opinions, was his between 1944 and 1983, when he gave up the assignment.

Strout also wrote magazine articles that appeared in *The New Yorker* and *Reader's Digest*. He often voiced his views of the horror of warfare and the inefficiency of Congress and other governmental units. He covered many Congressional hearings, including Kefauver's crime study, Senator Joe McCarthy's hearings, and the U-2 spy episode; and he has covered every president since Warren Harding.

He co-authored *Farewell to Model T* and wrote *TRB: Views and Perspectives on the Presidency*.

Strout won a special Pulitzer citation in 1978 and the University of Missouri Journalism Medal in 1974, the same year he won the Sidney Hillman Foundation Award. He has also been honored by the National Press Club and Sigma Delta Chi and has received the George Polk Memorial Award.

**SUGAR, Bert R.** (1937– )
The *Ring* magazine has been Bert Sugar's project since he became its editor and publisher in 1979. Before that, Sugar worked with a number of advertising agencies in New York City.

Sugar's contacts with magazines began in 1970 when he was the president, publisher, and editor of Champion Sports Publishing Co. Three years later, he was editor-in-chief of *Argosy* and *Imported Car Performance* magazines, and after a year with an advertising agency, he again took over *The Ring* magazine in 1979. He has been active in sports as co-founder of the Black Athletes Hall of Fame. He established the Joe Lapcheck Award, and in 1968, he won the Media Award from *Media Scope*. He has also won other citations.

In addition to his magazine articles, Sugar has written many books, including *Sting Like a Bee*; *Inside Boxing*; *The Sports Collectors Bible*; *The Assassination Chain*; *The Horseplayer's Guide to Winning System*; *Who Was Harry Steinfeldt? And Other Trivia Questions*; *The Life and Times of Harry Houdini*; *Classic Baseball Cards*; *The Thrill of Victory*; *Hit the Sign and Win a Free Suit of Clothes from Harry Finkelstein*; *The Book of Sports Quotes*; *Collectibles: The Nostalgia Collectors Bible*; *The Ring Record Book*; *The Great Fights*; *Baseball Trivia*; and *The Pictorial History of Wrestling*.

**SULKIN, Sidney** (1918– )

Sidney Sulkin was with the Voice of America during World War II and in Europe with SHAEF in 1945. He was Scandinavian correspondent for CBS News from 1945 to 1947, before returning to America where he worked briefly on WCCO in Minneapolis before another tour with the Voice of America in Washington (1949–53). In Washington, he joined the National Issues Committee and then in 1955, the *Changing Times*, beginning a long association with its owners, the Kiplinger Washington Editors.

Sulkin has contributed short stories, poems, and articles to magazines and has written several books, including *The Family Man*; *Complete Planning for College*; and *Gate of Lions*, which won a poetry award in 1980. He also wrote one play, *The Other Side of Babylon*, and co-edited *For Your Freedom and Ours*.

**SULLIVAN, Edward Vincent** (1902–1974)

Ed Sullivan became well known as a New York newspaper columnist from 1928 until his death, and for the "Ed Sullivan Show," and its predecessor, "The Toast of the Town," from 1948 to 1971.

From his high school years on, Sullivan was an omnivorous reader, with a photographic memory that served him throughout his career. During these early years he wrote sports stories for the *Port Chester Daily Item*, 1918–19, and then joined the *Hartford Post*. In 1920, he was with the *New York Evening Mail*, the *World*, four years later, and then the *Morning Telegraph*.

Sullivan was associated with Bernarr Macfadden's *New York Graphic* from 1927 and 1929. He started as the tabloid's sports editor, but when Walter Winchell left to join the Hearst-owned *Daily Mirror*, Sullivan became the *Graphic*'s Broadway columnist. Through this column, which he took to the *Daily News* in 1932, Sullivan sponsored many benefit performances and variety shows.

That same year, 1932, Sullivan began his first radio show and eventually brought to the air such men as Irving Berlin, Jack Benny, George M. Cohan, Florenz Ziegfeld, and Jack Pearl. He had his "Ed Sullivan Entertains" radio show in 1942. During World War II, he staged benefit shows for the Army Emergency Relief and the Red Cross and also put on shows for wounded servicemen. He was cited on four occasions by the government for such events.

During one of the Harvest Moon Balls, sponsored by the *Daily News*, Sullivan's talents as the master of ceremonies were observed by a CBS executive. Shortly after that, he became the network's "Toast of the Town" master of ceremonies.

Sullivan had a "talent for spotting fresh personalities and brought many individuals to television"; these included the Beatles and Elvis Presley. In 1968, he was named Showman of the Century in the television industry.

**SULLIVAN, Walter Seagar, Jr.** (1918– )
As science editor for the *New York Times* since 1964, Walter Sullivan has been frequently cited for his outstanding writing.

Sullivan first joined the *Times* in 1940 as a copyboy. He later became a Far East correspondent and, from 1951 to 1952, covered the United Nations. After four years in Germany, he returned to New York and started his science editorship. He was chief science writer, then science news editor, and finally science editor. He served in the Navy during World War II and shortly after the conflict he returned to the *Times* and covered Admiral Richard Byrd's fourth expedition to Antarctica. Later he crossed the Gobi desert, went to Shanghai, and covered the Korean War.

Among his awards are the George Polk Memorial and three from the Westinghouse-AAAS group. The American Institute of Physics, the American Chemical Society, and the U.S. Steel Foundation have all honored his work. The American Society of Managing Editors and the National Association of Science Writers have also honored him.

His books include *Quest for a Continent*; *White Land of Adventure: The Story of the Antarctica* and *The Polar Regions*, both for children; *Assault on the Unknown: The International Geophysical Year*; *We Are Not Alone: The Search for Intelligent Life on Other Worlds*; *Scientists at Work: The Creative Process of Scientific Research*; *Continents in Motion*; and *Black Holes, the Edge of Space, the End of Time*. He edited *America's Race for the Moon*.

**SULZBERGER Family**
Adolph S. Ochs (1858–1935) moved from Chattanooga to New York in 1896 and acquired the ailing *New York Times*. Today his heirs direct the *Times* and their worth has been estimated between $100 to $200 million by *Quill* magazine; *Forbes*, in 1983, set it at $300 million, minimum. His descendants include Iphigene Ochs Sulzberger, Arthur O. Sulzberger, Marian Sulzberger Heiskell, Ruth Sulzberger Holmberg, and Judith Sulzberger Levinson.

In 1983, the New York Times Company's revenues passed the billion-dollar mark for the first time. In this year, the corporation owned thirty regional newspapers, four magazines, television stations and cable operations, and a book publishing firm. Arthur Ochs Sulzberger, the chairman, received the Parsons School of Design Award that year "as publisher of the newspaper most noted for its general excellence and far-flung influence. On this particular occasion we call attention to the leading role that the *New York Times* plays in both national and international fashion and to the worldwide recognition and respect accorded to it for the quality and authority of its fashion news reportage." This is merely one of numerous awards the *Times* has accumulated through the years.

Arthur Hays Sulzberger (1891–1968) was the *Times*' publisher from 1935 to 1961 and chairman of the board from 1957 to 1968. He was active in many associations. Iphigene Ochs became his wife in 1917 and they had four children, including Arthur Ochs Sulzberger (1926– ). Arthur Hays Sulzberger retired in 1961.

Iphigene Sulzberger (1917– ) was described by Dana Thomas as "the symbol that binds the past to the present, is the queen mother, proud, witty, exuberant." To her "nothing is impossible." For years, she sponsored the *Times*' College and School Service Division.

Arthur Ochs Sulzberger (1926– ), better known as "Punch," joined the *Times*' organization in 1951 and became president and publisher in 1963. Dana Thomas described him as "easy-going and low-keyed in his relationships; at the same time he can display a sharp independence, even ruthlessness in his decision-making." His 1962 experiment with a West Coast edition of the *Times* was not the most successful of the company's projects. Arthur Sulzberger served in the Marine Corps during World War II.

Arthur O. Sulzberger, Jr. has worked in many capacities with the organization, including advertising sales, Washington correspondent, reporting, and metropolitan desk editor.

**SWAYZE, John Cameron, Sr.** (1906– )

The "Camel News Caravan" went on the air over the NBC Network in 1949, with John Cameron Swayze as the announcer. As Al Westin wrote, Swayze's broadcast "was the first to recognize the need for its own film crews and a larger staff dedicated solely to television news."

Swayze began his career on the *Kansas City Journal Post* (Missouri) and as a news commentator on stations KMBC and WHB in the thirties. By 1940, he was a member of the news staff of KMCC, and in 1946, news and special events director for NBC in Hollywood.

By 1947, Swayze was with NBC in New York as radio and television commentator, a position he held until 1956. He is better known to today's television viewers for his Timex watch commercials.

In 1979, he wrote *The Art of Living*.

**SWEET, John Howard** (1907– )

John Sweet followed David Lawrence as the publisher of *U.S. News & World Report*. Early in his career, Sweet worked as an assistant circulation manager for the American Medical Association's publications (1926–29) and in a similar role for *Traffic World* (1929–37). Next, he became vice-president of Poor's Publishing Co., and from 1940 to 1942, he was with Dickie Raymond Inc.

Sweet joined *U.S. News* in 1946 as circulation director. He became executive vice-president in 1951 and president in 1959. He was publisher from 1951 to 1978 and chief operating officer from 1971 to 1981.

**SWINTON, Stanley M.** (1919–1982)
During his student days at the University of Michigan, Stan Swinton worked on the *Detroit Free Press* and for the United Press. However, the rest of his life was with the Associated Press, which he joined in Detroit in 1940. After Army service in World War II, during which time he was a combat correspondent for *Stars and Stripes* in the European Theater, he became an AP correspondent in the Philippines, Indonesia and Indochina. He also served in Southeast Asia and the Middle East before a year in Korea.

After several years in Italy, Swinton became general news editor, and subsequently, head of the AP World Service and moved to the vice-presidency of AP Ltd. in 1964. He remained a practicing journalist to the end.

He also taught at his alma mater, the University of Michigan, which awarded him the Regents' Outstanding Achievement Award in 1966 and its Sequicentennial Award in 1967. He also won the Maria Moors Cabot Prize for distinguished contributions to the advancement of Inter-American understanding.

His books include *Heartbreak Ridge*; *The Stars and Stripes*; *How I Got That Story*; and *Crisis in International News Policies and Prospects*.

**SZEP, Paul Michael** (1941– )
As editorial cartoonist for the *Boston Globe* since 1966, Paul Szep won the Pulitzer Prize in 1974 and again in 1977. Born in Canada, Szep was a sports cartoonist for the *Hamilton Spectator* (1958–61) and graphics designer for the *Financial Post* in Toronto (1965–66). He served several years with the Royal Canadian Army.

In addition to his Pulitzers, Szep has been cited on two occasions by Sigma Delta Chi and on other occasions by the Boston Junior Chamber of Commerce and the Headliner Club. He won the Reuben Award in 1979.

Szep's books include *In Search of Sacred Cows*; *Keep Your Left Hand High*; *At This Point in Time*; *The Harder They Fall*; *Unvote for a New America*; *Them Damned Pictures*; and *Warts and All*.

**SZULC, Tad** (1926– )
Born in Poland, Tad Szulc came to the United States in 1947, after working for the Associated Press in Brazil (1945–46). From 1949 to 1953, he worked for the United Press at the United Nations. He then moved to the *New York Times*.

Szulc has been the *Times*' Latin American correspondent and has served two tours in the Washington Bureau and tours in Spain, Portugal, and Eastern Europe. He has been a commentator on foreign policy since 1972.

Among his awards are six from the Overseas Press Club, plus the Maria Moors Cabot Gold Medal for the best book on foreign affairs.

His books include *Twilight of the Tyrants*; *The Cuban Invasion*; *The Winds of Revolution*; *Dominican Diary*; *Latin America*; *Bombs of Palomares*; *United States and the Caribbean*; *Czechoslovakia since World War II*; *Portrait of Spain*; *Compulsive Spy*; *The Strange Case of E. Howard Hunt*; *The Energy Crisis*; *Innocents at Home*; and *The Illusion of Peace.*

**TAISHOFF, Sol Joseph** (1904– )

Sol Taishoff established *Broadcasting Magazine* in 1931 and has continued with the publishing firm since, holding positions from editor to chairman. From 1920 to 1921, Taishoff was a copyboy with the Associated Press in its Washington Bureau. He worked for the wire service until 1926 as a telegraph operator and later a member of the news staff.

Taishoff became a reporter in 1926 on the *U.S. Daily*, one of the forerunners to today's *U.S. News & World Report*. He spent five years with the publication. During part of that time, he was also radio editor of the Consolidated Press, a service operated by David Lawrence, who owned the *U.S. Daily*.

In 1953, the University of Missouri awarded him its Journalism Medal. He has also been honored by the National Association of Broadcasters and was given a special citation by the International Radio and Television Society. Taishoff won the Paul White Memorial Award in 1967 from the Radio Television News Directors Association. He has also served as president of Broadcast Pioneers and Sigma Delta Chi.

**TALBURT, Harold M.** (1895–1966)

From 1916 to 1922, Harold Talburt was a cartoonist with the old *Toledo News-Bee* (Ohio). In 1922, he began a lifelong association with the Scripps-Howard Newspaper Alliance.

Talburt received a Pulitzer Prize for his cartooning in 1933. He also contributed cartoons to *Collier's* and the *American*. Among other awards Talburt received, were an award from the Freedoms Foundation and the Christopher Gold Medal.

**TALESE, Gay** (1932– )

In the media world, *The Kingdom and the Power* is recognized as an excellent "inside story" of the *New York Times*. For those not interested in journalism, *Thy Neighbor's Wife* reflects another world. Both books were written by Gay Talese, considered by many to be among the pioneers of the "New Journalism."

Talese, who joined the *New York Times* in 1953, originally applied for a job at the *Herald Tribune*, the *News*, the *Post*, and other New York newspapers, believing he had a better chance with any of them than with the *Times*. The *Times*, however, hired him as a copyboy and two years later he became a reporter. During much of that time, however, he was in the Army.

Talese wrote features for the *Times Magazine* and a 1955 story on Nita Naldi, a silent screen actress living in obscurity in Manhattan, started his trend to new themes and a different approach. His features covered city life, forgotten heroes and heroines, and anonymous individuals. In 1959, he took over as the *Times*' chief human interest writer.

From such stories Talese published his first book, *New York: A Serendipiter's Journey*.

The "New Journalism" era began, according to Tom Wolfe, with Talese's profile of Joe Lewis, "The King As a Middle Aged Man," in *Esquire* magazine in 1962. Talese continued this technique with stories about Joshua Logan, Frank Sinatra, and others. Several of his *Esquire* stories were written while he was with the *Times*, but in 1965 he left newspaper work to focus on books.

Talese's second book was *The Bridge*, which he later admitted disappointed him. It concerned the building of the Verrazano-Narrows Bridge, and Talese once told Rich Koster, "I did a 4-by-8 painting when I could have done the side of a cathedral." His next book, *The Overreachers*, was another collection of articles.

*The Kingdom and the Power* appeared in 1969 and to some critics it was "far and away the best book about an American newspaper ever published." Next Talese turned to the Mafia, and after six years of research, *Honor Thy Father* appeared. Another collection arrived under the title *Fame and Obscurity*.

In 1980, *Thy Neighbor's Wife* arrived after years of research. Some chapters were printed earlier in *Esquire*, including "The Erotic History of Hugh Hefner." The magazine discussed his writing of this book in late 1979, quoting Talese as saying, "What I've tried to do, writing, rewriting, and rewriting again, is to make the reading effortless. That's the hardest part. Clarity is what I want, and ease. This can include long sentences but ones the reader does not have to stop in and go back over to get the sense."

**TARBELL, Ida Minerva** (1857–1944)

Prior to her studies at the Sorbonne and Collège de France in 1891–1894, Ida Tarbell began her association with journalism as editor of the *Chantauquan*, 1883–1891.

Upon her return from France, Tarbell began her long association with *McClure's Magazine*, 1894–1906, where her first story was about Napoleon. Then she was with the *American* magazine from 1906 to 1915. In these publications Tarbell became noted for her muckraking articles that highlighted this era in the nation's history. She was long active in regard to the role of women in society, having developed her reformist zeal in France.

Tarbell served with several governmental agencies, including the woman's commission of the Council of National Defense; President Wilson's Industrial Conference; President Harding's Unemployment Conference;

National Women's Committee on Mobilization for Human Needs, and others.

Among her books are collections of her articles from *McClure's* and *American*. She also wrote *Short Life of Napoleon Bonaparte*; *Life of Madame Roland*; *Early Life of Abraham Lincoln*; *Life of Abraham Lincoln*; *History of the Standard Oil Co.*; *He Knew Lincoln*; *Father Abraham*; *The Tariff in Our Times*; *The Business of Being a Woman*; *The Ways of Women*; *New Ideals in Business*; *The Rising of the Tide*; *In Lincoln's Chair*; *Boy Scouts' Life of Lincoln*; *He Knew Lincoln, and Other Billy Brown Stories*; *In The Footsteps of Lincoln*; *Life of Judge Gary*; *A Reporter for Lincoln*; *Owen D. Young—A New Type of Industrial Leader*; *The Nationalizing of Business, 1878–98*; and *All in the Day's Work*, her autobiography.

**TATARIAN, Roger** (1916– )
Roger Tatarian has spent most of his years in journalism with the United Press International, working for the wire service from 1938 to 1972. He has worked in Fresno and San Francisco, California; Phoenix, Arizona; and Washington and London, as well as Italy; from 1949 to 1959, he was general manager for European news.

Later Tatarian was managing editor for the service in New York, moving up the ladder to the editor's position by 1965. He retired in 1972 and since that time he has been a journalism professor at California State University at Fresno. He has also been a consultant on UNESCO committees.

Ohio University awarded Tatarian its journalism award in 1968, and in 1979, the California Newspaper Publishers Association named him the Outstanding Journalism Professor in that state. He has also won the Lovejoy Award and has been named a Sigma Delta Chi fellow.

**TAYLOR Family**
Shortly after the *Boston Globe* was established in 1872, a member of the Taylor family took control. Since that time, the Taylors have continued to publish the *Globe*, which, in recent years, has won many awards, including the Pulitzer Prize for public service in 1966.

This Pulitzer, the first to be won by a Boston newspaper in nearly half a century, was in recognition of the newspaper's success in blocking the appointment of Francis X. Morrissey to the federal bench.

Charles Henry Taylor (1846–1921) had served as a printer on the *Boston Daily Traveller* when the *Globe* was established. He also served in the Civil War. By 1873, he was editor and general manager of the newspapers. He was publisher and president at the time of his death.

William O. Taylor (1871–1955) took over in 1921 and operated the *Globe* until his death in 1955.

Another William O. Taylor (1932– ) has been with the newspaper since 1956, serving in varied capacities and eventually becoming president and publisher. He has been active in local projects, working especially with the Handicapped Children, Boys' Club, and Settlement programs.

William Davis Taylor (1908– ) has been with the *Globe* since 1931, first as treasurer; then general manager and publisher, since 1955; and chairman of the board, since 1963. In 1983, he received a special government award from the Health and Human Services Department for his volunteer work to help organize private sector support against alcohol abuse. In 1975, he received the Lovejoy Award.

John I. Taylor has been president of the firm since 1963.

**TEAGUE, Bob** ( – )
Ten years in print journalism helped prepare Bob Teague for his current career in broadcasting. He was a reporter on the *Milwaukee Journal* (Wisconsin) and then the *New York Times* before he joined WNBC-TV in New York.

Teague once said he viewed television and newspaper work as being similar, adding, "The little movies I present on the tube each day can alleviate tension in a troubled neighborhood, initiate government action to ease the plight of a hungry family, bring heat to a cold tenament, launch official investigations on corrupt institutions, destroy popular misconceptions, reduce con artists' chance of fleecing unsuspecting sheep."

In his latest book (1982), Teague complained that "reporters and anchors are graded periodically on sex appeal, via galvanic skin tests, which measure emotional response of viewers by the amount of sweat on the skin at a given moment under questioning."

Teague's books include *Climate of Candor*; *Letters to a Black Boy*; *K-13 Super Spy*; *K-13 Super Spy in Outer Space*; and *Live and Off-Color: News Biz*.

**TER HORST, Jerald Franklin** (1922– )
Michigan and the nation's capital have been the center of Jerald Ter Horst's career. He became interested in journalism while a student at Michigan State in the early Forties and gained national recognition when President Gerald Ford, from Michigan, named him his press secretary in 1974.

After World War II service in the Marine Corps, Ter Horst became a reporter on the *Grand Rapids Press*, in 1946, and covered Ford's campaign for Congress, in 1948. In 1951, he was recalled for duty in Korea, but returned to the *Detroit News* in 1953, where he remained until 1974.

Ter Horst became the *News'* correspondent in Washington in 1958 and bureau chief in 1961. He went with President John Kennedy to Germany in 1963, Johnson to Southeast Asia in 1966, and President Richard Nixon on European tours in 1969 and 1970; he later went to China and Russia. He was with Kennedy in Dallas in 1963.

When Ter Horst became the presidential press secretary, his colleagues had great hopes for better relations with the White House. He told reporters, "This is going to be a professional operation, not a political one." But Ter Horst resigned when Ford granted Nixon a pardon. He termed the act "gross favoritism" as well as "a travesty of our system of justice."

Ter Horst rejoined the *Detroit News* and from 1974 to 1981 his column was syndicated. Since that time he has been the Washington director of public affairs for the Ford Motor Co.

His books include *Gerald Ford and Future of the Presidency* and *The Flying White House: The Story of Air Force One.*

**THIMMESCH, Nicholas Palen** (1927– )
Since 1969, Nicholas Thimmesch has been a syndicated columnist for the Los Angeles Times Syndicate, and since 1981, he has been the resident journalist of the American Enterprise Institute in Washington. Thimmesch began as a reporter in 1950 on the *Davenport Times* (Iowa). In 1953, he was with the *Des Moines Register* (Iowa), and in 1955, with *Time* magazine, where he remained until 1967. For two years he was chief of *Newsday*'s Washington Bureau.

Thimmesch was with the Mutual Radio Network's "Reporter's Roundup" and, from 1981 to 1982, he was a commentator for the Cable News Network. For several years he was a contributing editor on the *New York* magazine.

He co-authored a book, *Robert Kennedy at 40*, and wrote *The Bobby Kennedy Nobody Knows* and *Condition of Republicanism.*

**THOMAS, Bob** (1922?– )
For more than four decades, Hollywood has been Bob Thomas' beat for the Associated Press. He has been in the Los Angeles area since 1944; his only other newspaper experience had been seven months on a Fresno paper.

Despite a career covering the "stars," Thomas considers his biggest story to be the coverage of the assassination of Robert Kennedy in Los Angeles in 1968. He helped the AP gain a 10-minute world beat, which brought the service a National Headliner Award.

In an *Editor & Publisher* 1983 interview on his 40th year with the AP, Thomas said Marilyn Monroe became one of his best sources for information. "I look for stories with a strange angle—something editors will pick and be able to put a headline on."

Thomas has written some 25 books, including biographies of many Hollywood "greats," such as *Irving Thalberg, Selznick, Winchell, Marlon, Joan Crawford, King Cohn, The Massie Case, Flesh Merchants, The Heart of Hollywood, The Road to Hollywood* (with Bob Hope), two books on Walt Disney and others.

**THOMAS, Helen** (1920– )
"I don't think I had any illusions that it would be an easy road," Helen Thomas said about selecting a career in journalism that has taken her to the deanship of the White House correspondents. As such, she closes presidential press conferences with the traditional "Thank You, Mr. President."

Thomas worked briefly on the *Washington Daily News* before she joined the United Press in 1943. There she originally wrote radio broadcasts, but soon shifted to the White House when John F. Kennedy moved in. She once told a reporter that chief executives "have to be accountable. Otherwise, they don't serve the people well. And we have to be responsible, or we don't serve the people well."

When the National Press Club opened its membership to women, Thomas became its first woman officer. She is the only woman to have headed the White House Correspondents Association and was the first woman member of the Gridiron Club. She has been called a feminist, but she says, "I believe in liberation for men, too."

Thomas has traveled extensively with the presidents, including Kennedy, Johnson, Nixon, and Ford. In 1960, she covered Jackie Kennedy during the campaign. She reports on much of this in her book *Dateline: White House.* She also has a weekly syndicated column, "Backstairs at the White House."

Thomas has won many awards, including, for example, the Aldo Beckman Award in 1982 for her White House coverage.

**THOMAS, Lowell** (1892–1981)

Truly a pioneer in radio news commentary, Lowell Thomas started in this medium in 1930, and he was heard frequently over the air until his death.

The *Literary Digest* sponsored a daily CBS news broadcast in 1930, and Thomas was selected to replace the late Floyd Gibbons. His closing line became an American legend, "So long until tomorrow." In 1932, he joined NBC and for 15 years had the same sponsor, the Sun Oil Co.

In the mid-thirties, he was the voice of the Movietone News-reel. In 1939, he handled the first televised news programs for NBC. During World War II, he traveled around the world, sending back vivid descriptions of the events, places, and personalities he encountered.

In 1947, Thomas returned to CBS, and in 1949, he made his famous visit to the forbidden capital of Lhasa in Tibet. These trips generally were reported in fuller detail in the more than 40 books Thomas wrote. Some of these include the following: *With Lawrence in Arabia*, a 1923 bestseller; *Count Luckner, the Sea Devil*; *Beyond Khyber Pass*; *The First World Flight*; *The Boys' Life of Colonel Lawrence*; *Raiders of the Deep*; *The Hero of Vincennes*; *India: Land of the Black Pagoda*; *Kabluk of the Eskimos*; *Born to Raise Hell*; *Adventure among Immortals*; *Seeing Japan with Lowell Thomas*; *How to Keep Mentally Fit*; *Pageant of Adventure*; *Pageant of Life*; *Pageant of Romance*; *Stand Fast for Freedom*; and *These Men Should Never Die.*

Thomas continued to write books, including *Back to Mandalay*; *The New York Thruway Story*; *Seven Wonders of the World*; *The St. Lawrence Seaway Story*; *History as You Heard It*; *The Vital Spark: 101 Outstanding Lives*; *Sir Hubert Wilkins: His World of Adventure*; *More Great True Adventures*, written with his son; *More Great True Adventures*; *Lowell Thomas' Book of the High Mountains*; and *Famous First Flights That Changed History*, also with his son. He editored or co-authored such books as *Cavalcade of Europe: A Handbook of Information on 22 Countries by 14 Noted Overseas Correspondents*; *Great True Adventures*; and *Burma Jack.* In 1976, he wrote *Good Evening Everybody: From Cripple Creek to Samarkand.*

According to *Contemporary Authors*, Thomas originated the "Cinerama" wide-screen concept in 1953.

**THOMOPOULOS, Anthony D.** ( - )
In mid-1983, Tony Thomopoulos became president of the ABC Broadcast Group. For some time, he had been president of ABC Entertainment. These titles represent his achievements after more than 20 years in broadcasting.

Thomopoulos began with the NBC Network in 1959 as a mailroom clerk. He later became involved with international sales for the network and was director of foreign sales in 1964 for Four Star Entertainment Corp., a syndication and production company. From 1970 to 1971, he was with RCA.

After his RCA and Selecta Vision work, he joined ABC in 1973. Five years later he succeeded Fred Silverman, who moved to NBC.

Thomopoulos has been credited with placing ABC Entertainment in the top position in sign-on-to-sign-off averages. His "Good Morning, America" has been the leader of the early shows.

**THOMPSON, Dorothy** (1894–1961)
An early worker in the woman's suffrage movement, and active in social work in New York in the 1915 era, Dorothy Thompson started her newspaper career in 1920 as a foreign correspondent with the *Philadelphia Public Ledger* and *New York Evening Post*, then owned by the Curtis-Martin Newspapers Inc.

Throughout her career, Thompson was a columnist, lecturer, and radio commentator, and at one time the wife of another well-known writer, Sinclair Lewis. From 1936 to 1941, her column was handled by the New York Herald Tribune Syndicate, from 1941 to 1958, by the Bell Syndicate. From 1937 on, she was an editorial writer for the *Ladies' Home Journal*.

She also wrote the following books: *The New Russia*; *Political Guide*; *Once on Christmas*; *I Saw Hitler*; *Listen, Hans!*; and *The Courage to be Happy*.

**THOMPSON, Edward K.** (1907– )
Edward K. Thompson, in 1981, became the consultant to the secretary of the Smithsonian Institute. Earlier, in 1969, he started the *Smithsonian Magazine*, serving as editor and publisher until 1981 and making it of the nation's leading monthly publications when it passed the million circulation mark within five years.

Thompson began his newspaper career as editor of the *Foster County Independent* in Carrington, North Dakota, in 1927. Later that year, he became city editor of the *Fargo Morning Forum* and soon was picture editor and assistant news editor of the *Milwaukee Journal* (Wisconsin), where he remained for a decade.

His magazine career started with *Life*, in 1937, as associate editor and, in 1945, assistant managing editor. He was managing editor in 1961 and editor from 1961 to 1968. During World War II, he served in the Air Force and received the Legion of Merit. He also spent 1968 as a special assistant to the Secretary of State.

The National Press Photographers Association named him "Editor of the Year" in 1968, the same year he was selected for the North Dakota Hall of Fame. In 1973, he was the recipient of the Joseph Henry Medal from the Smithsonian. He once described the *Smithsonian* magazine as "about things in which the Smithsonian is interested, might be interested, or *ought* to be interested."

**THOMPSON, Edward T.** (1928– )

A lifelong career with magazines has brought Edward T. Thompson the title editor-in-chief of *Reader's Digest*. As noted earlier, Thompson's father, Edward K., had a successful career in the same medium, especially with *Life* and *Smithsonian* magazines.

Edward T. Thompson trained as an engineer, and then worked for the Mobil Oil Co. in Texas from 1952 to 1955 before he joined *Chemical Engineering* magazine as managing editor in New York. After a year there, he became the associate editor of *Fortune* and, four years later, he joined *Reader's Digest*.

His comments on writing appeared in an International Paper Co. advertisement in 1980, which was widely reprinted and read in schools across the nation. Among his words of advice to would-be writers were these: "Don't write to a level higher than your readers' knowledge of it." He urged persons to avoid jargon but use such "first degree words" as "face" rather than "visage" or "countenance."

**THOMPSON, Hunter** (1939– )

The "mad-dog prince of Gonzo journalism" is one of the many titles that have been applied to Hunter Thompson, a member of the "New Journalism" crowd and still a controversial reporter. For many years he wrote for *Rolling Stone* magazine.

Thompson served in the Air Force from 1956 to 1958; after his discharge, he worked briefly on the *Middletown Record* (New York) and as a *Time* magazine trainee. Another brief tour was with a bowling magazine in Puerto Rico.

Travel occupied several years of Thompson's life in the early Sixties. Some of his dispatches from South America appeared in the *National Observer*, a Dow-Jones weekly publication. But when he wanted to cover the Berkeley "Free Speech" movement in California, the publication resisted, and so they parted. From 1964 to 1966, Thompson was the West Coast correspondent for *The Nation*.

Thompson wrote articles and books about the radical elements in the West. Some appeared in the *New York Times Magazine* and *The Nation*. His experiences traveling with the Hell's Angels were recalled in stories and later in a 1966 book under that title. He also wrote *Fear and Loathing in Las Vegas* and *Fear and Loathing: On the Campaign Trail '72*.

His "Gonzo journalism" has been described as having an "intensely adversary, anti-Establishment quality." *The Curse of Lono*, which appeared in 1984, was termed another "Gonzo-style" book. Thompson and *Rolling Stone* joined forces in 1970, but parted in 1981. He also wrote for *High Times*. Other books include the *Great Shark Hunt*; *Buffalo Room*; and *Kona Stories*.

**THURBER, James** (1894–1961)

Although James Thurber began as a newspaper reporter, he became more famous as a cartoonist and a magazine writer, and will be better remembered for his many books.

Thurber worked on his hometown *Columbus Dispatch* (Ohio) as a reporter from 1920 to 1924. He worked for the *Chicago Tribune* in Paris from 1924 to 1925 and for the *New York Post* in 1926. Then he started a lifelong association with *The New Yorker*. He had sold magazine articles during his newspaper days.

Thurber was also a playwright, and is remembered for *The Secret Life of Walter Mitty* and *Male Animal*, which he co-wrote with Elliott Nugent. He also wrote *A Thurber Carnival*, a book which became a play. A television show was based on Thurber's writings and cartoons.

Known widely for his cartoons that featured dogs, Thurber told *Life* magazine in 1940 that he drew these as "a form of nervous relaxation—I did them swiftly, almost absently, and threw them away. It was years before I learned to my astonishment that they could be sold. Then I tried to draw slowly and carefully but my colleague, E.B. White put a stop to that. 'If you ever become good,' he said, 'you'd be mediocre.' I went back to rapidity."

Among his books are the following, including several written with a co-author: *If Grant Had Been Drinking at Appomattox*; *Is Sex Necessary? or Why Do You Feel the Way You Do*; *The Years with Ross*; *The Battle of the Sexes*, which was made into a movie; *My Life and Hard Times*; *The Seal in the Bedroom and Other Predicaments*; *The Middle-Aged Man on the Flying Trapese*; *Let Your Mind Alone!*; *The Owl in the Attic and Other Perplexities*; *The Last Flower*; *Fables for Our Time*; *My World and Welcome to It*, a theme used in a television show; *Many Moons*; *Men, Women and Dogs*; *The Great Quillow*; *The White Deer*; *The Beast in Me and Other Animals*; *The 13 Clocks*; *The Thurber Album*; *Thurber Country*; *Thurber's Dogs*; *Further Fables for Our Time*; *The Wonderful O*; *Alarms and Diversions*; *Lanterns and Lances*; *Credos and Curios*; and *Thurber and Company*.

**TOPPING, Seymour** (1921– )

"The emphasis in the future will be on quality, on newspapers that provide services that can't be matched electronically—comprehensive foreign and national coverage, business and financial coverage."

Such is the forecast for the future in print by Seymour Topping, managing editor of The *New York Times* since 1977.

Topping worked for the International News Service from 1946 to 1947, reporting the civil war in China. In 1948, he started an 11-year tour with the

Associated Press, working in Berlin before joining the *Times* in 1959. On the *Times*, he was chief correspondent in Moscow, 1960–63, and in Southeast Asia, 1963–66. For three years, he was the foreign editor.

From 1969 to 1976, he was the assistant managing editor and then deputy managing editor and, since 1977, the managing editor. In 1968, his alma mater, the University of Missouri, awarded him its Journalism Medal. He served in the Army in World War II and has written *Journey between Two Chinas*.

**TOTH, Robert Charles** (1928– )
After service in the Marines, 1946–48, and another two years with the Army Ordnance Department as an engineer, Robert Toth became a reporter on the *Providence Journal* (Rhode Island) in 1955. By 1957, he was reporting science stories for the *New York Herald Tribune*.

Toth was with the *New York Times* from 1962 to 1963 before joining the *Los Angeles Times*, where he continues today. He directed the *Times*' London Bureau, 1965–70 and then became diplomatic and later White House correspondent. The *Times* sent him to head the Moscow Bureau in 1974, but he returned to the Washington Bureau in 1977.

A graduate of Columbia University, Toth was a Pulitzer Traveling Scholar in 1955 from the School of Journalism. In 1977, the Overseas Press Club and Sigma Delta Chi both honored him, and the next year he received the George Polk Memorial Award for his foreign reporting. Columbia University gave him its alumni award in 1978.

**TRIMBLE, Vance Henry** (1913– )
After a long career with Scripps-Howard, Vance Trimble edited the group's handbook in 1981. In 1960, he won the Pulitzer Prize, the Raymond Clapper Award, and the Sigma Delta Chi Award for his Washington reporting.

Trimble began as a reporter on the *Okemah Daily Leader* (Oklahoma) in 1928 and later worked for newspapers in Okmulgee, Muskogee, and Tulsa. In 1974, he was named to the Oklahoma Journalism Hall of Fame.

Trimble began a long association with the *Houston Press* (Texas) in 1939, starting as a reporter and rising to managing editor on this Scripps-Howard newspaper. He moved to the Scripps-Howard Newspaper Alliance in Washington as news editor in 1955, remaining there until he became editor of the *Covington Post and Times-Star* (Kentucky), where he worked until his retirement in 1979. He was a trustee of the Scripps-Howard Foundation.

**TROAN, John** (1918– )
For nearly half a century, John Troan has been associated with the newspaper industry, first working on the *Scranton Tribune* during summers while attending Pennsylvania State University.

Troan's first full-time position was with the *Pittsburgh Press* in 1937. A decade later, he was the science editor, by 1966 associate editor, and by 1967 editor. During his tour as science editor, Troan reported on the development of Dr. Jonas Salk's polio vaccine that was "created" at the University of Pittsburgh.

Between 1958 and 1966, he was the medical and science writer for the Scripps-Howard Newspaper Alliance. Since 1967, he has been a trustee for Science Service.

For his public service, Troan was named one of Pittsburgh's 100 Outstanding Young Men by *Time* magazine in 1953, and in 1956 and 1966 the Pittsburgh Junior Chamber of Commerce named him the Man of the Year in Communications. He was president of the National Association of Science Writers and has been honored by other scientific groups.

He served in the Navy, 1944–46.

**TROHAN, Walter** (1903– )

Walter Trohan's newspaper life has evolved around the *Chicago Tribune*, which he joined in 1929 and remained with until 1971. Before joining the *Tribune*, he worked several years in the city with the *Daily Calumet* and the City News Bureau.

During his last 11 years with the *Tribune*, Trohan was a columnist. For 20 years, 1949 to 1969, he was chief of the Washington Bureau. He covered many major stories for the newspaper, both in the United States and abroad.

From time to time, Trohan was a news commentator on both the *Tribune*-owned station WGN and the Mutual Broadcasting System. He was president of the White House Press Correspondents in 1939 and the Gridiron Club in 1967. He has been named to the Sigma Delta Chi Washington Hall of Fame.

Trohan wrote *Political Animals* and edited *The Jim Farley Story* and *The Roosevelt Years.*

Lloyd Wendt, in his history of the *Tribune*, notes that Trohan was brilliant, with "the added capacity to so infuriate bureaucrats with his questions that he could lead them into outbursts against their own interests." He won the Beck Award twice for outstanding work on the *Tribune.*

**TROUT, Robert** (1908– )

Robert Trout began his broadcasting career, first without pay, on the Mt. Vernon Hills, Virginia station WJSV. The station later joined CBS, moved to Washington, and became WTOP.

By 1935, he was with WABC in New York City; two years later, he covered the George III coronation in London. Among his many programs were "The World Today" and "Headlines and Bylines." He was in London in 1941 and covered D-Day in 1944. When President Franklin D. Roosevelt died, Trout ad-libbed for 25 minutes on the man's career.

Trout joined the NBC Network in 1958, but returned to CBS in 1962.

**TRUDEAU, Garry** (1948– )

"Doonesbury" began in the *Yale Daily News*. This comic strip by Garry Trudeau has been extremely popular, especially among younger readers, and has appeared in some 700 newspapers. In 1982, Trudeau took

20 months off to devote more time to a musical comedy and other projects. The strip returned in late 1984.

In reporting on the musical comedy's opening in late 1983, *New York Times* critic, Frank Rich, wrote: "The qualities that have made Garry Trudeau's comic strip 'Doonesbury' a national treasure are all present in the musical-comedy version at the Biltmore Theater." On Broadway, Trudeau has continued with his political satire, capturing "with admirable accuracy Trudeau's class '60 kids," according to *Newsweek*'s review. It has been updated to include comments about President Ronald Reagan.

During his career, Trudeau has been "studied" by media, with *Time* giving him nearly six pages in 1976, under the title "Drawing and Quartering for Fun and Profit." Trudeau won the 1974 Pulitzer Prize, the first for cartooning to a non-editorial-page artist. Early in its history, the comic strip was termed "the best satire that's come along in a long time" by a writer who knows good satire, Art Buchwald.

"Doonesbury" is said to come from "doone," Yale slang for a good natured fool according to one source, while a term for out to lunch from another. The second syllable comes from Pillsbury, a college roommate of Trudeau's who came from the flour-fortune family.

In October 1970, the strip went nationwide, syndicated by an up-and-coming operation near Kansas City, McMeel and Andrews, now the Universal Press Syndicate. Trudeau's political comments often place him in hot water. He once drew the Kent State killings, placing the blame for the massacre on Attorney General John Mitchell. He has had problems with lawyers and other groups, and from time to time newspapers will withhold certain panels. The women's movement has been well represented, especially through Joanie Caucus.

Trudeau's many books include *Still a Few Bugs in the System*; *The President Is a Lot Smarter Than You Think*; *But This War Had Such Promise*; *Call Me When You Find America*; *Guilty, Guilty, Guilty!*; *Dare To Be Great*; *Ms. Caucus*; *What Do We Have for the Witnesses*; *The Fireside Watergate*; *Trout Fishing in the Reflecting Pool*; *Don't Ever Change Boopsie*; *I Have No Son*; *Speaking of Inalienable Rights, Amy*; *Wouldn't a Gremlin Have Been More Sensible?*; *As the Kid Goes for Broke*; *The People's Doonesbury*; *Sid*, and *Doonesbury Dossier, The Reagan Years.*

Trudeau follows a trend established earlier by Al Capp through his "Li'l Abner" and Walt Kelly in "Pogo." Both used their strips as political forums.

**TUNNEY, Kelly Smith** ( - )

Kelly Smith Tunney, in late 1983, became the first woman in the history of the 135-year-old Associated Press to become an assistant general manager. She works with AP president and general manager, Keith Fuller, in areas concerned with corporate communications, public relations, promotion, advertising, and special projects.

*Editor & Publisher* reported that Tunney "is the eighth assistant general manager presently holding the title at international headquarters" in New York. She started her association with the news service in Miami in 1962 before joining AP Newsfeatures in New York and Washington. She also has served AP abroad, including covering the Vietnam War in 1967.

Tunney worked in Los Angeles in 1968 and in New York as director of media relations in 1981. Her husband, Jay R. Tunney, is an international shipping and trade executive and the son of the late Gene Tunney.

**TUOHY, William Klaus** (1926– )

For his reporting of the Vietnam War, William Tuohy won the Pulitzer Prize for international coverage in 1969 and the Overseas Press Club Award the next year. Earlier he won a National Headliner Award for his Vietnam work.

Tuohy began his newspaper career as a copyboy on the *San Francisco Chronicle* in 1952, becoming night city editor before he left in 1959 to join *Newsweek*. He eventually became a foreign correspondent for this weekly magazine.

In 1966, Tuohy joined the *Los Angeles Times*, where he remains. He has served in the Middle East and in Rome, and since 1977 he has been chief of the *Times*' London Bureau.

He served in the Navy, 1944–46.

**TURNER, Robert Edward III** (1938– )

Ted Turner has been termed the "King of Cable News" as well as the "Mouth of the South." He began his Cable News Network in 1980, after having acquired the Atlanta Braves baseball team in 1976 and the Atlanta Hawks basketball team in 1977. *Quill* magazine, in 1982, estimated his wealth at between $100 and $200 million.

To sportsmen he may be better known as the 1977 winner of the America Cup with his yacht *Courageous*. He also owns the Turner Broadcasting Co.

"I'd like to bring shows like those shows back to television. Shows like "Playhouse 90," "See It Now," and others. Programs weren't as antisocial as they are now," Turner once said. He has been interviewed by *Playboy* in 1977 and again in 1983.

In his mid-twenties, Turner acquired a failing UHF station, WTCG, now WTBS, in Atlanta, with its wrestling shows and reruns. He then took over an ailing baseball team, continuing his great interest in sports. In 1983, he acquired the Satellite News Channels for $25 million.

*Playboy* referred to him as "the fast-talking, colorful sybarite from Georgia who charmed or outraged nearly everyone he met." In the last *Playboy* interview by Peter Ross Range, Turner was described as "a free-enterprising press mogul who stands for certain kinds of censorship, the public moralizer who is hypocritical in his private life, the promoter of nonviolence who combines personal meanness with uncontrolled outbursts of physical destruction."

Range added, "Turner aspires to *power*. He has money; he has achieved fame; he has won big at sports; and he has broken through in the news business when all said he would fail. Power is the only challenge left to him."

His network station has won a United Nations award for a documentary on population control. A biography by Christian Williams apparently sets the book's theme in the title: *Lead, Follow, or Get Out of the Way: The Story of Ted Turner.*

**VAIL, Thomas Van Husen** (1926– )
Thomas Vail, who was born in Cleveland, has spent his journalism career on the *News* and *Plain Dealer* there. Since 1957, he has been on the *Plain Dealer*, reaching the presidency in 1970.

Before joining the *Plain Dealer*, Vail worked from 1949 to 1957 as a reporter and political editor on the *News*. He also worked with the Art Gravure Corp. in Ohio and, from 1968 to 1974, was a director for the Associated Press.

Vail was Cleveland Man of the Year in 1976. Earlier he was given the National Human Relations Award for his civic activities. In 1983, he was appointed to the President's Advisory Council on Private Sector Initiatives, a 39-member group.

He served in the Navy during World War II.

**VALERIANI, Richard G.** (1932– )
In 1957, Richard Valeriani was a reporter on *The Trentonian* (New Jersey) before joining the Associated Press where he worked until 1961, including several years as the wire service's correspondent in Havana.

Valeriani turned to broadcasting in 1961, when he joined NBC-TV News and has covered Washington for the network since 1964. In 1976, he moderated the second Carter–Ford debate. In 1965, he received the Overseas Press Club award for best radio reporting.

Valeriani wrote *Travels with Henry*.

He served in the Army, 1955–56.

**VAN ANDA, Carr V.** (1864–1945)
"The chief architect of the superior news department" of the *New York Times* is the best description of Carr Van Anda, who served as managing editor of this daily newspaper for twenty years.

Van Anda began his journalistic career as a typesetter on the *Cleveland Herald* in 1883, moving to telegraph editor, and later to the *Plain Dealer* before he joined the *Balitmore Sun* as night editor in 1886. After two years there he moved to New York where he worked on the *Sun* until he joined the *Times* in 1904.

Among Van Anda's major achievements with the *Times* was his handling of the sinking of the *Titanic* in 1912.

For a brief time Van Anda attended Ohio University. Today this university awards an annual prize in his name.

**VAN BUREN, Abigail** (1918– )
"Dear Abby," a syndicated newspaper column, is read daily by millions of Americans. Created by Pauline Esther Friedman Phillips, the column began in the *San Francisco Chronicle* in 1956.

Her twin sister, Esther Pauline Landers, writes the "Ann Landers" column, a similar advice service that also appears in hundreds of newspapers. Between the two sisters, their comments are read by the majority of American newspaper readers.

Van Buren submitted samples of her writing to the *Chronicle* and so impressed the editors that they started the "Dear Abby" column. She created her writing name, Abigail Van Buren.

Among her books are *Dear Abby*; *Dear Teen-ager*; and *Dear Abby on Marriage*. Some of her books have been translated into other languages. She helps support many national organizations, such as Goodwill Industries, National Planned Parenthood, and the American Educational Council.

**VANDERBILT, Amy** (1908–1974)
Starting in the late Twenties, Amy Vanderbilt held various jobs involving public relations and advertising. For example, she was business manager for *American Spectator* and was briefly associated with Tower Magazines. For a time she was with Publicity Associates, becoming president in 1940.

Amy Vanderbilt began her noted syndicated column, "Etiquette," in 1954. It continued until her death in 1974. During that time she also wrote articles for *McCall's*, the *Ladies' Home Journal*, and encyclopedias, as well as other publications. Between 1954 and 1960 she had a television show, "It's Good Taste," and from 1960 to 1962 a radio show, "The Right Thing To Do."

*Amy Vanderbilt's Complete Book of Etiquette* has been a bestseller for years, with frequent updating. She also wrote *Amy Vanderbilt's Everyday Etiquette* and *Amy Vanderbilt's Complete Cook Book*.

**VANDERCOOK, John W.** (1902–1963)
An actor, author, reporter, and commentator, John W. Vandercook was involved in many activities around the world. He was an actor before joining the *Columbus Citizen* in 1921. He then worked on the *Washington News* and *Baltimore Post* until 1923.

Vandercook was associated with Macfadden Publications from 1923 to 1925, serving the last year as feature editor for the tabloid *Graphic*.

In 1940, Vandercook joined the NBC Network as a staff commentator, a position he held until 1946. He was with the Liberty Broadcasting Co., 1951–52, and the ABC network, 1953–61. He was involved in many explorations around the world.

He wrote many books over a period of years; these included *Tom-Tom*; *Black Majesty*; *The Fools' Parade*; *Forty Stay In*; *Murder in Trinidad*; *Murder in Fiji*; *Dark Island*; *Caribbee Cruise*; *King Cane*; *Empress of the Dusk*; *One Day More*; *Great Sailor*; *Murder in Haiti*; and *Murder in New Guinea*. He also wrote many magazine articles.

**VAN HORNE, Harriet** (1920– )
A longtime radio and television critic, Harriet Van Horne, in 1942, was a columnist on the *New York World-Telegram* and, later, the *New York Post*.

Before this, she had worked for newspapers in Rochester, New York and Greenwich, Connecticut.

In 1947, Van Horne had her own television interview show. Currently she is syndicated by the New York Times Syndicate and appears on television as a panelist. She also appears as an analyst on radio news programs. In addition to magazine articles, she has written *Never Go Anywhere without a Pencil.*

**VANOCUR, Sander** (1928- )

Sander Vanocur began his newspaper career in 1954 in England as a *Manchester Guardian* reporter following two years of Army service. He also had a weekly news analysis program on the British Broadcasting Company. In addition, he wrote for the *London Observer* and was a stringer for the CBS Network in London.

Vanocur's American career began in 1955 when he became a *New York Times* reporter. Two years later, he was in broadcasting as an NBC News correspondent in Washington. Vanocur was moved in 1958 to Chicago, where he once said, "I spent most of my time in hotels and airplanes."

In 1971, Vanocur joined the Public Broadcasting Service, where he remained until 1977. For two years of that period, he was also a television columnist for the *Washington Post.* From 1977 to 1980, he was with ABC News and Sports as vice-president of special reporting units, and since 1980, he has been chief "Overview" correspondent for the network.

Vanocur was given the Broadcast Leadership Award from the Yale Broadcasting Co. in 1962.

**VARGAS, Joaquin Alberto** (1895–1982)

The "Vargas" girls became a major morale booster for American GIs during World War II. Alberto Vargas created these "luscious, slinky" girls who appeared for three decades, first in *Esquire*, in 1940, and later in *Playboy*, in 1956, where more than 160 of his paintings have been printed. He once said he "never found a substitute for a beautiful girl" to paint.

Vargas was called "one of the giants of American illustration" in 1979. Earlier in his career, Vargas sketched the stars of the Ziegfeld Follies to appear on posters promoting this Broadway show.

Born in Peru of wealthy parents, Vargas' father wanted him to study photography. In Europe, however, he drew beautiful women "for my own pleasure," he said later.

A collection of his works appeared under the title *Vargas* in 1981. These include the pictures from *Playboy.*

**VERONIS, John James** (1923- )

John Veronis and Nicholas H. Charney became known in the magazine industry for their founding of the *Psychology Today* and for their less-successful operation on *Saturday Review.*

Veronis was associated with *Popular Science, Field and Stream*, and *Woman's Day* in New York City between 1948 and 1952. For the next six years, he was with *American Home* before he joined the Curtis Publishing

Co. He remained there until 1964, serving at one time or another as publisher of *American Home*, publisher of *Ladies' Home Journal*, and president of the Curtis magazine division.

From 1964 to 1966, Veronis was president of Veronis Publishing Co., and then, for a year, was with the Interpublic Group of Companies in New York. He became the co-founder of *Psychology Today* in 1967. From 1967 to 1971, he was president of Communications/Research/Machines, Inc.

With *Saturday Review* in 1972, Veronis and Charney changed the format to include four monthlies (Education, Science, Arts, Society) rather than the traditional weekly editions. Charney replaced Norman Cousins, who had made the magazine a success, as editor; within a year the magazine filed for bankruptcy.

Veronis offered guidance to *Essence* magazine when it began in 1970, along with other magazine industry leaders. Later he became president of *Book Digest* magazine, which has since disappeared from the publishing scene. Currently Veronis is with the PV Publishing Co., Inc., in New York.

**VITTORINI, Carlo** (1929– )
"One of the most recognized names in publishing," Carlo Vittorini has been president and chief executive officer of *Parade* magazine since 1979. Before joining this newspaper-distributed publication, Vittorini worked with Chilton Publications, 1950–51, and *Farm Journal*, 1952–53, both in Philadelphia (Pennsylvania).

Between 1953 and 1960, Vittorini was in advertising and sales, with the *Saturday Evening Post* before joining *Look* for five years. He was said to have been the "youngest ad sales representative ever hired by the old *Saturday Evening Post*."

Eventually Vittorini became president of Charter Publishing Co., which then included *Redbook*, the *Ladies' Home Journal*, and *Sport*. He was briefly president of Harlequin Magazine, Inc.

According to Ira Ellenthal, writing in *Folio* magazine in 1983, "Vittorini has remained in each post long enough to leave his imprint." He added, "Vittorini has several specialities," from writing, to sales, to composition and production, and all phases of advertising. "*Parade* is now a much improved magazine in many respects."

**VON HOFFMAN, Nicholas** (1929– )
"A literate, witty writer who views life from the far left" is one of many descriptive comments about Nicholas Von Hoffman, a longtime columnist for the *Washington Post*.

Von Hoffman worked for a foundation in Chicago before entering newspaper work, with the *Chicago Daily News* in 1963. In three years, he was with the *Post*, remaining in Washington for a decade. On the *Post* he wrote not to please, but more to prod, and sometimes to outrage, according to *Post* executive Ben Bradlee.

Mrs. Katharine Graham told *Post* historian Chalmers Roberts that Von Hoffman "almost alone among American journalists, is telling us what it is in the minds of the vast youthful segment of our nation which we little understand but often greatly resent when its misunderstanding of us threatens the fabric of the society."

Among his many books are *Mississippi Notebook*; *Multiversity*; *We Are The People Our Parents Warned Us against*; *Two, Three, Many More*; *Left at the Post*; *Fireside Watergate* and *Tales from the Margaret Mead Taproom* (both with Garry Trudeau); and *Make-Believe Presidents: Illusions of Power from McKinley to Carter.*

**VOSBURGH, Frederick G.** (1904– )
After nearly 37 years with the *National Geographic* magazine, Frederick Vosburgh retired in 1970 as its editor. He remains with the Society's Board of Trustees and its Committee for Research and Exploration.

Vosburgh worked on Syracuse newspapers from 1922 to 1926 before he joined the Associated Press in Washington in 1927. For the wire service he covered sports and later the Senate, the State Department, and such major events as the World Economic Conference in London. He joined *National Geographic* in 1933.

By 1951, Vosburgh was assistant editor; by 1956, senior assistant editor; by 1957, associate editor; and by 1967, editor. His *National Geographic* subjects for more than 20 major articles "ranged from the Everglades to postwar Berlin and Japan, from jet airplanes to fireflies."

Among his awards was one from his alma mater, Syracuse University, in 1963, the George Arents Pioneer Medal for "excellence in magazine journalism." The Syracuse School of Public Communications gave him its journalism medal in 1969. He also won the Freedoms Foundation Medal and the American Association for the Advancement of Science–George Westinghouse Writing Award.

He served in the Air Force in World War II.

**VREELAND, Diana** (1903?– )
As a fashion journalist, Diana Vreeland has been *Vogue* magazine's editor since 1962. In 1971, she became a consulting editor. Truman Capote once termed her one of the "very few great original women." Vreeland has also been called the "high priestess of American fashion since the 1940s."

She was raised in Paris and once recalled that "our parents spent their days having a good time. They never contributed a bloody thing, and they and all their friends lived the life of Riley." Her parents came to America in 1914 and settled in New York City, where Diana made her debut in 1922.

After her marriage, Vreeland worked first on a free-lance basis for *Harper's Bazaar.* She wrote a column, "Why don't you . . . ?" Started in 1936, the column was described in *Current Biography* as "An offbeat advice column combining snob appeal and luxurious fantasy, it asked its readers why they did not do such things as 'turn your old ermine coat into a bathrobe.'" She wrote about the "jet set" and the "beautiful people."

Vreeland's background prepared her for fashion and high society. Her years with *Harper's Bazaar* prepared her to be an editor. She stayed with this magazine until 1962, when she moved to its archrival, *Vogue.* She remained there until 1971, when the Condé Nast Corporation called for new leadership, hoping to reverse *Vogue*'s declining ad revenues.

In 1963, she won the New York Fashion Designers Award; she has also been awarded the French Legion of Honor. Her autobiography, *D.V.*, was a 1984 bestseller. It was edited by George Plimpton and Christopher Hemphill.

**WAGNER, Frederick Earl** (1941– )
"Grin and Bear it" has been a popular comic cartoon since it was first syndicated in 1974. Frederick Wagner began his drawing career in his home city of Memphis, Tennessee, as an artist and manager of a specialties firm involved in custom wall decor and interiors.

In 1967, Wagner was in Orlando, as artist and manager of Florestone of Florida. Two years later, he was an editorial artist on the *Orlando Sentinel Star*, where he continues.

Wagner has won several citations for his cartoons, including the Greater Orlando Press Club's best editorial cartoon in 1971. *Editor and Publisher* cited him in 1976 for having the best color illustration, and that same year, the Florida Magazine Association gave him an award for best graphics.

**WALKER, Mort** (1923– )
More than 100,000,000 newspaper readers around the world each day read and laugh at something Mort Walker has drawn that appears on the comic page. Generally, it will be the "Beetle Bailey" comic strip. However, it might also be "Hi and Lois" or "Sam's Strip" or "Boner's Ark" or, possibly, "Sam and Silo." He created all of these, with assistants working with him.

At the age of 15, Walker drew a strip for the *Kansas City Journal*.

When he was in his teens, Walker also worked for the Hallmark Greeting Card Co. in Kansas City as a designer. He later served in the Army in World War II and once described Beetle as "the Army's worst private who has retired the title permanently"; Lt. Fuzz is more like his creator, Walker.

After the war, Walker worked with the Dell Publishing Co. and then free-lanced, selling his cartoons to the *Saturday Evening Post* and other publications. In 1950, he created "Beetle Bailey," which has been syndicated since that time by King Features.

Walker once said, "I love my work. I'd draw cartoons for nothing if I had to." Even as a kid, he said, he "wanted to make it big as a cartoonist and New York was glamorous to me." He said "Beetle Bailey" "began as a college strip based on the guys I knew at the University of Missouri before and after World War II." While at the University, he edited the campus humor magazine, *Show-Me*.

Walker has been instrumental in establishing the Museum of Cartoon Art and Hall of Fame in Greenwich, Connecticut, which is now open to the public. Among his many books are *Beetle Bailey and Sarge*; *Trixie*; *National Cartoon Society Album*; *Beetle Bailey and Friends*; *Sam's Strip Lives*;

*Fall Out Laughing*; *Hi and Lois*; *Most*; *Land of Lost Things*; *Backstage at the Strips*; and *The Best of Beetle Bailey*. He has contributed to many anthologies and textbooks.

**WALKER, Stanley** (1898–1962)
*City Editor*, for years, was read by young, would-be journalists seeking more knowledge about the excitement that came with "big time" newspaper work.

Stanley Walker, who wrote *City Editor*, had worked on the *Austin American* and the *Dallas Morning News* (Texas) during World War I before moving to New York as a reporter and rewrite man on the *Herald* in 1920. Six years later he was night city editor and then city editor from 1928 to 1935.

Later, Walker worked on the *New York Mirror*, *American*, *The New Yorker*, *New York Woman*, and from 1937 to 1939, he was an editorial writer for the *Herald-Tribune*. He worked on the *Philadelphia Evening Public Ledger* from 1939 to 1940.

Walker also wrote *The Night Club Era*; *Mrs. Astor's Horse*; *Dewey: An American of This Century*; *Journey toward the Sunlight*; *The Story of the Dominican Republic and Its People*; and *Home in Texas*.

**WALLACE, DeWitt** (1889–1981)
**WALLACE, Lila Bell** (1889–1984)
In 1922, *Reader's Digest* appeared on the American market. Since that time, this magazine has become the most widely circulated publication in the world, reaching untold millions.

Started on borrowed money used to print the initial dummy, the Wallaces, DeWitt and Lila Bell, developed "The Little Magazine" into an operation worth between $200 and $300 million, according to a *Quill* magazine report in 1982. Most of the profits go to a foundation, which has distributed millions to humanities, medicine, art, and religious projects through the years.

DeWitt Wallace served in the Army during World War I. There he developed the idea of condensing articles from the major magazines and, thus, offering readers a variety of topics. He studied magazines in the St. Paul public library. Before entering service, Wallace had worked in the city with Brown and Bigelow, and after the war he worked with Westinghouse Electric and Manufacturing Co.

The Wallaces, both children of Presbyterian ministers, were married in 1921 in Pleasantville, New York, long the mailing address for *Reader's Digest*, which now has beautiful offices in nearby Chappaqua.

Among this magazine's innovations is its reprinting policy. When the monthly printed "And Sudden Death," a vivid account of automobile accidents, the demand for copies was so great that the publication started reprinting its leading stories. In 1938, the first international edition, in London, was started. The American edition started carrying advertisements in 1955.

The magazine has long been considered conservative, although in recent years it has become more balanced. For example, the Nixons were good friends of the Wallaces and both the President and his wife, Pat, wrote for the magazine. Later, however, the *Reader's Digest* printed a two-part article by Theodore H. White, "Breach of Faith: The Fall of Richard Nixon."

In addition to the magazine, the firm operates a condensed book club; it also publishes books and has produced motion pictures.

For their contributions to the nation, the Wallaces were presented the Medal of Freedom in 1972, the highest United States honor for a civilian. Earlier, they had won the Theodore Roosevelt Association Award and citations from Syracuse and Missouri universities and from the Volunteers of America. Mrs. Wallace maintained a strong interest in art, interior decorating, gardening, and the restoration of old homes.

**WALLACE, Mike** (1918– )

Known to millions of television viewers as one of the "probers" on the CBS "60 Minutes" show each Sunday evening, Mike Wallace has been called "unquestionably the toughest and probably the most fearsome interviewer on television." Av Westin wrote that "Wallace is probably the best-known 'confrontation' interviewer on television. He is a relentless questioner, and he does a lot of homework before he goes into action."

"Wallace is stretched too thin, with his 26 pieces a year for 60 minutes and his documentary work for the network," according to Mark Ribowsky, writing in *TV Guide* in 1983. Another 1983 *TV Guide* article, this by John Weisman, noted that "Wallace still exudes the energy of a man decades younger. But he is not indestructible. How much longer can he take the pace?"

Wallace worked his way through the University of Michigan and made his radio debut in Detroit. He was a narrator on "The Lone Ranger" and "The Green Hornet." In 1941, he was with the *Chicago Sun* and, in addition, did some acting. After Navy service in World War II, he continued his role as moderator and narrator of shows. He even produced some commercials. He and his second wife had a "Mike and Buff" show on CBS-TV in New York, which ended in 1954 when they divorced.

In 1955, Wallace was with the Dumont network, with WABD-TV in New York. He handled news and interviews on "Night Beat." By 1957, he was on ABC with "The Mike Wallace Interview," called a "fresh" and "stimulating" addition to the air. The show continued for 18 months. After another local reporting assignment, he joined Westinghouse Broadcasting Co. in 1960 and later worked with David Wolper's "Biography" series, which was syndicated independently.

Wallace was with CBS News in 1963, first with the "Morning News with Mike Wallace" and then with other CBS productions. In 1968, "60 Minutes" premiered, eventually gaining its prime time Sunday slot.

He wrote a book, *Mike Wallace Asks: Highlights from Forty-Six Controversial Interviews*. *Close Encounters* with Gary Paul Gates, appeared in 1984.

Among his awards are the Carr Van Anda Award from Ohio University, the Alfred I. du Pont Award from Columbia University, several Emmys, and a Sigma Delta Chi citation.

**WALSH, Denny Jan** (1935- )
In 1969, Denny Walsh won a Pulitzer Prize for exposing corruption in St. Louis where he was a reporter on the *Globe-Democrat.* He had joined the morning newspaper in 1961 and when the award was announced, he was writing similar stories for *Life* magazine, 1968–73.

While at *Life,* he created a controversy over a story that implied corruption involving the St. Louis mayor and organized crime. Walsh later spent a year with the *New York Times* before going to California where he joined the *Sacramento Bee.*

Walsh also received the Con Lee Kelliher Award from the St. Louis Sigma Delta Chi chapter in 1962. The American Political Science Association Award came in 1963, and a Sigma Delta Chi national award in 1968. He won first prize from the San Francisco Press Club in 1977 for his reporting.

Walsh served in the Marine Corps, 1954–58.

**WALSH, John A.** (1945- )
Few journalists have had the varied experiences that John A. Walsh has had since he left the University of Missouri in 1970 to join *Newsday.* At the University, he was the sports editor for the school's daily newspaper and an assistant professor.

At *Newsday,* Walsh held several positions, including the co-editorship of the weekend magazine section. He also worked in sports. From 1973 to 1974, Walsh was managing editor of *Rolling Stone* magazine, but according to one account, Walsh "was out of his depth in *Rolling Stone*'s turbulent waters" and was fired within a year. After this experience, he free lanced for several years.

For two years, 1977–79, Walsh was assignment editor for the Style Section of the *Washington Post.* From there he moved to the *Post*-owned *Newsweek* as editor of the new ventures development, becoming responsible for the development of the sports magazine, *Inside Sports,* which he eventually edited from its start in late 1979 to its demise in 1982.

In 1983, Walsh became senior executive editor for The Sports Network, a unit of Group W Satellite Communications.

He edited a book, *Life and Death of the SLA,* and wrote *Tatooits.*

**WALTERS, Barbara** (1931- )
Although her first ambition was to be an actress, according to Barbara Matusow's book on television, Barbara Walters has become the nation's most respected woman interviewer on the air, and, according to many viewers, the nation's top interviewer. It was through her efforts that Sadat and Begin talked and later met with President Jimmy Carter at Camp David.

Walters began as a writer-producer on WNBC-TV and later with WPIX and CBS-TV. She joined the "Today Show" in 1961 and from 1963 to 1974 was a regular panel member. She was co-host, 1974–76.

In 1976, she joined ABC Evening News and, according to James Brady in *Advertising Age,* "the chemistry between Barbara and Harry Reasoner never did work out. True, Barbara's *forte* isn't sitting there reading copy off a teleprompter. True, she wasn't Walter Cronkite. But what she was, and is, is a hell of a newsman, a first-rate journalist with a first-rate record." Av Westin said ABC believed Walters "could attract a vast audience to the 'Evening News.'" He also wrote that Walters is another of television's great interviewers. "She manages to ask the questions that are on the minds of everyone. She is not afraid of probing and putting the indelicate subject before her guest."

She has won many awards. In 1975, in addition to her Emmy, she was recognized by the National Association of Television Program Executives and the American Jewish Committee Institute of Human Relations. She later won the Hubert H. Humphrey Freedom Prize from the Anti-Defamation League–B'nai B'rith in 1978 and the Matrix Award from the New York Women in Communications in 1977.

*Harper's Bazaar* named her among the 100 Women of Accomplishment and the *Ladies' Home Journal* named her among the nation's 75 Most Important Women. In 1974, she was the Woman of the Year in Communications and the Women of the Year selected by Theta Sigma Phi. She was also among *Time*'s 200 Leaders of the Future. The Illinois Broadcasters Association named a scholarship in her honor in 1975.

She wrote one book, *How to Talk with Practically Anybody about Practically Anything*. She has also written for major magazines.

**WARNER, Albert Lyman** (1903–1971)

Between 1929 and 1971, Albert Warner was associated with newspapers, broadcasting, and magazines. He began his career on the *Brooklyn Daily Eagle* in 1924 and, two years later, was with the *New York Times* as its Albany legislative correspondent. In 1930, he was in the Washington Bureau of the *New York Herald Tribune*, serving as chief from 1936 to 1939.

Warner was with the four major networks between 1939 and 1953: He was Washington correspondent and commentator for CBS, 1939–42; chief of the Washington News Bureau for MBS, 1945–49; with ABC, 1949–50 and 1954–56; and with NBC Three Star Extra, 1950–53.

Warner pioneered in broadcasting Congressional hearings. For his work, he received Sigma Delta Chi's first annual award for radio writing in 1940.

**WECHSBERG, Joseph** (1907–1983)

Joe Wechsberg saw his first copy of *The New Yorker* magazine in 1939. He began to write for this weekly in 1943 and was a staff member by 1949. In *The New Yorker*'s obituary it was noted that Wechsberg "had an intense curiosity about how things worked and how people behaved; he was a natural absorber of sounds and sights and facts; he took nothing for granted; detail enchanted him."

As a staffer, Wechsberg wrote more than one hundred pieces, as well as many profiles of prominent individuals and travel articles. He won the Sidney Hill Foundation magazine award in 1953.

Wechsberg also practiced law and was a musician, both are reflected in some of the following books he wrote: *The Best Things in Life*; *Journey through the Land of Eloquent Silence*; *The Merchant Bankers*; *Vienna, My Vienna*; *The Voices*; *The First Time Around*; *Prague, the Mystical City*; *The*

*Opera; The Glory of the Violin; The Waltz Emperors; Verdi; Dream Towns of Europe; In Leningrad; Schubert: His Life, His Work, His Time; The Vienna I Knew; Looking for a Bluebird; Homecoming; Sweet and Sour; The Continental Touch; Blue Trout and Black Truffles: The Peregrinations of an Epicure; The Self-Betrayed; Avalanche; Red Plush and Black Velvet*; and *Dining at the Pavillion.*

**WEHRWEIN, Austin Carl** (1916– )
Austin Wehrwein has had a varied career in journalism as an international reporter, a financial editor, and an editorial writer.

Wehrwein worked in Washington for the United Press, 1941–43 and 1946–48, reporting from London, Copenhagen, Oslo, and Stockholm. He served in the Air Force, 1943–45, and briefly was with the *Stars & Stripes* in Shanghai.

From 1951 to 1953, Wehrwein was a financial writer on the *Milwaukee Journal* (Wisconsin) and then moved to Chicago with Time Inc. for two years. After a year with the *Chicago Sun-Times* as financial editor, Wehrwein became the *New York Times'* Chicago Bureau chief, a position he held until 1966. Since 1966, he has been editorial writer for the *Minneapolis Star* (Minnesota).

He won a Pulitzer for international reporting in 1953, and has been honored by his alma mater, the University of Wisconsin, with its Distinguished Journalism Award. He has also been recognized by the American Bar Association with awards in 1968, 1969, and 1971.

**WEIL, Louis A. III** (1905– )
Louis Weil joined the Gannett Company in Rochester, New York in the corporate development program in 1971. Two years later, he was executive vice-president of the Westchester Rockland Newspapers and, shortly after that, president and publisher.

Weil was vice-president of development from 1979 to 1983, when he became senior vice-president of Planning and Development of the Gannett operations. He also is in charge of the firm's Project S, a task force exploring spinoffs and synergies that may exist within Gannett.

In his early years, Weil was president and director of Federated Publications, Inc., with newspapers in Indiana, Idaho, Michigan, and Washington. He was publisher of the *Grand Rapids Herald* (Michigan) and the *Lafayette Journal and Courier* (Indiana) before he joined Gannett.

Among his professional activities, Weil has been president of the New York State Publishers Association and the Inland Daily Press Association. He is active in the American Newspaper Publishers Association programs, as well as in Westchester area civic projects.

In 1960, he received a Distinguished Service to Journalism citation from the University of Minnesota.

**WELLES, Chris** ( – )
Chris Welles began as a reporter in 1962 for *Life* magazine. Three years later, he was its business editor. By 1968, he was business editor for the *Saturday Evening Post*, which closed in 1969. Until he joined the *Times* he

was a free-lance writer. One of his articles in *Institutional Investor* won the runner-up honor in the University of Missouri 1983 business writing contest.

In 1983, Welles became a business and finance writer for the *Los Angeles Times.*

However, Welles had earlier demonstrated his knowledge of the business world by winning the National Magazine, the G. M. Loeb, the University of Missouri, and the John H. Hancock business writing awards. Among Welles' books are *The Elusive Bonanza: The Story of Oil Shale*; *The Last Days of the Club* (about Wall Street and the Stock Exchange); and *Conflicts of Interest: Nonprofit Institutions.*

Welles has also been associated with the Columbia University Graduate School of Journalism in the Walter Bagehot Fellowship Program in Economics and Business Journalism.

**WENDT, Lloyd** (1908– )

Born in South Dakota, Lloyd Wendt began his reporting career on the *Sioux Falls Press* in 1927. He later worked in Sioux Falls on the *Daily Argus-Leader* and taught journalism at Sioux Falls College.

Wendt's Chicago career began on the *Tribune* in 1934. Wendt moved up on the *Tribune*, became Sunday editor by 1961, and associate editor and then editor of the *Tribune*-owned *American.* He was publisher of the tabloid *Today*, formerly the *American*, from 1969 to 1974.

Since 1977 he has been a free-lance writer. Among his many books he wrote, or co-authored with Herman Kogan, are *Lords of the Levee*; *Gunners Get Glory*; *Bright Tomorrow*; *Bet a Million*; *Give the Lady What She Wants*; *Big Bill of Chicago*; and *Chicago: A Pictorial History.* In 1979, he wrote *The Chicago Tribune, The Rise of a Great American Newspaper*, a definitive history of this daily.

**WENNER, Jann** (1946– )

Jann Wenner's career has been the *Rolling Stone* magazine, which he established in 1967 at the age of 21. He has also been associated with *Look*, *Outside*, and *San Francisco* magazines. *Rolling Stone*, however, was his successful entry into the magazine world. He has won National Magazine Awards in 1970 and 1977 for this periodical.

*Rolling Stone* is a product of the Age of Aquarius, the anti-Vietnam riots, and possibly, the underground press, although it was never really a part of this newspaper world. Wenner was a University of California at Berkeley student during much of the "excitement" of the 1960s.

As a preteen, Wenner published a neighborhood mimeographed newspaper. After dropping out of college, he worked on the *Sunday Ramparts.* He borrowed money to start *Rolling Stone*, about which Wenner once wrote that it "is not just about music, but also about the things and attitudes that music embraces." It offered more "straight" news than did the underground publications.

Dana Thomas called the initial issue "a cross between a journalist enterprise and a psychedelic nightmare." It survived on a youth audience and advertisements from music firms. Never a "hippie" magazine, in 1976 its headquarters were moved from San Francisco to New York City.

In 1979, Wenner was with the revived *Look* magazine for several editions. He started *Outside* in the late Seventies, but later sold it to *Mariah* magazine. Other short-time projects were *Earth Times* and *Rolling Stone College Papers.* He gained greater national recognition after profiles appeared in *Time*, *Newsweek*, *New York*, *New Times*, and other publications. Wenner also operates Straight Arrow Publishers.

**WESTIN, Avran Robert** (1929- )

Av Westin's broadcasting career began in the late Forties when he was a mailboy and copyboy during the summers with the CBS Network. By 1950, he was a writer for CBS News, moving to a reporter's status, news editor, director, and from 1958 to 1967, a producer-director. Westin wrote that in the early days to him "television was a sideshow. It was locked into studios, unable to get to the scene of news stories quickly."

During some of that time he was in Europe for CBS. He was also involved with starting "Morning News with Mike Wallace" for the network and he worked with Fred Friendly on "CBS Reports." Between 1967 and 1969, Westin was director of Public Broadcasting Laboratory, NET, which was financed by the Ford Foundation.

Westin's career with the ABC Network began in 1969, as executive producer of the "Evening News" and "Weekend News," for which he sought brevity and clarity in coverage. Other appointments during his ABC years include the vice-presidency for news documentaries, 1973–76, and since 1979, vice-president for program development.

His many awards include a 1969 Peabody for "Where We Stand-Part Two." That same year, he won the Polk Memorial Award and the Ohio State Institute Radio and Television award for "The Population Explosion." He also has won the Albert Lasker Foundation Award for special medical journalism. He won Emmy awards for best documentary writing in 1959 and 1968 and the School Bell Award from NEA in 1964. Another Emmy Award was won in 1972 for the coverage of President Richard Nixon's China trip. Also in 1972, he won a Christopher Award for "Heroes and Heroin," which focused on addiction among servicemen in Southeast Asia.

Westin once said he didn't expect to surpass CBS "Evening News," "CBS and Cronkite are like God and mother. They're unbeatable." In his book, *News-Watch*, he wrote: "Twenty-four hours of news must somehow be squeezed into 24 minutes. There must always be contradictions and compromises. It is accomplished with elaborate electronic gadgetry and a host of people who have been trained for specific tasks." He offered his Rule of Pragmatism: "Pragmatism increases in inverse proportion to the amount of time left before air."

Westin concluded that "there are shortcomings in the way we do things on American television news broadcasts. The individuals who decide what you see and hear on television and radio newscasts are probably more powerful than newspaper editors and book publishers these days."

**WHELAN, James Robert** (1933- )

From 1952 to 1968, James Whelan was with the United Press International, working from Buffalo to Argentina, Venezuela, and Puerto Rico and in other localities.

Whelan was associated with ITT World Directions for two years before he became the Latin American correspondent for Scripps-Howard Newspaper Alliance in Washington, 1970–71. He then joined the *Miami News* (Florida) as managing editor, where he remained for two years. After a year as a free-lance writer, he became president, editor, and publisher of the Hialeah Publishing Co. in 1975.

Later, Whelan was with the Panax Corporation in Washington as vice-president and editorial director, moving west to the *Sacramento Union* (California) in 1980. He returned to Washington in 1981 as editor and publisher of the newly established *Times*.

Among Whelan's awards are the Golden Press from the American Legion Auxiliary and its Florida group, the Overseas Press Club Award, and the Unity Award for outstanding journalism, from Lincoln University in Missouri.

He has written *Through the American Looking Glass*; *Central America's Crisis*; and *Allende: Death of a Marxist Dream*. He has been a guest lecturer at several institutions, including Boston and Miami universities.

**WHICHARD, David** (1928- )

A third-generation North Carolina publisher, David Whichard took over the presidency of the Southern Newspaper Publishers Association in 1983. More than a century earlier, his grandfather had established the *Greenville Daily Reflector*.

Whichard worked on the *Reflector* as a youth and, after graduation from the University of North Carolina and service in the Navy, he became a full-time reporter in 1948. By the mid-Sixties he was editor.

In an interview with Celeste Huenergard for *Editor & Publisher* in late 1983, Whichard voiced his fear of the Reagan Administration and its attitude toward the press, as displayed that fall in Granada. "And look at their other efforts to stop news leaks, to initiate lie detector tests and the new rules they have promulgated for classifying information. I'm concerned about the little fences I see going up between the people in office and what's going on."

On the University of North Carolina Board of Governors, Whichard has also been active in Greenville projects and associations.

**WHITE, E.B.** (1899–1985)

After graduation from Cornell, E.B. White moved west and worked on the *Seattle Times* (Washington) for a year before he traveled to the Aleutian Islands and the Arctic as a messboy. Eventually, he reached New York.

Soon after *The New Yorker* was started in 1925, White began to contribute articles. In 1926, he was a regular staffer, and for 12 years he wrote essays for "Notes and Comments." From 1938 to 1943, White contributed to *Harper's* through a column, "One Man's Meat." In 1945, he returned to *The New Yorker*.

In 1963, White received the Presidential Medal of Freedom, as well as the Gold medal from the American Academy of Arts and Letters. He also won awards for his children's books and, in 1978, received a special Pulitzer Prize.

Among his books are *The Lady Is Cold*; *Is Sex Necessary?* (with James Thurber); *Every Day Is Saturday*; *The Fox of Peapack*; *Quo Vadimus*; *One Man's Meat*; *Stuart Little*; *The Wild Flag*; *Here Is New York*; *Charlotte's Web*; *The Second Tree from the Corner*; *The Points of My Compass*; *The Trumpet of the Swan*; *Letters of E.B. White*; *Essays of E.B. White*; and *Poems and Sketches of E.B. White*. He edited *Ho Hum* and *Another Ho Hum*. He also revised William Struck Jr.'s *The Elements of Style* through several editions. White and his wife, Katharine, co-edited *A Subtreasury of American Humor* in 1941.

White served in the Army in World War I.

**WHITE, Gordon Eliot** (1933- )
A stringer's job for the *Nassau Daily Review-Star*, in Rockville Centre, Long Island (New York) was the starting point for Gordon White, who in 1949, joined the *Freeport Leader*. He also worked on the *Ithaca Evening News* (New York) and as photographer and editorial writer for the *Cornell Daily Sun* while attending Cornell.

By 1958, White was a copy editor on the *American Banker*. For several years, he was the Washington correspondent for the *Chicago American* before taking his current position in 1961 as Washington Bureau chief for the *Deseret News* (Salt Lake City). In 1976, he obtained an exclusive interview with President Gerald Ford.

White, who won first prize in newspaper photography from Sigma Delta Chi in 1954, also won the Raymond Clapper Memorial Award in 1978 and recognition from the National Press Club for his coverage of the Executive Department and the White House in 1977. He has been cited by the Associated Press for his coverage of the Idaho region.

**WHITE, Robert M. II** (1915- )
Few small-town newspaper publishers earn national reputations such as William Allen White, of Emporia, Kansas, achieved. Robert M. White, II, is one of the exceptions. A third-generation newsman, White followed his grandfather (Colonel Robert M. White) and his father (L. Mitchell White) as editor-publisher of the *Mexico Ledger* (Missouri). The family acquired the *Ledger* in 1879.

Born in Mexico, White was graduated from Washington and Lee University in 1938. Although he worked briefly for the United Press in Kansas City, White's most prestigious assignment outside of his long career in his hometown was with the *New York Herald Tribune*, where he was editor from 1959 to 1961. His other exposure to "big-time journalism" was as editorial consultant to the *Chicago Sun-Times* from 1956 to 1959.

White has held many offices in the Inland Press Association, the American Society of Newspaper Editors, the American Newspaper Publishers Association, and the Missouri Press Association. He was president of some of these organizations.

After World War II, when he won the Bronze Star for service in the Pacific, White returned to the *Ledger*. Since then he has visited Russia, The People's Republic of China, the Middle East, and other areas with delegations from the media or the government.

White won the Sigma Delta Chi Wells Key Award, and on two occasions, the National Newspaper Association Award for outstanding editorial writing. The New York Silurians cited him for best editorial published in that city, and the University of Missouri School of Journalism gave him its Journalism Medal; he was the first third-generation winner.

White has served as a Pulitzer Prize juror and with the Lovejoy Journalism Award Jury. In 1983, he won the Ralph D. Casey Minnesota Award for distinguished service in journalism.

**WHITE, Theodore** (1915– )

Ted White, a journalist and an historian, has been successful in merging these two roles. His four volumes *The Making of a President* (published in connection with elections in 1960, 1964, 1968, and 1972), are among the best-read books concerning this nation's political history.

Starting as a newsboy selling newspapers on streetcars in Boston, White won a traveling fellowship, and on his trip around the world, stopped in China, where he free-lanced for the *Boston Globe* and the *Manchester Guardian*, before *Time* magazine hired him to cover World War II.

White returned to America in 1946 and wrote his first book, *Thunder Out of China*, with Annalee Jacoby. In 1947, he joined the *New Republic* as a senior editor, but resigned six months later. For a time he free lanced articles for magazines and edited *The Stilwell Papers*.

In 1948, White was in Paris, working for the Overseas News Agency and *The Reporter*. He then wrote *Fire in the Ashes: Europe in Mid-Century*. Back in the United States, White worked for *The Reporter* and *Collier's* and began his intensive coverage of presidential campaigns. He also wrote his first novel, *The Mountain Road*, followed in 1960 by *The View from the Fortieth Floor*.

White early considered Nixon "one of the major Presidents," but later wrote *Breach of Faith: The Fall of Richard Nixon*. He has won many prizes, including the Pulitzer in 1962. Other recognition has come with the Sidney Hillman, Benjamin Franklin, Ted V. Rodgers, and Sigma Delta Chi awards. He won an Emmy in 1964 for the best television show and another in 1967 for best documentary on television. A recent book is *In Search of History: A Personal Adventure*. Nine of his books have been either Book-of-the-Month Club or Literary Guild selections.

**WHITE, William Allen** (1868–1944)

Through one editorial, "What's the Matter with Kansas?" William Allen White made his hometown, Emporia, Kansas, famous, made his name as one of the best known small-town journalists in America, and became an influence in journalism for decades. On the political scene following this 1896 editorial, he suggested Kansas was "following the false gods of Populism instead of building factories." He became a "citizen of America and a spokesman for its small towns," according to journalism historians, Edwin and Michael Emery.

While attending the University of Kansas, Allen was a printer, a reporter, and a correspondent for the *Kansas City Journal*. After he left Kansas, where the school of journalism bears his name today, White worked on the *Kansas City Star* until he acquired the *Emporia Gazette* in 1895.

White was long active in the Republican Party. He was a close friend of many presidents, especially Theodore Roosevelt. He was termed "the patient liberal" by some although to others he seemed contradictory. At the turn of the century he was a "muckraker," writing for such magazines as *McClure's* and *American*.

During World War I White was an observer for the Red Cross in Europe. In 1940 he headed the Committee to Defend America by Aiding the Allies. He served in 1938 as president of the American Society of Newspaper Editors and was on the Pulitzer Awards Committee. He won a Pulitzer Prize in 1922 for editorial writing and later a gold medal from the Theodore Roosevelt Memorial Assn. His essay on the death of his daughter, "Mary White," was widely reproduced and, long after White's death, it was turned into a television production.

Among White's books are the following: *The Citizen's Business*; *The Real Issue and Other Stories*; *The Court of Boyville*; *Stratagems and Spoils*; *In Our Town*; *A Certain Rich Man*; *The Old Order Changeth*; *God's Puppets*; *In the Heart of a Fool*; *The Martial Adventures of Henry and Me*; *Life of Woodrow Wilson*; *Calvin Coolidge: The Man Who Is President*; *Masks in a Pageant*; *A Puritan in Babylon*; *The Changing West: An Economic Theory About Our Golden Age*; and, eventually, his *Autobiography*.

**WHITE, William Lindsay** (1900–1973)

The son of William Allen White (1868–1944) became a successful newspaperman after starting as a reporter on the family-owned *Emporia Gazette* (Kansas). During the latter part of his career, from 1944 to 1973, he was the *Gazette*'s editor and publisher.

Meanwhile, White had a varied career away from the *Gazette*. He worked briefly on the *Washington Post*, in 1935, and on *Fortune*, in 1937. During World War II, he reported for a group of daily newspapers and at times represented the CBS Network. He also served as a roving editor for *Reader's Digest*.

White served as an overseer at Harvard and as director for both the Theodore Roosevelt Memorial Association and Freedom House. He, like his father, was active in Republican Party affairs.

Among his books are *What People Said*; *Zero Hour*; *Journey for Margaret*; *They Were Expendable*; *Queens Die Proudly*; *Report on the Russians*; *Report on the Germans*; *Lost Boundaries*; *Land of Milk and Honey*; *Bernard Baruch*; *Back*

*Down the Ridge*; *The Captives of Korea*; *The Little Toy Dog*; and *Report on the Asians*.

**WHITEHEAD, Donald Ford** (1908–1981)
Don Whitehead won a Pulitzer Prize in 1950 for international reporting from Korea and another in 1952 for national reporting of the Eisenhower trip to Korea.

After studying journalism and working on the student newspaper at the University of Kentucky, Whitehead worked on the *La Follette Weekly Press* (Tennessee); and in 1930, he became editor of the *Harlan Daily Enterprise* (Kentucky), moving, in 1934, to the *Knoxville Journal*. The next year he became night editor for the Associated Press in the AP Memphis office.

He was a feature writer for the AP in New York City, and then a war correspondent in the Eastern Theater of Operations. He landed with the Allied forces on Normandy Beach on D-Day and later won the Army Medal of Freedom.

After Europe, Whitehead was AP Hawaii Bureau chief from 1945 through 1948, reporting on the atomic bomb tests in Bikini. In 1950, he reported from Korea and continued with the AP until 1956, when he joined the *New York Herald Tribune*. From 1957 to 1981, he was a columnist for the *Knoxville News-Sentinel*.

Whitehead wrote many books, including *The FBI Story*; *Journey into Crime*; *Border Guard*; *The FBI Story for Young Readers*; *The Dow Story*; *Attack on Terror*; and *The FBI against the Ku Klux Klan in Mississippi*.

**WHITING, John Randolph** (1914– )
In the mid-Thirties, John Whiting was a reporter on newspapers in Ohio and in New York State. Between 1936 and 1946, he was with the *Literary Digest*, *Time*, *Click*, and *Popular Photography*.

Whiting edited *Science Illustrated*, 1947–49 and was publisher and editor of *Flower Grower* magazine, 1949–60. He spent the next five years as executive vice-president of Popular Science Publishing Co and was president of Communigraphics Consultants, 1966–67, and publisher of *Motor Boating* and *Sailing* magazines, 1967–75. Since 1975, he has been manager of the Hearst Magazine division of motor boating and sailing books.

With such a varied background, Whiting has won varied honors. He is past president of both the International Association of Boating Writers and the Garden Writers Association, and won an editor's award from the American Seed Trade Association.

He has written *Photography Is a Language* and has edited and co-authored other books in this field.

**WHITNEY, John Hay** (1904–1982)
John Hay Whitney was a successful capitalist and sportsman, yet his inability to keep the *New York Herald Tribune* alive was a major disappointment to him.

He was chairman of Whitney Communications and at one time or another had an interest in twenty-five small newspapers, five television stations, six radio stations, and the International Herald Tribune Co. He had become publisher of the *Herald Tribune* in 1957, and ran it until 1966, when it became the short-lived *World-Journal Tribune*.

Whitney was United States ambassador to Great Britain in 1956, returning to America in 1961. He held many public and business positions during his varied career.

Whitney was given the Yale Medal award and, later, the Albert Einstein Commemorative honor, along with the Benjamin Franklin and the Lovejoy awards. He was honored by France and Britain.

**WHITNEY, Ruth** (1928– )

For more than 15 years, Ruth Whitney has led *Glamour* magazine to its greatest success, with a circulation approaching two million. Depending on monthly readership surveys, Whitney knew what her readers want and then sought to meet that need.

A mark of Whitney's success is her 1981 National Magazine Award in the category of general excellence for magazines with circulation of more than one million.

Whitney was a copywriter with Time Inc. in circulation from 1949 to 1953 before she moved to *Better Living*. Three years later, she was associate editor and later executive editor for *Seventeen*, between 1953 and 1962. Then she moved to *Glamour* as editor-in-chief. In 1980, she received the Matrix Award from Women in Communications, Inc. for outstanding achievement in the magazine world.

Ira Ellenthal, writing in *Folio* in late 1982, recalls how Whitney introduced many new sections to *Glamour*, such as "Washington Report," "Good Listening," "Car Buyers Guide," and "How to Get More For Your Money." He added that "Whitney has fine tuned *Glamour*'s content to reflect women's diversifying interests." Whitney said she "wouldn't swap being editor here for being editor anywhere."

**WHITTEN, Leslie Hunter, Jr.** (1928– )

Les Whitten has been senior associate and investigator for columnist Jack Anderson since 1969. During that time Whitten worked on the Watergate, ABSCAM, Carter, and congressional scandal stories, as well as other major stories.

Whitten was a newsman with Radio Free Europe, 1952–57; he was then briefly with the International News Service before going to United Press International in 1958. He worked for the *Washington Post* from 1958 to 1963, when he joined the Hearst Newspapers, working up to assistant chief of the Washington Bureau, from 1966 to 1969.

"I think that ethics is a question for us [investigative reporters] because we're not really in it for the money in this business. Some of us make money as a result of having been in it, but I think all of us are sort of drunk on the First Amendment," Whitten said.

He has received the Edgerton Award from the American Civil Liberties Union and an earlier honorable mention for public service from the Washington Newspaper Guild.

He wrote *Progeny of the Adder; Moon of the Wolf; Pinion, the Golden Eagle; The Abyss; F. Lee Bailey; The Alchemist; Conflict of Interest; Sometimes a Hero*; and *A Washington Cycle.*

He was in the Army from 1946 to 1948.

**WHITTINGHAM, Charles A.** (1930– )
When *Life* was re-established in 1978, Charles Whittingham was the publisher. He called this new *Life* a "really bold magazine," with its high quality paper and its large page size that permitted better use of pictures.

Whittingham worked for the McCall Corporation in Chicago from 1956 to 1959, when he began his long association with Time Inc., first in that city. By 1962, he was the publisher's representative for *Fortune* in New York City before being sent, three years later, to manage the San Francisco office.

Returning to New York in 1969, Whittingham was assistant to the publisher for *Fortune*, and between 1970 and 1978, he was the assistant publisher before taking his present position with *Life.*

**WHITTLE, H. Christopher** ( – )
As co-owner with Phillip W. Moffitt of the 13–30 Corporation in Knoxville, Tennessee, Christopher Whittle today is also one of the owners of *Esquire* magazine.

In Nashville, these two men developed periodicals for persons between the ages of 13 and 30, including *Nutshell, Graduate, 18 Almanac,* and *New Marriage.* They are distributed through high schools and colleges across the nation. The firm also prepares special editions of a single topic for a single advertiser, with the editorial content directed to a specific audience.

**WICKER, Thomas Grey** (1926– )
Tom Wicker's early years were spent in North Carolina, first as the executive director of the Southern Pines Chamber of Commerce, 1948–49, and, later in 1949, as editor of the weekly *Sandhill Citizen* in Aberdeen. Between 1949 and 1959, Wicker worked on the *Lumberton Robesonian* and the *Winston-Salem Journal*, where he was copy editor, sports editor, Sunday feature editor, Washington correspondent, and editorial writer.

He served in the Navy, 1952–54, and then spent a year, 1957–58, as a Nieman Fellow at Harvard. For a brief time, he was associate editor of the *Nashville Tennessean.*

In 1960, Wicker joined the *New York Times.* Gay Talese, in *The Kingdom and the Power*, notes that Wicker's first attempt to join the *Times'* reportorial staff was marred by his beard. "Nobody on the *Times'* reportorial staff then wore a beard except a foreign correspondent recently returned from Turkey, and he was quickly transferred to Jersey City." Yet Wicker did become one of "James Reston's Boys," and four years later was the

Washington Bureau chief. Wicker became associate editor of the *Times* in 1968.

Vice-President Spiro Agnew once attacked Wicker for his "irresponsibility and thoughtlessness." Time, apparently, has determined who was right in this instance.

**WIGGINS, James Russell** (1903– )
James Wiggins "fought with presidents, bureaucrats, and Congress to establish access to the news as a constitutional right of the press; there, he disdained anything that smacked of stealing government secrets for publication," according to Chalmers Roberts, *Washington Post* historian. "He was as ardent a believer in and advocate of a free press and 'the people's right to know' as journalism has ever produced."

Wiggins began as a reporter in 1922 for the *Crock County Star* in Luverne, Minesota. He became its publisher and editor, before selling it in 1930 and joining the staff of the *St. Paul Dispatch-Pioneer Press*, where he was editorial writer, Washington correspondent, managing editor, and editor. From 1946 to 1947, he was an assistant to the publisher of the *New York Times* before joining the *Washington Post* in 1947 as managing editor. Six years later, he added the title of vice-president. As more titles were added, Wiggins became *Post* editor and executive vice-president from 1960 to 1968.

The next year, he was United States ambassador to the United Nations. Since 1969, he has been editor and publisher of the *Ellsworth American* (Maine).

Among his awards are the Lovejoy, John Peter Zenger, and Golden Key of the National Association of School Administrators and the University of Missouri Journalism Medal. He is past president of both the American Society of Newspaper Editors and the American Antiquarian Society. He wrote *Freedom or Secrecy* and contributed to *Civil Rights, the Constitution, and the Courts.*

During World War II, he served in the Air Force.

**WILL, George F.** (1941– )
As a Pulitzer Prize winning conservative columnist, George Will may be better known to millions of television viewers for his role on shows such as "Agronsky & Company," and on Public Television. During the 1980 political conventions, he worked for the ABC Network as a commentator.

Will's latest book, *Statecraft as Soulcraft—What Government Does*, calls for a "contemplative, a philosophic turn of mind." A reviewer, Bruce R. Sievers, noted Will's "central thesis, that American society is rooted [to its detriment] in economic self-interestedness and laissez-faire individualism, is an indictment of contemporary conservatism and liberalism alike."

In 1983, nearly 400 newspapers carried Will's syndicated column. When it was revealed that Will had assisted Ronald Reagan in preparing for his 1980 debates with Jimmy Carter, about 10 newspapers dropped the column. Most others, however, agreed with Edwin Guthman, editor of the

*Philadelphia Inquirer*, that Will is "a good writer. And we've understood from the beginning that he has a close relationship with the administration."

Will received his Ph.D. from Princeton, writing his dissertation on the First Amendment. During his college years he ceased being a liberal and became a conservative. In 1970, after several teaching appointments, Will became an aide to Republican Senator Gordon Allott of Colorado, and in 1973, he began his writing career, as the Washington editor for William Buckley's *National Review*. Two years later, he started a column on the Op-Ed page of the *Washington Post*.

Later, he wrote a column for *Newsweek*. Will once wrote in that magazine that "a journalist's duty is to see politicians steadily and see them whole. To have intelligent sympathy with them, it helps to know a few as friends."

**WILLIAMS, Nick** ( – )

Nick Williams' lifelong career with the *Los Angeles Times* where, in 1958, he became editor has placed him among the great editors of this century.

From the beginning of his editorship, Williams was determined to turn the newspaper away from its close ties with the Republican Party, once writing an in-depth study of the John Birch Society, which resulted in 15,000 cancellations.

Setting out with Otis Chandler to make the paper the best in the nation, he increased the pay for staffers and provided better coverage for readers.

David Halberstam referred to Williams as "a very deceptive man. He did not look or seem like a man destined to be the great editor of a powerful expanding national newspaper." He called Williams "perhaps the ablest major American newspaper editor of his generation," a person with great political skill who has moved the *Times* from "right to center."

**WILLIAMS, Betty Anne** ( – )

President Ronald Reagan congratulated Betty Anne Williams in late 1983 upon her appointment as the first Black president of the Washington Press Club. Originally named the Women's National Press Club, this longtime Washington group started to admit men to membership in the 1970s.

The Reverend Jesse L. Jackson, who installed Williams in her new office, "told the audience there has been more progress for Black people in athletics, the church, and other fields than in journalism," according to an account in *Editor & Publisher*.

Williams said one of her early scoops was learning from Congressman Wayne Hays of Ohio that "Elizabeth Ray could not type." Ray had been on Hays' payroll as a secretary. Williams has been with the Associated Press since her graduation from the University of South Carolina. She worked 20 months in Columbia, South Carolina before moving to the Associated Press Washington Bureau in 1974.

**WILLS, Garry** (1934– )
Garry Wills has been called a "brilliant and scholarly political journalist and essayist." In his *Confessions of a Conservative*, he said he was "a Catholic cold warrior." During his career in education he taught at St. Louis University, Xavier University in Cincinnati, Johns Hopkins, Union College, and since 1980, Northwestern University.

Wills contributed to the *National Review* in the late 1950s and worked for a time on the *Richmond News Leader*. He also contributed to *Esquire* from 1967 to 1970, and since 1970 he has been a columnist for the Universal Press Syndicate. He has developed a number of his magazine stories into books.

Wills' books include *Chesterton: Man and Mask*; *Politics and Catholic Freedom*; *Roman Culture*; *Jack Ruby*; *Second Civil War for Armageddon*; *Nixon Agonistes*; *Bare Ruined Choirs*; *Doubt, Prophecy and Radical Religions*; *Inventing America: Jefferson's Declaration of Independence*; *At Button's: Confessions of a Conservative*; *Explaining America: The Federalist*; and *The Kennedy Imprisonment: A Meditation on Power*. He also has written pamphlets about the Bible for younger readers.

**WILSON, Earl** (1907– )
For nearly half a century, Earl Wilson reported on New York's "Great White Way" through his syndicated newspaper column, "It Happened Last Night." When Wilson stepped down from writing in 1983, he said his final report was number 11, 424.

In announcing his retirement, Wilson wrote, "I've been my own legman for 40 years but now my legs are tired and I want to sit and rest a while." Also, Parkinson's disease had hit him several years earlier.

Wilson believed his most memorable columns were "breaking the stories of Marilyn Monroe's romance with Arthur Miller and her later divorce from the playwright." Wilson also helped a young, struggling Woody Allen get one of his first paying jobs.

According to *Editor & Publisher*, Wilson also felt he was the first to break as a news story the discovery of the Salk polio vaccine. He learned about it while interviewing an actress for another story.

Among his books are *Jungle Performers*; *I Am Gazing into My 8-Ball*; *Pike's Peek or Bust*; *Let 'Em Eat Cheese Cake*; *Look Who's Abroad Now*; *Earl Wilson's New York*; *The Show Business Nobody Knows*; *Show Business Laid Bare*; *Sinatra*; and *Hot Times*. He also wrote for magazines. In his column he frequently referred to the "B.W.," his Beautiful Wife.

**WILSON, Lyle Campbell** (1899–1967)
Although Lyle Wilson's reporting career paralleled the growth of the United Press, he started as a reporter for the *Daily Oklahoman* in 1920. Within two years he had joined the UP, working in London.

Wilson moved back to New York City as cable editor in 1924, and three years later he was in Washington, where he spent the rest of his career. From 1933 to 1942, he directed the Washington Bureau through the Depression and the start of World War II. From 1943 to 1964, he was the general manager of the news service. Eventually Wilson became vice president and, for a time, he wrote a column for the news service.

Among Wilson's awards was one from the Atlantic City Headliner Club for consistent Washington correspondence. The University of Missouri honored him in 1940 with its Journalism Medal, and Sigma Delta Chi made him a Fellow of the Society.

**WILSON, Phyllis Starr** (1928– )
Phyllis Wilson worked for the New Orleans Coca-Cola Co. in 1949 as a receptionist and assistant on the firm's house organ. Soon she was with *Weird Tales* magazine in New York in 1950; she became a secretary at Condè Nast Publications in 1951.

Wilson moved up to become a researcher and writer for *Vogue*, working there until 1962, when she moved to *Glamour* as a writer. She also edited *Glamour's Health and Beauty Book.* Again she moved up, to senior editor and then managing editor before she joined the new magazine, *Self*, in 1977 as editor-in-chief.

She won a J.C. Penney–University of Missouri Journalism Award for her medical writing in 1969. In 1982, she was honored in New York as one of the Outstanding Women in Communications.

**WILSON, Richard Lawson** (1905–1981)
A long-time member of the Cowles Publications, Richard Wilson worked on the *Des Moines Register* (Iowa) from 1922 to 1923, and for the *St. Louis Globe-Democrat* (Missouri) for less than a year. He later returned to the *Register* and in 1930 became city editor. He became the Washington correspondent for the *Register and Tribune* in 1933. From 1938 to 1970, he was the Washington Bureau chief for Cowles.

While in Washington Wilson won the Pulitzer Prize for distinguished reporting of national affairs in 1954; the same year he was honored with the Sigma Delta Chi and Headliner awards. He has also won other honors.

Wilson is a past president of both the National Press Club and the Gridiron Club.

He wrote *Setting the Course* and *A New Road for America*, along with magazine articles. For many years he has had a syndicated newspaper column.

**WINCHELL, Walter** (1897–1972)
At the peak of his career, Walter Winchell attracted 90 percent of all radio listeners to his Sunday evening broadcasts that usually started, "Mr. and Mrs. America and all the ships at sea." At the same time, he had some 50 million readers of his syndicated newspaper column, which contained more gossip than now found in the widely circulated weekly tabloids on the nation's newsstands and in the supermarkets.

Winchell's real name was spelled with the single "l" and his Uncle George was one of the founders of the American Stock Exchange. His father was a salesman who taught him to "ask questions and learn. . . .

People who laugh at people who want to learn are the ones who are ignorant."

Winchell, a classmate of George Jessel early in school, was exposed to the stage, movies, *Variety* magazine, and many of the greats of all times. For years he was a friend of the noted writer, Damon Runyon, and established the Runyon Fund to fight cancer after his death. Winchell paid all of the administrative costs of the fund for years.

He first wrote for *The Vaudeville News*, a two-man operation, with Glenn Condon. In 1924, he joined Bernarr Macfadden's *Evening Graphic* for $100 a week. Four years later, he was lured to Hearst's *Mirror* at five times that salary. Winchell later wrote that for years he earned more than a million a year, with much of this coming from the radio broadcast. He and "Jergens Lotion," one of his sponsors, were together for 16 years. Winchell also credited "My Girl Friday" with helping his programs and columns succeed.

Winchell was a friend of celebrities, politicians, gangsters, and presidents. He had his enemies, and from time to time editors would delete portions of his columns. Lucille Ball once said she learned she was pregnant from Winchell before she learned it from her doctor. No individual radio commentator or columnist has the saturation of the potential audience that Winchell had at his peak.

**WINSHIP, Thomas** (1920– )

Since 1965, Tom Winship as editor of the *Boston Globe* has been credited with providing much of the impetus that has moved this newspaper into the Top Ten in America.

"I hope newspapers will never be satisfied with what we do for our readers. But I think one of our current failures is not ever addressing, let alone satisfying, the needs of a large segment of our readership—specifically, the non-white and the very poor white readers," Winship wrote in 1983.

During World War II, Winship was with the Coast Guard in the European Theater of Operations. After the war, Winship became a *Globe* reporter in 1945 and, in 1956, the daily's Washington correspondent. In 1965, he went back to Boston as the editor.

**WINTER, Ruth Grosman** (1930– )

Starting in 1955 with the *Houston Press*, Ruth Winter worked on the *Newark Star Ledger* in 1955 and became its science editor from 1956 to 1969. Later she joined the Los Angeles Times Syndicate, and since 1981 she has been with the Register and Tribune Syndicate.

Currently she has several columns, including "Beat the Clock," "Vitamins," "Celebrities at Midlife," "Currently with Ruth Winter," and "Medical Breakthroughs."

Winter's awards provide a good indication of her subject matter. They include awards from the Arthritis Foundation on two occasions and other awards from the American Dental Association and the American Society of Anesthesiologists. Upsala College named her its Alumnus of the Year and the New Jersey Daily Newspaper Women honored her twice, as Woman of the Year and as Woman of Achievement. She is a past president of the American Society of Journalists and Authors.

Among her many books are *Poisons in Your Food; How to Reduce Your Medical Bills; A Consumer's Dictionary of Food Additives; Vitamin E: The Miracle Worker; So You Have Sinus Trouble; Ageless Aging; So You Have a Pain in the Neck; A Consumer's Dictionary of Cosmetic Ingredients; Don't Panic; The Fragile Bond: Marriage in the '70's; Triumph Over Tension; The Smell Book: Scent, Sex and Society; Scent Talk Among Animals; Cancer Causing Agents: A Preventive Guide*; and *The Great Self-Improvement Sourcebook.*

**WISMER, Harry** (1913–1967)
While attending Michigan State University in the mid-thirties, Harry Wismer began a broadcasting career that continued for decades. He was first sports director of the university station, and from 1935 to 1940, he held the same position with Detroit stations WJR and WXYZ.

Wismer moved to the NBC Blue Network in New York in 1941 as a sports announcer, and two years later he was sports director for the ABC Network there. After 1952, he was involved with several stations in executive positions. He was also asssociated with the Yankee Radio Network and the Don Lee Network.

He was chairman of the American Football League in Dallas from 1959 to 1963.

Wismer won the Ernie Pyle Plaque in 1947 and received recognition from the Junior Chamber of Commerce, the Marine Corps, the American Legion, the Veterans of Foreign Wars, the Helms Foundation, the National Conference of Christians and Jews, and other organizations.

**WITCOVER, Jules** (1927– )
After working on newspapers in Hackensack, New Jersey, Providence, Rhode Island, and Newark, New Jersey for four years, Jules Witcover moved to Washington where he has been reporting since 1953. He has covered the capitol for the Newhouse National News Service and the *Los Angeles Times.* In 1973, he joined the *Washington Post.* He has covered all the presidential campaigns since 1960.

Witcover has been a columnist since 1968 and he has co-authored a syndicated column with Jack W. Germond since 1977.

His books include *85 Days: The Last Campaign of Richard Kennedy; The Resurrection of Richard Nixon; White Knight: The Rise of Spiro Agnew*; and *The Main Chance.* He has co-authored *A Heartbeat Away: The Investigation and Resignation of Vice-President Spiro T. Agnew*, with Richard Cohen and *Blue Smoke & Mirrors: How Reagan Won and Why Carter Lost the Election of 1980*, with Jack Germond. He also has written many magazine articles.

**WOLFE, Tom (Thomas Kennerly, Jr.)** (1931– )
Tom Wolfe, often dressed out in his "whites," has been credited by some individuals with creating the "nonfiction novel," although he credits himself more with what has been called the "New Journalism."

Wolfe wrote that in the 1960s it was discovered "it just might be possible to write journalism that would read like a novel." He considered Gay Talese's "Joe Lewis: The King as a Middle-Aged Man" an article that could be reworked to read as a short story.

From 1956 to 1958, Wolfe was a reporter with the *Springfield Union* (Massachusetts); from 1959 to 1962, he was the Latin American correspondent for the *Washington Post.* He moved to the *New York Herald Tribune* in 1962 to work until it became the *World-Journal Tribune* in 1966 and for the next year when the *WJT* died. From 1968 to 1976, Wolfe was a contributing editor for *New York* magazine; since 1977, he has been with *Esquire.* In recent years, he has been a contributing artist for *Harper's* magazine. Wolfe, who has illustrated some of his books with line drawings, has had his art exhibited in New York galleries.

Wolfe won a Front Page Award for humor and foreign news reporting from the Washington Newspaper Guild and an award of excellence from the Society of Magazine Writers. His book, *The New Journalism,* won the Frank Luther Mott-Kappa Tau Alpha Research Award in Journalism. Other books, which include several collections of his magazine articles, are *The Kandy-Kolored Tangerine-Flake Streamline Baby*; *The Electric Kool-Aid Acid Test*; *The Pump House Gang*; *Radical Chic and Mau-mauing the Flak Catchers*; *The Painted Word*; *Mauve Gloves and Madmen, Clutter and Vine*; and *The Right Stuff,* which became a controversial motion picture in 1983. In 1984 he started a novel in *Rolling Stone* magazine, writing each installment as it was due in print.

**WOODRUFF, Judy** (1946- )

Judy Woodruff has been in broadcasting since her first job as news announcer and reporter on an Atlanta, Georgia station, WAGA-TV, from 1970 to 1975. She next joined NBC News in Atlanta and in 1977 became the network's White House correspondent. She later moved to the MacNeil/Lehrer Newshour in 1983.

While in Atlanta, Woodruff was given the Leadership Award by the Women in Communications, Inc. She won an Emmy in 1975. She has also worked with the University of Georgia School of Journalism and the Atlanta Camp Fire Girls.

She has written a book, *This Is Judy Woodruff at the White House.*

**WOODS, Howard B.** (1917–1976)

Howard Woods worked for many leading Black newspapers after service as associate director of the United States Information Agency in Washington, 1965–67. He became editor-in-chief of Sengstacke Newspapers, in 1967, and he was editor and publisher of the *St. Louis Sentinel* (Missouri) from 1968 to 1981.

During his St. Louis career, Woods was a newscaster and commentator on local radio and television stations, and at times he had his own interview shows. He was also heavily involved in local activities.

In 1965, he received the Outstanding Achievement in Journalism Honor from Lincoln University of Missouri. He also received the National

Shriners' Citizens Achievement Award and recognition from the National Newspaper Publishers Association and the Mound City Press Club.

**WOODWARD, Robert U.** (1943– )
Robert Woodward and Carl Bernstein will long be remembered for their reporting and exposure of the Watergate episode while they were reporters on the *Washington Post.* From this also came their book, *All the President's Men*, which was made into a motion picture, and *The Final Days.* His biography, *Wired: The Short Life and Fast Times of John Belushi*, became a 1984 bestseller.

Woodward had been on the *Post*'s staff for only nine months when he was teamed with Bernstein to probe the Watergate incident. The rest is history. Woodward has been described as a "smooth, subtle interrogator."

He has won the George Polk Memorial, the Drew Pearson Foundation, the Heywood Broun, the Sidney Hillman, and the Sigma Delta Chi awards.

He co-authored *The Brethren.*

**WORDEN, Helen** (1896– )
Among the many writing assignments performed by Helen Worden (Mrs. W.W. Cranmer) was the continuation of the Dorothy Dix column from 1960 to 1964, after the death of the creator.

Worden began her newspaper career in 1926 with the New York *Sunday World.* She was the *World*'s society editor later, and by 1935 a columnist for the Scripps Howard Syndicate, a position she held until 1944 when she worked for *Reader's Digest* and *Liberty* magazines, 1944–47.

The following two years, 1947–49, she was with the *New York Herald Tribune* as a columnist. She was associate editor of *Collier's* from 1951 to 1956. Worden was honored by the New York Newspaper Women's Club for best news features.

Among Worden's books are *The Real New York*; *Round Manhattan's Rim*; *Society Circus*; *Here Is New York*; *Out of the World*; *Many Sinners and a Few Saints*; and *High Chair at Rector's.* She contributed to *The Boudoir Companion* and co-authored *Etiquette.*

She was long active in New York projects, such as the Opera, the Dramatist's Guild, the Historical Society, the New York Botanical Garden, and the New York Public Library.

**WREDE, John G.** (1932– )
John Wrede was with McGraw-Hill Publications for more than 20 years before becoming president of the firm in 1983.

Previously, Wrede had been president of the firm's Information Systems Co. for three years. While in college Wrede had considered the ministry, but then obtained a position with the McGraw-Hill *Architectual Record.* He was a classified advertising trainee in Boston before he joined McGraw-Hill's *Chemical Week*, where he eventually became publisher.

**WRIGHT, Don** ( - )
"I must simplify an issue to the point where the message comes through in a way they can understand. Then I want to agree or disagree to the extent that they get furious or enthusiastic enough to come back tomorrow."

So Don Wright explains his role as a political cartoonist for the *Miami News* (Florida), according to journalism historian Ernest Hynds. Wright's cartoons are distributed by the Tribune Company Syndicate.

Wright won the Pulitzer Prize for his cartooning, in 1966 and again in 1980. He also won the 1982 Inter-American Press Association Tom Wallace Award for commentary about Latin-American politics. In 1983, he was the first editorial cartoonist to win the Robert F. Kennedy Memorial Journalism Award.

**WYMAN, Tom** (1929- )
Before taking over the Columbia Broadcast System as president and chief operating officer in 1980, Tom Wyman had a varied background in the business world.

Wyman was a management trainee with a New York bank, and then joined the Nestle Company in marketing and new products operations, eventually working for the firm in Switzerland. He moved to Polaroid, in 1965, and spent a decade with the company until he became president of the Green Giant Co., in 1974. He later spent 1979–80 with the Pillsbury Company.

Active in civic affairs, Wyman is a trustee for several organizations.

He served in the Army during the Korean War.

**YATES, Floyd (Bill)** (1921- )
Bill Yates has created several comics, including "Professor Phumble" and "Benjy." During the Fifties, Yates worked for humor and movie magazines and was also an editor and art director for the *Hew Haw* magazine, for the CBS Network, and the Charlton Publishing Co.

While attending the University of Texas, Yates edited the humor magazine and later edited the National Cartoonists Society's publication. "Professor Phumble" was syndicated from 1960 to 1978; "Benjy" was syndicated from 1950 to 1960. Since 1980, Yates has been the comics editor for King Features Syndicate. His cartoons have also appeared in magazines and other newspapers.

In addition to lecturing on cartooning, Yates has drawn the Ronald McDonald comic books.

He served in the Navy during World War II.

**YOUNG, Chic (Murat Bernard)** (1901–1973)
"Blondie" has been one of the world's most popular comic strips since it was created in 1930 by Chic Young. Since 1963, it has been drawn by his son, Dean Wayne Young.

Young studied in art schools in Chicago, New York, and Cleveland and he worked with the Newspaper Enterprise Association in Cleveland, 1920–

21. He moved to the Bell Syndicate in 1921, and after 1923 his strip was handled by the King Features Syndicate.

Young began with "Dumb Dora" in 1924. He stopped this when he turned to "Blondie." More than 1,600 newspapers around the world carried the strip while he was drawing it.

**YOUNG, P. Bernard** (1884–1962)
One of the successful pioneer Black journalists, Bernard Young took over as editor and publisher of the *Norfolk Journal and Guide* (Virginia) in 1910 and continued in this operation until his death 52 years later.

Young was involved in many local and civic activities in the Norfolk area. From 1943 to 1947, he was vice-president of the Southern Regional Council. He also received several honorary university degrees.

**YOUNG, Robert Francis** (1919– )
Bob Young's early career involved a greater emphasis on the business than on journalism, such as a Street & Smith Publishing Co. salesman's position, 1947–49. He was next with *Look*, also as a salesman, until 1955. He then worked with Benton & Bowles advertising agency, until he joined *Family Circle* as publisher in 1968.

Young became president of *Family Circle* in 1975 and was also a director of the New York Times Media Co., which owns the magazine. He increased the magazine's publishing frequency to a unique 17 issues a year, starting in 1979.

Young, who served in the Air Force during World War II, once told *Madison Avenue Magazine* that he "was challenged and appreciated at the same time [in his latest task]. And that feels good."

**ZAGORIA, Sam** (1919– )
Since 1984 Sam Zagoria has been the ombudsman for the *Washington Post*, following a long career with newspapers and with the Federal Government. Zagoria joined the *New Brunswick Daily Home News* (New Jersey) in 1940. The next year he was with the New Jersey Defense Council in Trenton and in 1942 he was there with the Federal Office of Government Reports.

Zagoria returned to newspaper work as a reported for the *Washington Post* in 1946, a position he held until he became an administrative assistant to Senator Clifford P. Case in 1955. After ten years with the senator, Zagoria returned to government work as a member of the National Labor Relations Board. He became a member of the U.S. Consumer Product Safety Commission in 1978 and six years later returned to the *Post* to assume his present position.

In World War II Zagoria was with the Air Force. In 1954 he was a Nieman fellow at Harvard.

**ZEIGLER, Ronald L.** (1940– )
Ron Zeigler, who became better known to the American public when he was the press secretary for President Richard Nixon, became president of

the National Association of Truck Stop Operators in 1980. In some ways the two jobs are similar since, Zeigler said, "If I do nothing more, I'm going to communicate the best I can to the public at large and to anyone who will listen that this is an industry made up of fine men and women."

Zeigler earned a marketing degree from the University of Southern California in 1961 and then worked with the Republican State Central Committee. He joined Nixon's campaign for the governorship of California in 1962. He then joined the J. Walter Thompson advertising agency, but took a leave in 1968 to rejoin Nixon.

After he handled the transition from the Nixon to the Ford administration, Zeigler joined the Sysk & Hennessy engineering firm.

In media circles, Zeigler is best remembered for calling the Watergate break-in a "third-rate burglary attempt" and for his reference to its coverage as the "shoddiest type of journalism." Zeigler later apologized to Bob Woodward and Carl Bernstein, who broke the Watergate story.

**ZEKMAN, Pamela Lois** (1944– )

Investigative reporting in the Chicago area has brought two Pulitzer Prizes, plus many other awards, to Pamela Lois Zekman.

She began as a social worker in Cook County, Illinois, and then turned to journalism, working with the City News Bureau from 1966 to 1970. For five years (1970–75), she was with the *Chicago Tribune*, and for the next six years, the *Sun-Times*.

Zekman turned to television in 1981 as an investigative reporter for station WBBM-TV. Her many awards recognize the type of subjects she probed during her career in the city.

Her Pulitzers, for example, resulted from in-depth reporting on vote frauds and hospital abuse. She has won awards from both press services (UPI and AP), as well as two awards from the Inland Daily Press Association. Other recognition came from the National Headliner Club and Sigma Delta Chi. Northern Illinois University named her the Journalist of the Year in 1979.

Zekman investigated illegal baby selling, as well as problems in the currency exchange situation. She also probed a home for retarded children. Slumlords were also subjected to one of her incisive studies. Her married name is Mrs. Fredric Soll.

**ZUCKERMAN, Mortimer B.** (1937– )

Although Mortimer Zuckerman has become involved in the media world, he made his fortune as a real estate tycoon.

Zuckerman acquired the Atlantic Monthly Co. in 1980 and serves as its president and chairman of the board. His other interests are investments and banking. He has served as president of the board of trustees of the Sidney Farber Cancer Institute in Boston and has been on the boards of hospitals and educational institutions.

In 1984, he bought *U.S. News and World Report.*

# Index